EDUCATION 96/97

Twenty-Third Edition

Assignment:
Make Up 3ʳᵈ Questions
from each unit.

Editor

Fred Schultz
University of Akron

Fred Schultz, professor of education at the University of Akron, attended Indiana University to earn a B.S. in social science education in 1962, an M.S. in the history and philosophy of education in 1966, and a Ph.D. in the history and philosophy of education and American studies in 1969. His B.A. in Spanish was conferred from the University of Akron in May 1985. He is actively involved in researching the development and history of American education with a primary focus on the history of ideas and social philosophy of education. He also likes to study languages.

A Library of Information from the Public Press

Article 21 is Good
And Easy

CO-AZV-891

Cover illustration by Mike Eagle

**Dushkin Publishing Group/
Brown & Benchmark Publishers
Sluice Dock, Guilford, Connecticut 06437**

The Annual Editions Series

Annual Editions is a series of over 65 volumes designed to provide the reader with convenient, low-cost access to a wide range of current, carefully selected articles from some of the most important magazines, newspapers, and journals published today. Annual Editions are updated on an annual basis through a continuous monitoring of over 300 periodical sources. All Annual Editions have a number of features designed to make them particularly useful, including topic guides, annotated tables of contents, unit overviews, and indexes. For the teacher using Annual Editions in the classroom, an Instructor's Resource Guide with test questions is available for each volume.

VOLUMES AVAILABLE

Abnormal Psychology
Africa
Aging
American Foreign Policy
American Government
American History, Pre-Civil War
American History, Post-Civil War
American Public Policy
Anthropology
Archaeology
Biopsychology
Business Ethics
Child Growth and Development
China
Comparative Politics
Computers in Education
Computers in Society
Criminal Justice
Developing World
Deviant Behavior
Drugs, Society, and Behavior
Dying, Death, and Bereavement
Early Childhood Education
Economics
Educating Exceptional Children
Education
Educational Psychology
Environment
Geography
Global Issues
Health
Human Development
Human Resources
Human Sexuality

India and South Asia
International Business
Japan and the Pacific Rim
Latin America
Life Management
Macroeconomics
Management
Marketing
Marriage and Family
Mass Media
Microeconomics
Middle East and the Islamic World
Multicultural Education
Nutrition
Personal Growth and Behavior
Physical Anthropology
Psychology
Public Administration
Race and Ethnic Relations
Russia, the Eurasian Republics, and Central/Eastern Europe
Social Problems
Sociology
State and Local Government
Urban Society
Western Civilization, Pre-Reformation
Western Civilization, Post-Reformation
Western Europe
World History, Pre-Modern
World History, Modern
World Politics

Cataloging in Publication Data
Main entry under title: Annual editions: Education. 1996/97.
  1. Education—Periodicals. I. Schultz, Fred, *comp*. II. Title: Education.
370'.5   73-78580   ISBN 0–697–31571–1

Twenty-Third Edition

Printed in the United States of America

Printed on Recycled Paper

Editors/ Advisory Board

EDITOR

Fred Schultz
University of Akron

Members of the Advisory Board are instrumental in the final selection of articles for each edition of Annual Editions. Their review of articles for content, level, currentness, and appropriateness provides critical direction to the editor and staff. We think you'll find their careful consideration well reflected in this volume.

ADVISORY BOARD

Timothy J. Bergen
University of South Carolina

Kenneth Bower
College of Charleston

Lynn M. Burlbaw
Texas A & M University

Anthony A. DeFalco
Long Island University

Lloyd Duck
George Mason University

Jennifer J. Endicott
University of Central Oklahoma

Stephanie Evans
California State University
Los Angeles

Robert V. Farrell
Florida International University

Robert Gates
Bloomsburg University

William G. J. Goetter
Eastern Washington University

J. Merrell Hansen
Brigham Young University

Walter H. Klar
Framingham State College

Lawrence D. Klein
Central Connecticut State University

Margaret A. Laughlin
University of Wisconsin
Green Bay

Robert Leahy
Stetson University

James Wm. Noll
University of Maryland
College Park

G. Patrick O'Neill
Brock University

Charlene S. Plowcha
Mansfield University

Arthea J.S. Reed
University of North Carolina

Max L. Ruhl
Northwest Missouri State University

Quirico S. Samonte, Jr.
Eastern Michigan University

Robert J. Taggart
University of Delaware

Robert Welker
Wittenberg University

To the Reader

In publishing ANNUAL EDITIONS we recognize the enormous role played by the magazines, newspapers, and journals of the *public press* in providing current, first-rate educational information in a broad spectrum of interest areas. Within the articles, the best scientists, practitioners, researchers, and commentators draw issues into new perspective as accepted theories and viewpoints are called into account by new events, recent discoveries change old facts, and fresh debate breaks out over important controversies.

Many of the articles resulting from this enormous editorial effort are appropriate for students, researchers, and professionals seeking accurate, current material to help bridge the gap between principles and theories and the real world. These articles, however, become more useful for study when those of lasting value are carefully *collected, organized, indexed,* and *reproduced* in a *low-cost format,* which provides easy and permanent access when the material is needed. That is the role played by ANNUAL EDITIONS. Under the direction of each volume's *Editor,* who is an expert in the subject area, and with the guidance of an *Advisory Board,* we seek each year to provide in each ANNUAL EDITION a current, well-balanced, carefully selected collection of the best of the public press for your study and enjoyment.

We think you'll find this volume useful, and we hope you'll take a moment to let us know what you think.

Public concerns regarding the education of elementary and secondary students in the United States continue to center around certain key issues as *Annual Editions: Education 96/97* goes to press. There have been important shifts in the attitudes of some major organizations toward public schooling in recent months. The debate over whether all public monies should go to the public schools or whether public tax dollars for education should follow the student into either public or private schools has again intensified. The school "choice" debate is heating up even more. "Charter schools" are anticipated for more public schools to enable them to attempt very innovative approaches to elementary and secondary curricula and instruction. Citizens and teachers are very concerned over violence in the schools and the need for character education, as well as the teaching of methods of nonviolent conflict resolution to students. People within and outside of the teaching profession are also concerned about what specific moral and cultural canons the public schools ought to champion. Several new approaches to schooling are described in this year's edition. There is a great deal of experimental innovation going on in American elementary and secondary schools. Debates regarding academic tracking of students and inclusion continue. Interest in the quality of education is being voiced by many individuals and organizations as elementary and secondary schools strive for excellence.

American communities are intensely interested in local school politics and school funding issues. Not only the 27th Annual *Phi Delta Kappa/*Gallup poll of public attitudes toward the public schools but other essays in this edition reflect these interests and concerns as well. There continues to be healthy dialogue about and competition for the support of the various "publics" involved in public schooling.

The essays reflect spirited criticism as well as spirited defense of our public schools. There are competing, and very differing, school reform agendas being discussed, as has been the case for years now. Democratic publics tend to debate and disagree on important issues affecting public institutions and resources. All of this occurs as the United States continues to experience fundamentally important demographic shifts in its cultural makeup. In 1993 the cultural composition of the United States indicated that 30 percent of all American school children were from cultural minority groups. By the year 2000, it is estimated that 43 percent of the overall student body will be comprised of students from minority cultural backgrounds. Minority student populations are growing at a much faster rate than traditional Caucasian populations. Many scholars argue that the distinction between majority and minority school populations is being steadily eroded and will become meaningless by the year 2030.

Dialogue and compromise are the order of the day. The many interest groups within the educational field reflect a broad spectrum of viewpoints ranging from various behaviorist and cognitive developmental perspectives to humanistic ones. The agendas and interests of students, parents, state/provincial governments, and the corporate world compose the many differing views on how people should learn.

In assembling this volume, we make every effort to stay in touch with movements in educational studies and with the social forces at work in schools. Members of the advisory board contribute valuable insights, and the production and editorial staffs at Dushkin Publishing Group/Brown & Benchmark Publishers coordinate our efforts. Through this process we collect a wide range of articles on a variety of topics relevant to education in North America.

The readings in *Annual Editions: Education 96/97* explore the social and academic goals of education, the current condition of the nation's educational systems, the teaching profession, and the future of American education. In addition, these selections address the issues of change and the moral and ethical foundations of schooling. As always, we would like you to help us improve this volume. Please rate the material in this edition on the postage-paid form provided at the back of this book and send it to us. We care about what you think. Give us the feedback that we need.

Fred Schultz
Editor

Contents

Unit 1

How Others See Us and How We See Ourselves

Six articles examine today's most significant educational issues: the debate over privatization, the quality of schools, and the current public opinion about U.S. schools.

The concepts in bold italics are developed in the article. For further expansion please refer to the Topic Guide and the Index.

Unit 2

Rethinking and Changing the Educative Effort

Seven articles discuss the tension between ideals and socioeconomic reality at work in today's educational system.

The concepts in bold italics are developed in the article. For further expansion please refer to the Topic Guide and the Index.

Unit 3

Striving for Excellence: The Drive for Quality

Five selections examine the debate over achieving excellence in education by addressing issues relating to questions of how best to teach and how best to test.

Unit 4

Morality and Values in Education

Five articles examine the role of American schools in teaching morality and social values.

The concepts in bold italics are developed in the article. For further expansion please refer to the Topic Guide and the Index.

Unit 5

Managing Life in Classrooms

Four selections consider the importance of building effective teacher-student and student-student relationships in the classrooms.

Unit 6

Equal Opportunity in Education

Six articles discuss issues relating to fairness and justice for students from all cultural backgrounds and how curricula should respond to culturally pluralistic student populations.

The concepts in bold italics are developed in the article. For further expansion please refer to the Topic Guide and the Index.

Unit
7

Serving Special Needs and Concerns

Eight articles examine some of the important aspects of
special educational needs and building cooperative
learning communities in the classroom setting.

The concepts in bold italics are developed in the article. For further expansion please refer to the Topic Guide and the Index.

Unit 8

The Profession of Teaching Today

Seven articles assess the current state of teaching in U.S. schools and how well today's teachers approach subject matter learning.

Unit 9

A Look to the Future

Four articles look at new forms of schooling that break from traditional conceptions of education in America.

The concepts in bold italics are developed in the article. For further expansion please refer to the Topic Guide and the Index.

Topic Guide

This topic guide suggests how the selections in this book relate to topics of traditional concern to students and professionals involved with the study of education. It is useful for locating articles that relate to each other for reading and research. The guide is arranged alphabetically according to topic. Articles may, of course, treat topics that do not appear in the topic guide. In turn, entries in the topic guide do not necessarily constitute a comprehensive listing of all the contents of each selection.

TOPIC AREA	TREATED IN	TOPIC AREA	TREATED IN
Adolescents and Schooling	12. Evolving Strategy for Middle Grade Reform 30. *Turning Points* Revisited	Equal Educational Opportunity	28. Challenging the Myths about Multicultural Education 29. Time to See, Tell, and Do about Bigotry and Racism 30. *Turning Points* Revisited 31. Canon Debate 32. Investing in Our Children 33. AAUW Report: How Schools Shortchange Girls
American Association of University Women (AAUW)	33. AAUW Report: How Schools Shortchange Girls		
Basic Education	4. Public School Lifts Kids off New York's Mean Streets	Ethics and Education	21. Return of Character Education
Change and Restructuring Education	7. Shifting the *Target* of Educational Reform 8. How Our Schools Could Be 9. Class of Their Own 10. Rebel with a Cause 12. Evolving Strategy for Middle Grade Reform	Eurocentric Curriculum (The "Canon Debate")	31. Canon Debate
		Excellence in Education	7. Shifting the *Target* of Educational Reform 14. Towards Excellence in Education 15. Not All Standards Are Created Equal 16. Wrong Problem, Wrong Solution 17. Somebody's Children 18. Making America's Schools Work
Channel One	37. Commercialization of Youth		
Choice in Schooling	17. Somebody's Children		
Classroom Management	24. Routines and the First Few Weeks of Class 25. Waging Peace in Our Schools 26. How to Create Discipline Problems 27. Lesson Plan Approach for Dealing with School Discipline	Family Values	20. A De-Moralized Society 22. What Are Your Family Values? 23. Teaching Values
		Federal Programming in Education	14. Towards Excellence in Education
Coalition of Essential Schools	13. On Lasting School Reform	Full-Service Schooling	3. Full-Service Schools
Community Service	32. Investing in Our Children	Future of Education	49. Philosophy of Education for the Year 2000 50. Preparing for the 21st Century 51. Searching for Terms 52. Plug-In School
Conflict Resolution	1. Education for Conflict Resolution 25. Waging Peace in Our Schools		
Discipline in Schools	24. Routines and the First Few Weeks of Class 25. Waging Peace in Our Schools 26. How to Create Discipline Problems 27. Lesson Plan Approach for Dealing with School Discipline	Gallup Poll	6. 27th Annual Phi Delta Kappa/Gallup Poll
		Gender and Schools	33. AAUW Report: How Schools Shortchange Girls
		Good Teaching	8. How Our Schools Could Be 9. Class of Their Own 24. Routines and the First Few Weeks of Class 42. Reflection and Teaching 43. Phase II: Implementing a Design for Learning 44. Toward Lives Worth Sharing 45. About Instruction
Economic Education	38. Enhancing K–12 Economic Education with Contemporary Information Resources		
Environmental and Global Education	50. Preparing for the 21st Century		
		Home Schooling	34. Home Sweet School

TOPIC AREA	TREATED IN	TOPIC AREA	TREATED IN
Management of Schools	2. Will Schools Ever Get Better?	**Renewal in Education**	1. Education for Conflict Resolution 4. Public School Lifts Kids off New York's Mean Streets 7. Shifting the *Target* of Educational Reform
"Means-Tested" School Choice	17. Somebody's Children	**Sex Education**	41. Everyone Is an Exception
Morality and Education	19. Morally Defensible Mission for Schools in the 21st Century 20. De-Moralized Society 21. Return of Character Education 22. What Are Your Family Values?	**Social Mission of Schools**	1. Education for Conflict Resolution 5. America Skips School 19. Morally Defensible Mission for Schools in the 21st Century 21. Return of Character Education 49. Philosophy of Education for the Year 2000
Multicultural Education	28. Challenging the Myths about Multicultural Education 31. Canon Debate		
Nonviolent Conflict Resolution in Schools	1. Education for Conflict Resolution 25. Waging Peace in Our Schools	**Standards in Education**	15. Not All Standards Are Created Equal 16. Wrong Problem, Wrong Solution 17. Somebody's Children
Pressures on Schools	48. Challenges to the Public School Curriculum 49. Philosophy of Education for the Year 2000	**Teaching**	24. Routines and the First Few Weeks of Class 25. Waging Peace in Our Schools 26. How to Create Discipline Problems 27. Lesson Plan Approach for Dealing with School Discipline 42. Reflection and Teaching 43. Phase II: Implementing a Design for Learning 44. Toward Lives Worth Sharing 45. About Instruction
Profession of Teaching	36. Blackboard Bungle 42. Reflection and Teaching 43. Phase II: Implementing a Design for Learning 44. Toward Lives Worth Sharing 45. About Instruction 46. Cultural Revolution 47. How to Make Detracking Work 48. Challenges to the Public School Curriculum		
		Technology and Learning	52. Plug-In School
Professional Development	36. Blackboard Bungle 46. Cultural Revolution	**Tracking**	40. Blowing up the Tracks 47. How to Make Detracking Work
Public Perceptions of Schools	1. Education for Conflict Resolution 2. Will Schools Ever Get Better? 3. Full-Service Schools 4. Public School Lifts Kids off New York's Mean Streets 5. America Skips School 6. 27th Annual Phi Delta Kappa/Gallup Poll	**Values and Teaching**	19. Morally Defensible Mission for Schools in the 21st Century 20. De-Moralized Society 21. Return of Character Education 22. What Are Your Family Values?
		Violence and Education	1. Education for Conflict Resolution 25. Waging Peace in Our Schools 39. Violence as a Public Health Issue for Children
Racism and Bigotry	29. Time to See, Tell, and Do about Bigotry and Racism	**Western Canon Debate and Multicultural Education**	31. Canon Debate
Reflective Teaching	42. Reflection and Teaching		
		Year-Round School	35. Year-Round School
Reform of Schools	7. Shifting the *Target* of Educational Reform 8. How Our Schools Could Be 9. Class of Their Own 10. Rebel with a Cause 12. Evolving Strategy for Middle Grade Reform	**Young Adolescents in America**	12. Evolving Strategy for Middle Grade Reform 30. *Turning Points* Revisited

How Others See Us and How We See Ourselves

The United States has great interest in policy issues regarding greater accountability to the public for what goes on in schools. Also, there is public concern for the safety of American school students, especially in the larger urban school systems. We are possibly the most culturally pluralistic nation in the world, and we are becoming even more culturally pluralistic as a national population. David Hamburg raises the issue of learning to live together peacefully and looks at what the roles of educators ought to be in teaching students nonviolent conflict resolution skills. Many educators as well as students are concerned about such issues.

The recently elected conservative majority in Congress appears to be supporting some policy options for parents in sending their children to school. We may be approaching a historic moment in our national history regarding the public funding of education and the choices parents might be given for the education of their children. The essays in other units of this volume describe and explore some of these options and the lines of reasoning for them. We are not far from a truly historic turning point regarding new options for educating American youth. Financial as well as qualitative considerations are being debated. Scholars in many fields of study and journalists and legislators are asking how we can make our nation's schools more effective, as well as how we might optimize American parents' sense of control over how their children are to be educated.

Democratic societies have always enjoyed spirited dialogue and debate over the purposes of their public institutions. Aristotle noted in his *Politics* that citizens of Athens could not seem to agree as to the purposes of education. He noted further that many of the city's youth questioned traditional values. So has it been wherever people have been free. Yet this reality of democratic life in no way excuses us from our continuing civic duty to address directly, and with our best resources, the intellectual and social well-being of our youth. Young people "read" certain adult behaviors well; they see it as hypocrisy when the adult community wants certain standards and values to be taught in schools but rewards other, often opposite behaviors in society. Dialogue regarding what it means to speak of "literacy" in democratic com-

munities continues. Our students read much from our daily activities and our many information sources, and they form their own shrewd analyses of what social values actually do prevail in society. How to help young people develop their intellectual potential as well as to become perceptive students of and participants in democratic traditions are major public concerns. These have always been primary concerns to democratic educators.

Concerns regarding the quality of public schooling can also be seen in the social context of the dramatic demographic changes currently taking place in North America and especially in the United States, which is experiencing the second largest wave of immigration in its history. Cuts in federal government funding over the past 12 years of such important early educational programs as Head Start have created a situation in some areas of the nation, such as in West Virginia, where only about one in three eligible children from poverty-level homes can have a place in Head Start programs. In addition, school dropout rates, adult and youth illiteracy, the increasing rate of teenage pregnancy, and several interrelated health and security issues in schools cause continued public concern.

There is public uncertainty as well regarding whether or not state and provincial legislators will or should accept a greater state government role in funding needed changes in the schools. Intense controversy continues among citizens about the quality and adequacy of our schools. Meanwhile, the plight of many children is getting worse, not better. Some have estimated that a child is molested or neglected in the United States every 47 seconds; a student drops out of school every 8 seconds. More than a third of the children have no health insurance coverage. Our litany of tragedies affecting our nation's children and teenagers could be extended, but the message is clear. There is grave, serious business yet to be attended to by the social service and educational agencies that try to serve American youth. People are impatient to see some fundamental efforts made to meet the basic educational needs of young people. The problems are the greatest in major cities and in more isolated rural areas. Public perceptions of the schools are affected by high levels of economic deprivation among large minority sectors of the population and by the economic pressures that our interdependent world economy produces as a result of international competition for the world's markets.

Studies conducted in the past few years, particularly the Carnegie Corporation's study of adolescents in the United States, document the plight of millions of young persons in North America. Some authors point out that although there was much talk about educational change in the 1990s, those changes were only marginal and cosmetic at best. States responded by demanding more course work and tougher exit standards from school. The underlying causes of poor academic achievement have received no more attention. With still more than 25 percent of school children in the United States living at or below the poverty level, and almost a third of them in more economically and socially vulnerable nontraditional family settings, the overall social situation for many young persons continues to be difficult. The public wants more effective governmental responses to public needs.

Alternative approaches to attracting new and talented teachers have received sympathetic support among some sectors of the public, but these alternative teacher certification approaches have met with stiff opposition from large segments of the incumbent school staff systems. Many states are exploring and experimenting with such programs at the urging of government and business leaders. Yet many of these alternative programs appear to be too superficial and are failing to teach the candidates in these programs the new knowledge base on teaching and learning that has been developed in recent years.

So, in the face of major demographic shifts and of the persistence of many long-term social problems, the public watches how schools respond to new as well as old challenges. In recent years, these challenges have aggravated rather than allayed much public concern about the efficacy of public schooling. Various political, cultural, corporate, and philanthropic interests continue to articulate alternative educational agendas. At the same time, the incumbents in the system respond with their own educational agendas that reflect their views from the inside. Overall, it is surely the well-being and the academic progress of students that are the chief motivating forces behind the recommendations of all well-meaning interest groups in this dialogue.

Looking Ahead: Challenge Questions

What educational issues are of greatest concern to citizens today?

What ought to be the policy directions of national and state governments regarding educational reform?

What are the most important problems blocking efforts to improve educational standards? How can we best build a national public consensus regarding the structure and purposes of schooling?

What social factors encourage at-risk students to drop out of school early?

What are the differences between the myth and the reality of U.S. schooling? Have the schools done anything right? Support your answer.

How can we most accurately assess public perceptions of the educational system?

What is the functional effect of public opinion on national public policy regarding educational development?

What generalizations concerning public schools in the United States can be drawn from the *Phi Delta Kappa* / Gallup poll data?

—F. S.

Education for Conflict Resolution

In the fall of 1994, Mikhail S. Gorbachev, former president of the Soviet Union, reflected on a decade of intensive involvement with political leaders all over the world. One of his outstanding conclusions was the large extent to which they see "brute force" as their ultimate validation. His observation, based on abundant experience, highlights a long-standing, historically deadly inclination of leaders of many kinds from many places to interpret their mandate as being strong, tough, aggressive, even violent. For all too many, this is indeed the essence of leadership.

Gorbachev, in control of a vast nuclear arsenal, not to speak of immense power in conventional, chemical, and biological weapons, was wise enough not to interpret his own leadership in terms of brute force. But the world is full of leaders who do. More and more often, they will have massive killing power at their disposal in the twenty-first century. Look at the scale of slaughter in Rwanda with penny-ante weapons!

It is time to take seriously the remark of Archibald MacLeish in the aftermath of World War II: "Since wars begin in the minds of men, it is in the minds of men that the defenses of peace must be constructed." He was writing about the mission of the emerging international institutions that were vividly mindful of the carnage of World War II and the Holocaust, but his words apply to the furious small wars of today.

Can We Learn to Live Together?

The human species seems to have a virtuoso capacity for making harsh distinctions between groups and for justifying violence on whatever scale the technology of the time permits. Moreover, fanatical behavior has a dangerous way of recurring across time and locations. Such behavior is old, but what is historically new and very threatening is the destructive power of our weaponry and its ongoing worldwide spread. Also new is the technology that permits rapid, vivid, widely broadcast justifications for violence. In such a

NOTE: *The president's annual essay is a personal statement representing his own views. It does not necessarily reflect the foundation's policies. This essay is based on a presentation made in June 1994 at a Nobel symposium in Sweden. This symposium will be published in a book edited by Professor David Magnusson, Stockholm University, titled* Individual Development Over the Lifespan.

From the Carnegie Corporation Annual Report, *Report of the President,* 1994, pp. 4-15. Reprinted by permission of the Carnegie Corporation of New York, 437 Madison Avenue, New York, NY 10022.

world, human conflict is a subject that deserves the most careful and searching inquiry. It is a subject par excellence for public understanding. Yet today's education has little to say on the subject. Worse still, education almost everywhere has ethnocentric orientations.

Can we do better? Can we educate ourselves to avoid conflict or peacefully resolve it? Is it possible for us to modify our attitudes and orientations so that we practice greater tolerance and mutual aid at home and in the world? Perhaps it is unlikely. But the stakes are so high now that even a modest gain on this goal would be exceedingly valuable. This essay explores a few, and only a very few, of the possibilities brought to light by recent inquiry and innovation. The examples are meant to be evocative — better ones may well be available. They are meant to move this subject higher on the world's agenda.

INSIGHTS INTO INTERGROUP HOSTILITY

The challenge is immense. Both in field studies and experimental research by social scientists, the evidence is very strong: We humans are remarkably prone to form partisan distinctions between our own and other groups, to develop a marked preference for our own group, to accept favorable evaluations of the products and performances of the in-group, and to make unfavorable evaluations of other groups that go far beyond the objective evidence or the requirements of a situation. Indeed, it seems difficult for us to avoid making invidious distinctions even when we want to.

Orientations of ethnocentrism and prejudice are rooted in our ancient past and were probably once adaptive. Over the millennia, our estimate of personal worth if not our very survival has been built on the sense of belonging to a

7

valued group—a sense that seems to go hand in glove with the impulse to assign negative value to those who are not of our group. Both these tendencies historically have been reinforced by parental and social education beginning in early childhood in nearly every human society.

Today, reinforcement occurs at home, in the schools, in the streets, and in the mass media. The cumulative effect of widespread frustrating conditions also exacerbates the development of prejudice and stereotyped thinking. Political firebrands put gasoline on the embers. Worldwide, the education received from multiple sources is still remarkably ethnocentric. In some places ethnocentrism and prejudice are inflamed by official propaganda, the cultivation of religious stereotypes, and political demagoguery, leading to intergroup violence that is justified in the name of some putatively high purpose.

The global outburst of intergroup violence, with its explosive mixture of ethnic, religious, and national strivings, is badly in need of illumination. People everywhere need to understand why we behave as we do, what dangerous legacy we carry with us, and how we can convert fear to hope.

MUST CHILDREN GROW UP HATEFUL? A DEVELOPMENTAL PERSPECTIVE

Education, via the family, schools, the media, and community organizations, must be turned into a force for reducing intergroup conflict. It must serve to enlarge our social identifications in light of common characteristics and superordinate goals. It must seek a basis for fundamental human identification across a diversity of cultures in the face of manifest conflict. We *are,* in fact, a single, interdependent, meaningfully attached, worldwide species.

The question is whether human beings can learn more constructive orientations toward those outside their group while maintaining the values of group allegiance and identity. From an examination of a great deal of laboratory and field research, it seems reasonable to believe that, in spite of very bad habits from the past, we can indeed learn new habits of mind.

There is an extensive body of research on intergroup contact that bears on this question. For example, experiments have demonstrated that the *extent* of contact between groups that are negatively oriented toward one another is *not* the most important factor in achieving a more constructive orientation. Much depends on whether the contact occurs under favorable conditions. If there is an aura of mutual suspicion, if the parties are highly competitive or are not supported by relevant authorities, or if contact occurs on the basis of very unequal status, then it is not likely to be helpful, whatever the amount of exposure. Contact under unfavorable conditions can stir up old tensions and reinforce stereotypes.

On the other hand, if there is friendly contact in the context of equal status, especially if such contact is supported by relevant authorities, and if the contact is embedded in cooperative activity and fostered by a mutual aid ethic, then there is likely to be a strong positive outcome. Under these conditions, the more contact the better. Such contact is then associated with improved attitudes between previously suspicious or hostile groups as well as with constructive changes in patterns of interaction between them.

Other experiments demonstrate the power of shared, highly valued superordinate goals that can only be achieved by cooperative effort. Such goals can override the differences that people bring to the situation and often have a powerful, unifying effect. Classic experiments readily made strangers at a boys' camp into enemies by isolating them from one another and heightening competition. But when powerful superordinate goals were introduced, enemies were transformed into friends.

These experiments have been replicated in work with business executives and other professionals with similar results. So the effect is certainly not limited to children and youth. Indeed, the findings have pointed to the beneficial effects of working cooperatively under conditions that lead people to formulate a new, inclusive group, going beyond the subgroups with which they entered the situation. Such effects are particularly strong when there are tangibly successful outcomes of cooperation—for example, clear rewards from cooperative learning. They have important implications for child rearing and education.

DEVELOPING CONSTRUCTIVE ORIENTATIONS IN CHILDHOOD AND ADOLESCENCE

Ameliorating the problem of intergroup relations rests upon finding better ways to foster child and adolescent development. This fact should present crucial new opportunities to educate young people in conflict resolution and in mutual accommodation.

Pivotal educational institutions such as the family, schools, community-based organizations, and the media have the power to shape attitudes and skills toward decent human relations or toward hatred and violence. If they really wish to be constructive, such organizations need to utilize the findings from research on intergroup relations and conflict resolution. They can use this knowledge in fostering positive reciprocity, cross-cutting relations, superordinate goals, and mutual aid.

Education everywhere needs to convey an accurate concept of a single, highly interdependent, worldwide species—a vast extended family sharing fundamental human similarities and a fragile planet. The give-and-take fostered within groups can be extended far beyond childhood to relations between adults and to larger units of organization, even covering international relations.

All research-based knowledge of human conflict, the diversity of our species, and the paths to mutual accommodation constitutes grist for the education mill. What follows is a sketch of some possibilities for making use of many different educational vehicles for learning to live together within nations and across national boundaries.

FOSTERING PROSOCIAL BEHAVIOR IN EARLY LIFE

In the context of secure attachment and valued adult models, provided by either a cohesive family or a more extended social support network, a child can learn certain social norms that are conducive to tolerance and a mutual aid ethic. Children can learn to take turns, share with others, cooperate (especially in learning and problem solving), and help others in everyday life as well as in times of stress.

These norms, though established on a simple basis in the first few years of life, open the way toward constructive human relationships that can have significance throughout the life span. Their practice earns respect from others, provides gratification, and increases confidence and competence. For this reason, both family care and early intervention programs need to take account of the factors that influence the development of attachment and prosocial behavior. This is important in parent education, in child care centers, and in preschool education.

There is research evidence, both from direct observation and experimental studies, that settings that promote the requirements and expectations of prosocial behavior do in fact strengthen such behavior. For example, children who are responsible for tasks helpful to family maintenance, as in caring for younger siblings, are generally found to be more altruistic than children who do not have these prosocial experiences.

In experimental studies, typically an adult (presumably much like a parent) demonstrates a prosocial act like sharing toys, coins, or candy that have been won in a game. The sharing is with someone else who is said to be in need though not present in the experimental situation. The adult plays the game and models the sharing before leaving the child to play. The results are clear. Children exposed to such modeling, when compared to similar children in control groups, tend to show the behavior manifested by the models, whether it be honesty, generosity, or altruism. Given the child's pervasive exposure to parents and teachers, the potential for observational learning in this sphere as in others is very great. Prosocial behavior is particularly significant in adaptation because it is likely to open up new opportunities for the growing child, strengthen human relationships, and contribute to the building of self-esteem.

EMPATHY TRAINING

Empathy, defined as a shared emotional response between observer and subject, may be expressed as "putting oneself in the shoes of another person." Empathy training has been tested with eight- to ten-year-olds in elementary school classrooms. In one program, children were given thirty hours of exercises in small groups of four to six. Activities were designed to increase their skill in identifying emotional responses and in taking the perspective of another. The intervention group was compared with two kinds of control groups.

The participants in empathy training showed more prosocial behavior, less aggression, and more positive self-concept than did children in either control group. This elementary school training model may provide a guide for the enhancement of empathy in other contexts—for example, in learning to take the perspective of other ethnic or religious groups. In any event, responding empathically in potential conflict situations helps to reduce hateful outcomes.

A FRAMEWORK FOR CONFLICT RESOLUTION IN THE SCHOOLS

Much of what schools can accomplish is similar to what parents can do—employ positive disciplinary practices, be democratic in procedure, teach the capacity for responsible decision making, foster cooperative learning procedures, and guide children in prosocial behavior in the various spheres of their lives. They can convey in interesting ways the truth of human diversity and the humanity we all share. They can convey the fascination of other cultures, making understanding and respect a core attribute of their outlook on the world—including the capacity to interact effectively in the emerging global economy.

Professor Morton Deutsch of Teachers College, Columbia University, a distinguished scholar in conflict resolution, has delineated programs that schools can use to promote attitudes, values, and knowledge that will help children develop constructive relations throughout their lives. Such programs include cooperative learning, conflict resolution training, the constructive use of controversy in teaching, and the creation of dispute resolution centers.

In his view, constructive conflict resolution is characterized by cooperation, good communication, perception of similarity in beliefs and values among the parties, acceptance of the other's legitimacy, problem-centered negotiations, mutual trust and confidence, and information sharing. Destructive conflicts, in contrast, are characterized by harsh competition, poor communication, coercive tactics, suspicion, perception of basic differences in values, an orientation to increasing power differences, challenges to the legitimacy of other parties, and personal insecurity.

Efforts to educate on these matters are most effective where there is a substantial, in-depth curriculum with repeated opportunities to learn and practice cooperative conflict resolution skills. Students gain a realistic understanding of the amount of violence in society and the deadly consequences of such violence. They learn that violence begets violence, that there are healthy and unhealthy ways to express anger, and that nonviolent alternatives to dealing with conflict are available and will always be useful to them.

COOPERATIVE LEARNING

A substantial body of information during the past two decades has been generated from research on cooperative learning. These efforts stem in part from a desire to find alternatives to the usual lecture mode and to involve students actively in the learning process. They are inspired, moreover, by a mutual aid ethic and appreciation for student diversity. In cooperative learning, the traditional classroom of one teacher and many students is reorganized into heterogeneous groups of four or five students who work together to learn a particular subject matter, for instance, mathematics.

Research has demonstrated that student achievement is at least as high—and often higher

— in cooperative learning activities as it is in traditional classroom activities. At the same time, cooperative learning methods promote positive interpersonal relations, motivation to learn, and self-esteem. These benefits are obtained in middle grade schools and also high schools, for various subject areas and for a wide range of tasks and activities.

In my view, there are several overlapping yet distinctive concepts of cooperative learning that offer a powerful set of skills and assets for later life: learning to work together; learning that everyone can contribute in some way; learning that everyone is good at something; learning to appreciate diversity in various attributes; learning complementarity of skills and a division of labor; learning a mutual aid ethic. There is good reason why cooperative learning has lately stimulated so much interest. It deserves more widespread utilization along with continuing research to broaden its applicability.

EARLY ADOLESCENCE: LEARNING LIFE SKILLS

The Carnegie Council on Adolescent Development's Working Group on Life Skills Training, chaired by Dr. Beatrix Hamburg, in 1990 provided the factual basis and organizing principles on which such interventions can be based. It also described a variety of exemplary programs.

One category of life skills is being assertive. An example of assertiveness is knowing how to take advantage of opportunities — for example, how to use community resources such as health and social services or job training. Another aspect is knowing how to resist pressure or intimidation by peers and others to take drugs, carry weapons, or make irresponsible decisions about sex — and how to do this without spoiling relationships or isolating oneself. Yet another aspect of assertiveness is knowing how to resolve conflict in ways that make use of the full range of nonviolent opportunities that exist. Such skills can be taught not only in schools but in community organizations.

Required community service in high schools, indeed even in middle grade schools, can also be helpful in the shaping of responsible, sharing, altruistic behavior. It is important to have serious reflection on such community service experience, to analyze its implications, and to learn ways to benefit from setbacks. *How* we help others is crucial. "Help" must not imply superiority over others but rather convey a sense of being full members of the community, sharing a common fate as human beings together. This orientation can usefully be an important part of parent education as well. As the development of parental competence increasingly comes to be based on explicit courses of education and preparation for parenthood, the elements of caring for others, of reciprocity and of mutual understanding must be a key part of the task.

VIOLENCE PREVENTION IN ADOLESCENCE

A public health perspective suggests that the prevention strategies that have been successful in dealing with other behavior-related health problems, such as smoking, may be applicable to the problem of adolescent violence. Adolescent experimentation with behavior patterns and values offers an opportunity to develop alternatives to violent responses. A pioneering example is provided by the Boston Violence Prevention Program — a multi-institutional initiative with the goal of reducing fights, assaults, and intentional injuries among adolescents. It trains providers in diverse community settings in a violence prevention curriculum, promotes incorporation of this curriculum into service delivery, and creates a community consensus supportive of violence prevention. The program targets two poor Boston neighborhoods characterized by high violence rates. Its four principal components are curriculum development, community-based prevention education, clinical treatment services, and a media campaign.

The curriculum was first developed in 1983 by Dr. Deborah Prothrow-Stith. It acknowledged anger as a normal and potentially constructive emotion; alerted students to their high risk of being a perpetrator or victim of violence; helped students find alternatives to fighting by discussing potential gains and losses; offered positive ways to deal with anger and arguments; encouraged students to analyze the precursors of fighting and to practice alternative conflict resolution by playing different roles; and created a classroom climate that is nonviolent.

During the initial stages of curriculum development, it became clear that intervention in the schools alone was insufficient. In 1986 a community-based component was initiated in which community educators provided violence prevention training to youth-serving agencies. Additional materials included informational flyers, a videotape, a rap song, cartoon characters, church sermons, and Sunday school sessions.

The project seeks to reach as many community settings as possible, including multi-service centers, recreation programs, housing developments, police stations and courts, religious institutions, neighborhood health centers, and schools. There is a referral network for health, education, and social services. The community campaign has produced television and radio public service announcements, posters, and T-shirts using the slogan, "Friends for life don't let friends fight." It focuses on peer influences and the responsibility that friends have for helping to defuse conflict situations. It also includes a public television documentary.

Violence prevention efforts of such a systematic and extensive sort are very recent. It would be surprising if the first efforts were highly successful, because of the great complexity and difficulty of the tasks in terribly impaired neighborhoods. One clear finding is that the adolescents—and especially disadvantaged males—are urgently in need of dependable life skills and constructive social supports that foster health, education, and decent human relationships.

TELEVISION AND PROSOCIAL BEHAVIOR

Research has established causal relationships between children's viewing of either aggressive or prosocial behavior on television and their subsequent behavior. Children as young as two years old are facile at imitating televised behaviors. Television violence can affect a child's behavior at an early age and the effects can extend into adolescence. In general, the relationship between television violence and subsequent viewer behavior holds in a variety of countries. Cross-national studies show this in countries as diverse as Australia, Finland, Israel, the Netherlands, Poland, and the United States.

There is some research evidence that television need not be a school for violence—that it can be used in a way that reduces intergroup hostility. The relevant professions need to encourage the constructive use of this powerful tool to promote compassionate understanding, nonviolent problem solving, and decent intergroup relations.

Television can portray human diversity while highlighting shared human experiences. It can teach skills that are important for the social development of children and do so in a way that both entertains and educates. So far we have had only glimpses of its potential for reducing intergroup hostility.

Professor Gerald Lesser at Harvard University has summarized features of the children's educational television program, "Sesame Street," that are of interest in this context. The program originated in the United States in 1969 and appears today in 100 other countries. Each program is fitted to the language, culture, and traditions of a particular nation. The atmosphere of respect for differences permeates all of the many versions of "Sesame Street."

Research from a variety of countries is encouraging. For example, the Canadian version of "Sesame Street" shows many sympathetic instances of English- and French-speaking children playing together. Children who see these examples of cross-group friendships are more likely to form such friendships on their own than are children who do not see them. The same is true for Dutch, Moroccan, Turkish, and Surinamese children who see "Sesame Street" in Holland. The findings suggest that appealing and constructive examples of social tolerance help young children to learn such behavior. These are tantalizing results, making us wish for a wide range of similar programming and experimentation.

LEARNING FROM ALL KINDS OF CONFLICTS

Processes of conflict resolution in any sphere should be examined for their implications in other spheres. It may well be that understanding of the processes of conflict resolution between groups *within* a nation will concomitantly enhance our ability to reduce conflict *between* nations — and vice versa.

Are there lessons to be learned from decent human relations in various spheres of life? Abundant experience and study at the level of interpersonal relations and small-group and community relations provide a way of thinking about decent relations between large groups and even nations. What are the major requirements?

1. Each party needs a basis for self-respect, a sense of belonging in a valued group, and a distinctive identity.

2. Each party needs dependability of communication with the other.

3. Each party needs from the other a recognition of some shared interests and the fact of interdependence.

4. Each needs civil discourse, including the ability to understand the perspective of the other — even if they do not always agree. Disagreements can also be considered in a civil way. And both parties need to keep in mind their common humanity even — and especially — in times of adversity.

5. Each party has the possibility of earning the respect of the other — in a differentiated way, admiring some attributes but not others.

6. Boundaries for competition and disagreement can be recognized, even if they are sometimes dimly seen.

7. When boundaries fundamentally have to do with violence, each party can seriously consider and reconsider from time to time the balance between interests of self and the interests of the other.

Such concepts of decent human relations have considerable operational significance in daily living. On the whole, they serve the human species well at various levels of social organization. Could we learn to utilize them in relations between ethnic groups and even adversarial powers? The experience of ending the Cold War suggests that this may be possible.

ROLE OF THE INTERNATIONAL COMMUNITY

The growing threat of prejudicial ethnocentrism as a path to hatred, violence, and mass killing has to emerge as one of the major educational challenges of the next century, with international institutions playing an important role. The international community can be a powerful force in broad public education on the entire problem of intergroup violence. It can help and reward conflict resolution leaders, build education systems worldwide, and provide useful, sensitive, early intervention.

It is of utmost importance for contending parties throughout the world to be educated on the nature, scope, and consequences of ethnocentric violence, particularly the action-reaction cycles in such violence, with the buildup of revenge motives; the tendency to assume hatred as an organizing principle for life and death; and the slippery slope of proliferation, escalation, and addiction to hatred and killing that emerges so readily in festering intergroup conflict.

Adversaries need to grasp how violent extremists and fanatics tend to take increasing control of the situation; they need to face up to the probable degradation of life — even annihilation — that will occur for all concerned in areas of intense fighting. The international community must make these dangers clear and vivid in the minds of populations involved in potential hot spots.

The policy community in much of the world is not deeply familiar with the principles and techniques of conflict resolution. It must become so, with the United Nations and the Secretary General playing one of the leading roles. The United Nations, respected widely throughout the world, could do more than it has done historically to educate publics to the need and possibilities for resolving conflicts without violence. The

Secretary General has a bully pulpit of formidable proportions.

Among other initiatives, the U.N. can sponsor world leadership seminars in cooperation with qualified nongovernmental organizations such as universities and research institutes. These leadership seminars might well include new heads of state, new foreign ministers, and new defense ministers.

Ongoing leadership seminars could also clarify how the U.N. and other institutions and organizations can help. Given the contemporary climate, it is singularly important that such seminars deal objectively and in a penetrating way with problems of nationalism, ethnocentrism, prejudice, hatred, and violence. Through the leadership seminars and a wider array of publications, the U.N. can make available the world's experience bearing on conflicts in general and on particular conflicts; on the responsible handling of weapons by governmental leaders and policymakers; on the likely consequences of weapons build-up, especially weapons of mass destruction; on the skills, knowledge base, and prestige properly associated with successful conflict resolution; on economic development, including the new uses of science and technology for development; and on cooperative behavior in the world community, including the handling of grievances.

THE GLOBAL REACH OF RADIO AND TELEVISION

The role of media is a powerful one, for better and for worse. Books, films, music, television, and radio all carry a variety of messages, both cognitive and emotional. The power of the mass media, and particularly television, has revised our concept of what constitutes reality.

Television directs attention to a subject beyond any previous medium's ability. It has the power to focus on one situation and instantly raise the world's awareness. Unfortunately, this power can be and often is used to exacerbate conflict. Terrorists, for instance, have long recognized the power of television to give a small, fanatical group international exposure to their cause.

Political power is more and more associated with media coverage. The primacy of television's linkage with political power was well demonstrated in the recent revolutionary events in Eastern Europe and the former Soviet republics, when control of television output was at the center of the struggle.

Television has immense latent capacity as a force for global transformation. The medium is deeply international, readily crossing boundaries. Each side in a war may be able to watch the other's television broadcasts. In divided Germany, most East Germans watched West German television, which provided an effective antidote to Communist government propaganda. With new digital technologies and more powerful satellites, it will be increasingly difficult to isolate a country from the global media. Cable News Network already has had a powerful effect through its global news distribution and extensive use of live broadcasting from sites on every continent. Although this was most vivid during the Gulf war, it is a daily fact of life on a global basis.

Television has great potential for reducing tensions between countries. It can be used to demystify the adversary and improve understanding. A Cold War example was provided by U.S.-Soviet spacebridge programs—live, unedited discussion between the two countries made possible by satellites and simultaneous translation. Starting in 1983, U.S.-Soviet spacebridges linked ordinary American and Soviet citizens in an effort to overcome stereotypes. Beginning before the Gorbachev era, they provided an opening to his policy of glasnost. Later, Internews' "Capital to Capital" program, broadcast simultaneously on ABC and on Soviet and Eastern European television, joined members of Congress and the Supreme Soviet for uncensored debate on arms control, human rights, and the future of Europe. These spacebridge programs were seen by 200 million people at a time. Ted Koppel's "Nightline" program on ABC was dynamic in settings of this sort, especially between the U.S. and South Africa and between the U.S. and the Soviet Union. The dramatic "Nightline" town meeting between Palestinians and Israelis in 1988 showed how television can foster reasonable dialogue on tender issues even among old adversaries.

Independent, pluralistic media are vital for democracy. They are the main vehicles for clarifying issues and for the public to understand candidates. In the first post-Soviet Ukrainian election, President Leonid Kravchuk had total control over television throughout the process, whereas other candidates had hardly any access to it. Such elections cannot be considered free and fair. International election monitors must therefore observe access to the media as well as the voting itself.

Radio is exceedingly important because it reaches virtually everyone everywhere almost all the time. Hate radio has been all too effective in inciting violence—remember its role in Rwanda and Bosnia. What about reconciliation radio?

How can the international community foster education via the mass media with respect to prejudice, ethnocentrism, and conflict resolution? Leaders like the extremists in the former Yugoslavia reap political gain from stirring intense hatred among their people. The world is full of ethnic entrepreneurs and skillful demagogues putting acid on the scars, playing on ethnocentric sentiments for their own political purposes, and utilizing electronic media to get their messages across. By doing so they gain power, wealth, and high status. Is it possible to go over the heads of such leaders to educate their publics directly about paths to conflict resolution? After all, it is the rank-and-file citizenry that absorbs the terrible beating of these wars, not the leadership.

Can television and radio help in preventing or coping with deadly conflict within nations? What would be involved in such education? First and foremost, conveying the consequences of continuing on the path of hatred and violence. Television and radio could illuminate slaughter in various areas, both nearby and far away, where ethnocentric violence has gone unchecked and where the consequences for all participants have been far more dreadful than envisioned in the initial phase when wishful thinking predominated. Let adversaries see the disastrous course they are on now, one that others have fol-lowed, and how much worse it can get the [...] ther it is pursued. Let them not be shielded [...] the consequences of atrocities in the way [...] Germans were in the events of the Holoca[...]

Conflict areas need independent tele[...] and radio news channels broadcasting thr[...] out the region. Mass media communicatio[...] only about the consequences of ethnocentric violence, but also about the possibilities for conflict resolution, and the willingness of the international community to help, should become a vital component of the problem-solving machinery in ethnic conflicts.

Television and radio can also be useful in conflict resolution by clarifying how others have succeeded in achieving it: documentaries, for example, on the experiences of Western Europe after World War II, or programs on the transformation of Germany and Japan without revenge by the United States. Let those in hot spots learn about the best of what conflict resolution, civilized human relationships, and democratic institutions have done in the twentieth century and could do for them in the twenty-first.

In principle, it should even be possible to establish a nongovernmental International Educational Telecommunications System that would effectively link organizations in many nations to sources of creative audiovisual learning materials. There could be an active pool of material over a wide range of content and format generated for a variety of purposes, mainly on peace and democracy, in rich and poor countries alike.

Financing might be provided to the new system through a mix of governmental and private funds from many nations. The highest standards could be ensured by an international commission of impeccable standing. The system would both provide venture capital for creative programming and carefully select the best available material from the world's broadcasting storehouse.

It might present basic concepts, processes, and institutions on a level perhaps comparable to that of National Public Radio in the United States or the British Broadcasting Corporation in the United Kingdom. This could be done in a variety of languages and adapted to many cultures. In a relatively short time, it might be feasible to enhance the level of understanding throughout the world of what is involved in democracy and its potential benefits for all — especially in providing reliable ways of coping with ubiquitous human conflicts without resorting to mass violence.

CONCLUDING COMMENT

Let me close with a crucial question for the human future: Can human groups achieve internal cohesion, self-respect, and adaptive effectiveness without promoting hatred and violence? Altogether, we need to strengthen research and education on child development, prejudice, ethnocentrism, and conflict resolution to find out. We must generate new knowledge and explore vigorously the application of such knowledge to urgent problems in contemporary society.

Nowhere should the responsibility for promoting social tolerance be taken more seriously than among leaders of nations — not only in government but in business and media and other powerful institutions. They bear a heavy responsibility, all too often evaded, for utilizing the vehicles of mass education for constructive purposes. They can convey in words and actions an agenda for cooperation, caring, and decent human relations.

There is little in our very long history as a species to prepare us for this world we have suddenly made. Perhaps we cannot cope with it — witness Bosnia and Rwanda. Still, it is not too late for a paradigm shift in our outlook toward human conflict. Perhaps it is something like learning that the earth is not flat. Such a shift in child development and education throughout the world might at long last make it possible for human groups to learn to live together in peace and mutual benefit.

David C. Hamburg

President

Carnegie Corporation
of New York

Will Schools Ever Get Better?

Enrollments are up, money is tight—but there's hope

Americans are fed up with their public schools. Businesses complain that too many job applicants can't read, write, or do simple arithmetic. Parents fear that the schools have become violent cesspools where gangs run amok and that teachers are more concerned with their pensions than their classrooms. Economists fret that a weak school system is hurting the ability of the U.S. to compete in the global economy. And despite modest improvements in test scores, U.S. students still rank far behind most of their international peers in science and math.

And the woes of public schools may be about to get even deeper. Over the rest of the decade, the nation's schools will face a financial crunch that will be far worse than almost anyone had projected. Tight budgets will mean overcrowded classrooms, less individual attention, deferred maintenance, and elimination of such "frills" as music, art, and sports. And schools will have difficulty paying for the computers and other information technology needed to prepare young Americans for the new workplace.

Public schools have frittered away vast sums without much visible improvement in student performance

---

At the root of this school squeeze is an enrollment boom that has caught educators by surprise. Originally, the student population was supposed to rise by some 3 million students in the 1990s (chart). Instead, immigration and higher-than-expected birthrates have fueled a student rush that will add more than 7 million students to the schools by the year 2000, with more to come after that. The school population is rising as fast as it did during the baby-boom years of the 1960s.

But this is not the 1960s, and overcrowded school systems can't expect big wads of tax dollars to bail them out. There's no help in sight from Congress, where Republicans have already proposed cutting federal spending on education. And times are tight on the state and local level as well: Schools already take more than one-third of state and local spending on goods and services, and taxpayers are increasingly unwilling to pour

billions more into a system that is widely perceived as having failed.

Indeed, the schools are in large part responsible for their own financial problems. Only 52% of every school dollar actually gets into the classroom in a typical large school district, according to Bruce Cooper of Fordham University, working with the accounting firm Coopers & Lybrand (chart, page 19).

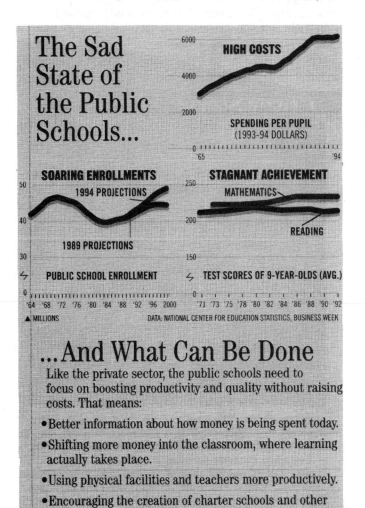

The Sad State of the Public Schools...

HIGH COSTS

SPENDING PER PUPIL (1993-94 DOLLARS)

SOARING ENROLLMENTS
1994 PROJECTIONS
1989 PROJECTIONS
PUBLIC SCHOOL ENROLLMENT

STAGNANT ACHIEVEMENT
MATHEMATICS
READING
TEST SCORES OF 9-YEAR-OLDS (AVG.)

▲ MILLIONS   DATA: NATIONAL CENTER FOR EDUCATION STATISTICS, BUSINESS WEEK

...And What Can Be Done

Like the private sector, the public schools need to focus on boosting productivity and quality without raising costs. That means:

● Better information about how money is being spent today.

● Shifting more money into the classroom, where learning actually takes place.

● Using physical facilities and teachers more productively.

● Encouraging the creation of charter schools and other alternatives to the current system in order to increase competition.

DATA: BUSINESS WEEK

How Public Education Costs Stack Up

Spending by all levels of government, fiscal year 1995*

	BILLIONS OF DOLLARS
HEALTH CARE	$450
EDUCATION	345
ELEMENTARY/HIGH SCHOOL 267	
POSTSECONDARY 78	
SOCIAL SECURITY	336
DEFENSE	272
CRIMINAL JUSTICE	100
HIGHWAYS	80

*Estimated   DATA: OMB, COMMERCE DEPARTMENT, BUSINESS WEEK

And the schools have frittered away vast sums without much visible improvement in student performance. Per-pupil expenditures, adjusted for inflation, have risen more than 25% over the past 10 years. "A lot of money being spent in the schools is wasted," says Eric A. Hanushek, an education economist at the University of Rochester. "What we do know is the problem of inefficient use of resources seems to be everywhere."

If there is a problem with bloated and inefficient government, public education must be a big part of it. The country spends nearly $270 billion a year on public elementary and secondary education, making that one of the largest government expenditures (table, this page). And the 6 million people working for the public schools account for about 30% of all civilian government employment.

Schools, long used to speaking the language of education—curriculum, test scores, standards—need to start talking about the issues of cost and efficiency. U.S. corporations have become more productive by getting rid of needless layers of management and focusing instead on improving efficiency on the factory floor or the back office. In the same way, public schools have to get more of their funds to the place where the process of learning actually occurs: the classroom. "One of the key concepts shared between the best schools and the best companies is a clear focus on the customer," says Katherine M. Hudson, chief executive of W. H. Brady Co., a Milwaukee manufacturer. "In the schools, that's the student."

Public education can benefit from the hard lessons learned by U.S. corporations in recent years. For one, it's now drummed into the bones of every successful corporate manager that productivity and quality cannot be improved without accurate information about current operations. But that's a place where the schools fall down badly. The vast majority of school districts cannot answer the obvious question: How much money is actually getting to the classroom? "We keep pumping in more and more money, but we don't know where it goes when it gets into the system," says Cooper. "It's like swinging an ax in the dark."

The second lesson from the private sector is the importance of competition, which pushes schools to innovate and to break down rigid regulations and work rules. That can mean a voucher system, as in Milwaukee, where low-income parents can get money to send their children to private school. Or it can mean allowing parents, teachers, and organizations such as universities to set up "charter" schools—new public schools, but outside the existing bureaucracy. A new study by economist Caroline M. Hoxby of Harvard University shows that the availability of more school choices can lead to lower spending and higher student achievement. Indeed, competition can accomplish the goal of improving education without the need for top-down standards or rules.

BREAKING POINT. And the schools must learn to make better use of their physical and human resources, just as Corporate America has. Rather than building expensive new schools, overcrowded school districts need to consider alternatives such as shifting to year-round classes or using converted surplus office or retail space. And the almost 3 million teachers in the public school systems can be used more effectively. For example, educational research shows clearly that spending on early education can pay off big—yet high schools still have an average pupil-teacher ratio 19% lower than elementary schools. "We need to think about using those teaching resources differently," says Lawrence O. Picus, an education specialist at the University of Southern California.

Certainly, business as usual is no longer an option. The combination of soaring enrollments and tight finances means that pupil-teacher ratios are on the rise for the first time in the postwar era. And the school squeeze will hit some states harder than others. A new analysis by BUSINESS WEEK shows that the states facing the toughest school squeeze over the rest of the decade are California, New Jersey, and Maryland (chart, next page). These are states where weak economic growth is combined with fast-growing student populations.

As enrollments rise, schools across the country will come under increasing pressure to curtail spending. Take Prince William County, Va., where hopes for a new source of tax revenue were dashed when Walt Disney Co. abandoned plans to build a historical theme park there. Student enrollments have risen by 12% over the past five years even as the county's economy has slowed, forcing the county to cut its school budget by 6% over the next three years. "We're now at the point where cuts will start to affect our instructional programs," says Robert A. Ferrebee, associate superintendent for management at the county school district. Pupil-teacher ratios have already risen, and some other cuts being contemplated include shortening the high school day, imposing user fees for high school sports, and cutting out elementary music.

"PRETTY GRIM." Some areas have become the victims of their own success. Vancouver, Wash., a largely blue-collar town of some 65,000, has become a mecca for young families, drawn by the plethora of jobs at Hewlett-Packard Co. and other high-tech plants in the area. As a result, the school population had skyrocketed, compelling the town to spend nearly $60 million in 1990 to build three new schools and renovate five old ones. By 1994, the new schools were already overcrowded, and voters

Where the School Squeeze Will Hurt the Most

The School Squeeze Index measures the projected gap between the growth in school spending and the growth in real personal income, 1994-2000*

CALIFORNIA
NEW JERSEY
MARYLAND
ALASKA
HAWAII
DELAWARE
NEW YORK
CONNECTICUT
WASHINGTON
MICHIGAN
NORTH CAROLINA
VIRGINIA

SCHOOL SQUEEZE INDEX

0   2   4   6   8   10   12   14

*Assuming a 2% annual increase in real spending per pupil

DATA: NATIONAL CENTER FOR EDUCATION STATISTICS, DRI/McGRAW-HILL, BUSINESS WEEK

approved an additional $135 million in school bonds. But with enrollment expected to rise 30% over the next seven years and the state school-construction fund running dry, that may not be enough. "Even with the financial commitment the community has already made, we can hardly keep up," says Tom Hagley, assistant to Vancouver's superintendent of schools. "We're bursting at the seams."

And a flood of immigrants is imposing enormous costs on the school system in places such as Southern California, New York City, and South Florida. For example, school enrollment in Dade County, Fla.—which includes Miami and Miami Beach—has gone up by 40% over the past 10 years, far exceeding the growth in population. The reason? The retirees who once made up a big piece of the county's population are "re-retiring" to locales farther north and being replaced by young families, including many immigrants. As a result, Dade's school budget has soared 60% since 1989.

The financial problems for the schools go far beyond the enrollment growth. Many school districts across the country have deferred essential maintenance on their buildings. According to a new report from the General Accounting Office, the U.S. would have to spend $112 billion to repair or upgrade schools. That's certainly true in Escondido Union School District in northern San Diego County, where 30% of the district's students are in portable classrooms—relocatable double-wide trailers with leaky roofs and holes in the floors. "It's pretty grim here when it rains," says Jane Gawronski, superintendent of the district. Nevertheless, on Mar. 7, Escondido

voters rejected a $52.5 million bond issue that would have paid for renovations and new buildings.

In addition, schools face the expensive prospect of moving into the computer age. That includes not simply the computers—which the schools can often get relatively cheaply—but the wiring and telephone lines required to support them and the space to put them in. And as Corporate America has found, the continuing costs of software and technical support for information technology far exceed the initial investment. "It's tough enough for schools to get the initial money, let alone plan for upgrading," says Darryl Toney, who manages Oracle Systems Corp.'s educational programs.

BLACK HOLES. The school squeeze is forcing districts to make hard choices as to where to spend their money. In recent years, public policy—on both the federal and state level—has emphasized helping disadvantaged students and districts. Out of the $20 billion that the federal government provides for elementary and secondary education, the bulk goes for disadvantaged or handicapped students. And federal law requires schools to provide costly special education to a growing number of students.

Also, prodded by the courts, New Jersey, Texas, Michigan, Missouri, and others have passed reforms in school financing to bring up spending in the poorest school districts, sometimes at the expense of more well-to-do areas. For example, Michigan decently shifted from relying on local property taxes to finance schools—which favors the high-income districts—to using a statewide sales tax. The state also capped spending growth in the richer districts to give their poorer cousins a chance to catch up. Birmingham School District, one of the state's wealthiest districts, will only be able to boost per-pupil spending by 1.6% this year, while Shelby Public Schools in low-income Oceana County will be able to raise spending by 6%.

Still, while more equitable financing may be a good start, it's definitely not enough. Over the past 20 years, a virtual army of academic researchers has examined the question of whether spending more money raises student performance. The result? At best, simply throwing money at the schools has a marginal impact. The money has to be spent well for it to matter.

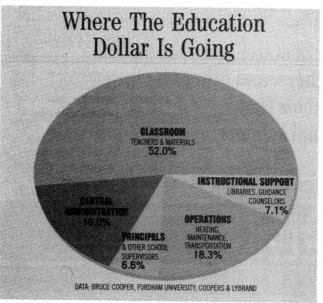

Where The Education Dollar Is Going

CLASSROOM
TEACHERS & MATERIALS
52.0%

INSTRUCTIONAL SUPPORT
LIBRARIES, GUIDANCE COUNSELORS
7.1%

CENTRAL ADMINISTRATION
16.0%

OPERATIONS
HEATING, MAINTENANCE, TRANSPORTATION
18.3%

PRINCIPALS
& OTHER SCHOOL SUPERVISORS
6.6%

DATA: BRUCE COOPER, FORDHAM UNIVERSITY; COOPERS & LYBRAND

Indeed, many voters believe that their school dollars are going into a black hole. "Virtually all school districts lack credibility inside and outside the district," says Sheree Speakman, partner at Coopers & Lybrand.

So with money tight, the first priority is to get control of spending. As a result, more and more school districts are moving to "site-based reporting," which was first developed by Cooper of Fordham University and is now being nationally distributed by Coopers & Lybrand and the U.S. Chamber of Commerce. This accounting system shows where the money is going: instruction vs. support services, or central administration vs. individual schools (chart, previous page).

Site-based reporting has been applied to more than 50 school districts nationwide, including New York City, where it showed that out of total spending of almost $8,000 per pupil per year, only $44 was budgeted for classroom materials. And the new system gives school districts benchmarks for seeing where their expenditures are excessive or falling short.

For example, when the Nashville public schools crunched the numbers, they discovered—much to their surprise that they were spending 24% of their budget on operations such as maintenance, compared with 18% for a typical large school district (chart, previous page). The result? A program to bring down operating costs. Now the district is using site-based reporting to help set spending policy. "We have a goal of increasing yearly the percentage of our operational budget that goes into direct instructional spending," says Edward Taylor, assistant superintendent for the Metro Nashville Public Schools.

FEW REWARDS. The new system also shows what parents have always suspected: Even within the same district, some schools do a much better job than others in using money wisely. One school may get 30% to the classroom, while just six blocks away, another school gets 80% to the classroom. With this information, "you can target the children who aren't getting the education," says Cooper. "You can do that kind of precision bombing because you know where the money is."

And the frontline production workers—the teachers—may also benefit, if the improved information is used to increase the amount spent in the classroom. That's why teacher unions are cautiously supportive of the new system. "This will get us a long way toward understanding how to be more efficient," says Jewell Gould, director of research for the American Federation of Teachers.

Certainly, current funding can be used more efficiently. For example, school districts often put up expensive new buildings when existing space could be used better. About 1,200 schools nationwide—mainly in California—now run year-round, increasing student capacity by 30% to 50%. And in Minnesota, some new charter schools are saving money by sharing facilities with the local housing authority or recreation center and by reusing existing retail space.

And teaching resources can also be directed more effectively. It's well-known, for example, that the early years of schooling are critical: A student who slips behind when reading is being taught has little chance to catch up. However, most school districts direct far more resources to high schools, with their athletic programs and specialized courses. That's why Missouri

structured its aid program so that districts have a financial incentive to reduce class size in the lower grades.

And within schools, new programs are showing how to reallocate existing money to better uses. For example, Success for All, a program developed by Robert Slavin of Johns Hopkins University, uses intensive tutoring to keep students from falling behind in the early grades. Now being used in about 200 schools in 20 states, it costs about $1,500 per student—but Slavin points out that poor districts, which need the program the most, can cover most of those costs by using funds that schools already get from the federal government for disadvantaged kids.

But even when such programs work, they are hard to sustain, because they typically demand increased effort from teachers and principals and more parental involvement. Moreover, schools have few incentives, financial or otherwise, for better performance. "People who do a good job get no rewards, compared to people who do a mediocre or poor job," says Hanushek.

BUREAUCRACY BLASTERS. One possibility is to create alternatives to the current public schools and let competition create pressure for both educational and financial reform. At one extreme are vouchers allowing students to attend the private or public school of their choice. The only voucher system now in use is in Milwaukee. But five other states are currently considering similar programs, focused mainly on low-income families. "When targeted at low-income families, folks who had been wary—minorities and Democrats—have been coming out of the woodwork," according to Jeanne Allen, president of the Washington-based Center for Education Reform, a pro-voucher group.

An increasing number of states are allowing parents, teachers, and others to set up "charter" schools that compete with traditional schools

---

But proposals to use vouchers often stir up enormous political opposition, as does privatization—allowing private profit-making companies to run public schools. The fear is that private schools would skim the best students off, leaving the public schools with the dregs.

Instead, an increasing number of states—including Minnesota, Michigan, and Massachusetts—are encouraging a more limited form of competition by allowing parents, teachers, and other groups to set up "charter" schools. A charter school is a public school, in the sense that it has to meet certain standards and not discriminate in admissions. At the same time, it's independent of the traditional school system.

Charter schools typically receive funding from the state for each pupil. But because they must attract students who are not obligated to attend, they have an incentive to spend the money in ways that will actually improve education. And charter schools also benefit by running leaner. "We can get by" on less money, says Nancy Miller, a teacher at the Minnesota Country School, a charter school in its first year in LeSeuer, Minn.,

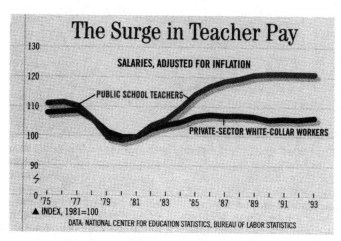

The Surge in Teacher Pay

SALARIES, ADJUSTED FOR INFLATION

PUBLIC SCHOOL TEACHERS

PRIVATE-SECTOR WHITE-COLLAR WORKERS

130
120
110
100
90
0
'75 '77 '79 '81 '83 '85 '87 '89 '91 '93
▲ INDEX, 1981=100

DATA: NATIONAL CENTER FOR EDUCATION STATISTICS, BUREAU OF LABOR STATISTICS

"because we don't build up all the bureaucracy traditional public schools do." With no administrators, Minnesota Country School can afford to spend more on new technology.

"INCENTIVES." And charter schools can also serve as a catalyst, pushing the existing public schools to offer new programs and improve existing ones. That's what happened in Boston last year, with the passage of a state law allowing charter schools. Faced with the unsettling prospect of competition, the Boston teacher's union agreed to the creation of new "pilot" schools, free of union and school board rules. "Charter schools provide new incentives for school districts to become more responsive and entrepreneurial," says Joseph Nathan, director of the Center for School Change at the University of Minnesota.

Competitive pressure may also lead to increased teacher productivity, which is critical in light of the rise in teacher salaries (chart). That's what's happening in Wilkensburg, Pa., a suburb of Pittsburgh, where Alternative Public Schools, a private corporation, has offered to run an elementary school at the same per-pupil cost but for longer hours and more days per year. The counterproposal from the local teacher's union: They would work 10 additional days a year, without any increase in pay.

In some cases, entire school districts are remaking themselves. Take Calvert County Public Schools in Maryland, where enrollment is skyrocketing at a time when state funding is tight. The traditional school model won't work, according to William Moloney, superintendent of the district. Instead, the district plans to restructure its elementary schools: Teachers will stay with the same kids two years, and schools will strive for a climate of work, discipline, and values. "Those things don't cost a lot, but they're tremendously important," says Moloney. "These changes will bring us more education for less money."

The U.S. needs to encourage these sorts of initiatives. Is there a risk that some of these new programs will go astray? Sure. But just as beleaguered American companies were able to increase the quality and lower the cost of what they made, so, too, can the public schools learn how to provide a better education for America's children.

By Michael J. Mandel in New York, with Richard A. Melcher in Milwaukee, Dori Jones Yang in Seattle, Mike McNamee in Washington, and bureau reports

FULL-SERVICE SCHOOLS: IDEAL AS REALITY

IN HER STUDY OF SCHOOLS THAT offer an extensive array of "add-on" social service programs, author Joy Dryfoos found two particularly outstanding models of service to their communities. Located at opposite ends of the country — New York City and Modesto, California — these schools may differ in the structure of their services, but they have in common the fact that both were created "from scratch," with new principals and new facilities, and are situated in poor neighborhoods with large ethnic and immigrant populations.

Salome Ureña

Located in upper Manhattan, Washington Heights' new middle school, IS 218, or Salome Ureña (SUMA), named after a Latina poet, is the serendipitous product of two resources that came together in the late 1980s: a round of capital spending by the city's School Construction Authority and a commitment by the Children's Aid Society (CAS), one of the city's oldest and largest nonprofit social service agencies.

The new building was designed to serve as a community center as well as a school, with such features as "zoned" areas, outdoor lighting to assure safe accessibility at night for community functions, and air conditioning as an antidote to New York's sweltering summers. The innovative educational structure of four "academies" not only gives students an early anchor for their lives, but it also provides a natural framework for after-school programs, which, in addition to offering traditional tutoring, direct students to special projects in their areas of interest, from the performing arts to business.

From the outset, SUMA acknowl-edged the strong ethnic base of the community, and its programs consequently reflect the population's particular needs. Dominican community organizations were consulted in planning after-school and family programs; the celebration of the Dominican national holiday was occasion for a school fair. Language training beyond the middle school curriculum is multidimensional: students and parents have taught local precinct police officers Spanish, while parents are enrolled in English as a Second Language classes at the family institute.

While the value of an institution such as SUMA seems obvious, the establishment of this "full-service" school came about only through an extraordinary level of commitment and cooperation among a voluntary agency, a local school district, and community-based organizations. Its success has depended in large measure on the effectiveness of an unusual administrative structure in which responsibilities are shared by the school principal and the CAS community school site director.

Hanshaw

Another approach to full service was employed by Hanshaw Middle School in Modesto, a northern California city of 175,000 whose socioeconomic foundation of traditional agriculture has evolved into modern agribusiness, its changing labor force reflecting a new ethnic mix. The vision of its founding principal Chuck Vidal, Hanshaw was designed after he conducted a door-to-door survey of residents in the disadvantaged neighborhood where a new school was to be built. Among the population of poor Hispanics and recent immigrants from Cambodia and Laos, many students were deficient in English. Yet family ambitions ran high: Parents wanted their children to go to a school that would put them on the college track. In 1991 Hanshaw started up in its new $13 million campus-like complex, featuring specialized facilities for music, arts, and crafts as well as auditoriums and a gymnasium. Vidal installed an interdisciplinary curriculum that features team teaching and cooperative learning among students. Their college goals are reinforced by links to several campuses in the California State University system, each university supporting a designated student group and welcoming the students to campus visits.

From the start, Hanshaw's primary focus was quality education. As student and community needs became clearer, social services were added, along with a school nurse, a mental health clinician, and aides to assist the immigrant populations. But Hanshaw had no coordinated approach to providing full services until it secured two operational grants from California's Healthy Start program, which requires a 25 percent match by applicant localities.

With its state grant complemented by resources from community agencies, Hanshaw set a budget of $400,000 per year for three years, concentrating its resources on a center for health and dental care and an interagency case management team linking students and families to a variety of social service agencies. Hanshaw appears to be living up to its full-service concept; the key measure of success will be whether its first graduates reach the ranks of higher education.

[**Editor's note:** See Annual Editions article 11, "Schools That Do More Than Teach," for more information on Joy G. Dryfoos.]

From *Carnegie Quarterly*, Fall 1994/Winter 1995, p. 9. Reprinted by permission of the Carnegie Corporation of New York, 437 Madison Avenue, New York, NY 10022.

Unit 3

Answers

#14 Self-Discipline, Motivation, & Ability to interact with others

#15 "Human growth and Development", "environmental steward ship", and "Cultural and creative endeavors"

#16 Standards & Assessment

#17 New schools will open to supply the Demand for good education

#18 No single overarching reform can solve the problems of every school

Unit 4

19 To Encourage the growth of competent, caring, Loving and lovable people.

20 because they need Help from the community, Churches, Ect...

21 To Help them become smart & To Help them become good

22 In Attitudes & beliefs

23 For community & moral support

unit 5

#24 Setting out expectations clearly & explicitly.

#25 2,000 Students

#26 Teaches them to procrastinate & use all the warnings the can

#27 The teachers Attitude

Answers

Article #12

1) Preparing American youth for the 21st century

2) Most all Conventional practice in traditional JR. Highs, Intermediate & middle schools

Article #13

1) To Have outcomes

2) People Don't see much value in the Approach thats Being pushed. They Don't Relate them to their children.

Unit 2

Answers

Article # 7 A's

1) Increased population
2) 1.5%

Article #8

1) It Doesn't capture there intelectual or demonstrative
capasities, there care for others, to Imagine How
others think + feel, or to be prepared to speak up + Be Heard
2) Cultivating mental & moral Habits.

Article #9

1) Oct of 94 what was the count of public schools
2) There are no start up funds, No Building provided, no guarentee
the school district will support you, & Local unions make it
Tough to recruit teachers

Article #10

1) A private, profit For-profit onginazation that calls itself
th "National Teacher Corps" and recruits, trains and places recent
graduates from top colleges & universities to Make a 2yr commitment
to teach in poor inner-city & Rural schools.
2) They Rely Heavily on judging people & Are not Realy Qualified to

Article #11

1) School Based Health Clinics
2) A wide Range of Help from Crisis intervention for
families under the greatest strain to social skills training
for young people

unit 1   Answers

① I.1 yes
  .2 Having the contact occur under favorable conditions
  II .1 The 60's Baby boom
  2) Clasrooms: Teachers + Materials
  III Volentary Agencies, a local school District,
      and Community - Based organizations
  IV To teach Key words + phrases that everyone needs
     to know to understand what you read or see on
     the television.
② I.1 More than 90million
  2) Because the advertizement on +V & Bill boards
     show you every way you can get wealthy accept
     by Going to school

  VI 1) They believed prayer would improve the behavior
     of students.
  2) what is the biggest problem Facing Local public
     schools? Lack of Disaplin

Public School Lifts Kids Off New York's Mean Streets

Pairing a curriculum that stresses general knowledge with students from one of the poorest neighborhoods in the Bronx, the Mohegan School is breaking the mold in public education. But critics of the program claim it is 'Eurocentric,' makes no allowances for differences among students and encourages passivity.

Stephen Goode

Tracy Torres is standing before her first-grade class, asking her 20 students to name an animal that eats meat. "An alligator," shouts one boy, bouncing on the edge of his seat with his hand raised high.

"What do we call animals that eat meat?" Torres asks, without a pause. "Carnivores," the class says in unison.

"What do we call animals like elephants that eat leaves and grass?"

"Herbivores!"

"And what are animals that eat meat and vegetables?" she asks.

"Omnivores!" the class says, triumphantly.

Omnivore may be an unusual word in the vocabulary of a first-grader anywhere, but it is even more surprising that these are first-graders at the Mohegan School in the Bronx, located in one of the most down-and-out sections of New York City. A bleak area of run-down housing blocks and trash-strewn lots, the neighborhood has the highest percentage of reported child abuse in the New York school system. Crack and other drugs are rampant, and "Most Wanted in the Bronx" posters are taped to the streetlight poles. All of Mohegan's students come from poor families, and many are in foster homes.

But despite all this, the school has developed one of the best records among New York public schools in recent years. Last year, Mohegan student scores on standardized reading tests climbed by more than 13 percent, with a similar improvement in math scores.

That's a dramatic change from a decade ago, when many of Mohegan's 1,000 or so students didn't even make it to high school. Now, Mohegan regularly places students in local parochial high schools (which are widely regarded as superior to their public counterparts), and one student recently was accepted at Brooklyn Technical, one of the most competitive public high schools in the city.

Students benefit *from shiny floors and pretty walls — and an overhauled staff.*

Mohegan's success can be attributed largely to its dynamic, hands-on principal, Jeffrey Litt, who has been running the school since June 1988. Litt is a maverick administrator who doesn't easily take no for an answer. "I would not want to be my own immediate supervisor," he says. At Mohegan, Litt is everywhere. During lunchtime, he helps the cafeteria staff serve food — his voice joining in the din of the large room where the students are fed in shifts. Dedication takes its toll. "I'm filled with Advil and antacid," he says jokingly. "I have a bottle of Maalox handy."

But it is the school's curriculum that separates it from all other public schools in the city as well as most throughout the nation. Three years ago, Mohegan adopted the Core Knowledge curriculum, a program that stresses vocabulary and general knowledge, in the belief that there are words, phrases and facts that every person needs to know to understand what he or she reads in the newspaper or sees on television. It is a program that goes against the grain of many current education theories, which stress multiculturalism and learning "skills" and condemn approaches that emphasize memorizing large amounts of information.

Litt first encountered Core Knowledge in 1991, more than two years after he'd arrived at Mohegan. At the instigation of longtime friend Carlos Medina — a senior fellow at the Center for Education Innovation at the Manhattan Institute — Litt attended a lecture by University of Virginia English Professor E.D. Hirsch, the man who originated the Core Knowledge idea.

For Litt, it was love at first sight. He regards Core Knowledge as "the great equalizer," a way of ensuring students can leave Mohegan and start high school on the same playing field as kids from more privileged families.

With disadvantaged, inner-city kids, he says, "you can't assume there will be museums on the weekends for them, or that there will be a library at home or magazine subscriptions. Don't assume they're getting nursery rhymes the rest of us hear at our parent's knees, because they probably are not."

In anything kids read throughout their lives, says Litt, the authors will assume the readers possess a certain amount of knowledge. As an example, he cites an article on the Supreme Court. To comprehend what is read, a reader must know what that court is and what its functions are. The reader also must know something about the nature of the federal legal system, and who sits on the court.

"If I have a student in my office who is generally well-behaved and he has done something wrong, I want him to be able to understand when I say, 'What are you, Dr. Jekyll and Mr. Hyde?'" So the students read the works of Robert Louis Stevenson as well as other classics.

Teachers are careful to develop themes in the curriculum and to help the students clearly see the connections between different kinds of information. Thus, when they take up the Industrial Revolution, they read Charles Dickens' *Oliver Twist*, which gives them a vivid picture of life in 19th-century London and of an underclass victimized by the excesses of that society. To learn about the differences between the House and Senate, the students perform a musical skit about the Constitutional Convention and the debates that went into creating the two houses of Congress.

What Mohegan is doing, Litt claims, is "creating an educated child."

Critics of Core Knowledge claim that it is "Eurocentric" and has no place in a school like Mohegan, with its large minority student body. But Litt says that simply isn't true. Core Knowledge makes up only 50 percent of the curriculum — which leaves the faculty free to play with the other half and include information on Latino and African-American history and culture, for example.

And Litt has instituted what he calls an "individualized education plan" to counter another criticism of Core Knowledge — that it makes no allowance for individual differences among students and their varying interests and abilities. Mohegan teachers meet Saturday mornings to develop ways to deal with individual students. No single student is expected to master the information presented in class in exactly the same way another student will master it.

Says the Manhattan Institute's Medina, "The end result is that they have a sense of power over words and meanings they otherwise would not have. They are empowered with knowledge. The kids are exposed to what made America what it is."

Core Knowledge critics also claim the curriculum encourages passivity: Students have little opportunity to exercise "creative input." But Litt insists that anyone who spends five minutes at the school would be hard-pressed to find evidence of passivity. "Creative noise is good," he says, noting that Mohegan students tend to be loudly competitive — especially when playing "Jeopardy" in class. And when students stumble over words when reading aloud, or fail to recognize a word, the other students speak up quickly.

How did Litt turn Mohegan around so dramatically? Changing the school's atmosphere was the big first step. When Litt first arrived there six years ago, the hallways reeked of urine and there was graffiti everywhere. A fire had damaged the principal's office. Litt rolled up his sleeves and set about to help clean up the mess. These days, the buffed marble floor of the lobby at Mohegan shines, and the halls and stairwells are freshly painted in bright colors.

But the changes have not been merely cosmetic. In the two years before Litt's arrival, Mohegan went through five acting principals. Morale was low, and teachers often called in sick. It was "the worst teaching staff

in the system," says Litt, made up largely of ineffective, burned-out people. During the next two years he got rid of three-quarters of the staff, hiring a number of replacements right out of college (and many of them without degrees in education). Litt was after young women and men in their 20s and 30s who would be open to the experiment and willing to put in extra hours to make the school successful.

There was more. Litt says he "begged for permission" to extend Mohegan, then a K-6 school, through the seventh and eighth grades — and got it. Litt didn't want the training he hoped Mohegan would give its students to be undermined by the standard junior high school experience in the Bronx, which he compares to a "mugging."

Days begin with singing "The Star-Spangled Banner," followed by the African-American song "Lift Every Voice and Sing" and the Puerto Rican anthem, "La Borinquena."

Classroom walls have signs that read, "Don't Call Out, Raise Your Hand" and "Follow Directions." Students invariably are polite to visitors, and they line up in an orderly fashion to leave classrooms. The sense of discipline is central to the school's success. "It is the way we take the street-kid stuff out of them," says Litt, adding, "the only exposure my kids are going to have to the police is as police officers, maybe as attorneys.

> Litt 'begged for permission' to extend Mohegan through the seventh and eighth grades — and got it. He didn't want the Mohegan training to be undermined by the standard junior high school experience in the Bronx, which he compares to a 'mugging.'

They won't be out there committing crime."

A big dose of self-esteem is part of

the Mohegan experience, and Litt and the faculty don't stint on praise. "I tell them, 'You're the best. You're Mohegan,'" says Litt, and adds, "We don't hesitate to say I love you." Clotheslines span the school's hallways and classrooms dangling student art, book reviews and other projects. "We're the kitchen refrigerator here," explains Litt. "They probably can't put anything on display at home. So we put it on display for them."

Part of the program he has brought to Mohegan has sixth-, seventh- and eighth-graders participating in career oriented programs such as "law and government," in which professionals such as a district attorney and a Bronx Supreme Court judge come to the school and talk to the students. Pupils enrolled in the "Health and Medicine" class go to St. Barnabas Hospital every Monday, where they are rotated among departments to learn about health care jobs.

The downside at Mohegan is that come the eighth grade and graduation, students must leave, and many of them will go to high schools in the Bronx where disorder and violence are the norm. Parents report to Litt that their children are prey to students who want their sneakers, money or bus passes, and their vulnerability haunts Litt, who hopes to expand Mohegan to include the high school grades.

While much of Mohegan's success depends on Litt's commitment and enormous energy, Medina says that the school's achievements can be duplicated elsewhere. Good teachers and a dedicated principal are important, he says, but so is a curriculum "that excites them to do things out of the ordinary."

The excitement has begun to spread. Teachers and administrators at six other New York elementary schools — three in Manhattan and one each in the Bronx, Brooklyn and

Queens — are interested in following Mohegan's example and adopting the curriculum — despite nay-saying among skeptical principals and superintendents. "You certainly take your gibes from other administrators," says Litt, explaining their resistance to new ideas. "You make people angry. Success is not well-received."

Meanwhile, on walls near Litt's office, framed awards herald the school's success, including an "A+" award from President Bush for "breaking the mold" in education. Letters from some of the many Mohegan visitors are posted, too, for the kids to see. Says one of the letters, "The most striking feature is how genuinely happy your students are to be in school."

Says Litt with pride, "You can look around here, and you wouldn't believe you're in the New York City public school system."

Core Knowledge: A Stroke of Genius

Core Knowledge is the brainchild of E.D. Hirsch, a University of Virginia English professor and the author of the 1987 best-seller *Cultural Literacy: What Every American Needs to Know*.

Hirsch followed his widely discussed book with *What Your First Grader Needs to Know* and *What Your Second Grader Needs to Know*. He also set up the Charlottesville, Va.-based Core Knowledge Foundation to help spread his views and make available information on Core Knowledge.

Hirsch's notion is simple: He argues that there is a body of knowledge that children should master to join the ranks of the educated, and it is the duty of schools to convey that knowledge to students.

The Core Knowledge curriculum includes a lot of emphasis on vocabulary, as well as on idiomatic expressions such as "on tenterhooks" and "you can't judge a book by its cover." Hirsch believes students should gain familiarity with topics such as world civilization, American civilization, language arts, geography, mathematics and the natural sciences.

No educational theorist, Hirsch leaves the details of teaching up to the teachers who adopt Core Knowledge. In 1990, Three Oaks Elementary School in Ft. Myers, Fla., was the first to do so. Since then, approximately 150 schools around the country have taken up Core Knowledge, and more plan to introduce the program. For many who use the curriculum, says Carlos Medina of the Manhattan Institute, "It is the cutting edge in education, because they see the students mastering a body of material and happy that they are mastering it."

— SG

AMERICA SKIPS SCHOOL

Why we talk so much
about education and do so little

Benjamin R. Barber

Benjamin R. Barber is Whitman Professor of Political Science and Director of the Whitman Center at Rutgers University and the author of many books including Strong Democracy *(1984),* An Aristocracy of Everyone *(1992), and* Jihad Versus McWorld *(Times Books, 1995).*

On September 8, the day most of the nation's children were scheduled to return to school, the Department of Education Statistics issued a report, commissioned by Congress, on adult literacy and numeracy in the United States. The results? More than 90 million adult Americans lacked simple literacy. Fewer than 20 percent of those surveyed could compare two metaphors in a poem; not 4 percent could calculate the cost of carpeting at a given price for a room of a given size, using a calculator. As the DOE report was being issued, as if to echo its findings, two of the nation's largest school systems had delayed their openings: in New York,. to remove asbestos from aging buildings; in Chicago, because of a battle over the budget.

Inspired by the report and the delays, pundits once again began chanting the familiar litany of the education crisis. We've heard it all many times before: 130,000 children bring guns along with their pencils and books to school each morning; juvenile arrests for murder increased by 85 percent from 1987 to 1991; more than 3,000 youngsters will drop out today and every day for the rest of the school year, until about 600,000 are lost by June—in many urban schools, perhaps half the enrollment. A lot of the dropouts will end up in prison, which is a surer bet for young black males than college: one in four will pass through the correctional system, and at least two out of three of those will be dropouts.

In quiet counterpoint to those staggering facts is another set of statistics: teachers make less than accountants, architects, doctors, lawyers, engineers, judges, health professionals, auditors, and surveyors. They can earn higher

THE YOUNG, WITH THEIR KEEN NOSES FOR HYPOCRISY, ARE IN FACT ADEPT READERS—BUT NOT OF BOOKS. WHAT THEY READ SO ACUTELY ARE THE SOCIAL SIGNALS EMANATING FROM THE WORLD IN WHICH THEY WILL HAVE TO MAKE A LIVING

salaries teaching in Berlin, Tokyo, Ottawa, or Amsterdam than in New York or Chicago. American children are in school only about 180 days a year, as against 240 days or more for children in Europe or Japan. The richest school districts (school financing is local, not federal) spend twice as much per student as poorer ones do. The poorer ones seem almost beyond help: children with venereal disease or AIDS (2.5 million adolescents annually contract a sexually transmitted disease), gangs in the schoolyard, drugs in the classroom, children doing babies instead of homework, playground firefights featuring Uzis and Glocks.

Clearly, the social contract that obliges adults to pay taxes so that children can be educated is in imminent danger of collapse. Yet for all the astonishing statistics, more astonishing still is that no one seems to be listening. The education crisis is kind of like violence on television: the worse it gets the more inert we become, and the more of it we require to rekindle our attention. We've had a "crisis" every dozen years or so at least since the launch of *Sputnik*, in 1957, when American schools were accused of falling behind the world standard in science education. Just ten years ago, the National Commission on Excellence in Education warned that America's pedagogical inattention was putting America "at risk." What the commission called "a rising tide of mediocrity" was imperiling "our very future as a Nation and a people." What was happening to education was an "act of war."

Since then, countless reports have been issued decrying the condition of our educational system, the DOE report being only the most recent. They have come from every side, Republican as well as Democrat, from the private sector as well as the public. Yet for all the talk, little happens. At times, the schools look more like they are being dismantled than rebuilt. How can this be? If Americans over a broad political spectrum regard education as vital, why has nothing been done?

I have spent thirty years as a scholar examining the nature of democracy, and even more as a citizen optimistically celebrating its possibilities, but today I am increasingly persuaded that the reason for the country's inaction is that Americans do not really care about education—the country has grown comfortable with the game of "let's pretend we care."

As America's educational system crumbles, the pundits, instead of looking for solutions, search busily for scapegoats. Some assail the teachers—those "Profscam" pedagogues trained in the licentious Sixties who, as aging hippies, are supposedly still subverting the schools—for producing a dire illiteracy. Others turn on the kids themselves, so that at the same moment as we are transferring our responsibilities to the shoulders of the next generation, we are blaming them for our own generation's most conspicuous failures. Allan Bloom was typical of the many recent critics who have condemned the young as vapid, lazy, selfish, complacent, self-seeking, materialistic, small-minded, apathetic, greedy, and, of course, illiterate. E. D. Hirsch in his *Cultural Literacy* and Diane Ravitch and Chester E. Finn Jr. in their *What Do Our Seventeen-Year-Olds Know?* have lambasted the schools, the teachers, and the children for betraying the adult generation from which they were to inherit, the critics seemed confident, a precious cultural legacy.

How this captious literature reeks of hypocrisy! How sanctimonious all the hand-wringing over still another "education crisis" seems. Are we ourselves really so literate? Are our kids stupid or smart for ignoring what we preach and copying what we practice? The young, with their keen noses for hypocrisy, are in fact adept readers—but not of books. They are society-smart rather than school-smart, and what they read so acutely are the social signals emanating from the world in which they will have to make a living. Their teachers in that world, the nation's true pedagogues, are television, advertising, movies, politics, and the celebrity domains they define. We prattle about deficient schools and the gullible youngsters they turn out, so vulnerable to the siren song of drugs, but think nothing of letting the advertisers into the classroom to fashion what an *Advertising Age* essay calls "brand and product loyalties through classroom-centered, peer-powered lifestyle patterning."

Our kids spend 900 hours a year in school (the ones who go to school) and from 1,200 to 1,800 hours a year in front of the television set. From which are they likely to learn more? Critics such as Hirsch and Ravitch want to find out what our seventeen-year-olds know, but it's really pretty simple: they know exactly what our forty-seven-year-olds know and teach them by example—on television, in the boardroom, around Washington, on Madison Avenue, in Hollywood. The very first lesson smart kids learn is that it is much more important to heed what society teaches implicitly by its deeds and reward structures than what school teaches explicitly in its lesson plans and civic sermons. Here is a test for adults that may help reveal what the kids see when they look at our world.

REAL-WORLD CULTURAL LITERACY

1. According to television, having fun in America means

   a) going blond
   b) drinking Pepsi
   c) playing Nintendo
   d) wearing Air Jordans
   e) reading Mark Twain

2. A good way to prepare for a high-income career and to acquire status in our society is to

   a) win a slam-dunk contest
   b) take over a company and sell off its assets
   c) start a successful rock band
   d) earn a professional degree
   e) become a kindergarten teacher

3. Book publishers are financially rewarded today for publishing

   a) mega-cookbooks
   b) mega–cat books
   c) megabooks by Michael Crichton
   d) megabooks by John Grisham
   e) mini-books by Voltaire

4. A major California bank that advertised "no previous credit history required" in inviting Berkeley students to apply for Visa cards nonetheless turned down one group of applicants because

   a) their parents had poor credit histories
   b) they had never held jobs
   c) they had outstanding student loans
   d) they were "humanities majors"

5. Colleges and universities are financially rewarded today for

   a) supporting bowl-quality football teams
   b) forging research relationships with large corporations
   c) sustaining professional programs in law and business
   d) stroking wealthy alumni
   e) fostering outstanding philosophy departments

6. Familiarity with *Henry IV, Part II* is likely to be of vital importance in

   a) planning a corporate takeover
   b) evaluating budget cuts in the Department of Education
   c) initiating a medical-malpractice lawsuit
   d) writing an impressive job résumé
   e) taking a test on what our seventeen-year-olds know

WE THINK NOTHING OF LETTING ADVERTISERS INTO THE CLASSROOM TO FASHION WHAT AN *ADVERTISING AGE* ESSAY CALLS "BRAND AND PRODUCT LOYALTIES THROUGH CLASSROOM-CENTERED, PEER-POWERED LIFESTYLE PATTERNING"

SCHOOLS CAN AND
SHOULD LEAD, BUT WHEN
THEY CONFRONT A SOCIETY
THAT IN EVERY INSTANCE TELLS
A STORY EXACTLY OPPOSITE
TO THE ONE THEY ARE TEACHING,
THEIR JOB BECOMES IMPOSSIBLE

7. To help the young learn that "history is a living thing," Scholastic, Inc., a publisher of school magazines and paperbacks, recently distributed to 40,000 junior and senior high-school classrooms

  a) a complimentary video of the award-winning series *The Civil War*
  b) free copies of Plato's *Dialogues*
  c) an abridgment of Alexis de Tocqueville's *Democracy in America*
  d) a wall-size Periodic Table of the Elements
  e) gratis copies of Billy Joel's hit single "We Didn't Start the Fire" (which recounts history via a vaguely chronological list of warbled celebrity names)

My sample of forty-seven-year-olds scored very well on the test. Not surprisingly, so did their seventeen-year-old children. (For each question, either the last entry is correct or all responses are correct *except* the last one.) The results of the test reveal again the deep hypocrisy that runs through our lamentations about education. The illiteracy of the young turns out to be our own reflected back to us with embarrassing force. We honor ambition, we reward greed, we celebrate materialism, we worship acquisitiveness, we cherish success, and we commercialize the classroom—and then we bark at the young about the gentle arts of the spirit. We recommend history to the kids but rarely consult it ourselves. We make a fuss about ethics but are satisfied to see it taught as an "add-on," as in "ethics in medicine" or "ethics in business"—as if Sunday morning in church could compensate for uninterrupted sinning from Monday to Saturday.

The children are onto this game. They know that if we really valued schooling, we'd pay teachers what we pay stockbrokers; if we valued books, we'd spend a little something on the libraries so that adults could read, too; if we valued citizenship, we'd give national service and civic education more than pilot status; if we valued children, we wouldn't let them be abused, manipulated, impoverished, and killed in their beds by gang-war cross fire and stray bullets. Schools can and should lead, but when they confront a society that in every instance tells a story exactly opposite to the one they are supposed to be teaching, their job becomes impossible. When the society undoes each workday what the school tries to do each school day, schooling can't make much of a difference.

Inner-city children are not the only ones who are learning the wrong lessons. TV sends the same messages to everyone, and the success of Donald Trump, Pete Rose, Henry Kravis, or George Steinbrenner makes them potent role models, whatever their values. Teen dropouts are not blind; teen drug sellers are not deaf; teen college students who avoid the humanities in favor of pre-business or pre-law are not stupid. Being apt pupils of reality, they learn their lessons well. If they see a man with a rubber arm and an empty head who can throw a ball at 95 miles per hour pulling down millions of dollars a year while a dedicated primary-school teacher is getting crumbs, they will avoid careers in teaching even if they can't make the major leagues. If they observe their government spending up to $35,000 a year to keep a young black behind bars but a fraction of that to keep him in school, they will write off school (and probably write off blacks as well).

Our children's illiteracy is merely our own, which they assume with commendable prowess. They know what we have taught them all too well: there is nothing in Homer or Virginia Woolf, in Shakespeare or Toni Morrison, that will advantage them in climbing to the top of the American heap. Academic credentials may still count, but schooling in and of itself is for losers. Bookworms. Nerds. Inner-city rappers and fraternity-house wise guys are in full agreement about that. The point is to start pulling down the big bucks. Some kids just go into business earlier than others. Dropping out is the national pastime, if by dropping out we mean giving up the precious things of the mind and the spirit in which America shows so little interest and for which it offers so little payback. While the professors argue about whether to teach the ancient history of a putatively white Athens or the ancient history of a putatively black Egypt, the kids are watching televised political campaigns driven by mindless image-mongering and inflammatory polemics that ignore history altogether. Why, then, are we so surprised when our students dismiss the debate over the origins of civilization, whether Eurocentric or Afrocentric, and concentrate on cash-and-carry careers? Isn't the choice a tribute not to their ignorance but to their adaptive intelligence? Although we can hardly be proud of ourselves for what we are teaching them, we should at least be proud of them for how well they've learned our lessons.

Not all Americans have stopped caring about the schools, however. In the final irony of the educational endgame, cynical entrepreneurs like Chris Whittle are insinuating television into the classroom itself, bribing impoverished school boards by offering free TV sets on which they can show advertising for children—sold to sponsors at premium rates. Whittle, the mergers and acquisitions mogul of education, is trying to get rich off the poverty of public schools and the fears of parents. Can he really believe advertising in the schools enhances education? Or is he helping to corrupt public schools in ways that will make parents even more anxious to use vouchers for private schools—which might one day be run by Whittle's latest entrepreneurial venture, the Edison Project.

According to Lifetime Learning Systems, an educational-software company, "kids spend 40 percent of each day . . . where traditional advertising can't reach them." Not to worry, says Lifetime Learning in an *Advertising Age* promo: "Now, you can enter the classroom through custom-made learning materials created with your specific marketing objectives in mind. Communicate with young spenders directly and, through them, their teachers and families as well." If we redefine young learners as "young spenders," are the young really to be blamed for acting like mindless consumers? Can they become young spenders and still become young critical thinkers, let alone informed citizens? If we are willing to give TV cartoons the government's imprimatur as "educational television" (as we did a few years ago, until the FCC changed its mind), can we blame kids for educating themselves on television trash?

Everyone can agree that we should educate our children to be something more than young spenders molded by "lifestyle patterning." But what should the goals of the classroom be? In recent years it has been fashionable to define the educational crisis in terms of global competition and minimal competence, as if schools were no more than vocational institutions. Although it has talked sensibly about education, the Clinton Administration has leaned toward this approach, under the tutelage of Secretary of Labor Robert Reich.

The classroom, however, should not be merely a trade school. The fundamental task of education in a democracy is what Tocqueville once called the apprenticeship of liberty: learning to be free. I wonder whether Americans still believe liberty has to be learned and that its skills are worth learning. Or have they been deluded by two centuries of rhetoric into thinking that freedom is "natural" and can be taken for granted?

The claim that all men are born free, upon which America was founded, is at best a promising fiction. In real life, as every parent knows, children are born fragile, born needy, born ignorant, born unformed, born weak, born foolish, born dependent—born in chains. We acquire our freedom over time, if at all. Embedded in families, clans, communities, and nations, we must learn to be free. We may be natural consumers and born narcissists, but citizens have to be made. Liberal-arts education actually means education in the arts of liberty; the "servile arts" were the trades learned by unfree men in the Middle Ages, the vocational education of their day. Perhaps this is why Thomas Jefferson preferred to memorialize his founding of the University of Virginia on his tombstone rather than his two terms as president; it is certainly why he viewed his Bill for the More General Diffusion of Knowledge in Virginia as a centerpiece of his career (although it failed passage as legislation—times were perhaps not so different). John Adams, too, boasted regularly about Mas-

IN RECENT YEARS IT HAS BEEN FASHIONABLE TO DEFINE THE EDUCATIONAL CRISIS IN TERMS OF GLOBAL COMPETITION AND MINIMAL COMPETENCE, AS IF SCHOOLS WERE MERELY VOCATIONAL INSTITUTIONS. BUT THE CLASSROOM SHOULD NOT BE MERELY A TRADE SCHOOL

SECURITY GUARDS AND
METAL DETECTORS ARE POOR
SURROGATES FOR CIVILITY, AND
THEY MAKE OUR SCHOOLS LOOK
INCREASINGLY LIKE PRISONS
(THOUGH THEY MAY BE LESS SAFE
THAN PRISONS)

sachusetts's high literacy rates and publicly funded education.

Jefferson and Adams both understood that the Bill of Rights offered little protection in a nation without informed citizens. Once educated, however, a people was safe from even the subtlest tyrannies. Jefferson's democratic proclivities rested on his conviction that education could turn a people into a safe refuge—indeed "the only safe depository" for the ultimate powers of society. "Cherish therefore the spirit of our people," he wrote to Edward Carrington in 1787, "and keep alive their attention. Do not be severe upon their errors, but reclaim them by enlightening them. If once they become inattentive to public affairs, you and I and Congress and Assemblies, judges and governors, shall all become wolves."

The logic of democracy begins with public education, proceeds to informed citizenship, and comes to fruition in the securing of rights and liberties. We have been nominally democratic for so long that we presume it is our natural condition rather than the product of persistent effort and tenacious responsibility. We have decoupled rights from civic responsibilities and severed citizenship from education on the false assumption that citizens just happen. We have forgotten that the "public" in public schools means not just paid for by the public but procreative of the very idea of a public. Public schools are how a public—a citizenry—is forged and how young, selfish individuals turn into conscientious, community-minded citizens.

Among the several literacies that have attracted the anxious attention of commentators, civic literacy has been the least visible. Yet this is the fundamental literacy by which we live in a civil society. It encompasses the competence to participate in democratic communities, the ability to think critically and act with deliberation in a pluralistic world, and the empathy to identify sufficiently with others to live with them despite conflicts of interest and differences in character. At the most elementary level, what our children suffer from most, whether they're hurling racial epithets from fraternity porches or shooting one another down in schoolyards, is the absence of civility. Security guards and metal detectors are poor surrogates for civility, and they make our schools look increasingly like prisons (though they may be less safe than prisons). Jefferson thought schools would produce free men: we prove him right by putting dropouts in jail.

Civility is a work of the imagination, for it is through the imagination that we render others sufficiently like ourselves for them to become subjects of tolerance and respect, if not always affection. Democracy is anything but a "natural" form of association. It is an extraordinary and rare contrivance of cultivated imagination. Give the uneducated the right to participate in making collective decisions, and what results is not democracy but, at best, mob rule: the government of private prejudice once known as the tyranny of opinion. For Jefferson, the difference between the democratic temperance he admired in agrarian America and the rule of the rabble he condemned when viewing the social unrest of Europe's teeming cities was quite simply education. Madison had hoped to "filter" out popular passion through the device of representation. Jefferson saw in education a filter that could be installed within each individual, giving to each the capacity to rule prudently. Education creates a ruling aristocracy constrained by temperance and wisdom; when that education is public and universal, it is an aristocracy to which all can belong. At its best, the American dream of a free and equal society governed by judicious citizens has been this dream of an aristocracy of everyone.

To dream this dream of freedom is easy, but to secure it is difficult as well as expensive. Notwithstanding their lamentations, Americans do not appear ready to pay the price. There is no magic bullet for education. But I no longer can accept that the problem lies in the lack of consensus about remedies—in a dearth of solutions. There is no shortage of debate over how to repair our educational infrastructure. National standards or more local control? Vouchers or better public schools? More parental involvement or more teacher autonomy? A greater federal presence (only 5 or 6 percent of the nation's education budget is federally funded) or fairer local school taxes? More multicultural diversity or more emphasis on what Americans share in common? These are honest disputes. But I am convinced that the problem is simpler and more fundamental. Twenty years ago, writer and activist Frances Moore Lappé captured the essence of the world food crisis when she argued that starvation was caused not by a scarcity of food but by a global scarcity in democracy. The education crisis has the same genealogy. It stems from a dearth of democracy: an absence of democratic will and a consequent refusal to take our children, our schools, and our future seriously.

Most educators, even while they quarrel among themselves, will agree that a genuine commitment to any one of a number of different solutions could help enormously. Most agree that although money can't by itself solve problems, without money few problems can be solved. Money also can't win wars or put men in space, but it is the crucial facilitator. It is also how America has traditionally announced, We are serious about this!

If we were serious, we would raise teachers' salaries to levels that would attract the best young professionals in our society: starting lawyers get from $70,000 to $80,000—why don't starting kindergarten teachers get the same? Is their role in vouchsafing our future less significant? And although there is evidence suggesting that an increase in general educational expenditures doesn't translate automatically into better schools, there is also evidence that an increase aimed specifically at instructional services does. Can we really take in earnest the chattering devotion to excellence of a country so wedded in practice to mediocrity, a nation so ready to relegate teachers—conservators of our common future—to the professional backwaters?

If we were serious, we would upgrade physical facilities so that every school met the minimum standards of our better suburban institutions. Good buildings do not equal good education, but can any education at all take place in leaky, broken-down habitats of the kind described by Jonathan Kozol in his *Savage Inequalities*? If money is not a critical factor, why are our most successful suburban school districts funded at nearly twice the level of our inner-city schools? Being even at the starting line cannot guarantee that the runners will win or even finish the race, but not being even pretty much assures failure. We would rectify the balance not by penalizing wealthier communities but by bringing poorer communities up to standard, perhaps by finding other sources of funding for our schools besides property taxes.

If we were serious, we'd extend the school year by a month or two so that learning could take place throughout the year. We'd reduce class size (which means more teachers) and nurture more cooperative learning so that kids could become actively responsible for their own education and that of their classmates. Perhaps most important, we'd raise standards and make teachers and students responsible for them. There are two ways to breed success: to lower standards so that everybody "passes" in a way that loses all meaning in the real world; and to raise standards and then meet them, so that school success translates into success beyond the classroom. From Confucian China to Imperial England, great nations have built their success in the world upon an education of excellence. The challenge in a democracy is to find a way to maintain excellence while extending educational opportunity to everyone.

Finally, if we were serious, parents, teachers, and students would be the real players while administrators, politicians, and experts would be secondary, at best advisers whose chief skill ought to be knowing when and how to facilitate the work of teachers and then get out of the way. If the Democrats can clean up federal government bureaucracy (the Gore plan), perhaps we can do the same for educational bureaucracy. In New York up to half of the city's teachers occupy jobs outside the classroom. No other enterprise is run that way: Half the soldiers at company headquarters? Half the cops at stationhouse desks? Half the working force in the assistant manager's office? Once the teachers are back in the classroom, they will need to be given more autonomy, more professional responsibility for the success or failure of their

JEFFERSON SAW IN EDUCATION A FILTER THAT COULD BE INSTALLED WITHIN EACH INDIVIDUAL, GIVING TO EACH THE CAPACITY TO RULE PRUDENTLY; UNIVERSAL AND PUBLIC EDUCATION CREATES AN ARISTOCRACY TO WHICH ALL CAN BELONG

EVEN AS OUR LOWER SCHOOLS ARE AMONG THE WORST IN THE WESTERN WORLD, OUR GRADUATE INSTITUTIONS ARE AMONG THE BEST, PARTLY BECAUSE CORPORATE AMERICA BACKS UP STATE AND FEDERAL PRIORITIES IN THIS CRUCIAL DOMAIN

students. And parents will have to be drawn in not just because they have rights or because they are politically potent but because they have responsibilities and their children are unlikely to learn without parental engagement. How to define the parental role in the classroom would become serious business for educators.

Some Americans will say this is unrealistic. Times are tough, money's short, and the public is fed up with almost all of its public institutions: the schools are just one more frustrating disappointment. With all the goodwill in the world, it is still hard to know how schools can cure the ills that stem from the failure of so many other institutions. Saying we want education to come first won't put it first.

America, however, has historically been able to accomplish what it sets its mind to. When we wish it and will it, what we wish and will has happened. Our successes are willed; our failures seem to happen when will is absent. There are, of course, those who benefit from the bankruptcy of public education and the failure of democracy. But their blame is no greater than our own: in a world where doing nothing has such dire consequences, complacency has become a greater sin than malevolence.

In wartime, whenever we have known why we were fighting and believed in the cause, we have prevailed. Because we believe in profits, we are consummate salespersons and efficacious entrepreneurs. Because we love sports, ours are the dream teams. Why can't a Chicago junior high school be as good as the Chicago Bulls? Because we cherish individuality and mobility, we have created a magnificent (if costly) car culture and the world's largest automotive consumer market. Even as our lower schools are among the worst in the Western world, our graduate institutions are among the very best— because professional training in medicine, law, and technology is vital to our ambitions and because corporate America backs up state and federal priorities in this crucial domain. Look at the things we do well and observe how very well we do them: those are the things that as a nation we have willed.

Then observe what we do badly and ask yourself, Is it because the challenge is too great? Or is it because, finally, we aren't really serious? Would we will an end to the carnage and do whatever it took—more cops, state militias, federal marshals, the Marines?—if the dying children were white and middle class? Or is it a disdain for the young—white, brown, and black— that inures us to the pain? Why are we so sensitive to the retirees whose future (however foreshortened) we are quick to guarantee—don't worry, no reduced cost-of-living allowances, no taxes on social security except for the well-off—and so callous to the young? Have you noticed how health care is on every politician's agenda and education on no one's?

To me, the conclusion is inescapable: we are not serious. We have given up on the public schools because we have given up on the kids; and we have given up on the kids because we have given up on the future—perhaps because it looks too multicolored or too dim or too hard. "Liberty," said Jean-Jacques Rousseau, "is a food easy to eat but hard to digest." America is suffering from a bad case of indigestion. Finally, in giving up on the future, we have given up on democracy. Certainly there will be no liberty, no equality, no social justice without democracy, and there will be no democracy without citizens and the schools that forge civic identity and democratic responsibility. If I am wrong (I'd like to be), my error will be easy to discern, for before the year is out we will put education first on the nation's agenda. We will put it ahead of the deficit, for if the future is finished before it starts, the deficit doesn't matter. Ahead of defense, for without democracy, what liberties will be left to defend? Ahead of all the other public issues and public goods, for without public education there can be no public and hence no truly public issues or public goods to advance. When the polemics are spent and we are through hyperventilating about the crisis in education, there is only one question worth asking: are we serious? If we are, we can begin by honoring that old folk homily and put our money where for much too long our common American mouth has been. Our kids, for once, might even be grateful.

<u>THE 27TH ANNUAL</u>

Phi Delta Kappa/Gallup Poll
Of the Public's Attitudes
Toward the Public Schools

Stanley M. Elam and Lowell C. Rose

Illustrations by Joe Lee

THE 1995 Phi Delta Kappa/Gallup Poll of the Public's Attitudes Toward the Public Schools, number 27 in the annual series, features in-depth exploration of a number of significant national education issues. Among these are the public's grading of its schools; its level of awareness of educational issues; participation by the federal, state, and local governments in policy and financial decisions involving local schools; public and nonpublic school choice; higher achievement standards for students; inclusion of special education students in regular classrooms; financial assistance for college attendance; school prayer; the biggest problems facing the schools; violence in the schools; and ways of dealing with disruptive students.

A summary of the important findings follows:

■ People continue to rate the schools in their own communities much higher than they rate the nation's schools. And the closer people get to the schools, the higher the ratings. Almost two-thirds (65%) of public school parents assign a grade of A or B to the school their oldest child attends.

■ Lack of discipline and lack of financial support are viewed as the major problems facing the schools. Fighting/violence/gangs, tied for first in the list of problems a year ago, is now third, followed by the use of drugs.

■ People view lack of parental control and the breakdown of family life as the major causes of what they see as an increase in school violence. Interestingly, however, public opinion follows the same pattern with regard to violence in schools as it does with regard to grading the schools. The closer people are to the schools in question and the more contact they have with them, the less likely they are to view violence as a serious problem.

■ People do not generally believe that students who are guilty of disruptive behavior or violence in school should be expelled. Instead, a majority opts for transfer to separate facilities where students can be given special attention.

■ The poll results call into question the extent of public support for inclusion programs. The clear preference is for placing students with learning problems in special classrooms.

■ There continues to be strong public support for the introduction of higher academic standards

STANLEY M. ELAM is contributing editor of the Phi Delta Kappan. He was Kappan editor from 1956 through 1980 and has been coordinating Phi Delta Kappa's polling program since his retirement. LOWELL C. ROSE is executive director of Phi Delta Kappa.

From *Phi Delta Kappan*, September 1995, pp. 41-56. © 1995 by Phi Delta Kappa, Inc. Reprinted by permission.

into the public schools, something the public has favored for many years. Higher standards as a requirement for graduation are also favored — even if this means that fewer students would graduate.

■ The desire for a constitutional amendment permitting spoken prayer in the schools continues to be strong. The public is surprisingly ecumenical with regard to the nature of such prayer, believing that all religions should be accommodated. However, the strongest support is for a moment of silence to be used as each individual chooses.

■ Support for choice within the public schools is strong; however, choice whereby students attend private schools at public expense is opposed. Moreover, people believe that private schools that accept public funds should be subject to regulation by public authorities.

■ The public favors the kind of devolution of authority from federal to state to local governments that the Republican-controlled Congress is now trying to bring about — even if the transferring of authority means that less federal money would be available for local schools.

■ Americans place a high value on a college education, with most expressing the hope and the belief that their oldest child will attend college. However, a significant number are concerned about their ability to pay for that college education in light of increasing costs.

■ The public strongly supports government financial assistance for those with the ability but not the money to attend college. This assistance includes scholarships and grants, work-study programs, and low-interest loans.

■ The public is opposed to providing educational services at public expense for the children of illegal immigrants.

■ Parents indicate considerable involvement with the schools.

Almost three-fourths of the 55 questions in this year's poll are new. The responses to each question are presented and discussed in the following pages.

Grading the Public Schools

Beginning in 1974, respondents to the Phi Delta Kappa/ Gallup education polls have been asked to rate the public schools on a scale of A to F. At first only the "local public schools" were rated. After 1981, people were also asked to rate the "nation's public schools." In 1986 parents were asked to grade the public school their oldest child was attending. Last year still another question was added, this one asking respondents to grade the public schools attended by children "in your neighborhood."

The pattern of responses over the years is enlightening. The closer respondents are to the schools they are asked to grade, the higher the grades they give them. This has been true in every year since 1986. This year, 65% of parents award their oldest child's school either an A or a B. The grades given neighborhood schools are also high, but lower than those given by parents to their oldest child's school. Meanwhile, only 20% of the public award the nation's schools a grade of A or B.

Over the years these ratings of the local schools have been surprisingly stable, despite largely negative media coverage of the public schools and frequent charges that they are failing. Approval ratings hold up even though the percentage of parents with children in school, the group likely to give the highest ratings, has dropped from 41.5% in 1974 to about 27% today.

(This factor could well explain a drop of five percentage points, between 1984 and 1995, in the number of A's and B's awarded the nation's public schools.)

This year poll planners decided to shed new light on the phenomenon of high local ratings and low national ratings; 517 of the 1,311 respondents rated the nation's schools lower than their local schools. Given a list of 11 possible reasons for the differences, these 517 made a significant number-one choice: the local schools place more emphasis on high academic achievement. Not far behind were the perceptions that local schools have fewer disciplinary problems and less racial and ethnic conflict. The last table in this section lists all the reasons why respondents distinguished between local school quality and quality of schools in the nation as a whole.

The first question:

Students are often given the grades A, B, C, D, and FAIL to denote the quality of their work. Suppose the public schools themselves, in this community, were graded in the same way. What grade would you give the public schools here — A, B, C, D, or FAIL?

	National Totals %	No Children In School %	Public School Parents %	Nonpublic School Parents %
A & B	41	38	49	23
A	8	6	12	6
B	33	32	37	17
C	37	38	34	40
D	12	11	12	23
FAIL	5	5	4	10
Don't know	5	8	1	4

Ratings Given the Local Public Schools

	1995 %	1994 %	1993 %	1992 %	1991 %	1990 %	1989 %	1988 %	1987 %	1986 %	1985 %
A & B	41	44	47	40	42	41	43	40	43	41	43
A	8	9	10	9	10	8	8	9	12	11	9
B	33	35	37	31	32	33	35	31	31	30	34
C	37	30	31	33	33	34	33	34	30	28	30
D	12	14	11	12	10	12	11	10	9	11	10
FAIL	5	7	4	5	5	5	4	4	4	5	4
Don't know	5	5	7	10	10	8	9	12	14	15	13

The second question:

How about the public schools in the nation as a whole? What grade would you give the public schools nationally — A, B, C, D, or FAIL?

	National Totals %	No Children In School %	Public School Parents %	Nonpublic School Parents %
A & B	20	21	18	8
A	2	2	2	*
B	18	19	16	8
C	50	51	47	63
D	17	17	18	18
FAIL	4	4	4	4
Don't know	9	7	13	7

*Less than one-half of 1%.

Ratings Given the Nation's Public Schools

	1995 %	1994 %	1993 %	1992 %	1991 %	1990 %	1989 %	1988 %	1987 %	1986 %	1985 %
A & B	20	22	19	18	21	21	22	23	26	28	27
A	2	2	2	2	2	2	2	3	4	3	3
B	18	20	17	16	19	19	20	20	22	25	24
C	50	49	48	48	47	49	47	48	44	41	43
D	17	17	17	18	13	16	15	13	11	10	12
FAIL	4	6	4	4	5	4	4	3	2	5	3
Don't know	9	6	12	12	14	10	12	13	17	16	15

The third question (asked of parents with children in the public schools):

Using the A, B, C, D, FAIL scale again, what grade would you give the school your oldest child attends?

Ratings Given School Oldest Child Attends

	1995 %	1994 %	1993 %	1992 %	1991 %	1990 %	1989 %	1988 %	1987 %	1986 %
A & B	65	70	72	64	73	72	71	70	69	65
A	27	28	27	22	29	27	25	22	28	28
B	38	42	45	42	44	45	46	48	41	37
C	23	22	18	24	21	19	19	22	20	26
D	8	6	5	6	2	5	5	3	5	4
FAIL	3	1	2	4	4	2	1	2	2	2
Don't know	1	1	3	2	*	2	4	3	4	3

*Less than one-half of 1%.

The fourth question:

How about the public schools attended by children from your neighborhood? What grade would you give them — A, B, C, D, or FAIL?

Ratings Given Neighborhood Schools

	National Totals '95 %	National Totals '94 %	No Children In School '95 %	No Children In School '94 %	Public School Parents '95 %	Public School Parents '94 %	Nonpublic School Parents '95 %	Nonpublic School Parents '94 %
A & B	48	50	47	46	52	60	31	39
A	12	12	9	10	18	16	6	11
B	36	38	38	36	34	44	25	28
C	30	30	28	30	32	29	47	35
D	9	9	10	10	8	7	14	12
FAIL	4	6	4	7	4	3	7	8
Don't know	9	5	11	7	4	1	1	6

The fifth question (asked of the 517 respondents who graded the schools in their community higher than the public schools nationally):

To indicate why you grade the public schools in your community higher than the public schools nationally, would you say whether you agree or disagree with the following statements?

Reasons for Rating Local Schools Higher	National Totals* Agree %	National Totals* Disagree %	No Children In School* Agree %	No Children In School* Disagree %	Public School Parents* Agree %	Public School Parents* Disagree %
The local schools:						
Place more emphasis on high academic achievement	79	15	80	13	77	19
Have better discipline and less crime and violence	74	22	75	20	74	24
Have fewer racial and ethnic disturbances involving students	74	22	75	21	72	25
Provide better programs for slow learners and the physically handicapped	70	19	70	17	69	21
Send a higher percentage of their graduates to college	69	18	70	17	66	19
Have better, more varied academic courses	68	21	68	21	69	20
Have fewer dropouts	68	22	70	22	65	23
Have better teachers	67	22	67	21	66	24
Offer better sports and athletic and extracurricular programs	67	24	70	21	62	28
Provide better programs for the gifted and talented	64	27	64	26	64	29
Have more money to spend per pupil	44	44	46	41	39	50

*To find the percentage of "don't knows" or refusals, add agree and disagree columns and subtract from 100%.

Awareness of National Education Issues

To determine the public's awareness of current issues in education, poll respondents were offered a list of nine education issues that have been accorded considerable attention by the media in recent years and then were asked to indicate how much they had heard or read about each issue.

Judging by the responses, the public is distressingly uninformed about the education scene in America today. Student violence and ways to deal with it was by far the issue about which the public had heard or read the most. The table below lists the nine issues in order of familiarity to the public.

The issue about which the public had heard or read the least was charter schools, which are already being tested in more than a dozen states. And despite long exposure to the issue, the public does not feel knowledgeable about school choice.

The question:

Here are some national education issues that are currently being discussed and debated. As I read off each issue, would you tell me whether you have heard or read about that issue a great deal, a fair amount, not very much, or not at all?

	How Much Heard or Read				
	A Great Deal	A Fair Amount	Not Very Much	Not at All	Don't Know
The amount of student violence in the public schools, including possible ways to deal with it	56	27	11	6	*
A proposed amendment to the U.S. Constitution permitting spoken prayer in the public schools	44	33	16	7	*
National testing programs to measure the academic achievement of public school students	25	38	23	14	*
Public school choice; that is, allowing public school children to attend any public school of their own or their parents' choice	23	30	25	22	*
Private school choice; that is, allowing parents to send their children to private or church-related schools at taxpayers' expense	22	29	22	27	*
The federal and state governments' efforts to raise achievement standards of public schools nationwide	20	36	28	16	*
Providing federal funds for education to the states in the form of "block grants"	19	26	27	27	1
The debate over what should be taught in U.S. history courses in the public schools	12	24	33	30	1
Charter schools, which would permit some public schools to operate independently, free from certain state restrictions	6	17	31	46	*

*Less than one-half of 1%.

School-Based Health and Social Services

In 1993 people told Gallup interviewers that they would like the public schools to provide health and social services to students. In most cases, these sometimes costly programs were approved by overwhelming margins. Exams to detect sight and hearing defects were approved by 92% of respondents; free or low-cost lunches, by 87%; inoculations, by 84%; and after-school care for children of working parents, by 62%.

Thus it was no surprise that 91% of respondents to this year's poll considered "serving the emotional and health needs of students" very important or somewhat important. Only 3% considered this role for the schools not important at all. Women (69%), nonwhites (80%), those aged 18-29 (74%), and Democrats (74%) were somewhat more likely to view this role for the schools as very important than were men (59%), whites (61%), those aged 50 and over (59%), and Republicans (56%).

The question:

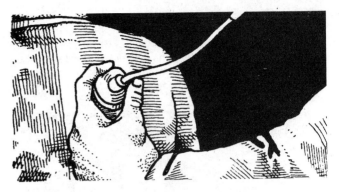

In addition to their educational role, how important do you think it is for the public schools to serve the emotional and health needs of students?

	National Totals %	No Children In School %	Public School Parents %	Nonpublic School Parents %
Very important	64	63	69	52
Somewhat important	27	28	24	35
Not very important	5	6	4	3
Not important at all	3	2	2	6
Don't know	1	1	1	4

Federal, State, and Local Roles

Americans have been consistently skeptical of centralized government power. This skepticism seems to lie behind answers to a number of poll questions related to the locus of authority in public education. The responses show that public sentiment strongly favors local control over federal or even state control.

The first three questions:

Thinking about the future, would you like to see the federal government in Washington have more influence or less influence in determining the educational programs of the local public schools?

How about the state government? Would you like the state government to have more influence or less influence in determining the educational programs of the local schools?

How about the local government? Would you like the local government to have more influence or less influence in determining the educational programs of the local schools?

	Federal Government			State Government			Local Government		
	1995 %	1987 %	1986 %	1995 %	1987 %	1986 %	1995 %	1987 %	1986 %
More influence	28	37	26	52	55	45	64	62	57
Less influence	64	39	53	37	21	32	24	15	17
Same amount	5	14	12	8	15	16	8	15	17
Don't know	3	10	9	3	9	7	4	8	9

This year 36% of Democrats but only 19% of Republicans favored more federal influence. Nonwhite respondents (51%) were much more in favor of greater federal influence than were whites (23%). Nonwhites were also more favorable toward increased influence for other levels of government. For example, 62% of nonwhites, but only 49% of whites, favored more state influence, and 72% of nonwhites, compared with 62% of whites, want to see local government have more influence in school matters. Urban dwellers were more likely (34%) than suburbanites (24%) and rural residents (23%) to favor more federal influence.

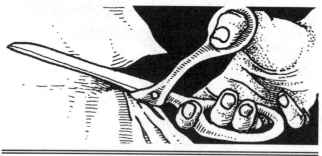

Financing Education

The next five questions had to do with federal and state relations in the expenditure of federal education funds, an issue with which Congress is now wrestling.

The first question:

In your opinion, should your state have more say in the way money from federal education programs is spent in your state, less say, or about the same as now?

	National Totals %	No Children In School %	Public School Parents %	Nonpublic School Parents %
More say	48	48	46	47
Less say	12	11	15	11
About the same as now	37	38	36	40
Don't know	3	3	3	2

The second question (asked of those who said the state should have more say):

What if giving your state more say means that less money from the federal government would be available to the state for education? Do you think your state should have more say in the way money from federal education programs is spent, if it means less money would be available, or not?

	National Totals %	No Children In School %	Public School Parents %	Nonpublic School Parents %
Yes, more say	64	67	58	54
No	30	27	37	27
Don't know	6	6	5	19

Party affiliation was the only striking demographic difference in the responses to this question. Seventy percent of Republicans were willing to give up some federal money if it meant more say for the state. Only 52% of Democrats felt the same way.

The third question:

When the federal government appropriates money for educational programs, it usually requires the schools that receive this money to spend it as the federal government directs. Should or should not this be changed to permit local school authorities to decide how the money is to be spent?

	National Totals		No Children In School		Public School Parents		Nonpublic School Parents	
	'95 %	'77 %	'95 %	'77 %	'95 %	'77 %	'95 %	'77 %
Yes, should be changed	70	62	71	60	70	65	72	67
No, should not be changed	26	29	24	29	27	29	19	27
Don't know/ no answer	4	9	5	11	3	6	9	6

Again, it was Republicans rather than Democrats who most strongly supported this change: Republicans, 77% in favor; Democrats, 63% in favor.

Although the public generally supports greater say at the local level, its response to a question dealing with a specific "block grant" proposal shows deep division.

The fourth question:

When federal money is turned over to the states with no strings attached as to how it should be spent, it is called a "block grant." One proposed block grant would, over time, reduce the amount of money in the federal school lunch program in exchange for giving the states more say in how the money is spent. Are you in favor of or opposed to this block grant?

	National Totals %	No Children In School %	Public School Parents %	Nonpublic School Parents %
Favor	45	46	42	32
Oppose	47	45	51	57
Don't know	8	9	7	11

Demographic categories in which there were significant differences of opinion are summarized below:

	Favor %	Oppose %	Don't Know %
National Totals	45	47	8
Race			
White	47	44	9
Nonwhite	34	61	5
Politics			
Republicans	59	30	11
Democrats	33	60	7
Independents	41	51	8

The fifth question:

Last year, federal aid-to-education programs were changed to give the local public schools more say, in exchange for bringing students to higher levels of academic achievement. Do you favor or oppose this change?

	National Totals %	No Children In School %	Public School Parents %	Nonpublic School Parents %
Favor	86	86	85	85
Oppose	10	10	11	9
Don't know	4	4	4	6

Public and Private School Choice

Beginning in 1989, these polls have tracked public opinion on the issue of giving parents a choice of the public school their children attend, regardless of where they live. Sentiment has consistently favored this form of choice. By 1990 several states had begun experimenting with choice plans involving the public schools, and the idea had the backing of President Bush and the U.S. Department of Education. Today, more than half of the states have passed laws permitting some form of public school choice, and others are considering such laws.

Plans that include choice of a private school to attend at public expense are an entirely different matter, however. This year's poll shows that approximately two-thirds of the public opposes such plans. While this figure represents strong opposition, it is not as strong as it was in 1993, when 74% of the public expressed opposition.

However, among the 13 different demographic groups routinely tracked in this poll, not one shows a majority favoring private school choice at public expense. Even Roman Catholics and nonpublic school parents oppose the idea: Catholics 54% to 44% and nonpublic school parents 51% to 44%.

The first question:

Do you favor or oppose allowing students and their parents to choose which public schools in the community the students attend, regardless of where they live?

	National Totals %	No Children In School %	Public School Parents %	Nonpublic School Parents %
Favor	69	69	69	78
Oppose	28	28	29	21
Don't know	3	3	2	1

National Totals				
1995 %	1993 %	1991 %	1990 %	1989 %
Favor	69	65	62	62	60

	1995 %	1993 %	1991 %	1990 %	1989 %
Favor	69	65	62	62	60
Oppose	28	33	33	31	31
Don't know	3	2	5	7	9

The second question:

Do you favor or oppose allowing students and parents to choose a private school to attend at public expense?

	National Totals %	No Children In School %	Public School Parents %	Nonpublic School Parents %
Favor	33	30	38	44
Oppose	65	68	59	51
Don't know	2	2	3	5

National Totals		
1995 %	1993 %	1991 %
Favor	33	24	26

	1995 %	1993 %	1991 %
Favor	33	24	26
Oppose	65	74	68
Don't know	2	2	6

Answers to the next question probably explain the reluctance of Roman Catholics and nonpublic school parents to approve the idea of private school choice at public expense.

The third question:

Do you think private schools that accept government tuition payments for these students should be accountable to public authorities or not?

National Totals		
	1995 %	1993 %
Yes, should be accountable	73	63
No, should not be accountable	24	34
Don't know	3	3

Higher Standards

Republicans and Democrats in the federal government, along with state governors of both parties, have embraced the need for higher standards of academic achievement in the nation's schools.

A dozen associations representing the academic disciplines have spent long hours and millions of dollars drafting a mountain of standards. Most of these groups had completed their work by the end of the 1994-95 school year.

But the national standards movement is not proceeding as swiftly now as anticipated. There are increasing questions and controversy. *Education Week* has summarized these as follows: Who should set standards, and who has the right to say whether they are good enough? Are the proposed standards really for all children, from the gifted and talented to those with special needs? Will all students have access to the instruction and resources they need to meet the standards? Will the standards dictate a national curriculum in a country that has a strong tradition of local control in education? What role, if any, should the federal government have played in developing standards? And are the emerging documents both politically balanced and academically rigorous?

These polls have dealt with the standards issue on several occasions. In 1989 and 1991, for example, people were asked whether they favored or opposed requiring their local schools to conform to national achievement standards and goals. By a margin of 70% to 19% in 1989 and 81% to 12% in 1991, they favored this strategy. In both years 77% also favored using standardized national tests to determine whether students were meeting these national standards. It is no surprise, then, that the vast majority of respondents in this year's poll (87%) favor setting higher standards in the basic subjects than are now required in order to move from grade to grade. Nearly as many (84%) favor setting higher standards for high school graduation.

The questions:

Would you favor or oppose setting higher standards than are now required about what students should know and be able to do in the basic subjects — that is, math, history, English, and science — for promotion from grade to grade?

Would you favor or oppose requiring the students in the public schools in your community to meet higher standards than are now required in math, English, history, and science in order to graduate from high school?

Higher Standards	National Totals		No Children In School		Public School Parents		Nonpublic School Parents	
	For Promotion %	For Graduation %	For Promotion %	For Graduation %	For Promotion %	For Graduation %	For Promotion %	For Graduation %
Favor	87	84	88	85	84	82	89	94
Oppose	10	13	8	12	14	17	5	6
Don't know	3	3	4	3	2	1	6	*

*Less than one-half of 1%.

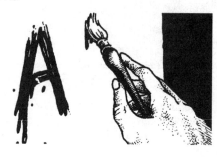

Possible Effects of Higher Standards

The possible effects of raising standards are being widely debated today. Such leaders as Albert Shanker of the American Federation of Teachers have fought for a get-tough attitude, saying children need to understand that the quality of their school achievement has serious consequences for later life. In order to sample public opinion on various questions related to the possible effects of higher standards, four questions were asked in this poll.

The first question:

Some people say that raising achievement standards will encourage students from low-income backgrounds to do better in school. Others say that raising standards will put these students at such a disadvantage that they will become discouraged about school or will even drop out. Do you think that raising achievement standards will encourage students from poor backgrounds to do better in school, or will it cause them to become discouraged or to drop out?

	National Totals		No Children In School		Public School Parents		Nonpublic School Parents	
	'95 %	'87 %	'95 %	'87 %	'95 %	'87 %	'95 %	'87 %
Yes, encourage	60	52	63	52	53	51	67	60
No, discourage	29	30	27	27	36	37	26	28
Don't know	11	18	10	21	11	12	7	12

Nationally, a surprising 60% of the respondents thought that raising standards would encourage low-income students to do better in school, but there were many doubters, particularly among parents of public school children. Moreover, one-tenth of the respondents didn't venture an answer. There were no statistically significant differences by race in the responses to this question.

The second question:

Would you favor stricter requirements for high school graduation, even if it meant that significantly fewer students would graduate than is now the case?

	National Totals		No Children In School		Public School Parents		Nonpublic School Parents	
	'95 %	'86 %	'95 %	'86 %	'95 %	'86 %	'95 %	'86 %
Yes	65	68	67	68	59	68	78	77
No	29	23	27	22	34	26	21	18
Don't know	6	9	6	10	7	6	1	5

There were no significant differences by race on this question, and other demographic differences were small.

The third question:

Thinking about kindergarten through grade 3, would you favor or oppose setting standards for what students in these grades should know and be able to do in various subjects?

	National Totals %	No Children In School %	Public School Parents %	Nonpublic School Parents %
Favor	78	78	76	83
Oppose	20	19	22	16
Don't know	2	3	2	1

Three times before, the Phi Delta Kappa/Gallup polls have asked respondents if they approve of promoting students to the next grade only if they can pass examinations. In 1978, 68% were in favor; in 1983, 75% were in favor; in 1990, 67% were in favor. This year people were asked a similar question, but this time the examinations were described as "standardized" and "national." Support remained strong.

The fourth question:

Do you favor or oppose requiring students in the public schools in this community to pass standardized, national examinations for promotion from grade to grade?

	National Totals %	No Children In School %	Public School Parents %	Nonpublic School Parents %
Favor	65	65	64	66
Oppose	32	31	34	33
Don't know	3	4	2	1

	National Totals			
	1995 %	1990 %	1983 %	1978 %
Favor	65	67	75	68
Oppose	32	29	20	27
Don't know	3	4	5	5

Is U.S. History Adequately Taught?

Standards for the teaching of U.S. history, released late in 1994, illustrate some of the difficulties of the standards movement. A storm of controversy greeted the release of the history standards. Yet the schools bear much of the burden of acquainting the younger generation with their national historical heritage. Commercial television has devoted more time to the O.J. Simpson trial this year than to the entire history of America. Even PBS has devoted little time to American history recently, beyond a few such programs as Ken Burns' Civil War series.

While poll designers felt it would be futile to try to explore popular feeling about the controversy over history standards — after all, it was confined mainly to professional ranks — two questions were asked.

The first question:

In your opinion, is U.S. history being taught more accurately and realistically than when you were in school, or not?

	National Totals %	No Children In School %	Public School Parents %	Nonpublic School Parents %
More accurately	33	31	39	27
Less accurately	37	37	36	39
No difference	8	8	8	9
Don't know	22	24	17	25

The results show that people are almost evenly divided on the issue of whether history teaching is more or less accurate than in the past, with a sizable number saying that they don't know. There were some interesting differences in demographic groups.

	More Accurately %	Less Accurately %	No Difference %	Don't Know %
National Totals	33	37	8	22
Race				
White	31	37	8	24
Nonwhite	45	38	5	12
Age				
18-29 years	38	30	9	23
50-64 years	27	45	6	22
65 and older	20	55	4	21

The second question:

In your opinion, is U.S. history being taught with too much emphasis on the positive aspects of the nation's history and its successes, too much emphasis on the negative aspects of the nation's history and its failures, or with about the right balance?

	National Totals %	No Children In School %	Public School Parents %	Nonpublic School Parents %
Too positive	17	17	17	19
Too negative	18	18	17	25
Right balance	48	46	52	44
Don't know	17	19	14	12

Half of the public feels that the current balance is about right, while groups of almost equal size feel that the teaching of history is too positive or too negative. Once again, a few demographic differences surfaced.

	Too Positive %	Too Negative %	Right Balance %	Don't Know %
National Totals	17	18	48	17
Race				
White	16	18	48	18
Nonwhite	21	19	47	13
Age				
18-29 years	28	13	49	10
50 and older	7	23	45	25
Politics				
Republicans	11	28	44	17
Democrats	19	16	47	18
Independents	21	12	51	16
Education				
Total college	21	18	44	17
Total high school	12	18	53	17

Special Education

Since 1975, when Congress passed the first version of what is now the Individuals with Disabilities Education Act, special education has come under attack from various sources. State and local districts are hard put to meet the staggering costs of a "free and appropriate education" for all of the 5.2 million U.S. students now classified as being in some way handicapped or disabled. More recently, the merits of inclusion — placing handicapped students in classes with nonhandicapped students — have been hotly debated.

Four questions in the current poll explored public attitudes on these issues. Well-informed or not, most respondents were

willing to express an opinion on them. The first question, on who should pay, was first asked in 1977, shortly after the disabilities act became law. Some eight of 10 respondents said then (and a similar number say today) that the federal government should pay the attendant costs. These costs have escalated as more and more students have been classified as "disabled."

The next three questions explored public attitudes toward including students with learning problems in the same classes with other students and asked what the likely effects would be on other students and on the students with learning problems themselves. Two-thirds of the respondents believed that children with learning problems should be placed in special classes. If students with learning problems are included in the same classrooms with other students, 37% of the respondents believed that the effect of their inclusion on other students would be negative, while 36% thought that it would not make much difference. A plurality of respondents (40%) thought that inclusion would have a negative effect on the students with learning problems themselves. Clearly, the proponents of greater inclusion have a public relations problem.

The first question:

Services for physically and mentally handicapped students cost more than regular school services. When the local schools are required to provide these special services by the federal government, should the federal government pay the extra cost, or not?

	National Totals		No Children In School		Public School Parents		Nonpublic School Parents	
	'95 %	'77 %	'95 %	'77 %	'95 %	'77 %	'95 %	'77 %
Yes, should	84	82	82	80	89	85	89	84
No, should not	12	11	14	12	9	9	10	14
Don't know	4	7	4	8	2	6	1	2

The second question:

In your opinion, should children with learning problems be put in the same classes with other students, or should they be put in special classes of their own?

	National Totals %	No Children In School %	Public School Parents %	Nonpublic School Parents %
Yes, same classrooms	26	25	29	25
No, special classes	66	68	62	66
Don't know	8	7	9	9

There were very few significant differences in responses by category of respondent. However, the older the person interviewed, the less likely he or she was to approve of inclusion. Only 15% of persons over age 65 favored the idea, while 34% of 18- to 29-year-olds did.

The third question:

Do you think that including children with learning problems in the same classrooms with other students would have a positive effect on the other students, a negative effect, or would it not make much difference?

	National Totals %	No Children In School %	Public School Parents %	Nonpublic School Parents %
Positive effect	23	21	25	26
Negative effect	37	38	35	39
Would make little difference	36	37	35	34
Don't know	4	4	5	1

The fourth question:

How about children with learning problems them-

selves? Do you think including them in classes with other students would have a positive effect on the children with learning problems, a negative effect, or would it not make much difference?

	National Totals %	No Children In School %	Public School Parents %	Nonpublic School Parents %
Positive effect	38	35	44	42
Negative effect	40	43	35	43
Would make little difference	17	17	16	11
Don't know	5	5	5	4

Paying for a College Education

Economist Richard Hokenson predicts a 33% increase in the number of young people who will enter college by the year 2010. This will tend to hold down tuition increases, he says, because many college operating costs are fixed. Still, by 2010 the cost of tuition for one year at a state university may well be more than $15,000 per student — and the average tuition at private schools more than $66,000 — in today's dollars. That increase may well price many families out of the market.

The new AmeriCorps program promoted by President Clinton to give moderate-income students an opportunity to trade public service for some college aid now has only about 20,000 members because of inadequate funding, and it may experience further cuts by the Republican-controlled Congress.

Five questions in the current poll probed public attitudes toward college education and the difficulties of paying for it.

The first question:

Many high school graduates cannot afford to attend college, although they may have the ability and desire to do so. When students have the ability and desire to attend college but not enough money, would you favor or oppose more state or federal assistance to enable them to attend?

	National Totals		No Children In School		Public School Parents		Nonpublic School Parents	
	'95 %	'89 %	'95 %	'89 %	'95 %	'89 %	'95 %	'89 %
Favor	86	83	83	82	92	87	87	83
Oppose	12	13	15	14	7	11	11	14
Don't know	2	4	2	4	1	2	2	3

The second question:

There are several forms of state or federal assistance that might be provided to a student who has the ability but not enough money to attend college. As I read off each form of assistance, one at a time, would you tell me whether you would favor or oppose this form of assistance?

	National Totals		No Children In School	Public School Parents	Nonpublic School Parents
	'95 %	'89 %	'95 %	'95 %	'95 %
More scholarships and grants					
Favor	89	94	88	91	89
Oppose	10	4	11	8	7
Don't know	1	2	1	1	4
More work-study programs					
Favor	93	94	93	94	88
Oppose	5	3	5	5	12
Don't know	2	3	2	1	*
More low-interest loans					
Favor	90	93	89	93	94
Oppose	9	5	10	7	6
Don't know	1	2	1	*	*

*Less than one-half of 1%.

In 1995, as in 1982, an overwhelming majority of respondents wanted their children to attend college, as the figures below suggest. Indeed, the desire is almost universal today: 98% state that they would like their oldest child to attend college, a figure that includes at least 90% of every demographic group. Despite increases in college costs in recent years, the vast majority of parents believe their children will indeed attend college; some two-thirds believe that it is very likely or somewhat likely that they can pay the costs themselves.

The third question:

Would you like to have your oldest child go on to college after graduating from high school?

	Public School Parents		Nonpublic School Parents	
	1995 %	1982 %	1995 %	1982 %
Yes	98	87	98	84
No	1	5	*	6
Don't know	1	8	2	10

*Less than one-half of 1%.

The fourth question:

Do you think he or she will go to college?

	Public School Parents		Nonpublic School Parents	
	1995 %	1982 %	1995 %	1982 %
Yes	82	57	85	67
No	12	19	8	15
Don't know	6	24	7	18

The fifth question:

How likely do you think it is that you or your family will be able to pay for college for your oldest child?

	National Totals %	Public School Parents %	Nonpublic School Parents %
Very likely	30	29	43
Somewhat likely	39	39	37
Not too likely	17	17	14
Not at all likely	12	13	5
Don't know	2	2	1

Should Spoken Prayer be Allowed?

Nine questions in this poll, including several never previously asked in the series, probed aspects of the issue of prayer in the public schools. The responses add a great deal to our knowledge of public opinion on this currently important topic.

For the first time in many years, Congress is seriously considering action. The Christian Coalition, credited by *Time* magazine with "providing the winning margin for perhaps half of the Republicans' 52-seat gain in the House of Representatives last fall and a sizable portion of their nine-seat pickup in the Senate," supports a constitutional amendment "to protect religious expression."

The 1984 Phi Delta Kappa/Gallup poll asked two questions about a then-proposed constitutional amendment that would allow prayer in the public schools. The first question revealed that 93% of the public at that time were aware of the proposed amendment — exactly the same proportion who said this year that they had heard or read about the issue. When asked in 1995 whether they favored or opposed such an amendment, the responses closely paralleled those of 1984. This was true even though *only* those claiming awareness of the proposed amendment were asked the question in 1984, while all respondents were asked the question this year.

The first question:

An amendment to the U.S. Constitution has been proposed that would permit prayers to be spoken in the public schools. Do you favor or oppose this amendment?

	National Totals		No Children In School		Public School Parents		Nonpublic School Parents	
	'95 %	'84 %	'95 %	'84 %	'95 %	'84 %	'95 %	'84 %
Favor	71	69	68	68	75	73	74	68
Oppose	25	24	28	25	20	21	23	21
Don't know	4	7	4	7	5	6	3	11

In 1995, as in 1984, those with at least some college (65% in favor), those 18 to 29 years of age (63%), and those living in the West (58%) supported the amendment least, though they, too, supported it. It received highest support in the South (80%) and among those in the lowest income group (88%).

The current poll revealed that a majority (65%) of people favoring the amendment felt very strongly about it, and 30% felt fairly strongly. A smaller majority (54%) of those who opposed the amendment also felt very strongly about the issue, and 34% felt fairly strongly. Although 74% thought that only a small percentage of parents with children in the local public schools would be offended by an amendment permitting spoken prayer, 55% thought such prayer should not be permitted in a community where a large percentage of parents *would* be offended.

Interestingly, those who supported an amendment allowing spoken prayer were only about one-third as likely (13% to 44%) as those who opposed the amendment to feel that a large percentage of parents would be offended if spoken prayer were allowed in the schools. In addition, by a close margin (53% to 44%) those who favored the amendment would allow prayer in the schools *even if* it were to offend a large percentage of parents.

The most interesting finding, perhaps, was the opinion, held by more than half of the respondents (including those who opposed public school prayer), that the introduction of spoken prayer would *improve the behavior of students*; 24% said "a great deal," and 31% said "somewhat."

A sizable majority (70%) of respondents said that they would prefer a moment of silence or silent prayer to spoken prayer (24%).* Somewhat surprisingly, even advocates of the amendment preferred a moment of silence to spoken prayer. Of those who favored the amendment, 64% preferred a moment of silence, and 32% preferred spoken prayer. Furthermore, even those who strongly favored the amendment preferred a moment of silence to spoken prayer (55% preferred silence, whereas 41% preferred spoken prayer).

Asked if school prayers should be basically Christian, a large majority (81%) said no. A majority (73%) favored allowing Jewish, Muslim, or Hindu prayers as well as Christian prayers, by students professing those faiths.

*A CBS News/New York Times poll taken recently showed that "the majority of Americans — 55% — did not know that a child's right to pray privately in school is constitutionally protected. Many probably do not know, either, that the Supreme Court struck down Alabama's moment-of-silence law in 1985, terming it a constitutional establishment of religion.

The second question (asked only of those who favored an amendment):

How strongly do you favor this amendment?

| | National Totals | |
	1995 %	1984 %
Very strongly	65	61
Fairly strongly	30	34
Not at all strongly	5	5
Don't know	*	*

*Less than one-half of 1%.

The third question (asked only of those who opposed an amendment):

How strongly do you oppose this amendment?

| | National Totals | |
	1995 %	1984 %
Very strongly	54	49
Fairly strongly	34	38
Not at all strongly	12	12
Don't know	*	1

*Less than one-half of 1%.

The fourth question:

Thinking about the local situation, what percentage of parents of students in the local public schools do you think would be offended if spoken prayer were permitted?

	National Totals %	No Children In School %	Public School Parents %	Nonpublic School Parents %
A large percentage	21	21	23	16
A small percentage	74	74	72	73
Don't know	5	5	5	11

The fifth question:

Do you think spoken prayer should be permitted in the local public schools if it offends a large percentage of parents?

	National Totals %	No Children In School %	Public School Parents %	Nonpublic School Parents %
Yes, should be permitted	41	41	41	40
No, should not be permitted	55	56	55	49
Don't know	4	3	4	11

The sixth question:

Do you think that the introduction of spoken prayer in the local public schools would improve the behavior of the students a great deal, somewhat, very little, or not at all?

	National Totals %	No Children In School %	Public School Parents %	Nonpublic School Parents %
A great deal	24	22	26	25
Somewhat	31	30	34	42
Very little	20	21	19	17
Not at all	24	26	21	16
Don't know	1	1	*	*

*Less than one-half of 1%.

The seventh question:

If you had a choice, which would you prefer in the local public schools — spoken prayer, a moment of silence for contemplation or silent prayer, neither, or both?

	National Totals %	No Children In School %	Public School Parents %	Nonpublic School Parents %
Spoken prayer	24	22	27	25
A moment of silence	70	72	67	65
Neither	3	3	3	3
Both	2	2	3	6
Don't know	1	1	*	1

*Less than one-half of 1%.

The eighth question:

Suppose spoken prayers were allowed in the local public schools. Do you believe that the prayers should be basically Christian, reflecting Christian beliefs and values, or should the prayers reflect all major religions, including Christianity?

	National Totals %	No Children In School %	Public School Parents %	Nonpublic School Parents %
Should reflect Christian beliefs and values	13	11	17	28
Should reflect all major religions	81	82	78	65
Neither of these	4	5	3	5
Don't know	2	2	2	2

The ninth question:

Again, suppose spoken prayers were allowed in the public schools in this community. In addition to Christian prayers, would you favor or oppose allowing spoken Jewish, Muslim, or Hindu prayers by students of these faiths?

	National Totals %	No Children In School %	Public School Parents %	Nonpublic School Parents %
Favor	73	72	73	71
Oppose	20	20	21	25
Neither	4	4	4	2
Don't know	3	4	2	2

Benefits for Children of Illegal Immigrants

Whether the children of illegal immigrants should receive such public benefits as free education is a sharply divisive issue in many states. Whether denying such benefits is constitutionally permissible is currently being tested in court in California.

People differ on this issue by race, by political party affiliation, and by income level. A sizable national majority (67%) opposed providing such benefits, but a significant percentage (47%) of nonwhites were in favor, while 46% were opposed. (This poll did not attempt to discover whether respondents knew that the children of illegal immigrants born in the U.S. are automatically U.S. citizens and therefore eligible for free public education and other social benefits.)

The question:

Are you in favor of or opposed to providing free public education, school lunches, and other benefits to children of immigrants who are in the United States illegally?

	In Favor %	Opposed %	Don't Know %
National Totals	**28**	**67**	**5**
Race			
Whites	24	72	4
Nonwhites	47	46	7
Politics			
Republicans	17	78	5
Democrats	37	57	6
Independents	30	66	4
Income			
$50,000 and over	24	72	4
Under $10,000	43	52	5

Biggest Problems Facing Local Public Schools

As in 18 of the 26 prior Phi Delta Kappa/Gallup polls, "lack of discipline" was judged this year to be the biggest problem faced by local public schools. Fifteen percent of all respondents mentioned discipline or lack of student control, while 9% listed fighting/violence/gangs as a major problem. Last year fighting/violence/gangs was mentioned by 18%, tying with discipline. Lack of proper financial support came in second as a problem this year; it was mentioned by 11% of respondents. Financial problems have topped the list twice, in 1971 and in 1993. Drug abuse headed the list from 1986 through 1991.

Other problems in order of frequency of mention in the current poll were drug abuse, 7%; standards or quality of education offered, 4%; overcrowded schools, 3%; lack of respect for teachers/authority/students, 3%; and lack of family structure and problems of home life, 3%. No other problem was listed by more than 2% of those polled.

The question:

What do you think are the biggest problems with which the public schools of this community must deal?

	National Totals '95 %	National Totals '94 %	No Children In School '95 %	No Children In School '94 %	Public School Parents '95 %	Public School Parents '94 %	Nonpublic School Parents '95 %	Nonpublic School Parents '94 %
Lack of discipline	15	18	17	18	11	17	18	22
Lack of proper financial support	11	13	10	12	12	16	3	9
Fighting/violence/gangs	9	18	9	19	8	16	8	17
Drug abuse	7	11	7	11	7	13	8	7
Standards/quality of education	4	8	4	8	4	5	4	11
Overcrowded schools	3	7	3	5	5	11	3	10
Lack of respect	3	3	3	2	4	3	6	1
Lack of family structure/problems of home life	3	5	3	5	1	3	5	4
Crime/vandalism	2	4	2	5	2	4	2	3
Integration/segregation, racial discrimination	2	3	2	3	2	2	*	2
Difficulty in getting good teachers	2	3	2	4	3	2	*	2
Management of funds/programs	2	*	2	*	2	*	3	*
Parents' lack of support/interest	2	3	2	4	2	2	3	3
Pupils' lack of interest/truancy/poor attitudes	2	3	2	3	1	3	2	5
Poor curriculum/low curriculum standards	2	3	2	2	1	3	1	2
There are no problems	3	1	2	1	6	2	2	2
Miscellaneous**	4	9	5	9	3	8	3	13
Don't know	11	11	12	12	10	9	6	11

*Less than one-half of 1%.

**A total of 29 different kinds of problems were mentioned by fewer than 2% of the 1995 respondents.

(Figures add to more than 100% because of multiple answers.)

This year a variation on the "biggest problems" question was put to parents of public school children. In addition to identifying problems of the "local public schools," these parents were asked what they considered to be the biggest problems of the school *attended by their oldest child.* Answers were not dramatically different from those to questions seeking perceptions of problems of local community schools. For example, fighting/violence/gangs led the list, and discipline was tied for second with peer pressure and drug abuse. Lack of proper financial support got fewer mentions, however.

The question (asked of public school parents):

What do you think are the biggest problems with which the public school attended by your oldest child must deal?

	Public School Parents %
Fighting/violence/gangs	9
Peer pressure	8
Drug abuse	8
Lack of discipline/control	8
Lack of proper financial support	7
Overcrowded schools	4
Lack of respect	4
There are no problems	9
Don't know	10

No other problem accounted for more than 2% of responses.

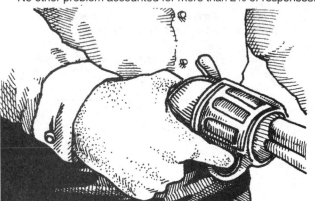

The Incidence of Student Violence in School

The causes of an undeniable spurt in crime and violence perpetrated by young people and the nature of effective treatment of this pathology constitute one of the most complex, puzzling, and intractable problems of our time. While a poll of the public is unlikely to help much in the quest for answers, it can alert educators to prevailing attitudes and perhaps suggest information campaigns to counter misinformation or misunderstanding.

Building on earlier poll findings, the current poll asked respondents to speculate on six questions related to student violence and its possible causes and cures. The questions and the findings follow.

The first question:

Just your impression — would you say that student violence in the public schools in your community has increased a great deal in recent years, increased some, declined some, declined a great deal, or remained about the same?

The second question:

How about in the pubic schools nationwide? Is it your impression that student violence in the public schools nationwide has increased a great deal in recent years, increased some, declined some, declined a great deal, or remained about the same?

The third question (asked of public school parents):

How about the public school attended by your oldest child? Is it your impression that student violence in this school has increased a great deal, increased some, declined some, declined a great deal, or remained about the same?

	In Local Public Schools %	In the Nation's Public Schools %	In School Attended by Oldest Child %
Increased a great deal	37	68	15
Increased some	30	21	26
Declined some	5	2	7
Declined a great deal	1	1	4
Remained about the same	25	6	43
Don't know	2	2	5

The responses to these three questions suggest two obvious conclusions. First, a vast majority of the public believes that violence in the public schools is increasing, not only in the nation's schools (89%) but in the local schools (67%) as well. Second, the closer one is to the public schools, the less likely one is to believe there has been a great increase. (Eleven percent of parents even believe that there has been at least some decrease in violence in the school attended by their oldest child, and a surprising 43% see no change.) People living in urban areas (47%) and in the West (48%) were most likely to think violence has increased greatly in their local schools.

People with children in *private* or *church-related* schools were much more likely than others to perceive a great increase in violence in the *public* schools locally (50%) and nationally (77%).

The National Association of Secondary School Principals reported last May that "three million crimes occur in or near school property each year. Such violence deprives students of their rights to quality education." Irrespective of rate increases or decreases, this is far too much crime for a civilized society to tolerate among its youth.

Because the 1994 Phi Delta Kappa/Gallup poll showed that, for the first time in the poll's history, people viewed violence and poor discipline as overwhelmingly the most serious problems in their local public schools — 18% named each of them — the 1995 poll probed this area with three more questions.

The fourth question:

What, in your opinion, are the major causes of student violence in the public schools?

	National Totals %	No Children In School %	Public School Parents %	Nonpublic School Parents %
Lack of parental control/ discipline/supervision/ involvement/values	24	26	18	21
Lack of family structure/ problems of family life/ poverty	20	22	16	31
Drug related	13	13	13	9
Pupils' attitudes/boredom/ disrespect/lack of self-esteem	6	5	8	6
Gang related	5	5	7	4
Integration/segregation problems; racial disputes	4	3	6	6
TV/movies/pop music/news media	3	3	3	3
Availability of guns/weapons	3	3	2	1

No other category accounted for more than 2% of responses. Only 6% of all respondents failed to answer the question.

Note that none of these so-called causes constitute a criticism of schools or school personnel. The public obviously believes itself to be at fault. While a logician might be able to show that some of the thinking behind these responses is weak, there is no doubt that people — including parents — blame themselves for violence in the schools.

The last questions in this section of the poll had to do with two major strategies for dealing with disruptive or violent students.

The fifth question:

Suppose a student in a public school in this community were guilty of continually disruptive behavior in school. Which one of these two approaches would you prefer — expelling the student from school or transferring the student to a separate facility for special attention?

	National Totals %	No Children In School %	Public School Parents %	Nonpublic School Parents %
Expulsion	20	21	18	16
Transfer	77	76	79	82
Neither	2	2	2	1
Don't know	1	1	1	1

The sixth question:

Suppose a student in a public school in this community were guilty of violence against another student or a teacher. Which one of these two approaches would you prefer — expelling the student from school or transferring the student to a separate facility for special attention?

	National Totals %	No Children In School %	Public School Parents %	Nonpublic School Parents %
Expulsion	31	33	30	32
Transfer	66	64	67	68
Neither	2	2	2	*
Don't know	1	1	1	*

*Less than one-half of 1%.

Generally, demographic differences were not statistically significant.

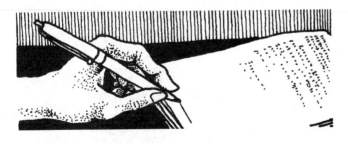

Parent Involvement

One of the two national goals recently added to the original six by the President and the state governors urges parents to become more closely involved in their children's education. Answers to the following question suggest that parent involvement may already be at a fairly high level.

The question (asked of public school parents):

During the past school year — that is, since last September — which of the following, if any, have you yourself done?

	Public School Parents %
Made sure your children attended school	98
Made sure that books were available for your children to read	97
Made sure that homework assigned to any of your children was completed	95
Read and/or discussed a school assignment with any of your children	94
Met with any teacher or administrator about any of your children	90
Read a book to, or with, any of your children	80
Placed definite limits on the kind of TV any of your children watch	79
Placed definite limits on the amount of TV any of your children watch	74
Attended a school board meeting	38

Public school parents were then asked about their willingness to spell out everyone's responsibilities with regard to their children's education.

The question:

Thinking about the public school attended by your oldest child, would you yourself be willing or not willing to sign a contract which would specify everyone's responsibilities — the school's, your child's, and yours as a parent?

An overwhelming 89% answered this question in the affirmative. Only 9% said they would be unwilling to sign such a contract. There were no statistically significant differences among respondent categories. This response suggests that the movement to draw up such formal contracts could expand rapidly.

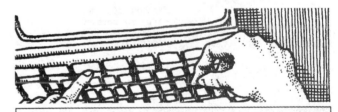

Conducting Your Own Poll

The Phi Delta Kappa Center for Professional Development and Services makes available PACE (Polling Attitudes of the Community on Education) materials to enable nonspecialists to conduct scientific polls of attitude and opinion on education. The PACE manual provides detailed information on constructing questionnaires, sampling, interviewing, and analyzing data. It also includes updated census figures and new material on conducting a telephone survey. The price is $55.

For information about using PACE materials, write or phone Phillip Harris at Phi Delta Kappa, P.O. Box 789, Bloomington, IN 47402-0789. Ph. 800/766-1156.

Sampling Tolerances

In interpreting survey results, it should be borne in mind that all sample surveys are subject to sampling error, i.e., the extent to which the results may differ from what would be obtained if the whole population surveyed had been interviewed. The size of such sampling error depends largely on the number of interviews.

1. HOW OTHERS SEE US AND HOW WE SEE OURSELVES

The following tables may be used in estimating the sampling error of any percentage in this report. The computed allowances have taken into account the effect of the sample design upon sampling error. They may be interpreted as indicating the range (plus or minus the figure shown) within which the results of repeated samplings in the same time period could be expected to vary 95% of the time, assuming the same sampling procedure, the same interviewers, and the same questionnaire.

The first table shows how much allowance should be made for the sampling error of a percentage:

Recommended Allowance for Sampling Error of a Percentage

In Percentage Points
(at 95 in 100 confidence level)*

	Sample Size						
	1,500	1,000	750	600	400	200	100
Percentages near 10	2	2	3	3	4	5	8
Percentages near 20	3	3	4	4	5	7	10
Percentages near 30	3	4	4	5	6	8	12
Percentages near 40	3	4	5	5	6	9	12
Percentages near 50	3	4	5	5	6	9	13
Percentages near 60	3	4	5	5	6	9	12
Percentages near 70	3	4	4	5	6	8	12
Percentages near 80	3	3	4	4	5	7	10
Percentages near 90	2	2	3	3	4	5	8

*The chances are 95 in 100 that the sampling error is not larger than the figures shown.

The table would be used in the following manner: Let us say that a reported percentage is 33 for a group that includes 1,000 respondents. We go to the row for "percentages near 30" in the table and across to the column headed "1,000."

The number at this point is 4, which means that the 33% obtained in the sample is subject to a sampling error of plus or minus four points. In other words, it is very probable (95 chances out of 100) that the true figure would be somewhere between 29% and 37%, with the most likely figure the 33% obtained.

In comparing survey results in two samples, such as, for example, men and women, the question arises as to how large a difference between them must be before one can be reasonably sure that it reflects a real difference. In the tables below, the number of points that must be allowed for in such comparisons is indicated.

Two tables are provided. One is for percentages near 20 or 80; the other, for percentages near 50. For percentages in between, the error to be allowed for lies between those shown in the two tables.

Recommended Allowance for Sampling Error of the Difference

In Percentage Points
(at 95 in 100 confidence level)*

TABLE A	Percentages near 20 or percentages near 80					
Size of Sample	1,500	1,000	750	600	400	200
1,500	4					
1,000	4	5				
750	5	5	5			
600	5	5	6	6		
400	6	6	6	7	7	
200	8	8	8	8	9	10

TABLE B	Percentages near 50					
Size of Sample	1,500	1,000	750	600	400	200
1,500	5					
1,000	5	6				
750	6	6	7			
600	6	7	7	7		
400	7	8	8	8	9	
200	10	10	10	10	11	13

*The chances are 95 in 100 that the sampling error is not larger than the figures shown.

Here is an example of how the tables would be used: Let us say that 50% of men respond a certain way and 40% of women respond that way also, for a difference of 10 percentage points between them. Can we say with any assurance that the 10-point difference reflects a real difference between men and women on the question? Let us consider a sample that contains approximately 750 men and 750 women.

Since the percentages are near 50, we consult Table B, and, since the two samples are about 750 persons each, we look for the number in the column headed "750," which is also in the row designated "750." We find the number 7 here. This means that the allowance for error should be seven points and that, in concluding that the percentage among men is somewhere between three and 17 points higher than the percentage among women, we should be wrong only about 5% of the time. In other words, we can conclude with considerable confidence that a difference exists in the direction observed and that it amounts to at least three percentage points.

If, in another case, men's responses amount to 22%, say, and women's to 24%, we consult Table A, because these percentages are near 20. We look in the column headed "750" and see that the number is 5. Obviously, then, the two-point difference is inconclusive.

Research Procedure

The Sample. The sample used in this survey embraced a total of 1,311 adults (18 years of age and older). A description of the sample and methodology can be found at the end of this report.

Time of Interviewing. The fieldwork for this study was conducted during the period of 25 May to 15 June 1995.

The Report. In the tables used in this report, "Nonpublic School Parents" includes parents of students who attend parochial schools and parents of students who attend private or independent schools.

Due allowance must be made for statistical variation, especially in the case of findings for groups consisting of relatively few respondents, e.g., nonpublic school parents.

The findings of this report apply only to the U.S. as a whole and not to individual communities. Local surveys, using the same questions, can be conducted to determine how local areas compare with the national norm.

Composition of the Sample

Adults	%
No children in school	66
Public school parents	32*
Nonpublic school parents	5*

*Total exceeds 34% because some parents have children attending more than one kind of school.

Sex	%
Men	45
Women	55

Race	%
White	81
Nonwhite	18
Undesignated	1

Age	%
18-29 years	21
30-49 years	46
50 and over	33

Occupation	%
(Chief Wage Earner)	
Business and professional	33
Clerical and sales	9
Manual labor	31
Nonlabor force	1
Farm	*
Undesignated	26

Income	%
$40,000 and over	39
$30,000-$39,999	16
$20,000-$29,999	18
$10,000-$19,999	12
Under $10,000	7
Undesignated	8

Region	%
East	24
Midwest	24
South	32
West	20

Community Size	%
Urban	39
Suburban	41
Rural	19
Undesignated	1

Education	%
Total college	59
College graduate	23
College incomplete	36
Total high school	41
High school graduate	30
High school incomplete	11

*Less than one-half of 1%.

Design of the Sample

For the 1995 survey the Gallup Organization used its standard national telephone sample, i.e., an unclustered, directory-assisted, random-digit telephone sample, based on a proportionate stratified sampling design.

The random-digit aspect of the sample was used to avoid "listing" bias. Numerous studies have shown that households with unlisted telephone numbers are different in important ways from listed households. "Unlistedness" is due to household mobility or to customer requests to prevent publication of the telephone number.

To avoid this source of bias, a random-digit procedure designed to provide representation of both listed and unlisted (including not-yet-listed) numbers was used.

Telephone numbers for the continental United States were stratified into four regions of the country and, within each region, further stratified into three size-of-community strata.

Only working banks of telephone numbers were selected. Eliminating non-working banks from the sample increased the likelihood that any sample telephone number would be associated with a residence.

The sample of telephone numbers produced by the described method is representative of all telephone households within the continental United States.

Within each contacted household, an interview was sought with the youngest man 18 years of age or older who was at home. If no man was home, an interview was sought with the oldest woman at home. This method of respondent selection within households produced an age distribution by sex that closely approximates the age distribution by sex of the total population.

Up to three calls were made to each selected telephone number to complete an interview. The time of day and the day of the week for callbacks were varied so as to maximize the chances of finding a respondent at home. All interviews were conducted on weekends or weekday evenings in order to contact potential repondents among the working population.

The final sample was weighted so that the distribution of the sample matched current estimates derived from the U.S. Census Bureau's Current Population Survey (CPS) for the adult population living in telephone households in the continental U.S.

As has been the case in recent years in the Phi Delta Kappa/Gallup poll series, parents of public school children were oversampled in the 1995 poll. This procedure produced a large enough sample to ensure that findings reported for "public school parents" are statistically significant.

How to Order the Poll

The minimum order for reprints of the published version of the Phi Delta Kappa/Gallup education poll is 25 copies for $10. Additional copies are 25 cents each. This price includes postage for delivery (at the library rate). Where possible, enclose a check or money order. Address your order to Phi Delta Kappa, P.O. Box 789, Bloomington, IN 47402. Ph. 800/766-1156.

If faster delivery is desired, do not include a remittance with your order. You will be billed at the above rates plus any additional cost involved in the method of delivery. Persons who wish to order the 437-page document that is the basis for this report should contact Phi Delta Kappa, P.O. Box 789, Bloomington, IN 47402. Ph. 800/766-1156. The price is $95, postage included.

Acknowledgments

Twelve educators served on a panel that rated and offered comments on questions offered for use in the 1995 Phi Delta Kappa/Gallup poll. They are: Patricia Bolaños, principal, The Key Renaissance School, Indianapolis; John E. Coons, professor of law emeritus, University of California, Berkeley; Leo Freiwald, teacher, Benjamin Franklin Elementary School, Dade County, Fla.; Michael W. Kirst, professor of education, Stanford University, Stanford, Calif.; Chris Pipho, division director, Information Clearinghouse/State Relations, Education Commission of the States, Denver; Richard Morland, chairman emeritus, Department of Education, Stetson University, DeLand, Fla.; Diane Ravitch, senior research scholar, New York University; Phillip C. Schlechty, president and CEO, Center for Leadership in School Reform, Louisville, Ky.; Eric Schaps, president, Developmental Studies Center, Oakland, Calif.; Robert Schiller, superintendent of public instruction, Michigan Department of Education, East Lansing; Robert Slavin, co-director, Center for Research on Students Placed at Risk, Johns Hopkins University, Baltimore; and Robert F. Sexton, executive director, Prichard Committee for Academic Excellence, Lexington, Ky.

Another group met with Alec Gallup in Indianapolis in late February to discuss poll questions. They included the two co-authors of this report and the following persons: Pauline Gough, editor, *Phi Delta Kappan*; John F. Jennings, director, Center on National Education Policy, Washington, D.C.; Arliss Roaden, board member, Phi Delta Kappa Educational Foundation, Nashville, Tenn.; and Sandra Weith, director, Phi Delta Kappa Administrative Center.

Phi Delta Kappa is indebted to all of these people for their excellent advice. It should be noted, however, that Lowell Rose and Stanley Elam are responsible for the final form in which the questions were asked and for the way in which answers were interpreted.

Rethinking and Changing the Educative Effort

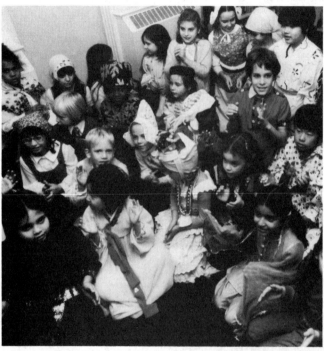

The dialogue regarding how to rethink and restructure the priorities of educational services in the United States is continuing; this is not surprising. There has been discussion relating to this theme in every generation of American history. There is debate regarding whether the focus for change and reform in education today should be on restructuring how teachers are prepared or on researching the changing conditions of many American youth today and how to help them better meet the challenges in their lives.

The articles in this unit reflect a wide range of opinions on these concerns. Several new and exciting ideas are being proposed as to how we might rethink the idea of school to encompass much more variety in school learning communities and to meet a broader range of the academic and social needs of today's youth.

American educators could have a much better sense of their own past as a profession, and the public could have a better sense of understanding the history of public education. In the United States, a fundamental cycle of similar ideas and practices reappears in school curricula every so many years. The decades of the 1970s and 1980s witnessed the rise of "behavioral objectives" and "management by objectives," and the 1990s have brought us "outcome-based education" and "benchmarking" in educational discourse within the public school system's leadership. These are related behavioral concepts focusing on measurable ways to pinpoint and evaluate the results of educational efforts. Why do we seem to reinvent the wheel of educational thought and practice every so many decades? This is an important question worth addressing. Many of our ideas about change and reform in educational practice have been wrongheaded. There is in the mid-1990s a stronger focus on more qualitative, as opposed to empirical, means of assessing the outcomes of our educative efforts; yet state departments of education still insist on external, objective assessments and verifications of students' mastery of predetermined academic skills. How does this affect the development of creative, imaginative teaching in schools? We are not sure; but all of us in the education system are concerned, and many of us believe that there really are some new and generative ideas to help students learn basic intellectual skills and content.

The essays in this and later units of this volume explore some of these ideas. There are a variety of myths about what did or did not happen in some "golden age" of our educational past. Our current realities in the field of education reflect very differing conceptions of how schooling ought to change. It is difficult to generalize reliably regarding school quality across several decades because of several factors; high schools, for instance, were more selective in 1900, when only 7 percent of American youth graduated from them, whereas today we encourage as many youth as are able to graduate from high school. The social purposes of schooling have been broadened; now we want all youth to complete some form of higher education.

We have to consider the social and ideological differences among those representing opposing school reform agendas for change. The differences over how and in what directions change is to occur in our educational systems rest on which educational values are to prevail. These values form the bases for differing conceptions of the purposes of schooling. Thus, the differing agendas for change in American education have to be positioned within the context of the different ideological value systems that underpin each alternative agenda for change.

There are several currently contending (and frequently conceptually conflicting) strategies for restructuring life in schools as well as the options open to parents in choosing the schools that they want their children to attend. On the one hand, we have to find ways to empower students and teachers to improve the quality of academic life in classrooms. On the other hand, there appear to be powerful forces contending over whether control of educational services should be even more centralized or more decentralized (site-based). Those who favor greater parental and teacher control of schools support greater decentralized site management and community control conceptions of school governance. Yet the ratio of teachers to nonteaching personnel (administrators, counselors, school psychologists, and others) continues to decline as public school system bureaucracies become more and more "top heavy."

In this unit, we consider the efforts to reconceive, redefine, and reconstruct existing patterns of curricula and instruction at the elementary and secondary levels of schooling and compare them with the efforts to rethink existing conflicting patterns of teacher education. There is a broad spectrum of dialogue developing in North America, the British Commonwealth, Russia, Central Eurasia, and other areas of the world regarding the redirecting of the learning opportunities for all its citizens.

Prospective teachers here are being encouraged to question their own individual educational experiences as part of the process of their becoming what all communities view as rural institutions. We must acknowledge that our values affect our ideas about curriculum content and the purpose of educating others. This is perceived as vitally important in the developing dialogue over liberating all students' capacities to function as independent inquirers. The dramatic economic and demographic changes in our society necessitate a fundamental reconceptualization of how schools ought to respond to the many social contexts in which they are located. This effort to reassess and reconceive the education of others is a vital part of broader reform efforts in society as well as a dynamic dialectic in its own right. How can schools, for instance, better reflect the varied communities of interest that they serve? What must they do to become

better perceived as just and equitable places in which all young people can seek to achieve learning and self-fulfillment?

This is not the first period in which our citizens have searched their minds and souls to redirect, reconstruct, and, if necessary, deconstruct their understandings regarding formal educational systems. The debate over what ought to be the conceptual and structural underpinnings of national educational opportunity structures has continued since the first mass educational system was formed in the nineteenth century.

When we think of continuity and change, we think of the conceptual balance between cherished traditions and innovations that will facilitate learning without compromising cherished core values and standards. When we think of change in education, we are reminded of such great educational experiments of earlier times as John Dewey's Laboratory School at the University of Chicago, Maria Montessori's Casi di Bambini (children's houses), and A. S. Neill's controversial Summerhill School in England as well as many other innovative experiments in learning theories. Our own time has seen similarly dramatic experimentation.

Each of the essays in this unit relates directly to the conceptual tension involved in reconceiving how educational development should proceed in response to all these dramatic social and economic changes in society.

Looking Ahead: Challenge Questions

What are some issues in the debate regarding educational reform?

What social, political, and economic pressures are placed on our public school systems?

Why are comparisons made of the school performance of students from different nations, and what can be learned from these comparisons? What are some limitations of such comparisons?

Should the focus of educational reform be on changing the ways educators are prepared, changing needs of students, or both? What are some imaginative new models of schools?

How do we build communities of learners?

—F. S.

Shifting the *Target* of Educational Reform

Reformers should take aim at students instead of educators to improve the status quo in education.

William E. Klingele

William E. Klingele is currently professor and dean of the College of Education at the University of Akron.

We slumped at round tables, more than 200 of us, all teacher educators representing thirty-eight colleges and universities from across the state. A few blocks away in the capital city, an approximately equal number of school administrators were meeting for the same purpose, planning for educational reform. A provocative thought entered my mind. The focus of each meeting involved what we could do to educators to improve the almost "hopeless" state of public education. As my mind drifted, I envisioned an educational mythology where both groups, school administrators and teacher educators, came together in the Universal Temple of Educational and Cultural Hiatus (UTEACH), to sacrifice an educator to the gods in the name of educational reform.

The processional was impressive. Leaders in education marched in academic regalia, *A Nation at Risk* under their arms, as the teacher of the year was led to the sacrificial altar. A few protesting teachers mingled about outside, humbled with tattered targets on their backs, prohibited from entering the temple of educational reform.

The testimony was eloquent. The Secretary of Education was heavily armed with world statistics that defined the devastation in American public education. I wondered if the Secretary of Defense was equally critical of our U.S. Armed Services. And the Attorney General: was the same type of criticism being fired at our legal profession? I wondered if the Secretary of Labor found any problems with the labor force. I hadn't heard of any. I wondered why the Attorney General was a lawyer, the Secretary of Labor was an economist, the Surgeon General was a physician, and the Secretary of Education was a politician.

The most successful business leaders in America joined in the sacrificial ceremonies. They identified their corporate views of the new American school, how they could lead us there, and what we had to do to educators to get there.

Radio and television talk shows were programmed into the arena. "The schools don't teach reading and writing anymore," and "schools aren't any good anymore," and "teachers don't teach anymore," and numerous other commonly heard statements were being promoted as replacements for "In God We Trust" on the U.S. coin.

As my mind drifted, the scene began to focus and I began to question: Is the teacher the problem? Has the teacher changed that much? Could the source of the problem be somewhere else? And should the solution to the problem be shifted somewhere else? Perhaps we do not really need to sacrifice educators to the gods of reform in order to strengthen American education. What is the source of the problem in American education?

It's the Student, Stupid

By borrowing a popular method of expression, one can call attention to what may be considered quite obvious by many. The changing nature of the student is the source of the problem in American education today. Education must focus on students rather than

   From *Educational Horizons*, Summer 1994, pp. 196-200. © 1994 by Pi Lambda Theta, Inc. Reprinted by permission.

teachers. Educational reform efforts must be shifted from what we need to do to teachers to what we need to do for students to realistically facilitate learning. Current efforts involve government, commissions, and task forces setting goals, legislatures placing demands on schools, and educational leaders deciding what needs to be done to teachers, all with the purpose of increasing test scores. If teachers were truly empowered in this process, the needed focus of change—the student—would become evident.

Teachers and education in general cannot realistically overcome student social, personal, physical, and psychological problems, the solution to which is prerequisite to improved learning. Teachers are experts in the teaching-learning process, not social workers, security officers, health care professionals, psychologists, or support figures for students without parent or guardian supervision. It will take a continuing collaborative

---

The changing nature of the student is the source of the problem in American education today.

---

effort from all external environmental forces that affect the learning of many of today's students if schools are to be held accountable for the success of all students. It

should be noted that many schools are truly successful with the majority of today's students, those that happen to have environmental support forces in place.

In his book *Beyond the Schools*, Harold Hodgkinson identifies many of the problems that affect the success of schools.

- Each year, about 350,000 children are born to women who were addicted to cocaine during pregnancy. The survivors have strikingly short attention spans, poor coordination, and other physical problems—in addition to being drug addicted themselves.
- About 40,000 children annually are born with alcohol-related birth defects, which can cause a range of impairments, from retardation and hypersensitivity to language problems.
- About 6.7 percent, or 260,000 children, are born each year with lower-than-normal birth weights. These babies are one-and-a-half times as likely to need special education services.
- In 1987, 2.2 million reports of child abuse or neglect were made to child protective service agencies. This was triple the number in 1976.
- Fifteen million children are now reared by single mothers, whose average income is about $11,000—$1,000 above the poverty line.
- At least 2 million children of school age have no adult supervision after school.
- One-fourth of pregnant mothers receive no physical care of any sort during the crucial first trimester. About 20 percent of today's handicapped children would not be handicapped if their mothers had received just one physical examination in the first trimester.

- Since 1987, one-fourth of all preschool children in the United States have lived in poverty.

What we do as educators in schools cannot overcome many of the external factors affecting educational success. The educational success of many students is more dependent on what occurs outside the schools than what occurs inside the schools. Educators alone cannot solve the problems of many of today's students. Solving many of these problems is a prerequisite to educational success. The one category of mankind that has more influence on learning than the teacher is the learner. The learner is a product of an environment. A supportive, problem-free environment facilitates educational success. The learner and the environment that produces the learner should be the target for reform.

The Current Focus

A quick survey of the history of American education reveals that schools have done essentially what was expected of them. They have attempted to educate all of the school-age population, including those with severe and profound handicaps, different languages, different levels of language proficiency, and different cultural levels, with or without parental support. All schools, through teachers, are teaching youngsters despite the environmental obstacles created by child abuse, addictive drugs, television, movies, and numerous other forces. Depending on the nature of the student and the adequacy of resources, however, most schools are successful.

Educators have consistently initiated new approaches to schooling. Most have come and gone with minimal affect at best. Many current approaches involve quick-fix panaceas through technology, total quality management, choice, excessive testing, extended school year, and site-based management. Some may lead to the improvement of learning, but will not in the long-run impact education in the manner that is being demanded. There is no reason to believe that an unmotivated, undersupported, and problem-plagued student who is currently learning very little will learn more than very little if the school year is lengthened or he is tested excessively.

The quality of education in the United States needs to be improved. Success toward improvement will evolve, however, only through a total quality student focus. For many students this will require new support from families, community, and health care agencies, and perhaps students themselves will need to assume some responsibility for learning.

Schools Are Successful

In spite of the popularity of "education bashing" and the misdirected focus of reform, education in America is successful. In general, teachers are doing a good job teaching, often under less than adequate conditions and with few incentives. Most adequately funded schools are providing a quality education for most students. Not all students can avail themselves of the education provided for one or more of a long list of reasons outside the control of the school.

The successes of American schools appear less than obvious to the American public. Thus, critics generally decry the "fact" that American students are performing less adequately on tests today than in the past. Studies comparing test scores of yesteryear with current test scores, however, reveal that current test scores are better.

Studies by psychologist James Flynn in a 1987 *Psychology Bulletin* show that test scores have increased significantly. Today's students average about fourteen IQ points higher than their grandparents, and about seven IQ points higher than their parents. The number of students expected to have IQs of 130 or above is now seven times greater than it was for the generation that is now retiring.

It is often noted that Scholastic Achievement Test (SAT) scores have declined 3.3 percent since 1965. This is due, however, to the much greater numbers of students in the bottom 60 percent of their classes who are taking the tests since the 1960s. It could be argued that the successes of American schools are directly responsible for this phenomenon. These successes have caused the overall decline due to the increase in educational opportunities for more diverse groups in this country.

United Nations Educational, Scientific, and Cultural Organization (UNESCO) data have shown that educators have indeed done more with less. In 1988 dollars, the United States ranked ninth among sixteen industrialized nations in per pupil expenditures for grades K-12, 14 percent less than Germany, 13 percent less than Japan, and 5 percent less than Switzerland. Thirteen of the sixteen industrialized nations spent a greater percentage of per capita income on K-12 education than did the United States. This debunks the common criticism that American schools are too expensive and that the United States spends more money on education than any other country of the world, and achieves less.

What Can Be Done

Teachers are teaching, schools are changing, education is improving, so why are so many students not learning? Focusing on the student will identify why students are not learning and may differ widely from one student to the next. Long-term success of education will depend on a total student-community of learning approach. Again, we must concentrate on the student, not "fixing" the teacher.

If education is to improve significantly, it will require full collaboration from a community of learning impactors. The leadership must come from the schools. Educators must become the coordinators of the total student-community of learning approach, taking the lead at all levels of government and within the profession. In turn, educators must be given the freedom to deliver a moral education stressing the values that Americans share, to teach human dignity, tolerance, peaceful resolutions to conflicts, the benefits of democracy, truth, work ethics, the values of our American democracy, self-reliance, and perhaps most important, responsibility. And in addition, the values associated with the American family must be returned to America through the schooling process. In effect, schools today must become actively involved in changing society in a manner that will impact learning in schools tomorrow.

Moral education in the terms identified here will continue to face opposition by special interest groups that do not want concepts that "should be taught in the home" being taught in the school. Parents will want to influence schools more

Each student must have the support of a parent or substitute support figure who is legally responsible for the student in school.

directly if they are to become more actively involved and held responsible. Agencies, community groups, service organizations, and other key community impactors will want more influence on the schools. Educators should welcome this interest and concern and apply the principles of a moral education as processes for involvement are implemented. The values of our American democracy, for example, can be applied to the process for ensuring equal representation and majority rule as the community of learning impactors comes together in the best interest of students.

The media must voluntarily take on responsibility for societal improvement, thus facilitating the future of school success. Television and the movies could have a tremendous impact on learning by emphasizing the same values being taught in schools. Current programming, it could be argued, is doing just the opposite.

Government must reduce the bureaucracy that inhibits educational improvements. It must provide the flexibility for change and provide the leadership and financial support, and focus legislation on students rather than educators.

Businesses must provide the tax base for supporting education. Robert Reich, a Harvard political economist and Secretary of Labor, states in a 1987 book that the corporate share of local property tax revenues dropped from 45 percent in 1957 to 16 percent in 1987. Property tax is the primary funding source for schools. While corporate executives are criticizing the schools, and some are even serving on commissions to reform education, they are successfully lobbying for tax breaks and subsidies from state and local governments. This, in turn, decreases the real support for educational improvement.

In addition, business must begin to invest in PK-12 education in much the same way that they support higher education. Corporate contributions to education are focused primarily on higher education. Only 1.5 percent of corporate contributions to education in 1989 was directed toward K-12 education. The model is in place. School districts must proceed with activities that capitalize on private support as colleges and universities have for many years.

Agencies, both public and private, must join schools in the education of our youth. Health care and social service agencies must allocate support to schools by serving the needs of youth outside the schools so that learning can occur inside the schools. If all students were provided adequate health care and social services, reform in American schools would occur in the greatest of proportions.

Each student must have the support of a parent or substitute support figure who is legally responsible for the student in school. In turn, parents and support figures must be involved in the decision-making at the local school level. This collaboration, too, can have a significant impact on the reform of American education.

Efforts to implement such changes range from state-wide initiatives demonstrated in Kentucky and Ohio to single-school projects like Decker School in Barberton, Ohio. Decker School involves Barberton City Schools, Akron Children's Hospital, and the University of Akron in a total student-community learning environment that focuses on an interprofessional model for educating youth. K-16 collaboration projects initiated by the American Association of Higher Education are examples of another approach to total student-community learning.

Many states are making progress in the strengthening of our educational systems. They are recognizing the need for family support and inter-agency collaboration. Much of this effort still involves cure, and cure is needed in the short term. However, in the long term, the most acceptable solution can be realized only through prevention. Prevention will be realized only through a concentrated focus on the student in a total student-community learning environment that molds our society as it educates our youth.

How Our Schools Could Be

Although the reasons for the current national concern about schooling may have little to do with democracy, the reforms described here by Ms. Meier have everything to do with it.

Deborah Meier

DEBORAH MEIER was the director of Central Park East schools in New York City from 1974 to 1994. She is the author of The Power of Their Ideas *(Beacon Press, 1995) and is a senior fellow with the Annenberg Institute.*

W E STAND poised between two alternative visions of the schools of tomorrow. The tough part is that these two visions are often espoused by the same people, and teachers and citizens alike are led to believe that both can be carried out simultaneously. In fact, they stand in chilling contrast to each other.

One vision rests on the assumption that top-down support for bottom-up change — which everyone is rhetorically for — means that the top does the critical intellectual work, defining purposes and content as well as how to measure them, and the bottom does the "nuts and bolts," the "how-to" — a sort of "men's work" versus "women's work" division of labor.

The second vision rests on a different assumption — that the only top-down reforms that are useful are those that help to create and sustain self-governing learning communities. When schools see themselves as membership communities, not service organizations, parents and teachers discuss ideas, argue about purposes, and exercise judgment, because taking responsibility for making important decisions is at the heart of what it means to be well-educated. Students can't learn unless the adults who must show them the way practice what they preach.

The Goals 2000 national education agenda, with its focus on setting measurable goals and standards, is weighted down with assumptions that the top does the critical intellectual work and the bottom is left with doing the how-to. But that second camp, with its alternative assumptions of what schools could be, is showing a surprising capacity to thrive these days. At least for a time. I've been told that I'm ignoring the train that's already left the station and is coming down the line, the "do-it-or-else" express. But if history is any guide, such fast-track solutions often turn out to be expensive dead ends.

Can we post a counter-mandate to the "all students will" dicta being invented by expert, university-based task forces? Let me propose a mandate saying, "Standards shall be phased in only as fast as the school, the district, and the state can bring

their adult staff members up to the standards they expect of all 18-year-old students." That might delay the train just a little.

We in New York have historically lived under the imposition of an awesome array of local and state curricular mandates and outcomes assessments. (Except for private schools, which were always free to ignore them and always have.) Every so often someone gets the idea to create still another set, generally laid right on top of the old ones, and then moves on to other things. New York teachers are experienced and inventive saboteurs of the best and worst of such plans. Our state is home therefore to some of the greatest as well as some of the worst of schools.

But the second alternative described above is staring us in the face. And it is gathering surprising national momentum, even from such unexpected (for old cynics like me) places as the New York State Board of Regents (New York's state board of education). The state authorities are now embarked on a new and more promising approach, as are the governor, the mayor, and the local New York City board of education — despite contradictions all over the place. That so many are now marching to a different drummer in the name of a different vision of "systemic" reform is heartening. This different vision has the support this time around not only of child-centered romantics like me, but also of hardheaded corporate and management reformers, such as the folks who invented the team approach to building the Saturn car or the Deming way of managing businesses.

We also have some hardheaded history of school reform to point to, on a scale that should make it hard to dismiss this "other" way as suitable only for the brave and the foolish, the maverick and the exceptional. It's no longer "alternative," but almost mainstream.

When a handful of like-minded teachers in East Harlem's Community School District No. 4 started a "progressive, open education" elementary school, Central Park East, in 1974, we were encouraged by the then district superintendent, Anthony Alvarado, to pay little heed to rules and regulations. We were told to create the kind of school we believed would work for the children of District 4. This revolutionary autonomy, which in local circles was referred to alternatively as "creative compliance" and "creative noncompliance," was simply a public and collaborative version of what many of us had long done behind closed doors.

Central Park East, along with more than 30 other small schools of choice begun by District 4 during the next 10 years, was and remains an amazing success story. We lived a somewhat lonely existence for a decade, but today both the Central Park East schools and the District 4 "way" have been roughly replicated in dozens of New York City school districts and are now part of accepted citywide reform plans. What the schools that have adopted this model share is a way of looking at children that is reminiscent of good kindergarten practice. Or, put another way, they operate according to what we know about how human beings learn, and they are guided by a deep-seated respect for all the parties involved — parents, teachers, and students.

Kindergarten is the one place — for many children it may be the last place — where such mutual respect has been a traditional norm (if not always practiced). A kindergarten teacher, for example, is expected to know children well, even if they don't hand in their homework, finish their Friday tests, or pay attention. Kindergarten teachers know that learning must be personalized, because kids come that way — no two alike. They know that parents and the community must be partners, or kids will be shortchanged. Kindergarten teachers know that part of their job description is to help children learn to become more self-reliant — starting with tying their shoes and going to the bathroom on their own.

Alas, it is the last time that children are given such independence, that they are encouraged to make choices and allowed to move about on their own. Having learned to use the bathroom by themselves at age 5, at age 6 they're required to wait until the whole class lines up at bathroom time. In kindergarten, parents and teachers meet to talk and often have one another's phone numbers. After that, communication is mainly one-way and impersonal. In kindergarten, we design our rooms for real work, not just passive listening. We put things in the room that we have reason to believe will appeal to children, things that will grab their interests and engage their minds and hearts. The older that children get, the less we take into account the importance of their own interests, their own active learning. In kindergarten, teachers are editors, critics, cheerleaders, and caretakers, not just lecturers or deliverers of instruction. What Theodore Sizer calls "coaching" is second nature to the kindergarten teacher, who takes for granted that her job description includes curriculum development as well as ongoing assessment.

But what's true for students is also true for teachers: they have less and less authority, responsibility, and independence as their charges get older — until, of course, the students make it into college or graduate school. Then both teachers and students go back to kindergarten.

It was Sizer who, when he came to visit our school, pointed out to us that the kindergarten principles of Central Park East were the same principles he was espousing for the nation's high schools. He suggested that we start a secondary school, beginning with seventh-graders, as a continuation of our elementary school. It was 1984 — the right moment for such an idea. And even though community school districts in New York City are not supposed to operate high schools, the idea was approved. Central Park East would just keep going from kindergarten through the 12th grade.

So we made the decision to see if we could use the principles of a good kindergarten as the basis for running a good high school. We opened Central Park East Secondary School in 1985 with a seventh grade and grew one grade a year each year thereafter.

We were not without great trepidation. Running through our minds were thoughts such as: Dare we? Could we take on teenagers? Aren't teenagers impossible to handle? I had spent a lot of years avoiding adolescents in groups of more than two, and I realized that it would be hard to build a secondary school without bumping into them in groups of at least three. We also knew that high school kids wouldn't like to be compared to kindergartners — or even sixth-graders. We needed to create new rituals that symbolized their new maturity. Finally, we were aware that, as the school was "growing up," it meant that we needed to be concerned about the expectations at the other end — what colleges and employers might want. Was there such a thing as being *too* nurturing or giving kids too much independence and too great a sense of empowerment?

One thing we very much wanted was to get away from the contemporary mode of breaking everything down into discrete bits and pieces — whether subject matter or "thinking skills." We were determined to keep intact the elementary school tradition of respect for the wholeness of both subject matter and human learning. We were looking for ways to build a school that offered youngsters a deep and rich curriculum that would inspire them with the desire to know more — that would cause them to fall in love with books and with stories of the past, that would instill in them a sense of wonder at how much there is to learn.

We also saw schools as models of the possibilities of democratic life. Although students' classroom lives could certainly be made more democratic than traditional schools encouraged, we saw it as equally important that the school lives of *adults* be made more democratic. It seemed unlikely that we could foster democratic values in our school unless the adults had significant rights within their workplace. We wanted not just good individual classrooms but a good school.

Another priority for us was creating a setting in which all members of the community were expected to engage in the discussion of ideas and in the "having of their own wonderful ideas," as Eleanor Duckworth has put it. Indeed, one of our most prominently stated, up-front aims was the cultivation of what we came to call "Habits of Mind" — habits that apply to all academic and nonacademic subject matter and to all thoughtful human activities. The five we came up with are not exhaustive, but they suggest the kinds of questions that we believed a well-educated person raises about his or her world.

- How do we know what we think we know? What's our evidence? How credible is it?
- Whose viewpoint are we hearing, reading, seeing? What other viewpoints might there be if we changed our position — our perspective?
- How is one thing connected to another? Is there a pattern here?
- How else might it have been? What if? Supposing that?
- What difference does it make? Who cares?

In order to carry out our basic mission of teaching students to use their minds well and preparing them to live productive, socially useful, and personally satisfying lives, we approach curriculum with these habits as the backdrop and specific "essential" questions at the core. Clearly, we can't depend on textbooks. Many courses don't use them at all, except perhaps as reference books. We cover less and, we hope, uncover a lot more. We integrate different academic disciplines — history with literature, science with math. In the jargon of the Coalition of Essential Schools, this is the "less is more" principle. We spend, for example, two years on biology, mostly focused on a few central biological issues, and two years on American history — and we don't pretend to cover it.

We do more "hands-on" experimental work. We expect kids to read many different sources on the same subject, to use the library a lot, to write a lot (preferably on a computer), and to think and discuss their ideas with many different people. We expect them to share their knowledge with one another and to work in groups as well as on their own. Our curriculum is designed to reinforce the connection between "school" knowledge and "real world" knowledge and to include multiple perspectives.

Most of our students do take most of the standard city and state competency tests, and we provide coaching for such tests, as well as for the SAT. But we don't see these tests as a measuring rod. They capture neither essential intellectual competence nor the demonstrated capacity of our students to use their knowledge, to care for others, to imagine how others think and feel, and to be prepared to speak up and be heard. These skills are no less crit-

ical, no less rigorous. They are part of the "hard" stuff.

Twenty years of documented evidence — regarding high school graduation, dropout rates, and college acceptances, for example — are hard to dispute. The Central Park East schools are demonstrably successful. Over 90% of the graduates of the elementary school go on to earn high school diplomas, and 90% of those who enter the high school not only receive high school diplomas but go on to college — nearly double the rate for the city as a whole. Furthermore, it is hard to attribute our remarkable statistics to having selected an elite or favored group. The student body of both the elementary and the high schools has always been about 40% Hispanic, 45% African American, and 15% other (Asian and white). Over two-thirds are poor enough to be eligible for free or reduced-price lunches, and at least 20% are labeled as "special ed" or "handicapped." They come to us looking remarkably like the assortment of students in the city as a whole. They leave, however, with substantially greater life choices.

But, proud as we are of these schools, we do not see what we do as the "best or only way" to educate children. As Seymour Fliegel, a former deputy superintendent in District 4, has put it, "The aim here has been to create a system that — instead of trying to fit all students into some standardized school — has a school to fit every student in this district. No kid gets left out, no kid gets lost. Every kid is important, every kid can learn if you put him or her in the right environment. But since kids have this huge range of different needs, different interests, and different ways of learning, we've got to have a wide diversity of schools."

While it has taken time for the District 4 ideas to catch on and for Central Park East's particular approach to spread, today both are "in the mainstream." Everyone is imitating the system of choice used in District 4, and there are more than 50 small public schools in New York City created in this tradition. Plans are afoot to vastly increase this number over the next five years. There are also plans to introduce innovations that will better match these new, less standardized approaches to teaching and learning with the ways in which we hold schools accountable.

It is clear that choice plans will require creative revisions in our current rules and regulations. As schools develop a variety of obviously different solutions, it will not

be possible to assign students to schools by street address or lottery. Parents and children will have to be involved in making choices about which school they think will best suit the student's needs, talents, and interests. Eventually all school districts may wish to develop schools of choice, even as they may also (as in District 4) give priority to parents on the basis of residence. Another way of lessening the transportation problems that are inherent in many choice plans is to locate several small schools in the same building.

The crucial decision made in the District 4 "revolution" of two decades ago was to create a broad and diverse set of new schools, not to reform existing schools. This meant that the district could focus on encouraging schoolpeople to innovate, instead of on monitoring them for compliance with district-mandated reforms. The next phase will do well not to ignore the lessons learned: it's easier to design a new school culture than to change an existing one. And it's the *whole* school culture — not this or that program — that stands in the way of learning.

The role of parents in the new schools was another central issue. Choice offered a way of providing for increased professional decision making without pitting parents and teachers against one another in a useless power struggle. Furthermore, small schools of choice offered everyone — teachers and families — vastly more time to meet together and work out differences through both formal and informal structures. The time needed is considerable but worth it. One top-down mandate we'd have no trouble with would be legislation requiring employers to provide time off for parents to attend school meetings.

Indeed, no school can complete its educational task without the support and trust of a student's family. Such trust rests on mutual respect and is never a luxury. Without it, the schools are crippled — and all the more so where differences in race, religion, and language between school staff and community are greatest. Young people sent to school with a message of distrust for the motives and methods of the school are fighting an uphill battle. They are always warily looking for hidden traps. And they will find plenty of them, since teachers too often don't hear the mixed messages they send out regarding their respect for children's families and communities.

Teachers rate "parental indifference"

as their number-one complaint. That's a misreading of what keeps parents and teachers apart. Unless and until the two groups feel able to join together as advocates for the common good of youngsters, such apparent "indifference" will remain. We will not create serious educational breakthroughs until we can meet as allies.

Schoolpeople must learn to share with parents some of the autonomy associated with what are now being called "charter" schools: the control over administrative, curricular, staffing, and fiscal matters that allows them to pursue their own special approach to the education of children and young people.

We need such small autonomous schools so that democratic governance systems become possible — so that it doesn't seem silly to talk of "everyone" getting together. Just as the Empire State Building contains dozens of companies, so our big school buildings could contain many schools. They could contain schools, furthermore, serving different age groups. They might hire a building manager to deal solely with building matters, as the Empire State Building does. But the educational life of each school would remain distinct and independent. Simple changes that are impossible to make in a mega-school can be decided in one afternoon and implemented the next morning in a small school. You can even dispense with all permanent committees and representative bodies if you get your numbers right. It's our guess that a few hundred students with a faculty of under 20 is about optimum size for effective, democratic schooling. (Those figures don't preclude a half dozen or more schools in one building.)

Teachers will not have a major impact on the way students use their minds until teachers come to know how their students' minds are working — one by one. Teachers cannot help young people make sense of things if they do not have time to answer their students' questions — and time to really hear the questions. They cannot improve a student's writing if there isn't time to read it, reflect on it, and then occasionally meet with the student to talk it over together. They cannot find ways to connect new ideas with old ones if they have no control over curriculum or pacing. Nor can they influence the values and aspirations of young people if they cannot shape the tone and value system of their classrooms and schools.

But what about the loud cries for "accountability" that play such a major role in the support of top-down schemes? Who will tell us if it's "world class"? How will we know for sure how students stack up against one another nationally and internationally in the great race to see who's first?

Small, self-governed schools are at an advantage when it comes to being accountable to their own *immediate* community — parents, students, and fellow staff members. But we need to turn our attention to the question of how schools that set out to be independent and idiosyncratic can meet the legitimate demands for broader accountability to taxpayers. We've built our current system of public accountability on the basis of the factory-model school with its interchangeable parts. It's no wonder that we get almost no useful or honest information back. The task that lies ahead of us is to respond to democratically established norms for equity, access, outcomes, and fiscal integrity without sacrificing our educational principles. Given that few if any of these legitimate needs are currently being met, we need not expect a miracle answer as we design our better mousetraps. We're not catching any mice now. But that doesn't mean that mousetraps are not needed.

The danger here is that we will cramp the needed innovations with overambitious demands for accountability. Practical realism must prevail. Changes in the daily conduct of schooling — whether they relate to new curriculum or pedagogy or just to new ways of collaborating and governing — are hard, slow, and above all immensely time-consuming; they require a level of trust and patience that goes beyond that to which we are accustomed.

The structural reforms — changes in size, the role of choice, and shifts in power relationships — may be hard to make. But to some degree these are the changes that can be "imposed" from above. The trouble is that they merely lay the foundation for the slow and steady work that will have an actual impact on young people's intellectual and moral development. That's the tough realization. Some claim we can't afford such slow changes. They are wrong. There is nothing faster. If we try to go faster we may get somewhere faster — but not where we need to go.

Vandalism, assault, truancy, and apathy on the part of students cannot be eliminated by more of the same — metal detectors, identification cards, automated lateness calls, automatic expulsions and holdovers. Instead, these ills require an assault by schoolpeople on the culture of anonymity that permeates youngsters' lives. Our children need stable personal relationships more than ever, and our schools offer such relationships less than ever.

Although the reasons for the current national concern about schooling may have little to do with democracy, the reforms described here have everything to do with it. Giving wider choices and more power to those who are closest to the classroom are not reforms that appeal to busy legislators, politicians, and central board officials. Such reforms seem too messy and too hard to track. They cannot be initiated on Monday and measured on Friday. They require fewer constraints, fewer rules — not more of them. They require asking why it matters and who cares — not lists of 465 skills, facts, and concepts multiplied by the number of disciplines academia can invent. They require initiating a debate in this nation that might shake us to the roots, a debate about what we value so dearly that we incarcerate our children for 12 years to make sure they've "got it." There *has* to be a better reason than to house them while we're busy, to keep them from taking our jobs, or merely to socialize them into packs or sort them into their proper pecking order.

A democratic society has a right to insist that the central function of schooling is to cultivate the mental and moral habits that a modern democracy requires. These include openness to other viewpoints, the capacity to sustain uncertainty, the ability to act on partial knowledge, and the inclination to step into the shoes of others — all habits that can be uncomfortable to have but, it is hoped, hard to shake. Until we face the fundamental question of the purpose of schooling, it makes little sense to keep asking for better tools to measure what we haven't agreed about. "What's it for?" the young ask often enough. It's time adults took the question seriously. There are no silver bullets when it comes to raising children right, no fast-track solutions with guaranteed cures. The only sensible course involves hard work, keeping your eyes on the prize, and lots of patience for the disagreements that inevitably arise.

A CLASS OF THEIR OWN

Bucking bureaucracy, brashly independent public schools have much to teach about saving education

Claudia Wallis

RON HELMER'S TWO-CAR GARAGE ISN'T much to look at, but the modest structure set amid the cornfields and ranch homes of exurban Freeland, Michigan, harbors a revolution. Inside the garage and spilling over into what was Helmer's living room is the Northlane Math and Science Academy, a new kind of public school. In these unconventional quarters, Helmer, a veteran teacher and school administrator, and two other teachers are attempting to guide 39 students, ages 6 to 12, toward a better understanding of their world via a very active brand of learning.

On a recent day, the youngest children gathered around the small pond in Helmer's backyard, collecting water samples and aquatic plants for study. In the former living room, an older group struggled with the intricacies of urban planning—where to put the power plants, whether to build a highway, how big to make the municipal hospital—by playing a complex computer game called SimCity 2000 on the school's five new Macintoshes. Members of a third group could be found in the garage, sanding and sawing to create kid-size furniture of their own design.

Like other Michigan public schools, Northlane Academy gets its funding—a total of $175,500—from the state lottery and sales taxes. But because the school belongs to a new category of independent "charter schools"—one of nine that have opened in Michigan this fall—Helmer, as principal, is free to spend the money as he sees fit—on those Macs, for example—without interference or oversight from the local board of education. He is also free to depart from the public-school curriculum, which he regards as about a mile long and an inch deep. Northlane, he vows, will teach kids to think and understand rather than learning by rote. "Here we're not so concerned with being able to name the three capitals of South Africa as we are with why South Africa has three capitals; with understanding the cul-

tural, economic and political forces that created those capitals."

It's an approach that so far seems to be going over well with Northlane's young scholars. Sidney Tessin, 10, excitedly tells how her class dissected walnuts and discussed the ways vascular and nonvascular plants differ. In her old public school, "we talked about plants," she says, "but never about *why* there are vascular and nonvascular plants." Nick Reisinger, a freckled 12-year-old, chimes in: "Here we get to talk about things instead of just listening to some boring teacher. I don't feel like 'Duh, what am I doing here?' anymore."

THE CHARTER-SCHOOL MOVEMENT IS NOT YET big. Just 11 states, beginning with Minnesota in 1991, have passed laws permitting the creation of autonomous public schools like Northlane; a dozen more have similar laws in the works. Most states have restricted the number of these schools (100 in California, 25 in Massachusetts) in an attempt to appease teachers' unions and other opponents. Nevertheless, the charter movement is being heralded as the latest and best hope for a public-education system that has failed to deliver for too many children and cannot compete internationally.

"Charters can bring real innovation into the classroom and challenge other public schools to raise their standards," insists Massachusetts Governor William Weld. Parents are clearly eager for alternatives: just consider the growth of the home-schooling movement, which now involves half a million children. Where charter schools have opened, they are thronged with applicants. Where they have not, parents and educators are moving mountains to create them, either from scratch or from a frayed cloth of old public schools.

Take this other scene from the revolution. In the hardscrabble barrio of Pacoima near Los Angeles lies the Vaughn Next Century Learning Center. Of its 1,107 students, 931 are Hispanics who speak limited English; 95% are so poor they qualify for free breakfast and lunch. Four years ago, Vaughn was

just another failing inner-city elementary school: test scores were among the lowest in the state, 24 of the 40-odd faculty members had quit in the previous two years, and the principal had resigned after anonymous death threats. Yvonne Chan, the new principal, was determined to turn things around.

Possessed of enough energy and drive to power a locomotive, Chan was nonetheless hindered at every turn by the inertial drag of school bureaucracy. California's education code runs to 6,000-plus pages. Most of it seems designed to generate more paper: local schools are required to send reams of forms to district offices before they can fix a broken window, change the school menu, take a class on a field trip or buy new textbooks. To make real innovations, Chan found herself perpetually fighting for waivers. In 1992, when California enacted a charter-school law, Chan was one of the first to apply. "We wanted the waiver of all waivers," she explains. "The charter takes the handcuffs off the principal, the teacher and the parents—the people who know the kids best. In return, we are held responsible for how kids do."

Granted charter status last fall, Vaughn Next Century, with a budget of $4.6 million, became a case study in how to take the money and run—in the direction of greater efficiency and higher student achievement. Chan totally revamped spending. She put services like payroll and provisioning the cafeteria out for competitive bids; she reorganized special education. By year's end she had managed to run up a $1.2 million surplus, which she proceeded to plow back into the school. She added new computers, an after-school soccer program and, most important, more teachers, so that the number of students per teacher dropped from 33 to 27. To relieve overcrowding, the school broke ground this month for a new 14-classroom complex.

As for academic achievement, in the four years since Chan has been principal, test scores have risen markedly. She believes that with charter status, further gains will come fast. For one thing, Chan has far more control over her staff and their duties than do principals working under union and district rules, including the power to hire and fire. Teachers at Vaughn work longer hours than they did before the school went charter, but they are paid more and given more authority. Every faculty member serves on one of eight parent-teacher committees that meet weekly and essentially run the school. "We don't want people who just clock in and out," says Chan. "This is not business as usual."

Nor is it for parents, who must sign a three-page contract committing them to be involved in their child's education and to volunteer 30 hours in the school. Most seem pleased to be involved and amazed to be consulted on matters of substance. Says parent Nina Uribe: "It has been a beautiful change."

AMERICAN SCHOOLS DO NOT TURN ON A dime. Yes, they are buffeted regularly by the passing winds of reform (as any teacher will attest). Those breezes usually leave behind another layer of managers in the central office, another mandatory service to be provided to the needy few, another couple of hundred pages of education code telling teachers what they should do and when. But the basic structure remains the same. It is a structure forged in the early industrial age: the school as factory turning out regulation graduates, with teachers as laborers, principals as foremen, and supervisors as well, supervisors, running every detail from the curricular to the custodial in a strictly top-down fashion.

It is this time-honored structure that the charter-school movement seeks to challenge, if not topple, by placing authority in the individual school, freeing it from the bureaucracy. The nation's 140 charter schools come in every size, shape and flavor. Some have a special emphasis, as Northlane does on science; others serve a special population—dropouts, for instance. But whatever their mission or philosophy, they reflect the growing recognition that fundamental change is needed in American education and that to make it, schools must break free of stultifying regulation and bureaucracy. Fifty years of top-down reform have not done the trick.

This realization has found expression in other forms as well. In cities like New York, Philadelphia and Chicago, reform-minded administrators have not waited for state legislatures to act. They have seized the initiative to create scores of charter-like high schools and middle schools—small alternative schools that operate independently of district rules. In New York City, veteran principal and school reformer Deborah Meier is one of a group using a $25 million grant from the Annenberg Foundation to raise the number of such schools from 50 to 100. The goal, she says, "is to demonstrate that public schools can be creative, idiosyncratic, interesting places of academic excellence without losing their publicness."

A handful of other places—notably Baltimore, Maryland, and Hartford, Connecticut—are experimenting with a far more radical way to circumvent bureaucracy: hiring a for-profit company to run their schools. "The idea," says Baltimore schools superintendent Walter Amprey, "is to have a company ready for true accountability that offers a way to pierce the bureaucracy and gives us a model that, if we have the will and courage, could change the collective culture of failure" in urban schools.

"All of these are efforts to bust up the system," says Linda Darling-Hammond, co-director of the National Center for Restructuring Education, Schools and Teaching at Columbia University's Teachers College. "Right now we are trying to do a once-in-a-century reform of education. This is a transforming era. These efforts reflect the frustration people have with a perceived public-school bureaucracy that is very, very entrenched in a way of doing things that cannot meet our needs in the future."

The frustration has been building for years. During the Reagan Administration, a federal study group tripped alarms with the dire 1983 report *A Nation At Risk*. It was the first of a series of major reports showing how poorly American students stack up in math, science and other subjects against their foreign peers and future competitors in the global economy. Throughout the 1980s, school districts increased spending and in many places granted substantial salary raises to teachers. The benefits have been hard to discern.

By the 1990s the talk was all of bureaucratic bloat and poor return on investment. According to a now infamous 1992 report by the Educational Testing Service, the U.S. spends a greater percentage of its gross national product on education (7.5%) than any other country except Israel, and yet is outperformed in math and science among 13-year-olds by more than 10 nations, including Hungary, Taiwan and the former Soviet Union. Other studies indicate that a rather small percentage of the $275 billion spent this year on U.S. public education will actually wind up in the classroom. In 1950 two-thirds of school spending went for classroom instruction; by 1990 the proportion had shrunk to less than half. Administrative outlays had meanwhile doubled from 4% to 8%.

In an era when business has been shedding layers of middle management and adhering to the late management guru W. Edwards Deming's notion of pushing responsibility down the line to those who know the customer best, it does not take a lot of imagination to see that the nation's public education systems need to do the same. In education, those who know the customer—students and their parents—best are the people who work at the neighborhood school. Not the folks in the central office.

Charter-school advocates, particularly the more conservative among them, have another agenda beyond efficiency and reform. Many see charter schools as a way to bring some diversity and options into an arena where traditionally there have been none. "Education is the only place in American life where there is no choice," argues Chester Finn, who served as Assistant Secretary of Education under President Reagan and is a founding partner of the Edison Project, a for-profit education company that has contracts to open three Massachusetts charter schools next fall. "We don't tell poor people what to eat; we give them food stamps. We don't tell them which doctor to go to; they have Medicaid cards." And yet when it comes to schools, says Finn, only the rich can "buy their way out, by moving into a certain neighborhood or choosing private schools." Charters, if there were enough of them, would offer a choice of schools to the less well-off.

In this sense, the charter movement is heir to the more radical voucher movement popularized in the 1980s. Voucher advocates want to break up the "public-education monopoly" by letting parents spend their allotment of public-school dollars as they wish—even on private or parochial schools. Charters are a kinder, gentler, more politically palatable way to provide parents with some measure of choice, albeit within the public system.

They are not, however, palatable to everyone. Not one charter bill has passed a state legislature without controversy. The reason: charter schools take money right out of the pockets of their rivals—the conventional public schools. In most states, the money simply follows the student. Thus, if the district spends $5,000 a year per pupil, and 30 children choose to attend the new charter instead of the local middle school, as much as $150,000—depending on district administrative costs and categorical grants—would go directly to the charter rather than the other district schools.

That prospect distresses many supporters of public education, including the hugely influential teachers' unions. Unions also oppose provisions in many state charter laws that free these special schools from collective bargaining agreements. In California the unions are fighting attempts to expand the state's popular charter schools beyond the current cap of 100. Meanwhile, the Michigan Education Association, having spent a fortune trying to block the state's 1993 charter-school act, is making Republican Governor John Engler's advocacy of that law an issue in his current campaign for re-election.

The M.E.A., along with the American Civil Liberties Union and others, has actually taken legal action to overturn Michigan's rather liberal charter law. Michigan is unusual in allowing private schools to apply for charter status. In fact, most of Mich-

WHEN PUBLIC SCHOOLS GO PRIVATE

For more than five years, the Rev. Norman Handy has been watching the Harlem Park Community School in Baltimore, Maryland. The fortress-like building, set amid the open-air drugmarkets and boarded-up houses of one of the city's worst neighborhoods, is right across the street from his Unity Methodist Church. The view has not been pretty.

Up until two years ago, says Handy, the brick structure was not only decrepit but crawling with rats and mice and "roaches so big you could feel the critters move under your foot." Academically, the school, which serves 2,051 students—prekindergarten through the eighth grade—was in just as bad shape. On any given day, he relates, a significant number of the kids were on "disciplinary removal," hanging out unsupervised and causing trouble on the block. "I would intervene in a street fight four or five times a week," says Handy. "Every morning the white students, especially the girls, would wait until after 9 a.m. to show up, because of gang violence against them."

In 1992 Baltimore's new school superintendent, Walter Amprey, proposed a novel way of dealing with the problems at Harlem Park and eight other city schools: let someone else run them. Amprey proposed giving a five-year, $125-million contract to Education Alternatives, Inc., a Minneapolis, Minnesota, corporation that operated three schools in three states. Handy was among many citizens who opposed the plan: "I saw it as a subterfuge to subvert the educational process and to experiment with African-American children."

Amprey's plan prevailed, and now Handy is a convert. Today he says, "That building is an oasis in a desert of poverty, drug addiction and violence." E.A.I. invested $1.1 million up front in material

improvements, computers and other supplies. It moved quickly to clean and repair the schools and take charge of security. Maintenance and financial management were contracted out for greater efficiency.

The Minnesota firm also instituted its teaching program, called "Tesseract," a name derived from a magical pathway in the children's classic *A Wrinkle in Time*. The program requires teachers to analyze each student's learning style and then devise an individualized plan and goals. It emphasizes parental involvement, the use of computers and continual encouragement. Posters bearing upbeat slogans abound in Tesseract schools: "Go for It!"; "Every Child Has Gifts and Talents."

The visible improvements in E.A.I. schools helped persuade the Board of Education in Hartford, Connecticut, to sign the firm to a $200 million contract earlier this month, under which it will manage the citywide system of 32 schools and 26,000 students. As in Baltimore, the decision was preceded by battles.

Chief among the critics of E.A.I. are members of the Baltimore and Hartford teachers' unions, who are, among other things, unhappy over the dismissal of Baltimore's experienced (and unionized) classroom aides. E.A.I. replaced them with recent college graduates who receive low pay and no benefits, and who tend toward high turnover. "You train them and they may be gone in six weeks," complains a teacher. Some opponents are unhappy with E.A.I.'s policy of mainstreaming nearly all special-education kids into regular classes—a measure they regard as a cost-cutting trick that shortchanges some kids.

But the most serious criticisms concern educational performance. According to figures released by the Baltimore schools last week, test scores in reading and math

have dropped slightly in the eight Tesseract elementary schools, while they rose a bit in the rest of the system. On the other hand, attendance at E.A.I schools was up. Stunned by the report, E.A.I. immediately dispatched a team of eight independent experts to Baltimore to re-examine the test data. Company officials point out that, to begin with, E.A.I. had been handed some of the city's lowest performing schools. In addition, E.A.I.'s test takers include more special-ed kids than at other schools. A third argument: student turnover rates at the schools are very high (30% of students present in September are gone by June). "Does Tesseract work?" asks E.A.I.'s Philip Geiger. "To know that, the kids have to have been in the program." Amprey insists that "we need five years and maybe more, but we know enough to say that this concept will work."

But the larger issue for defenders of E.A.I. is whether private corporations have any business making profits off public schools in the first place. E.A.I. chairman John Golle likes to point out that plenty of companies already do: the textbook industry, private bus companies, food services, even plumbers and electricians. Bringing in professional management makes sense, he insists. "We have asked well-meaning, competent educators to supervise the fixing of the boiler room and analyze cash flow—things they are not educated in." Most important, Golle notes, a private company is accountable. "You can cancel us and show us the door after we've invested millions up front in your district." Indeed, if test scores don't begin to rise, that may be just what Baltimore will do.

—By Claudia Wallis. Reported by Richard N. Ostling/Baltimore

igan's first charters were granted to former private schools. The M.E.A. argues that these schools are not truly public and cannot legally receive public funds. Last week a Michigan judge sent a chill through the charter community by temporarily holding up disbursement of $11 million in state funding until the matter is resolved.

In most states charter laws are quite weak; they actually make it difficult to create a charter school. There are no start-up funds, no buildings provided, no guarantee of support services from the school district. Local unions often add to the obstacles, making it tough to recruit teachers.

Though state education officials recognize the problems, coming up with seed money for charters is not easy, given the political opposition. A tiny bit of help may come from the Federal Government: a $6 million development fund for charter schools is included in the $11 billion school-reauthorization bill signed last week.

Meanwhile the experience of Clementina Durón in Oakland, California, is all too typical. When Durón, a public-school principal, joined with a group of Latino parents to form a charter middle school in the low-income barrio of Jingletown, they faced open hostility from the district school

board and union. The district refused to allow the proposed school to participate in its self-insurance program, which would have cost only $400. Instead, Durón had to pay $10,000 for private liability insurance. Nor was the district willing to share its legal services or payroll department. The attitude, says Durón, was " 'You guys want to run your own school, then you do the whole thing. Go ahead and fall on your faces.' "

The founders of Jingletown charter nearly did, but they were motivated to persevere. For years, the tight-knit community had watched its youngsters graduate happily from the local elementary school only to get lost in huge, anonymous and gang-ridden junior highs. They craved an alternative. Still, it was not until Aug. 20, 1993, three weeks before school was to start, that the district approved Jingletown's opening. The local Roman Catholic diocese agreed to provide a small park as a temporary site, and during the next few weeks, Jingletown parents feverishly dug ditches for electrical lines and sewers. They arranged to rent eight trailer-like portable classrooms for the school's 120 sixth- and seventh-graders, but when classes began, the sewer lines were still incomplete. "For three weeks, kids had nowhere to go to the bathroom," recalls Durón. "We had to knock on doors in the neighborhood. I'd take kids 10 at a time."

Miraculously, Jingletown is now in its second year, though still in need of a permanent home. Parents are pleased with the small classes and individual attention. "This school is a necessity," says Durón. "We are driven by commitment and passion."

COMMITMENT AND PASSION CAN BUILD A school, but will that school succeed educationally? Will charter schools produce graduates that are better equipped for success in society, as their advocates hope?

It is too early to measure the success of charter schools. But for all their diversity, it is interesting to note that many seem to be embracing a very similar set of pedagogical principles. First, reduce class size. Make sure parents are heavily involved. (Contracts with parents are a common feature.) Just as important, keep school size small, particularly in the inner city, where kids desperately need a sense of family and personal commitment from adults. Encourage active hands-on learning, in part through the intelligent use of technology. For older kids, drop the traditional switching of gears and classrooms from math to social studies to biology every 45 minutes and substitute lengthier classes that teach across disciplines.

These principles have proved successful in experimental schools of the past. "The tragedy of American education is not that we don't know what to do," observes Dominique Browning of the Edison Project, which has devised an elaborately ambitious plan for its schools. "There are countless studies in countless classrooms that show what works. The problem is getting it done on a big enough scale to make a real impact."

But the best intentions and cleverest plans can run aground in practice. The opening year of Michigan's University Middle School, a charter school for inner-city kids in Detroit, was an unmitigated disaster. The inexperienced staff of white, suburban-raised teachers had no idea how to relate to the kids, and vice versa. Insufficient supervision meant that students were hanging out windows and riding elevators all day long. The 90-min. classes failed to hold their attention. Midway through last year, the principal quit in despair.

With a strict new discipline code, University Middle School is off to a better start this fall. Still, critics of charter schools are worried that there is insufficient oversight, and experience will probably prove them right. There is, however, one important check on the performance of these new schools: most states grant charters for a maximum of five years. If the school fails to measure up, the charter will not be renewed.

Even if charter schools do succeed individually, the bigger question is, Will they make a difference to American education at large? Charter proponents argue that their schools are laboratories for change, places that will shine as examples and inspirations to the rest of the school system.

A number of experienced educational reformers have their doubts. "We have this romantic view that if we can show a successful pilot school, others will follow. Not true!" says Linda Darling-Hammond, noting that decades of successful magnet schools and model schools have not transformed the system. "Ordinary schools don't have the material resources—the funds, the faculty—to emulate the charters," she says. And it doesn't help that some school districts are so much poorer than others. "Unless you equalize spending, there's no hope of reforming schools at the bottom of the range."

Some critics go so far as to say that charter schools will actually hurt public-school systems by drawing away talent and money; they benefit the few at the expense of the many. "If state mandates are really such an impediment to the 1.6 million public-school students in Michigan, then why not remove them for all of us?" asks M.E.A. president Julius Maddox. Such concerns temper the general enthusiasm for charter schools expressed by U.S. Secretary of Education Richard Riley, who as a Democrat is closely attentive to the union view: "We don't want to take our attention off the great majority of schools. We need to make all schools more challenging and engaging."

But given how hard it is to start just one small charter school, how will it be possible to remake the entire system? In New York City, Meier hopes to show the way by building a new citywide support system for independent public schools. "We want to create a system that cherishes their idiosyncratic qualities, that encourages them to be entrepreneurial and creative and in which we invent some new forms of accountability." Without it, she fears, charter schools will be nothing more than "cute exceptions."

But maybe not. Minnesota doesn't have many charter schools, but it does have the longest experience with them. Educators there say the schools have had an influence well beyond their numbers. In several towns and cities, education officials have been spurred to reform by the mere prospect that a charter school would open in town.

In Forest Lake, a suburb of St. Paul, after facing down a group of parents who wanted to charter a Montessori program, the local school board decided to form such a program of its own. In the small college town of Northfield, the threat of secession by a charter group led the district to create a Spanish-language immersion program for first- and second-graders, introduce multiage classrooms and enrich the math program for middle-schoolers. "The charter made it easier to change things," admits Northfield superintendent Charles Kyte. "If we weren't progressive enough and didn't change, then somebody else would come along and do it for us."

Such change is inevitable in the view of Ray Budde, a retired University of Massachusetts professor of school administration who is credited with inventing the charter-school idea. "If you see kids leaving you and money leaving you and you're criticized about the job you're doing, you're going to respond," he says. "This is a wake-up call for the Establishment: the old organization doesn't fit the times. It's like the Berlin Wall—it's got to come down. But it's going to take 10 or 20 years for something new to emerge."

In the meantime, parents want better schools *now*. And in spite of the obstacles, they are organizing charter schools in droves and flocking to what few exist. Principal David Lehman of West Michigan Academy of Environmental Science, near Grand Rapids, has a sheaf of applications several inches thick for the year 1997, though his school has no track record. This summer he got a letter from Amy and Ron Larva of Grand Rapids. Their child was not yet born, they wrote, but they wanted to reserve a kindergarten spot for the year 2000.

—With reporting by Margot Hornblower/Los Angeles, Ratu Kamlani and Richard N. Ostling/New York and Scott Norvell/Minneapolis

Rebel With a Cause

ROCHELLE L. STANFIELD

Five years ago, fresh out of Princeton University, Wendy Kopp formed Teach for America to get some of the best and the brightest of the nation's college graduates interested in teaching. But now she's pushing for a more radical overhaul of the system.

Wendy Kopp is a young woman who makes no small plans. Even so, her latest undertaking is a doozy: She wants to revolutionize the teaching profession.

"Our whole mission is to build within the profession of teaching a talent pool which is unparalleled," she said in a recent interview. "We're committed to effect systemic change in the way all teachers are brought into the profession."

Teach for America, Kopp's five-year-old organization, aims to recruit the smartest and most committed college graduates into teaching. How? By bringing about a complete overhaul of the way teachers are trained and licensed to teach in public schools, Kopp said.

Many of the nation's brightest students disparage traditional education courses in college as "Mickey Mouse." Teach for America proposes to let teachers learn on the job with the support of a mentor. States require prospective teachers to have passed a certain number of college education courses before they can get a license, which is usually called a "certificate." Kopp wants states to license solely on teaching performance. "I'm convinced we are going to figure out the best way to develop teachers," she said.

The education establishment isn't quite sure what to make of Kopp and her organization. Many longtime activists in the teacher preparation arena, after all, have been working furiously toward the same basic goals—recruiting top students, improving teacher education and reforming state licensing practices—for at least 10 years, since before the 27-year-old Kopp graduated from high school. And the federal government has made professional development for teachers a high priority in the Goals 2000: Educate America Act, which President Clinton signed earlier this year, and in the reauthorization of the 1965 Elementary and Secondary Education Act.

Nonetheless, most education experts say that they welcome Kopp's enthusiasm, energy and commitment. Some add, cautiously, that they simply want to make sure that Kopp's ideas are subjected to the same rigorous scientific evaluations that mainstream notions must survive. A few are hostile to the upstart Kopp and resent all the publicity that she gets.

"This initiative is receiving attention out of proportion to its actual impact now or in the future," Arthur E. Wise, the president of the National Council for Accreditation of Teacher Education, said in an interview.

And Linda Darling-Hammond, a respected professor of education at Columbia University's Teachers College, recently gave Teach for America an F in an article for the September issue of *Phi Delta Kappan*, a widely read magazine for educators. "Extremely costly, plagued by questionable fiscal practices, exhibiting continuing problems with training and management and unable to prepare most of its recruits to succeed in the classroom, Teach for America demonstrates once again why quick fixes don't change systems," she wrote.

In a 14-page response to Darling-Hammond's article, Kopp branded it "filled with inaccuracies, unsubstantiated statements and mischaracterizations of our efforts" and said that the author had "made no effort to understand our program and the assumptions on which it is based, nor to gauge its quality and impact in an objective or scientific manner."

Teach for America recruits about 500 new teachers a year. Public elementary and secondary schools hire 150,000-

175,000 new teachers a year to fill out the nation's complement of about 2.5 million.

But, surprisingly, just about everybody takes Kopp and her compatriots seriously. Clinton has praised Teach for America, and Kopp has won several big-time service awards. Stories about Teach for America have been in all the major news media. The organization's roster of corporate and foundation backers includes all the important names.

The open question is how much of the attention and recognition flows from the merit of Kopp's ideas and how much from her considerable skills at public relations and fund raising.

"Don't underestimate them," said William L. Smith, a former U.S. commissioner of education (the top federal education official before the Education Department was established). "They are the most sophisticated, entrepreneurial and enterprising group of young leaders that I've ever seen, and they are going to stir up some kind of pot."

All this derives from Kopp's Teach for America, a private, not-for-profit organization that calls itself the "National Teacher Corps" and recruits, trains and places recent graduates from top colleges and universities who make a two-year commitment to teach in poor inner-city and rural schools. In June, the Clinton Administration's Corporation for National Service awarded Teach for America a $2 million grant.

Kopp proposed Teach for America in her 1989 undergraduate thesis for Princeton University. After she graduated that June, she got Mobil Corp. to ante up $26,000 and Union Carbide Corp. to provide office space in Manhattan. And she took off.

Teach for America Inc., Kopp said, is now a holding organization with a $9 million budget, 18 offices around the country, a 100-member staff and two new subsidiaries with some very ambitious ideas. The subsidiaries, TEACH! and Teacher Assessment for Licensure, are planning to market a recruitment, selection and training package to school districts and a new teacher licensing test to states for the school year that begins in the autumn of 1995. Kopp and her colleagues said that they are deep in negotiations with several prospective buyers.

With these two ventures, however, Kopp and Teach for America may have overreached, at least as far as the admiring education establishment is concerned. It's one thing to mobilize the best and the brightest college graduates to help out in the poorest schools for two years as a national service project. It's quite another matter to mess with the fundamentals of pedagogy and the legal strictures for licensing.

"We've got a lot of day-to-day substitute [teachers] in Philadelphia, for example, who may or may not have an interest in children," said Frederica F. Haas, the director of the Bureau of Teacher Preparation and Certification for the Pennsylvania Education Department. "I have to say to myself, 'Would I want [a] Teach for America [corps member], somebody coming out of Brown University, the cream of the crop, who may not have a lot of pedagogical understanding and skill but has the incentive to make a difference?' And I want to say, 'Yeah!' "

But when it comes to having Teach for America make sweeping changes in the basic structure of teacher preparation and licensing, Haas added, "for this whole blanket kind of thing, I'd have to say, 'No, I don't think so.' "

LEARNING ON THE JOB

Teach for America is about learning on the job—and that's what the organization has done in its first five years.

Kopp created Teach for America with a lot of enthusiasm and self-confidence but no teaching experience or knowledge about the teaching profession.

She got the idea for the project at a conference of business leaders and college students in 1988 that was sponsored by the Foundation for Student Communication, a student organization she headed at Princeton. After graduating from college, she solicited funds from the business contacts she'd made, set up a network of recruiters on top college campuses and got a handful of school districts to agree to accept the recruits as teachers in positions that the schools couldn't fill with regular teachers (to mollify the teachers' unions, which feared displacement of their members).

In the summer of 1990, Kopp gathered her recruits in Los Angeles for a two-month pep rally on excellence in education accompanied by practice teaching in the Los Angeles schools. In September, the recruits fanned out to school districts in five states—and hit a cultural and professional brick wall. Not only were they unprepared for the conditions they encountered in the schools, some of Teach for America's recruits have said, they also weren't prepared to teach.

"We were operating under the assumption that we would build them into a corps and that the school districts and the local schools of education would provide whatever support and development they needed," Kopp recently recalled. "What we found was that most of the school systems provided very little support, and the corps members were very frustrated by the courses they were taking in the schools of education."

And so Kopp went back to the drawing board and redesigned her teacher preparation system into a two-year residency program to coincide with the two-year commitment that recruits make.

For summer 1994, Teach for America ran a summer school in Houston with a four-week institute on teaching techniques combined with carefully supervised teaching in the school. During their two years on the job in their schools, Kopp's troops have a mentor, an experienced teacher on the Teach for America staff.

Kopp said that her residency program is ready to go on the road. And so she launched TEACH! to do that. "TEACH! is seeking contracts where a district actually pays us to recruit, select and train teachers for them," Richard Barth, its president, said in an interview. "That is a very important paradigm shift."

No more will Teach for America be limited to filling vacancies that certified teachers don't want. It plans to go mainstream. And here is where many professional educators switch from indulgent cheering to cautious scrutiny.

Professionals in teacher education acknowledge that many education courses have been Mickey Mouse—unrealistic, unhelpful lessons in pedagogical arcana. But they insist that the profession is improving education schools from within. And they warn of the danger of throwing out academic training if teaching is to be considered a real profession.

"What it means to have a profession is having a careful program of [academic] preparation," said Wise of the National Council for Accreditation of Teacher Education. "Teacher education used to be terrible and it still is terrible in some places. But it is not universally terrible, and it is not terrible in the 500 schools that we accredit. We propose to fix it rather than end-run it."

There are about 1,300 education schools across the nation. About 800 apply to Wise's organization for accreditation, a kind of seal of approval. Only 500 get it.

Kopp's program stresses hands-on experience for teacher trainees and in-the-school support for novice teachers, two elements that have been gaining favor with professional educators.

Linking up teacher education with real live classrooms is an essential—but still rare—practice, said Marshall S. Smith, the Education undersecretary and a former dean of the Stanford University School of Education. "The [education schools] have to involve [the student teachers] in a hands-on way so they have a strong sense of the nature and content and strategies that they need to teach," he said. "A few institutions do that, but most of them still have a long way to go."

School systems and education schools, he added, "have really been isolated from each other."

One of the eight national education goals in the Goals 2000 law is professional development for teachers. And in reauthorizing the Elementary and Secondary Education Act, Congress has agreed to encourage all schools—and require some—to spend at least 10 per cent of their budgets on helping teachers to improve their teaching techniques.

"The support notion ties in very nicely with the professional development provisions," David G. Imig, the executive director of the American Association of Colleges of Teacher Education, said in an interview. "These are elements in what Wendy has done that we applaud. We think they are very positive."

On the other hand, all that is known about the Teach for America method is anecdotal. No one has scientifically compared the process or the results with traditional teacher education.

"One of the questions I have is, how can we collect reliable evaluation data so we can know if this method is really working," Sharon P. Robinson, the assistant Education secretary for educational research and improvement, said.

Among the reasons no one knows how well Teach for America works, according to Darling-Hammond, is that Kopp won't allow objective evaluations. "A former [Teach for America] board member states that it may never be possible to subject the program to a rigorous analysis because Kopp will not allow scrutiny and pushes out those who raise questions," she wrote in her recent article for *Phi Delta Kappan*.

The anecdotal assessments of Teach for America have been adulatory. But that may be because the organization's screening process has been so highly selective that only the brightest and most committed recent graduates participate.

"They are young people with the commitment and the drive to seek excellence, so their whole existence is focused on doing the best job they can," Joseph D. Taylor, the assistant superintendent for human resources of the Oakland Unified School District, said in an interview. Taylor, a big booster of Teach for America, has employed about 40 of its recruits a year for the past four years in the Oakland schools. Drive and native intelligence make up for their lack of pedagogical knowledge and teaching practice, he said.

That may work for the hotshots in Teach for America, others say, but what about the average college graduates who will continue to constitute the overwhelming bulk of those who enter teaching?

Another question is cost. "The cost per participant is fairly substantial," Robin-son said. "We don't really have any reliable data about the staying power of these new entrants over the staying power of those who go through more-traditional programs that might be, in fact, less expensive."

TEACH! will charge school districts $8,000 for each teacher it recruits and trains. The $8,000 is almost half again as much as the cost of tuition, room and board for one year at a typical state university where a liberal arts graduate could get a master's degree in teaching.

The $8,000 will support, among other things, a Teach for America mentor who will supervise the work of 20 novice teachers. TEACH!'s Barth said that a mentor for high school teachers would be an experienced high school teacher. But what if the 20 novices are split among several disciplines—English, social studies, mathematics and biology, for example? Educational research now shows that different disciplines call for different teaching strategies. How can a single mentor possibly teach all of them?

"They also have to have mentoring with the school," Barth said. "That's how they would pick that up."

THE LICENSING GAME

No one can become a regular public school teacher without a state license or certificate. And so Kopp's second new venture seeks to break into the licensing game.

Schools of education have a monopoly in this field. States issue certificates to applicants who have the requisite number of education credits from a recognized college or university and who pass a test—often the National Teachers Examination, which is supplied by Princeton (N.J.)-based Educational Testing Service (ETS), which also supplies the Scholastic Assessment Test (SAT) and other standardized examinations.

Because many school districts have teacher shortages, some states have granted exceptions—generally called emergency certificates—so that they can maintain a teacher in every classroom. Teach for America's recruits now get an emergency certificate that lets them teach for the two years of their contract.

Teach for America is lobbying the states to accept TEACH!'s professional residency program instead of academic course work. That's not quite as bold as it sounds. Some states already have an alternative certification procedure for those who come to teaching from other professions. In most cases, however, alternative certificates require some academic course work in education. Teach for America wants to bypass all the academic course work. It also wants its teachers to receive a regular certificate.

But that's only the beginning. Teach for America's licensure project also wants to get into the testing business.

Traditionally, the certification test was a standardized multiple-choice examination based on education course work in college. Teach for America wants to turn it into a performance-based examination, assessing not what you learned about pedagogy but how well you teach.

Performance-based testing is the latest fashion at all levels of education. The Goals 2000 reform movement encourages schools to institute performance-based testing of students. The states, ETS and other test publishers have been working on a performance-based test for teachers since before Teach for America was formed.

ETS, for example, has invested $30 million over the past five years to develop a performance-based test called Praxis. "To do it right is very, very expensive," said Catherine Havrilesky, who heads the project for ETS.

Even so, Praxis has come in for considerable criticism as too narrow and not sufficiently reliable. As a result, the states are working on their own version. A task force of the Council of Chief State School Officers has been working on the problem since 1987. So far, it's developed 10 standards of performance for new teachers. M. Jean Miller, the director of the task force, figures that it will take another three to five years to get a performance-based assessment "up and running."

Teach for America has brashly rushed into this business. It developed an assessment "portfolio" that includes evaluations by the new teachers themselves, along with their principals and mentors, videotapes of them in action and samples of their students' work.

"We actually used that portfolio and field-tested it with about 200 Teach for America corps members nationwide," said Ian Rowe, who heads the Teach for America licensure venture. "It was very effective."

Darling-Hammond doesn't think so. "The portfolio process offers no guidance in learning to teach and provides no standards for evaluating teaching," she wrote in her article for *Phi Delta Kappan*. "The 'performance-based assessment' plan is a reflection of the jargon-ridden, content-free gobbledygook for which education is often criticized . . . no conception of high-quality teaching underlies the jargon."

Kopp responded that Darling-Hammond "does not understand either the manner in which we intend to use the instrument nor the way in which it works."

Teach for America plans to market the portfolio to states for use in 1995. But even some of the organization's most ardent admirers are saying "Whoa!"

"It would be very foolish for them to invest in this," said Imig of the teacher education colleges group.

"Their performance assessments relied heavily on the judgments of people I could not tell were qualified to make those judgments," said Bella Rosenberg, an assistant to the president of the American Federation of Teachers. "They just assumed it was a lot easier to develop performance assessments than I happen to know it is."

"I warned them when they first started that they've got to use the systems that are there," said Smith, the former education commissioner. "They can't expect to change them, because they are but a small piece of the action."

Such warnings aren't likely to slow down Kopp, who says that she's out to change the teaching profession and doesn't intend to let anything or anybody stand in her way. It's thus no surprise that the only thing other than Teach for America listed on her résumé is an extracurricular interest: running.

SCHOOLS THAT DO MORE THAN TEACH

HY JOHNNY CAN'T READ — or write, or do his sums — is just as much a concern of parents and community leaders today as it was nearly four decades ago when the Soviet Union's surprise launch of Sputnik turned the spotlight on the country's deficits in education, particularly in math and science. But today, schools are increasingly called on to fill a more comprehensive role in the development of productive adults. In addition to providing instruction, they must help to close the gaps left by the erosion of traditional family and social structures through a variety of school-based or school-related social services, especially health care.

In what might seem to be an idealized scenario, the familiar neighborhood school is transformed into a "full-service" institution, where a conventional — or innovative — daytime curriculum for youngsters is only one activity in what amounts to a community center serving a broader population than children and youth. These are ambitious objectives, to be sure, but not beyond possibility even in the current dampened climate for new public

spending, as author Joy G. Dryfoos points out in her most recent book.

In *Full-Service Schools: A Revolution in Health and Social Services for Children, Youth, and Families* (San Francisco: Jossey-Bass Publishers, 310 pp. $25.00), Dryfoos expands on her earlier studies of young adolescents, arguing that, without services to assure the health and well-being of the growing number of at-risk children and youth, the chances of their ever doing well in the classroom are poor. Indeed, communities can no longer afford *not* to meet this challenge. The transformation is possible, she concludes, if school administrations and their governing bodies design institutions that are responsive to the needs of the local communities and gain their support and if they tap resources from public, private, and not-for-profit sectors.

The number of schools nationwide that might qualify as models of "full service" is still small [see Annual Editions article 3, "Full-Service Schools: Ideal as Reality." **Ed.**] The most common social service facility, often the core of a more extensive network of services, is the school-based health clinic. These clinics

provide essential health care services for children from disadvantaged social environments. They address health-related problems that directly bear on a child's success in school and later life: teen pregnancy, substance abuse, and violent and suicidal behaviors.

An Old Idea

The idea of locating social services, in particular health clinics, within a school setting is a surprisingly old one. In tracing the history of such ventures, Dryfoos links their use to societal needs — from the outbreak of smallpox in the 1870s to the great wave of immigration at the turn of the century (and the consequent need to screen new arrivals for infectious disease) to the current threat of substance abuse and sexually transmitted diseases among teenage populations.

Dryfoos's approach in examining both narrow and broad programs of in-school services is essentially descriptive and anecdotal in the best narrative sense. Drawing on studies of successful programs and the recommendations of experts in educational reform, adolescent development, and family welfare, she outlines her vision of the

From *Carnegie Quarterly,* Fall 1994/Winter 1995, pp. 6-8. Reprinted by permission of the Carnegie Corporation of New York, 437 Madison Avenue, New York, NY 10022.

"model" full-service school — whose services range from crisis intervention for families under the greatest strain to social skills training for young people preparing for the adult world.

The model naturally varies according to identified needs of the school and community population, taking into account the accessibility of services in the community and the willingness of contracting agencies to provide services within the school. But the result is a kind of settlement house within a school.

Meeting Adolescent Needs

How great is the actual need for "full-service" schools? Concentrating her survey on middle school and high school populations, Dryfoos figures that, of the seven million young people categorized as being at high risk, only about one-tenth have access to health and social services in the school setting, primarily through the 600 schools in which clinics have been established. "Very needy" are the 16,250 schools in which more than half the students qualify for free or subsidized lunches. Of these, she says, 6,500 have such overwhelmingly large populations of poor students that they should be given top priority in the establishment of clinics and social service centers.

Dryfoos's study is particularly helpful in describing how communities can muster the financial support required to transform existing institutions or construct entirely new ones. Two full-service schools described in some detail, Salome Ureña Middle Academies (SUMA) in New York City and Hanshaw Middle School in Modesto, California (see sidebar p.9), were literally built from scratch, their innovative curricula and networks of in-school social services developed in conjunction with the commitment of capital expenditures for new buildings by local school authorities. In order to offer programs that would make them full-service schools, each sought additional resources from public, private, and not-for-profit institutions.

The full-service program at SUMA,

a new middle school in upper Manhattan, was made possible by foundation grants and public programs collected through the Children's Aid Society. The annual budget of $800,000 funds a health center, a family resource center, social services, and an after-school program. With an enrollment of 1,200, that works out to less than $1,000 per student, a veritable bargain in the cost-burdened structure of public education.

Such broad community support is not typical. A subtle barrier to making the full-service school a reality is the failure of educators and community leaders to elaborate in detail their vision of what the new institution should be and then adequately follow through by seeking technical assistance to set up the management structures needed to run such complex programs. They must design appropriate systems of accounting, quality control, medical protocols (in the case of health clinics), personnel management and community outreach. Ordinary school administration will not do.

Future Prospects

Nonetheless, in the case where a school system adopts only a limited approach to providing social services, incremental funds may be more readily available and outside agencies more willing to provide services on the school site than educators might expect. Medicaid funds may be tapped to establish school-based health services, for example, where there is a sufficient proportion of eligible students in a school system, *provided* administrators painstakingly construct the program to meet bureaucratic requirements of managed care and thereafter successfully wrestle with complicated billing procedures.

Other public sources of funds are available for different programs. The U.S. Department of Education distributes more than $6 billion annually to school districts for special programs that serve needy populations. State and county health agencies may provide both funding and personnel for school clinics. In the private sector, individuals, industry, and nonprofit organiza-

tions have provided significant resources for programs to assure quality education, from industrialist Eugene Lang's "I Have a Dream" incentive program to keep disadvantaged students on the college-bound track, to business "partnerships" that help orient students to the workplace. These might be tapped.

Individual and community initiatives such as these can do much to enrich the school years of at-risk children. But the large-scale installation of even narrowly defined social services that Dryfoos envisions would require a massive injection of public funds. To initiate the 16,000 health clinics that she says are needed would cost a minimum of $1.6 billion, a significant amount of which could be redirected from existing federal programs.

Although the political pendulum in Washington has swung since Dryfoos completed her study, and the fiscal purse strings are consequently tighter than ever, she remains upbeat about the prospects for innovation. "Adversity brings people together," she observes. The close cooperation among teachers and administrators, public officials, community leaders, and parents that is required for full-service schools under the best of conditions may actually blossom when the environment seems rather hostile to new investment in social capital. "Public outrage over program cuts and politicians' insensitivity to the needs of families and children are making people more determined than ever to change the institutions they can," says Dryfoos. She hopes that her book will provide not only practical information but also inspiration for community organizations and public agencies that have not been extensively involved in school-based social service programs before.

— MAGGIE McCOMAS

For information:

Joy G. Dryfoos, 20 Circle Drive, Hastings-on-Hudson, NY 10706. See also, Adolescents at Risk, *by Joy Dryfoos (New York: Oxford University Press, 1990).*

AN EVOLVING STRATEGY FOR MIDDLE GRADE REFORM

ANTHONY W. JACKSON

The publication in 1989 of *Turning Points: Preparing American Youth for the 21st Century,* by the Carnegie Council on Adolescent Development's Task Force on Education of Young Adolescents, marked the beginning of Carnegie Corporation's effort to stimulate systemwide reform of middle grade schools, a pivotal yet often neglected segment of American education.

Turning Points provides a set of principles for school restructuring that challenge virtually all of conventional practice in traditional junior high, intermediate, and middle schools.

Soon after the report's release, the Corporation began the Middle Grade School State Policy Initiative, a program of grants to states to stimulate statewide changes in middle grade educational policy and practice. The initiative's focus on states reflects the view that, while it is essential to reform individual schools, creating the capacity for broad reform requires state-level action. Designed as a "top-down, bottom-up" reform strategy, the goals of the initiative are to:

▶ promote widespread implementation of *Turning Points* reform principles through changes in state policies that encourage local schools to adopt promising practices;

▶ target restructuring efforts on schools serving those most in need — educationally disadvantaged youth.

In the nearly three years of the initiative, participating states' strides toward comprehensive reform have been impressive. At the level of policy, a substantial number of states are implementing comprehensive middle grade policy statements.

At the local level, networks of middle grade schools undergoing transformation are actively engaged in implementing *Turning Points'* recommendations in nearly all the states. Many of these schools have established supportive relationships with universities, community and youth-serving organizations, and health and social service agencies.

But do the *Turning Points* principles produce better outcomes for middle grade students? Early results from Corporation-supported research being conducted by Robert Felner, director of the Center for Prevention Research and Development at the University of Illinois, are extremely encouraging. Initial

---

GOOD NEWS ON REFORM

In the late 1980s, in advance of *Turning Points*, California launched a middle school reform program, Caught in the Middle, in part supported by Carnegie Corporation. In December 1992, the California Department of Education reported that the latest California Assessment Program of all the state's eighth-grade students registered an increase in the average scores (a combination of reading, writing, math, science, and history) of eleven points since 1986.

Math and science scores alone have gone up by seventeen and fifteen points, respectively. The news is even better when it is considered that the tests included a very substantial enrollment of new immigrants, many with limited knowledge of English.

From *Carnegie Quarterly,* Spring 1993, pp. 6-7. Reprinted by permission of the Carnegie Corporation of New York, 437 Madison Avenue, New York, NY 10022.

findings show significant improvements in students' reading, mathematics, and language arts achievement, in students' ratings of the supportiveness of the school environment, and in teachers' ratings of students' behavioral adjustment.

In the most recent, third, phase of the initiative, states will concentrate on two critical but undeveloped elements of middle grade reform: the integration of health and education for young adolescents and the reform of curriculum, instruction, and student performance assessment. Some states have addressed one or both of these issues well, but the overall need for greater, sustained work in both areas is reflected in *Turning Points: States in Action,* the interim report of the Council of Chief State School Officers, the Corporation's partner in providing technical assistance to the initiative.

In each of the two key areas of reform, the states' work will address specific objectives that reflect the views of experts in education and health on the major elements of systemwide reform at the state and local levels. Directing states' work toward these objectives, in part, reflects a lesson learned nearly two years ago: that states often need assistance in defining outcomes for comprehensive reform and in weaving these together into a coherent plan.

The objectives that will guide states over the next two years focus primarily on the establishment of statewide standards for the health and education of young adolescents and on building state agencies' capacity to support schools and communities in designing effective programs for middle grade students.

Professional development is a consistent theme. Health objectives include linking health and social services to schools, effective methods for gathering information on health, and providing training and technical assistance to schools and health agencies.

State-level change can create the conditions for innovation, but reform ultimately does or does not occur in individual schools. The initiative will continue to target the transformation of groups of schools, especially in disadvantaged communities. The goal is to create schools that promote intellectual achievement and healthy development for all young adolescents.

A Look to the Future

Middle grade reform continues to gain momentum, supported by the Corporation's initiative and by other foundations, state and local education agencies, professional organizations and unions, and, not least of all, teachers, students, and parents. Efforts are currently under way in several other states in the initiative, in addition to Illinois, to gather data on the implementation of *Turning Points'* recommendations.

Another strategy may involve creating or strengthening professional and community-based organizations and university-affiliated research and development institutions to augment governmental agencies' efforts to stimulate reform.

Action by the federal government to promote educational reform could speed progress. In its objectives and methods of targeting states' work, the Corporation's middle grade initiative is similar to recent federal proposals that provide a framework for educational reform. Over the next two years, the initiative as an experiment in state-based, systemwide reform may both benefit from, and inform, federally sponsored efforts.

STATES RECEIVING MIDDLE GRADE SCHOOL STATE POLICY INITIATIVE THIRD-ROUND GRANTS			
State	**Amount**	**State**	**Amount**
Arkansas	$190,000	New Mexico	$260,000
California	$360,000	New York	$260,000
Colorado	$190,000	North Dakota	$260,000
Connecticut	$360,000	Rhode Island	$260,000
Delaware	$260,000	South Carolina	$360,000
Illinois	$360,000	Texas	$190,000
Maryland	$190,000	Vermont	$360,000
Massachusetts	$360,000		

On Lasting School Reform:
A Conversation with Ted Sizer

Previous reforms amounted to fine-tuning a Model T, says Ted Sizer. Lasting reform requires creating a climate for local educators and community members to craft their own improvement strategies.

John O'Neil

Ted Sizer is Director of the Annenberg Institute for School Reform and Chairman of the Coalition of Essential Schools, Brown University, Providence, RI 02912. **John O'Neil** is Senior Editor of *Educational Leadership*.

During the 1980s, many states felt they had the answer for what ailed schools: tougher graduation requirements, more stringent teacher licensing, and so on. Do you think those kinds of reforms had much of an impact?

The evidence shows that they didn't. The poor kids did poorly and the richer kids did better. And that's not surprising. Those "reforms" were like ordering the Model T to drive 60 miles per hour. You can order all you want, but unless you change the vehicle, right down to how the engine's organized, you're not going to go 60 miles per hour. Too many reforms never questioned some basic assumptions about how schools are organized. How are you going to teach youngsters—inner-city youngsters—to read and write better in a high school if each teacher is responsible for 175 of them? People who made those policies have not understood the necessity of fundamentally reshaping

the way schools run. They may have changed the hubcaps on the problem, but it's still a Model T.

You launched the Coalition of Essential Schools during this era of state-led, top-down reforms. How is the Coalition strategy different from some of the other reforms?

One of the joys of this work is you find all sorts of friends, people marching to similar drummers all over the country. Still, there are two differences between what we're trying to do and what some of the other national projects are working for. One is that we focus on high schools, and many of the national reform efforts focus on younger kids.

Second, we start from the assumption that good schools are unique. In order to be good, a school has to reflect its own community. And therefore, we offer no model. There's nothing that you just "put into place," nothing to "implement." Our research suggests that you're not going to get significant, long-term reform unless you have subtle but powerful support and collaboration among teachers, students, and the families of those students in a particular community. Without that, you can get short-term changes in instruction, but you won't get at the heart of reform—which is

the willingness of the kids to work hard on important things.

That means the important decisions have to be made by the people right there. This frustrates researchers who want to look at how this design works in practice, because each community does things in its own fashion. But we strongly believe that you have to look at reform school-by-school-by-school.

How much has the Coalition grown?

We started with five schools in 1984, and it's now pushing 800. But that's a misleading figure in the sense that some schools are still exploring the idea, some schools have a plan and are putting it into effect, and a small number of schools, maybe no more than 50, have had a plan in effect long enough to make some judgments about how they're different.

What are some of the characteristics of the Coalition schools that have changed their practices in fruitful ways?

They tend to be smaller schools, which means that the key people—the superintendent, principals, teachers, parents, and influential community members—know one another. This means that the agreements and the fights are among people who face each other, and that's important.

Do you mean the schools themselves are small, or that the communities are small?

Both. But that's no surprise, because school administration involves personalities as much as classrooms. I just hadn't thought about it hard enough earlier, that the notion of small scale applied to the functioning of the school as much as it did to the pedagogy.

What else characterizes the most successful Coalition schools?

One of the things that has emerged as most critical—and also the most difficult to accomplish—is reducing the load of students assigned to each teacher. When you get that number down, even if nothing else changes, you see an effect on the kids. The kids show up. They complain because they can't get away with anonymity any more, but they show up.

You've said that teachers really shouldn't have more than a total of 80 students assigned to them. But how do they do that? I'm sure some would say it must take a lot of extra money.

Well, you can do it with extra money, but there isn't a lot of extra money around. Basically, you do it by simplifying and focusing the program and by creating teams of teachers. Take an example: I'm a history teacher and you're an English teacher, and we each have 160 students. So I take 80 students and teach both subjects, and so do you. Without increasing the budget a dime, we each see half as many students for twice as long each day. And since I'm the history major, and you're an English major, I have to submit to your scrutiny on the curriculum in your field, and vice versa.

I can see how that might work in elementary or middle school, but what about high school? The academic demands are much higher there.

Well, people say that, but you'll find that what I just described is characteristic of strong colleges. The amount of focused collective teaching that I'm familiar with here at Brown University, at its best, bears a strong resemblance to good middle school philosophy. It's only the senior high schools that somehow dismiss this.

What else seems to be pushing reform in the successful Coalition schools?

Clearly, the exhibition is very powerful. As soon as you have to describe the curriculum in terms of what the kids can show that they can do, that forces you to make a lot of curricular decisions that previously were swept under the rug. Most curriculums are made up of lists; they are not made up of examples of powerful intellectual work by kids. When you really focus on what kids should be able to demonstrate, you realize that the lists are not only rather meaningless, they're also far too long.

Specifically, what happens when you say that the goal is to prepare kids to be able to do the kind of work required to exhibit, not to cover the textbook from beginning to end?

I'll give you an example from my own field. Let's say that in a U.S. history course, we're concerned whether a youngster can take an unfamiliar Supreme Court decision, read it, figure out the constitutional issues, make some educated judgments about what time that particular case may have emerged on the court's docket, and come to some reasonable point of view on the constitutional question, as if he or she were a Justice of the Supreme Court.

What does this imply for the curriculum? Well a lot of kids now study *Marbury v. Madison* or *Brown v. Board of Education*, but very few can really use their knowledge of constitutional philosophy. That's very demanding. So the faculty realizes that if they're going to prepare kids to do that kind of rigorous work, it's going

to take more time than is normally available. They have to be more focused about what they teach; that's where you back into this "less-is-more" issue.

And some of the Coalition schools have been able to pare down the curriculum to a more manageable size?

Yes, but it's very difficult. Particularly when higher authorities designate committees to put together these goals, standards, and assessments. But the people on these committees usually never have to teach this stuff. As a result, they come up with these gargantuan lists preceded with fiery rhetoric, which heads schools in the wrong direction. That's why so many teachers are cynical about committee-written goals and standards.

You've been skeptical about the movement to create national standards, which some believe is the biggest reform going. Why?

For a variety of reasons. One, which I mentioned earlier, has to do with the importance of making sure that the politics of the community are brought to bear. Say I'm a parent. If I really don't like what's being taught, I want to be able to look in the eye of the administrator who has the ability to change the curriculum. That's not going to happen if decisions are made by a committee of people far away from the community.

My other objection is that national standards still avoid the really bloody issue of turning the Model T into a Ford Taurus. Once again, it's piling this stuff on the schools instead of hitching up our trousers and getting on with the tough work.

It does seem that some of the content standards originating from these national groups are going to be quite lengthy and, perhaps, overwhelming to schools.

While recognizing and appreciating the good will behind all that work, most of us who have taught a long time look at the national standards and sag. This is particularly true of those who are teaching high school kids living under terrible conditions. You know, one-fifth to one-third of our kids are growing up in conditions of danger and misery. So you read these lists, and you look at the kid who has just watched his brother get shot, and you say: Where is the country going?

But some would say that's a reason for having national standards. That the standards held for poor kids right now are so low, and that since there's no local incentive to raise standards, national standards are necessary.

Right, well, that's fine, so we'll write some documents.

But why aren't these kids performing well? Take what could be a national standard that any reasonable school would accept: that high school kids should be able to read a reasonably complicated op-ed piece in the local newspaper and tell you what it says. A lot of kids can't do that. So you have to ask: Is it the lack of the standard, or is it something else? My research and the research of many other people say it's something else.

Let's talk about some other reforms. For example, many see outcome-based education as a promising reform, although it's been mired in controversy the last year or two. Do you see the Coalition as being an example of OBE?

Any education is outcome-based. The whole point of education is to have outcomes. Those kids come to my class in order to change. So all education is outcome-based.

The question is what are the outcomes and who sets them? My view is that they should be set at the levels closest to the parents and kids. Levels of government above the local community should provide all sorts of examples of high-level work; they should create an intense conversation about good work. But ultimately, decisions about outcomes should remain at the local level, where a sense of real-

ism and respect for the local situation is present.

These are not new ideas, obviously. The idea of the exhibition, for example, was retrieved from the practices of the late 18th century American Academy, where a student would have to exhibit mastery in front of the public in order to get a learning certificate. That's an outcome-based concept, but it's not outcomes set in some distant capital by an unelected committee of people who are never held accountable.

School choice—in its many incarnations—is another reform that some are advocating. Do you see choice as a viable way to promote school reform?

Well, first remember that a major sector of Americans have always had choice. Those who are the wealthiest can pick where to live on the basis of the quality in the public schools. If it's good for the rich, it seems to me, it's good for the poor.

As a teacher, I would always prefer to teach kids who elected to be with me. Having taught classes like mandatory freshman English and also basic courses that students elected to take, I think my relationship with the students was better when they had some choice. I was also a principal of a school of choice, and it changed my whole relationship with the parents. I had to be much more attentive to the parents, because my budget depended on their support.

If you look at the Coalition schools that have really been on the move, they have been disproportionately schools of choice. Because nobody has to go there. Choice encourages people to experiment. People call it risk-taking: to me, nothing is riskier than leaving high schools the way they are. But the burden is always on those who favor choice.

Do you think choice might be able to encourage reform even in the schools that aren't schools of choice? In other words, can choice leverage broader improvement?

Choice can have an indirect and a direct influence. The indirect influence is that choice can create some sense of urgency in the existing schools. Right now, a lot of schools feel they don't have to pay much attention to their kids, 'cause they're the only shop in town. Around the country, I've seen again and again how choice can undermine the complacency of a monopoly. And I hate to admit that such complacency exists, but it does.

Many educators see choice as a threat, though. They think it will mean a loss of support, closing schools, and so on.

Well, where the charter schools, or schools of choice within the public sector, seem to flourish best is in districts where there is a rapidly growing student population. In fact, it isn't a threat; all it means is that new schools have to be built, and the school board and the superintendent say that these new schools are going to be different. If these schools of choice are different in the right direction, the kids will benefit, and nobody's losing their job. So of course that resonates back on the old schools.

You mentioned the power of exhibitions. Many people now see performance assessment as an important reform strategy. On the other hand, there seems to be something of a backlash against these alternatives to conventional testing ...

The problem may not be the assessment strategy, but the insistence that it be done on a mass scale. Most people—even those who scream at me in meetings—think it's quite reasonable to look very carefully at and assess the written work of a child. And portfolio assessment is nothing more than taking the real work of a child seriously and looking at it over time, instead of just relying on some 30-minute writing sample.

The problem is when you try to move from that to making comparisons between Johnny Jones in this school and Suzi Smith in that school. That's extremely difficult work, because reasonable people disagree over the quality of writing of an interesting paper. It's really tough to be consistent in grading when you get into rigorous academics. So what we have to do is to develop a system where we trust the people who know the kids.

Some people perceive that outside examiners are objective, but that teachers make subjective judgments about their students' achievement.

Still, if you're very sick, who do you listen to—the physician who's tended you for some time or the circuit rider who shows up and says: "Let me look at the charts. Now cut his arm off."

Recently, there's been an outcry among the public over some of the proposed school reforms. Communities that send lots of kids to college seem to feel that schools don't really need a whole lot of reform. And they're skeptical of reform efforts like alternative assessment or integrating the curriculum, for example.

It turns on the role of the colleges and what they require for admission. If the colleges say they don't care whether there's any connection between the math and physics courses my son takes in school, I wouldn't press for an integrated curriculum. What is slowly happening—in a number of states and colleges, and particularly within the College Board itself—is an agonizing reappraisal of how the colleges present themselves to the schools. Most serious scholars will say that you can no longer constructively separate chemistry, physics, biology, mathematics, and technology. The Amer-

ican Association for the Advancement of Science's Project 2061 shows the necessary and powerful interconnection of those subjects. So some colleges are saying, "We had better get behind AAAS; we've got to get the signal out that we shouldn't just be requiring more of the same."

The Coalition has been touched, hasn't it, by public protests over not just OBE but other reforms that educators sincerely think will improve schools?

Yes, we've taken our lumps.

The Coalition schools that have faced these kinds of protests have handled it by being ahead of the curve. That is, superintendents, principals, and, in particular, school board members, have given thought to who in their communities might have a different kind of agenda, who in their communities might find certain expressions of school policy offensive. And they have made sure that the committees of parents, teachers, and students at the high schools are strong. And, you know, they make sure that the superintendent goes to Rotary, the Chamber of Commerce, and so on.

So, as in the case of a couple of communities I know well, when questions arose, the school committee actually held a communitywide referendum on the changes the schools were undertaking. What happened was that the very noisy, well-orchestrated criticism of a very few people was buried.

You have to realize, though, that these were very savvy superintendents; they wouldn't have dared to do that unless they had really made sure

that the community understood what was going on, was behind it, and was prepared to protect it.

We're beginning a second decade of sustained interest in school reform. Some recent initiatives—for example, charter schools and the experiments in having private companies manage public schools—seem to suggest an impatience with the lack of real reform that has occurred. Are there successes to point to?

Anyone who looks at Fred Wiseman's film [*High School II*] can see that some schools are truly managing to change things in ways that improve the quality of teaching and learning. These kinds of successes are rarely reported by the media.

I read an editorial in the *Boston Globe* about all the things President Clinton has done: nothing about education. One reason, I think, that the public is disinterested in school reform as it is widely defined in the media is that they really don't see much value in the approach that's being pushed. They're not so much against reforms they hear about, but they don't see them as speaking to their particular kids.

Education is a very emotional enterprise for parents concerned about their children. If you remember that, you don't start reform by appointing a governor's commission on school standards, even though that may be a worthy thing to do. My experience is that there's a lot of public interest in reform when you get down to local people and local issues. And that's where reform has got to take place.

Striving for Excellence: The Drive for Quality

There are several very incisive analyses of why American educators' efforts to achieve excellence in schooling have frequently failed to achieve their goals. Today some very fascinating proposals are being offered as to how we might better conceive of what is possible in the drive to achieve qualitative improvement in the academic achievement of students. The current debate regarding excellence in education clearly reflects parents' concerns for more choices in how they attempt to school their children. The new conservative majority in the Congress of the United States has been hearing some proposals for how to realize higher levels of academic achievement of American students. The role of the federal government in providing stimuli for educational development in the states is being thoroughly reassessed. Various assumptions that have been prevalent since the 1960s as to how to encourage qualitative improvement of student achievement are being reevaluated.

The debate over which educational standards are the best ones for American students continues. Many authors of recent essays and reports believe that excellence can be best achieved by creating new models of schooling that give both parents and students more control over the types of school environments available to them. Many believe that more money is not a guarantor of quality in schooling. Imaginative academic programming and greater citizen choice can guarantee at least a greater variety of options open to parents who are concerned about their children's academic progress in school.

We all want the best quality of life that we can attain, and we each desire the opportunity for an education that will optimize our chances to achieve our objectives. The rhetoric on excellence and quality in schooling has been heated, and numerous opposing conceptions of how schools can achieve these goals have been presented for public consideration in recent years. The debate over how to achieve such qualitative improvement has led to the realization of improved academic achievement goals on the part of students, as well as to major changes in how teacher education programs are structured. But we also are beginning to see some fascinating alternatives open to us if we have the will to make them happen.

In the decade of the 1980s, those reforms instituted to encourage the qualitative growth in the conduct of schooling tended to be what education historian David Tyack referred to in *The One Best System* (Harvard University Press, 1974) as "structural" reforms. Structural reforms consisted of demands for standardized testing of students and teaching, reorganization of teacher education programs, legalized actions to provide alternative routes into the teaching profession, efforts to recruit more people into teaching, and laws to enable greater parental choice as to where their children may attend school. These structural reforms cannot, however, as Tyack noted as early as 1974, in and of themselves produce higher levels of student achievement. We need to explore a broader range of the essential purposes of schooling, which will require our redefining what it means to be a literate person. We need also to reconsider what we mean by the "quality" of education and to reassess the essential purposes of schooling our children.

When we speak of quality and excellence as aims of education, we must remember that these terms encompass aesthetic and affective, as well as cognitive, processes. Young people cannot achieve that full range of intellectual capacity to solve problems on their own simply by being obedient and by memorizing data. How students encounter their teachers in classrooms and how teachers interact with their students are concerns that encompass aesthetic as well as cognitive dimensions.

There is a real need in the 1990s to enforce intellectual (cognitive) standards and yet also to make schools more creative places in which to learn—places where students will yearn to explore, to imagine, and to hope.

Compared to the United States, European nations appear to achieve more qualitative assessments of students' skills in mathematics and the sciences, in written essay examinations in the humanities and social sciences, and in the routine oral examinations given by committees of teachers to students as they exit secondary schools. Perhaps this is not avoidable, due to the obvious necessity of some form of governmental financing of our school systems. Policy development for schooling needs to be tempered by even more "bottom-up," grassroots efforts to improve the quality of schools that are now under way in many communities in North America. New and imaginative inquiry and assessment strategies need to be developed by teachers working in their classrooms, and they must nurture the support of professional colleagues and parents.

Excellence is the goal; the means to achieve it is what is in dispute. There is a new dimension to the debate over assessment of academic achievement of elementary and secondary school students. In addition, the struggle continues of conflicting academic (as well as

political) interests in the quest to improve the quality of preparation of our future teachers, and we need to sort these issues out as well.

No conscientious educator would oppose the idea of excellence in education. The problem in gaining consensus over how to attain it is that excellence of both teacher and student performance is always defined against some preset standards. Which standards of assessment should prevail? The current debate over excellence in teacher education clearly demonstrates how conflicting academic values can lead to conflicting programmatic recommendations for educational reform.

The 1980s provided educators with many insightful individual and commissioned evaluations of ways to improve the educational system at all levels. Some of the reports addressed higher education concerns (particularly relating to general studies requirements and teacher education), but most of them focused on the academic performance problems of elementary and secondary school students. From literally dozens of such reports, some common themes developed. Some have been challenged by professional teaching organizations as being too heavily laden with hidden business and political agendas. The rhetoric on school reform extends to the educators in teacher education who are not in agreement either.

What forms of teacher education and in-service re-education are needed? Who pays for these programmatic options? Where and how will funds be raised or redirected from other priorities to pay for this? Will the "streaming and tracking" model of secondary school student placement that exists in Europe be adopted? How can we best assess academic performance? Can we commit to a more heterogeneous grouping of students and to mainstreaming handicapped students in our schools? Many individual, private, and governmental reform efforts did *not* address these questions.

Other industrialized nations champion the need for alternative secondary schools to prepare their young people for a range of life goals and civic work. The American dream of the common school translated into what has become the comprehensive high school of the twentieth century. But does it provide all the people with alternative diploma options? If not, what is the next step? What must be changed? For one, concepts related to our educational goals must be clarified and political motivation must be separated from the realities of student performance. We must clarify our goals. We must get a clearer picture of "what knowledge is of most worth."

Looking Ahead: Challenge Questions

Identify some of the different points of view on achieving excellence in education. What value conflicts can be easily defined?

Do teachers see educational reform in the same light as governmental, philanthropic, and corporate-based school reform groups? On what matters would they agree and disagree?

What can we learn from other nations regarding excellence in education?

What are the minimum academic standards that all high school graduates should meet?

What are some assumptions about achieving excellence in student achievement that you would challenge?

What can educators do to improve the quality of student learning?

Have there been flaws in American federal government programs aimed at encouraging the states to take certain educational initiatives in the past 30 years? If so, what are they?

What choices ought parents and students have in their efforts to optimize the quality of educational services they receive?

—F. S.

Towards Excellence in Education

Chester E. Finn, Jr.

Chester E. Finn, Jr., is John M. Olin Fellow at Hudson Institute and served as an assistant secretary of education from 1985 to 1988.

The battle lines over education reform have been drawn. Republican presidential candidates urge that the 15-year-old Department of Education be scrapped, and several members of Congress have already introduced "abolition" bills. A huge ruckus has arisen over federal interference, national standards, outcome-based education, and the Clinton Administration's *Goals 2000* program. Meanwhile, the Clinton Administration seeks $30.7 billion in fiscal year (FY) 1996 to fund the Department of Education's 250-odd programs. That is not a vast sum by contemporary Washington standards, but it works out to nearly $500 for every school and university student in the land. It is not unreasonable to ask what sort of return we can expect on this investment in relation to the problems plaguing American education today.

The House Budget Committee recently asked me to reflect on that question. Here is the answer I offered: If Congress wants to strengthen the quality, productivity, and efficiency of American education, as well as the performance of students passing through it, then further investment in the current array of federal programs is not a promising use of resources. With rare exception, these programs were designed for wholly different purposes—expansion of access, promotion of equality, and extension of services—and there is no evidence that efforts to adapt them to goals of quality and excellence have succeeded. Strategies formulated to increase the *quantity* of educational services available to people cannot be counted upon to boost the *quality* or performance of an education system in which mediocrity has long since overtaken scarcity as the central problem in need of solution.

Moreover, as the years have passed, those quantity-serving programs have been captured by educational "providers" and do not reliably serve the interests of quality-minded "consumers." They were designed for an era when it was believed that states, communities, and families could not be trusted to do the right thing, and that Washington and its experts should therefore set rules and make decisions. Today, however, the heavy hand of Uncle Sam deters more reform in education than it fosters.

FROM QUANTITY TO QUALITY

There is a long-standing, if rather academic, argument about whether education is a "private good" or a "public good." If it were strictly the former, individuals would profit from obtaining more schooling, but the larger society would not. In such a circumstance, all spending on education should be private, not courtesy of the taxpayer or government at any level. (We could view automobile ownership in this way. We expect people who want cars to muster the private means to purchase them in the marketplace.)

If, on the other hand, all benefit from education accrues to the larger society, and none to persons receiving it, it would be foolish for individuals to spend anything out-of-pocket to receive better schooling. All support of education would properly come from "public" resources. (This is how we think about national defense and highway construction.)

We find most Americans between these two poles, recognizing that education confers both private gain and public benefit. This is also where most analysts come down. Their consensus is well stated in *Making Schools Work* (Brookings Institution, 1994), by University of Rochester economics professor Eric A. Hanushek and a panel of education economists:

> A look at the history of the twentieth century suggests that schooling has generally been a good investment. . . .

The average earnings of workers with a high school education remain significantly above those of the less educated, and the earnings of workers with a college education now dwarf those of the high school educated.... Society as a whole also benefits from education. The nation is strengthened economically by having workers with more and better skills.... The more educated are more prone to vote in local and national elections, and a better-informed and more responsible electorate improves the workings of a democratic society. Increases in the level of education also are associated with reductions in crime.

Education has also helped to achieve both greater social equality and greater equity in the distribution of economic resources.... [F]or our purposes it is safe to say that education has been a good investment both for society and for individuals.

The context of that investment has changed, however. Adding resources for education was straightforward, so long as the goal was purchasing more of it, and the money served to enlarge or equalize the delivery system. At the turn of the century, just 6 percent of American adults had finished high school. By 1967, half of the adult population was walking around with diplomas. About 94 percent of today's young people complete high school sooner or later. Getting to that point required a vast expansion of the supply of education, which cost a great deal of money. But elementary and secondary schooling is now readily available to all who want it.

Much the same situation obtains in higher education. Sixty-two percent of high-school graduates proceed immediately to college. By the time Americans reach their early forties, 56 percent have had some college education and 28 percent possess a bachelor's degree. A large majority of American campuses are essentially "open-admission" institutions. Indeed, the hunger of colleges and universities for enough warm bodies to fill all the places in the vast post-secondary education industry now aggravates the low standards of our primary and secondary schools. So ample is access to educational services that it has begun to undermine their quality. That is why, as we approach the limits of growth in the quantity of education, further societal gains need to come from improving its performance. The central reason that the nation is "at risk" today is not because we are not supplying enough education but because our students are not absorbing enough of it.

The United States can take pride in having mustered the will and the means to solve the problems of equitable access and sufficient services. The question now is whether we can steel ourselves for the more difficult challenges of performance and efficiency.

THE FEDERAL ROLE IN EDUCATION

The U.S. Constitution never mentions the word "education," whereas it is embedded in the constitutions of all 50 states. Yet today, the federal government is deeply engaged in many aspects of education. Besides the Department of Education's hundreds of programs, many other departments and agencies are involved, from Health and Human Services (Head Start, financial aid for medical students, etc.), Labor (sundry job training schemes), and the National Endowment for the Humanities to the National Science Foundation and even the Pentagon. Across the government, education support in FY 1994 totaled $68 billion in "on-budget" outlays and nearly $20 billion more in "non-federal funds generated by federal programs" (most of the latter being private capital for government-guaranteed loans to college students).

Though the seeds of federal involvement were sown in the nineteenth century, the federal government's present role in education was shaped during the mid-1960s. Most of today's federal programs and activities in education continue to reflect the priorities, assumptions, and values of that era: an expansive national government that spends whatever is needed to supply resources to people who lack them; ending inequality and poverty by redistributing opportunity and services through a thousand federal programs, shaped and run by professionals; and the sublime confidence that "Washington knows best." Above all, the architects of the education programs of the 1960s believed that the nation's education problems were problems of shortage—and that their solutions lay in boosting the supply of education services and the access of those who had been deprived.

One need not dispute this mid-1960s reasoning. There were genuine access and equity problems at the time, and it was not unreasonable to enlist the national government in their solution. But the world has changed in the last three decades, and with it the essential nature of the education problems facing the United States. Yet, today, we still find ourselves with programs conceived for yesterday's purposes. Though "quality" has recently entered the rhetoric of federal program managers and advocates, those programs were not designed to meet this criterion. Moreover, there's little reason to believe that they will successfully make the switch from quantity to quality. That would be like entering a milk truck in the Indianapolis 500; it will not do well in this setting because it was not built for speed.

Let me set forth five aging assumptions that underlie most Department of Education programs and activities, followed by the new realities that they ignore. All five come straight from the social-reform handbook of the mid-1960s.

(1) The great problem of American education is that some people get more of it than others do. Access must be expanded and underwritten, particularly for needy groups (the poor, the handicapped, minorities, non-English speakers, etc.) that are not receiving enough services

and have in some cases been denied them. Because states and localities are not meeting these needs and cannot be trusted to do so, it is the federal government's obligation to intervene.

Today, access is virtually universal, but the quality of what children have access to is mediocre, expectations are low, and results are unsatisfactory. Federal interventions have created perverse incentives (such as classifying more and more children as "disabled") and have impeded bold reform efforts such as school choice.

(2) States and communities are stodgy, miserly, sometimes discriminatory, and ignorant about good research and practice. The federal government needs to foster innovation, justice, and the dissemination of knowledge.

Today, states and communities are taking the lead in transforming the schools, but federal policies often get in their way. Moreover, in an age of CD-ROMs, on-line information services, faxes, e-mail, cable television, conference-calling, and widespread travel, stage and local educators have easy access to all the knowledge and expertise they can use.

(3) A unified, centrally managed, and essentially monopolistic public school system is the best way to distribute resources according to national priorities and is, accordingly, the proper focus of federal policy and programs.

This assumption goes back to the "scientific-management" ideas of the 1920s and to the belief that "public" schools mean schools run by government agencies. Today, however, many people understand public education as a network of schools that all *serve* the public but may be organized and run in a thousand different ways. Federal programs, however, discriminate against such alternatives as non-government schools, charter schools, and home-schooling.

(4) Redistributing resources from people, states, and regions that have more to those with less is both a proper function of the national government and a way to improve education. Hence, poverty and other gauges of "neediness" should be the primary basis for receiving federal education aid.

As with welfare, the redistributionist ethic has had perverse effects within federal education programs, such as "punishing" schools and individuals that pull themselves out of ignorance and poverty. Moreover, our single-minded focus on "equality" has softened or erased standards lest some fail to meet them.

(5) Experts know best. The professionals who deliver education are, therefore, Washington's primary clients, even though the resources are provided in the name of needy consumers.

Consumers now have very different ideas about education reform than do the "experts," and many would make different decisions about the use of resources if they could. The federal government's deference to "producers" is not confined to education, of course, but here, as in other fields, it serves to shore up the status quo, keep power with the "establishment," and deter radical change. It also underwrites bureaucracy, subsidizes the very organizations that lobby it for more money, and pumps billions into the bank accounts of middle-class professionals.

FOUR FAILURES

These hoary assumptions still guide the expenditure of nearly all of the money that Uncle Sam spends on education. Yet, there is no evidence that the average American child will learn more, that the typical school will become more productive, or that the quality of American education as a whole will improve as a result of continuing such "investment" policies. Let me briefly discuss four examples.

Title I. This is the largest single program at the Department of Education, accounting for $7.4 billion in the Clinton budget request. It has changed its name a couple of times and gone through eight major reauthorizations (most recently in 1994), but the essential program dates to 1965. Close to $90 billion has been spent since its inception. The underlying rationale was, and remains, meeting the "special educational needs of educationally deprived children" by providing their schools with additional money to be used for "compensatory" services such as tutoring.

Cautionary notes were sounded at the outset, especially about the shift of power and control to Washington. In their "minority views" on the 1965 bill, for example, eight Republicans termed it "the most direct and far-reaching intrusion of Federal authority into our local school systems ever proposed in a bill before Congress. They were not crying wolf. They had spotted an essential characteristic of Great Society programs, here applied to the nation's schools:

> At first reading, this bill appears to leave approval of local programs to the State education agency, where the power belongs. However, there is inserted (hidden, almost) a power in the U.S. Commissioner of Education to require that such approval be consistent with basic criteria formulated by him. This effectively robs the State agency, or the local schools for that matter, of any real authority to shape the programs. This centralization of power in the U.S. Office of Education runs throughout the bill.

Thirty years later, that precise situation still obtains, except that the money is greater and the stakes are higher. What was then an "Office" is now a full-fledged cabinet department, the statutory language is far more prescriptive, and the accompanying regulations are truly voluminous.

But have poor children *learned* $90 billion more during these three decades? The Department of Education was refreshingly candid in September 1993, when it explained why the program should (again) be reformed by arguing that it was not accomplishing much:

> Chapter 1* is no longer closing the gap between disadvantaged students and others. . . . The progress of Chapter 1 participants on standardized tests and on criterion-referenced tests was no better than that of nonparticipants with similar backgrounds and prior achievement. More generally, the relative performance of students in very high-poverty schools . . . actually declines from the early to the later grades. . . . Chapter 1 has little effect on the regular program of instruction. . . . Chapter 1 frequently does not contribute to high-quality instruction. . . . Chapter 1 is not generally tied to state and local reform efforts. . . .

The authors of that report, and of myriad other evaluations over the years, naturally intended their gloomy conclusions to justify still more changes in the federal program. In this instance, the 103rd Congress agreed to some (though not all) of the amendments sought by the Administration, and President Clinton's FY 1996 budget justification predictably asserted that the program will henceforth be more effective.

Possibly. But it is well to take a step back and ask whether this much-revised federal education program does not, in one key respect, resemble the oft-reformed welfare program: Washington policy makers have tried time and again to revamp it so that it will actually accomplish its intended purposes, yet none of these repairs, now spanning several decades, has solved the basic problem. Should we try yet again to reform this education program in Washington, pouring more resources into it, only to discover again in a few years' time that the program is still ineffective? Or should we consider an altogether different strategy?

The sums involved here are substantial. If the money requested for FY 1996 were targeted to the lowest-achieving 10 percent of U.S. students, it would work out to almost $1500 apiece—enough to pay the tuition at most Catholic schools, even without state and local funds. If targeted to the lowest achieving fifth, it would amount to about $750 each—about what private firms charge for boosting the Scholastic Aptitude Test scores of upper-middle-class high-school students.

THE "TRACKING" FALLACY

Vocational Education. The Department of Education requested $1.2 billion for vocational education in 1996, not including $200 million—plus a like sum for the Labor Department—for its newly enacted "school-to-work" program and not including other billions for job training and tuition aid. Federal vocational-education outlays since 1960 total about $25 billion.

This program's antecedents can be traced to World War I, when the Smith-Hughes Act provided funds to

states to underwrite the salaries of teachers and others involved with preparing young people for industry, agriculture, and home economics. Federal vocational-education programs have been amended many times since, but they still partake of what can be termed the "tracking" assumption, namely, that some young people are headed for college, others for the job market, and that the education provided to the two groups should be fundamentally different.

That way of running the schools may have been suited to an industrial economy when only a small elite needed a solid liberal education in order for the nation to prosper, and when people quickly settled into career paths from which they seldom veered. Today, however, most people have several different careers. Just about everyone needs substantial knowledge and strong skills to handle the challenges of the post-industrial economy and the information age. Also, practically everyone needs the habits, self-discipline, motivation, and ability to interact with others that modern workplaces require.

Separately tracked vocational programs, in other words, have no proper place in today's schools. A unified curriculum that sets the same challenges and standards for everyone is indicated, and it should be taught as engagingly as possible (not excluding the kinds of practical problems and real-world applications once associated only with "vocational" courses).

Besides, today's vocational students are not learning much. According to the 1994 National Assessment of Vocational Education conducted by the Department of Education, academic-track students score at about the seventy-first percentile on standardized achievement tests, while the average score of vocational students is at the thirty-fourth percentile. One study found that "students give up some achievement gains by foregoing academic courses and taking vocational courses instead." Academic-track students even score higher than vocational students *on a test of industrial-arts knowledge.*

The formidable "vocational-education establishment" resists fundamental change. Yet such change is exactly what is needed. Even the Clinton Administration seems to have recognized this, as it begins to bypass vocational education in favor of its new "school-to-work" program and, remarkably, to replace traditional job-training programs with vouchers that consumers can use as they see fit. Why, then, also spend one billion-plus each year on the discredited approach of vocational training?

Bilingual Education. Washington's involvement with bilingual education dates to 1968. Approximately $3.5 billion in federal funds will have been spent for this by the end of FY 1995. For 1996, the administration asked for $300 million, a 20 percent increase. As federal programs go, this is not a huge sum, but bilingual education is a classic example of the corruption of a well-intentioned impulse and the seizure of a federal

---

*The Title 1 program is here referred to as "Chapter 1," a usage common during the 1980s and early 1990s. The 103rd Congress restored "Title 1" as the standard reference.

program by special interests. Above all, it's an example of a program that does not accomplish what most voters and taxpayers think it is meant to do. In reality, it does not even try.

The typical taxpayer supposes that the focus of this program is on teaching English as quickly as possible to immigrant and refugee children who arrive in the United States speaking another language. But that isn't how most bilingual educators see it, and is not, in fact, how the federal program operates. The program attempts to reinforce the child's original culture and native language, using that language as the primary vehicle of instruction and only very gradually developing English fluency. In other words, many bilingual educators are more interested in sustaining the ethnolinguistic, cultural, and political distinctiveness of immigrant populations than in aiding their rapid assimilation into the "mainstream."

Federal bilingual-education programs advance these agendas with money, experts, regulations, and legitimacy. It is never said baldly, of course, but a studied ambiguity has been present since the beginning. The congressional policy statement introducing the 1968 Bilingual Education Act, for example, never stated that the objective of the program was rapid English fluency. Rather, it spoke of "new and imaginative elementary and secondary school programs designed to meet" the "special educational needs of the large numbers of children of limited English-speaking ability in the United States."

Today, a close reading of the Administration's 1996 budget justification reveals *not a word about English fluency.* Instead, it talks of "high-quality instructional programs for recently arrived immigrants and other limited English proficient (LEP) students." Indeed, Congress has capped how much money can be used for the kinds of programs that promote rapid English fluency, often called "English immersion" or "English-as-a-second-language" (ESL) approaches. Only 25 cents of the federal bilingual dollar may be spent for such programs. At least 75 cents must be used for the approach commonly called "transitional bilingual education," in which the native language is used as the main instructional medium.

What difference does it make? A recent study by the New York City Board of Education found that youngsters enrolled in ESL programs acquired English faster, and were able to "test out" of the program sooner, than those enrolled in the "bilingual" programs favored by the federal government. (This finding held even when initial language facility was factored in.) And an analysis of the research literature by Boston University political scientist Christine Rossell found that most studies show "transitional" bilingual programs to be "no different or worse than ... doing nothing." Yet that's where the lion's share of the federal money goes.

LABORATORY WASTE

Regional Educational Laboratories. This is a small program, just $40 million in 1996, but it is another classic case in point. For 30 years, the federal government has been supporting this array of "middleman" institutions. Total expenditures come to more than half a billion dollars (not counting other federal funds that the laboratories have won). Total benefit: practically nothing.

It's not easy even to explain what a "regional educational laboratory" is meant to be or do. Their designers in the mid-1960s (notably President Johnson's Task Force on Education, chaired by John W. Gardner, who later served as Secretary of Health, Education and Welfare) visualized organizations that "would develop and disseminate ideas and programs for improving educational practices throughout the country." They seemed to have something like Los Alamos in mind, describing the new organizations as "akin to the great national laboratories of the Atomic Energy Commission."

What emerged instead was a collection of 10 small, nonprofit organizations spread across the country, which undertook a mishmash of research, dissemination, and technical-assistance activities, aimed mostly at state and local education agencies. It was assumed that states and communities lacked access to good information, could not end this drought for themselves, and needed help from intermediaries created and underwritten by the federal government. This was plausible 30 years ago, when many state and local education agencies had meager research capabilities, information could not be obtained by searching a CD-ROM disk or going on-line with a distant expert, and "regional" organizations were thought necessary to narrow the distance between communities and the nation as a whole.

Doubts arose early, however. In the early 1970s, Dean Francis Chase of the University of Chicago's School of Education observed that the laboratories

> were going in all directions—service-oriented, research-oriented, giving grants to people who couldn't have gotten them in national competition, some behaving like state departments of education, others behaving like weak schools of education. A lot of trial and error.

That is pretty much the situation today. Some of the research undertaken by the laboratories is useful; much is not. (After conducting the most careful examination in their history, University of Michigan scholar Maris Vinovskis in 1993 found "serious conceptual and statistical limitations" and "flawed and misleading analyses" in a great amount of the laboratories' research work.) As a whole, the program has outlived whatever justification it once had. Today, the country is awash in organizations that supply education policy makers and practitioners with information, advice, and technical assistance. They do such a good job that most of their recipients can now readily obtain more information than they can absorb.

Meanwhile, the laboratories entrenched themselves with the help of powerful lobbyists and congressional protectors. They have enjoyed an appropriations "earmark" or "set-aside" every year. They managed to get through their first two decades without even having to compete for the contracts through which their main federal subventions flow. Competitions were finally held in 1985 and 1990, but so formidable is the laboratories' power and the presumption of their continuing monopoly that few invested the energy to vie with the incumbents. Another such competition—leading to another five-or-more-year contract—has recently begun. Once again, however, nobody expects more than one or two of the present laboratories to face any challengers.

Federal funding of the regional educational laboratories is a textbook instance of what Senator Daniel P. Moynihan (D-N.Y.) has termed "feeding the sparrows by feeding the horses." The putative beneficiaries are schoolchildren who need to learn more. Yet, the money actually goes to well-paid professionals, sitting in comfortable offices far distant from the classroom, insulating themselves from most of the changes in American education and devoting much of their energy to ensuring that their federal gravy train does not halt on the tracks.

REAL REFORM NEEDED

Plenty of other examples could be cited, but they point to the same conclusion: The central policy problem posed by the Department of Education is that it has not adapted itself to the changing nature of our educational dilemmas.

A strong case can be made (and has been by former education secretaries William Bennett and Lamar Alexander) that the federal role in education should be virtually eliminated—and the Department of Education dismantled. A powerful argument can also be made that responsibility, authority, and resources for education should move from Washington to the states, communities, and families. Insofar as any federal involvement with education remains, it should be wholly recast around today's needs rather than those of the mid-1960s. It should be constructed around productivity, efficiency, accountability, and pluralism. It should reward performance rather than subsidize the delivery of services. Its primary clients should be consumers, not producers. Its chief implementers should be governors and mayors, not education professionals. Its watchword should be quality, not quantity.

Unfortunately, what the Department of Education will actually do with most of the money it will get for FY 1996 is diametrically opposed to these criteria. This is not because the department is evil, but because its culture, traditions, values, procedures, governing statutes, and constituencies all press in the opposite direction. If Congress wants to reverse its direction, an immense undertaking awaits—one that is manifestly worthwhile and long overdue.

Not All Standards Are Created Equal

An emphasis on academic content is one of ten criteria that the American Federation of Teachers considers essential to high-quality standards for student achievement.

Matthew Gandal for the AFT

Matthew Gandal is Senior Associate, Educational Issues Department, American Federation of Teachers, 555 New Jersey Ave., N.W., Washington, DC 20001-2079.

For more than a decade, the education community has taken a hard look at the quality of our schools. We've put energy and resources into reform ideas such as site-based management and model schools programs, but none of our efforts has paid off in terms of significant gains in student performance—at least not beyond a handful of successful schools. Over the last several years, a more promising idea has been making its way through statehouses and schools, an idea that has received national, bipartisan support: school reform based on rigorous academic standards for students.

Both Goals 2000 and the new Title I (formerly Chapter 1) require states to establish clear standards for student achievement and to refocus their educational efforts around these standards. They also require states to develop assessments to measure progress toward these standards and strategies to help

students meet them. The basic premise here is that once these standards and monitoring practices are up and running, teachers and schools can be freed from traditionally burdensome rules and given the flexibility to determine the best ways to help their students achieve at higher levels.

Standards will serve as the critical foundation for a wide-ranging set of reforms, and the caliber of those standards will have a serious impact on the quality of the overall improvements. States that move ahead with changes in curriculum, assessment, professional development, and teacher education before they've developed—or refined—the standards that should drive these changes will be putting the cart before the horse. And if states rush through the process of setting standards in order to begin work in these other areas, chances are the quality of their standards will suffer.

How can states make sure that the

standards they develop are of sufficiently high quality? By first adopting some sensible criteria that can guide their work. The following 10 criteria were developed by the Educational Issues Department of the American Federation of Teachers. We consider these to be essential characteristics of good standards.

1. Standards must focus on academics.

Improving students' academic performance should be the central mission of all our educational arrangements, and forging agreement around the academic content of the curriculum and our expectations for our children is the essential first step.

But there are some who would rather have standards focus on social and behavioral issues than on academics. Across the country, we've watched debates and legislative battles unfold around proposed education standards or "outcomes" that stray from or avoid academics. These efforts, frequently referred to as "outcome-based education" or "OBE," are being challenged and defeated, not only by religious fundamentalists but also by other concerned citizens.

In several states, the intense negative reaction to nonacademic standards resulted in the substantial revision or defeat of the entire reform package. For example, in 1992, Virginia Governor Douglas Wilder abandoned the complete draft set of "Common Core of Learning" standards, and in Pennsylvania, strong opposition prompted the state to significantly amend its draft "Student Learning Outcomes":

> All students demonstrate caregiving skills and evaluate, in all settings, appropriate child care practices necessary to nurture children based on child development theory. *(Pennsylvania's Student Learning Outcomes, Draft 1991)*

> [A] student who is becoming a fulfilled individual uses the fundamental skills of thinking, problem solving, communicating, quantifying, and collaborating ... to analyze personal strengths and limitations to improve behaviors, capabilities, and plans. *(Virginia's Common Core of Learning, Draft 1992)*

In contrast, the following excerpt from proposed history standards developed by the National Center for History in the Schools is clearly grounded in academic content:

> Students would be able to demonstrate understanding of the causes of the American Revolution by:

> ■ Comparing the arguments advanced by defenders and opponents of the new imperial policy on the traditional rights of English people and the legitimacy of asking the colonies to pay a share of the costs of empire....

> ■ Analyzing the connection between political ideas and economic interests and comparing the ideas and interests of different groups. Reconstructing the arguments among patriots and loyalists about independence and drawing conclusions about how the decision to declare independence was reached.

Standards will serve as the critical foundation for a wide-ranging set of reforms.

Although it makes sense to organize our education system around the results—or outcomes—we hope it will produce, OBE's treatment of academic knowledge as a low priority doesn't sit well with many teachers and parents. OBE proponents have served as key consultants to several state education departments, and in each case the so-called "reform" proposal that resulted was met with significant opposition largely because of the nonacademic and controversial nature of the standards. Now, in a number of states, those opposed to any kind of standards development are trying to pin the "OBE" label on whatever effort is under way in an attempt to taint it. Terminology, however, is not at the heart of the matter. In the end, it's the content of the standards that must be kept center stage.

One final note: Schools certainly have a role to play in helping students develop compassion, honesty, self-discipline, and other traits essential to good behavior and strong character. The standards-setting process can contribute to that mission by ensuring that all students have access to a solid academic curriculum, because moral education is a natural by-product of a good curriculum. Schools can also contribute to the moral education of the young in other ways—for example, through their discipline policies; through their decisions about what to award and recognize; and by the example they set as a community that both expects and honors those virtues. These matters, however, do not lend themselves well to the standards-setting mechanism but, rather, are best taken up as teachers, parents, and the local or school community come together to find common ground in their hopes for their children.

2. Standards must be grounded in the core disciplines.

Some educators have thought it best to move away from traditional subject areas and create interdisciplinary expectations for students. "Human growth and development," "environmental stewardship," and "cultural and creative endeavors" are just some "subject areas" that have replaced math, science, history, and English. Proponents of this approach argue that solutions to real-world problems cannot be based on one or another discipline, so, therefore, neither should standards.

This argument belies the purpose of standards, which is to focus our educational systems on what is most essential for students to learn, not to prescribe how the material should be taught. At its best, interdisciplinary education can be an effective approach to teaching the knowledge and skills that arise from the disciplines. But its value depends on a firm grounding in the subjects themselves. Strong standards in each of the core disciplines will ensure that interdisciplinary approaches reflect the depth and integrity of the disciplines involved.

When standards-setters abandon the disciplines, content suffers. Standards become vaguely worded and loosely connected, making the job of curriculum designers, assessment developers, and teachers all but impossible.

3. Standards must be specific enough to assure the development of a common core curriculum.

In addition to being academic and subject-based, a good set of standards should also outline the essential knowledge and skills that all students should learn in each subject area. Such standards would guarantee that all students, regardless of background or neighborhood, are exposed to a common core of learning.

A strong common core would help us put an end to the unequal, uninspiring curriculums that many disadvantaged kids get locked into from an early age. And it would make life much easier on students who move from one school to another and often find themselves either way ahead or behind the rest of the class. In addition, teachers would have a much clearer idea of what their students learned the year before, so they would not have to waste so much class time reteaching previously covered material.

Finally, a strong common core would enable us to continue to forge a strong common culture, to preserve what unites us without diminishing the unique strength that flows from our diversity.

Requiring a common core would not, of course, limit students who chose to pursue advanced-level high school courses in any of the academic subjects. Nor would it prevent a fruitful integration of the academic core with vocational or technical education at the upper secondary level. But to the extent that a common core was established through most of the high school years—which is the practice abroad—we would ensure that *all* students are given a more equal chance to become well-educated citizens.

If standards are to set forth the content of a common core, and if they are to be used by teachers, curriculum and assessment developers, textbook publishers, and others, they must be specific enough to guide these people in their activities. With a common core in hand, we could—as other industrialized countries have done—end the need for every teacher to reinvent the wheel. Like other professions, we could begin to accrue a more focused body of knowledge, a portfolio of good practice, of materials and options that teachers and teacher educators could adapt, add to, and refine. But this is possible only if there is broad agreement on what is most essential to learn.

Unfortunately, many states' standards offer the barest guidance as to what should be covered. Some fit entire subjects on a single page. Others don't distinguish between what elementary and secondary students should learn. Though it has received a lot of attention for its many recent reform efforts, Kentucky is an example of a state whose stan-

dards are not specific enough to guide local districts toward a core curriculum and matching content-based assessments. Each subject area contains only 5–10 standards, and many are vague and vacuous. Here, for example, are three of seven statements that compose Kentucky's entire list of social studies standards:

> Students understand the democratic principles of justice, equality, responsibility, and freedom and apply them to real-life situations.

> Students can accurately describe various forms of government and analyze issues that relate to the rights and responsibilities of citizens in a democracy.

> Students understand, analyze, and interpret historical events, conditions, trends, and issues to develop historical perspective.

In contrast, California provides its standards in terms of grade-by-grade curriculum frameworks, thus offering substantial, clear guidance to all players in the educational system. Here is an excerpt from the History/Social Science Framework describing what 11th graders should understand about the Great Depression:

> Students should assess the likely causes of the Depression and examine its effects on ordinary people in different parts of the nation through use of historical materials. They should recognize the way in which natural drought combined with unwise agricultural practices to cause the Dust Bowl, a major factor in the economic and cultural chaos of the 1930s. They should see the linkage between severe economic distress and social turmoil. Photographs, films, newspaper accounts, interviews with persons who lived in the period, as well as paintings and novels (such as John Steinbeck's *Grapes of Wrath*) will help students understand this critical era.

> The administration of Franklin D. Roosevelt and his New Deal should be studied as an example of the government's response to economic crisis. The efforts of the Roosevelt Administration to alleviate the crisis through the creation of social welfare programs, regulatory agencies, and economic planning bureaus should be carefully assessed.

How specific should standards be? It helps to keep in mind why we are setting standards and how they will be used. Here are some questions worth asking about the standards in your state:

■ Are the standards organized by grade levels or age bands, or do they in some way clearly delineate the differences in expectations for students at different levels?

■ Are the standards clear and specific enough to guide the development of curriculum frameworks that would describe the core units to be covered in every grade?

■ If a state were to adopt these standards but give districts the responsibility for fleshing them out into a curriculum, what are the chances that students across the state would be learning the same core curriculum?

■ If a student moved from one district to another or from school to school within a district, would these standards ease the move to a new grade in a new school without putting him or her too far ahead or behind the other students?

■ If a textbook publisher and an assessment developer were to use the standards in their work, is it likely that the text and the test would be well aligned?

4. Standards must be manageable given the constraints of time.

Neither standards nor the resulting common core curriculum should try to cover everything. A core curriculum should probably constitute somewhere between 60 and 80 percent of the academic curriculum; the rest can be filled in by local districts, schools, and teachers.

It's important not to draw the wrong conclusion here. There is nothing sacred about the ways schools apportion their time at present. According to *Prisoners of Time*, the 1994 report by the National Education Commission on Time and Learning, American schools spend about half as much time on academics as their counterparts overseas. There is no reason why this figure should be so low, and standards

How specific should standards be? It helps to keep in mind why we are setting standards and how they will be used.

are the first necessary step toward initiating some changes in school schedules.

As states begin to adopt standards, standards-setters will need to exhibit restraint in the face of competing demands for time in the curriculum—both within and among the disciplines. Their job is to determine what is *essential* for students to learn. A laundry list that satisfies everyone will leave teachers right where they are now—facing the impossible task of trying to rush through overstuffed textbooks and ridiculously long sets of curriculum objectives.

5. Standards must be rigorous and world-class.

The national education goals call for American students to be first in the world in math and science by the turn of the century. States and professional associations that are setting standards often repeat the mantras "world-class," "rigorous," and "challenging" to describe what they are doing. But what do these words really mean?

If standards truly are rigorous and world-class, they should stand up to some tough but sensible questions:

■ Do they reflect various levels of knowledge and skills comparable to what students in high-achieving countries are expected to master?

■ Which countries did the standards-setters use as a basis for comparison, and what documents did they look at to determine their standards?

■ Will the standards lead to a core curriculum for all students—those headed for college and those headed for work—as demanding as in France or Japan?

■ Will they result in assessments for the college-bound as rigorous as the German *Abitur*, the French *baccalauréat* exams, the British A-levels, or the Japanese university entrance exams?

■ Did the standards-setters refer to

internationally benchmarked curriculums and exams such as those of the International Baccalaureate program?

■ Did the standards-setters refer to the best programs and resources available in the United States, such as the College Board's Advanced Placement exams and Achievement tests, or the curriculum frameworks used in California?

Information on other countries is not easy to get hold of. One thing is certain, though: nothing will be accomplished by setting standards that are too low. Without honest international benchmarking, we will be captives of our own parochial notions of what students can accomplish, and low standards will be the result.

6. Standards must evaluate performance.

In any profession, specific standards are developed in order to motivate and measure performance. Whether you look at the medical boards that prospective doctors must pass or the time trials for drivers to qualify for the Indianapolis 500—performance is never dealt with in the abstract. Indy racers, for example, are not simply told that "very fast driving" will qualify them for the big race. They know exactly what times they need to beat, and they plan their strategies accordingly.

It should be the same for education standards. An influential report recently commissioned by the National Education Goals Panel[1] asserted that a complete set of standards should describe both what students should know and be able to do *and* how well they must know and do it. The report separated these functions into two distinct categories. *Content* standards define the knowledge (the most important and enduring ideas, concepts, issues, dilemmas, and information) and skills (the ways of thinking, working, communicating, reasoning, and investigating) essential to each discipline.

Performance standards indicate how competent a student demonstration must be to indicate attainment of the content standards—or "how good is good enough?"

It is safe to say that none of the standards documents we've seen—whether from the national standards groups, states, or other professional associations—fully incorporates performance standards as defined in the Goals Panel report. States will find this a particular problem when they try to develop assessments, because performance standards are essential to gauging whether the content standards are met.

A few states may be on the right track. Colorado, for example, has created a good set of content standards and will soon develop performance levels and assessments for each of those standards. So, not only will Colorado have a history standard that requires 4th graders to "understand the difference between a democracy and an autocracy," but the state will follow that with a performance standard that establishes how *well* students must understand that difference and how they can demonstrate that understanding. It will be interesting to watch this work develop.

A single standard would either have to be set low enough for most to pass or too high for many to reach.

7. Standards must include multiple performance levels.

When we speak of students being held to world-class standards, does that mean we should expect them all to achieve at the levels reached by the top students in other countries? Of course not. France and Germany have high standards for all their students, but they don't expect all to meet the *same* standard. It's just not realistic to expect the same from everyone.

There is nothing wrong with admitting this, and students know it very well. We need multiple standards that set expectations to match different aspirations and achievements. A single standard would either have to be set low enough for most to pass, which does nothing to raise student achievement, or too high for many to reach, which only turns students off to the idea of hard work. The trick is to set standards that are within reach, but still require dedication and hard work—to stretch all kids to their potential.

We can establish challenging standards without sacrificing rigor by developing multiple levels of achievement for each content standard. For example, students could work to reach "proficient," "advanced," or "expert" levels. This is how the National Assessment of Educational Progress reports its findings, and how California's Golden State Exams are scored.

Another approach could be to require all students to meet a common standard for graduation from high school, but also to create higher standards for students who attain that initial level earlier or who wish to qualify for more selective higher education. This is similar to the way that education systems in some foreign countries operate.

8. Standards must combine knowledge *and* skills.

There is a terrible myth in education that has a tendency to confuse important decisions affecting curriculum and which is threatening to strangle the standards movement. The theory goes something like this: Knowledge is dynamic, always changing, whereas the need to apply knowledge is constant. What is most important for students to learn are skills such as problem solving, decision making, and higher-order thinking, so that they can react to any situation, gain and use whatever knowledge they need, and not waste their time learning facts and theories that may turn out to be irrelevant in their lives. Who can be sure of how much specific knowledge each person will need in the real world anyway?

An overstatement, of course—but not by much. At the root of this myth

is a false dichotomy between knowledge and skills. And what it is leading to are standards that neglect the subject matter (the facts, ideas, concepts, issues, and information) of the traditional academic disciplines that is needed to develop the skills in the first place. Consider the following very general "skills" standard from Oregon:

> A student will demonstrate the ability to think critically, creatively, and reflectively in making decisions and solving problems. (*Oregon's Certificate of Initial Mastery, 1991*)

Standards such as this one leave unanswered just what students are to solve, decide, or think about. What kind of guidance do such skills examples give to teachers and others in education? "Critical thinking" cannot be taught in the abstract. It can be developed, however, by having students analyze the contradiction, for example, between the principle expressed in the Declaration of Independence that "all men are created equal" and the existence of slavery at the time. But a skill that is cut free from content and context is meaningless—and impossible to teach or assess.

An overemphasis on generic skills and processes seems to be a particular trend in states that allow local control of the *entire* curriculum. In essence, this is a way for states to avoid making judgments about the core content of the curriculum. But as discussed earlier, vague standards do not ensure that all kids are given a challenging curriculum, nor can they lead to assessments that reveal the depth and breadth of student knowledge.

9. Standards must not dictate how the material should be taught.

Good standards are designed to guide, not limit, instruction. If, for example, a set of standards includes teaching activities, they should be there for illustrative purposes only. Standards must not be allowed to infringe on teachers' professional responsibilities, their ability to choose particular methods and to design lessons and courses in ways that reflect the best available research and which are best suited to their students' needs and to their own strengths and teaching styles.

10. Standards must be written clearly.

Part of the challenge states will face with Goals 2000 and standards-setting is how to generate broad public support. It is important, therefore, that standards be written clearly enough for parents, students, and interested community members to understand—indeed, to be inspired by. Otherwise, standards-writers will risk alienating the very people whose trust and support they need. Sometimes, something as simple as a word or phrase that has no meaning to parents can cause a problem. Here are some questions for writers of standards to consider:

- Are the standards clear enough for teachers to understand what is required of them and their students?
- Are they clear enough for parents to understand what is expected of their children and to monitor their progress?
- Do the standards send a coherent message to employers and colleges as to what students will know and be able to do when they leave high school?
- Will the students themselves be able to read the standards and get a clear idea of what is expected of them?

If the answer to any of these questions is "no," your work is not done.

The Threshold of a Great Opportunity

Subject matter standards and a common core to the curriculum are new concepts in American education, and people—including many educators—are automatically skeptical of new ideas in the field. Considering the fads and failures of the past, this skepticism is healthy. But the American Federation of Teachers and others believe that if we develop rigorous and usable standards and shape intelligent Goals 2000 plans, we have a real opportunity to turn things around in our schools. Such an effort is certainly a more palatable and responsible strategy than turning the schools over to the whim of the market.

[1]*Promises to Keep: Creating High Standards for American Students*, a report to the National Education Goals Panel by the Technical Planning Group on the Review of Education Standards, November 15, 1993.

Editor's note: This article was adapted with permission from the fall 1994 issue of *American Educator*, the quarterly magazine of the American Federation of Teachers.

Response

Wrong Problem,
Wrong Solution

Kenneth R. Howe

Kenneth R. Howe is Associate Professor, School of Education, University of Colorado at Boulder, Campus Box 249, Boulder, CO 80309.

Better academic standards are a minuscule element of effective reform.

John Dewey advised us to avoid the trap of "either-or" thinking, and I take this advice very seriously. Although I am certainly no fan of the standards movement, its advocates have some truth on their side. In particular, we need to get much clearer about just what we are trying to accomplish in public education and just what would constitute success. On this general point, then, I agree with Matthew Gandal. I also agree that we ought not turn public education over to the "whim of the market." Here is where our agreement ends.

The Wrong Solution

Gandal himself abandons the process of negotiating shared ideals, though for different reasons than those who would abandon it to market-driven choice. In the face of significant controversy about what the curriculum

Gandal's call for "world-class standards" finds its roots in the crisis rhetoric that has dominated since *A Nation at Risk*.

should include—controversy strongly rooted in legitimate concerns about race, class, and gender bias—Gandal advocates including only what he calls "academic" content. Accordingly, he reasons that the traditional disciplines are to be the only object of standards and assessments.

Where is the negotiation? Gandal relies on "the public outcry" over including "nonacademic" aims in the curriculum (particularly the public reception of OBE) as evidence that his proposal is democratic. Readers must evaluate for themselves the accuracy of Gandal's portrayal of what the public expects of its schools. But even if it is accurate, don't educators have a responsibility to challenge the public

when it is headed in the wrong direction? In this connection, why does Gandal see fit to take a swipe at school choice in the face of significant public support for it?

As it turns out, Gandal does not wish to exclude nonacademic aims from schooling altogether—only from the arena of standards and assessment. Moral character, an appreciation for diversity, and the capacity to integrate knowledge are acceptable aims for schools to pursue, he says. Unlike the disciplines, however, they can somehow take care of themselves. I find this highly unlikely, particularly when they must compete with the disciplines for which standards and assessments exist.

In any case, by acknowledging that they should be included, Gandal becomes ensnared in his own logic. According to his thinking, are not rigorous standards necessary to foster learning of the kind we want? Why not start with these aims and let the disciplines take care of *themselves*? Why not at least add these aims to the disciplinary ones? (This, by the way, is what I take one of the main tenets of OBE to be.) Gandal simply begs these questions.

The Wrong Problem

Recounting the failed reforms of the last decade or so, Gandal then touts "school reform based on rigorous academic standards" as "a more promising idea" that can "turn things around in our schools." Granted, better standards can contribute to improving education, but it is difficult to see how they can be anything more than a very small piece of effective educational reform. Consider the conditions that Jonathan Kozol documents in *Savage Inequalities*, in which some children are taught in bathrooms and others must use hand-me-down textbooks. Better educational standards can eliminate low achievement under these conditions no more effectively than better nutritional standards can eliminate hunger under famine conditions.

Providing the means of attaining the standards is required in each case.

This kind of observation is one of the major justifications for including "opportunity to learn" standards in proposals like Goals 2000. Such standards are intended to ensure that all students have an adequate opportunity to achieve "content" and "performance" standards. And they are required not only to ensure effectiveness but equity as well. It is unfair to hold students and educators responsible for achieving content and performance standards if they must strive to do so under conditions that render success virtually impossible.

Gandal is completely silent about opportunity to learn standards, and, save passing reference to "exposing" the disadvantaged to a good curriculum, he has nothing to say about the problem they are designed to address. Indeed, AFT President Albert Shanker has been openly dismissive of opportunity to learn standards. Why the AFT would want

to take such a position I am not sure. I can only say that it is wholly inadequate from the viewpoint of those who see greater equality as essential to educational reform.

I conclude with a related observation about international benchmarking. Gandal's call for "world-class standards" finds its roots in the crisis rhetoric that has dominated since *A Nation at Risk*. If a crisis exists (which many educational scholars deny, at least by historical standards), it would be best identified with the vast inequality that currently threatens our democratic aspirations. High-performing U.S. students do well on international comparisons; the largest differences are to be found *within* U.S. public education. International benchmarking—the overemphasis on standards in general—thus serves to divert attention from the most pressing problem facing public education today: the need to provide a much larger, more diverse population with *genuine* opportunities to learn.

Somebody's Children

Expanding Educational Opportunities

for *All* America's Children

Diane Ravitch

Diane Ravitch, a nonresident senior fellow in the Brookings Governmental Studies program, is a senior research fellow at New York University. She is the author, most recently, of National Standards in American Education: A Citizen's Guide *(Brookings, 1994). This article is adapted from "Somebody's Children," in* Social Policies for Children, *edited by Irwin Garfinkel, Jennifer Hochschild, and Sara McLanahan (Brookings, 1995).*

LAST FEBRUARY, IN A SPEECH ON THE "STATE OF AMERICAN EDUCATION," Secretary of Education Richard Riley gave America's schools a mixed report card. Some schools, he said, are "excellent, some are improving, some have the remarkable capacity to change for the better." Some, though, "should never be called schools at all."

That last phrase is chilling: schools that "should never be called schools at all." Who attends these schools? African-American and Hispanic children, probably; children from very poor families, probably, many headed by a single parent struggling to make ends meet.

Somebody's children are compelled—some would say, condemned—to attend schools that most teachers shun, if they can, in neighborhoods that people of means avoid, if possible. *Somebody's children* go to those schools. Not mine. Not Secretary Riley's. Not President Clinton's nor Vice President Gore's. Not the children of urban mayors or school superintendents or teachers.

During the course of his speech, Riley invoked John Dewey: "What the best and wisest parent wants for his [and, may I say her] child, that must be [what] the community wants for all of its children. Any other ideal for our schools . . . destroys our democracy."

What would the best and wisest parents do if their children were zoned into schools that are unsafe and educationally bankrupt? They would—if they could—move to a different neighborhood or put their children into private schools. That is what the president did.

But *somebody's children* are required to go to those schools. Parents who don't have the money to move to a better neighborhood or to put their child into a private school have been told that they must stay there no matter how bad the school is. If they are parents with

Arguments for Means-tested Choice

The strong objections many people have to school choice do not apply to a means-tested choice program. Following are the primary objections raised by choice opponents—and Diane Ravitch's response to them.

1. A CHOICE PROGRAM WOULD DESTROY THE PUBLIC SCHOOL SYSTEM. Opponents of choice fear that if choice were available to all children, huge numbers would leave public education altogether. Such fears are groundless. A Carnegie Foundation for the Advancement of Teaching poll found that only 19 percent of all public school parents would like to send their children to a private school. In a means-tested system, many of these families, of course, would not qualify for scholarships. The public schools would probably enroll 80 percent or more of all students—instead of today's 90 percent. Far from being destroyed, the public school system would be strengthened because it would be able to shut down bad schools.

2. THERE IS NO PRECEDENT FOR ALLOWING STUDENTS TO USE GOVERNMENT FUNDS FOR PRIVATE OR RELIGIOUS INSTITUTIONS. Not true. For many years government-provided Pell grants have enabled college students to attend the school of their choice. The resulting system of higher education is believed by most people to be the best and most pluralistic in the world. The government does not care whether the school attended by a Pell grant student is public, private, or religious as long as it is accredited and approved by its state. Eighty percent of Pell students enroll in public institutions, no doubt because they cost less than private ones. The same dynamic would hold in K-12 education. In addition, religious schools already receive public funds to educate handicapped children and to run Headstart centers.

3. IT WOULD BE UNCONSTITUTIONAL FOR THE GOVERNMENT TO FINANCE RELIGIOUS SCHOOLS. Again, not true. It would be unconstitutional only if a public authority provided funds *directly* to religious schools. Financial aid that goes to parents to spend at the school of their choice would not violate the principle of separation of church and state. A 1971 court ruling established a three-prong test to determine the constitutionality of legislation affecting church-state issues. The statute must have a secular legislative purpose; its principal effect must neither advance nor inhibit religion; and it must not foster "an excessive governmental entanglement with religion." A law that grants funds to parents, not to religious schools, would meet all three requirements. In 1986 a unanimous Supreme Court upheld the grant of state aid to a blind student attending a Bible college in preparation for being a minister. In 1993 the Court ruled a public school district could provide a sign language interpreter for a deaf student in a Catholic high school. In both cases the ruling turned on the fact that the parents had made the choice.

4. A CHOICE SYSTEM WOULD PUT AN INTOLERABLE BURDEN ON ALREADY STRAINED STATE AND LOCAL BUDGETS. A means-tested choice program would involve measurable, predictable, and limited spending. It would cost the public no more than states now spend for children in public schools.

A full choice program may actually be a money-saver on capital expenditures. U.S. school enrollments are again on the rise. By 2004 they are expected to grow 13 percent in grades K–8, 24 percent in grades 9–12. Public officials must make a choice: either invest billions of dollars to build new schools or use fully all existing facilities. Officials can do the latter through a choice system that is well organized, well supervised, and coordinated with existing public schools.

5. A CHOICE PROGRAM WOULD "CREAM OFF" THE BEST STUDENTS, LEAVING PUBLIC SCHOOLS WITH THE POOREST AND MOST DIFFICULT STUDENTS. In a means-tested choice program, scholarships would be given only to the poorest students in the worst schools. *Good* schools in big cities will not be hurt by a means-tested choice program; they are likely to get many more applicants. Their students do not want to leave; their parents know they are getting a good education.

motivation and energy, they are told by school officials and policymakers that they must stay right where they are because they are the kind of parents who might someday help to improve that dreadful school. The people who tell them this would not keep their own child in that school for even a day.

For policymakers and academics, working toward reform "someday" may be appropriate. But for parents it is an outrageous proposition. Parents have children who live today, here and now. They cannot wait around to see whether the school will get better in five or ten years.

As Dewey suggested, we must project our passion for our own children's welfare onto those desperate parents. They love their children as much as we love ours. They worry about their children's future—and they know how much the odds are stacked against them. They should not be expected to wait patiently for the eventual transformation of the failing schools their children are required to attend each day. We would not thus sacrifice our own children. Why must they?

We Can't Wait for "Someday"

What can we do—and do *quickly*—for the children now attending schools that should not be called schools? The best solution I see is for states, cities, or the federal government to provide means-tested scholarships to needy families, who may use them to send their children to the school of their choice, be it public, independent, or religious.

The size of the scholarship should vary in relation to family income. The needier the child, the larger the grant. For the neediest, the grant should be at least equal to the state average per pupil expenditure, possibly larger. Children with disabilities should receive the full amount of financial aid to which they would be entitled under state and federal law. Since funds will necessarily be limited, highest priority for such scholarships should go to children who are now enrolled in schools identified by public authorities as the worst in the district. The number and size of such scholarships can be strictly controlled by public authorities to gauge the cost and consequences—though the number and size must not be so small as to render the program meaningless.

This proposal is not new. Others have made it before. It is, however, new for me.

For years I could not make up my mind about the issue of school choice. Unlike some supporters of choice, I harbor no animus toward the public schools. I attended public schools in Houston, Texas, for 13 years. I consider myself a friend and supporter of public education. But several things have overcome my hesitation about choice. First and foremost is that many years—and wave after wave of reforms—have passed, leaving the most desperate inner-city schools fundamentally unchanged. Trying harder has helped some schools, but the worst are untouched.

Certain personal experiences were also decisive. While in London in the fall of 1992 I visited one of Britain's "grant-maintained" schools—schools where parents have voted to leave the jurisdiction of the local board of education and receive public funding directly from the national government. The school I visited was a Roman Catholic girls' school, most of whose students were members of racial minorities. The nun who showed me around was in street dress, as were the teachers. The money that had once gone to the local school board (about 15 percent of the school's budget) now went directly to the school. The added funds helped build a new science laboratory, make long-deferred repairs, and hire more teachers. For the first time in its history, the school was allowed to select its own food supplier. No longer the last link in a bureaucratic chain, the staff

6. A CHOICE PROGRAM COULD WORSEN SEGRE-GATION IN BIG-CITY DISTRICTS. Providing means-tested scholarships to African-American and Hispanic students enrolled in completely segregated inner-city schools may well reduce segregation. It cannot make it worse.

7. A CHOICE PROGRAM COULD USE PUBLIC FUNDS TO SUPPORT SCHOOLS THAT TEACH BIZARRE RELIGIOUS AND RACIAL IDEAS. This potential problem would be easy to solve. Schools that violate civil rights laws or that teach racial or religious hatred would not be eligible to receive public scholarships. And schools that accept public scholarships would have to prepare their students to pass state subject-matter assessments at rates no worse than comparable public schools.

8. NONPUBLIC SCHOOLS MAY SHUN STUDENTS WITH HANDICAPPING CONDITIONS. Students with special needs should be eligible for a scholarship to go where their needs can best be met. If the scholarship is large enough, new schools will be created to meet the needs of these children. The Supreme Court has already ruled that parents of disabled students have the right to a free publicly financed education in the private sector if the state cannot provide it.

9. HOW CAN PUBLIC AUTHORITIES HOLD NON-PUBLIC SCHOOLS ACCOUNTABLE? Public authorities will find it easier to ensure the accountability of both nonpublic schools and public schools under a means-tested choice program. They now have no leverage over failing public schools. They cannot punish them by taking away money; that only makes matters worse. They have tried—without success—threatening to take the schools over or to send in monitors. If authorities could offer scholarships to students trapped in terrible schools, it would give them leverage over those schools while protecting the students. In a means-tested choice system, if nonpublic schools and public charter schools fail to meet their contractual obligations, officials can revoke their charter or their eligibility to receive public scholarships.

10. IT IS SOCIALLY DIVISIVE TO ALLOW STU-DENTS TO ATTEND SCHOOLS WITH DIFFERENT VALUES. Actually, our most divisive school-related conflicts occur because we impose a single set of state-defined values on everyone in public schools. School boards make decisions in the school made their own decisions. In classroom after classroom I saw teenage girls preparing for the national examinations in an atmosphere that was orderly, cheerful, and well-maintained. I vividly recall the guide's comment: "You can always tell a grant-maintained school by the smell of fresh paint."

Separation of Church and State?

That visit raised some questions. In the United States opposition to funding nonpublic schools, especially religious schools, is powerful. Admitting any demonstration of religious faith into the public school is anathema. We have been told for years that using any public funds in a religious school violates the constitutional principle of separation of church and state. Why?

No other developed democracy that shares our ideals has such a "wall of separation." Every other Western nation provides state aid to religious and other private schools. Denmark's government, for example, directly funds nonstate schools so that parents can exercise religious and political freedom. Only a tiny minority—about 5.6 percent—choose to attend such schools.

Why do we alone adamantly refuse any public funding for children who attend religious schools? And why only at the primary and secondary level? Why is Mary Jones—a young woman from an impoverished family—ineligible for public funds when she is an 18-year-old senior at St. Mary's Academy, yet eligible for a federal Pell grant when she is an 18-year-old freshman at St. Mary's College? Is it fair to deny free education to needy citizens whose religious convictions make it impossible for them to send their children to secular state schools? Why is public funding available only to schools that exclude religious values? Why is there free speech in public schools for all controversial views except religious ideas?

Although the rise of the American common school during the 19th century is often traced to efforts to create secular schools, in fact the goal of the evangelical Protestant reformers behind the movement was to deny public funds to Catholic schools and to assure that public funds went solely to nondenominational Protestant schools. And they succeeded. Well into the 20th century, students in nonsectarian public schools read the Protestant Bible, sang Protestant hymns, recited Protestant prayers, and learned a Protestant version of European history.

As historian Lloyd Jorgenson notes in *The State and the Nonpublic School, 1825–1925*, common school reformers did not claim that it was unconstitutional to spend public funds in Catholic schools. Instead, they passed state laws to prevent it. They did not invoke the principle of separation of church and state. Rather, they charged that Catholicism was a "menace to republican institutions and must be curbed." In short, America's common school ideology is rooted firmly in anti-Catholic bigotry.

All Our Children

The resulting theory of public education developed over the years is unnecessarily constricted. Public education, in current theory, happens only in schools operated and controlled by the government. Yet what should concern us is the education of the public—all the public. And what should concern us most is the education of children who are at risk, whether they go to a public school or not.

The best way to provide educational opportunity for poor children in urban areas is to make available means-tested scholarships with priority for children who are enrolled in schools with a long-term record of poor performance, to be used in the schools of their choice. If the scholarships are generous enough, many schools will welcome scholarship students, and new schools will open to supply the demand for good education.

that are deeply offensive to some families. Those of us who are liberal and secular feel comforted when our side wins and frightened when the other side wins. Yet why must people who are not liberal and secular submit their children to values they find oppressive? Under a means-tested choice program, schools should differ from each other in a variety of ways, so long as they respect the Constitution and the laws of the state and satisfy the state's educational standards. Permitting diversity of values may well prove less divisive in the end.

11. HOW WILL NEWCOMERS TO THE UNITED STATES BE ASSIMILATED TO THE MAINSTREAM IF THEY GO TO ETHNIC OR RELIGIOUS SCHOOLS? Most new immigrants will continue to choose traditional public schools because they are free, convenient, and satisfactory to most parents. Those who do not choose public schools do not threaten the stability of the nation. There is no reason to believe that children who attend non-public schools are any less civic-minded as adults than those who attend public schools. In fact, the public schools may not be the primary means of civic assimilation in our society. American society itself—its laws, its cultural pluralism, its openness, its tolerance for diversity, its encouragement of freedom of expression—may be the most effective instrument of social assimilation. Our commitment to pluralism and diversity should be strong enough to tolerate the few devout separatists who do not wish to assimilate.

Even the best schools cannot do everything to protect at-risk young people from the pressures that threaten them—from poverty, teen pregnancy, drug and alcohol abuse, AIDS, homelessness, violence. Even the best schools cannot by themselves end poverty—although children who do not get a good education are likely to endure a lifetime of poverty. Even the best schools cannot by themselves create jobs or improve housing conditions or stop the violence on the streets. But schools can and must nurture and guide the young people who are growing up in a milieu fraught with peril.

The anonymous comprehensive high school, for example—a hallmark of American education for most of this century—cannot meet the needs of endangered youngsters in the cities. Those children need individual support and nurturance. They need schools that work closely with their families. They need schools where many adults know their names and care about them, know when they are absent, know when they have a problem, think about their future, and talk frequently to their parents or guardian.

Whether public or private, the most successful urban schools share certain characteristics. Paul Hill calls them "high schools with character." Theodore Sizer calls them "thoughtful places." In their recent book about Catholic education, Anthony Bryk, Valerie Lee, and Peter Holland describe the caring community created by Catholic schools. All have in common a sense of purpose, a mission,

an identity of their own. And all function *in loco parentis*, with the knowledge and assent of parents who welcome a partnership with the school.

There are two ways to create more such schools. One is to provide means-tested scholarships to poor children, allowing them to attend any school that accepts public accountability for educational standards and civil rights laws. The other is to promote the spread of charter schools and special-purpose public schools managed under contract by institutions, parents, and teachers. The charter school movement is spreading rapidly. It has already been adopted in nearly a dozen states, is being considered by nearly a dozen more, and has been endorsed by the National School Boards Association. It is a politically practical strategy that avoids the inevitable constitutional problems that will accompany any choice plan that includes private and religious schools. But the two strategies are not alternatives. Rather, they are complementary ways to create a more diverse, pluralistic system of good schools from which parents and students may choose. One creates demand for special-purpose schools by supplying scholarships, the other creates a new supply by encouraging the spread of special-purpose schools.

Both strategies would expand educational opportunities for poor children. I argue the case for choice involving both state and non-state schools for two reasons. First, opening choice to all schools will rapidly expand the supply of places available. Second, including private and religious schools, so long as they are willing to comply with state standards, is a matter of justice. It is not *just* to compel poor children to attend bad schools. It is not *just* to prohibit poor families from sending their children to the school of their choice, even if that school has a religious affiliation. It is not *just* to deny free schooling to poor families with strong religious convictions, any more than it would be just to prohibit the use of federal scholarships in nonpublic universities like Notre Dame, Marymount, or Yeshiva. It is not *just* that there is no realistic way to close schools that students and their parents would abandon if they could.

What a Means-Tested Choice Program Could Do

What difference could a means-tested choice program make in the life of children now compelled to attend schools that should never be called schools? First, and most important, it would free those children to move to better schools—public, private, or religious. As the charter school movement spreads across the country, opportunities for students to move to small, purposeful schools are increasing. A model school created by Wayne State University in Detroit was heavily oversubscribed. Rice University in Houston was inundated with applications for a new school near its campus. Catholic schools have a strong track record, especially with disadvantaged urban students, who have a lower dropout rate and higher test scores than their peers in public schools. One reason for the difference is that students in Catholic schools are much likelier to be placed in college preparatory programs, regardless of race or social class. In 1990, 66 percent of high school sophomores in Catholic schools—and only 39 percent in public schools—were on a college-bound track.

Second, a means-tested choice program could strengthen the role of families in the lives of these children by giving parents a greater say in their children's education. Parent participation is certainly much greater in Catholic schools than in public schools, and it is probably greater in "focus" public schools than in ordinary public schools. Parents of children in Catholic schools are twice as likely as public school parents to belong to and participate in the PTA. Parents of poor black students in Catholic schools participate in the PTA at much higher levels than their counterparts in public schools. The act of choosing a school seems to make parents feel more responsible and become more involved.

Finally, means-tested scholarships will enable students to attend schools where teachers and parents share values and agree on a code of conduct. Participating in a close, consensual community will help nurture youngsters and shelter them from the dangers of the street. Most public schools, now operating on the basis of hierarchical, bureaucratic rules and regulations, fail to engage students as members of a community. Means-tested scholarships will enable eligible students to attend a school where there is focus, mission, and identity. Only in such a setting can students who are now alienated begin to see themselves as responsible participants, surrounded by adults and other students who are affected by their decisions and actions. Under the current system, there is no incentive to establish new focus schools. In a choice program, the incentive is to create many such schools.

Everybody's Children

Perhaps more than the people of any other nation, Americans value the freedom to choose, to make their own decisions, to manage their own lives. Children growing up in neighborhoods their parents cannot leave, attending schools no one would willingly attend, have no choice at all—about a matter of enormous consequence in their lives.

The goal of my proposal is to create a diverse, pluralistic system of schools with many different kinds of sponsors, all dedicated to educating the public and all monitored by state agencies responsible for assuring both equity and excellence. *Nobody's children* should be compelled to attend a bad public school. A good school system must offer equal education opportunity to *everybody's children*.

MAKING AMERICA'S SCHOOLS WORK

This Time Money Is Not the Answer

Eric A. Hanushek

Eric A. Hanushek, professor of economics and public policy at the
University of Rochester, is the author of Making Schools Work:
Improving Performance and Controlling Costs *(Brookings, 1994),*
a project of the Panel of the Economics of Educational Reform.

No one is happy with America's schools. Students, parents, politicians all call for schools to do a better job. The news media regularly report the failures of U.S. education, whether in the poor showing of American students in international test score competition or in the deficiencies of graduates entering the workplace.

Often the blame is placed on tightfisted government officials and taxpayers. Teachers' salaries, it is said, are too low. Class sizes are too big. The school year is too short. Educational reformers emphasize the need for renewed commitment to schooling—a commitment that is often translated into an appeal for expanded resources for schools.

But in fact, the nation has been spending more and more to achieve results that are no better and perhaps worse. Between 1960 and 1990, while student performance on such tests as the SAT and the National Assessment of Educational Progress faltered, real (inflation-adjusted) public spending on elementary and secondary education in the United States rose from just over $50 billion to almost $190 billion. Real per-student spending more than tripled—from $1,454 in 1960 to $4,622 in 1990.

Surprisingly, the increased costs, combined with public dissatisfaction with school performance, have aroused few protests or demands to stop the growth in spending. One explanation for the public's silence may be that the dramatic 1970–90 drop in the school-age population masked overall spending increases by offsetting much of the rise in per pupil instructional costs. But if that is the case, trouble lurks on the horizon. For the population of school-age children is on the rise again, and with it, fiscal pressures.

America's lunar-landing approach to school reform—devote sufficient energy and resources to the problem and the nation will crack it—is not sustainable. Education faces stiff competition for society's limited resources. The nation will not, indeed cannot, continue to spend more and more on education to achieve flat or falling performance.

More Money, Better Schools?

Nor is there any *reason* to continue to pour ever more money into the schools, given their current organization. Over the past quarter century researchers have made the surprising discovery that there is little systematic relationship between school resources and student performance. For every study that finds that increases in basic school resources promote higher achievement, another study shows just the opposite.

Take class size, for example. The intuitively appealing idea that smaller classes will improve student learning is a perennial cornerstone of educational reform. As a result, the pupil-teacher ratio in American schools is always on the decline. The ratio, which stood at 35–1 in 1890, fell to 28–1 in 1940, 20–1 in 1970, and less than 16–1 in 1990.

From *The Brookings Review*, Fall 1994, pp. 10-13. © 1994 by the Brookings Institution. Reprinted by permission.

But econometric and experimental evidence shows vividly that across-the-board reductions in class size are unlikely to yield discernible gains in overall student achievement. That is not to say that small classes are never useful. Some situations may lend themselves to smaller classes, while others can accommodate larger classes. For example, individual tutorial programs can substantially improve the achievement of poorly performing primary school students, while other students in various situations can be placed in larger classes without jeopardizing their achievement—so holding overall cost constant. Indeed, in Japan teachers and administrators expressly trade large class sizes for more time for teacher preparation. But so far, U.S. schools have made little effort to learn which uses of resources, for smaller classes or other purposes, best promote student achievement.

As the public school system is now organized, some schools appear to use money and resources effectively, but others do not. In fact, resources are spent ineffectively so often that there is simply no reason to expect overall improvement from increased resources. School administrators today are not monitoring the performance of their programs or the effectiveness of resource use. Schools have no way to know what does and does not work. What's more, few incentives push toward improved schooling and higher student performance.

Put the Money Where It Works

The highest priority for America's schools today is to use existing resources more efficiently. When economists try to interject the economic principle of efficiency into the education debate, however, they often meet with stout resistance—largely because of misunderstandings. Efficiency does not mean that educators should undertake a relentless drive to cut costs. Rather, it means that they should measure both the costs and benefits of various approaches to education—and choose the approach that maximizes the excess of benefits over costs. In simplest terms, funds devoted to schools should be put to their best possible use. If two programs are competing for limited funds, put the money into the one that achieves the best results. If a program does not improve student performance, do not fund it.

These notions are so commonsensical that resistance to them would seem out of the question. But as America's schools are now run, virtually no one in them has a serious interest in improving performance or conserving resources. And all are reluctant to face the uncertainty that change would entail.

The best way to improve performance is to establish mechanisms that directly reward improvement. In general, school systems can be run in two ways: through regulation and through performance incentives. Regulation is a centralized command and control system. Central management creates a system of rules. Results can be satisfactory if the rules are appropriate and useful, if the schools can be adequately monitored, and if punishments for violating rules are sufficient to ensure that rules are obeyed. Performance

Photography by Leo De Wys

incentives, on the other hand, rely more on rewards within a decentralized system of decisionmaking. Central management specifies its goals and rewards those who achieve them. Typically, incentive systems specify what is to be achieved and leave it up to the agent to decide how, while regulatory regimes attempt to specify both what and how.

Today's schools rely far more heavily on regulation that on incentives, even though education is inherently a highly decentralized activity. Almost all productive work is done in classrooms. It is next to impossible to create a single set of regulations capable of identifying, hiring, and mobilizing America's almost 3 million teachers. Still, despite the evident difficulty of applying strong regulatory regimes to education, schools today make little use of performance incentives—with results that are all too evident.

People respond to incentives, be they financial, emotional, or some other form. When rewarded for an action, people do it. Students, teachers, and other school personnel are no different. Moreover, every organization, either implicitly or explicitly, sets up incentives for action. Unfortunately, few incentives within today's schools relate to student performance. If school reform is to work, that must change.

Learning about Incentives

It is not enough simply to exhort schools to "use performance incentives." Performance incentives come in many forms, and incentives that work in one school system may not work in another. If there is a single, glaring lesson to be learned from past attempts at school reform, it is that no single overarching reform can solve the problems of every school. Policymakers must decentralize school systems to allow local decisionmakers to devise programs appropriate for their situations. They must also help provide the discipline to ensure that those programs are effective.

The school reform landscape is dotted with proposals for new programs of educational incentives. The ideas behind them are conceptually appealing, but so far we have little experience with the programs in practice. Somewhat hesitantly, schools have begun to experiment with a variety of new programs that differ both in how they define "good" performance and how they reward it. For example, charter schools enable teachers to set up new schools to try out new educational ideas in exchange for performance commitments. School choice and educational vouchers give students and their parents an important voice in determining whether schools are good by allowing them to decide which to attend. Merit pay for teachers and principals, together with attempts to contract educational services to private firms, provide still other performance definitions and incentives.

Applications of these new programs have, nonetheless, been very limited. All will need to be tested far more widely, and much greater effort will have to go into evaluating their performance and disseminating information about their results. The field of medicine has made great strides by wide and systematic experiments to test the efficacy of new treatments and publicize their success or failure. Schools should do likewise.

In some ways the discussion about performance incentives has become confused with notions of decentralized decisionmaking. Considerable legislation and local change has been devoted to promoting decentralized decisions through such means as site-based management or semi-autonomous subdistricts. But decentralization alone is not enough—for it has been tried widely and has frequently failed to lead to general improvement. Decentralization must be combined with well-crafted performance incentives based on clear definitions of good performance. These definitions, in turn, require agreement on the goals and objectives of schools.

Measurement and Evaluation

An essential ingredient of reform will therefore be clear measurement of student performance—a subject that is itself controversial. Naturally, people differ on what they think schools should accomplish, on how those things are best evaluated, and, ultimately, on what part of student performance should be attributed to schools.

The starting point must be a plain delineation of goals and objectives. While defining a good education is politically difficult, performance in core academic areas should be paramount. If schools fail to prepare students properly with basic literacy, numeracy, and analytical skills, they will never be judged successful.

One aspect of performance measurement that is being hotly debated is the appropriateness of currently available standardized tests. Many participants in that debate, however, can agree on three points. First, good measures of student performance are essential to educational improvement. Second, while the appropriate testing instrument depends considerably on the purpose of measurement, existing tests, though far from perfect, do provide useful information in assessing schools' performance. Third, although test measurements can and should be improved, evaluation of schools should not await development of the perfect instrument.

One confusion about performance measurement involves judging the contribution of schools. When student test scores are made public, many people immediately judge the performance of schools solely on the basis of these scores, implicitly ignoring the fact that student performance is the result of much more than just the schools. Inevitably it involves a mixture of schooling, education in the home, innate abilities, and the like. Thus, for example, a teacher or school that must deal with students unprepared for their current grade level should not be penalized for poor student preparation. Instead, attention should be focused on what the teacher or school contributes—on their value-added to learning. This focus is particularly appropriate when student performance is incorporated in incentive systems. Concentrating on value-added is also essential to program evaluations that attempt to uncover effective approaches to schooling. Indeed, when value-added is appropriately measured, we may well find that some schools with high average scores are really contributing little to students' performance and vice versa.

Altered Roles

Moving toward a school system that uses resources effectively, emphasizes incentives, and recognizes the importance of evaluation will require all participants to take on new roles and responsibilities, which will, of course, vary across states and districts.

Teachers, perhaps the most important element of our schooling system, must take an active part in improving schools. Yet teaching under a new system based on performance incentives and decentralized decisionmaking promises different challenges—and requires new experience, training, and expectations—than teaching today. One way to introduce changes into teaching without completely alienating current teachers is two-tier employment contracts. New teachers' contracts would offer fewer tenure guarantees, more risks, and greater flexibility and rewards. Existing teachers could either continue under existing employment rules for tenure, pay, and work conditions or opt for the new-style contract. The expectations that today's teachers had when they entered the profession cannot be arbitrarily revoked if we expect schools to improve.

State governments should put aside many of their old tasks—laying down school curricula and procedures—and instead promote local experimentation with new incentive systems and then help produce and disseminate evaluation results. States should define performance standards and explicit student goals. Finally, states share with the federal government a role in ensuring equality of opportunity. Disadvantaged students may well require additional resources, even when all schools are using resources effectively. Moreover, states must monitor the performance of local districts. When performance is unacceptably low, states must intervene through school choice programs or voucher systems that will enable students in poorly performing districts to move to better schools elsewhere.

The federal government should join states in setting goals and standards, developing performance information, supporting evaluation, and disseminating results. It should also take the lead in supporting supplemental programs for disadvantaged and minority students. (Programs for the disadvantaged should themselves follow the same guidelines as all other programs but may also involve expansions of earlier childhood education, integrated health and nutrition programs, and other supplemental interventions.)

Local school districts' responsibilities—making curricular choices and managing teacher and administrative personnel—would remain nominally the same but would actually change significantly if states removed many of their restrictions on instruction and organization. Moreover, if major decisions devolved to local schools, new emphasis would be placed on management and leadership.

Businesses too could take on a new role. While businesses frequently lament the quality of workers being turned out by the schools, they have never worked closely with schools in defining the skills and abilities they want. Closer consultation with schools, perhaps coupled with long-term hiring relationships, could aid both schools and businesses. Moreover, businesses could give students valuable incentives to perform well in school by making it clear that hiring decisions are based on school transcripts. And experienced business managers might have much to teach schools about how to manage performance incentives.

Finally, parents, who often have few opportunities to play an active part in schools today, would have a crucial role in many incentive-based systems of school management. Systems of choice require parents to decide which school offers the best opportunities for their children. Systems of decentralized management give parents a chance to become more actively involved in running schools, and indeed may require it.

An Overriding Perspective

Reforming America's schools does not require more money. On the contrary, the cause of reform will best be advanced by holding overall real spending constant. Schools must acquire the discipline imposed by economic efficiency. They must learn to consider trade-offs among programs and operations. They must learn to evaluate performance and eliminate programs that are not working. They must learn to seek out and expand on productive incentive structures and organizational approaches. In short, they must make better use of existing resources.

Inefficiencies in the current structure of schools are widespread, but there is little interest or pressure to eliminate them. Where such interest exists, it is often thwarted by regulations or contract restrictions that do not permit reasonable adjustments in personnel, classroom organization, the use of new technologies or other approaches that might improve performance for existing spending. If America's schools are to improve, they must embrace the basic principles of economics, with its attention to effectiveness of expenditures and to establishing appropriate incentives.

In the long run, the nation may find it appropriate to increase school spending. It is simply hard to tell at this point. But it is clear that expanding resources first and looking for reform second is likely to lead only to a more expensive system, not a better one.

Morality and Values in Education

There is a serious moral crisis facing young Americans as well as older ones. Children and teenagers are growing to adulthood in many communities where they witness the use of excessive violence frequently, where they are either sexually exploited themselves or witness sexual exploitation, where they are exposed to sexually transmitted diseases, such as the AIDS virus, and where they are affected by other serious social situations that raise fundamental ethical issues. This year's edition of this volume opened with David Hamburg's presidential address for the Carnegie Corporation for 1994 (received by me in early 1995), in which he documented the rising tide of violence in America. He discussed how schools could take part in teaching young people nonviolent conflict resolution strategies. As this edition was being prepared, a three-year-old girl had been murdered by a youth gang in a California city. There is terrible frustration and anger among some American youth, and we must address how educators can teach moral standards and ethical decision-making skills. This is no longer simply something desirable that we might do; it has become something that we *must* do. How it is to be done is currently the subject of a national dialogue.

Students need to develop a sense of genuine caring both for themselves and others. They need to learn alternatives to violence and human exploitation. Teachers need to be examples of morally responsible, caring, and loving persons who use reason and compassion in solving problems in school. Mean teachers will produce in their students the idea that it will be "OK" to be mean and brutish when they are finally in authority. Our children need moral examples in their classrooms whom they can truly admire and respect. Such teachers will exemplify self-respect and self-discipline and will encourage these values in their students; there is no room for compromise in maintaining classroom order and control. The levels of social violence in the United States are much higher than in western Europe or the British Commonwealth.

The essays in the unit reflect on these issues. An article comparing changes in British and American moral standards since the mid-Victorian period to the recent past is written by Gertrude Himmelfarb. Her work documents the changes in American public morals since the mid-nineteenth century. The other essays in this unit document the concerns of many persons regarding current American standards of public morality.

Some teachers describe their concern that students need to develop a stronger sense of character rooted in a more defensible system of values. Other teachers express concern that they cannot "do everything" and are hesitant to instruct on morality and values. Most believe that they must do something to help students become reasoning and ethical decision makers.

What teachers perceive to be worthwhile and defensible behavior informs our reflections on what we as educators should teach. We are conscious immediately of some of the values that inform our behavior, but we may not be aware of all that informs our preferences. Values that we hold without being conscious of them are referred to as tacit values—values derived indirectly after reasoned reflection on our thoughts about teaching and learning. Much of our knowledge about teaching is tacit knowledge, which we need to bring into conscious cognition by analyzing the concepts that "drive" our practice. We need to acknowledge how all our values inform and influence our thoughts about teaching.

Teachers need to help students develop within themselves a sense of critical social consciousness and a genuine concern for social justice. The debate on this issue continues in professional literature. Insight into the nature of moral decision making should be taught in the context of real current and past social problems and should lead students to develop their own skills in social analysis relating to the ethical dilemmas of human beings.

There is a need for teachers to develop principles of professional practice that will enable them to respond reasonably to the many ethical dilemmas that they now face. A knowledge base on how teachers derive their knowledge of professional ethics is developing; further study of how teachers' values shape their professional practice is very important. Educational systems at all levels are based on the desirability to teach certain fundamental beliefs and the disciplines of knowledge (however they may be organized in different cultures). School curricula are based on certain moral assumptions (secular or religious) as to the worth of knowledge—the belief that certain forms of knowledge are more worthy than others. Schooling should not only transmit national and cultural heritages, including our intellectual heritage; it is also a fundamentally moral enterprise in which students need to learn how to develop tenable moral standards in the contexts of their own visions of the world.

The controversy over teaching morality deals with more than just the tensions between secular and religious interests in society, although acknowledging such tensions is valuable. Moral education is also more than a debate over the merits of methods used to teach students to make morally sound, ethical choices in their lives, although this also is critically important and ought to be done. Thus we argue that the construction of educational processes and the decisions about the substantive content of school curricula are also moral issues as well as epistemological ones having to do with how we discover, verify, and transmit knowledge.

One of the most compelling responsibilities of both Canadian and U.S. schools is the responsibility of preparing young persons for their moral duties as free citizens of free nations. The Canadian and U.S. governments have always wanted their schools to teach the principles of civic morality based on their respective constitutional traditions. Indeed, when the public school movement began in the United States in the 1830s and 1840s, the concept of universal public schooling as a mechanism for instilling a sense of national identity and civic morality was supported. In every nation, school curricula have certain value preferences imbedded in them.

Do teachers have a responsibility to respond to student requests for information on sexuality, sexual morality, sexually transmitted diseases, and so on? Or should they deny these requests? For whom do the schools exist? Is a teacher's primary responsibility to his or her client, the student, or to the student's parents? Do secondary school students have the right to study and to inquire into subjects not in officially sanctioned curricula? What are the moral issues surrounding censorship of student reading material? What ethical questions are raised by arbitrarily withholding information regarding alternative viewpoints on controversial topics?

Teachers cannot hide all of their moral preferences. They can, however, learn to conduct just and open discussions of moral topics without succumbing to the temptation to indoctrinate students with their own views.

Teaching students to respect all people, to revere the sanctity of life, to uphold the right of every citizen to dissent, to believe in the equality of all people before the law, to cherish the freedom to learn, and to respect the right of all people to their own convictions—these are principles of democracy and ideals worthy of being cherished. An understanding of the processes of ethical decision making is needed by the citizens of any free nation; thus, this process should be taught in a free nation's schools.

What part ought the schooling experience play in the formation of such things as character, informed compassion, conscience, honor, and respect for self and others? From Socrates onward (and, no doubt, before him), we have wrestled with these concerns. Aristotle noted in his *Politics* that there was no consensus as to what the purposes of education should be in Athens, that people disputed what Athenian youth ought to be taught by their teachers, and that youth did not always address their elders with respect. Our present situation is far more serious than the one Aristotle confronted in fifth-century B.C. Athens. The issue of public morality and the question of how best to educate for individually and collectively responsible social behavior are matters of great significance in North America today.

The essays in this unit constitute a comprehensive overview of moral education with considerable historical and textual interpretation. Topics covered include public pressures on schools and the social responsibilities of schools. This unit can be used in courses dealing with the historical or philosophical foundations of education.

Looking Ahead: Challenge Questions

What is moral education? Why do so many people wish to see a form of moral education in schools?

Are there certain values about which most of us can agree? Should they be taught in schools? Why or why not?

Should local communities have total control of the content of moral instruction in their schools, as they did in the nineteenth century?

What is the difference between indoctrination and instruction?

Is there a national consensus concerning the form that moral education should take in schools? Is such a consensus likely if it does not now exist?

What attitudes and skills are most important to a responsible approach to moral decision making?

What can teachers do to help students become more caring, morally responsible persons?

—F. S.

A Morally Defensible Mission for Schools in the 21st Century

Education should be organized around themes of care rather than around the traditional disciplines, Ms. Noddings asserts, and she provides recommendations on how to begin.

Nel Noddings

NEL NODDINGS is Lee Jacks Professor of Child Education at Stanford University. She is the author of The Challenge to Care in Schools *(Teachers College Press, 1992), from which this article has been adapted.*

Illustration by Mario Noché

SOCIAL CHANGES in the years since World War II have been enormous. We have seen changes in work patterns, in residential stability, in styles of housing, in sexual habits, in dress, in manners, in language, in music, in entertainment, and — perhaps most important of all — in family arrangements. While schools have responded, albeit sluggishly, to technological changes with various additions to the curriculum and narrowly prescribed methods of instruction, they have largely ignored massive social changes. When they *have* responded, they have done so in piecemeal fashion, addressing isolated bits of the problem. Thus, recognizing that some children come to school hungry, schools provide meals for poor children. Alarmed by the increase in teenage pregnancies and sexually transmitted diseases, schools provide sex education. Many more examples could be offered,

but no one of these nor any collection of them adequately meets the educational needs of today's students.

What do we want for our children? What do they need from education, and what does our society need? The popular response today is that students need more

academic training, that the country needs more people with greater mathematical and scientific competence, that a more adequate academic preparation will save people from poverty, crime, and other evils of current society. Most of these claims are either false or, at best, only partly true.

For example, we do *not* need more physicists and mathematicians; many people already highly trained in these fields are unable to find work. The vast majority of adults do *not* use algebra in their work, and forcing all students to study it is a simplistic response to the real issues of equity and mathematical literacy. Just as clearly, more education will not save people from poverty unless a sufficient number of unfortunate people either reject that education or are squeezed out of it. Poverty is a *social* problem. No person who does honest, useful work — regardless of his or her educational attainments — should live in poverty. A society that allows this to happen is not an educational failure; it is a moral failure.

Our society does not need to make its children first in the world in mathematics and science. It needs to care for its children — to reduce violence, to respect honest work of every kind, to reward excellence at every level, to ensure a place for every child and emerging adult in the economic and social world, to produce people who can care competently for their own families and contribute effectively to their communities. In direct opposition to the current emphasis on academic standards, a national curriculum, and national assessment, I have argued that our main educational aim should be to encourage the growth of competent, caring, loving, and lovable people.[1]

At the present time, it is obvious that our main educational purpose is not the moral one of producing caring people but a relentless — and, as it turns out, hapless — drive for academic adequacy. I am certainly not going to argue for academic *in*adequacy, but I will try to persuade readers that a reordering of priorities is essential. All children must learn to care for other human beings, and all must find an ultimate concern in some center of care: care for self, for intimate others, for associates and acquaintances, for distant others, for animals, for plants and the physical environment, for objects and instruments, and for ideas. Within each of these centers, we can find many themes on which to build courses, topical seminars, projects, reading lists, and dialogue.

Today the curriculum is organized almost entirely around the last center, ideas, but it is so poorly put together that important ideas are often swamped by facts and skills. Even those students who might find a genuine center of care in some arena of ideas — say mathematics or literature — are sorely disappointed. In trying to teach everyone what we once taught only a few, we have wound up teaching everyone inadequately. Further, we have not bothered to ask whether the traditional education so highly treasured was ever the best education for anyone.

I have argued that liberal education (defined as a set of traditional disciplines) is an outmoded and dangerous model of education for today's young. The popular slogan today is "All children can learn!" To insist, however, that all children should get the same dose of academic English, social studies, science, and mathematics invites an important question unaddressed by the sloganeers: Why should children learn what we insist they "can" learn? Is this the material people really need to live intelligently, morally, and happily? Or are arguments for traditional liberal education badly mistaken? Worse, are they perhaps mere political maneuverings?

My argument against liberal education is not a complaint against literature, history, physical science, mathematics, or any other subject. It is an argument, first, against an ideology of control that forces all students to study a particular, narrowly prescribed curriculum devoid of content they might truly care about. Second, it is an argument in favor of greater respect for a wonderful range of human capacities now largely ignored in schools. Third, it is an argument against the persistent undervaluing of skills, attitudes, and capacities traditionally associated with women. This last point is an argument that has been eloquently made by Jane Roland Martin, whose article appears elsewhere in this issue.

What do we want for our children? Most of us hope that our children will find someone to love, find useful work they enjoy or at least do not hate, establish a family, and maintain bonds with friends and relatives. These hopes are part of our interest in shaping an acceptable child.[2] What kind of mates, parents, friends, and neighbors will our children be?

I would hope that all our children — both girls and boys — would be prepared to do the work of attentive love. This work must be done in every family situation, whether the family is conventionally or unconventionally constituted. Both men and women, if they choose to be parents, should participate in the joys and responsibilities of direct parenting, of acting as psychological parent. Too often, women have complained about bearing this responsibility almost entirely. When men volunteer to help with child care or help with housework, the very language suggests that the tasks are women's responsibilities. Men "help" in tasks they do not perceive as their own. That has to change.

In education today, there is great concern about women's participation in mathematics and science. Some researchers even refer to something called the "problem of women and mathematics." Women's lack of success or low rate of participation in fields long dominated by men is seen as a problem to be treated by educational means. But researchers do not seem to see a problem in men's low rate of participation in nursing, elementary school teaching, or full-time parenting. Our society values activities traditionally associated with men above those traditionally associated with women.[3]

The new education I envision puts a very high valuation on the traditional occupations of women. Care for children, the aged, and the ill must be shared by all capable adults, not just women, and everyone should understand that these activities bring special rewards as well as burdens. Work with children can be especially rewarding and provides an opportunity to enjoy childhood vicariously. For example, I have often wondered why high school students are not more often invited to revisit the literature of childhood in their high school English classes. A careful study of fairy tales, augmented by essays on their psychology, might be more exciting and more generally useful than, for example, the study of *Hamlet*. When we consider the natural interest we have in ourselves — past, present, and future — it is clear that literature that allows us to look forward and backward is wonderful. Further, the study of fairy tales would provide opportunities for lessons in geography, history, art, and music.

Our children should learn something about life cycles and stages. When I was in high school, my Latin class read Cicero's essay "On Old Age." With all his talk of wisdom — of milk, honey, wine, and cheese; of meditating in the afternoon breeze — I was convinced that old age had its own romance. Looking at the present condition of many elderly people, I see more than enough horror to balance whatever romance there may be. But studies of early childhood, adulthood, and old age (with or without Latin) seem central to education for real life. Further, active association with people of all ages should be encouraged. Again, one can see connections with standard subjects — statistical studies in math; the history and sociology of welfare, medical care, and family life; geographical and cultural differences. We see, also, that the need for such studies has increased as a result of the social changes discussed earlier. Home life does not provide the experience in these areas that it once did.

Relations with intimate others are the beginning and one of the significant ends of moral life. If we regard our relations with intimate others as central in moral life, then we must provide all our children with practice in caring. Children can work together formally and informally on a host of school projects, and, as they get older, they can help younger children, contribute to the care of buildings and grounds, and eventually — under careful supervision — do volunteer work in the community. Looking at Howard Gardner's multiple intelligences, we see that children can contribute useful service in a wide variety of ways; some have artistic talents, some interpersonal gifts, some athletic or kinesthetic abilities, some spiritual gifts.[4]

A moral policy, a defensible mission, for education recognizes a multiplicity of human capacities and interests. Instead of preparing everyone for college in the name of democracy and equality, schools should instill in students a respect for all forms of honest work done well.[5] Preparation for the world of work, for parenting, and for civic responsibility is essential for all students. All of us must work, but few of us do the sort of work implied by preparation in algebra and geometry. Almost all of us enter into intimate relationships, but schools largely ignore the centrality of such interests in our lives. And although most of us become parents, evidence suggests that we are not very good at parenting — and again the schools largely ignore this huge human task.

When I suggest that a morally defensible mission for education necessarily focuses on matters of human caring, people sometimes agree but fear the loss of an intellectual mission for the schools. There are at least two powerful responses to this fear. First, anyone who supposes that the current drive for uniformity in standards, curriculum, and assessment represents an intellectual agenda needs to reflect on the matter. Indeed, many thoughtful educators insist that such moves are truly anti-intellectual, discouraging critical thinking, creativity, and novelty. Second, and more important from the perspective adopted here, a curriculum centered on themes of care can be as richly intellec-

tual as we and our students want to make it. Those of us advocating genuine reform — indeed, transformation — will surely be accused of anti-intellectualism, just as John Dewey was in the middle of this century. But the accusation is false, and we should have the courage to face it down.

Examples of themes that are especially important to young people are love and friendship. Both can be studied in intellectual depth, but the crucial emphasis should be on the relevance of the subjects to self-understanding and growth. Friends are especially important to teenagers, and they need guidance in making and maintaining friendships.

Aristotle wrote eloquently on friendship, and he assessed it as central in moral life. In the *Nicomachean Ethics*, Aristotle wrote that the main criterion of friendship is that a friend wishes a friend well for his or her own sake. When we befriend others, we want good things for them not because those things may enhance our welfare but because they are good for our friends. Aristotle organized friendships into various categories: those motivated by common business or political purposes, those maintained by common recreational interests, and those created by mutual admiration of the other's virtue. The last was, for Aristotle, the highest form of friendship and, of course, the one most likely to endure.

How do friendships occur? What draws people together? Here students should have opportunities to see how far Aristotle's description will carry them. They should hear about Damon and Pythias, of course. But they should also examine some incongruous friendships: Huck and Jim in Mark Twain's *Adventures of Huckleberry Finn*; Miss Celie and Shug in Alice Walker's *Color Purple*; Lenny and George in John Steinbeck's *Of Mice and Men*; Jane and Maudie in Doris Lessing's *Diaries of Jane Somers*. What do each of these characters give to the friendship? Can friendship be part of a personal quest for fulfillment? When does a personal objective go too far and negate Aristotle's basic criterion?

Another issue to be considered is, When should moral principles outweigh the demands of friendship? The question is often cast this way, even though many of us find the wording misleading. What the questioner wants us to consider is whether we should protect friends who have done something morally wrong. A few years ago, there was a terrifying local example of this problem when a teen-

age boy killed a girl and bragged about it to his friends. His friends, in what they interpreted as an act of loyalty, did not even report the murder.

From the perspective of caring, there is no inherent conflict between moral requirements and friendship, because, as Aristotle teaches us, we have a primary obligation to promote our friends' moral growth. But lots of concrete conflicts can arise when we have to consider exactly what to do. Instead of juggling principles as we might when we say, "Friendship is more important than a little theft" or "Murder is more important than friendship," we begin by asking ourselves whether our friends have committed caring acts. If they have not, something has to be done. In the case of something as horrible as murder, the act must be reported. But true friends would also go beyond initial judgment and action to ask how they might follow through with appropriate help for the murderer. When we adopt caring as an ethical approach, our moral work has just begun where other approaches end. Caring requires staying-with, or what Ruddick has called "holding." We do not let our friends fall if we can help it, and if they do, we hold on and pull them back up.

Gender differences in friendship patterns should also be discussed. It may be harder for males to reject relationships in which they are pushed to do socially unacceptable acts, because those acts are often used as tests of manhood. Females, by contrast, find it more difficult to separate themselves from abusive relationships. In both cases, young people have to learn not only to take appropriate responsibility for the moral growth of others but also to insist that others accept responsibility for their own behavior. It is often a fine line, and — since there are no formulas to assist us — we remain vulnerable in all our moral relations.

A TRANSFORMATION of the sort envisioned here requires organizational and structural changes to support the changes in curriculum and instruction. It requires a move away from the ideology of control, from the mistaken notion that ironhanded accountability will ensure the outcomes we identify as desirable. It won't just happen. We should have learned by now that both children and adults can accomplish wonderful things in an atmosphere of love and trust and that they will (if they are healthy) resist — sometimes to their own detriment — in environments of coercion.

(Because I would like to present for discussion my basic recommendations for both structural and curricular changes) I will risk setting them forth here in a skeletal form. Of course, I cannot describe and defend the recommendations adequately in so brief a space, but here is a summary.

The traditional organization of schooling is intellectually and morally inadequate for contemporary society. We live in an age troubled by social problems that force us to reconsider what we do in schools. Too many of us think that we can improve education by merely designing a better curriculum, finding and implementing a better form of instruction, or instituting a better form of classroom management. These things won't work.

We need to give up the notion of *a single* ideal of the educated person and replace it with a multiplicity of models designed to accommodate the multiple capacities and interests of students. We need to recognize multiple identities. For example, an 11th-grader may be a black, a woman, a teenager, a Smith, an American, a New Yorker, a Methodist, a person who loves math, and so on. As she exercises these identities, she may use different languages, adopt different postures, and relate differently to those around her. But whoever she is at a given moment, whatever she is engaged in, she needs — as we all do — to be cared for. Her need for care may require formal respect, informal interaction, expert advice, just a flicker of recognition, or sustained affection. To give the care she needs requires a set of capacities in each of us to which schools give too little attention.

I have argued that education should be organized around themes of care rather than around the traditional disciplines. All students should be engaged in a general education that guides them in caring for self, intimate others, global others, plants, animals, the environment, objects and instruments, and ideas. Moral life so defined should be frankly embraced as the main goal of education. Such an aim does not work against intellectual development or academic achievement. Rather, it supplies a firm foundation for both.

How can we begin? Here is what I think we must do:

1. *Be clear and unapologetic about our goal.* The main aim of education should be to produce competent, caring, loving, and lovable people.

2. *Take care of affiliative needs.* We must keep students and teachers together (by mutual consent) for several years, and we must keep students together when possible. We should also strive to keep students in the same building for considerable periods of time and help students to think of the school as theirs. Finally, we must legitimize time spent in building relations of care and trust.

3. *Relax the impulse to control.* We need to give teachers and students more responsibility to exercise judgment. At the same time we must get rid of competitive grading and reduce the amount of testing that we do. Those well-designed tests that remain should be used to assess whether people can competently handle the tasks they want to undertake. We also need to encourage teachers to explore material with students. We don't have to know everything to teach well.

In short, we need to define expertise more broadly and instrumentally. For example, a biology teacher should be able to teach whatever mathematics is involved in biology, while a social studies teacher should be able to teach whatever mathematics is required in that subject. We must encourage self-evaluation and teach students how to do it competently, and we must also involve students in governing their own classrooms and schools. Making such changes means that we accept the challenge to care by teaching well the things that students want to learn.

4. *Get rid of program hierarchies.* This will take time, but we must begin now to provide excellent programs for *all* our children. Programs for the noncollege-bound should be just as rich, desirable, and rigorous as those for the college-bound.

We must abandon uniform requirements for college entrance. What a student wants to do or to study should guide what is required by way of preparation. Here we should not worry greatly about students who "change their minds." Right now we are afraid that, if students prepare for something particular, they may change their minds and all that preparation will be wasted. Thus we busily prepare them uniformly for nothing. We forget that, when people have a goal in mind, they learn well and that, even if they change their minds, they may have acquired the skills and habits of mind they will need for further learning. The one essential point is that we give all students what all students need — genuine opportunities to explore the questions central to human life.

5. *Give at least part of every day to themes of care.* We should discuss existential questions — including spiritual matters — freely. Moreover, we need to help students learn to treat each other ethically by giving them practice in caring. We must help students understand how groups and individuals create rivals and enemies and help them learn how to "be on both sides." We should encourage a way of caring for animals, plants, and the environment that is consistent with caring for humans, and we should also encourage caring for the human-made world. Students need to feel at home in technical, natural, and cultural worlds, and educators must cultivate wonder and appreciation for the human-made world.

6. *Teach students that caring in every domain implies competence.* When we care, we accept the responsibility to work continuously on our competence so that the recipient of our care — person, animal, object, or idea — is enhanced. There is nothing mushy about caring. It is the strong, resilient backbone of human life.

1. Nel Noddings, *The Challenge to Care in Schools* (New York: Teachers College Press, 1992).

2. Sara Ruddick, "Maternal Thinking," *Feminist Studies*, vol. 6, 1980, pp. 342-67.

3. For an extended and powerful argument on this issue, see Jane Roland Martin, *Reclaiming a Conversation* (New Haven, Conn.: Yale University Press, 1985).

4. Howard Gardner, *Frames of Mind* (New York: Basic Books, 1983).

5. John Gardner, *Excellence: Can We Be Equal and Excellent Too?* (New York: Harper, 1961).

A DE-MORALIZED SOCIETY: THE BRITISH/AMERICAN EXPERIENCE

GERTRUDE HIMMELFARB

Gertrude Himmelfarb is professor emeritus of history at the City University of New York. She is the author of numerous books, including The Idea of Poverty, The New History and the Old, *and* On Looking Into the Abyss.

"THE PAST is a foreign country," it has been said. But it is not an unrecognizable country. Indeed, we sometimes experience a "shock of recognition" as we confront some aspect of the past in the present. One does not need to have had a Victorian grandmother, as did Margaret Thatcher, to be reminded of "Victorian values." One does not even have to be English; "Victorian America," as it has been called, was not all that different, at least in terms of values, from Victorian England. Vestigial remains of that Victorianism are everywhere around us. And memories of them persist, even when the realities are gone, rather like an amputated limb that still seems to throb when the weather is bad.

How can we not think of our present condition when we read Thomas Carlyle on the "Condition of England" one hundred and fifty years ago? While his contemporaries were debating "the standard of living question"—the "pessimists" arguing that the standard of living of the working classes had declined in that early period of industrialism, and the "optimists" that it had improved—Carlyle reformulated the issue to read, "the condition of England question." That question, he insisted, could not be resolved by citing "figures of arithmetic" about wages and prices. What was important was the "condition" and "disposition" of the people: their beliefs and feelings, their sense of right and wrong, the attitudes and habits that would dispose them either to a "wholesome composure, frugality, and prosperity," or to an "acrid unrest, recklessness, gin-drinking and gradual ruin."

In fact, the Victorians did have "figures of arithmetic" dealing with the condition and disposition of the people as well as their economic state. These "moral statistics" or "social statistics," as they called them, dealt with crime, illiteracy, illegitimacy, drunkenness, pauperism, vagrancy. If they did not have, as we do, statistics on drugs, divorce, or teenage suicide, it is because these problems were then so negligible as not to constitute "social problems."

It is in this historical context that we may address our own "condition of the people question." And it is by comparison with the Victorians that we may find even more cause for alarm. For the current moral statistics are not only more troubling than those a century ago; they constitute a trend that bodes even worse for the future than for the present. Where the Victorians had the satisfaction of witnessing a significant improvement in their moral and social condition, we are confronting a considerable deterioration in ours.

The 'Moral Statistics': Illegitimacy

In nineteenth-century England, the illegitimacy ratio—the proportion of out-of-wedlock births to total births—rose from a little over 5 percent at the beginning of the century to a peak of 7 percent in 1845. It then fell steadily until it was less than 4 percent at the turn of the century. In East London, the poorest section of the city, the figures are even more dramatic, for illegitimacy was consistently well below the average: 4.5 percent in mid-century and 3 percent by the end of the century. Apart from a temporary increase during both world wars, the ratio continued to hover around 5 percent until 1960. It then began to rise: to over 8 percent in 1970, 12 percent in 1980, and then precipitously, to more than 32 percent by the end of 1992—a two-and-one-half-times increase in the last decade alone and a sixfold rise in three decades. In 1981, a married woman was half as likely to have a child as she was in 1901, while an unmarried woman was three times as likely. (See Figure 1).

From *American Educator,* Winter 1994/95, pp. 14-21, 40-43. Originally from *The Public Interest,* Fall 1994. Adapted from *The De-Moralization of Society: From Victorian Virtues to Modern Values* by Gertrude Himmelfarb, published by Alfred A. Knopf, Inc. © 1995 by Gertrude Himmelfarb. Reprinted by permission.

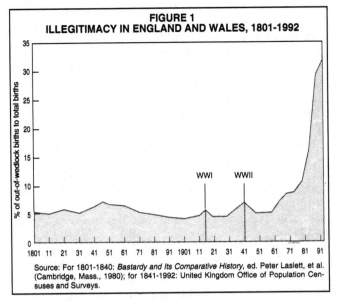

FIGURE 1
ILLEGITIMACY IN ENGLAND AND WALES, 1801-1992

Source: For 1801-1840: *Bastardy and Its Comparative History*, ed. Peter Laslett, et al. (Cambridge, Mass., 1980); for 1841-1992: United Kingdom Office of Population Censuses and Surveys.

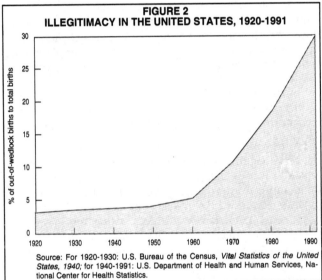

FIGURE 2
ILLEGITIMACY IN THE UNITED STATES, 1920-1991

Source: For 1920-1930: U.S. Bureau of the Census, *Vital Statistics of the United States, 1940;* for 1940-1991: U.S. Department of Health and Human Services, National Center for Health Statistics.

In the United States, the figures are no less dramatic. Starting at 3 percent in 1920 (the first year for which there are national statistics), the illegitimacy ratio rose gradually to slightly over 5 percent by 1960, after which it grew rapidly: to almost 11 percent in 1970, over 18 percent in 1980, and 30 percent by 1991—a tenfold increase from 1920 and a sixfold increase from 1960. For whites alone, the ratio went up only slightly between 1920 and 1960 (from 1.5 percent to a little over 2 percent) and then advanced at an even steeper rate than that of blacks: to almost 6 percent in 1970, 11 percent in 1980, and nearly 22 percent in 1991—fourteen times the 1920 figure and eleven times that of 1960. If the black illegitimacy ratio did not accelerate as much, it was because it started at a higher level: from 12 percent in 1920 to 22 percent in 1960, over 37 percent in 1970, 55 percent in 1980, and 68 percent by 1991. (See Figure 2.)

Teenage illegitimacy has earned the United States the dubious distinction of ranking first among all industrialized nations, the rate having tripled between 1960

and 1991. In 1990, one in ten teenage girls got pregnant, half of them giving birth and the other half having abortions. England is second only to the United States in teenage illegitimacy, but the rate of increase in the past three decades has been even more rapid. In both countries, teenagers are far more "sexually active" (as the current expression has it) than ever before, and at an earlier age. In 1970, 5 percent of fifteen-year-old girls in the United States had had sexual intercourse; in 1988, 25 percent had.

The 'Moral Statistics': Crime

Public opinion polls in both England and the United States show crime as the major concern of the people, and for good reason, as the statistics suggest. Again, the historical pattern is dramatic and disquieting. In England between 1857 and 1901, the rate of indictable offenses (serious offenses, not including simple assault, drunkenness, vagrancy, and the like) decreased from about 480 per 100,000 population to 250— a decline of almost 50 percent in four decades. The absolute numbers are even more graphic: While the population grew from about 19 million to 33 million, the number of serious crimes fell from 92,000 to 81,000. Moreover, 1857 was not the peak year; it is simply the year when the most reliable and consistent series of statistics starts. The decline (earlier statistics suggest) started in the mid or late 1840s—at about the same time as the beginning of the decline in illegitimacy. It is also interesting that just as the illegitimacy ratio in the middle of the century was lower in the metropolis than in the rest of the country, so was the crime rate.

The considerable decrease of crime in England is often attributed to the establishment of the police force, first in London in 1829, then in the counties, and by 1856, in the country at large. Although this undoubtedly had the effect of deterring crime, it also improved the recording of crime and the apprehension of criminals, which makes the lower crime rates even more notable. One criminologist, analyzing these statistics, concludes that deterrence alone cannot account for the decline, that the explanation has to be sought in "heavy generalizations about the 'civilizing' effects of religion, education, and environmental reform."

The low crime rate persisted until shortly before the First World War when it rose very slightly. It fell during the war and started a steady rise in the mid-twenties, reaching 400 per 100,000 population in 1931 (somewhat less than the 1861 rate) and 900 in 1941. During the Second World War, unlike the First (and contrary to popular opinion), crime increased, levelling off or declining slightly in the early 1950s. The largest rise started in the mid-fifties, from under 1,000 in 1955 to 1,750 in 1961, 3,400 in 1971, 5,600 in 1981, and a staggering 10,000 in 1991—ten times the rate of 1955 and forty times that of 1901. Violent crimes alone almost doubled in each decade after 1950. (See Figure 3.) (On the eve of this rise, in 1955, the anthropologist Geoffrey Gorer remarked upon the extraordinary degree of civility exhibited in England, where "football crowds are as orderly

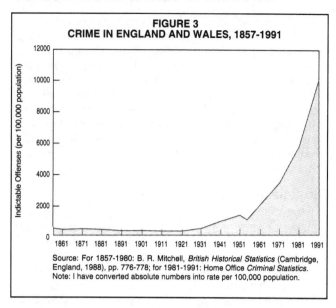

FIGURE 3
CRIME IN ENGLAND AND WALES, 1857-1991

Source: For 1857-1980: B. R. Mitchell, *British Historical Statistics* (Cambridge, England, 1988), pp. 776-778; for 1981-1991: Home Office *Criminal Statistics*.
Note: I have converted absolute numbers into rate per 100,000 population.

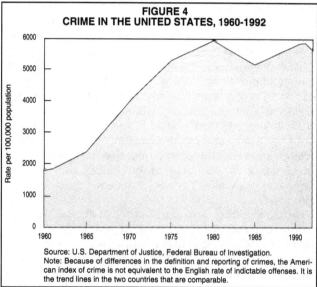

FIGURE 4
CRIME IN THE UNITED STATES, 1960-1992

Source: U.S. Department of Justice, Federal Bureau of Investigation.
Note: Because of differences in the definition and reporting of crimes, the American index of crime is not equivalent to the English rate of indictable offenses. It is the trend lines in the two countries that are comparable.

as church meetings." Within a few years, those games became notorious as the scene of mayhem and riots.)

There are no national crime statistics for the United States for the nineteenth century and only partial ones (for homicides) for the early twentieth century. Local statistics, however, suggest that, as in England, the decrease in crime started in the latter part of the nineteenth century (except for a few years following the Civil War) and continued into the early twentieth century. There was even a decline of homicides in the larger cities, where they were most common; in Philadelphia, the rate fell from 3.3 per 100,000 population in mid-century to 2.1 by the end of the century.

National crime statistics became available only in 1960, when the rate was under 1,900 per 100,000 population. That figure doubled within the decade and tripled by 1980. A decline in the early 1980s, from almost 6,000 to 5,200, was followed by an increase to 5,800 in 1990; the latest figure, for 1992, is somewhat under 5,700. The rate of violent crime (murder, rape, robbery, and aggravated assault) followed a similar pattern, except that the increase after 1985 was more precipitous and continued until 1992, making for an almost fivefold rise from 1960. In 1987, the Department of Justice estimated that eight of every ten Americans would be a victim of violent crime at least once in their lives. (See Figure 4.)*

Homicide statistics go back to the beginning of the century, when the national rate was 1.2 per 100,000 population. That figure skyrocketed during prohibition, reaching as high as 9.7 by one account (6.5 by another) in 1933, when prohibition was repealed. The rate dropped to between five and six during the 1940s and to under five in the fifties and early sixties. In the mid-sixties, it started to climb rapidly, more than doubling between 1965 and 1980. A decline in the early eighties was followed by another rise; in 1991 it was just short of its 1980 peak. The rate among blacks, especially in the cities, was considerably higher than among whites—at one point in the 1920s as much as eight times higher. In the 1970s and early 1980s, the black rate fell by more than one-fourth (from over 40 to under 30), while the white rate rose by one-third (from 4.3 to 5.6); since then, however, the rate for young black males tripled while that for young white males rose by 50 percent. Homicide is now the leading cause of death among black youths.

For all kinds of crimes the figures for blacks are far higher than for whites—for blacks both as the victims and the perpetrators of crime. Criminologists have coined the term "criminogenic" to describe this phenomenon:

> In essence, the inner city has become a criminogenic community, a place where the social forces that create predatory criminals are far more numerous and overwhelmingly stronger than the social forces that create virtuous citizens. At core, the problem is that most inner-city children grow up surrounded by teenagers and adults who are themselves deviant, delinquent, or criminal. At best, these teenagers and adults misshape the characters and lives of the young in their midst. At worst, they abuse, neglect, or criminally prey upon the young.

More Moral Statistics

There are brave souls, inveterate optimists, who try to put the best gloss on the statistics. But it is not much consolation to be told that the overall crime rate in the United States has declined slightly from its peak in the early 1980s if the violent crime rate has risen in the same period—and increased still more among juveniles and girls (an ominous trend, since the teenage population is also growing). Nor that the divorce rate has fallen somewhat in the past decade, if it had doubled in the previous two decades; if more parents are co-habitating without benefit of marriage (the rate in the United States has increased sixfold since 1970); and if more children are

---

*Because of differences in the definition and reporting of crimes, the American index of crime is not equivalent to the English rate of indictable offenses. The English rate of 10,000 in 1991 does not mean that England experienced almost twice as many crimes per capita as America did. It is the trend lines in both countries that are significant, and those lines are comparable.

born out of wedlock and living with single parents. (In 1970, one out of ten families was headed by a single parent; in 1990, three out of ten were). Nor that the white illegitimacy ratio is considerably lower than the black, if the white ratio is rapidly approaching the black ratio of a few decades ago, when Daniel Patrick Moynihan wrote his percipient report about the breakdown of the black family. (The black ratio in 1964, when that report was issued, was 24.5 percent; the white ratio now is 22 percent. In 1964, 50 percent of black teenage mothers were single; in 1991, 55 percent of white teenage mothers were single.)

Nor is it reassuring to be told that two-thirds of new welfare recipients are off the rolls within two years, if half of those soon return, and a quarter of all recipients are on for more than eight years. Nor that divorced mothers leave the welfare rolls after an average of five years, if never-married mothers remain for more than nine years, and unmarried mothers who bore their children as teenagers stay on for ten or more years. (Forty-three percent of the longest-term welfare recipients started their families as unwed teenagers.)

Nor is the cause of racial equality promoted by the news of an emerging "white underclass," smaller and less conspicuous than the black (partly because it is more dispersed) but rapidly increasing. If, as has been conclusively demonstrated, the single-parent family is the most important factor associated with the "pathology of poverty"—welfare dependency, crime, drugs, illiteracy, homelessness—a white illegitimacy ratio of 22 percent, and twice that for white women below the poverty line, signifies a new and dangerous trend. In England, Charles

> *We are constantly beseeched to be "nonjudgmental," to be wary of crediting our beliefs with any greater validity than anyone else's.*

Murray has shown, a similar underclass is developing with twice the illegitimacy of the rest of the population; there it is a purely class rather than racial phenomenon.

Redefining Deviancy

The English sociologist Christie Davies has described a "U-curve model of deviance," which applies to both Britain and the United States. The curve shows the drop in crime, violence, illegitimacy, and alcoholism in the last half of the nineteenth century, reaching a low at the turn of the century, and a sharp rise in the latter part of the twentieth century. The curve is actually more skewed than this image suggests. It might more accurately be described as a "J-curve," for the height of deviancy in the nineteenth century was considerably lower than it is today—an illegitimacy ratio of 7 percent in England in the mid-nineteenth century, compared with over 32 percent toward the end of the twentieth; or a crime rate of about 500 per 100,000 population then compared with 10,000 now.

In his *American Scholar* essay, "Defining Deviancy Down," Senator Moynihan has taken the idea of deviancy a step further by describing the downward curve of the concept of deviancy. What was once regarded as deviant behavior is no longer so regarded; what was once deemed abnormal has been normalized. As deviancy is defined downward, so the threshold of deviancy rises: Behavior once stigmatized as deviant is now tolerated and even sanctioned. Mental patients, no longer institutionalized, are now treated, and appear in the statistics, not as mentally incapacitated but as "homeless." Divorce and illegitimacy, once seen as betokening the breakdown of the family, are now viewed more benignly; illegitimacy has been officially rebaptized as "nonmarital childbearing," and divorced and unmarried mothers are lumped together in the category of "single-parent families." And violent crime has become so endemic that we have practically become inured to it. The St. Valentine's Day Massacre in Chicago in 1929, when four gangsters killed seven other gangsters, shocked the nation and became legendary, immortalized in encyclopedias and history books; in Los Angeles today, James Q. Wilson observes, as many people are killed every weekend.

It is ironic to recall that only a short while ago criminologists were accounting for the rise of the crime rates in terms of our "sensitization to violence." As a result of the century-long decline of violence, they reasoned, we had become more sensitive to "residual violence"; thus, more crimes were being reported and apprehended. This "residual violence" has by now become so overwhelming that, as Moynihan points out, we are being desensitized to it.

Charles Krauthammer has proposed a complementary concept in his *New Republic* essay, "Defining Deviancy Up." As deviancy is normalized, so the normal becomes deviant. The kind of family that has been regarded for centuries as natural and moral—the "bourgeois" family, as it is invidiously called—is now seen as pathological, concealing behind the façade of respectability the new "original sin," child abuse. While crime is underreported because we have become desensitized to it, child abuse is overreported, including fantasies imagined (often inspired by therapists and social workers) long after the supposed events. Similarly, rape has been "defined up" as "date rape," to include sexual relations that the participants themselves may not at the time have perceived as rape.

The combined effect of defining deviancy up and defining it down has been to normalize and legitimate what was once regarded as abnormal and illegitimate, and, conversely, to stigmatize and discredit what was once normal and respectable. This process too, has occurred with startling rapidity. One might expect that attitudes and values would lag behind the reality, that people would continue to pay lip service to the moral principles they were brought up with, even while violating those principles in practice. What is startling about the 1960s "sexual revolution," as it has properly been called, is how revolutionary it was, in sensibility as well as reality. In 1965, 69 percent of American women and

65 percent of men under the age of thirty said that pre-marital sex was always or almost always wrong; in 1972, those figures plummeted to 24 percent and 21 percent. For women over the age of thirty, the figures dropped from 91 percent to 62 percent, and for men from 62 percent to 47 percent—this in seven short years. Thus language, sensibility, and social policy conspire together to redefine deviancy.

Understanding the Causes

For a long time, social critics and policy makers found it hard to face up to the realities of our moral condition, in spite of the evidence of statistics. They criticized the statistics themselves or tried to explain them away. The crime figures, they said, reflect not a real increase in crime but an increase in the reporting of crime; or the increase is a temporary aberration, a blip on the demographic curve representing the "baby boomers" who would soon outgrow their infantile, antisocial behavior; or criminal behavior is a cry for help from individuals seeking recognition and self-esteem; or crime is the unfortunate result of poverty, unemployment, and racism, to be overcome by a more generous welfare system, a more equitable distribution of wealth, and a more aggressive drive against discrimination.

These explanations have some plausibility. The rise and fall of crime sometimes, but not always, corresponds to the increase and decrease of the age group most prone to criminal behavior. And there is an occasional, but not consistent, relation between crime and economic depression and poverty. In England in the 1890s, in a period of severe unemployment, crime (including property crime) fell. Indeed, the inverse relationship between crime and poverty at the end of the nineteenth century suggests, as one study put it, that "poverty-based crime" had given way to "prosperity-based crime."

In the twentieth century, the correlation between crime and unemployment has been no less erratic. While crime did increase in England during the depression of the 1930s, that increase had started some years earlier. A graph of unemployment and crime between 1950 and 1980 shows no significant correlation in the first fifteen years and only a rough correlation thereafter. The crime figures, a Home Office bulletin concludes, would correspond equally well, or even better, with other kinds of data. "Indeed, the consumption of alcohol, the consumption of ice cream, the number of cars on the road, and the Gross National Product are highly correlated with rising crime over 1950-1980."

The situation is similar in the United States. In the high-unemployment years of 1949, 1958 and 1961, when unemployment was 6 or 7 percent, crime was less than 2 percent; in the low-unemployment years of 1966 to 1969, with unemployment between 3 and 4 percent, crime was almost 4 percent. Today in the inner cities there is a correlation between unemployment and crime, but it may be argued that it is not so much unemployment that causes crime as a culture that denigrates or discourages employment, making crime seem more nor-

Schools Seek Help To Stop Violent Acts

By Robert O'Harrow, Jr.

Fairfax County [Virginia] school officials, anxious about a rising number of assaults, weapon confiscations and incidents such as the recent drive-by shooting at J.E.B. Stuart High School, are acknowledging they cannot handle school violence problems alone and are appealing to the community for help.

Reflecting a growing national concern over the impact of violence on education, county officials have begun to form twenty-three school-community groups to try to reach out to parents, police, and other residents for solutions to violence in classrooms and near schools.

During one organizational meeting at Stuart on Wednesday night, dozens of Fairfax parents, educators, police officers, and community activists swapped ideas and fretted about rising gang activity.

One man suggested sending delegations of parents and educators to troubled neighborhoods near the school. A mother appealed for more hallway guards to make her teenage daughter feel safer. Someone else talked about starting a newsletter to circulate ideas about violence prevention.

School officials said they welcomed any and all suggestions.

"I don't have the National Guard to go around the perimeter" of campus, Stuart Principal Nancy Weisgerber said during the meeting. "The only way we can fight this is by working together.... We cannot do it alone."

School officials nationwide say that increases in weapons, fights, gangs, and drug use on campuses are community problems that educators can't hope to solve alone. And increasingly, they are turning to programs similar to Fairfax's in search of solutions.

"We've seen it in every part of the country, in rich and poor schools," said William Modzeleski, director of drug planning and outreach for the U.S. Department of Education. "Schools need to break down the isolation and insulation."

In Prince George's County [Maryland], school officials have developed strong ties with churches, public housing groups and tenant associations, and they regularly hold off-campus seminars on ways to stop youth violence.

Montgomery County [Maryland] officials have been working closely with a volunteer group called Voices Versus Violence, which held more than a dozen town meetings last spring with parents, students, teachers, religious leaders, police, and others.

mal, natural, and desirable than employment. The "culture of criminality," it is evident, is very different from the "culture of poverty" as we once understood that concept.

Nor can the decline of the two-parent family be attributed, as is sometimes suggested, to the economic recession of recent times. Neither illegitimacy nor divorce increased during the far more serious depression of the 1930s—or, for that matter, in previous depressions, either in England or in the United States. In England in the 1980s, illegitimacy actually increased more in areas where the employment situation improved than in those where it got worse. Nor is there a correlation between illegitimacy and poverty; in the latter part of the nineteenth century, illegitimacy was significantly lower in the East End of London than in the rest of the country. Today there is a correlation between illegitimacy and poverty, but not a causal one; just as crime has become part of the culture of poverty, so has the single-parent family.

The Language of Morality

These realities have been difficult to confront because they violate the dominant ethos, which assumes that moral progress is a necessary byproduct of material progress. It seems incomprehensible that in this age of free, compulsory education, illiteracy should be a problem, not among immigrants but among native-born Americans; or illegitimacy, at a time when sex education, birth control, and abortion are widely available. Even

Violent crime has become so endemic that we have practically become inured to it.

more important is the suspicion of the very idea of morality. Moral principles, still more moral judgments, are thought to be at best an intellectual embarrassment, at worst evidence of an illiberal and repressive disposition. It is this reluctance to speak the language of morality, far more than any specific values, that separates us from the Victorians.

Most of us are uncomfortable with the idea of making moral judgments even in our private lives, let alone with the "intrusion," as we say, of moral judgments into public affairs. We are uncomfortable not only because we have come to feel that we have no right to make such judgments and impose them upon others, but because we have no confidence in the judgments themselves, no assurance that our principles are true and right for us, let alone for others. We are constantly beseeched to be "nonjudgmental," to be wary of crediting our beliefs with any greater validity than anyone else's, to be conscious of how "Eurocentric" and "culture bound" we are. *Chacun à son goût,* we say of morals, as of taste; indeed, morals have become a matter of taste.

Public officials in particular shy away from the word "immoral," lest they be accused of racism, sexism, or elitism. When members of the president's Cabinet were

Montgomery school security officials also plan to broaden contacts with parent and minority groups when they finish adding security teams to all twenty-one secondary schools this year.

The initiative in Fairfax is one of the most far-reaching in the region, and it follows several years of increasing trouble with weapons, gang fights, and assaults.

The number of recommendations for expulsions considered by the School Board, for example, increased from fourteen in the 1985-86 school year to 133 last year.

This school year has been marred by an unprecedented amount of gunfire. In September, two teenagers were wounded while watching a fight after a Lake Braddock football game, when a bystander pulled out a handgun and started shooting. On Nov. 3, a man riding in a car fired a gun several times near Stuart shortly after classes had ended. No one was

injured, but one of the bullets shattered a window in the school gym. Police described both incidents as gang related.

Officials hope to head off future incidents by creating the community groups that will come up with ideas for safer schools and redirect teenagers regarded as prone to violence or involved with drinking or drugs.

With the help of about $425,000 in federal grants, volunteers from schools, churches, business and parents groups have been receiving training this year on how to organize themselves and prevent violence. Eventually, each group will involve students.

At Wednesday's meeting of the new Stuart Circle Community Coalition, parents wanted to start by talking about the recent shooting. While many were still aggrieved by the incident, others, such as Togi Foldvary, wanted to talk about why their children dismissed it as nothing particularly important.

"She said, 'Mom, get used to it. That's the way it is,'" Foldvary said of her fourteen-year-old daughter, Melissa, a freshman at Stuart. "We can't accept it. They're growing up with it. It's a natural part of their lives."

Gerald Jackson, a senior probation officer in Fairfax, said the group will be critical to the school.

"This is a crucial time in the history of the community," said Jackson, who helped organize the group.

But others seemed skeptical.

"I'm all in favor of community involvement, but I personally don't know. What kind of leverage do you have?" asked Thomas Grossman, the parent of a senior. "Who do you leverage?"

———

Robert O'Harrow, Jr. is a staff writer for The Washington Post. *This article is reprinted with permission from the November 18, 1994, issue of that newspaper.*

asked if it is immoral for people to have children out of wedlock, they drew back from that distasteful phrase. The Secretary of Health and Human Services replied, "I don't like to put this in moral terms, but I do believe that having children out of wedlock is just wrong." The Surgeon General was more forthright: "No. Everyone has different moral standards . . . . You can't impose your standards on someone else."

It is not only our political and cultural leaders who are prone to this failure of moral nerve. Everyone has been infected by it, to one degree or another. A moving testimonial to this comes from an unlikely source: Richard Hoggart, the British literary critic and very much a man of the left, not given to celebrating Victorian values. It was in the course of criticizing a book espousing traditional virtues that Hoggart observed about his own hometown:

> In Hunslet, a working-class district of Leeds, within which I was brought up, old people will still enunciate, as guides to living, the moral rules they learned at Sunday School and Chapel. Then they almost always add, these days: "But it's only my opinion, of course." A late-twentieth century insurance clause, a recognition that times have changed towards the always shiftingly relativist. In that same

council estate, any idea of parental guidance has in many homes been lost. Most of the children there live in, take for granted, a violent, jungle world.

De-moralizing Social Policy

In Victorian England, moral principles and judgments were as much a part of social discourse as of private discourse, and as much a part of public policy as of personal life. They were not only deeply ingrained in tradition, they were also imbedded in two powerful strains of Victorian thought: Utilitarianism on the one hand, Evangelicalism and Methodism on the other. These may not have been philosophically compatible, but in practice they complemented and reinforced each other, the Benthamite calculus of pleasure and pain, rewards and punishments, being the secular equivalent of the virtues and vices that Evangelicalism and Methodism derived from religion.

It was this alliance of a secular ethos and a religious one that determined social policy, so that every measure of poor relief or philanthropy, for example, had to justify itself by showing that it would promote the moral as well as the material well-being of the poor. The distinction between pauper and poor, the stigma attached to

Talk Shows 'Normalize' Deviant Behavior

PHIL, SALLY and Oprah's increasing reliance on bizarre tales of deviance and pathology could have a dangerous consequence: a society numb to once obvious maxims of right and wrong, say two Penn State professors.

"In their competition for audience share, ratings, and profits, television talk shows co-opt deviant subcultures, break taboos and eventually, through repeated, non-judgmental exposure, make it all seem banal and ordinary," write Drs. Vicki Abt and Mel Seesholtz in *The Journal of Popular Culture.*

Abt and Seesholtz's research on television talk shows, titled "The Shameless World of Phil, Sally, and Oprah: Television Talk Shows and the Deconstructing of Society," appeared in the journal's summer 1994 edition.

Abt, professor of sociology, and Seesholtz, assistant professor of English, both at Penn State's Ogontz campus in suburban Philadelphia, spent six months studying the program content of sixty talk shows, watching twenty

episodes each of television's three most visible daytime talk shows: "The Donahue Show," "The Sally Jessy Raphael Show," and "The Oprah Winfrey Show."

"The implication of this research is that television talk shows obliterate the boundaries that society has created between issues of good and evil, public and private, shame and pride," said Abt. "Our culture used to give us boundaries. Today, there are no boundaries. Nothing is forbidden any more. Society's conventions are flouted with impunity. Television emphasizes the deviant so that it becomes normal. If you are really normal, no one cares."

Talk show hosts, meanwhile, continue to rationalize their programs' sensational focus by claiming to serve a valuable role in educating the public. The article cites specific instances when talk-show hosts "use pseudo-professional phrasing to mask voyeurism."

For instance: "I ask this question not to pry in your business, but to educate parents in our audience."
—Oprah, talking to a female guest

who claims to have been sexually abused by her father. And during the same program: "This is a country that doesn't recognize child abuse, and that's why we're doing this show."

Such proclamations, the article says, strain credulity, given the ". . . countless similar talk shows on the same subject." Talk shows have also created a culture of "victims" who are rarely held accountable for their actions, according to Abt and Seesholtz.

"Rather than being mortified, ashamed or trying to hide their stigma, guests willingly and eagerly discuss their child molesting, sexual quirks and criminal records in an effort to seek 'understanding' for their particular disease," they note.

According to talk show ideology, "people now are sick," Abt says, "rather than possibly being irresponsible, weak people.... They are not to blame for anything. These shows destroy the whole notion that people are responsible for their behavior."
—*Pennsylvania State University Department of Public Information*

the "abled-bodied pauper," indeed, the word "pauper" itself, today seem invidious and inhumane. At the time, however, they were the result of a conscious moral decision: an effort to discourage dependency and preserve the respectability of the independent poor, while providing at least minimal sustenance for the indigent.

In recent decades, we have so completely rejected any kind of moral calculus that we have deliberately, systematically divorced welfare from moral sanctions or incentives. This reflects in part the theory that society is responsible for all social problems and should therefore assume the task of solving them; and in part the prevailing spirit of relativism, which makes it difficult to pass any moral judgments or impose any moral conditions upon the recipients of relief. We are now confronting the consequences of this policy of moral neutrality. Having made the most valiant attempt to "objectify" the problem of poverty, to see it as the product of impersonal economic and social forces, we are discovering that the economic and social aspects of that problem are inseparable from the moral and personal ones. And having made the most determined effort to devise social policies that are "value free," we find that these policies imperil both the moral and the material well-being of their intended beneficiaries.

In de-moralizing social policy—divorcing it from any moral criteria, requirements, even expectations—we have demoralized, in the more familiar sense, both the individuals receiving relief and society as a whole. Our welfare system is counterproductive not only because it aggravates the problem of welfare, creating more incentives to enter and remain within it than to try to avoid or escape from it. It also has the effect of exacerbating other, more serious, social problems, so that chronic dependency has become an integral part of the larger phenomenon of "social pathology."

The Supplemental Security Income program is a case in point. Introduced in 1972 to provide a minimum income for the blind, the elderly, and the disabled poor, the program has been extended to drug addicts and alcoholics as the result of an earlier ruling defining "substance abusers" as "disabled" and therefore eligible for public assistance. Apart from encouraging these "disabilities" ("vices," the Victorians would have called them), the program has the effect of rewarding those who remain addicts or alcoholics while penalizing (by cutting off funds) those who try to overcome their addiction. This is the reverse of the principle of "less eligibility" that was the keystone of Victorian social policy: the principle that the dependent poor be in a less "eligible," less desirable, condition than the independent poor. One might say that we are now operating under a principle of "more eligibility," the recipient of relief being in a more favorable position than the self-supporting person.

Just as many intellectuals, social critics, and policy makers were reluctant for so long to credit the unpalatable facts about crime, illegitimacy, or dependency, so they find it difficult to appreciate the extent to which these facts themselves are a function of values—the extent to which "social pathology" is a function of "moral pathology" and social policy a function of moral principle.

Victims of the Upperclass

The moral divide has become a class divide. The same people who have long resisted the realities of social life also find it difficult to sympathize with those, among the working classes especially, who feel acutely threatened by a social order that they perceive to be in an acute state of disorder. (The very word "order" now sounds archaic.) The "new class," as it has been called, is not, in fact, all that new; it is by now firmly established in the media, the academy, the professions, and the government. In its denigration of "bourgeois values" and the "Puritan ethic," the new class has legitimized, as it were, the values of the underclass and illegitimized those of the working class, who are still committed to bourgeois values, the Puritan ethic, and other such benighted ideas.

In a powerfully argued book, Myron Magnet has analyzed the dual revolution that led to this strange alliance between what he calls the "Haves" and the "Have-Nots." The first was a social revolution, intended to liberate the poor from the political, economic, and racial oppression that kept them in bondage. The second was a cultural revolution, liberating them (as the Haves themselves were being liberated) from the moral restraints of bourgeois values. The first created the welfare programs of the Great Society, which provided counter-incentives to leaving poverty. And the second disparaged the behavior and attitudes that traditionally made for economic improvement—"deferral of gratification, sobriety, thrift, dogged industry, and so on through the whole catalogue of antique-sounding bourgeois virtues." Together these revolutions had the unintended effect of miring the poor in their poverty—a poverty even more demoralizing and self-perpetuating than the old poverty.

The underclass is not only the victim of its own culture, the "culture of poverty." It is also the victim of the upperclass culture around it. The kind of "delinquency" that a white suburban teenager can absorb with relative (only relative) impunity may be literally fatal to a black inner-city teenager. Similarly, the child in a single-parent family headed by an affluent professional woman is obviously in a very different condition from the child (more often, children) of a woman on welfare. The effects of the culture, however, are felt at all levels. It was only a matter of time before there should have emerged a white underclass with much the same pathology as the black. And not only a white underclass but a white upper class; the most affluent suburbs are beginning to exhibit the same pathological symptoms: teenage alcoholism, drug addiction, crime, and illegitimacy.

By now this "liberated," anti-bourgeois ethic no longer seems so liberating. The social realities have become so egregious that it is now finally permissible to speak of the need for "family values." President Clinton himself has put the official seal of approval on family values, even going so far as to concede—a year after the event—that there were "a lot of very good things" in Quayle's famous speech about family values (although he was quick to add that the "Murphy Brown thing" was a mistake).

Beyond Economic Incentives

If liberals have much rethinking to do, so do conservatives, for the familiar conservative responses to social problems are inadequate to the present situation. It is not enough to say that if only the failed welfare policies are abandoned and the resources of the free market released, economic growth and incentives will break the cycle of dependency and produce stable families. There is an element of truth in this view, but not the entire truth, for it underestimates the moral and cultural dimensions of the problem. In Britain as in America, more and more conservatives are returning to an older Burkean tradition, which appreciates the material advantages of a free-market economy (Edmund Burke himself was a disciple of Adam Smith) but also recognizes that such an economy does not automatically produce the moral and social goods that they value—that it may even subvert those goods.

For the promotion of moral values, conservatives have always looked to individuals, families, churches, communities, and all the other voluntary associations that Tocqueville saw as the genius of American society. Today they have more need than ever to do that, as the dominant culture—the "counterculture" of yesteryear—becomes increasingly uncongenial. They support "school choice," permitting parents to send their children to schools of their liking; or they employ private security guards to police their neighborhoods; or they form associations of fathers in inner cities to help fatherless children; or they create organizations like the Character Counts Coalition to encourage "Puritan" virtues and family values. They look, in short, to civil society to do what the state cannot do—or, more often, to undo the evil that the state has done.

Yet here, too, conservatives are caught in a bind, for the values imparted by the reigning culture have by now received the sanction of the state. This is reflected in the official rhetoric ("nonmarital childbearing" or "alternative lifestyle"), in mandated sexual instruction and the distribution of condoms in schools, in the prohibition of school prayer, in social policies that are determinedly "nonjudgmental," and in myriad other ways. Against such a pervasive system of state-supported values, the traditional conservative recourse to private groups and voluntary initiatives may seem inadequate.

Individuals, families, churches, and communities cannot operate in isolation, cannot long maintain values at odds with those legitimated by the state and popularized by the culture. It takes a great effort of will and intellect for the individual to decide for himself that something is immoral and to act on that belief when the law declares it legal and the culture deems it acceptable. It takes an even greater effort for parents to inculcate that belief in their children when school officials contravene it and authorize behavior in violation of it. Values, even traditional values, require legitimation. At the very least, they require not to be illegitimated. And in a secular society, that legitimation or illegitimation is in the hands of the dominant culture, the state, and the courts.

You cannot legislate morality, it is often said. Yet we have done just that. Civil rights legislation prohibiting racial discrimination has succeeded in proscribing racist conduct not only legally but morally as well. Today moral issues are constantly being legislated, adjudicated, or resolved by administrative fiat (by the educational estab-

lishment, for instance). Those who want to resist the dominant culture cannot merely opt out of it; it impinges too powerfully upon their lives. They may be obliged, however reluctantly, to invoke the power of the law and the state, if only to protect those private institutions and associations that are the best repositories of traditional values.

The Use and Abuse of History

One of the most effective weapons in the arsenal of the "counter-counterculture" is history—the memory not only of a time before the counterculture but also of the evolution of the counterculture itself. In 1968, the English playwright and member of Parliament A.P. Herbert had the satisfaction of witnessing the passage of the act he had sponsored abolishing censorship on the stage. Only two years later, he complained that what had started as a "worthy struggle for reasonable liberty for honest writers" had ended as the "right to represent copulation, veraciously, on the public stage." About the same time, a leading American civil liberties lawyer, Morris Ernst, was moved to protest that he had meant to ensure the publication of Joyce's *Ulysses,* not the public performance of sodomy.

In the last two decades, the movements for cultural and sexual liberation in both countries have progressed far beyond their original intentions. Yet, few people are able to resist their momentum or to recall their initial principles. In an unhistorical age such as ours, even the immediate past seems so remote as to be antediluvian; anything short of the present state of "liberation" is regarded as illiberal. And in a thoroughly relativistic age such as ours, any assertion of value—any distinction between the publication of *Ulysses* and the public performance of sodomy—is thought to be arbitrary and authoritarian.

It is in this situation that history may be instructive, to remind us of a time, not so long ago, when all societies, liberal as well as conservative, affirmed values very different from our own. (One need not go back to the Victorian age; several decades will suffice.) To say that history is instructive is not to suggest that it provides us with models for emulation. One could not, even if one so desired, emulate a society—Victorian society, for example—at a different stage of economic, technological, social, political, and cultural development. Moreover, if there is much in the ethos of our own times that one may deplore, there is no less in Victorian times. Late-Victorian society was more open, liberal, and humane than early-Victorian society, but it was less open, liberal, and humane than most people today would think desirable. Social, ethnic, and sexual discriminations, class rigidities and political inequalities, autocratic men, submissive women, and overly disciplined children, constraints, restrictions, and abuses of all kinds—there is enough to give pause to the most ardent Victoriaphile. Yet there is also much that might appeal to even a modern, liberated spirit.

Victorian Lessons

The main thing the Victorians can teach us is the importance of values—or, as they would have said, "virtues"—in our public as well as private lives. The Victorians were, candidly and proudly, "moralists." In recent decades, that has almost become a term of derision. Yet, contemplating our own society, we may be prepared to take a more appreciative view of Victorian moralism— of the "Puritan ethic" of work, thrift, temperance, cleanliness; of the idea of "respectability" that was as powerful among the working classes as among the middle classes; of the reverence for "home and hearth"; of the stigma attached to the "able-bodied pauper," as a deterrent to the "independent" worker; of the spirit of philanthropy that made it a moral duty on the part of the donors to give not only money but their own time and effort to the charitable cause, and a moral duty on the part of the recipients to try to "better themselves."

We may even be on the verge of assimilating some of that moralism into our own thinking. It is not only "values" that are being rediscovered but "virtues" as well. That long-neglected word is appearing in the most unlikely places: in books, newspaper columns, journal articles, and scholarly discourse. An article in the *Times Literary Supplement,* reporting on a spate of books and articles from "virtue revivalists" on both the right and the left of the political spectrum, observes that "even if the news that Virtue is back is not in itself particularly exciting to American pragmatism, the news that Virtue is good for you most emphatically is." The philosopher Martha Nussbaum, reviewing the state of Anglo-American philosophy, focuses upon the subject of "Virtue Revived," and her account suggests a return not to classical ethics but to something very like Victorian ethics: an ethics based on "virtue" rather than "principle," on "tradition and particularity" rather than "universality," on "local wisdom" rather than "theory," on the "concreteness of history" rather than an "ahistorical detached ethics."

If anything was lacking to give virtue the *imprimatur* of American liberalism, it was the endorsement of the White House, which came when Hillary Rodham Clinton declared her support for a "Politics of Virtue." If she is notably vague about the idea (and if, as even friendly critics have pointed out, some of her policies seem to belie it), her eagerness to embrace the term is itself significant.

In fact, the idea of virtue has been implicit in our thinking about social policy even while it was being denied. When we speak of the "social pathology" of crime, drugs, violence, illegitimacy, promiscuity, pornography, illiteracy, are we not making a moral judgment about that "pathology"? Or when we describe the "cycle of welfare dependency," or the "culture of poverty," or the "demoralization of the underclass," are we not defining that class and that culture in moral terms and finding them wanting in those terms? Or when we propose to replace the welfare system by a "workfare" system, or to provide "role models" for fatherless children, or to introduce "moral education" into the school curriculum, are we not testifying to the enduring importance of moral principles that we had, surely prematurely, consigned to the dustbin of history? Or when we are told that organizations are being formed in black communities to "inculcate values" in the children and that "the concept of self-help is reemerging," or that campaigns are being conducted among young people to promote sexual abstinence and

that "chastity seems to be making a comeback," are we not witnessing the return of those quintessentially Victorian virtues?

The Present Perspective

It cannot be said too often: No one, not even the most ardent "virtue revivalist," is proposing to revive Victorianism. Those "good-old"/"bad-old" days are irrevocably gone. Children are not about to return to that docile condition in which they are seen but not heard, nor workers to that deferential state where they tip their caps to their betters (a custom that was already becoming obsolete by the end of the nineteenth century). Nor are men and women going to retreat to their "separate spheres"; nor blacks and whites to a state of segregation and discrimination. But if the past cannot—and should not—be replicated, it can serve to put the present in better perspective.

In this perspective, it appears that the present, not the past, is the anomaly, the aberration. Those two powerful indexes of social pathology, illegitimacy and crime, show not only the disparity between the Victorian period and our own but also, more significantly, the endurance of the Victorian ethos long after the Victorian age—indeed, until well into the present century. The 4 to 5 percent illegitimacy ratio was sustained (in both Britain and the United States) until 1960—a time span that encompasses two world wars, the most serious depression in modern times, the traumatic experience of Nazism and Communism, the growth of a consumer economy that almost rivals the Industrial Revolution in its moral as well as material consequences, the continuing decline of the rural population, the unprecedented expansion of mass education and popular culture, and a host of other economic, political, social, and cultural changes. In this sense "Victorian values" may be said to have survived not only the formative years of industrialism and urbanism but some of the most disruptive experiences of our times.

It is from this perspective, not so much of the Victorians as of our own recent past, that we must come to terms with such facts as a sixfold rise of illegitimacy in only three decades (in both Britain and the United States),* or a nearly sixfold rise of crime in England and over threefold in the United States, or all the other indicators of social pathology that are no less disquieting. We are accustomed to speak of the sexual revolution of this period, but that revolution, we are now discovering, is part of a larger, and more ominous, moral revolution.

A Society's Ethos

The historical perspective is also useful in reminding us of our gains and losses—our considerable gains in

---

*The present illegitimacy ratio is not only unprecedented in the past two centuries; it is unprecedented, so far as we know, in American history going back to Colonial times, and in English history from Tudor times. The American evidence is scanty, but the English is more conclusive. English parish records in the mid-sixteenth century give an illegitimacy ratio of 2.4 percent; by the early seventeenth century it reached 3.4 percent; in the Cromwellian period it fell to 1 percent; during the eighteenth century it rose from 3.1 percent to 5.3 percent; it reached its peak of 7 percent in 1845, and then declined to under 4 percent by the end of the nineteenth century. It is against this background that the present rate of 32 percent must be viewed.

material goods, political liberty, social mobility, racial and sexual equality—and our no-less-considerable losses in moral well-being. There are those who say that it is all of a piece, that what we have lost is the necessary price of what we have gained. ("No pain, no gain," as the motto has it.) In this view, liberal democracy, capitalism, affluence, and modernity are thought to carry with them the "contradictions" that are their undoing. The very qualities that encourage economic and social progress—individuality, boldness, the spirit of enterprise and innovation—are said to undermine conventional manners and morals, traditions, and authorities. This echoes a famous passage in *The Communist Manifesto:*

> The bourgeoisie, wherever it has got the upper hand, has put an end to all feudal, patriarchal, idyllic relations. It has pitilessly torn asunder the motley feudal ties that bound man to his "natural superior," and has left no other bond between man and man then naked self-interest, than callous "cash payment." ... The bourgeoisie has torn away from the family its sentimental veil and has reduced the family relation to a mere money relation.

Marx was as wrong about this as he was about so many things. Victorian England was a crucial test case for him because it was the first country to experience the industrial-capitalist-bourgeois revolution in its most highly developed form. Yet, that revolution did not have the effects he attributed to it. It did not destroy all social relations, tear asunder the ties that bound man to man, strip from the family its sentimental veil, and reduce everything to "cash payment" (the "cash nexus," in other translations). It did not do this, in part because the free market was never as free or as pervasive as Marx thought (*laissez-faire,* historians now agree, was less rigorous, both in theory and in practice, that was once supposed); and in part because traditional values and institutions continued to play an important role in society, even in those industrial and urban areas most affected by the economic and social revolution.

Industrialism and urbanism—"modernism," as it is now known—so far from contributing to the de-moralization of the poor, seem to have had the opposite effect. At the end of the nineteenth century, England was a more civil, more pacific, more humane society than it had been in the beginning. "Middle-class" manners and morals had penetrated into large sections of the working classes. The traditional family was as firmly established as ever, even as women began to be liberated from their "separate sphere." And religion continued to thrive, in spite of the premature reports of its death.

If Victorian England did not succumb to the moral and cultural anarchy that are said to be the inevitable consequences of economic individualism, it is because of a powerful ethos that kept that individualism in check. For the Victorians, the individual, or "self," was the ally rather than the adversary of society. Self-help was seen in the context of the community as well as the family; among the working classes, this was reflected in the virtue of "neighbourliness," among the middle classes, of philanthropy. Self-interest stood not in opposition to the general interest but, as Adam Smith had it, as the instrument of the general interest. Self-discipline and self-control were thought of as the source of self-respect and self-betterment; and self-respect as the precondition for the respect and approbation of others. The individual, in short, was assumed to have responsibilities as well as rights, duties as well as privileges.

That Victorian "self" was very different from the "self" that is celebrated today. Unlike "self-help," "self-esteem" does not depend upon the individual's actions or achievements; it is presumed to adhere to the individual regardless of how he behaves or what he accomplishes. Moreover, it adheres to him regardless of the esteem in which he is held by others, unlike the Victorian's self-respect, which always entailed the respect of others. The current notions of self-fulfillment, self-expression, and self-realization derive from a self that does not have to prove itself by reference to any values, purposes, or persons outside itself—that simply is, and by reason of that alone deserves to be fulfilled and realized. This is truly a self divorced from others, narcissistic and solipsistic.

This is the final lesson we may learn from the Victorians: that the ethos of society, its moral and spiritual character, cannot be reduced to economic, material, political, or other factors, that values—or, better yet, virtues—are a determining factor in their own right; so far from being a "reflection," as the Marxist says, of the economic realities, they are themselves, as often as not, the crucial agent in shaping those realities. If in a period of rapid economic and social change, the Victorians showed a substantial improvement in their "condition" and "disposition," it may be that economic and social change do not necessarily result in personal and public disarray. If they could retain and even strengthen an ethos that had its roots in religion and tradition, it may be that we are not as constrained by the material conditions of our time as we have thought. A post-industrial economy, we may conclude, does not necessarily entail a postmodernist society or culture, still less a de-moralized society or culture.

The Return of Character Education

Concern over the moral condition of American society is prompting a reevaluation of the schools' role in teaching values.

Thomas Lickona

Thomas Lickona is a developmental psychologist and Professor, Education Department, State University of New York at Cortland, Cortland, NY 13045. He is author of *Educating for Character: How Our Schools Can Teach Respect and Responsibility* (New York: Bantam Books, 1991.)

To educate a person in mind and not in morals is to educate a menace to society.
—*Theodore Roosevelt*

Increasing numbers of people across the ideological spectrum believe that our society is in deep moral trouble. The disheartening signs are everywhere: the breakdown of the family; the deterioration of civility in everyday life; rampant greed at a time when one in five children is poor; an omnipresent sexual culture that fills our television and movie screens with sleaze, beckoning the young toward sexual activity at ever earlier ages; the enormous betrayal of children through sexual abuse; and the 1992 report of the National Research Council that says the United States is now *the* most violent of all industrialized nations.

As we become more aware of this societal crisis, the feeling grows that schools cannot be ethical bystanders. As a result, character education is making a comeback in American schools.

Early Character Education

Character Education is as old as education itself. Down through history, education has had two great goals: to help people become smart and to help them become good.

Acting on that belief, schools in the earliest days of our republic tackled character education head on—through discipline, the teacher's example, and the daily school curriculum. The Bible was the public schools' sourcebook for both moral and religious instruction. When struggles eventually arose over whose Bible to use and which doctrines to teach, William McGuffey stepped onto the stage in 1836 to offer his McGuffey Readers, ultimately to sell more than 100 million copies.

McGuffey retained many favorite Biblical stories but added poems, exhortations, and heroic tales. While children practiced their reading or arithmetic, they also learned lessons about honesty, love of neighbor, kindness to animals, hard work, thriftiness, patriotism, and courage.

Why Character Education Declined

In the 20th century, the consensus supporting character education began to crumble under the blows of several powerful forces.

Darwinism introduced a new metaphor—evolution—that led people to see all things, including morality, as being in flux.

The philosophy of logical positivism, arriving at American universities from Europe, asserted a radical distinction between *facts* (which could be scientifically proven) and *values* (which positivism held were mere expressions of feeling, not objective truth). As a result of positivism, morality was relativized and privatized—made to seem a matter of personal "value judgment," not a subject for public debate and transmission through the schools.

In the 1960s, a worldwide rise in personalism celebrated the worth, autonomy, and subjectivity of the person, emphasizing individual rights and freedom over responsibility. Personalism rightly protested societal oppression and injustice, but it also delegitimized moral authority, eroded belief in objective moral norms, turned people inward toward self-fulfillment, weakened social commitments (for example, to marriage and parenting), and fueled the socially destabilizing sexual revolution.

Finally, the rapidly intensifying pluralism of American society (Whose values should we teach?) and the increasing secularization of the public arena (Won't moral education violate the separation of church and state?), became two more barriers to achieving the moral consensus indispensable for character education in the public schools. Public schools retreated from their once central role as moral and character educators.

The 1970s saw a return of values education, but in new forms: values clarification and Kohlberg's moral-dilemma discussions. In different ways, both expressed the individualist spirit of the age. Values clarification said, don't impose values; help students choose their values freely. Kohlberg said, develop students' powers of moral reasoning so they can judge which values are better than others.

Each approach made contributions, but each had problems. Values clarification, though rich in methodology, failed to distinguish between personal preferences (truly a matter of free choice) and moral values (a matter of obligation). Kohlberg focused on moral reasoning, which is necessary but not sufficient for good character, and underestimated the school's role as a moral socializer.

The New Character Education

In the 1990s we are seeing the beginnings of a new character education movement, one which restores "good character" to his historical place as the central desirable outcome of the schools' moral enterprise. No one knows yet how broad or deep this movement is; we have no studies to tell us what percentage of schools are making what kind of effort. But something significant is afoot.

In July 1992, the Josephson Institute of Ethics called together more than 30 educational leaders representing state school boards, teachers' unions, universities, ethics centers, youth organizations, and religious groups. This diverse assemblage drafted the Aspen Declaration on Character Education, setting forth eight principles of character education.[1]

The Character Education Partnership was launched in March 1993, as a national coalition committed to putting character development at the top of the nation's educational agenda. Members include representatives from business, labor, government, youth, parents, faith communities, and the media.

The last two years have seen the publication of a spate of books—such as *Moral, Character, and Civic Education in the Elementary School, Why Johnny Can't Tell Right From Wrong,* and *Reclaiming Our Schools: A Handbook on Teaching Character, Academics, and Discipline*—that make the case for character education and describe promising programs around the country. A new periodical,

the *Journal of Character Education,* is devoted entirely to covering the field.[2]

Why Character Education Now?

Why this groundswell of interest in character education? There are at least three causes:

1. *The decline of the family.* The family, traditionally a child's primary moral teacher, is for vast numbers of children today failing to perform that role, thus creating a moral vacuum. In her recent book *When the Bough Breaks: The Cost of Neglecting Our Children,* economist Sylvia Hewlett documents that American children, rich and poor, suffer a level of neglect unique among developed nations (1991). Overall, child well-being has declined despite a decrease in the number of children per family, an increase in the educational level of parents, and historically high levels of public spending in education.

In "Dan Quayle Was Right," (April 1993) Barbara Dafoe Whitehead synthesizes the social science research on the decline of the two biological-parent family in America:

> If current trends continue, less than half of children born today will live continuously with their own mother and father throughout childhood.... An increasing number of children will experience family break-up two or even three times during childhood.

Children of marriages that end in divorce and children of single mothers are more likely to be poor, have emotional and behavioral problems, fail to achieve academically, get pregnant, abuse drugs and alcohol, get in trouble with the law, and be sexually and physically abused. Children in stepfamilies are generally worse off (more likely to be sexually abused, for example) than children in single-parent homes.

No one has felt the impact of family disruption more than schools. Whitehead writes:

> Across the nation, principals report a dramatic rise in the aggressive, acting-out behavior characteristic of children, especially boys, who are living in

single-parent families. Moreover, teachers find that many children are so upset and preoccupied by the explosive drama of their own family lives that they are unable to concentrate on such mundane matters as multiplication tables.

Family disintegration, then, drives the character education movement in two ways: schools have to teach the values kids aren't learning at home; and schools, in order to conduct teaching and learning, must become caring moral communities that help children from unhappy homes focus on their work, control their anger, feel cared about, and become responsible students.

2. *Troubling trends in youth character.* A second impetus for renewed character education is the sense that young people in general, not just those from fractured families, have been adversely affected by poor parenting (in intact as well as broken families); the wrong kind of adult role models; the sex, violence, and materialism portrayed in the mass media; and the pressures of the peer group. Evidence that this hostile moral environment is taking a toll on youth character can be found in 10 troubling trends: rising youth violence; increasing dishonesty (lying, cheating, and stealing); growing disrespect for authority; peer cruelty; a resurgence of bigotry on school campuses, from preschool through higher education; a decline in the work ethic; sexual precocity; a growing self-centeredness and declining civic responsibility; an increase in self-destructive behavior; and ethical illiteracy.

The statistics supporting these trends are overwhelming.[3] For example, the U.S. homicide rate for 15- to 24-year-old males is 7 times higher than Canada's and 40 times higher than Japan's. The U.S. has one of the highest teenage pregnancy rates, the highest teen abortion rate, and the highest level of drug use among young people in the developed world. Youth suicide has tripled in the past 25 years, and a survey of more than 2,000 Rhode Island students, grades six through nine, found that two out of three boys and one of two girls thought it "acceptable for a man to force sex on a woman" if they had been dating for six months or more (Kikuchi 1988).

3. *A recovery of shared, objectively important ethical values.* Moral decline in society has gotten bad enough to jolt us out of the privatism and relativism dominant in recent decades. We are recovering the wisdom that we do share a basic morality, essential for our survival; that adults must promote this morality by teaching the young, directly and indirectly, such values as respect, responsibility, trustworthiness, fairness, caring, and civic virtue; and that these values are not merely subjective preferences but that they have objective worth and a claim on our collective conscience.

Such values affirm our human dignity, promote the good of the individual and the common good, and protect our human rights. They meet the classic ethical tests of reversibility (Would you want to be treated this way?) and universalizability (Would you want all persons to act this way in a similar situation?). They define our responsibilities in a democracy, and they are recognized by all civilized people and taught by all enlightened creeds. *Not* to teach children these core ethical values is a grave moral failure.

What Character Education Must Do

In the face of a deteriorating social fabric, what must character education do to develop good character in the young?

First, it must have an adequate theory of what good character is, one which gives schools a clear idea of their goals. Character must be broadly conceived to encompass the cognitive, affective, and behavioral aspects of morality. Good character consists of knowing the good, desiring the good, and doing the good. Schools must help children *understand* the core values, *adopt* or commit to them, and then *act upon* them in their own lives.

The cognitive side of character includes at least six specific moral qualities: awareness of the moral dimensions of the situation at hand, knowing moral values and what they require of us in concrete cases, perspective-taking, moral reasoning, thoughtful decision-making, and moral self-knowledge. All these powers of rational moral thought are required for full moral maturity and citizenship in a democratic society.

People can be very smart about matters of right and wrong, however, and still choose the wrong. Moral education that is merely intellectual misses the crucial emotional side of character, which serves as the bridge between judgment and action. The emotional side includes at least the following qualities: conscience (the felt obligation to do what one judges to be right), self-respect, empathy, loving the good, self-control, and humility (a willingness to both recognize and correct our moral failings).

At times, we know what we should do, feel strongly that we should do it, yet still fail to translate moral judgment and feeling into effective moral behavior. Moral action, the third part of character, draws upon three additional moral qualities: competence (skills such as listening, communicating, and cooperating), will (which mobilizes our judgment and energy), and moral habit (a reliable inner disposition to respond to situations in a morally good way).

Developing Character

Once we have a comprehensive concept of character, we need a comprehensive approach to developing it. This approach tells schools to look at themselves through a moral lens and consider how virtually everything that goes on there affects the values and character of students. Then, plan how to use all phases of classroom and school life as deliberate tools of character development.

If schools wish to maximize their moral clout, make a lasting difference in students' character, and engage and develop all three parts of character

(knowing, feeling, and behavior), they need a comprehensive, holistic approach. Having a comprehensive approach includes asking, Do present school practices support, neglect, or contradict the school's professed values and character education aims?

In classroom practice, a comprehensive approach to character education calls upon the individual teacher to:

■ *Act as caregiver, model, and mentor,* treating students with love and respect, setting a good example, supporting positive social behavior, and correcting hurtful actions through one-on-one guidance and whole-class discussion;

■ *Create a moral community,* helping students know one another as persons, respect and care about one another, and feel valued membership in, and responsibility to, the group;

■ *Practice moral discipline,* using the creation and enforcement of rules as opportunities to foster moral reasoning, voluntary compliance with rules, and a respect for others;

■ *Create a democratic classroom environment,* involving students in decision making and the responsibility for making the classroom a good place to be and learn;

■ *Teach values through the curriculum,* using the ethically rich content of academic subjects (such as literature, history, and science), as well as outstanding programs (such as *Facing History and Ourselves*[4] and *The Heartwood Ethics Curriculum for Children*[5]), as vehicles for teaching values and examining moral questions;

■ *Use cooperative learning* to develop students' appreciation of others, perspective taking, and ability to work with others toward common goals;

■ *Develop the "conscience of craft"* by fostering students' appreciation of learning, capacity for hard work, commitment to excellence, and sense of work as affecting the lives of others;

■ *Encourage moral reflection* through reading, research, essay writing, journal keeping, discussion, and debate;

■ *Teach conflict resolution,* so that students acquire the essential moral skills of solving conflicts fairly and without force.

Besides making full use of the moral life of classrooms, a comprehensive approach calls upon the school *as a whole* to:

■ *Foster caring beyond the classroom,* using positive role models to inspire altruistic behavior and providing opportunities at every grade level to perform school and community service;

■ *Create a positive moral culture in the school,* developing a schoolwide ethos (through the leadership of the principal, discipline, a schoolwide sense of community, meaningful student government, a moral community among adults, and making time for moral concerns) that supports and amplifies the values taught in classrooms;

■ *Recruit parents and the community as partners in character education,* letting parents know that the school considers them their child's first and most important moral teacher, giving parents specific ways they can reinforce the values the school is trying to teach, and seeking the help of the community, churches, businesses, local government, and the media in promoting the core ethical values.

The Challenges Ahead

Whether character education will take hold in American schools remains to be seen. Among the factors that will determine the movement's long-range success are:

■ *Support for schools.* Can schools recruit the help they need from the other key formative institutions that shape the values of the young— including families, faith communities, and the media? Will public policy act

to strengthen and support families, and will parents make the stability of their families and the needs of their children their highest priority?

■ *The role of religion.* Both liberal and conservative groups are asking, How can students be sensitively engaged in considering the role of religion in the origins and moral development of our nation? How can students be encouraged to use their intellectual and moral resources, including their faith traditions, when confronting social issues (For example, what is my obligation to the poor?) and making personal moral decisions (For example, should I have sex before marriage?)?

■ *Moral leadership.* Many schools lack a positive, cohesive moral culture. Especially at the building level, it is absolutely essential to have moral leadership that sets, models, and consistently enforces high standards of respect and responsibility. Without a positive schoolwide ethos, teachers will feel demoralized in their individual efforts to teach good values.

■ *Teacher education.* Character education is far more complex than teaching math or reading; it requires personal growth as well as skills development. Yet teachers typically receive almost no preservice or inservice training in the moral aspects of their craft. Many teachers do not feel comfortable or competent in the values domain. How will teacher education colleges and school staff development programs meet this need?

"Character is destiny," wrote the ancient Greek philosopher Heraclitus. As we confront the causes of our deepest societal problems, whether in our intimate relationships or public institutions, questions of character loom large. As we close out a turbulent century and ready our schools for the next, educating for character

is a moral imperative if we care about the future of our society and our children.

---

[1]For a copy of the Aspen Declaration and the issue of *Ethics* magazine reporting on the conference, write the Josephson Institute of Ethics, 310 Washington Blvd., Suite 104, Marina del Rey, CA 90292.

[2]For information write Mark Kann, Editor, *The Journal of Character Education,* Jefferson Center for Character Education, 202 S. Lake Ave., Suite 240, Pasadena, CA 91101.

[3]For documentation of these youth trends, see T. Lickona, (1991), *Educating for Character:How Our Schools Can Teach Respect and Responsibility* (New York: Bantam Books).

[4]*Facing History and Ourselves* is an 8-week Holocaust curriculum for 8th graders. Write Facing History and Ourselves National Foundation, 25 Kennard Rd., Brookline, MA 02146.

[5]*The Heartwood Ethics Curriculum for Children* uses multicultural children's literature to teach universal values. Write The Heartwood Institute, 12300 Perry Highway, Wexford, PA 15090.

References

Benninga, J.S., ed. (1991). *Moral, Character, and Civic Education in the Elementary School.* New York: Teachers College Press.

Hewlett, S. (1991). *When the Bough Breaks: The Cost of Neglecting Our Children.* New York: Basic Books.

Kikuchi, J. (Fall 1988). "Rhode Island Develops Successful Intervention Program for Adolescents." *National Coalition Against Sexual Assault Newsletter.*

National Research Council. (1992). *Understanding and Preventing Violence.* Washington, D.C.: National Research Council.

Whitehead, B. D. (April 1993) "Dan Quayle Was Right." *The Atlantic* 271: 47-84.

Wynne, E. A., and K. Ryan. (1992). *Reclaiming Our Schools: A Handbook on Teaching Character, Academics, and Discipline.* New York: Merrill.

What are **your** family values?

Teaching kids right from wrong,

respect for others, and the value of work

is a tough job for today's parents. Tell us how you're doing it.

True family values are not found in a TV show or a political slogan. Values are the deeply held attitudes and beliefs that matter most to parents and that they hope to pass on to their own children. *Parents* want[ed] to know [about] values and how [they are] transmitt[ed] to kids.*

Answer questions by circling the number that best reflects your view.

1 **Which of the following positions is closest to your own in terms of parents' teaching their children values? (Choose one number only.)**
- I want my children to have values identical with or very similar to my own..1
- I want my children to have a firm set of values, but I don't mind if their values differ significantly from my own..(2)
- I am not so concerned about my children's values; it's more important that they get a good job, find a good mate, and so on...3
- Not sure..4

2 **Do parents need to make a special effort to ensure that their children acquire values, or do children automatically acquire the dominant values of the household in which they grow up?**
- Parents need to make a special effort.................................(1)
- Children automatically acquire values.................................2
- Not sure..3

3 **Do you think it's harder now for parents to instill values in their children than it was when you were growing up?**
- Yes..(1)
- No...2
- Not sure...3

4 **How important is it for parents to teach their children each of the following values? (Circle one number in each row.)**

	One of the most important	Important but not essential	Not very important	Not sure
Religious beliefs	(1)	2	3	4
The importance and necessity of hard work and delaying gratification	1	(2)	3	4
The importance of education	1	(2)	3	4
Basic ideas of right and wrong	(1)	2	3	4
The importance of each individual's achieving his or her full potential	(1)	2	3	4
Appreciation of art and culture	1	2	(3)	4
Tolerance for people of different races, ages, values, and so on	(1)	2	3	4
Standards concerning sexual behavior	(1)	2	3	4
Patriotism	1	(2)	3	4
The importance of marriage and family	(1)	2	3	4
The value of friendship	(1)	2	3	4
Good manners and appropriate social behavior	(1)	2	3	4
The importance of being financially independent and secure	1	(2)	3	4
The importance of ecology and of preserving our planet	1	(2)	3	4

4. MORALITY AND VALUES IN EDUCATION

5 At what age do you think parents should begin to teach their children values? (Circle one number only.)

1 year or younger........(1)	7 years old.................7
2 years old...............2	8 years old.................8
3 years old...............3	9 years old.................9
4 years old...............4	10 years or older..........0
5 years old...............5	Not sure...................X
6 years old...............6	

6 Please rate the influence of each of the following in transmitting values to kids. (Circle one number in each row.)

	A lot of influence	Some influence	No influence	Not sure
• School, teachers, and so on...............	(1)	2	3	4
• Participation in organized sports.......	1	(2)	3	4
• Nonschool activities, such as Scouts....................	1	(2)	3	4
• What parents tell their children about values, proper behavior, and so on.......	1	(2)	3	4
• The examples that parents set for their children by their actions..............	(1)	2	3	4
• Other family members....................	(1)	2	3	4
• Religious institutions......................	(1)	2	3	4
• Mass media (television, movies, popular music, and so on)....................	1	(2)	3	4
• Their peers, older kids, and so on ...	(1)	2	3	4

7 Over the last generation or so, have the values of our society declined, improved, or stayed about the same?

• Declined.................(1)	• Stayed the same...............3
• Improved 2	• Not sure.....................4

8 Over the next generation or so, will our society's values decline, improve, or stay about the same?

• Will decline.................1	• Will stay the same...........3
• Will improve.................2 *Hopefully*	• Not sure.....................(4)

9 Here are some changes in our society over the last few decades. Some people see them as destructive to traditional values. Other people might defend some of these changes, saying that they represent progress toward a more open, just society. What is your evaluation of these changes? Is each a change for the better, a change for the worse, or a change of no consequence one way or the other?

	Change for the better	Change for the worse	No consequence	Not sure
• Increasing number of women having children outside of marriage.....	1	2	3	4
• Increased emphasis on separation of church and state (such as prohibiting prayer in public schools)....................	1	2	3	4
• Increasing number of mothers who work outside the home...............	1	2	3	4
• Increasing number of children growing up in single-parent households....................	1	2	3	4
• Families spending less time together....................	1	2	3	4
• More is expected of children at an early age....................	1	2	3	4
• A decline in respect for authority in our society....................	1	2	3	4
• A change toward a more pluralistic society, with no one "right" way to live....................	1	2	3	4

• More liberal and permissive standards of sexual behavior...............	1	2	3	4
• Increased importance of popular music....................	1	2	3	4
• Increased presence and importance of TV and film....................	1	2	3	4
• Increased candor on the part of the media, such as reporting details of political leaders' and celebrities' private lives....................	1	2	3	4
• Increased likelihood that grown children live in a different part of the country from their parents..........	1	2	3	4

10 How old is your oldest child? _____ years old

11 What is the sex of this child? Male ....1 Female 2

12 Here are some different behaviors and lifestyles. Using a scale of 1 to 10, indicate how you would react to each behavior if it were something your oldest child did.

	Doesn't bother you at all								Extremely disturbing to you		Not sure
Your oldest child:	1	2	3	4	5	6	7	8	9	10	X
• Never got married..................	1	2	3	4	5	6	7	8	9	10	X
• Got divorced..................	1	2	3	4	5	6	7	8	9	10	X
• Lived with someone of the opposite sex without getting married..................	1	2	3	4	5	6	7	8	9	10	X
• Became an atheist..................	1	2	3	4	5	6	7	8	9	10	X
• Had a child outside of marriage..................	1	2	3	4	5	6	7	8	9	10	X
• Regarded people of other racial and ethnic groups as inferior and treated them accordingly..........	1	2	3	4	5	6	7	8	9	10	X
• Never had any children	1	2	3	4	5	6	7	8	9	10	X
• Lived with someone of the same sex in a homosexual relationship..................	1	2	3	4	5	6	7	8	9	10	X
• Was convicted of a white-collar crime, such as embezzlement..................	1	2	3	4	5	6	7	8	9	10	X
• Was convicted of a violent crime, such as assault..................	1	2	3	4	5	6	7	8	9	10	X
• Used illegal drugs..................	1	2	3	4	5	6	7	8	9	10	X
• Never finished high school.....	1	2	3	4	5	6	7	8	9	10	X
• Never had a good job	1	2	3	4	5	6	7	8	9	10	X
• Was interested only in making money..................	1	2	3	4	5	6	7	8	9	10	X

13 What do you think parents should teach their children about sexual behavior? (Circle one number only.)

• To abstain from sex before marriage...1	
• To abstain from sex until they're older (although not necessarily until they are married) 2	
• That sex is a personal issue and that their children should make their own decisions 3	
• Not sure...4	

14 Since some teenagers, regardless of what their parents tell them, will be sexually active, do you think that we should or should not teach them how to protect themselves from AIDS, other sexually transmitted diseases, and pregnancies through the use of condoms?
- Yes, we should teach teenagers about condoms 1
- No, we should not teach teenagers about condoms......................2
- Not sure..3

15 Have you or your spouse talked to your oldest child about each of the following topics?

	Yes	No	Not applicable
● Religious beliefs..................................	1	2	3
● The difference between right and wrong	1	2	3
● Sex from a factual point of view.........................	1	2	3
● Sex from an ethical point of view—the kind of sexual behavior that you expect from your child.........................	1	2	3
● Drug and alcohol abuse	1	2	3
● The importance of treating other people fairly and with compassion.........................	1	2	3
● The importance of hard work and persistence.........................	1	2	3
● Manners.........................	1	2	3

16 What is your policy regarding letting your oldest child watch TV? (Circle all that apply.)
- He or she can watch any programs as often as he or she likes.........1
- I limit the number of hours that he or she can watch TV...............2
- I must approve all programs that he or she watches.......................3
- Other... 4

17 Does your oldest child have a TV set in his or her room?
Yes.....................1   No 2

18 Would you say that your oldest child watches TV more than, less than, or about the same amount as you did when you were the same age?
- Oldest child watches more TV...1
- Oldest child watches less TV...2
- Oldest child watches about the same amount of TV 3
- Not applicable (child too young) 4

19 How often does your family participate in each of the following activities together?

	Several times a week or more	About once a week	Several times a month	About once a month	Several times a year	Less often or never	No answer
● Have dinner together..............	1	2	3	4	5	6	7
● Watch TV together..............	1	2	3	4	5	6	7
● Play games at home together....	1	2	3	4	5	6	7
● Read books or help with homework..........	1	2	3	4	5	6	7
● Go to religious services together..........	1	2	3	4	5	6	7
● Go out, such as to the movies or to a restaurant.....	1	2	3	4	5	6	7
● Talk to one another as a group............	1	2	3	4	5	6	7
● Take part in volunteer community service or activities.........	1	2	3	4	5	6	7
● See relatives together............	1	2	3	4	5	6	7
● Get together with neighbors or friends............	1	2	3	4	5	6	7

20 Would you say that you attend religious services less frequently than, more frequently than, or about as frequently as when you were a child?
- Attend less frequently now..1
- Attend more frequently now..2
- Attend about as often now...3

21 Which is the greater distance?
- The distance from your home to your mother's house....................1
- The distance from your mother's house to her mother's house when you were a child.............................2
- Not applicable or not sure 3

22 How often do you talk to your neighbors?
Frequently..............1   Occasionally..........2   Rarely or never 3

23 Is this frequency more often than, less often than, or about as often as when members of your family talked to neighbors during your childhood?
More often 1   About as often..........................3
Less often 2   Not sure 4

24 Please indicate the extent to which you agree or disagree with each of the following statements.

	Agree strongly	Agree somewhat	Disagree somewhat	Disagree strongly	Not sure
● It's harder today for parents to know what is right and wrong than it was when I was growing up...............1		2	3	4	5
● To be effective in governing behavior, values should be based on religious beliefs.............1		2	3	4	5
● Women should stay home to take care of preschool children, even if it means that the family will have to skimp to get by financially.......1		2	3	4	5
● For the sake of their children, couples with small children should not get divorced, even if both of them would prefer to do so.........1		2	3	4	5
● As a society, we've lost track of our basic values 1		2	3	4	5

25 Who lives in your household? (Circle all that apply.)
- Your spouse..1
- Your children...2
- One or more parents of yours or of your spouse 3
- Other relatives...4
- Other persons...5

26 Your sex: Male 1   Female 2

4. MORALITY AND VALUES IN EDUCATION

27 What is your <u>current</u> marital status?
(Circle one number only.)

Married once 1
Married two or more times 2
Separated...3
Divorced 4
Widowed 5
Never married 6

28 What is your current job status?

Not employed...1
Employed full-time 2
Employed part-time 3

(Answer question 29 only if you live with your spouse.)

29 What is your spouse's current job status?

Not employed...1
Employed full-time 2
Employed part-time 3

(Everyone should answer the following questions.)

30 In which of the following age categories do you belong?

Under 21.................1		41 to 50......................4	
21 to 30 2		51 to 60......................5	
31 to 40 3		61 and over................6	

31 What is the highest level of education that you have completed?

● Some high school or less..1
● Graduated from high
school, including vocational
or technical school...2
● Some college 3
● Graduated from a
four-year college...4
● Attended graduate school...5

*Note: Results of the survey can be found in the next *Annual Editions* article.

Teaching values

How 7,700 of you feel about ethics, manners, tolerance, sexuality, and religion—and what you want your kids to believe.

Jean Grasso Fitzpatrick

Jean Grasso Fitzpatrick, a psychotherapist and author, holds seminars on families' spiritual growth. Her latest book is Small Wonder: How to Answer Your Child's Impossible Questions About Life *(Viking).*

[In December 1994 *Parents* did a survey of its readers on family values (see *Annual Editions* 96/97, article 22). The results of that survey are presented here. **Ed.**]

When someone hurled rocks at the Hanukkah decorations in the window of Linda Brown's Philadelphia home, her 8-year-old son heard the glass shatter and tires screech as a car sped away. "My son was so terrified that he wanted to take down the decorations," Brown remembers, "but we told him it was important to stand strongly for who we are and what we believe in." Standing up for her own beliefs and values—and passing them on to her children—is a top priority, Brown told us in the letter she sent in response to our most recent survey, "What Are *Your* Family Values?" (December 1994). "I believe that if we can teach children to love, forgive, and be truthful, then our world will be a better place." In today's "do what feels right" culture, Brown wrote, "our children, unfortunately, are learning that not all people share our values. We tell them some children are not

being raised to appreciate all kinds of life. We tell them some kids aren't disciplined, or don't have parents to teach them."

More than 7,700 *Parents* readers wrote to tell us that you consider teaching your children values one of your most meaningful endeavors as parents, and a practical way to make a lasting contribution to society. Over 99 percent of you said that you want your children to have a firm set of values. You made it clear that you don't expect it to be easy; 94 percent of respondents told us parents need to make a special effort to instill values in their children. We heard from parents across the United States and Canada, from inner cities, suburbs, and farms. Stapled and clipped to thousands of surveys were letters, rich with readers' personal experiences and passionate feelings about values. Although 96 percent of the respondents were women, a number of

couples wrote letters to tell us they had chosen to fill out the questionnaire together, sparking some lively kitchen-table debates. And if you connect family values with a certain political or religious viewpoint, here's a surprise: *Parents'* survey showed that values can't be linked with any particular group. We heard from readers who described themselves as agnostics, committed Christians, Orthodox Jews, or Muslims; from parents who called themselves liberals or conservatives; from working couples, single mothers, and day-care workers.

When do values start?

Sixty percent of respondents told us values are learned at the age of 1 or younger. "I believe that the teaching of values begins from day one!" wrote Mary Beth Bennett, of Payette, Idaho, a mother

of three and a fourth-grade teacher. "Just as language is developed over a long period, a little at a time, so are values."

The overwhelming majority of you told us that what parents *do* is more important in teaching children values than what they say. "Even something as small as giving back excess change to the cashier is honesty, and children really take note," wrote Natalie Guild, of Delray Beach, Florida.

72% pre-approve the TV shows their children watch.

Sixty-one percent of respondents want their children to have values identical with or very similar to their own. This same group of parents was more likely to be disturbed if their children made different lifestyle choices as adults, such as living in a homosexual relationship, becoming an atheist, or having a child outside of marriage. "Alternative lifestyles come from lack of values, lack of basic knowledge of what is right and wrong, and not knowing their inherited biblical beginnings," wrote Valerie K. Southard, of Buford, Georgia, a mother of two sons. Yet of the 38 percent who answered, "I want my children to have a firm set of values, but I don't mind if their values differ significantly from my own," several letter writers explained that instilling values means much more than teaching specific dos and don'ts. To confront the challenges of a changing world, they told us, a child needs to develop the capacity to think clearly about issues.

"I will expect her own creative thinking to guide her," wrote Vanessa Collier, of Richmond, Virginia, whose daughter is 2. "After all, I won't always be there to tell her what to do."

Is it realistic to expect kids to have exactly the same values as their parents, or are we better off focusing on teaching them moral reasoning? "Unless you do say there are certain core values that you believe in, a kid thinks that everything is up for grabs," notes William Damon, author of *Greater Expectations: Overcoming the Culture of Indulgence in America's Homes and Schools* (Free Press) and director of the Center for the Study of Human Development, at Brown University. "But a child has to figure out what honesty, for example, means in his own life—not just memorize 'I'll never tell a lie.' "

Finding time.
When we listed changes in our society over the last few decades and asked you to evaluate them, 98 percent agreed that "families spending less time together" was a change for the worse. "After work, making dinner, getting kids ready for bed, and getting bags ready for day care for the next day, I don't seem to have the patience or energy to have the talks, the walks, the quiet moments with my kids," wrote Robin Wolfkill, of Des

Moines. "I am afraid my kids will not acquire my values because of *my* lifestyle."

In response to our question about whether women should stay home to take care of preschool children, even if it means that the family will have to skimp to get by financially, 59 percent of respondents agreed. (Several letter writers took us to task for saying "women" rather than "parent.") Yet 55 percent of mothers who responded to our poll are employed full- or part-time, and many told us that values are a central focus in their family lives and in child-care and scheduling decisions. "I've used good, family-oriented baby-sitters and preschools," wrote Patrice Berenato, of Hammonton, New Jersey, "My husband and I spend every evening and weekend doing activities with the children."

We also heard from dozens of caregivers who told us how important family values are to them—and that whether or not Mom or Dad is employed outside the home, parents' values have a powerful impact on kids. Wrote Shawna Ferguson, the mother of a 2-year-old boy and the office manager of a Salt Lake City day-care center, "If a parent doesn't care how the child treats others, chances are the parent doesn't treat others well."

Single parents.
Eighty-four percent of you rated the increased number of single-parent households today a negative influence. Only 7 percent of respondents were divorced or never married. "I see a lot of children every week, and those with stable households are the children who are successful in school," wrote Susan Delgardo, of Chico, California, a junior high school teacher and mother of four. "They have more security and happiness. They learn that families work together."

Yet several of you wrote in to protest media stereotypes of single parents—and

to tell us, based on your personal experience, that all families can instill values. "As a single parent, my mother raised four children (three boys and one girl)," wrote Primrose Walters, of the Bronx, New York. "Limits were set, the expectations were clear. . . . She taught us love for one another and for humanity. Today all four of us are responsible, productive, caring persons."

Television.
Only 42 percent of readers who responded to our survey said they limit the amount of TV their kids can watch, but 72 percent said they do preapprove their children's programs. "I think that for parents of young children, the number should be closer to 100 percent," comments Action for Children's Television founder Peggy Charren. "If you can't turn off the set when children are little, it's going to be a disaster when they get older."

Readers do place fewer restrictions on their older children, with more than 40 percent allowing children over the age of 11 to have a television in their own room and only 45 percent continuing to preapprove their programs. A few parents wrote letters defending television as a springboard for discussion of values. "I find that it provides an impetus for communication with my two teenagers," wrote Deborah Edmond, of Chicago. "I'm always questioning and challenging the 'status quo' of what the media presents."

Religion.
While 61 percent of readers polled said that to be effective in governing behavior, values should be based on religious beliefs, a significant minority—38 percent—disagreed. This, together with the findings that parents attend religious services slightly less frequently now than when they were children and that religious beliefs scored only 9th in

Top ten *values*

Which are the most important values to teach kids?

1. Basic ideas of right and wrong 98%

2. The importance of education 92%

3. Standards concerning sexual behavior 83%

4. Tolerance for people of different races, ages, values, and so on 82%

5. The importance of marriage and family 77%

6. The value of friendship 77%

7. Good manners and appropriate social behavior 75%

8. The importance of each individual's achieving his or her full potential 71%

9. Religious beliefs 63%

10. The importance and necessity of hard work and delaying gratification 60%

And the bottom three . . .
Readers found these values less important to teach: ecology and preserving our planet (43%), patriotism (29%), and an appreciation of art and culture (13%).

importance out of 14 values named, raises the question: Is religion declining in authority when it comes to teaching values?

"There has been a debunking of leaders in our society, a turning away from clergy and religious institutions," confirms Barbara Dafoe Whitehead, vice-president of the Institute for American Values, a nonpartisan research organization. "Many parents are religious without being committed to a particular denomination. They would rather buy a self-help book and sit in the woods," Whitehead notes, though, that as children get older, parents may turn to organized religion for community and moral support.

That's among the reasons Brooklyn, New York, mother Stacey Duke brings her 20-month-old daughter, Asari, to a Lutheran church almost every week. "We live in a transient city," she explained. "At church she'll know everyone and they'll know her as she grows up. It will give her stability." •

Even non-church members reported that a sense of everyday spirituality is important to them. "I'd rather have my children retain their sense of wonder than accept the words some men put in the mouth of God," wrote Don Ramie, of Fremont, California. "I've told my older daughters what I personally believe: The universe is a good and orderly place, God set it in motion with laws encouraging growth and refinement . . . they can't be happy if they're mean to others and only care about themselves."

Sexuality.

The "facts of life" may not have changed since we were children, but the sexual revolution has transformed parents' attitudes and advice to their kids. Only 42 percent of survey participants favored teaching children to abstain from sexual intercourse until marriage, and an overwhelming 86 percent believe children should be taught about condom use as protection from the virus that causes AIDS. In fact, 69 percent of parents who want to teach children to abstain from premarital sex nevertheless feel that kids

ought to be taught about condoms—an apparent recognition that children do not always follow parents' advice and need to learn to protect themselves.

When we asked respondents to tell us how strongly you would disapprove of your child's having a baby outside of marriage—using a scale of 1 to 10, with 10 indicating "extremely disturbing"—the average disapproval rating was a strong 7. Yet in your letters, several of you told us that your attitude would depend on your child's age: "My reaction would be completely different if this happened at age 15 or at age 30," wrote Christine Sweeney, mother of 2-year-old Bridget. "At age 15, a child would get in the way of her opportunities for education and experiences. By age 30, it would be a more conscious decision."

The decline in values.

More than three quarters of parents surveyed think it is harder now to transmit values to kids than was the case when they were growing up, and 90 percent agreed that values have declined over the last generation and that we've lost track of basic values. "My parents did not have to monitor my friends, books, movies, TV programs, or what was taught at school," wrote Cherry Eshom, of Cincinnati. "I feel that to teach my children the values I want them to have, I have to be far more involved."

"As a teacher in a large inner-city school, I have personally seen the decline of family life and values over the last decade," wrote Kathryn W. Lerner, of Milwaukee. "The children I teach have not learned (or have not been taught) the difference between right and wrong, but they have learned street survival. . . . They are exposed to drugs, alcohol, sex, and violence in their own homes and neighborhoods. . . . I don't know what the solution is. I do know that my students are suffering on a daily basis and need help."

On the other hand, several readers reminded us that the good old days were not all good. "A decline in family values?" asked Tracy Schroeder, of North Syracuse, New York, a mother of three. "This is one of my pet peeves! We are talking about a time when married couples stayed together no matter how unhappy they were, no matter how much abuse or adultery was going on . . . when women stayed at home, not because they wanted to but because it was 'their place' . . . when a black family moving into the neighborhood meant that the neighborhood was going downhill . . . when no one talked about abuse, rape, sexism, or racism. We kept it in the closet."

"I've witnessed a resurgence of family values, as 'Generation X'ers' become the heads of households," wrote Jason Hanold, of Lincoln, Nebraska. "Many of us were raised in homes during the late '60s and '70s by 'revolutionary-type' parents. . . . In my current home, the smells of pot-

Bad conduct

Parents would feel most distressed if their child:

Was convicted of a violent crime, such as assault 86%

Regarded people of other racial and ethnic groups as inferior and treated them accordingly 63%

Used illegal drugs 61%

Was convicted of a white-collar crime, such as embezzlement 61%

Never finished high school 60%

But parents would be less alarmed if their child:
Became an atheist (48%), lived with someone in a homosexual relationship (45%), had a child outside marriage (22%), lived with someone of the opposite sex without getting married (17%), got divorced (10%), never had any children (5%), never got married (3%).

pourri and home cooking have replaced the smells of incense and marijuana from my childhood home."

Working together.

When we asked which values you considered most important to teach children, you ranked "tolerance for people of different races, ages, values, and so on" fourth highest, with 82 percent calling it "one of the most important"—ahead of marriage and family, good manners, the necessity of hard work, and patriotism. Your dedication to tolerance, one of the basic values on which our democracy was founded, suggests that there is a real basis for thoughtful, constructive dialogue in this country. "When there's no room for sharing ideas, people start throwing ultimatums at one another," wrote Gorman and Crystal Rasmussen, who are raising their blended family in Austin, Texas. "Compromise, tolerance, and understanding can go a long way toward developing a nation with a good system of values."

Family time

Once a week or more, here's what parents and children do together.

98%
Have dinner as a family.

91%
Read books or help with homework.

91%
Watch television.

80%
Talk to one another as a group.

76%
Play games at home.

But for other traditional family activities, the frequency of participation was far lower: going to religious services together, 51%; seeing relatives together, 45%; getting together with neighbors or friends, 39%; going out to the movies or a restaurant, 35%; and taking part in volunteer community service, 11%.

Managing Life in Classrooms

All teachers have concerns regarding the quality of "life" in classroom settings. All teachers and students want to feel safe and accepted when they are in school. There exists today a reliable, effective knowledge base on classroom management and the prevention of disorder in schools. This knowledge base has been developed from hundreds of studies of teacher-student interaction and student-student interaction that have been conducted in schools in North America and Europe. We speak of managing life in classrooms because we now know that there are many factors that go into building effective teacher-student and student-student relationships. The traditional term *discipline* is too narrow and refers primarily only to teachers' reactions to undesired student behavior. We can better understand methods of managing student behavior when we look at the totality of what goes on in classrooms, with teacher responses to student behavior as a part of that totality. Teachers have tremendous responsibility for the emotional climate that is set in a classroom. Whether students feel secure and safe and whether they want to learn depend to an enormous extent on the psychological frame of mind of the teacher. Teachers must be able to manage their own selves first in order to manage effectively the development of a humane and caring classroom environment.

Teachers bear moral and ethical responsibilities for being witnesses to and examples of responsible social behavior in the classroom. There are many models of observing life in classrooms. When one speaks of life in classrooms, arranging the total physical environment of the room is a very important part of the teacher's planning for learning activities. Teachers need to expect the best work and behavior from students that they are capable of achieving. Respect and caring are attitudes that a teacher must communicate to receive them in return. Open lines of communication between teachers and students enhance the possibility for congenial, fair dialogical resolution of problems as they occur.

Developing a high level of task orientation among students and encouraging cooperative learning and shared task achievement will foster camaraderie and self-confidence among students. Shared decision making will build an *esprit de corps,* a sense of pride and confidence, which will feed on itself and blossom into high-quality performance. Good class morale, well-managed, never hurts academic achievement. The importance of emphasizing quality, of helping students to achieve levels of performance they can feel proud of having attained, and of encouraging positive dialogue among them leads them to take ownership in their individual educative efforts.

When that happens, they literally empower themselves to do their best.

When teachers (and prospective teachers) discuss what concerns them about their roles (and prospective roles) in the classroom, the issue of discipline, how to manage student behavior, will usually rank near or at the top of their lists. A teacher needs a clear understanding of what kinds of learning environments are most appropriate for the subject matter and ages of the students. Any person who wants to teach must also want his or her students to learn well, to acquire basic values of respect for others, and to become more effective citizens.

There is considerable debate among educators regarding certain approaches used in schools to achieve a form of order in classrooms that also develops respect for self and others. The dialogue about this point is spirited and informative. The bottom line for any effective and humane approach to discipline in the classroom, the necessary starting point, is the teacher's emotional balance and capacity for self-control. This precondition creates a further one—that the teacher wants to be in the classroom with his or her students in the first place. Unmotivated teachers cannot motivate students.

Helping young people learn the skills of self-control and motivation to become productive, contributing, and knowledgeable adult participants in society is one of the most important tasks that good teachers undertake. These are teachable and learnable skills; they do not relate to heredity or social conditions. They can be learned by any human being who wants to learn them and who is cognitively able to learn them. We know also that these skills are learnable by virtually all but the most severely cognitively disabled persons. There is a large knowledge base on how teachers can help students learn self-control. All that is required is the willingness of teachers to learn these skills themselves and to teach them to their students. No topic is more fundamentally related to any thorough examination of the social and cultural foundations of education. There are many sound techniques that new teachers can use to achieve success in managing students' classroom behavior, and they should not be afraid to ask colleagues questions and to develop peer support groups with whom they can work with confidence and trust.

Teachers' core ethical principles come into play when deciding what constitutes defensible and desirable standards of student conduct. As in medicine, realistic preventive techniques combined with humane but precise principles of procedure seem to be most effective. Teach-

ers need to realize that before they can control behavior, they must identify what student behaviors are desired in their classrooms. They need to reflect as well on the emotional tone and ethical principles implied by their own behaviors. To optimize their chances of achieving the classroom atmosphere that they wish, teachers must strive constantly for emotional balance within themselves; they must learn to be more accurate observers; and they must further develop just, fair strategies of intervention to aid students in learning self-control and good behavior. To repeat, a teacher is a good model of courtesy, respect, tact, and discretion. Children learn by observing how other persons behave and not just by being told how they are to behave. There is no substitute for positive, assertive teacher interaction with students in the classroom.

This unit addresses many of the topics covered in basic foundations courses. The selections shed light on classroom management issues, teacher leadership skills, the legal foundations of education, and the rights and responsibilities of teachers and students. In addition, the articles can be discussed in foundations courses involving curricula and instruction. This unit falls between the units on moral education and equal opportunity because it can be directly related to either or both of them.

Looking Ahead: Challenge Questions

What are some things that can be done to help students and teachers to feel safe in school?

What is a good technique for learning self-control?

What should be the behavioral standards in schools? On what factors should they be based?

Does peer mediation seem to be a workable approach? Why or why not?

What ethical issues may be raised in the management of student behavior in school settings?

What reliable information is available on the extent and severity of school discipline problems in North America? What sources contain such information?

What civil rights do students have? Do public schools have fewer rights than private schools in controlling student behavior problems? Why or why not? What are the rights of a teacher in managing student behavior?

Do any coercive approaches to behavioral management in schools work better than noncoercive ones?

Why is teacher self-control a major factor in just and effective classroom management strategies?

—F. S.

Routines and the First Few Weeks of Class

KEN APPLETON

Ken Appleton is a senior lecturer on the Faculty of Education, Central Queensland University, Rockhampton, Australia.

What is the best thing to do during the first few weeks with a class? This is an important question for beginning teachers (Amarel and Feiman-Nemser 1988) and an ongoing concern for many more experienced teachers. We have been told that, for effective learning in our classrooms, teachers need to be businesslike and task oriented, use suitable classroom management and organization strategies, and pace students briskly through the curriculum (Brophy 1988; Reynolds 1992). People who can quickly create smooth-running classes are obviously at an advantage, but how do we do it? Are there specific things we can do in the first few weeks of school that set the tone for the rest of the year?

A valuable strategy that I have found is the use of *routines*. A routine is a way of doing something in the classroom that both students and teacher have established (Gump 1969). Each routine should have its own set of explicit and implicit rules that are known to both teacher and students (Edwards and Mercer 1987). There can be a routine for entering a room and sitting, one for distributing books or worksheets, one for a teacher giving a lecture, one for a whole class discussion with students seated at desks, another for a whole class discussion with students seated more informally on a carpet, and so on. Most teachers use many routines, which are present in all teaching activities. However, I have found that high school teachers tend to use fewer routines than elementary teachers, possibly because they feel that students are already familiar with the desired routines (Brophy 1987).

Note that some routines, such as how a particular student workbook is to be organized, are very simple. Other routines, such as using equipment in a small group, are more complex. Some might be dependent on school policies, such as procedures for entering rooms.

Every lesson can consist of a series of routines, with transitions from one routine to another (Coles 1992). Any routine is independent of the task that students may be assigned, although particular tasks may be more clearly associated with certain routines (Coles 1992). For example, a science activity lesson would most likely be associated with using equipment in a small group routine, although the equipment could also be used in an individual seat work routine if that were possible.

Establishing Routines

Because each routine has its own set of rules and language that are common knowledge in the classroom, each routine becomes a "minisociety" of the classroom society. In one routine, the rules may allow students to talk to each other, but in another, such behavior is not permitted. To feel that they belong to the classroom, teachers and students must know the routines, the signals that initiate the routines, and the behaviors associated with each one. If someone does not know the rules, he or she clearly does not belong to the classroom, as student teachers know from teaching their first classes.

Teacher and students should be able to function at an automatic, subconscious level in all the routines to be used in a lesson. If the teacher has to continually remind students about expected behaviors, or if students are unsure about the expectations of their behavior and continually test the boundaries of the teacher's expectations, less time will be spent on task. A contributing factor to a well-ordered classroom, then, is how well and how quickly the routines have been identified and established so that they become automatic. The establishment of routines should be a high priority in the beginning of the year when a teacher faces a new class; many experienced teachers have learned to do this, but beginning teachers may be unfamiliar with the importance of routines and how to establish them (Reynolds 1992).

There are three key steps you should take to establish routines in a new class. First, identify all the routines you think you will use in your classroom. Write them down. You will find you quickly accumulate a long list

From *The Clearing House*, May/June 1995, pp. 293-296. © 1995 by the Helen Dwight Reid Educational Foundation. Reprinted by permission of Heldref Publications, 1319 Eighteenth Street, NW, Washington, DC 20036-1802.

(see table 1 for some examples). Second, for each routine, identify all the rules that you think should apply to that routine. Because these rules apply to both student and teacher behavior, make sure you know what *you*, as well as the students, should be doing in each routine. You will notice that some rules are common to many routines; these can be extracted as general classroom rules. Third, teach each routine to the class. Doing this is by no means simple, so let me elaborate.

The teaching of a routine involves the teacher's setting out his or her expectations clearly and explicitly.

The teacher can either make a set of explicit rules or have the students help to make them. A process of negotiation between teacher and students follows as the routine is worked out in practice, several times over a period of days. The teacher constantly emphasizes the expected rules, and the students constantly test the rules against experience. (If the teacher is inconsistent and shows that a particular rule applies only in some circumstances, the students will attempt to identify the circumstances when it applies and when it does not.) If the teacher continually shifts ground, then the students will

---

TABLE 1
Some Routines and Possible Associated Rules

Routine	Rules
Setting out of math workbooks	Pages are to be ruled before class begins. Fold the page once to the center, and rule a line down the fold with a ruler.
Teacher explaining at chalkboard	Students sit at their desks. All attend to the teacher; no other activity is permitted. No talking among students is permitted. Students respond to a teacher's question by raising their hands. The teacher selects who will speak. No student may get up from his or her seat without permission.
Individual seat work	Students sit at their desks. Students work on the set task from the chalkboard, book, or work sheet. No talking among students is permitted. Students requiring assistance raise their hands. Students are not permitted to leave their seats without permission.
Small group discussions	Students work in the small groups they are assigned to and sit as a group facing each other in a circle. Students may not change groups or visit other groups. The group of students works on the set task. Talking among students that is on task is encouraged. Off-task talking is discouraged. Overall noise levels must remain at an acceptable level. Groups requiring assistance must raise their hands and wait. Students should take turns and be polite when discussing.
Small group work with equipment	Students work in the small groups they are assigned to and sit facing each other in a circle. Students may not change groups or visit other groups. The group of students works on the set task. Talking among students that is on task is encouraged. Off-task talking is discouraged. Overall noise levels must remain at an acceptable level. Groups requiring assistance must raise their hands and wait. Equipment is collected/returned from the distribution points by one student from the group. Off-task use of the equipment is not permitted. Safety instructions must be strictly observed. The assigned roles of each student in the group must be adhered to.

not be able to identify the circumstances and there will be uncertainty about some rules. This situation is a minefield for the teacher, as the students ignore whatever rules they can.

The main task for a teacher during the first few weeks should be to establish the selected routines quickly and efficiently (Brophy 1987). Fortunately, the task is not as difficult as it first appears. After the first year of middle or high school, students will be familiar with the rudiments of many routines. However, you may want to introduce new ones, and the rules you want to apply might differ in some respects from the ones they are used to. So, for most routines, you only need to clarify your own version of some common routines. Of course, for new routines, you will have to start from the beginning. For example, if you like to use small group work, but the class has never done any, you will have to teach the routines associated with this type of activity. If you do not, the students will use the rules that apply to similar social situations where they interact with peers, such as those they follow on the playground. Note that if your emphasis is on teaching routines, it cannot be on teaching a lot of new content. However, you can use the time to find out what the students already know. You should endeavor to have the main routines established by the end of the first week.

Attending to Cultural Differences

What I have described works well if both the teacher and students belong to the same cultural group. Complications can occur if there are mixed cultural groups in the class. Because the classroom society is essentially a reflection of the dominant cultural group in the class, the routines will also reflect the behaviors and language of that group. Students from other cultural groups with different language and behavior patterns will have difficulty recognizing some of the expected behavior and language rules, let alone learning them (Philips 1983). Similarly, teachers might misinterpret students' behaviors and responses by using the teachers' own cultural cues rather than the cultural framework of the students (Contreras and Lee 1990). In such a situation, the students are at a considerable learning disadvantage unless the teacher can take appropriate steps to understand his or her students better (Cazden 1986).

What to do depends on the cultural blend of the classroom. If a majority of people in the class are from the same cultural group, the cultural mores of that group will be dominant in the classroom and will be reflected in the rules and behaviors for the routines established. If you belong to the dominant cultural group, there will be a minimum of problems in establishing the routines for the majority of students. Any minority group of students will have difficulties, however, unless you

- discover quickly the key social communication behaviors of the minority groups,

- modify expectations for behaviors in routines to incorporate the minority group behaviors,
- interpret the minority group's behaviors from its viewpoint rather than the viewpoint of the dominant group, and
- begin a teaching program to help the dominant group recognize and value the behaviors of the minority group and vice versa.

If your cultural origin is different from the dominant cultural group in the class, you will have great difficulty establishing routines unless they are based around the dominant group's communication behaviors. In this case, you should learn as much about the cultural group's communication behavior as soon as possible and modify the planned routines accordingly. For example, Australian Aboriginal children are much more concerned about the social group in a class than their Anglo counterparts (Malin 1990). They therefore spend considerable time monitoring the activities of other students, and they readily help someone in difficulty and delight in the achievements of others. An Anglo teacher in a dominant Aboriginal classroom who is trying to establish, say, an individual seat work routine drawn from his or her own cultural framework would feel considerable anger and frustration at the tendency of the students to gaze around, move to look at others' work, and make slow progress through the assigned work (Malin 1990). An uninformed teacher may interpret such behavior as naughtiness and/or laziness. However, if the teacher found out about these cultural behaviors and modified the rules for the routine to incorporate them, then his or her frustration would be considerably reduced, and the students would not suffer the learning disadvantage of being labeled naughty or lazy. Each cultural group represented in the classroom would still need to be acquainted with the communication behaviors of the other groups.

Consequences of Inadequately Established Routines

If you make the mistake of going into a new class without having thought out the details of all the routines you will use, you will find yourself constantly exposed as an apparently inexperienced or weak teacher. Within a few weeks I would expect you to begin experiencing problems with control and discipline. Some students in a mixed cultural class may become rebellious and resentful. This will happen because the students are unclear about the behavioral standards you expect in the routines you try to use, and your authority is eroded as a result of your ambiguity and apparent inexperience. The same problem exists for preservice teachers during the practicum. Within the first few days, they have to identify the routines that are already common knowledge to the supervising teacher and students; they then have to negotiate their own social position in each routine with both the teacher and students. Because the preservice teacher is effectively a new teacher, the students will test the rules for the routines to see if they still apply. If the preservice teacher shows ignorance of the rules or inconsistency in applying them, control problems will soon emerge. If this happens to preservice or beginning teachers, their first reaction is often to introduce control and discipline techniques, such as reward systems for good behavior. This will work for a while, but unless the underlying problem is addressed—that is, the teacher's failure to know and consistently apply the rules—further discipline problems will emerge. I do not find it surprising that the most common difficulty expressed by beginning teachers is control and discipline) (Pearson 1987; Reynolds 1992).

Conclusion

It is important to establish early with a new class the routines and associated rules that the teacher wants to use. Once that is done, (lessons simply become a string of known routines) where the behaviors of both students and teacher are common knowledge and appropriate behaviors are therefore automatically generated. In such a context, the teacher can deal with content efficiently and effectively, so the students' work is focused and on-task behavior is high. Discipline problems are reduced, and the students feel greater satisfaction in the purposeful learning environment generated.

REFERENCES

Amarel, M., and S. Feiman-Nemser. 1988. Prospective teachers' views of teaching and learning to teach. Paper presented at the Annual Meeting of the American Educational Research Association, New Orleans.

Brophy, J. 1987. Educating teachers about managing classrooms and students. Occasional Paper No. 115. East Lansing, Mich.: Michigan State University, Institute for Research on Teaching. ERIC Document No. ED285844.

———. 1988. Research on teacher effects: Uses and abuses. *Elementary School Journal* 89: 3–21.

Cazden, C. B. 1986. Classroom discourse. In *Handbook of research on teaching*, third ed., edited by M.C. Wittrock. New York: Macmillan.

Coles, B. 1992. Classroom behavior settings for science: What can pre-service teachers achieve? *Research in Science Education* 22: 81–90.

Contreras, A., and O. Lee. 1990. Differential treatment of students by middle school science teachers: Unintended cultural bias. Science Education 74: 433–44.

Edwards, D., and N. Mercer. 1987. *Common knowledge: The development of understanding in the classroom.* London: Routledge.

Gump, P. 1969. Intra-setting analysis: The third grade classroom as a special but instructive case. In *Naturalistic viewpoints in psychological research*, edited by E. Willems and H. Raush, 200–220. New York: Holt, Rinehart and Winston.

Malin, M. 1990. Why is life so hard for Aboriginal students in urban classrooms? *Aboriginal Child at School* 18(1): 9–29.

Pearson, J. 1987. The problems experienced by student teachers during teaching practice: A review of published research studies. *Journal of Teaching Practice* 7 (2): 1–20.

Philips, S. U. 1983. *The invisible culture: Communication in the classroom and community on the Warm Springs Indian Reservation.* New York: Longman.

Reynolds, A. 1992. What is competent beginning teaching? A review of the literature. *Review of Educational Research* 62: 1–35.

Waging Peace In Our Schools

Beginning with the Children

The good news is that, as big as the problem of violence is, we have the power to turn things around. Ms. Lantieri provides the details.

Linda Lantieri

LINDA LANTIERI is national director of the Resolving Conflict Creatively Program, sponsored by Educators for Social Responsibility. She is the co-author with Janet Dutrey of Peacing Our Schools Back Together *(Beacon Press), from which this article has been adapted.*

> If we are to reach real peace in this world . . . we shall have to begin with the children.
>
> — *Mahatma Gandhi*

RECENT events in our country have shaken us as never before. We have come to the realization that our society is in the midst of an epidemic of violence. Homicide has become the third leading cause of death for children between the ages of 5 and 14 and the leading cause of death for young African American men. If we count suicides, a gun takes the life of an American child every two hours.

In the last few years we have witnessed the killing of several students in the hallways of what was once a sacred place — the school. At my alma mater, Thomas Jefferson High School in New York City, one student shot and killed another and critically wounded a teacher. Similar incidents have been repeated in other schools throughout the country. The U.S. Department of Justice estimates that each day some 100,000 children carry guns to school. Each hour, more than 2,000 students are physically attacked on school grounds. And teachers suffer, too. Every hour, approximately 900 teachers are threatened, and nearly 40 are physically attacked.

No school seems immune. A 1993 Harris poll of students in grades 6 through 12 found widespread fear of violence at school. Moreover, this fear is not unreasonable. More than 400,000 violent crimes are reported in and around our nation's schools each year, with still more crimes going unreported.[2]

The toll this violence takes on our children's psyches is clear. More than one-third of the students in the Harris poll said that they believe their lives will be cut short by violence. Miguel Sánchez, a student from New York City, described his fear during the 1993 National Hearings on Violence and the Child in Washington, D.C.: "When I wake up in the morning, I ask myself, am I going to survive this day? So everyday I try to make it seem as if it is my last day on this Earth. So far, I've been lucky. I don't know when my luck is going to run out."

According to Carol Beck, former principal of Thomas Jefferson High School, more than 50% of the young people in that school have puncture wounds on their bodies. Many of our children in large cities are covering their ears to muffle the sound of gunshots in the night. They exhibit the same signs of post-traumatic stress syndrome that we observe in children who grow up in war-torn areas.

Why is this violence taking place? Deborah Prothrow-Stith, assistant dean at the Harvard University School of Public Health, has addressed that question, and her response may be hard for adults to swallow. Why are our children killing one another? *Because we are teaching them to.* Our society glamorizes violence.[3] Indeed, the media often portray the hero as one who chooses violence to get what he or she wants and needs.

"They say we are the future," observes 11-year-old Jessica, a student mediator at P.S. 261 in Brooklyn, New York. "But they treat us like we're nothing. On TV, it's sex, drugs, and violence — they're projecting that to kids. Practically all cartoons have something to do with guns or destruction."

The students at Thomas Jefferson High School went home after the shootings that left one student dead and a teacher wounded, and a few nights later on their televisions they saw "Saturday Night Live" portray the scenes at their school in a comedy skit. For the producers of the program, there were no tears, funerals, or images of kids crying in teachers' arms. Yet most adults are confused and appalled when they see young people commit violent acts with no apparent remorse. That's the bad news.

The good news is that, as big as the problem of violence is, we have the power to turn things around. Ten years ago, I co-founded the Resolving Conflict Creatively Program (RCCP) in New York City, and today I serve as national director of the program. In our work at the RCCP, we have found that violence is preventable. I visited Thomas Jefferson High School after the incident and had an intense discussion with 14 young people, several of whom had actually watched their schoolmate dying. In the first hour I learned a lot from them about the futility of the violence that surrounds them and the hopelessness they feel. They knew that violence was destroying them, but they saw no alternatives.

Then I began asking them whether, from the beginning to the end of this fatal dispute, there was anything anyone could have done differently. They identified eight or nine things — mainly done by bystanders — that had actually escalated the conflict in the hallway. What I was helping them to see was that the dispute that culminated in tragedy had escalated by the accumulation of many small acts. Young people often think these are things that no one has any control over, and that makes them feel helpless. When they step back and reflect, they begin to feel empowered.

A New Way of Fighting

"Mom," says 8-year-old Wayne, "the fifth-graders are learning a new way of fighting."

"Oh? What do you mean?"

"Well, when kids get mad, they don't hit each other. Other kids help them talk out the fight instead."

Wayne is referring to the student mediation process being established in his school as part of the RCCP. The program began in 1985 as a collaboration between the New York City Public Schools and Educators for Social Responsibility's New York City chapter. Now in its 10th year, RCCP educates for intergroup understanding, alternatives to violence, and creative conflict resolution among students, teachers, parents, and administrators in five school systems across the country: the New York City Public Schools, the Anchorage School District, the New Orleans Public Schools, the Vista Unified School District in Southern California, and the South Orange/Maplewood School District in New Jersey. Participants in the RCCP during the 1993-94 school year included 120,000 young people in more than 300 schools from a variety of communities. The RCCP is now the largest school-based program of its kind in the country. In September 1993 Educators for Social Responsibility established the RCCP National Center to support those national replication efforts already begun and to provide technical assistance to additional school systems in developing and implementing conflict resolution programs.

The world yearns for "a new way of fighting," one in which people can be strong without being mean. Conflict is part of life, and we wouldn't want to elim-

inate it even if we could. But we urgently need to find ways to end the violence between diverse groups of people that causes so much unnecessary pain and suffering. Through the RCCP, we are giving young people the important message that the Rambos of the world, far from being heroes, are pathetic because they can think of only one response to conflict. Young people in our program are beginning to see that the highest form of heroism is the passionate search for creative, nonviolent solutions to the problems of our pluralistic society. They are beginning to incorporate these ideas into their everyday lives, as in the following scene.

With tears streaming down her face, 7-year-old Veronica picks herself up from the asphalt of the playground and charges toward her friend Jasmine.

"Why'd you trip me?" she screams.

"I didn't trip you."

"Yes, you did, and I'm gonna trip you right back on your face!"

"Just try it, and see what happens!"

Suddenly two fifth-graders wearing bright blue T-shirts appear. Across the front and back of their shirts, the word *mediator* is emblazoned. "Excuse me!" says one. "My name is Jessica."

"And I'm Angel," says the other. "We're mediators. Would you like us to help solve this problem?"

"I guess so," the younger girls say grudgingly. Jessica and Angel first obtain the disputants' agreement to some ground rules (including no name-calling and no interrupting), and then the mediators suggest that they all move to a quieter area of the playground to talk things out.

"You'll speak first, Veronica," says Jessica. "But don't worry, Jasmine, you'll get your chance. Okay, Veronica, tell us what happened."

Within two minutes, the girls have solved their problem. Jasmine acknowledges that she tripped Veronica by accident as she was trying to tag her. She says she is sorry. Veronica agrees to accept the apology and to be Jasmine's friend again. After being congratulated by Angel and Jessica for solving their problem, the girls resume their game.

The RCCP Model

The RCCP is based on a relatively simple idea that is often hard to carry out: that people should listen to one another when there are problems and work toward peaceable solutions. The RCCP process encourages open discussion in a suppor-

tive atmosphere to help children and adults better understand conflict and its roots. Most important, the RCCP teaches students (as well as teachers, parents, and administrators) practical skills that enable them to find creative solutions to conflicts as they happen. The program helps young people realize that they have many choices for dealing with conflict other than passivity or aggression. They learn the skills needed to make those choices in their own lives, and they increase their understanding and appreciation of their own and other cultures.

By creating a "peaceable school" — a safe environment where students are encouraged to experiment with peaceful ways of resolving conflict — RCCP teachers strive to give their students a new image of what their world can be. For this to happen, however, the teachers themselves must change. They must learn and apply a new set of skills for heading off and resolving conflict. Even more difficult, they must adopt a new style of classroom management, one that fundamentally involves a sharing of power with students so that they can learn how to deal with their own disputes.

To this end, the RCCP's comprehensive approach includes the following com-

> We are seeing adults change first. We are seeing individual students change second, and then we are seeing whole schools change.

ponents: (1) a K-12 classroom curriculum, (2) professional training and ongoing technical assistance and support for teachers, (3) a student-led mediation program, (4) parent training, and (5) administrator training.

The price tag for the RCCP comes to just over $33 per student per year. To educators accustomed to buying packaged curricula that sell for a few hundred dollars, this figure might seem expensive. However, it is wise to bear in mind that the RCCP is much more than a curriculum. Rather, it is an intensive effort at school reform, with a strong emphasis on teacher training and professional development.

An Observable Impact

From the earliest days of the program, teachers have reported positive changes in their students and themselves as a result of introducing the RCCP into their schools. Tony Soll, a sixth-grade teacher at the Brooklyn New School, related one of his experiences with the program:

We had been discussing news articles, and I asked the students in my class to find stories in the newspapers about people solving conflicts. There were two boys in the class who were buddies but became enemies at least five times every day. The fighting would go on and on, and it was driving everybody crazy. One day they decided, on their own, to go out in the hall and write a peace treaty. They were afraid to get into an argument about the peace treaty, so they picked four other kids — not necessarily their best friends, but definitely people who would be dependable. They all went out into the hall and signed the peace treaty. (At that time, we hadn't even used the word *mediation*.) The treaty is still up on the wall. It belongs to the whole class now and serves as a reminder that you don't always have to fight.

A formal evaluation of the RCCP conducted in 1989-90 confirmed the teachers' impressions. Metis Associates, an independent evaluator, concluded in its report that the program had "an observable and quantifiable positive impact on students, participating staff, and classroom climate." The teachers reported that they devoted an average of seven periods per month to specific lessons on conflict resolution and that they were also infusing the concepts of conflict resolution into other aspects of the curriculum. They noted less physical violence in their classrooms, a decreased use of verbal putdowns in favor of more supportive comments, spontaneous student use of conflict resolution skills, and an increase in their students' self-esteem, leadership skills, and initiative. They also reported positive effects in themselves, particularly in their ability to handle angry students and to deal with conflict in general.

The RCCP in New York is currently involved in an in-depth, three-year evaluation of the program, funded by a grant from the federal Centers for Disease Control and Prevention.

A Way of Life

Learning conflict resolution skills is only one way to address the epidemic of violence in our society. Violence has many sources, as Ted Quant, co-director of the RCCP in New Orleans, points out: "I look at the violence and see that it is rooted in fear, rooted in injustice, rooted in poverty, racism, sexism, ageism, homophobia — all of these are examples of violence because all of them deny the basic humanity of our brothers and sisters and the children in this village we call Earth." Conflict resolution can help, but it will be most effective as part of a larger strategy. As one of our teachers put it, "The RCCP is more than a curriculum; it's a way of life."

Conflict resolution is not a quick fix. It takes time for adults to integrate conflict resolution concepts and a multicultural perspective into their own lives, it takes time for them to learn how to translate these concepts for students, and it takes time for even the most effective classroom instruction to have a significant impact. Some of the most successful teachers in the RCCP have observed that it sometimes takes months for youngsters to begin integrating concepts and skills in such a way that their behavior begins to change.

But we are seeing changes. We are seeing adults change first. We are seeing individual students change second, and then we are seeing whole schools change for the better. More than anything, we are demonstrating the power of nonviolence and showing that the right kind of intervention can turn us and our schools around. We *can* create violence-free zones in our nation's schools.

Imagine a child being born today who enters kindergarten in 1999 and begins to learn "another way of fighting." Imagine that, from that first day of school, this child experiences an atmosphere in which differences are accepted and nonviolent approaches to conflict are the norm. Imagine that, by the time the student reaches fifth grade, he or she is chosen by peers to be a mediator to settle disputes among classmates. And imagine that, by the time this young person enters high school, all students are walking through doors without metal detectors and are taking required classes in conflict resolution and intergroup relations. Finally, imagine that this young person will, for the rest of his or her life, have the courage to be a hero for peace and justice.

This imagined scenario is already taking place in the lives of thousands of young people across the nation. We have the preventive tools to begin to turn back the tide of bigotry and violence. Now we must put them to good use. Our children deserve a future in which their right to safety is reclaimed and their cultural diversity is celebrated.

1. *Cease Fire in the War Against Children* (Washington, D.C.: Children's Defense Fund, 1994).
2. Chancellor's Working Group on School-Based Violence Prevention, "Draft Report," New York City Board of Education, July 1994.
3. Deborah Prothrow-Stith and Michaele Weissman, *Deadly Consequences: How Violence Is Destroying Our Teenage Population and a Plan to Begin Solving the Problem* (New York: HarperCollins, 1991).

How to Create Discipline Problems

M. MARK WASICSKO and STEVEN M. ROSS

M. Mark Wasicsko is provost at Texas Wesleyan College in Fort Worth, Texas. Steven M. Ross is professor of education at Memphis State University.

Creating classroom discipline problems is easy. By following the ten simple rules listed you should be able to substantially improve your skill at this popular teacher pastime.

1. *Expect the worst from kids.* This will keep you on guard at all times.
2. *Never tell students what is expected of them.* Kids need to learn to figure things out for themselves.
3. *Punish and criticize kids often.* This better prepares them for real life.
4. *Punish the whole class when one student misbehaves.* All the other students were probably doing the same thing or at least thinking about doing it.
5. *Never give students privileges.* It makes students soft and they will just abuse privileges anyway.
6. *Punish every misbehavior you see.* If you don't, the students will take over.
7. *Threaten and warn kids often.* "If you aren't good, I'll keep you after school for the rest of your life."
8. *Use the same punishment for every student.* If it works for one it will work for all.
9. *Use school work as punishment.* "Okay, smarty, answer all the questions in the book for homework!"
10. *Maintain personal distance from students.* Familiarity breeds contempt, you know.

We doubt that teachers would deliberately follow any of these rules, but punishments are frequently dealt out without much thought about their effects. In this article we suggest that many discipline problems are caused and sustained by teachers who inadvertently use self-defeating discipline strategies. There are, we believe, several simple, concrete methods to reduce classroom discipline problems.

Expect the Best from Kids

That teachers' expectations play an important role in determining student behavior has long been known. One author remembers two teachers who, at first glance, appeared similar. Both were very strict, gave mountains of homework, and kept students busy from the first moment they entered the classroom. However, they differed in their expectations for students. One seemed to say, "I know I am hard on you, but it is because I know you can do the work." She was effective and was loved by students. The other conveyed her negative expectations, "If I don't keep these kids busy they will stab me in the back." Students did everything they could to live up to each teacher's expectations. Thus, by conveying negative attitudes toward students, many teachers create their own discipline problems.

A first step in reducing discipline problems is to demonstrate positive expectations toward students. This is relatively easy to do for "good" students but probably more necessary for the others. If you were lucky, you probably had a teacher or two who believed you were able and worthy, and expected you to be capable even when you presented evidence to the contrary. You probably looked up to these teachers and did whatever you could to please them (and possibly even became a teacher yourself as a result). Now is the time to return the favor. Expect the best from *each* of your students. Assume that *every* child, if given the chance, will act properly. And, most important, if students don't meet your expectations, *don't give up!* Some students will require much attention before they will begin to respond.

Make the Implicit Explicit

Many teachers increase the likelihood of discipline problems by not making their expectations about proper behavior clear and explicit. For example, how many times have you heard yourself saying, "Now class, BEHAVE!"? You assume everyone knows what you mean

This article originally appeared in the December 1982 issue of The Clearing House.

From *The Clearing House*, May/June 1994, pp. 248–251. © 1994 by the Helen Dwight Reid Educational Foundation. Reprinted by permission of Heldref Publications, 1319 Eighteenth Street, NW, Washington, DC 20036-1802.

by "behave." This assumption may not be reasonable. On the playground, for example, proper behavior means running, jumping, throwing things (preferably balls, not rocks), and cooperating with other students. Classroom teachers have different notions about proper behavior, but in few cases do teachers spell out their expectations carefully. Sad to say, most students must learn the meaning of "behave" by the process of elimination: "Don't look out the window. . . . Don't put hands on fellow students. . . . Don't put feet on the desk . . . don't . . . don't . . . don't . . . ."

A preferred approach would be to present rules for *proper* conduct on the front end (and try to phrase them positively: "Students should . . ."). The teacher (or the class) could prepare a poster on which rules are listed. In that way, rules are clear, explicit, and ever present in the classroom. If you want to increase the likelihood that rules will be followed, have students help make the rules. Research shows that when students feel responsible for rules, they make greater efforts to live by them.

Rewards, Yes! Punishments, No!

A major factor in creating classroom discipline problems is the overuse of punishments as an answer to misbehavior. While most teachers would agree with this statement, recent research indicates that punishments outweigh rewards by at least 10 to 1 in the typical classroom. The types of punishments identified include such old favorites as The Trip to the Office and "Write a million times, 'I will not. . . . '" But punishments also include the almost unconscious (but frequent) responses made for minor infractions: the "evil eye" stare of disapproval and the countless pleas to "Face front," "Stop talking," "Sit down!" and so on.

Punishments (both major and minor) have at least four consequences that frequently lead to increased classroom disruption: (1) Punishment brings attention to those who misbehave. We all know the adage, "The squeaky wheel gets greased." Good behavior frequently leaves a student nameless and unnoticed, but bad behavior can bring the undivided attention of the teacher before an audience of classmates! (2) Punishment has negative side effects such as aggression, depression, anxiety, or embarrassment. At the least, when a child is punished he feels worse about himself, about you and your class, or about school in general. He may even try to reduce the negative side effects by taking it out on another child or on school equipment. (3) Punishment only temporarily suppresses bad behavior. The teacher who rules with an iron ruler can have students who never misbehave in her presence, but who misbehave the moment she leaves the room or turns her back. (4) Punishment disrupts the continuity of your lessons and reduces the time spent on productive learning. These facts, and because punishments are usually not premeditated (and frequently do not address the real problems of misbehavior such as boredom, frustration,

or physical discomfort), usually work to increase classroom discipline problems rather than to reduce them.

In view of these factors, the preferred approach is to use rewards. Rewards bring attention to *good* behaviors: "Thank you for being prepared." Rewards provide an appropriate model for other students, and make students feel positive about themselves, about you, and about your class. Also, reinforcing positive behaviors reduces the inclination toward misbehavior and enhances the flow of your lesson. You stay on task, get more student participation, and accentuate the correct responses.

Let the Punishment Fit the Crime

When rewards are inappropriate, many teachers create discipline problems by using short-sighted or ineffective punishments. The classic example is the "whole class punishment." "Okay, I said if anyone talked there would be no recess, so we stay in today!" This approach frustrates students (especially the ones who were behaving properly) and causes more misbehavior.

Research indicates that punishments are most effective when they are the natural consequences of the behavior. For example, if a child breaks a window, it makes sense to punish him with clean-up responsibilities and by making him pay for damage. Having him write 1,000 times, "I will not break the window," or having him do extra math problems(!) does little to help him see the relationship between actions and consequences.

In reality, this is one of the hardest suggestions to follow. In many cases, the "natural consequences" are obscure ("Okay Steve, you hurt Carlton's feelings by calling him fat. For your punishment, you will make him feel better"). So, finding an appropriate punishment is often difficult. We suggest that after racking your brain, you consult with the offenders. They may be able to come up with a consequence that at least appears to them to be a fit punishment. In any case, nothing is lost for trying.

If You Must Punish, Remove Privileges

In the event that there are no natural consequences that can serve as punishments, the next best approach is to withdraw privileges. This type of punishment fits in well with the actual conditions in our society. In "real life" (located somewhere outside the school walls) privileges and responsibilities go hand in hand. People who do not act responsibly quickly lose freedoms and privileges. Classrooms provide a great opportunity to teach this lesson, but there is one catch: *There must be privileges to withdraw!* Many privileges already exist in classrooms and many more should be created. For example, students who finish their work neatly and on time can play an educational game, do an extra credit math sheet, work on homework, or earn points toward fun activities and free time. The possibilities are limitless. The important point, however, is that those who break the rules lose out on the privileges.

"Ignor"ance Is Bliss

One of the most effective ways to create troubles is to reward the very behaviors you want to eliminate. Many teachers do this inadvertently by giving attention to misbehaviors. For example, while one author was observing a kindergarten class, a child uttered an expletive after dropping a box of toys. The teachers quickly surrounded him and excitedly exclaimed, "That's nasty! Shame! Shame! Don't ever say that nasty word again!" All the while the other kids looked on with studied interest. So by lunch time, many of the other students were chanting, ". . . (expletive deleted) . . ." and the teachers were in a frenzy! Teachers create similar problems by bringing attention to note passing, gum chewing, and countless other minor transgressions. Such problems can usually be avoided by ignoring minor misbehaviors and, at a later time, talking to the student individually. Some minor misbehavior is probably being committed by at least one student during every second you teach! Your choice is to spend your time trying to correct (and bring attention to) each one *or* to go about the business of teaching.

Consistency Is the Best Policy

Another good way to create discipline problems is to be inconsistent with rules, assignments, and punishments. For example, one author's daughter was given 750 math problems to complete over the Christmas holidays. She spent many hours (which she would rather have spent playing with friends) completing the task. As it turned out, no one else completed the assignment, so the teacher extended the deadline by another week. In this case, the teacher was teaching students that it is all right to skip assignments. When events like this recur, the teacher loses credibility and students are taught to procrastinate, which they may continue to do throughout their lives.

Inconsistent punishment has a similar effect. By warning and rewarning students, teachers actually cultivate misbehavior. "The next time you do that, you're going to the office!" Five minutes pass and then, "I'm warning you, one more time and you are gone!" And later, "This is your last warning!" And finally, "Okay, I have had it with you, go stand in the hall!" In this instance, a student has learned that a punishment buys him/her a number of chances to misbehave (she/he might as well use them all), and that the actual punishment will be less severe than the promised one (not a bad deal).

To avoid the pitfalls of inconsistency, mean what you say, and, when you say it, follow through.

Know Each Student Well

Discipline problems can frequently be caused by punishing students we intended to reward and vice versa. When a student is told to clean up the classroom after school, is that a reward or punishment? It's hard to tell. As we all know, "One person's pleasure is another's poison."

One author remembers the difficulty he had with reading in the fourth grade. It made him so anxious that he would become sick just before reading period in the hope that he would be sent to the clinic, home, or anywhere other than to "the circle." One day, after helping the teacher straighten out the room before school, the teacher thanked him with, "Mark, you've been so helpful, you can be the first to read today." The author made sure he was never "helpful" enough to be so severely punished again.

The opposite happens just as often. For example, there are many class clowns who delight in such "punishments" as standing in the corner, leaving the room, or being called to the blackboard. The same author recalls having to stand in the school courtyard for punishment. He missed math, social studies, and English, and by the end of the day had entertained many classmates with tales of his escapades.

The key to reducing discipline problems is to know your students well; know what is rewarding and what is punishing for each.

Use School Work as Rewards

One of the worst sins a teacher can commit is to use school work as punishments. There is something sadly humorous about the language arts teacher who punishes students with, "Write 1,000 times, I will not. . . ." or the math teacher who assigns 100 problems as punishment. In cases like these we are actually punishing students with that which we want them to use and enjoy! Teachers can actually reduce discipline problems (and increase learning) by using their subjects as rewards. This is done in subtle and sometimes indirect ways, through making lessons meaningful, practical, and fun. If you are teaching about fractions, bring in pies and cakes and see how fast those kids can learn the difference between 1/2, 1/4, and 1/8. Reading teachers should allow free reading as a reward for good behavior. Math teachers can give extra credit math sheets (points to be added to the next test) when regular assignments are completed. The possibilities are endless and the results will be less misbehavior and a greater appreciation for both teacher and subject.

Treat Students with Love and Respect

The final suggestion for reducing discipline problems is to treat students kindly. It is no secret that people tend to respond with the same kind of treatment that they are given. If students are treated in a cold or impersonal manner, they are less likely to care if they cause you grief. If they are treated with warmth and respect they will want to treat you well in return. One of the best ways to show you care (and thus reduce discipline problems) is to surprise kids. After they have worked particularly hard, give them a treat. "You kids have worked so hard you may have 30 minutes extra recess." Or have a party one day for no good reason at all. Kids will come to think, "This school stuff isn't so bad after all!'' Be careful to keep the surprises unexpected. If kids come to expect them, surprises lose their effectiveness. Recently, one author heard a student pay a teacher the highest tribute. He said, ''She is more than just a teacher; she is our friend.'' Not surprisingly, this teacher is known for having few major discipline problems.

Final Thoughts

When talking about reducing discipline problems, we need to be careful not to suggest that they can or should be totally eliminated. When children are enthusiastic about learning, involved in what they are doing, and allowed to express themselves creatively, ''discipline problems'' are apt to occur. Albert Einstein is one of numerous examples of highly successful people who were labeled discipline problems in school. It was said of Einstein that he was ''the boy who knew not merely which monkey wrench to throw in the works, but also how best to throw it.'' This led to his expulsion from school because his ''presence in the class is disruptive and affects the other students.'' For dictators and tyrants, robot-like obedience is a major goal. For teachers, however, a much more critical objective is to help a classroom full of students reach their maximum potential as individuals.

The theme of this article has been that many teachers create their own discipline problems. Just as we teach the way we were taught, we tend to discipline with the same ineffectual methods that were used on us. By becoming aware of this and by following the simple suggestions presented above, learning and teaching can become more rewarding for all involved.

A Lesson Plan Approach for Dealing with School Discipline

JOHN R. BAN

John R. Ban is professor of education and coordinator of administrative programs at Indiana University Northwest in Gary, Indiana.

Teaching school poses no more formidable challenge than managing student behavior. Over the years, a cavalcade of devices has been marshalled by educators to discipline unruly students. Sometimes with inspiration, often times in desperation, teachers have resorted to a wide assortment of discipline methods—ranging from the hickory stick and dunce caps to bribery and capitulation. Whatever the tactic, it has not completely tamed the land of unsavory behavior.

Teacher remedies for discipline problems today can be grouped into two categories. One can be labeled reactive discipline. A fly-by-the-seat approach, it is the most common form of discipline used in the public schools. Teachers react when infractions occur by deciding what to do on the spot to handle them. Misbehavior is not anticipated; nor is the response planned to deal with it. With reactive disciplines, similar behavior outbursts merit different reactions depending on the individual student. By dealing with problem students on an individual basis, teachers demonstrate an inconsistency that undermines their credibility and authority. Presently, teachers resort to a mixture of reaction practices, most varying from day-to-day, from student to student, and from circumstance to circumstance. Reactive discipline is improvisation and impromptu classroom management. It is a form of free-lancing that may work fine in show business but is fraught with hidden dangers in dealing with aberrant children.

Proactive Discipline

An approach that offers better prospect for success is a proactive design of classroom management. Proactive discipline is predicated on the necessity for forethought, anticipation, preparation, and consistency with regard to teacher behavior and the consequences occasioned by student misbehavior. It is a system approach to discipline problems. Like any system, proactive discipline consists of components that can be learned. It rests on the belief that the surest road to resolving classroom management problems is through the establishment of a comprehensive system that can be activated when problems arise.

Several excellent proactive discipline systems have been developed for teachers and schools around the country. These include Canter's Assertive Discipline, Glasser's Reality Therapy, Gill and Heller's Diagnostic Discipline, Duke's Systematic Management Plan, and Alschuler's Social Literacy.

Most of these discipline plans argue for changes in school organization. Furthermore, they urge that the entire school staff follow the same discipline format. Admittedly, a system-wide discipline plan enjoys the best chance of success since it would reduce inconsistencies in teacher management techniques and lead to collaborative efforts on the part of all educators. A system-wide approach, however, may not be realizable in many schools.

While system-wide discipline plans have been implemented around the country, they have not been without problems. It is exceedingly difficult to convince all educators to adopt lock, stock, and barrel a single system of school discipline. The reason is that schools differ, classrooms differ, and so do teachers and students—making the typical school heterogeneous and unsusceptible to a uniform discipline approach.

Many teachers can be expected to feel uncomfortable with a mandated set of rules that circumscribes widely diverse elements of classroom organization. Their anxieties can be further compounded by a wide spectrum of idiosyncrasies in their instructional style. Dissimilarities in the learning habits of students present an additional problem in implementing universal behavior decrees.

One may inquire why teachers cannot accept a standardized discipline system when they willingly follow

This article originally appeared in the April 1982 issue of The Clearing House.

other school-wide requirements. The response to such an inquiry is that certain institutional requirements pertain to mechanics of operation, deal with things, and make organizational sense. Others do not. The directive of using one kind of report card or using a specific student attendance form, for instance, does not interfere with the infinite complexities of student conduct. Nor does it have a bearing on the fluid personal relationships between teacher and student.

Because a system-wide discipline plan may not be workable in many schools, a lesson plan approach to discipline is proposed here. This plan can be used either on a school-wide basis, which is preferable, or simply in a class-to-class situation. The lesson plan is a familiar instructional tool to all teachers. It is one in which they are skilled and which they employ daily. These features alone make it a palatable mechanism for strengthening discipline both within and outside the classroom.

Becoming involved in lesson planning for effective discipline can persuade teachers to employ a proactive approach in dealing with misbehavior. Just as teachers court trouble when they do not plan for instruction, they run the same risk when they do not prepare to handle discipline problems. If there is a chief weakness among teachers in dealing with discipline problems, it is their failure to design a synoptic strategy that addresses misbehavior before it happens.

Making the Lesson Plan

A lesson plan approach to discipline is predicated on several propositions: behavior in school should be an object for study in the classroom; instruction during the first week of school should center on conduct and its consequences; there should be a lesson plan prepared for this purpose; students should be involved in determining classroom rules; peer influence should be used as a force in molding conduct in school; a proper record-keeping system for misbehavior should comprise an essential part of a teacher's discipline system.

A lesson plan approach to discipline requires that the teacher set aside the teaching of subject matter during the first week of school. Instead, one should devote that time to "comportment training," teaching about not only behavior in general but also, more specifically, about behavior in educational institutions. One of the best sources for this lesson is the school's student conduct manual. Another is local school board policy relative to pupil behavior. Students should be encouraged to study in detail what the school system's student conduct code says about behavior, corporal punishment, suspension, expulsion, due process, student responsibilities, specific behavior offenses, and consequences for breaking certain rules. Students should be given the opportunity to explore the reasons behind these rules and express their reactions to them.

Understanding the role of rules or law in society is closely tied to any effective discipline system. Teachers should help students understand what schools are and why they need rules. Schools are institutions that handle, organize and are responsible for the learning of young people. They are learning communities made up of distinct groups (teachers, students, administrators, etc.) that are bound together by a common goal. Like other institutions, schools need rules to accomplish their goals. School rules have these functions: they guide behavior toward a particular end; ensure orderly processes; promote the common good; protect the rights of everyone; spell out responsibilities of all parties; provide lessons in living; and prepare youngsters for life in a society of law.

Central to a lesson plan on school discipline is involving students in assisting the teacher in instituting classroom rules. Classroom communities are stronger when all their members participate in designing rules for behavior. Substantial research indicates that people are more inclined to obey rules when they have had a significant part in determining them. Many authorities in school discipline are insisting that educators and students share in this function.

Student Involvement

In keeping with the points above, teachers should ask students to identify common behavior problems in school. In addition, the reasons for and consequences of these problems should be discussed. The students should formulate a behavior statement or rule that deals with these identified misbehaviors. To do this, teachers can divide students into committees that would report back to the class on their deliberations. Once these rules are amply debated and approved by the entire class, they should be promulgated. Promulgation can take the form of being posted on a bulletin board where they can serve as a constant reminder to students or prepared in a memo distributed to each student to take home for parental perusal and signature.

In too many classrooms student behavior is regulated solely by teacher authority, which students are eager to challenge. In classrooms where students have had a part in shaping the rules of behavior, the power of peer pressure will work to ensure student compliance with these rules.

A close companion to behavior restraints is temper management. How can one study proper conduct without examining measures for temper control? Yet few teachers treat this topic in a systematic way. Fewer still rally youngsters to establish temper management plans.

The first step in a temper management plan is student identification of those situations that cause a loss of temper. Students should be encouraged to monitor their angry responses during the day and acknowledge ways others handle hostility and aggression. Following this, students should make a value judgment of their temper loss, whether it was beneficial/harmful (good/bad) to them or others. It is important, too, that students associate consequences with unbridled anger.

Above all, students should have the opportunity to explore how exemplary people control their tempers. Teachers can then steer students to study, and even practice, suggested techniques of self-control, ranging from deep muscle relaxation to fantasizing pleasant scenes.

A basic feature of a lesson plan on discipline is to focus on behavior required of students outside the classroom. Some authorities on discipline point out that most of the unruly behavior in school occurs outside the classroom—in the halls, cafeteria, playground, washroom, and on school buses. This is the case in some schools but not all. Regardless, it is imperative that students know school rules regarding the behavior expected of them in extra-class areas. These rules should be studied in terms of their rationale, their place in the organization of the school, and their relationship to classroom rules.

Keeping records of student misbehavior is a necessary element in any effective classroom discipline system. Given the legal climate surrounding the schools and the rules of evidence inherent in student due process proceedings, teachers should establish a simple, easily retrievable log on discipline incidents in their classes. Once a discipline record plan is determined for the class, the teacher should notify students about it, explaining its purpose and rationale.

A discipline record form need not be sophisticated nor time consuming, but it should contain at least five categories that supply information sufficient for legal use. On a small note card, teachers could record the following: (a) *incident*—identifying the specific misbehavior; (b) *description*—specifying items like frequency, location or any unusual circumstance; (c)*impact*—shorthanding the effect of the misbehavior on students, learning, teacher, or school; (d) *corrective action*—recording action taken by the teacher to deal with misbehavior; (e) *follow-up*—monitoring the conduct of an unruly child over a period of time and assessing the effectiveness of the remedy employed.

In conjunction with the lesson plan approach to school discipline, teachers should schedule a private five-minute conference every three weeks with each student in class. These can be called HAT meetings (for How Are Things?). They are brief, time-out periods where the teacher demonstrates concern for youngsters through inquiring about how things are going for them in and out of class, where the teacher can volunteer assistance with personal or behavior problems, and where the teacher delivers an unmistakable message that he or she cares. Research at the University of Wisconsin Research and Development Center indicated that both

the behavior and performance of students improved with the use of periodic conferences between teacher and students.

Teacher Attitude

In the final analysis, the key to any effective discipline system is teacher attitude. A lesson plan on discipline merely establishes the structure and substance for managing student behavior. Teacher style supplies the essential ingredient for its successful implementation. If discipline is important to learning, and few would deny that it is, then the teacher must take time not only to preplan a classroom management system but also to convey an enthusiasm and disposition for making it work.

Substantial research has been done on teacher behaviors that hold down the incidence of student misbehavior. These behaviors afford valuable guidelines for teachers in becoming effective classroom managers. They include extensive planning for instruction, teaching classroom rules, helping students learn proper behavior in school, employing praise and positive reinforcement, sending out cues that the teacher cares, giving greater structure and focus to assignments, providing opportunities for students in on-task activities, monitoring regularly student performance, supplying continuous feedback to students regarding their work, and allowing a high degree of student participation in classroom affairs.

Teachers have to project a caring attitude, a deep concern for youngsters and a willingness to be fair but firm. They have to place heavy reliance on praise, trust, and encouragement. They have to demonstrate control over their own temper if they expect students to control theirs. In the delicate art of interpersonal relations, they have to model proper behavior in front of students. Above all, teachers must sharpen their skills in classroom management since success in their trade hinges on this simple fact. To expect teachers to survive in a classroom without behavior management skills is like expecting an artist to paint without a brush.

The problem of student discipline is a painful thorn in the flesh of public education. It appears that everyone is waiting for teachers to perform the extraction that supplies relief. Yet teachers are caught in a squeeze between rising expectation of their control of student behavior and organizational and community forces that make this a difficult task. Without waiting for outside help, teachers can address the discipline problem on their own. Discipline can be learned from studying it. The lesson plan approach comprises a convenient and effective instrument to promote responsible behavior among students. Even more, it is a teaching medium that all teachers could comfortably use.

Equality of Educational Opportunity

As we move toward the end of this century, there is an immense amount of unfinished business before us in the area of intercultural relations. America is becoming more and more multicultural with every passing decade. This requires steps to ensure that all of our educational opportunity structures remain open to all persons regardless of their cultural backgrounds. There is also unfinished business with regard to improving educational opportunities for girls and young women—gender issues in American education that are very real and directly related to the issue of equality of educational opportunity. In addition, issues of racial prejudice and bigotry still plague us in American education, even though there has been massive effort in many school systems to improve racial and intercultural relations. Many American adolescents are in crisis as their basic health and social needs are not adequately met and as their educational development is affected by crises in their personal lives. The essays in this unit reflect all of the above concerns plus other concerns related to providing equality of educational opportunity to all American youth. These essays attempt to clarify what multicultural education is and what it is not; they explore issues relating to how we can better improve the educational opportunity structures for a generation of American youth, many of whom live in constant crisis.

The "equity agenda," or social justice agenda, in the field of education is a complex matrix of gender- and culture-related issues aggravated by incredibly wide gaps in the social and economic opportunity structures available to citizens. We are each situated by cultural, gender-based, and socioeconomic factors in society; this is true of all persons everywhere. We have witnessed a great and glorious struggle for human rights in our nation. The struggle continues to deal more effectively with educational opportunity issues related to cultural diversity and gender.

The effort to improve equality of opportunity in the field of education relates to a wide range of both cultural and gender issues still confronting our society. Although there has been a great, truly historic, effort to achieve social justice in American society, our striving must continue. We need to see our social reality in the context of our "wholeness" as a culturally pluralistic society in which there remain unresolved issues in the field of edu-

cation for both cultural minorities and women. Women's issues and concerns have historically been part of the struggle for civil liberties. An overview of the executive summary of the American Association of University Women's (AAUW) report, "How Schools Shortchange Girls" (1992), is published in this unit to identify what can be done to treat female students more fairly in the educational system.

The "Western canon" is being challenged by advocates of multicultural perspectives in school curricula development. Multicultural educational programming, which will reflect the rapidly changing cultural demographics of North American schooling, is being fiercely advocated by some and strongly opposed by others. This controversy centers around several different issues regarding what it means to provide equality of opportunities for culturally diverse students. This debate is reflected in the essays in this unit. The traditional Western cultural content of general and social studies and language arts curricula is being challenged as Eurocentric.

Helping teachers to further broaden their cultural perspectives and to take a more global view of curricula content is something the advocates of culturally pluralistic approaches to curriculum development would like to see integrated into the entire elementary and secondary school curricula structure. North America is as multicultural a region of the world as exists anywhere. Our enormous cultural diversity encompasses populations from many indigenous "First Americans" as well as peoples from every European culture and from many Asian, African, and Latin American nations and the Central and South Pacific Island groups. There is spirited controversy over how to help *all* Americans to better understand our collective multicultural heritage. There are spirited defenders and opponents to the traditional Eurocentric curriculum.

The problem of inequality of educational opportunity is of great concern to American educators. One in four American children do not have all of their basic needs met and live under poverty conditions. Almost one in three live in single-parent homes, which in itself is no disadvantage—but under conditions of poverty, it often is. More and more concern is expressed over how to help children of poverty. The equity agenda of our time has to do with many issues related to gender, race, and ethnicity. All forms of social deprivation and discrimination are aggravated by great disparities in income and accumulated wealth. How can students be helped to have an equal opportunity to succeed in school? We have wrestled with this dilemma in educational policy development for decades. How can we advance the just cause of the educational interests of our young people more effectively?

Some of us are still proud to say that we are a nation of immigrants. As we became a new nation, powerful demographic and economic forces impacted upon the makeup of our population. In addition to the traditional minority/majority group relationships that evolved in the United States, new waves of immigrants today are again making concerns for achieving equality of opportunity in education as important as ever. In light of these vast sociological and demographic changes, we must remain true to our ideal of being a *pro*-multicultural democracy.

The social psychology of prejudice is something that psychiatrists, social psychologists, anthropologists, and sociologists have studied in great depth since the 1930s. Tolerance, acceptance, and a valuing of the unique worth of every person are teachable and learnable attitudes. A just society must be constantly challenged to find meaningful ways to raise human aspirations, to heal human

hurt, and to help in the task of optimizing every citizen's potential. Education is a vital component to that end. Teachers can incorporate into their lessons an emphasis on acceptance of difference, toleration of and respect for the beliefs of others, and the skills of reasoned debate and dialogue.

We must remain alert to keep our constitutional promises. Although it is not easy to maintain fair opportunity structures in a culturally pluralistic society, we must continually try.

The struggle for optimal representation of minority perspectives in the schools will be a matter of serious concern to educators for the foreseeable future. From the many court decisions upholding the rights of women and cultural minorities in the schools over the past 40 years has emerged a national consensus that we must strive for the greatest degree of equality in education as is possible. The triumph of constitutional law over prejudice and bigotry must continue.

As we look with hope to our future, we seek compassion in the classroom for our respective visions of the world.

Looking Ahead: Challenge Questions

How do you respond to calls for the integration of more multicultural content into school studies?

What do you know about how it feels to be poor? How do you think it would feel in school? How would you respond?

What is multicultural education? To what does the national debate over multiculturalism in the schools relate? What are the issues regarding it?

What is the "canon debate" about?

If you are a female, have you ever felt that you were discriminated against or, at the least, ignored?

If you are a male, have you ever felt that you were being favored?

How can schools address more effectively the issues of gender bias?

How do children learn to be prejudiced? How can they learn tolerance?

What academic freedoms should every teacher and student have?

—F. S.

Challenging the Myths About Multicultural Education

Carl A. Grant

Carl A. Grant is a professor with the College of Education, University of Wisconsin, Madison, and is President of the National Association for Multicultural Education.

Multiculturalism is becoming pervasive in most aspect of our lives because of a significant shift in the sociological paradigm of the United States. This shift has been created by three major forces.

The foremost of these forces is the changing population demographics of our nation. The population of the United States has increased more than 10 percent since 1980: there are now nearly 250 million people living in this country. Forty percent of the increase is due to immigration, mainly from Asia, the Caribbean, and Latin America. In addition, the birth rate of women of color is on the rise. The Population Reference Bureau has projected that by the year 2080 the United States may well be 24 percent Latino, 15 percent African American, and 12 percent Asian American. In other words, within the next 90 years, the white population may become a "minority."

The face of the workforce is also changing. The ethnic breakdown of the workforce in 1988 was: 41 percent native white males; 33 percent native white females; 10 percent native males of color; 9 percent native females of color; 4 percent immigrant males; and 3 percent immigrant females. The projections for workers entering the workforce between 1989 and 2000 are: 28 percent native white females; 21 percent native females of color; 21 percent native males of color; 12 percent immigrant males;

9 percent immigrant females; and 9 percent native white males (National Association of State Boards of Education, 1993).

Finally, our national ethic is changing from "individual" centeredness to the acceptance and affirmation of both groups and individuals. The rugged hard-working individual since colonial times has been portrayed as the hero and the contibutor to this country. The 1960s witnessed the rise and identification with groups—*e.g.*, ethnic/racial, women, lesbian and gay, physically challenged, and the poor. All of these groups demanded fairness and justice within and throughout all of society's formal and informal structures.

With the increasing pervasiveness of multicultural education have come myths, especially about what it is and what isn't. These myths often serve to impede or halt the progress of multicultural education. Consequently, important to challenging and correcting these myths is first providing a definition of multicultural education that can frame and provide a context for espousing these myths.

Definition of Multicultural Education

Multicultural education is a philosophical concept and an educational process. It is a concept built upon the philosophical ideals of freedom, justice, equality, equity, and human dignity that are contained in United States documents such as the Constitution and the Declaration of Independence. It recognizes, however, that equality and equity are not the same thing: equal access does not necessarily guarantee fairness.

Multicultural education is a process that takes place in schools and other edu-

cational institutions and informs all academic disciplines and others aspects of the curriculum. It prepares all students to work actively toward structural equality in the organizations and institutions of the United States. It helps students to develop positive self-concepts and to discover who they are, particularly in terms of their multiple group memberships. Multicultural education does this by providing knowledge about the history, culture, and contributions of the diverse groups that have shaped the history, politics, and culture of the United States.

Multicultural education acknowledges that the strength and richness of the United States lies in its human diversity. It demands a school staff that is multiracial and multiculturally literate, and that includes staff members who are fluent in more than one language. It demands a curriculum that organizes concepts and content around the contributions, perspectives, and experiences of the myriad of groups that are part of United States society. It confronts and seeks to bring about change of current social issues involving race, ethnicity, socioeconomic class, gender, and disability. It accomplishes this by providing instruction in a context that students are familiar with, and builds upon students' diverse learning styles. It teaches critical-thinking skills, as well as democratic decision making, social action, and empowerment skills. Finally, multicultural education is a total process; it cannot be truncated: all components of its definition must be in place in order for multicultural education to be genuine and viable.

This definition, I believe, encapsulates the articulated and published ideas and beliefs of many multicultural schol-

From *Multicultural Education*, Winter 1994, pp. 4-9. © 1994 by the National Association for Multicultural Education. Reprinted by permission.

ars, and is not far removed from what many other multiculturalists believe multicultural education to be.

Six Myths About Multicultural Education

There are numerous myths about multicultural education. The ones that are most frequently voiced are:

(1) It is both divisive and so conceptually weak that it does little to eliminate structural inequalities;

(2) It is unnecessary because the United States is a melting pot;

(3) Multiculturalism—and by extension multicultural education—and political correctness are the same thing;

(4) Multicultural education rejects the notion of a common culture;

(5) Multicultural education is a "minority thing;" and

(6) Multicultural education will impede learning the basic skills. These six myths will be the focus of my discussion.

Myth 1:
Multicultural education is divisive, and/or multicultural education is a weak educational concept that does not attempt to eliminate structural inequalities.

As multicultural education has grown as a philosophy and a practice, critics representing both radical and conservatives ideologies have opposed it.

Radical critics argue that multicultural education emphasizes individual choice over collective solidarity (Olneck, 1990); that it neglects to critique systems of oppression like race or class (Mattai, 1992) and structural inequalities; that it emphasizes "culture" over "race" (Jan Mohamed & Lloyd, 1987). Radical critics also argue that multicultural education's major purpose is to advocate prejudice reduction as a solution to inequality. Therefore, they argue, its purpose is naive and misdirected.

Conservative critics of multicultural education argue that the United States has always been "multicultural" so there is, in fact, no controversy. Ravitch (1990) writes, "The real issue on campus and in the classroom is not whether there will be multiculturalism, but what kind of multiculturalism will there be" (p. A44). Ravitch is against "particularism," *i.e.*, multicultural education that is defined as African American-centric, Arab American-centric, Latino-centric, and/or gender-centric.

Similarly, E. D. Hirsch (1987) believes that there is value in multicultural education because it "inoculates tolerance and provides a perspective on our own tradi-

tions and values." However, he adds, "It should not be allowed to supplant or interfere with our schools' responsibility to insure our children's mastery of American literate culture" (p. 18).

Although these conservative critics believe in multicultural education, their vision of multicultual education is one that adheres to traditional Western thought and ideology and seeks to perpetuate institutions as they presently exist.

Also, since many conservative critics believe that there is already adequate attention given to race, class, and gender in American life, they have harsh criticisms for proponents of multicultual education. They argue that multicultural education is a movement by a "cult" (Siegel, 1991), or it is ideas from former radical protesters of the 1960s (D'Souza, 1991). Further, these conservative critics argue that multi-cultural education is divisive (Balch, 1992; D'Souza, 1991), and that too much attention is given to race and ethnicity. The multicultural education now being proposed, they argue, will "disunite America" (Schlesinger, 1991) and lead to "balkanization" or "tribalism."

Both radical and conservative critics of multicultural education often leave their research skills, scholarship, and willingness to conduct a thorough review of the educational literature at the academy door. Most radical critiques of multicultural education seem to be written after reading (not studying) a few limited selections from the multicultural literature. For example, some (*e.g.*, Olneck, 1990) claim that dominant versions of multicultural education are divorced from sociopolitical interests, and that multicultural scholars see ethnic conflict as the result of negative attitudes and ignorance about manifestations of difference, which can be resolved by cultivating empathy, appreciation, and understanding.

It is for certain that these critics have not examined the work of Nieto (1992), Banks (1991), Banks and Banks (1989), Gay (1986), Gollnick and Chinn (1994), Grant (1988), Sleeter and Grant (1988) and Sleeter (1993). These authors point out that people of color, women, the disabled, and the poor are oppressed by racism, sexism, and classism, and that one goal of multicultural education is to empower students so that they may have the courage, knowledge, and wisdom to control their life circumstances and transform society.

Some of the radical scholars (*e.g.* McCarthy, 1990a) mainly quote from earlier publications on multicultural education, ignoring the context of time in which these publications were written, ignoring the conceptual evolution of multicultural

education, and ignoring the more recent essays on multicultural education. Also, these critics seem to read what they wish into the writings on multicultural education. For example, McCarthy (1990b) compares the argument put forth in Sleeter and Grant's (1989) "Education That Is Multicultural and Social Reconstructionist" approach to one of crosscultural competence for enhancing minority negotiation with mainstream society (p.49). This is difficult to understand, because a good deal of this approach is concerned with providing students with strategies for social action and developing self-empowerment (Sleeter & Grant, 1988, p. 201).

These misinterpretations of multicultual education by radical and conservative critics lead to continuous controversy, and undercut the influence that multicultural education can have on society. Paul Robeson Jr. (1993) tells us:

> The controversy over multiculturalism is not, as many claim, merely a manifestation of the politics of race and gender; rather, it is at the heart of a profound ideological struggle over the values of American culture and the nature of U. S. civilization. Above all it is a debate about whether the melting-pot culture, which is the foundation of the American way of life and imposes its Anglo-Saxon Protestant values on our society, should be replaced by a mosaic culture incorporating the values of the diverse groups that make up America's population. (p.1)

This statement by Robeson provides an excellent response to the conservative critics, but I believe the radical critics have somewhat of a different problem. Their problem is one of a need to understand that many multicultural educators are not simply interested in an education that will lead to the assimilation of student into society as it presently exists. Many multicultural educators are interested in changing the knowledge and power equation so that race, class, and gender groups that have previously been marginalized have equity and equality in all the structures of society.

Myth 2:
The United States is a Melting Pot for all U.S. citizens.

An increasing number of people are coming to the realization that the United States never was a melting pot. The argument they put forth is that people of color have not been able to "melt," and other groups, such as women, the physically challenged, lesbians and gay men, and the poor, have not been fully accepted into the mainstream of American society. Many realities—the glass ceiling in corporate America that prevents women and people of color from reaching top leadership positions; inequities in pay between men and women and between people of color and white people; the lockout of women, people of color, and the poor from much of the political system; and the increasing slide of the United States into a two-class society of "haves and have nots"—invalidate the melting pot thesis.

Robeson explains that the melting-pot is based upon the denial of group rights and a one-sided emphasis on "radical individualism," whereas the mosaic culture affirms group rights along with individual rights and emphasizes a balance between individual liberty and individual responsibility to the community. Robeson further adds:

> This difference underlies the conflicts between the melting pot and the mosaic over the issue of race, ethnicity, gender, and class, since the melting pot has traditionally used the denial of group rights to subordinate non Anglo-Saxon White ethnic groups, non-White, White women, and those who do not own property (*i.e.*, people who do not belong to the middle or upper class). (p.3)

Myth 3:
Multicultural Education and Political Correctness are the same thing.

Multicultural education is not a synonym for "political correctness." Many, educators and other members of society unknowingly connect Political Correctness to multicultural education. Hughes (1993) states:

> Much mud has been stirred up by the linkage of multiculturalism with political correctness. This has turned what ought to be a generous recognition of cultural diversity into a worthless symbolic program, clogged with lumped-radical jargon. Its offshoot is the rhetoric of cultural separatism. (p.83)

Political correctness, it is argued, is about doing the proper thing. Hughes (1993) also, says it is "political etiquette." Some conservative critics argue that political correctness is about speech repression. For example, penalizing students for using certain words on campus, that they would not be penalized for if they used these same words off campus. Cortes (1991), an observer of social history, explains:

> ...some campuses have instituted ill-conceived speech codes that have reached ludicrous extremes of attempting to micro-manage the "unacceptable." Such action have had the

unfortunate side effect of trivializing the critical issue of continuing campus bigotry, while at the same time casting a pall on the entire higher educational struggle against prejudice and for multicultural understanding.... (p.13)

Repressing the use of speech, or limiting the books that make up the "canon," leads many—especially those who are opposed to multicultural education, or who are unsure about its meaning—to view multicultural education and political correctness as one in the same. An example may help to illuminate this point.

I was recently told that many P. C. advocates would probably ban or discourage the reading of *Huckleberry Finn*. I was then asked what would I, an advocate of multicultural education, do about the use of this American classic in schools. My reply was that *Huckleberry Finn*, or *Tom Sawyer,* can be read but in so doing needs to be read in a "context." By context, I mean the teacher leading the discussion should have experience teaching from a multicultural perspective. This would include having introduced the students (before the reading of *Huckleberry Finn*) to a variety of literature, some of which features African Americans as heroes and heroines; some of which has explained the historical meaning of words and terms; some of which included a rounded view of other ethnic groups, including whites. I would also add that the sequencing of *Huckleberry Finn* is important. It may not be wise to have it as the first book the class reads. It should be read after a positive climate is established, and students have developed an attitude of sensitivity and respect for each other within groups and across groups.

Garcia and Pugh (1992) claim that "political correctness" serves the purpose of defining a political and intellectual perspective as an aberrant ideology and then attacking it as indoctrination" (p. 216). When multicultural education is reduced to P. C., Garcia and Pugh (1992) argue, "[it] undercuts the validity of pluralism as a universally shared experience," and I would add it minimizes the importance of women, the poor, the physically challenged, and lesbians and gay men.

Myth 4:
Multicultural Education Reject a Common Culture.

Multicultural education offers a way to achieve the **common** culture that doesn't presently exist. We all are aware that the United States is a land of many people, most of whose foreparents came from other countries, bringing different languages, customs, and religious beliefs. We are also aware that the United States' strength

and humanity come from its diverse people. Additionally, we are aware that from this "diversity" it is important that we create a "oneness" or a common culture. Peter Erickson, using the canon as the context for his argument, offers four reasons why multiculturalism is not fraying America, and why it can help us the achieve a common culture.

First, Erickson (1991) argues that traditionalists view the canon as made up of diverse, inconsistent elements, but whole in the sense of being conceived as a single entity. He states, "The basic unit of organization is single authors, however diverse; their diversity is expressed through the framework of a single literary tradition" (p. B2). Multicultural education, on the other hand, supports the acceptance and affirmation of multiple traditions. Erickson writes, "In a multicultural approach, the basic organizational component is not individual authors, but multiple traditions. Diversity is thus placed on a different conceptual foundation. This foundation implies that each minority tradition is a distinct cultural entity that cannot be dissolved into an overarching common tradition through the catalytic action of adding one or two minority authors to the established canon."

Second, multicultural education expands the idea of what constitutes "valid criticism." Criticism is not confined to the rules laid out by established classical authors. Erickson argues:

> Multicultural criticism...recognizes the possibility of a sharp criticism of Shakespeare that cuts through the mantle of his established position. Such criticism does not seek to eject Shakespeare from the canon, but proposes that Shakespeare no longer be viewed as an inviolable fixture. (p.B2)

Third, multiculturalists do not reject the idea of a common culture, as many opponents of multicultural education claim. Instead, "it [multiculturalism] opposes the traditionalist way of constructing a common culture through over-simplified appeals to a common heritage achieved by applying the principles of universalism and transcendence to peoples's differences" (p. B2). Erickson argues that for the multiculturalists, "common culture is not a given: it has to be created anew by engaging the cultural differences that are part of American Life" (p. B2).

Fourth, the common reader for the multiculturalist is shaped by "identity politics." In other words, the identity of the reader(s) needs to be taken into account if we are to understand the culture we hold in common. Similarly, race, class, and gender are active factors that must be acknowledged and deemed important to understanding and interpretations.

Myth 5:
Multicultural education is a "minority thing"

Many teachers and teacher educators see multicultural education as a "minority thing." They see it as mainly related to the school experiences of people of color. It is seen as an educational plan to help enhance the self-concept of students of color, especially African-American and Hispanic students, who many educators believe come

to school with a negative self-image. Also, it is viewed as an educational plan to help manage the behavior of these same students. Additionally, it is regarded as a curriculum innovation that seeks to include the culture and history of underrepresented groups in the American experience.

Conversely, multicultural education is not seen as important and necessary for whites. One reason for this is that many whites see the focus of multicultural as mainly race, and "race" is perceived nar-

rowly as a "black or brown" problem—a problem that black and brown people need to overcome (Omi &Howard, 1986). Often forgotten is the United States' history of slavery and discrimination and the need for whites to understand how they contribute to everyday racism (Essed, 1990). Although the social science literature is replete with arguments that "race" (and racism) is very much the white man's problem, and that its evilness works against **all** of United States' society (Myrdal, 1944; Report of the National Advisory Commis-

References and Resources

Balch, S. A. (Winter, 1992). Political correctness or public choice? *Educational Record*, 21-24.

Banks, J. A. (1991). Teaching strategies for ethnic studies (5th ed.) Boston, MA: Allyn & Bacon.

Banks J. A. & Banks C. A. M. (1989). (Eds.) *Multicultural education: Issues and perspectives*. Boston: Allyn & Bacon.

Brossard, C. A. (1994). Why do we avoid class in this sig? Why do we fail to integrate two or more topics across race, class, and gender, in our paper? "Critical examination of race, ethnicity, class and gender in education." *AERA SIG Newsletter*, 9: 1 (March 1994)

Cortes, C. (September/October, 1991). Pluribus & unum: The quest for community amid diversity. *Change: The Magazine of Higher Learning*. 8-13.

D'Souza, D. (1991). *Illiberal education: The politics of race and sex on campus*. New York: The Free Press.

Erickson, P. (June 26, 1991). Rather than reject a common culture, multiculturalism advocates a more complicated route by which to achieve it. *The Chronicle of Higher Education*. 37 (41). B1-B3.

Hirsh, E. D. (1987). *Cultural literacy*. New York: Houghton Mifflin p.18.

Essed, P. (1990). *Everyday racism*. Claremont, CA: Hunter House.

Fennema, E. & Franke, M. L. (1992). Teachers' knowledge and its impact. In D. A. Grouws (Ed.) *Handbook of research on mathematics teaching and learning*. New York: Macmillian.

Gay, G. (Winter, 1986). Another side of the educational apocalypse: Educating for being. *Journal of Educational Equity and Leadership*. 6 (4). 260-273.

Gay, G. (1990). "Achieving educational equality through curriculum desegregation," *Phi Delta Kappan*, 72(1).

Gollnick D. M. & Chinn, P. C. (1994). *Multicultural education in a pluralistic society* (4th ed.) New York: Merrill/Macmillan.

Gracia, J. & Pugh, S. L. (1992). Multicultural education in teacher preparation Programs: A political or an educational concept. *Phi Delta Kappan* 75 (3) 214-219.

Grant, C. A. (1977). *Multicultural education: Commitments, issues, and applications*. Association for Supervision and Curriculum Devlepment: Washington, D. C.

Grant, C. A. (1988). The persistent significance of race in schooling. *The Elementary School Journal*. 88 (5). 561-569.

Grant, C. A. & Sleeter, C. E. (1986). Race, class, and gender in education research: an arguement for integrative analysis. *Review of Educational Research*. 56: 2, summer.

Hughes, R. (1993). *Culture of complaint the fraying of America*. New York: Oxford University Press.

JanMohamed, A. & Lloyd, D. (1987). Introduction: Toward a theory of minority discourse. *Cultural Critique* 6, 5-12.

Mattai, P. R. (1992). Rethinking multicultural education: Has it lost its focus or is it being misused? *Journal of Negro Education* 61 (1), 65-77.

McCarthy, C. (1990a).Race and Education in the united states: The multicultural solution. *Interchange*, 21 (3) 45-55.

McCarthy, C. (1990b). *Race and curriculum*. London: Falmer.

National Association of State Boards of Education (1993). *The american tapestry educating a nation*. Alexandria, Va.: The National Association of State Boards of Education.

Miel, A. (1967). The shortchanged children of suburbia. Institute of Human Relations Press, The America Jewish Committee. New York: Institute of Human Relations Press.

Myrdal, G. (1944) *An american dilemma*. New York: Harper and Brothers.

Nieto, S. (1992). *Affirming diversity*. New York: Longman.

Olneck, M. (1990). The recurring dream: Symbolism and ideology in intercultural and multicultural education. *American Journal of Education* 98 (2), 147-174.

Omi, M. & Winanat, H. (1986). *Racial formation in the United states: From the 1960s to the 1980s*. New York: Routledge.

Ravich, D. (1990). Multiculturalism yes, particularism no. *The Chronicle of Higher Education*, October 24, 1990, p. A44.

Ringer, B. B. & Lawless, E. R. (1989). *Race, ethnicity, and society*. London, England: Routledge.

Robeson, P., Jr. (1993). Paul robeson, jr. speaks to america. New Brunswick, NJ: Rutgers University Press.

Schlesinger, A. Jr. (1991). *The disuniting of america*. Whittle Direct Books.

Siegel, F. (Feb. 18, 1991). The cult of multiculturalism. *The New Republic*.

Sleeter, C. E. (1992). *Keepers of the american dream: A study of staff development and multicultural education*. London, England: The Falmer Press.

Sleeter, C. E. & Grant, C. A. (1988). *Making choices for multicultural education*. New York: Merrill.

Suzuki, B. (1979). Multicultural education: What's it all about? *Integrated Education*.

Tocqueville, A. de (1969) Democracy in america. Garden City, NY: Doubleday and Co.

Trueba, H. T. (1991). Learning needs of minority children: Contributions of ethnography to educational research. In L. M. Malave & G. Duquette (Eds.), *Language, culture & cognition*. Clevedon, England: Multilingual Matters Ltd.

U. S. National Advisory Commission on Civil Disorders Report (1968). New York: Bantam Books.

sion on Civil Disorders, 1968; Tocqueville 1969), this point is too often ignored (Omi & Winant, 1986; Ringer & Lawless, 1989).

Also ignored when race is seen as the only foundational pillar of multicultural education is the attention scholars of multicultural education gave to discussing socioeconomic class issues (*e.g.*, control of wealth in society, discussion of the causes of poverty and homelessness), gender (*e.g.*, the gender-based glass ceiling in corporate America, treatment of girls in math and science class), disability (*e.g.*, the isolation or absence of the physically challenged in the classroom and at school events).

Additionally, when multicultural education is seen as only a "minority thing" whites are mis-educated. They are inclined to develop ethnocentric and prejudicial attitudes toward people of color when they are deprived of the opportunity to learn about the sociocultural, economic, and psychological factors that produce conditions of ethnic polarization, racial unrest, and hate crimes. As a result, they do not understand their responsibility to participate in eliminating the "isms" (Miel, 1967; Suzuke, 1979).

Further, when multicultural education is seen as a minority thing, the importance of analyzing the impact of race, class, and gender interactions which are important to multicultural education research is ignored or understated. For example, Grant and Sleeter (1986) reported that studies of cooperative learning that mainly paid attention to one status group (race) oversimplified the behavior analysis, and this oversimplification could contribute to perpetuation of gender and class basis. Similarly, (Bossard, 1994) discusses the importance of studying the interaction effects of race, class, and gender over time in order to understand and break down the negative institutionalized patterns of social life in school.

Myth 6:
Multicultural education will impede the teaching of the basics and preparation of students to live in a global technological society.

Learning the basics and being able to apply them to real life situations is essential to any quality educational program, and the purpose of multicultural education is to provide a high quality educational program for all students. Multicultural education includes curriculum and instructional approaches that place learning in a context that challenges students, while at the same time allowing them to have some familiarity with the learning context and the purpose for learning the content being taught (Gay, 1990; Trueba, 1991).

Much of the early multicultural curriculum in the 1970s and the early 1980s dealt with how to help teachers include or integrate multicultural education into the subject matter they teach daily. Reading and social studies especially received multicultural attention (Banks, 1979: Grant, 1977). More recently, beginning in the late 1980s, materials have been readily available to help teachers understand how to make their science and mathematics relate to their students' thinking and conceptual understanding (*e.g.*, Grant & Sleeter, 1989; Fennema and Franke, 1992)

The integration of multicultural education throughout the entire curriculum and instructional process is advocated to encourage students to learn the basics, understand that mathematics and science are tools that they can command, and that what they learn should give them greater control of their destiny.

Also important to multicultural education is developing the ability to listen to, appreciate, and critique different voices and stories. Development of these abilities, along with gaining an appreciation for differences, is essential to being able to successful live in the 21st century. Hughes (1993) reminds us:

> The future of America, in a globalized economy without a Cold War, will lie with people who can think and act with informed grace across ethnic, cultural, linguistic lines. (p.26)

Finally, it is clear that multicultural education is being challenged, but we should not be dismayed or discouraged by this challenge. Just a few years ago, only a few people were seriously discussing multicultural education or paying attention to its potential and possibilities. Positive circumstances and events for multicultural education are happening all across the United States. For example, the State of Maryland has recently passed a law for education in the State entitled "Education That Is Multicultural."

Finally, it is important to remember the words of Frederick Douglass:

> If there is no struggle, there is no progress. Those who profess to favor freedom, and yet deprecate agitation, are men who want crops without plowing up the ground. They want rain without thunder and lighting. They want the ocean without the awful roar of its many waters. This struggle may be a moral one; or it may be both moral and physical; but it must be a struggle. Power concedes nothing without a demand.

TIME TO SEE, TELL AND DO ABOUT BIGOTRY AND RACISM

Incidents of bigotry and racism are occurring at an alarming rate on our college campuses. The author suggests that these incidents are but surface manifestations of commonly held and well dispersed thoughts and feelings. Individuals are encouraged to heed the warning and to forcefully respond, if overwhelming crisis is to be avoided.

MICHAEL L. FISCHLER

Professor of Education and Director, Counseling & Human Relations Center, Plymouth State College of the University System of New Hampshire, Plymouth, NH 03264

Personal

Three horny men looking to tag-team young afro-american virgin...X5950, X7041, X5912

Three campus editors placed this ad in the personal section of their small town New England college newspaper. The reaction they got was mixed. A few people laughed. A few more searched for a "politically correct" response. A few less were frightened. More than a few were angry. Most just didn't care. The three editors claimed that the ad resulted from "late night 'pre-deadline' fatigue" and a "poor attempt at humor". They were put on probation, apologized, forced to "bleed" appropriately, assured the community that they had learned from their misdeed, then dutifully returned to their editorial responsibilities.

The story doesn't end there...Zen teaches us that crisis is almost always accompanied by opportunity. The personal did provide members of the campus community with an opportunity to more seriously consider the presence of racism and bigotry. Toward that end, students in my "multicultural education" class kept a "journal" and dutifully recorded day-to-day incidents involving racism and bigotry. Here is a sample of what they found:

"I'm loading out on my couch in front of the t.v. watching college football with a couple of fraternity brothers. I really get into college games and get vocal about it. Although I swear at players, I rarely involve their nationality. one of my buddies yells at the t.v., 'you dumb coon,

you couldn't catch AIDS if it was injected into you' (meaning he dropped the ball every time).

"When Channel 9 broadcasted the statement written in the campus paper, a snide remark was made from one of my friends: 'what's the problem? black bitches would love to get f--- by a white guy. Black chicks love it anyway they can get it."

In regard to an AIDS presentation on television: "Why don't we just take all the faggots and put them on a desert island somewhere and let them rot."

"My roommates call me a Jew because I don't spend money as freely as they do. It bothers me, but I don't really listen to them. I pay for everything at school whereas their parents are sending them money every week. I work so I can survive here so I don't just go out and blow my money. I am not tight at all. I just watch what I spend money on."

"I visited my girlfriend at...College with two of my friends, one black kid and one white kid. There was a fire alarm that was pulled and the security guard immediately blamed the black kid. When we walked out I distinctly saw the security guard bump into my black friend. We all got pissed off and they escorted us off campus."

"While talking with my friend about the infamous newspaper ad, my friend said, 'Why not, they always take out women."

"I heard a group of girls talking as I walked by... 'I want to scoop a black guy tonight, I hear they are better in bed'."

"While walking home after class a nice looking black female walks by. I heard two guys say, 'Look at that nigger girl'. I was shocked and felt bad for the girl even though she did not hear them."

"Those blacks are fine when they're alone. Then they seem real laid back, but when they get into a group they go crazy."

"My roommate asked if we knew why blacks don't play hockey. He then proceeded to tell us that genetically they have weak ankles and can't skate. After we all laughed we asked him where he got the information. He told us that he read it and left the room feeling uncomfortable."

It's apparent that the three misguided "editors" have no corner on racism or bigotry. For one ugly moment they held up a mirror which reflected not so much their own visage, but that of society's. They were the mailmen. They just delivered society's mail. What is striking is not only the presence of racism and bigotry, but that it's commonplace, and it is generally accepted. Bigoted language appears to be a normal part of everyday speech. It is shared openly and without anxiety. Few appear to be *aware* that anything's wrong.

For the bigot as well as the victim of bigotry, personal growth must begin with awareness. The event which creates the awareness is irrelevant. A "personal ad"...a racially motivated attack...interracial love. Events merely present starting points...opportunities for growth. Yet history is replete with starting points that become ending points...growth opportunities that become lost opportunities.

As citizens we must realize that bigoted/racist attitudes and behaviors are not only commonplace, they are firmly in place. They are prevalent on first choice and last choice college campuses. They are found in uptown shops and downtown bistros. They can be observed in homes that are blessed by the sounds of laughter, as well as those that are violated by the sounds of sirens. These attitudes and behaviors are steadfastly pushing our nation toward crisis. The question remains whether individuals will choose to recognize the dysphoria which surrounds them and respond appropriately, or whether the experiencing of overwhelming crisis will be a necessary ingredient in the development of a more profound level of consciousness and caring. One would hope that crisis, with all its accompanying pain and trauma could be avoided. Yet if crisis is to be avoided, both awareness and concerted action is necessary, and it is necessary now!

Direction for an effective response can be found in the well worn advice that concerned parents offer their beloved children as they venture off into a foreboding world:

See...*what is truly there. Your life may depend on it.*

Tell...*others when something is wrong. Do so quickly. Don't wait for a crisis.*

Do...*whatever is necessary to protect yourself...Be careful because we love you.*

It is time to embrace the wisdom of the concerned parent that lies deep within each of us. It is time to **see** clearly the ignorance, racism and bigotry that surrounds us, and that works relentlessly toward diminishing the quality of our lives. It is time to **tell** others what we see, and to do so quickly, struggling to avoid the emerging crisis. It is time to **do** not only what is the "necessary thing," but more importantly what is the "right thing". All of this is essential because we, as individuals and as a society need love far more than we need hate, intimacy far more than we need estrangement, and healing far more than we need hostility. It is time for each of us to leave the safety of the sidelines, and to resolutely step forward onto the field of emerging hopes and struggling dreams. It is time to **see**. It is time to **tell**. It is time to **do**.

TURNING POINTS REVISITED:
a new deal for adolescents

FRED M. HECHINGER

When public schools for young adolescents were created in the first decade of the twentieth century, it seemed a giant step forward: the American education establishment recognized that the onset of puberty affects youngsters' bodies and minds, the ways they think and behave. They seek greater independence from adults; they test the limits of adult authority; they explore; they argue; they challenge rules. They also need adult guidance—sometimes gentle, sometimes firm, but always understanding.

This, educators realized, called for a special educational response—one that would organize teaching differently from the elementary school, where typically one teacher was responsible for everything children were expected to learn, and that would also be distinct from the rather impersonal high school ruled through its academic departments. The junior high school was born.

In practice, junior high turned out to be *too* different from the elementary school and not different enough from the high school. It was unlike the nurturing elementary school and more like high school, where students moved from class to class, from subject to subject, from teacher to teacher. Straying from its original purpose, the junior high school often ignored children's personal academic and developmental strengths and problems. Many of its teachers were not trained to deal with young volatile adolescents.

In 1960, James Bryant Conant, former president of Harvard University, in his book, *Education in the Junior High School Years,* sharply criticized those flaws and called for new schools designed to respond to young adolescents' needs.

"In many ways," David A. Hamburg, president of Carnegie Corporation of New York, noted in *Today's Children: Creating a Future for a Generation in Crisis,* "[young adolescents] resemble a larger version of toddlers — having the newly acquired capacity for getting into all sorts of novel and risky situations, but all too little judgment and information on which to base decisions about how to handle themselves. Historically much of their information and world view was shaped by the nuclear and extended family: parents, older siblings, older peers, and various other relatives. Today, adolescents' information comes largely from the media and unrelated peers, and much of it clashes with parental expectations."

Nancie Atwell, a former eighth- grade English teacher who heads the Center for Teaching and Learning in Maine, wrote in her book, *In the Middle: Writing, Reading, and Learning with Adolescents,* "When I listen to my junior high students, their message to me is, 'We're willing to learn. We like to find out about things we didn't know before. But make it make sense. Let us learn together. And be involved and excited so that we can be involved and

excited.' When I hear educators talk about junior high, I hear a different message. I'm told to keep the lid on . . . and prepare my students for high school."

Clearly, the schools owed adolescents a new deal.

The Birth of Turning Points

In 1989, under the auspices of the Carnegie Council on Adolescent Development, the Task Force on Education of Young Adolescents produced *Turning Points: Preparing American Youth for the 21st Century.* The report describes the middle grade schools as "potentially society's most powerful force to recapture millions of youth adrift, and help every young person thrive. . . ." It urges restructuring of the middle grades as an antidote to the traditional junior high schools' forbidding size and cold impersonality; establishment of a trusted relationship between each young adolescent and a teacher or other adult; a forging of links between school and life, school and family, and school and community; and support of the intellectual, physical, mental, and emotional well-being of the whole child.

The prescriptions of *Turning Points* were aimed at freeing the middle grades from domination by the high schools and directing their full attention to the education and nurture of young adoles-

From *Carnegie Quarterly,* Spring 1993, pp. 1-5, 8-15. Reprinted by permission of the Carnegie Corporation of New York, 437 Madison Avenue, New York, NY 10022.

cents. They deal with the total school environment in which teenagers live and learn. They pay attention to the impact of adolescents' health on their intellectual capacity.

One important theme stressed in *Turning Points* is the intimate linkage of education and health. Explains Hamburg, "Children in poor health have dif-

> ## PREVENTIVE INTERVENTION
>
> "Before damaging behaviors are firmly established, there is an exceptional opportunity for preventive intervention to diminish later casualties in education and health."

ficulty learning. . . . Before damaging behaviors are firmly established, there is an exceptional opportunity for preventive intervention to diminish later casualties in education and health."

Turning Points recognizes the importance of youngsters' relationship with their teachers, who represent the adult world to them. It holds teachers responsible for more than the transmission of knowledge. "Our teachers are advocates for kids," says Gary Soto, principal of Southridge Middle School, in Fontana, California, one of the schools that has followed the new approach to teaching. Richard Roth, the assistant principal, declares, "You can teach teachers to teach, but you can't teach them to like kids."

Deborah Meier, director of Central Park East Secondary School, in East Harlem, summarizes the need for a student-friendly environment: "Kids need to be known and respected. So, first we created a culture for students."

Turning Points' recommendations for transforming middle grade schools are comprehensive. The report asks schools to:

▸ create small communities for learning . . . . The key elements of these communities are schools-within-schools or houses, with students and teachers grouped together as teams;

▸ teach a core academic program that results in students who are literate, including in the sciences, and who know how to think critically, lead a healthy life, behave ethically, and assume the responsibilities of citizenship in a pluralistic society;

▸ ensure success for all students through the elimination of tracking by achievement level;

▸ staff middle grade schools with teachers who are expert at teaching young adolescents;

▸ improve academic performance through the fostering of health and fitness of young adolescents;

▸ reengage families in the education of young adolescents;

▸ connect schools with communities — which together share responsibility for each middle grade student's success — through identifying service learning opportunities in the community.

Implementing the Recommendations

To follow up on its report, Carnegie Corporation in 1990 created the Middle Grade School State Policy Initiative (MGSSPI). The initiative provided $60,000 in planning grants to each of twenty-seven states, selected from proposals sent by nearly all states. The funds were matched by the recipient states to stimulate systemwide changes in middle grade policy and practice.

In 1991, fifteen of these states received continuation grants of up to $180,000, also matched by state funds.

Anthony W. Jackson, principal author of *Turning Points,* and the Corporation's program officer in charge of the initiative, reports that "states have worked diligently not to mandate reform but to create the conditions for reform at the local level."

MGSSPI does not aim merely at a restructuring of the schools, says Vivien Stewart, chair of Carnegie Corporation's Education and Healthy Development of Children and Youth program. "If the middle grades reform only affects school organization and does not improve what children learn and how they learn, it would not merit the label of true reform. There can be no reform without a focus on the curriculum."

"It was not our firm intention to continue the grant program beyond its first three years," says Hamburg. "But the amount and quality of states' work to restructure middle level education has convinced us that this work is at the vanguard of nationwide educational reform and must continue." In January 1993 the Corporation invited governors of the initially funded twenty-seven states to submit a proposal for a third round of awards of up to $360,000 each.

The proposed changes aim at a school organization that fosters academic achievement while giving all young adolescents the personal support of teams of teachers who know them as pupils, individuals, and members of families and communities.

"Teaming," a crucial part of the reform, is not to be confused with the "team teaching" that was widely recommended in the 1950s, in which two or more teachers taught in one classroom. In the *Turning Points* model, "teaming" means that three, four, or five teachers are jointly responsible for the education of a small, self-contained unit of as many as 150 students, forming a school within a school. Together, the team members plan the curriculum and address the students' academic, social, and emotional development. Under this system, every young teenager has a personal link to at least one of the team members. In the best of all worlds, the team might stay with its students for two or even three years.

As Jackson notes, the success of reforms will depend in large part on the creation of a spirit of cooperation among all parties — teachers, administrators, children and families — in designing a school that functions as a community. The challenge is to return to John Dewey's philosophy of serving "the whole child" — mind, body, and emotions — and to view the school itself as a democratic society in microcosm.

Moving in that direction is not easy in an institution that traditionally functions as a hierarchy in which the children are at the bottom of the pyramid. It is made even more difficult by the fact that few of those who deal with middle school children have been trained to understand, and develop a rapport with, young adolescents. Peter Scales, director of national initiatives at the Center for Early Adolescence, reports that only 17 percent of those who teach in the middle grades have had any special preparation for their task. Many did not intend to teach at that level, and almost one-third feel they are poorly prepared for such strategies as cooperative learning (children working together in groups); teaming by three or more teachers; heterogeneous grouping of children of different abilities learning together in the same classroom rather than in separate tracks; and communication with families and local communities.

Yet, Robert Felner, director of the Center for Prevention Research and Development at the University of Illinois and senior investigator of the evaluation of the Association of Illinois Middle Schools statewide reform initiative, reports that teachers in schools that are implementing the recommendations of *Turning Points* enjoy their work more and are more involved with their schools' decision making.

Students, too, are positive about the changes. Their scores on achievement tests are higher. They are less likely to be anxious and depressed. And there is less disruptive classroom behavior.

A Look at the Schools

The full story of change and improvement can best be told by what is happening in schools that are part of the Middle Grade School State Policy Initiative. A look at individual "lead" schools of the reform effort suggests how the new approaches affect what happens in classrooms, how far the

reforms have gone, what supports them or stands in their way, and how much is yet to be done.

Planning and preparation are crucial. Shereene Wilkerson, principal of Willis Jepson Middle School in Vacaville, California, not far from Sacramento, puts it simply: "The first year of teaming is like dating: Teachers worry that when they become part of an interdisciplinary team they will betray their subject. They have to discover the connecting points — if the kids are reading history, you are really an English teacher, too."

Principal Wilkerson, a tall, articulate woman who, earlier in her career, did a stint as a police officer, is a realist. She knows that some of the youngsters are gang members and that there is alcohol and illegal drug abuse. Fewer than half of the students are growing up with their biological parents.

Joy Swank, one of the early converts to teaming at Jepson, says: "I was practically lynched when I proposed it. Some of us didn't even like each other. But now, it's so much better. We talk about children's problems. I'm a kinder, gentler teacher now."

Jepson, a school of 880 seventh and eighth graders — 75 percent white — has divided the seventh grade into teams of about 160 students, each with four or five teachers, typically representing social studies, English, science and mathematics, and health.

Nukhet Anders, a former high school teacher, said of her new position at Jepson Middle School: "This is the last chance we can affect children's lives. Not only must we be good teachers in our respective disciplines, but we must also create a climate of 'an extended family' for our kids."

Early results from the experiment show that test scores have improved and the school's atmosphere has changed.

The Personal Touch

On a Wednesday morning at Baltimore's Canton Middle School, the Primary Assessment Committee is in session, as it is every Wednesday. Members are the school nurse, guidance counselor, a

mental health therapist, a school social worker, some teaching team members, the committee coordinator, and representatives of Baltimore's departments of juvenile and social services.

The committee deals with many of the students' problems — getting eyeglasses, hearing aids, and dental care, arranging counseling for emotional problems, providing medical care or family planning advice, finding the proper after-school program or vocational training.

On that recent Wednesday, the group was taking up referral forms from teachers about youngsters in need of help who are identified only by number.

"She'll do anything to get attention," begins the report on one twelve-year-old sixth grader. "She came in with a woman she said was her mother, but it turned out she had merely appealed to her on the street and persuaded her to come to school with her." The nurse said she would talk to the girl who had never come to the nearby school-related clinic. With a 3.8 grade average, the youngster's problems clearly were emotional rather than academic.

Often the group discovers serious past neglect. A sixth-grade boy failed a vision test administered in second grade, but there was no follow-up to help him. Now the health services affiliated with Canton will provide the remedy.

A little girl has complained of having terrifying nightmares that betray a fear of death and sexual molestation. Her parents have denied all knowledge of their child's problems, labeling her behavior as merely melodramatic. The school will try to persuade the parents that either they or the school must deal with the child's problems.

A sixth-grade boy has been eating dirt he scraped from the floor. At one point he wrapped an extension cord around his neck and held up a sign that said: "Help me."

Craig Spilman, the principal, urges: "Don't shut out that valuable resource [the teacher]. Get a substitute so the teacher who knows the child can take time off to talk with the boy."

"To attack academic problems first, before dealing with emotional and health problems, is putting the cart before the horse," Spilman says.

Students at risk of dropping out are placed into a "four and one" program — four days in school and one day on a job, with regular pay.

"At first, the money was the hook," the principal says. "In the long term, self-esteem becomes the hook."

His philosophy: "School must be a good place for children to come to. When nobody knows them, they get pushed out. Here we say, 'Come, we care about you.'"

Benefits of Continuity

Canton School acts as the coordinating center for the students' academic, physical, and emotional well-being. But, as some of the referrals show, it must still cope with inadequate communication between elementary, middle, and high school. Brunswick Middle School, perhaps because of its location in the relative rural isolation of Brunswick, Maryland, benefits from continuity by being part of a larger complex that links three schools from kindergarten to twelfth grade.

Brunswick serves grades six, seven, and eight. It is part of Community Agency School Services, which coordinates health, mental health, nursing, and police services, paying attention to problems of alcohol and illegal drug abuse, family planning, family conflicts, poverty, and homelessness. Lest students, teachers, or parents forget, a prominent wall chart in the hall spells out the goals of academic achievement and indicates where the school stands in reaching those goals.

But in a region of widespread white poverty, teenage pregnancies, and female-headed households, the availability of school-related health services is as important as the school's stress on academic excellence.

The reasons students need help, says Hal Mosser, the tall athletic principal, range from financial problems and from neglect to the emotional and mental consequences of neglect and abuse. Dealing

ELECTRONIC LINK

Baltimore's Canton Middle School has developed a telecommunications program that allows the school to communicate directly with every student's home. It can instantly inform parents that their child has not come to school or has been late. It allows a science teacher to explain a new program or let an English teacher urge parents to help children with their studies.

In addition, a twenty-four-hour homework hotline lets parents check on their children's assignments. Students who are regular latecomers get a programed wake-up call at six-thirty in the morning.

"Will effective use of this technology forge closer bonds between home and school?" asked Dr. Craig E. Spilman, Canton's principal. "Can something as simple as Alexander Graham Bell's telephone be a cutting-edge tool to improve America's schools? Who knows? But the lines are humming and the phones are ringing. . . ."

with them, he adds, calls for a community program, not just a school program.

"For youngsters who need something special," the principal continues, "we have a 'Different Drummer' program with a one-on-one approach and study groups with similar kids."

He has a word of caution for his colleagues elsewhere: "If you want to empower people, you better actually do it. Get them into making decisions. We discussed whether to get into the Carnegie initiative, and everybody took part in making the decision."

A Team-Created Curriculum

After the teachers in her school in East Harlem were organized into teams, principal Deborah Meier created what she calls "a culture" in which youngsters see adults dealing with ideas. "We formed a committee of adults," she says, "who work collectively to shape the curriculum

and select books and make all this visible to students. Kids become members of a genuine intellectual community."

"We give kids access to knowledgeable adults so that they may want to be like them some day," Meier says. The same teachers deal with the same students for two years.

Marcia Dains is a seventh-grade team member at Arroyo Junior High School. "I did not change the content of what I was teaching," she says, "but I rearranged it." For a curriculum that combines history, science, math, and English, she picked the study of Black Death (the bubonic plague). How did it affect history? The English class read Camus' *The Plague*. The science class discussed diseases. What causes them? What is the nature of new diseases like AIDS? The mathematics teacher interpreted health statistics and graphs.

Such coordination, Dains points out, permits teachers to reinforce each others' curriculum and lets students see the connection between subjects. During the weeks when the Black Death was studied, there were no academic failures

Students were involved with what they learned.

The effect on the teachers: "We are constantly talking with one another. We are reinforcing each others' curriculum."

But Dains warns that "interdisciplinary teaming does not work unless all team members really know their subjects."

Bret Harte Preparatory Intermediate School is located in South Central Los Angeles. Inside the school, the reforms are working well under the firm hand of principal Catherine C. Sumpter, an educator with high expectations of her students and a believer in strict discipline to keep them in line. Decisions are shared through a council that the school set up in 1981 and that in 1989 was included in the teachers' contract.

The present council is composed of seven teachers, an administrator, a clerical staff member, a student government officer, and four parents. It makes decisions on the instructional materials budget, textbooks, discipline, scheduling of events, and staff development.

Teaming at all levels breaks the enrollment of 1,180 sixth, seventh, and eighth graders into manageable units.

Unfortunately, Bret Harte cannot ignore its environment of violence, drugs, vandalism, and gangs. "All our children are at risk," Sumpter says sadly. When she talks of the dress code, the stress is on safety: no earrings for boys, no nose rings for girls.

Gangs try to recruit youngsters on their way to and from school, and the children's lives are in jeopardy whether they let themselves be pressured to join or refuse to join.

The school's heroine and role model is Yvonne Miranda, a petite twenty-six-year-old uniformed police officer, one of two officers assigned to Bret Harte by the Los Angeles Unified School Police Department. Officer Miranda expresses deep concern over the availability and access that kids have to weapons. She has lost more than twenty of her high school friends to violence and guns, she says. She would like to see drug- and gun-free zones around the school. Failing that, she does whatever she can to protect the children, sometimes walking them home if they are in danger.

Safe Haven-Limited

Half a continent from Bret Harte is Henry Suder Middle School in Chicago. In many ways, Suder represents much that is best about the *Turning Points* model. Its grades six, seven, and eight are a School Within a School that also houses preschool, kindergarten, and elementary school classes. What Suder, located just seven minutes west of the Loop, has in common with Bret Harte is an environment of danger. It is in an area that has not yet recovered from the riots of 1968 when much of the neighborhood went up in flames after the assassination of Dr. Martin Luther King.

The enrollment is 100 percent black; 95 percent of the children are entitled to free breakfast and lunch. There is no recess: once the children are in school they stay there for safety reasons.

The children, says one teacher, "teach us when to hit the floor if we hear gun fire from the nearby housing project." When a class of seventh graders is asked who knew somebody who has been killed or seriously injured, every hand goes up.

"We don't want to downplay academics, but there are social issues, too," says principal Brenda B. Daigre, a woman with an easy smile and a hearty laugh.

Visiting a father or relative in jail is part of the children's natural conversation. Kindergarten youngsters talk about drugs and sex. Many have very young mothers, perhaps only twelve years older than themselves, and no fathers in the house.

Daigre, who has been in the school for seventeen years, has had some of the mothers as pupils. She combines warmth with toughness. Her slogan: "No excuses and no exceptions."

Most of the parents, she says, want their children to be successful but don't know what to do about it. And so it becomes the school's task. Teams of teachers responsible for the education of small numbers of children provide the warmth and caring that the outside world denies them.

"We were departmentalized like high schools," Daigre recalls. "Then we brought in *Turning Points* and had everybody read it. We invited parents. We discussed what the school should be like. We had to let the whole school know what we would do."

The key, Daigre says, is to give these children of poverty and chaos a sense of self-esteem. She immerses the school in African and African American traditions and achievements. One unit deals with slavery, combining language arts, social studies, mathematics, and science, and using African American literature from slavery to Martin Luther King. Every year the principal takes ten students on a summer trip to Africa.

Attendance is "fantastic" now, the principal says with pride. "The children are actively learning."

The University of Illinois provides immunization and some health care as well as a twice-a-week guidance counselor. The board of education assigns a nurse and a psychological counselor once a week.

Without question, Suder has risen above the limits posed by the dismal environment. Principal Daigre is pleased with what has been achieved but, like many of her colleagues laboring under similar conditions, she still has a long wish list: more complete social and health services for children and parents; keeping the school open long beyond conventional hours; having a longer school day and year. "The kids lose too much during the long summer vacation," she says. "The school calendar is very inconsistent with what is expected of us."

IS CHARISMA NECESSARY?

To those who say that school reform requires charismatic leadership, especially by principals, David Hornbeck, who chaired the Task Force on Education of Young Adolescents, replies that the charismatic leader who stands out in front may not be the essential ingredient. Leadership, he emphasizes, can be exercised more quietly by those who have clear objectives and are able to share strategies of moving toward them.

Another View of Chicago

At the entrance to the Walter H. Dyett Middle School, there is an oversized drawing of Snoopy. His welcoming words: "Dyett School where the cool go to school." The school's motto: "Catch the Dream."

Dyett is in Chicago's Washington Park section, a nearly all-black community whose population ranges from poor to lower middle class. The spacious, brightly attractive, air-conditioned twenty-year-old school occupies four acres on about ten acres of park. Its 790 sixth, seventh, and eighth graders are divided into groups of about eighty, each instructed in all subjects by a team of three teachers that stays with the same youngsters throughout their three middle school years.

"Send the children to Dyett to have a vision," says an enthusiastic, fast-talking woman who is the school's volunteer community representative. "We create an environment where children want to be."

Stephen Blair, a sixth grader, confirms this. "Dyett is a very good school," he says. Others are not embarrassed to say that they love the principal, Yvonne Minor, a woman of great energy and charm.

Parents are involved in all school committees. Parent-trainers aim, Minor says, "at restoring excellence to black families so they can deal with their children."

The academic program is rigorous. It stresses reading, writing, and critical thinking, along with science and mathematics. The school has a radio studio, a fine arts component, Spanish and French programs, home economics and industrial arts, science and computer labs, and a student newspaper. Clubs include science, math, computer, library, poetry, and stock market.

When the sixth graders arrive, their average reading level is slightly above third grade, the principal says. At the end of the year, their average is fifth grade — still too low but a significant gain.

A California Way

Southridge Middle School in Fontana, California, is less than a two-hour drive from Bret Harte in Los Angeles; it might as well be another country. No thoughts about metal detectors here. The open campus on some forty acres fits the mind's image of California. So does principal Gary Soto — tall, informal, wearing a multicolored shirt.

Southridge is a new community, and the school reflects it. Its 1,200 students in grades six, seven, and eight represent the demography of the town: 46 percent Hispanic, 44 percent Caucasian, and 10 percent African American. Slightly more than one-third are classified as poor.

Modern suburban life faces problems that differ little from those of the cities: many parents commute to work and don't come home until seven o'clock. The youngsters face the usual adolescent risks.

"We don't claim that everything is wonderful," says Soto. "We have problems. But we embrace problems instead of avoiding them."

"Tremendous numbers of kids need help," Soto says. "You have to think they are all at high risk — they could go either way."

He leaves most of the management to the teachers. Units of about 150 to 180 youngsters are under the personal and academic care of a team of four teachers.

Soto takes pride in running a "progressive" school. As a key ingredient of the liberation of education from the traditional ways of judging students' progress, he has introduced three day-long, student-led conferences in November, January, and April, in which the youngsters demonstrate their knowledge before their parents.

"We hand out the traditional report cards at the end of the conference because by that time their importance has faded away," Soto says.

In a sixth-grade science class, groups of about six youngsters discuss their experiments at seven tables. Elsewhere small groups are engaged in learning techniques of conflict resolution. A seventh-grade history class discusses prehistoric art. All classrooms are filled with students' work, flowering plants, and artifacts related to the study at hand.

Every day after school, crews of students clean up the campus.

Attendance is 97 percent. Soto is convinced that the youngsters like being in school. The ultimate vindication, he says, comes when former students who have problems in high school come back to Southridge for help. "I believe that the emphasis of our concern should be with the success of students not only while they are with us but also after they finish school."

A Special Kind of Perfection

Intermediate School 218, more appropriately called Salome Urena Middle Academies, is located in New York's Washington Heights, lately a center for Dominican immigrants who constitute 32 percent of the population. The median annual income of the area is $12,477; 40 percent of the families have incomes below $10,000; 25 percent of the population is under the age of eighteen. The area is not served by any major youth organization. In recent years, it has become notorious for its thriving drug trade and a drug-related urban riot.

By contrast, I.S. 218 is an oasis of cheerful calm, a place where youngsters and, increasingly, their parents and other members of the community want to be and are welcome.

Although not part of Carnegie Corporation's middle grade reform initiative, the school has adopted many of its key recommendations. Special support comes from the Children's Aid Society, a nonprofit organization, which adds about $1,200 to the $5,500 per pupil expenditure provided by the city.

The school has rediscovered what some fifty years ago used to be known in New York as the All-Day Neighborhood School, open from dawn to past dusk and serving, along with the children, the entire community. What so long ago had been a common-sense response to the needs of poor immigrants fell victim to budget cuts and changing educational theories. Now the Children's Aid Society has responded to new realities: poor parents at work throughout the day; children in need of all-day care and safety; adults starved for an introduction to an unfamiliar language and strange customs.

The new institutional label, in New York and elsewhere, is "Community Schools."

I.S. 218 responds to the children's basic needs, starting with a dental office and the ministrations of a nurse practitioner. A community clinic and health care facility offer medical, immunization, nutrition, and other health and counseling services to children and parents.

The school is open from 7:00 a.m. until 10:00 p.m. An after-school program from 3:00 p.m. to 6:00 p.m. offers students a choice of voluntary pursuits of ideas and skills in computers, multimedia and environmental studies, in drama, dance, arts and crafts, music and photography, along with athletics. Tutorial programs provide individual and group study sessions in reading, math, English language, help with homework, and introduction to research skills.

Currently, about 500 of a total enrollment of 1,200 are regularly taking part in after-school activities. After 6:00 p.m., older teenagers are welcomed. To make all this possible, the school has a "night principal."

A bright meeting place with all the comforts of a living room and a constantly brewing coffee pot is open for parents to sit and chat and compare their children's accomplishments. A family resource center offers information and assistance in matters of immigration and naturalization; citizenship courses; employment workshops; housing; crisis intervention; health and parenting. Evening offerings include aerobics classes. A Fathers' Fitness program features basketball, softball, and other sports.

On a recent afternoon, a group of seventh graders was studying entrepreneurship. Each student proudly owns an attaché case-type business bag containing, among other items, a record book, a calculator, and an inexpensive clock. "Being on time is very important in business," one youngster says.

Together, these budding entrepreneurs manage the school's general store, which expects an annual revenue of some $50,000, with the children's "salaries" put into individual accounts for their college education in the future.

Principal Marc Kavarsky, a low-key but determined administrator, provided each of the building's four floors with a theme — math, science, and technology; community service; business studies; and the arts. Each floor, or academy, is subdivided into teams of teachers. Kavarsky has renamed the cafeteria the Dining Room. "We dine in dignity," he says.

One of the signs on the wall reads: "Think for yourself — your friends may be wrong."

"If there's a bad apple," the principal says, "we take the worm out." His aim, he adds, is to put an end to "the culture of failure" that so often misshapes urban education.

Adapting the Model to Realities

What has begun to emerge from these middle school reform efforts is not a single mold but a recognizable pattern of models. The teaming of teachers from different disciplines tends to create a new sense of responsibility for the students' development and a new sense of professionalism among the teachers. The curriculum begins to depend on the teams' creativity instead of being handed down by some distant tradition-bound authorities. Because the children no longer feel lost in a mass of anonymous bodies, they develop a sense of belonging — a membership in a community that cares. Instead of being allowed to fester, their academic, emotional, and physical problems are recognized by caring and knowledgeable adults. They are constantly helped to learn and to grow.

A middle grade school can reform itself internally but, ultimately, it cannot escape its setting. It can be an oasis of peace and learning for part — often too small a part — of the day. But set in a cultural desert, in an atmosphere of fear, in a subculture of drugs and violence, many schools are not waging their contest for the minds and hearts of the young adolescent on anything like a level playing field. Can an inner-city school in Chicago, surrounded by violent gangs, be compared with a forty-acre campus school in California, even when both are trying conscientiously to implement the *Turning Points* recommendations?

Some progress has been made in caring for adolescents' health, but the pace is slow. Even in some of the academically most successful schools, attention to students' physical and emotional developmental problems is too often left primarily to a part-time nurse. Most teachers appear to agree that many students are put at serious but unnecessary risk by the precarious state of their mental health.

The need for school-based or school-related health services is widely acknowledged, but their development remains far behind the pace of education reform.

Much confusion persists about the best way of judging students' progress. If traditional assessment is imposed on schools, usually in the form of standardized tests, teachers worry about the effect of an unconventional curriculum on students' test scores, even when they know that the students' actual knowledge has improved. This does not mean that goals and standards set for schools by state and national authorities can be ignored; it does mean that teachers in local schools should have much freedom in deciding how best to reach those goals and meet those standards.

Middle grade reform is breaking the old mold into which children are so often pressed like shapeless clay. The goal of the reform, as it emerges in successful schools, is to liberate teaching and learning. State and national authorities can help by reforming the tests by which students are judged.

The Larger Picture

Middle school reform must be part of a larger school reform, or it cannot succeed, believes principal Deborah Meier. So far, this is happening only sporadically and without any concerted plan. Modest progress has been made in forging a better link between the elementary and the middle grades. Some of the reorganized middle schools have made contact with the next cadre of elementary school

children and their teachers. In one ambitious program, middle grade students have been invited to serve as mentors to elementary school children to prepare them for what is ahead.

But many high school administrators and teachers are loath to abandon the departmentalized structure and are blocking the continuity of reform. Their students, who are still adolescents in need of personal attention, continue to rush from class to class. They remain submerged in the mass of oversized schools.

Under such conditions, middle schools are literally caught in the middle. Principals of the most successfully reformed middle schools express concern that some of their students' gains will be wiped out by a high school system that retains its impersonal ways, just as many of the gains of successful Head Start programs for four- and five-year-olds were wiped out when elementary schools failed to build on the children's earlier progress.

Could high schools adopt some of the key recommendations of *Turning Points*? Could they turn to teacher teaming and interdisciplinary teaching without loss of academic muscle and stature? Principals of successful middle schools answer those questions with an emphatic "yes." They point out that, under present conditions, large numbers of students drop out of the high schools. Moreover, the high schools suffer most from violent student behavior and vandalism, which many school reformers attribute to the schools' unwieldy size and the students' anonymity within them.

Another roadblock to a faster pace for school reform is the reluctance on the part of many educators to imitate crucial aspects of successful models. For example, the highly successful Dyett Middle School in Chicago is part of a cluster of six middle grade schools. So far, the other schools in the cluster appear reluctant to adopt what are Dyett's widely praised reforms.

Still, there is progress. Many states are making the best of opportunities to implement *Turning Points*' recommendations with help from Carnegie Corporation and other funding sources. In exemplary schools for young adoles-

cents, the promise of a better future is in the air: children learn by exploration rather than regurgitation; they respect their teachers and regard the school as a second (in some cases, only) home.

Twelve states have developed or actively implemented comprehensive middle grade policy statements approved by the state board of education or the legislature. Eleven states have established a middle grades unit within the state education agency where no such unit existed.

A number of schools have forged links to health and social service agencies. Such arrangements include the creation of a school-based clinic, employment of a physician's assistant through the state health department, or creation of a partnership with a group of family practice physicians.

URBAN PRESCRIPTION

Philip Coltoff, executive director of the Children's Aid Society, quotes the assessment by community leaders in New York City's Washington Heights area of children's needs in poor urban neighborhoods:

• Day and after-school care for children of all ages.

• Recreation programs and compensatory education for children and teens.

• Family counseling, especially dealing with parenting skills and child abuse prevention.

To cite a specific example, the Middle Grade School State Policy Initiative provided for the formation of the Task Force on Middle School Education in Texas, which, in 1991, challenged the education establishment to make the middle schools responsive to the special needs of young adolescents. As in a number of other states, this led to the creation of a Texas Middle School Network. Nineteen schools were identified to serve as leaders or mentors for the network. By May 1992, the number had increased to more than 400 schools. "Our three-year goal," says the Texas reform prospectus, "is to have all middle schools in the state join the Middle School Network."

At its best, networking extends beyond the schools to all agencies that deal with the needs of young adolescents. For example, in Maryland, the state education department established the School Improvement Action Team with representatives from the state departments of education, of health and mental hygiene, and of human resources.

In a slightly different version of networking, California selected a cadre of exemplary middle schools to serve as linchpins for statewide reform.

If there are to be different middle schools, there must also be differently prepared teachers. In Massachusetts, as in a number of other states, future teachers of young teenagers will spend significantly more time training for service in middle schools. New middle grade certification standards in Massachusetts will take effect in 1994.

Progress in these and many other states in building middle grade reform into the system promises a new deal for the nation's young adolescents. The creation of networks within and beyond the schools, to include health services, community agencies, and parents, opens the door to that crucial, but often lacking, element of school reform: the move from pilot project to general or at least widespread use.

As the impact of *Turning Points* and the middle grade school initiative is felt in improved academic achievement and in better health and less risky behavior, more formal assessment of the results will follow. At this early stage, the most

persuasive proof that the "new and improved" middle schools are meeting their goal is the start of a remarkable phenomenon — former students returning to their middle school teachers and principals for help and advice when they run into personal or academic problems in high school.

Several principals make it clear that they want the youngsters to look on their school as a place to come home to long after they leave it as students. If such attitudes spread, *Turning Points* will not merely have set in motion the reform of the middle grades, it will have shown the way toward the reform of all American education, from infancy to early adulthood. The watchword will be continuity in the service to children and youth.

For information:

Ruby Takanishi, Executive Director, Carnegie Council on Adolescent Development, 2400 N Street, N.W., 6th Floor, Washington, DC 20037. (202) 429-7979.

References

Atwell, Nancie. *In the Middle: Writing, Reading, and Learning with Adolescents.* New York: Boynton/ Cook, 1987.

Caught in the Middle: Educational Reform for Young Adolescents in California Public Schools. The Report of the Superintendent's Middle Grade Task Force. Sacramento, CA: California Department of Education, 1987.

Conant, James Bryant. *Education in the Junior High School Years.* Princeton, NJ: Education Testing Service, 1960.

Hamburg, David A. *Today's Children: Creating a Future for a Generation in Crisis.* New York: Times Books, 1992.

Hechinger, Fred M. *Fateful Choices: Healthy Youth for the 21st Century.* New York: Hill and Wang, 1993.

Lerner, Richard M., ed. *Early Adolescence: Perspectives on Research, Policy, and Intervention.* The Penn State Series on Child and Adolescent Development. Hillsdale, NJ: Lawrence Erlbaum Associates, 1993.

Lewis, Anne C. *Making it in the Middle: The Why and How of Excellent Schools for Young Urban Adolescents.* New York: The Edna McConnell Clark Foundation, 1990.

THE NEED FOR SPECIAL ATTENTION

Approximately 28 million youngsters fall into the age group served by middle or junior high schools and high schools, and 7 million — one in four — are considered at high risk of failing in school and engaging in such dangerous behavior as alcohol and illegal drug abuse, premature and unprotected sexual activity, and addiction to nicotine. They may become victims or perpetrators of violence. They may not be covered by insurance or have access to health care services. Another 7 million may be at moderate risk and therefore are a matter of serious concern as well. Because, as a group, adolescents are vulnerable, they need special attention in school.

6. EQUAL OPPORTUNITY IN EDUCATION

Turning Points: Preparing American Youth for the 21st Century. The Report of the Task Force on Education of Young Adolescents of the Carnegie Council on Adolescent Development. Washington, DC: Carnegie Council on Adolescent Development, 1989.

Turning Points: States in Action. An Interim Report of the Middle Grade School State Policy Initiative. Washington, DC: Council of Chief State School Officers, 1992.

MGSSPI State Products

Turning Points: State Network News. A Publication of the Council of Chief State School Officers Resource Center on Educational Equity. Washington, DC: Council of Chief State School Officers.

Magic in the Middle, 1993. Contact Susan Zelman, Massachusetts Department of Education, 350 Main Street, Malden, MA 02148.

Right in the Middle, 1991. Recommendations for the continued development of middle grade education in Connecticut. Contact Richard E. Lappert, Connecticut State Department of Education, P.O. Box 2219, Hartford, CT 06145.

Guidelines for Middle Level Education in Delaware: An Agenda for Success, 1991. Explains the provisions of Delaware's Middle Level Education Policy, adopted by the state board of education in April 1991. Contact Clifton Hutton, Delaware Department of Public Instruction, P.O. Box 1402, Townsend Building, Dover, DE 19903.

Right in the Middle, 1991. Plans for the transformation of education for young adolescents in Illinois. Contact Sheryl Poggi, Illinois State Board of Education, 100 North First Street, Springfield, IL 62777.

Betwixt and Between, 1992. Reports on the recommendations of Indiana's Middle Level Task Force on restructuring education for middle level students. Contact Betty Johnson, Indiana Department of Education, Room 229, State House, Indianapolis, IN 46204.

Middle Morphosis: Kentucky's Plan for Young Adolescents, 1991. Reports on Kentucky's plan to improve the education of young adolescents. Contact Betty Edwards, Kentucky Department of Education, 1806 Capital Plaza Tower, 500 Mero Street, Frankfort, KY 40601.

Task Force Report — What Matters in the Middle Grades: Recommendations for Maryland Middle Grades Education, 1987. Thirty-seven recommendations made by the middle level task force with rationales and research supporting each suggestion. Contact Antoinette Favazza, Maryland State Department of Education, 200 West Baltimore Street, Baltimore, MD 21201.

Moving Into Action: Middle Level Education in New Mexico, 1991. Report to the State Board of Education that presents findings and recommendations for middle level educational reform in New Mexico schools. Contact Richard LaPan, New Mexico State Department of Education, 300 Don Gaspar, Education Building, Santa Fe, NM 87501.

Regents Policy Statement on Middle Level Education and Schools with Middle Level Grades, 1989. Recommends policy changes for middle level education practices and outcomes. Contact David A. Payton, New York State Education Department, Room 212 EB, Albany, NY 12234.

Last Best Chance, 1990. Recommendations to improve middle level education for North Carolina in response to

Turning Points. Contact Frances Reaves, Department of Public Instruction, 301 North Wilmington, Raleigh, NC 27601.

Bridges for Young Adolescents — Governor's Task Force on Early Adolescence, 1992. Recommendations for building stronger bridges for families, school boards, and educators who work with adolescents in North Dakota. Contact Lowell Thompson, P.O. Box 7189, University Station, Grand Forks, ND 58202.

From the Margins to the Middle: A Call for Reform, 1991. Advocates a comprehensive and unified approach to middle level education through policy reform. Contact Ken Fish, Rhode Island Department of Elementary and Secondary Education, 22 Hayes Street, Providence, RI 02908.

Policy Statement on Middle Grade Education and Middle Grade Schools, 1991. Provides a framework for middle level education, passed unanimously by the state board of education in 1991. Contact Melody Johnson, Texas Education Agency, 1701 North Congress Avenue, Austin, TX 78701.

The Middle Matters: Transforming Education for Vermont's Young Adolescents, 1991. Provides direction for the development of middle grades programs in all Vermont schools. Contact Judy Carr, 28 Sleepy Hollow Road, Essex Junction, VT 05452.

Framework for Education in the Middle School Grades in Virginia, 1991. Describes desirable educational practices for Virginia students in grades 6-8. Contact Helen Stiff, Virginia Department of Education, P.O. Box 6-Q, Richmond, VA 23216.

The Canon Debate, Knowledge Construction, and Multicultural Education

JAMES A. BANKS

JAMES A. BANKS *is professor and director, Center for Multicultural Education, University of Washington, Seattle, WA 98195. He specializes in social studies education and multicultural education.*

I review the debate over multicultural education in this article, state that all knowledge reflects the values and interests of its creators, and illustrate how the debate between the multiculturalists and the Western traditionalists is rooted in their conflicting conceptions about the nature of knowledge and their divergent political and social interests. I present a typology that describes five types of knowledge and contend that each type should be a part of the school, college, and university curriculum.

Educational Researcher, Vol. 22, No. 5, pp. 4–14.

A heated and divisive national debate is taking place about what knowledge related to ethnic and cultural diversity should be taught in the school and university curriculum (Asante, 1991a; Asante & Ravitch, 1991; D'Souza, 1991; Glazer, 1991; Schlesinger, 1991; Woodward, 1991). This debate has heightened ethnic tension and confused many educators about the meaning of multicultural education. At least three different groups of scholars are participating in the canon debate: the Western traditionalists, the multiculturalists, and the Afrocentrists. Although there are a range of perspectives and views within each of these groups, all groups share a number of important assumptions and beliefs about the nature of diversity in the United States and about the role of educational institutions in a pluralistic society.

The Western traditionalists have initiated a national effort to defend the dominance of Western civilization in the school and university curriculum (Gray, 1991; Howe, 1991; Woodward, 1991). These scholars believe that Western history, literature, and culture are endangered in the school and university curriculum because of the push by feminists, ethnic minority scholars, and other multiculturalists for curriculum reform and transformation. The Western traditionalists have formed an organization called the National Association of Scholars to defend the dominance of Western civilization in the curriculum.

The multiculturalists believe that the school, college, and university curriculum marginalizes the experiences of people of color and of women (Butler & Walter, 1991; Gates, 1992; Grant, 1992; Sleeter, personal communication, October 26, 1991). They contend that the curriculum should be reformed so that it will more accurately reflect the histories and cultures of ethnic groups and women. Two organizations have been formed to promote issues related to ethnic and cultural diversity. Teachers for a Democratic Culture promotes ethnic studies and women studies at the university level. The National Association for Multicultural Education focuses on teacher education and multicultural education in the nation's schools.

The Afrocentrists maintain that African culture and history should be placed at the "center" of the curriculum in order to motivate African Americans students to learn and to help all students to understand the important role that Africa has played in the development of Western civilization (Asante, 1991a). Many mainstream multiculturalists are ambivalent about Afrocentrism, although few have publicly opposed it. This is in part because the Western traditionalists rarely distinguish the Afrocentrists from the multiculturalists and describe them as one group. Some multiculturalists may also perceive Afrocentric ideas as compatible with a broader concept of multicultural education.

The influence of the multiculturalists within schools and universities in the last 20 years has been substantial. Many school districts, state departments of education, local school districts, and private agencies have developed and implemented multicultural staff development programs, conferences, policies, and curricula (New York City Board of Education, 1990; New York State Department of Education, 1989, 1991; Sokol, 1990). Multicultural requirements, programs, and policies have also been implemented at many of the nation's leading research universities, including the University of California, Berkeley, Stanford University, The Pennsylvania State University, and the University of Wisconsin system. The success that the multiculturalists have had in implementing their ideas within schools and universities is probably a major reason that the Western traditionalists are trying to halt multicultural reforms in the nation's schools, colleges, and universities.

The debate between the Western traditionalists and the multiculturalists is consistent with the ideals of a democratic society. To date, however, it has resulted in little productive interaction between the Western traditionalists and the multiculturalists. Rather, each group has talked primarily to audiences it viewed as sympathetic to its ideologies and visions of the present and future (Franklin, 1991; Schlesinger, 1991). Because there has been little productive dialogue and exchange between the Western traditionalists and the multiculturalists, the debate has been polarized, and writers have frequently not conformed to the established rules of scholarship (D'Souza, 1991). A kind of forensic social science has developed (Rivlin, 1973), with each side stating briefs and then marshaling evidence to support its position. The debate has also taken place primarily in the popular press rather than in academic and scholarly journals.

Valuation and Knowledge Construction

I hope to make a positive contribution to the canon debate in this article by providing evidence for the claim that the positions of both the Western traditionalists and the multiculturalists reflect values, ideologies, political positions, and human interests. Each position also implies a kind of knowledge that should be taught in the school and university curriculum. I will present a typology of the kinds of knowledge that exist in society and in educational institutions. This typology is designed to help practicing educators and researchers to identify types of knowledge that reflect particular values, assumptions, perspectives, and ideological positions.

Teachers should help students to understand all types of knowledge. Students should be involved in the debates about knowledge construction and conflicting interpretations, such as the extent to which Egypt and Phoenicia influenced Greek civilization. Students should also be taught how to create their own interpretations of the past and present, as well as how to identify their own positions, interests, ideologies, and assumptions. Teachers should help students to become critical thinkers who have the knowledge, attitudes, skills, and commitments needed to participate in democratic action to help the nation close the gap between its ideals and its realities. Multicultural education is an education for functioning effectively in a pluralistic democratic society. Helping students to develop the knowledge, skills, and attitudes needed to participate in reflective civic action is one of its major goals (Banks, 1991).

I argue that students should study all five types of knowledge. However, my own work and philosophical position are within the transformative tradition in ethnic studies and multicultural education (Banks, 1988, 1991; Banks & Banks, 1989). This tradition links knowledge, social commitment, and action (Meier & Rudwick, 1986). A transformative, action-oriented curriculum, in my view, can best be implemented when students examine different types of knowledge in a democratic classroom where they can freely examine their perspectives and moral commitments.

The Nature of Knowledge

I am using knowledge in this article to mean the way a person explains or interprets reality. *The American Heritage Dictionary* (1983) defines knowledge as "familiarity, awareness, or understandings gained through experience or study. The sum or range of what has been perceived, discovered or inferred" (p. 384). My conceptualization of knowledge is broad and is used the way in which it is usually used in the sociology of knowledge literature to include ideas, values, and interpretations (Farganis, 1986). As postmodern theorists have pointed out, knowledge is socially constructed and reflects human interests, values, and action (Code, 1991; Foucault, 1972; S. Harding, 1991; Rorty, 1989). Although many complex factors influence the knowledge that is created by an individual or group, including the actuality of what occurred, the knowledge that people create is heavily influenced by their interpretations of their experiences and their positions within particular social, economic, and political systems and structures of a society.

In the Western empirical tradition, the ideal within each academic discipline is the formulation of knowledge without the influence of the researcher's personal or cultural characteristics (Greer, 1969; Kaplan, 1964). However, as critical and postmodern theorists have pointed out, personal, cultural, and social factors influence the formulation of knowledge even when objective knowledge is the ideal within a discipline (Cherryholmes, 1988; Foucault, 1972; Habermas, 1971; Rorty, 1989; Young, 1971). Often the researchers themselves are unaware of how their personal experiences and positions within society influence the knowledge they produce. Most mainstream historians were unaware of how their regional and cultural biases influenced their interpretation of the Reconstruction period until W. E. B. DuBois published a study that challenged the accepted and established interpretations of that historical period (DuBois, 1935/1962).

Positionality and Knowledge Construction

Positionality is an important concept that emerged out of feminist scholarship. Tetreault (1993) writes:

> Positionality means that important aspects of our identity, for example, our gender, our race, our class, our age . . . are markers of relational positions rather than essential qualities. Their effects and implications change according to context. Recently, feminist thinkers have seen knowledge as valid when it comes from an acknowledgment of the knower's specific position in any context, one always defined by gender, race, class and other variables. (p. 139)

Positionality reveals the importance of identifying the positions and frames of reference from which scholars and writers present their data, interpretations, analyses, and instruction (Anzaldúa, 1990; Ellsworth, 1989). The need for researchers and scholars to identify their ideological positions and normative assumptions in their works—an inherent part of feminist and ethnic studies scholarship—contrasts with the empirical paradigm that has dominated science and research in the United States (Code, 1991; S. Harding, 1991).

The assumption within the Western empirical paradigm is that the knowledge produced within it is neutral and objective and that its principles are universal. The effects of values, frames of references, and the normative positions of researchers and scholars are infrequently discussed within the traditional empirical paradigm that has dominated scholarship and teaching in American colleges and universities since the turn of the century. However, scholars such as Mydral (1944) and Clark (1965), prior to the feminist and ethnic studies movements, wrote about the need for scholars to recognize and state their normative positions and valuations and to become, in the apt words of Kenneth B. Clark, "involved observers." Myrdal stated that valuations are not just attached to research but permeate it. He wrote, "*There is no device for excluding biases in social sciences than to face the valuations and to introduce them as explicitly stated, specific, and sufficiently concretized value premises*" (p. 1043).

Postmodern and critical theorists such as Habermas (1971) and Giroux (1983), and feminist postmodern theorists such as Farganis (1986), Code (1991), and S. Harding (1991), have developed important critiques of empirical knowledge. They argue that despite its claims, modern science is not value-free but contains important human interests and normative assumptions that should be identified, discussed, and examined. Code (1991), a feminist epistemologist, states that academic knowledge is both subjective and objective and that both aspects should be recognized and discussed. Code states that we need to ask these kinds of questions: "Out of whose subjectivity has this ideal [of objectivity] grown? Whose standpoint, whose values does it represent?" (p. 70). She writes:

> The point of the questions is to discover how subjective and objective conditions together produce knowledge, values, and epistemology. It is neither to reject objectivity nor to glorify subjectivity in its stead. Knowledge is neither value-free nor value-neutral; the processes that produce it are themselves value-laden; and these values are open to evaluation. (p. 70)

In her book, *What Can She Know? Feminist Theory and the Construction of Knowledge,* Code (1991) raises the question, "Is the sex of the knower epistemologically significant?" (p. 7). She answers this question in the affirmative because of the ways in which gender influences how knowledge is constructed, interpreted, and institutionalized within U.S. society. The ethnic and cultural experiences of the knower are also epistemologically significant because these factors also influence knowledge construction, use, and interpretation in U.S. society.

Empirical scholarship has been limited by the assumptions and biases that are implicit within it (Code, 1991; Gordon, 1985; S. Harding, 1991). However, these biases and assumptions have been infrequently recognized by the scholars and researchers themselves and by the consumers of their works, such as other scholars, professors, teachers, and the general reader. The lack of recognition and identification of these biases, assumptions, perspectives, and points of view have frequently victimized people of color such as African Americans and American Indians because of the stereotypes and misconceptions that have been perpetuated about them in the historical and social science literature (Ladner, 1973; Phillips, 1918).

Gordon, Miller, and Rollock (1990) call the bias that results in the negative depiction of minority groups by mainstream social scientists "communicentric bias." They point out that mainstream social scientists have often viewed diversity as deviance and differences as deficits. An important outcome of the revisionist and transformative interpretations that have been produced by scholars working in feminist and ethnic studies is that many misconceptions and partial truths about women and ethnic groups have been viewed from different and more complete perspectives (Acuña, 1988; Blassingame, 1972; V. Harding, 1981; King & Mitchell, 1990; Merton, 1972).

More complete perspectives result in a closer approximation to the actuality of what occurred. In an important and influential essay, Merton (1972) notes that the perspectives of both "insiders" and "outsiders" are needed to enable social scientists to gain a complete view of social reality. Anna Julia Cooper, the African American educator, made a point similar to Merton's when she wrote about how the perspectives of women enlarged our vision (Cooper, 1892/1969, cited in Minnich, 1990, p. viii).

> The world has had to limp along with the wobbling gait and the one-sided hesitancy of a man with one eye. Suddenly the bandage is removed from the other eye and the whole body is filled with light. It sees a circle where before it saw a segment.

A Knowledge Typology

A description of the major types of knowledge can help teachers and curriculum specialists to identify perspectives and content needed to make the curriculum multicultural. Each of the types of knowledge described below reflects particular purposes, perspectives, experiences, goals, and human interests. Teaching students various types of knowledge can help them to better understand the perspectives of different racial, ethnic, and cultural groups as well as to develop their own versions and interpretations of issues and events.

I identify and describe five types of knowledge (see Table 1): (a) personal/cultural knowledge; (b) popular knowledge; (c) mainstream academic knowledge; (d) transformative academic knowledge; and (e) school knowledge. This is an ideal-type typology in the Weberian sense. The five categories approximate, but do not describe, reality in its total complexity. The categories are useful conceptual tools for thinking about knowledge and planning multicultural teaching. For example, although the categories can be conceptually distinguished, in reality they overlap and are interrelated in a dynamic way.

Since the 1960s, some of the findings and insights from transformative academic knowledge have been incorporated into mainstream academic knowledge and scholarship. Traditionally, students were taught in schools and universities that the land that became North America was a thinly populated wilderness when the Europeans arrived in the 16th century and that African Americans had made few contributions to the development of American civilization (mainstream academic knowledge). Some of the findings from transformative academic knowledge that challenged these conceptions have influenced mainstream academic scholarship and have been incorporated into mainstream college and school textbooks (Hoxie, no date; Thornton, 1987). Consequently, the relationship between the five categories of knowledge is dynamic and interactive rather than static (see Figure 1).

The Types of Knowledge

Personal and Cultural Knowledge

The concepts, explanations, and interpretations that students derive from personal experiences in their homes, families, and community cultures constitute personal and cultural

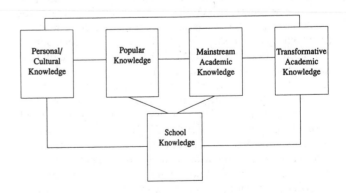

FIGURE 1. *The interrelationship of the types of knowledge. This figure illustrates that although the five types of knowledge discussed in this article are conceptually distinct, they are highly interrelated in a complex and dynamic way.*

Table 1

Types of Knowledge

Knowledge Type	Definition	Examples
Personal/cultural	The concepts, explanations, and interpretations that students derive from personal experiences in their homes, families, and community cultures.	Understandings by many African Americans and Hispanic students that highly individualistic behavior will be negatively sanctioned by many adults and peers in their cultural communities.
Popular	The facts, concepts, explanations, and interpretations that are institutionalized within the mass media and other institutions that are part of the popular culture.	Movies such as *Birth of a Nation, How the West Was Won,* and *Dances With Wolves.*
Mainstream academic	The concepts, paradigms, theories, and explanations that constitute traditional Western-centric knowledge in history and the behavioral and social sciences.	Ulrich B. Phillips, *American Negro Slavery;* Frederick Jackson Turner's frontier theory; Arthur R. Jensen's theory about Black and White intelligence.
Transformative academic	The facts, concepts, paradigms, themes, and explanations that challenge mainstream academic knowledge and expand and substantially revise established canons, paradigms, theories, explanations, and research methods. When transformative academic paradigms replace mainstream ones, a scientific revolution has occurred. What is more normal is that transformative academic paradigms coexist with established ones.	George Washington Williams, *History of the Negro Race in America;* W. E. B. DuBois, *Black Reconstruction;* Carter G. Woodson, *The Mis-education of the Negro;* Gerda Lerner, *The Majority Finds Its Past;* Rodolfo Acuña, *Occupied America: A History of Chicanos;* Herbert Gutman, *The Black Family in Slavery and Freedom 1750–1925.*
School	The facts, concepts, generalizations, and interpretations that are presented in textbooks, teacher's guides, other media forms, and lectures by teachers.	Lewis Paul Todd and Merle Curti, *Rise of the American Nation;* Richard C. Brown, Wilhelmena S. Robinson, & John Cunningham, *Let Freedom Ring: A United States History.*

knowledge. The assumptions, perspectives, and insights that students derive from their experiences in their homes and community cultures are used as screens to view and interpret the knowledge and experiences that they encounter in the school and in other institutions within the larger society.

Research and theory by Fordham and Ogbu (1986) indicate that low-income African American students often experience academic difficulties in the school because of the ways that cultural knowledge within their community conflicts with school knowledge, norms, and expectations. Fordham and Ogbu also state that the culture of many low-income African American students is oppositional to the school culture. These students believe that if they master the knowledge taught in the schools they will violate fictive kinship norms and run the risk of "acting White." Fordham (1988, 1991) has suggested that African American students who become high academic achievers resolve the conflict caused by the interaction of their personal cultural knowledge with the knowledge and norms within the schools by becoming "raceless" or by "ad hocing a culture."

Delpit (1988) has stated that African American students are often unfamiliar with school cultural knowledge regarding power relationships. They consequently experience academic and behavioral problems because of their failure to conform to established norms, rules, and expectations. She recommends that teachers help African American students learn the rules of power in the school culture by explicitly teaching them to the students. The cultural knowledge that many African American, Latino, and American Indian students bring to school conflict with school norms and values, with school knowledge, and with the ways that teachers interpret and mediate school knowledge. Student cultural knowledge and school knowledge often conflict on variables related to the ways that the individual should relate to and interact with the group (Hale-Benson, 1982; Ramírez & Castañeda, 1974; Shade, 1989), normative communication styles and interactions (Heath, 1983, Labov, 1975; Philips, 1983; Smitherman, 1977), and perspectives on the nature of U.S. history.

Personal and cultural knowledge is problematic when it conflicts with scientific ways of validating knowledge, is oppositional to the culture of the school, or challenges the main tenets and assumptions of mainstream academic knowledge. Much of the knowledge about out-groups that students learn from their home and community cultures consists of misconceptions, stereotypes, and partial truths (Milner, 1983). Most students in the United States are socialized within communities that are segregated along racial, ethnic, and social-class lines. Consequently, most American youths have few opportunities to learn firsthand about the cultures of people from different racial, ethnic, cultural, religious, and social-class groups.

The challenge that teachers face is how to make effective instructional use of the personal and cultural knowledge of students while at the same time helping them to reach beyond their own cultural boundaries. Although the school should recognize, validate, and make effective use of student personal and cultural knowledge in instruction, an important goal of education is to free students from their cultural and ethnic boundaries and enable them to cross cultural borders freely (Banks, 1988, 1991/1992).

In the past, the school has paid scant attention to the personal and cultural knowledge of students and has concentrated on teaching them school knowledge (Sleeter & Grant, 1991a). This practice has had different results for most White middle-class students, for most low-income students, and for most African American and Latino students. Because school knowledge is more consistent with the cultural experiences of most White middle-class students than for most other groups of students, these students have generally found the school a more comfortable place than have low-income students and most students of color—the majority of whom are also low income. A number of writers have described the ways in which many African American, American Indian, and Latino students find the school culture alienating and inconsistent with their cultural experiences, hopes, dreams, and struggles (Hale-Benson, 1982; Heath, 1983; Ramírez & Castañeda, 1974; Shade, 1989).

It is important for teachers to be aware of the personal and cultural knowledge of students when designing the curriculum for today's multicultural schools. Teachers can use student personal cultural knowledge as a vehicle to motivate students and as a foundation for teaching school knowledge. When teaching a unit on the Westward Movement to Lakota Sioux students, for example, the teacher can ask the students to make a list of their views about the Westward Movement, to relate family stories about the coming of the Whites to Lakota Sioux homelands, and to interview parents and grandparents about their perceptions of what happened when the Whites first occupied Indian lands. When teachers begin a unit on the Westward Movement with student personal cultural knowledge, they can increase student motivation as well as deepen their understanding of the schoolbook version (Wiggington, 1991/1992).

Popular Knowledge

Popular knowledge consists of the facts, interpretations, and beliefs that are institutionalized within television, movies, videos, records, and other forms of the mass media. Many of the tenets of popular knowledge are conveyed in subtle rather than obvious ways. Some examples of statements that constitute important themes in popular knowledge follow: (a) The United States is a powerful nation with unlimited opportunities for individuals who are willing to take advantage of them. (b) To succeed in the United States, an individual only has to work hard. You can realize your dreams in the United States if you are willing to work hard and pull yourself up by the bootstrap. (c) As a land of opportunity for all, the United States is a highly cohesive nation, whose ideals of equality and freedom are shared by all.

Most of the major tenets of American popular culture are widely shared and are deeply entrenched in U.S. society.

However, they are rarely explicitly articulated. Rather, they are presented in the media and in other sources in the forms of stories, anecdotes, news stories, and interpretations of current events (Cortés, 1991a, 1991b; Greenfield & Cortés, 1991).

Commercial entertainment films both reflect and perpetuate popular knowledge (Bogle, 1989; Cortés, 1991a, 1991b; Greenfield & Cortés, 1991). While preparing to write this article, I viewed an important and influential film that was directed by John Ford and released by MGM in 1962, *How the West Was Won*. I selected this film for review because the settlement of the West is a major theme in American culture and society about which there are many popular images, beliefs, myths, and misconceptions. In viewing the film, I was particularly interested in the images it depicted about the settlement of the West, about the people who were already in the West, and about those who went West looking for new opportunities.

Ford uses the Prescotts, a White family from Missouri bound for California, to tell his story. The film tells the story of three generations of this family. It focuses on the family's struggle to settle in the West. Indians, African Americans, and Mexicans are largely invisible in the film. Indians appear in the story when they attack the Prescott family during their long and perilous journey. The Mexicans appearing in the film are bandits who rob a train and are killed. The several African Americans in the film are in the background silently rowing a boat. At various points in the film, Indians are referred to as *hostile Indians* and as *squaws*.

How the West Was Won is a masterpiece in American popular culture. It not only depicts some of the major themes in American culture about the winning of the West; it reinforces and perpetuates dominant societal attitudes about ethnic groups and gives credence to the notion that the West was won by liberty-loving, hard-working people who pursued freedom for all. The film narrator states near its end, "[The movement West] produced a people free to dream, free to act, and free to mold their own destiny."

Mainstream Academic Knowledge

Mainstream academic knowledge consists of the concepts, paradigms, theories, and explanations that constitute traditional and established knowledge in the behavioral and social sciences. An important tenet within the mainstream academic paradigm is that there is a set of objective truths that can be verified through rigorous and objective research procedures that are uninfluenced by human interests, values, and perspectives (Greer, 1969; Kaplan, 1964; Sleeter, 1991). This empirical knowledge, uninfluenced by human values and interests, constitute a body of objective truths that should constitute the core of the school and university curriculum. Much of this objective knowledge originated in the West but is considered universal in nature and application.

Mainstream academic knowledge is the knowledge that multicultural critics such as Ravitch and Finn (1987), Hirsch (1987), and Bloom (1987) claim is threatened by the addition of content about women and ethnic minorities to the school and university curriculum. This knowledge reflects the established, Western-oriented canon that has historically dominated university research and teaching in the United States. Mainstream academic knowledge consists of the theories and interpretations that are internalized and accepted by most university researchers, academic societies, and organizations such as the American Historical Association, the American Sociological Association, the American Psychological Association, and the National Academy of Sciences.

It is important to point out, however, that an increasing number of university scholars are critical theorists and postmodernists who question the empirical paradigm that dominates Western science (Cherryholmes, 1988; Giroux, 1983; Rosenau, 1992). Many of these individuals are members of national academic organizations, such as the American Historical Association and the American Sociological Association. In most of these professional organizations, the postmodern scholars—made up of significant numbers of scholars of color and feminists—have formed caucuses and interest groups within the mainstream professional organizations.

No claim is made here that there is a uniformity of beliefs among mainstream academic scholars, but rather that there are dominant canons, paradigms, and theories that are accepted by the community of mainstream academic scholars and researchers. These established canons and paradigms are occasionally challenged within the mainstream academic community itself. However, they receive their most serious challenges from academics outside the mainstream, such as scholars within the transformative academic community whom I will describe later.

Mainstream academic knowledge, like the other forms of knowledge discussed in this article, is not static, but is dynamic, complex, and changing. Challenges to the dominant canons and paradigms within mainstream academic knowledge come from both within and without. These challenges lead to changes, reinterpretations, debates, disagreements and ultimately to paradigm shifts, new theories, and interpretations. Kuhn (1970) states that a scientific revolution takes place when a new paradigm emerges and replaces an existing one. What is more typical in education and the social sciences is that competing paradigms coexist, although particular ones might be more influential during certain times or periods.

We can examine the treatment of slavery within the mainstream academic community over time, or the treatment of the American Indian, to identify ways that mainstream academic knowledge has changed in important ways since the late 19th and early 20th centuries. Ulrich B. Phillips's highly influential book, *American Negro Slavery*, published in 1918, dominated the way Black slavery was interpreted until his views were challenged by researchers in the 1950s (Stampp, 1956). Phillips was a respected authority on the antebellum South and on slavery. His book, which became a historical classic, is essentially an apology for Southern slaveholders. A new paradigm about slavery was developed in the 1970s that drew heavily upon the slaves' view of their own experiences (Blassingame, 1972; Genovese, 1972; Gutman, 1976).

During the late 19th and early 20th centuries, the American Indian was portrayed in mainstream academic knowledge as either a noble or a hostile savage (Hoxie, 1988). Other notions that became institutionalized within mainstream academic knowledge include the idea that Columbus discovered America and that America was a thinly populated frontier when the Europeans arrived in the late 15th century. Frederick Jackson Turner (Turner, 1894/1989) argued that the frontier, which he regarded as a wilderness, was the main source of American democracy. Although Turner's thesis is now being highly criticized by revisionist historians, his essay established a conception of the West that has been highly influential in American mainstream scholarship, in the popular culture, and in schoolbooks. The conception of the West he depicted is still influential today in the school curriculum and in textbooks (Sleeter & Grant, 1991b).

These ideas also became institutionalized within mainstream academic knowledge: The slaves were happy and contented; most of the important ideas that became a part of American civilization came from Western Europe; and the history of the United States has been one of constantly expanding progress and increasing democracy. African slaves were needed to transform the United States from an empty wilderness into an industrial democratic civilization. The American Indians had to be Christianized and removed to reservations in order for this to occur.

Transformative Academic Knowledge

Transformative academic knowledge consists of concepts, paradigms, themes, and explanations that challenge mainstream academic knowledge and that expand the historical and literary canon. Transformative academic knowledge challenges some of the key assumptions that mainstream scholars make about the nature of knowledge. Transformative and mainstream academic knowledge is based on different epistemological assumptions about the nature of knowledge, about the influence of human interests and values on knowledge construction, and about the purpose of knowledge.

An important tenet of mainstream academic knowledge is that it is neutral, objective, and was uninfluenced by human interests and values. Transformative academic knowledge reflects postmodern assumptions and goals about the nature and goals of knowledge (Foucault, 1972; Rorty, 1989; Rosenau, 1992). Transformative academic scholars assume that knowledge is not neutral but is influenced by human interests, that all knowledge reflects the power and social relationships within society, and that an important purpose of knowledge construction is to help people improve society (Code, 1991, S. Harding, 1991; hooks & West, 1991; King & Mitchell, 1990; Minnich, 1990). Write King and Mitchell: "Like other praxis-oriented Critical approaches, the Afrocentric method seeks to enable people to understand social reality in order to change it. But its additional imperative is to transform the society's basic ethos" (p. 95).

These statements reflect some of the main ideas and concepts in transformative academic knowledge: Columbus did not discover America. The Indians had been living in this land for about 40,000 years when the Europeans arrived. Concepts such as "The European Discovery of America" and "The Westward Movement" need to be reconceptualized and viewed from the perspectives of different cultural and ethnic groups. The Lakota Sioux's homeland was not the West to them; it was the center of the universe. It was not the West for the Alaskans; it was South. It was East for the Japanese and North for the people who lived in Mexico. The history of the United States has not been one of continuous progress toward democratic ideals. Rather, the nation's history has been characterized by a cyclic quest for democracy and by conflict, struggle, violence, and exclusion (Acuña, 1988; Zinn, 1980). A major challenge that faces the nation is how to make its democratic ideals a reality for all.

Transformative academic knowledge has a long history in the United States. In 1882 and 1883, George Washington Williams (1849–1891) published, in two volumes, the first comprehensive history of African Americans in the United States, *A History of the Negro Race in America From 1619 to 1880* (Williams, 1982–1983/1968). Williams, like other African American scholars after him, decided to research and write about the Black experience because of the neglect of African Americans by mainstream historians and social scientists and because of the stereotypes and misconceptions about African Americans that appeared in mainstream scholarship.

W. E. B. DuBois (1868–1963) is probably the most prolific African American scholar in U.S. history. His published writings constitute 38 volumes (Aptheker, 1973). DuBois devoted his long and prolific career to the formulation of new data, concepts, and paradigms that could be used to reinterpret the Black experience and reveal the role that African Americans had played in the development of American society. His seminal works include *The Suppression of the African Slave Trade to the United States of America, 1638–1870,* the first volume of the Harvard Historical Studies (DuBois, 1896/1969). Perhaps his most discussed book is *Black Reconstruction in America: An Essay Toward a History of the Part Which Black Folk Played in the Attempt to Reconstruct Democracy in America, 1860–1880,* published in 1935 (1935/1962). In this book, DuBois challenged the accepted, institutionalized interpretations of Reconstruction and emphasized the accomplishments of the Reconstruction governments and legislatures, especially the establishment of free public schools.

Carter G. Woodson (1875–1950), the historian and educator who founded the Association for the Study of Negro Life and History and the *Journal of Negro History,* also challenged established paradigms about the treatment of African Americans in a series of important publications, including *The Mis-education of the Negro,* published in 1933. Woodson and Wesley (1922) published a highly successful college textbook that described the contributions that African Americans have made to American life, *The Negro in Our History.* This book was issued in 10 editions.

Transformative Scholarship Since the 1970s

Many scholars have produced significant research and theories since the early 1970s that have challenged and modified institutionalized stereotypes and misconceptions about ethnic minorities, formulated new concepts and paradigms, and forced mainstream scholars to rethink established interpretations. Much of the transformative academic knowledge that has been produced since the 1970s is becoming institutionalized within mainstream scholarship and within the school, college, and university curricula. In time, much of this scholarship will become mainstream, thus reflecting the highly interrelated nature of the types of knowledge conceptualized and described in this article.

Only a few examples of this new, transformative scholarship will be mentioned here because of the limited scope of this article. Howard Zinn's *A People's History of the United States* (1980): *Red, White and Black: The Peoples of Early America* by Gary B. Nash (1982): *The Signifying Monkey: A Theory of African-American Literacy Criticism* by Henry Louis Gates, Jr.

(1988); *Occupied America: A History of Chicanos* by Rodolfo Acuña (1988); *Iron Cages: Race and Culture in 19th-Century America* by Ronald T. Takaki (1979); and *The Sacred Hoop: Recovering the Feminine in American Indian Traditions* by Paul Gunn Allen (1986) are examples of important scholarship that has provided significant new perspectives on the experiences of ethnic groups in the United States and has helped us to transform our conceptions about the experiences of American ethnic groups. Readers acquainted with this scholarship will note that transformative scholarship has been produced by both European-American and ethnic minority scholars.

I will discuss two examples of how the new scholarship in ethnic studies has questioned traditional interpretations

---

Students should be given opportunities to investigate and determine how cultural assumptions, frames of references, perspectives, and the biases within a discipline influence the ways knowledge is constructed.

---

and stimulated a search for new explanations and paradigms since the 1950s. Since the pioneering work of E. Franklin Frazier (1939), social scientists had accepted the notion that the slave experience had destroyed the Black family and that the destruction of the African American family continued in the post–World War II period during Black migration to and settlement in northern cities. Moynihan (1965), in his controversial book, *The Negro Family in America: The Case for National Action,* used the broken Black family explanation in his analysis. Gutman (1976), in an important historical study of the African American family from 1750 to 1925, concluded that "despite a high rate of earlier involuntary marital breakup, large numbers of slave couples lived in long marriages, and most slaves lived in double-headed households" (p. xxii).

An important group of African and African American scholars have challenged established interpretations about the origin of Greek civilization and the extent to which Greek civilization was influenced by African cultures. These scholars include Diop (1974), Williams (1987), and Van Sertima (1988, 1989). Cheikh Anta Diop is one of the most influential African scholars who has challenged established interpretations about the origin of Greek civilization. In *Black Nations and Culture,* published in 1955 (summarized by Van Sertima, 1989), he sets forth an important thesis that states that Africa is an important root of Western civilization. Diop argues that Egypt "was the node and center of a vast web linking the strands of cultures and languages; that the light that crystallized at the center of this early world had been energized by the cultural electricity streaming from the heartland of Africa" (p. 8).

Since the work by Diop, Williams, and Van Sertima, traditional interpretations about the formation of Greek civilization has been challenged by Bernal (1987–1991), a professor of government at Cornell University. The earlier challenges to established interpretations by African and African Americans received little attention, except within the African American community. However, Bernal's work has received wide attention in the popular press and among classicists.

Bernal (1987–1991) argues that important aspects of Greek civilization originated in ancient Egypt and Phoenicia and that the ancient civilization of Egypt was essentially African. Bernal believes that the contributions of Egypt and Phoenicia to Greek civilization have been deliberately ignored by classical scholars because of their biased attitudes toward non-White peoples and Semites. Bernal has published two of four planned volumes of his study *Black Athena*. In Volume 2 he uses evidence from linguistics, archeology and ancient documents to substantiate his claim that "between 2100 and 1100 B.C., when Greek culture was born, the people of the Aegean borrowed, adapted or had thrust upon them deities and language, technologies and architectures, notions of justice and polis" from Egypt and Phoenicia (Begley, Chideya, & Wilson, 1991, p. 50). Because transformative academic knowledge, such as that constructed by Diop, Williams, Van Sertima, and Bernal, challenges the established paradigms as well as because of the tremendous gap between academic knowledge and school knowledge, it often has little influence on school knowledge.

School Knowledge

School knowledge consists of the facts, concepts, and generalizations presented in textbooks, teachers' guides, and the other forms of media designed for school use. School knowledge also consists of the teacher's mediation and interpretation of that knowledge. The textbook is the main source of school knowledge in the United States (Apple & Christian-Smith, 1991; Goodlad, 1984; Shaver, Davis, & Helburn, 1979). Studies of textbooks indicate that these are some of the major themes in school knowledge (Anyon, 1979, 1981; Sleeter & Grant, 1991b): (a) America's founding fathers, such as Washington and Jefferson, were highly moral, liberty-loving men who championed equality and justice for all Americans; (b) the United States is a nation with justice, liberty, and freedom for all; (c) social class divisions are not significant issues in the United States; (d) there are no significant gender, class, or racial divisions within U.S. society; and (e) ethnic groups of color and Whites interact largely in harmony in the United States.

Studies of textbooks that have been conducted by researchers such as Anyon (1979, 1981) and Sleeter and Grant (1991b) indicate that textbooks present a highly selective view of social reality, give students the idea that knowledge is static rather than dynamic, and encourage students to master isolated facts rather than to develop complex understandings of social reality. These studies also indicate that textbooks reinforce the dominant social, economic, and power arrangements within society. Students are encouraged to accept rather than to question these arrangements.

In their examination of the treatment of race, class, gender, and disability in textbooks, Sleeter and Grant (1991b) concluded that although textbooks had largely eliminated sexist language and had incorporated images of ethnic minorities into them, they failed to help students to develop an understanding of the complex cultures of ethnic groups, an understanding of racism, sexism and classism in American society, and described the United States as a nation that had largely overcome its problems. Sleeter & Grant write:

The vision of social relations that the textbooks we analyzed for the most part project is one of harmony and equal opportunity—anyone can do or become whatever he or she wants; problems among people are mainly individual in nature and in the end are resolved. (p. 99)

A number of powerful factors influence the development and production of school textbooks (Altbach, Kelly, Petrie, & Weis, 1991; FitzGerald, 1979). One of the most important is the publisher's perception of statements and images that might be controversial. When textbooks become controversial, school districts often refuse to adopt and to purchase them. When developing a textbook, the publisher and the authors must also consider the developmental and reading levels of the students, state and district guidelines about what subject matter textbooks should include, and recent trends and developments in a content field that teachers and administrators will expect the textbook to reflect and incorporate. Because of the number of constraints and influences on the development of textbooks, school knowledge often does not include in-depth discussions and analyses of some of the major problems in American society, such as racism, sexism, social-class stratification, and poverty (Anyon, 1979, 1981; Sleeter & Grant, 1991b). Consequently, school knowledge is influenced most heavily by mainstream academic knowledge and popular knowledge. Transformative academic knowledge usually has little direct influence on school knowledge. It usually affects school knowledge in a significant way only after it has become a part of mainstream and popular knowledge. Teachers must make special efforts to introduce transformative knowledge and perspectives to elementary and secondary school students.

Teaching Implications

Multicultural education involves changes in the total school environment in order to create equal educational opportunities for all students (Banks, 1991; Banks & Banks, 1989; Sleeter & Grant, 1987). However, in this article I have focused on only one of the important dimensions of multicultural education—the kinds of *knowledge* that should be taught in the multicultural curriculum. The five types of knowledge described above have important implications for planning and teaching a multicultural curriculum.

An important goal of multicultural teaching is to help students to understand how knowledge is constructed. Students should be given opportunities to investigate and determine how cultural assumptions, frames of references, perspectives, and the biases within a discipline influence the ways the knowledge is constructed. Students should also be given opportunities to create knowledge themselves and identify ways in which the knowledge they construct is influenced and limited by their personal assumptions, positions, and experiences.

I will use a unit on the Westward Movement to illustrate how teachers can use the knowledge categories described above to teach from a multicultural perspective. When beginning the unit, teachers can draw upon the students' personal and cultural knowledge about the Westward Movement. They can ask the students to make a list of ideas that come to mind when they think of "The West." To enable the students to determine how the popular culture depicts the West, teachers can ask the students to view and analyze the film discussed above, *How the West Was Won*. They can also ask them to view videos of more recently made films about the West and to make a list of its major themes and images. Teachers can summarize Turner's frontier theory to give students an idea of how an influential mainstream historian described and interpreted the West in the late 19th century and how this theory influenced generations of historians.

Teachers can present a transformative perspective on the West by showing the students the film *How the West Was Won and Honor Lost*, narrated by Marlon Brando. This film describes how the European Americans who went West, with the use of broken treaties and deceptions, invaded the land of the Indians and displaced them. Teachers may also ask the students to view segments of the popular film *Dances With Wolves* and to discuss how the depiction of Indians in this film reflects both mainstream and transformative perspectives on Indians in U.S. history and culture. Teachers can present the textbook account of the Westward Movement in the final part of the unit.

The main goals of presenting different kinds of knowledge are to help students understand how knowledge is constructed and how it reflects the social context in which it is created and to enable them to develop the understandings and skills needed to become knowledge builders themselves. An important goal of multicultural education is to transform the school curriculum so that students not only learn the knowledge that has been constructed by others, but learn how to critically analyze the knowledge they master and how to construct their own interpretations of the past, present, and future.

Several important factors related to teaching the types of knowledge have not been discussed in this article but need to be examined. One is the personal/cultural knowledge of the classroom teacher. The teachers, like the students, bring understandings, concepts, explanations, and interpretations to the classroom that result from their experiences in their homes, families, and community cultures. Most teachers in the United States are European American (87%) and female (72%) (Ordovensky, 1992). However, there is enormous diversity among European Americans that is mirrored in the backgrounds of the teacher population, including diversity related to religion, social class, region, and ethnic origin. The diversity within European Americans is rarely discussed in the social science literature (Alba, 1990) or within classrooms. However, the rich diversity among the cultures of teachers is an important factor that needs to be examined and discussed in the classroom. The 13% of U.S. teachers who are ethnic minorities can also enrich their classrooms by sharing their personal and cultural knowledge with their students and by helping them to understand how it mediates textbook knowledge. The multicultural classroom is a forum of multiple voices and perspectives. The voices of the teacher, of the textbook, of mainstream and transformative authors—and of the students—are important components of classroom discourse.

Teachers can share their cultural experiences and interpretations of events as a way to motivate students to share theirs. However, they should examine their racial and ethnic attitudes toward diverse groups before engaging in cultural sharing. A democratic classroom atmosphere must also be created. The students must view the classroom as a forum where multiple perspectives are valued. An open and democratic classroom will enable students to acquire the skills and abilities they need to examine conflicting knowledge claims and perspectives. Students must become critical consumers of knowledge as well as knowledge producers if they are to acquire the understandings and skills needed to function in the complex and diverse world of tomorrow. Only a broad and liberal multicultural education can prepare them for that world.

Notes

This article is adapted from a paper presented at the conference "Democracy and Education," sponsored by the Benton Center for Curriculum and Instruction, Department of Education, The University of Chicago, November 15–16, 1991, Chicago, Illinois. I am grateful to the following colleagues for helpful comments on an earlier draft of this article: Cherry A. McGee Banks, Carlos E. Cortés, Geneva Gay, Donna H. Kerr, Joyce E. King, Walter C. Parker, Pamela L. Grossman, and Christine E. Sleeter.

References

Acuña, R. (1988). *Occupied America: A history of Chicanos* (3rd ed.). New York: Harper & Row.

Alba, R. D. (1990). *Ethnic identity: The transformation of White America.* New Haven, CT: Yale University Press.

Allen, P. G. (1986). *The sacred hoop: Recovering the feminine in American Indian traditions.* Boston: Beacon Press.

Altbach, P. G., Kelly, G. P., Petrie, H. G., & Weis, L. (Eds.). (1991). *Textbooks in American Society.* Albany, NY: State University of New York Press.

The American heritage dictionary. (1983). New York: Dell.

Anyon, J. (1979). Ideology and United States history textbooks. *Harvard Educational Review, 49,* 361–386.

Anyon, J. (1981). Social class and school knowledge. *Curriculum Inquiry, 11,* 3–42.

Anzaldúa, G. (1990). Haciendo caras, una entrada: An introduction. in G. Anzaldúa (Ed.), *Making face, making soul: Haciendo caras* (pp. xv–xvii). San Francisco: Aunt Lute Foundation Books.

Apple, M. W., & Christian-Smith, L. K. (Eds.). (1991). *The politics of the textbook.* New York: Routledge.

Aptheker, H. (Ed.). (1973). *The collected published works of W. E. B. Dubois* (38 Vols.). Millwood, NY: Kraus.

Asante, M. K. (1991a). The Afrocentric idea in education. *The Journal of Negro Education, 60,* 170–180.

Asante, M. K. (1991b, September 23). Putting Africa at the center. *Newsweek, 118,* 46.

Asante, M. K., & Ravitch, D. (1991). Multiculturalism: An exchange. *The American Scholar, 60,* 267–275.

Banks, J. A. (1988). *Multiethnic education: Theory and practice* (2nd ed.). Boston: Allyn & Bacon.

Banks, J. A. (1991). *Teaching strategies for ethnic studies* (5th ed.). Boston: Allyn & Bacon.

Banks, J. A. (1991/1992). Multicultural education: For freedom's sake. *Educational Leadership, 49,* 32–36.

Banks, J. A., & Banks, C. A. M. (Eds.). (1989). *Multicultural education: Issues and perspectives.* Boston: Allyn & Bacon.

Begley, S., Chideya, F., & Wilson, L. (1991, September 23). Out of Egypt, Greece: Seeking the roots of Western civilization on the banks of the Nile. *Newsweek, 118,* 48–49.

Bernal, M. (1987–1991). *Black Athena: The Afroasiatic roots of classical civilization* (Vols. 1–2). London: Free Association Books.

Blassingame, J. W. (1972). *The slave community: Plantation life in the Antebellum South.* New York: Oxford University Press.

Bloom, A. (1987). *The closing of the American mind.* New York: Simon & Schuster.

Bogle, D. (1989). *Toms, coons, mulattoes, mammies & bucks: An interpretative history of Blacks in American films* (new expanded ed.). New York: Continuum.

Butler, J. E., & Walter, J. C. (1991). (Eds.). *Transforming the curriculum: Ethnic studies and women studies.* Albany, NY: State University of New York Press.

Cherryholmes, C. H. (1988). *Power and criticism: Poststructural investigations in education.* New York: Teachers College Press.

Clark, K. B. (1965). *Dark ghetto: Dilemmas of social power.* New York: Harper & Row.

Code, L. (1991). *What can she know? Feminist theory and the construction of knowledge.* Ithaca, NY: Cornell University Press.

Cooper, A. J. (1969). *A voice from the South.* New York: Negro Universities Press. (Original work published 1982)

Cortés, C. E. (1991a). Empowerment through media literacy. In C. E. Sleeter (Ed.), *Empowerment through multicultural education.* Albany: State University of New York Press.

Cortés, C. E. (1991b). Hollywood interracial love: Social taboo as screen titillation. In P. Loukides & L. K. Fuller (Eds.), *Beyond the stars II: Plot conventions in American popular film* (pp. 21–35). Bowling Green, OH: Bowling Green State University Press.

Delpit, L. D. (1988). The silenced dialogue: Power and pedagogy in educating other people's children. *Harvard Educational Review, 58,* 280–298.

Diop, C. A. (1974). *The African origin of civilization: Myth or reality?* New York: Lawrence Hill.

D'Souza, D. (1991). *Illiberal education: The politics of race and sex on campus.* New York: Free Press.

DuBois, W. E. B. (1962). *Black reconstruction in America 1860–1880: An essay toward a History of the part which Black folk played in the attempt to reconstruct democracy in America, 1860–1880.* New York: Atheneum. (Original work published 1935)

DuBois, W. E. B. (1969). *The suppression of the African slave trade to the United States of America, 1638–1870,* Baton Rouge, LA: Louisiana State University Press. (Original work published 1896)

Ellsworth, E. (1989). Why doesn't this feel empowering? Working through the repressive myths of critical pedagogy. *Harvard Educational Review, 59,* 297–324.

Farganis, S. (1986). *The social construction of the feminine character.* Totowa, NJ: Russell & Russell.

FitzGerald, F. (1979). *America revised: History schoolbooks in the twentieth century.* New York: Vintage.

Foucault, M. (1972). *The archaeology of knowledge and the discourse on language.* New York: Pantheon.

Fordham, S. (1988). Racelessness as a factor in Black students' school success: Pragmatic strategy or Pyrrhic victory? *Harvard Educational Review, 58,* 54–84.

Fordham, S. (1991). Racelessness in private schools: Should we deconstruct the racial and cultural identity of African-American adolescents? *Teachers College Record, 92,* 470–484.

Fordham, S., & Ogbu, J. (1986). Black students' school success: Coping with the burden of 'acting White.' *The Urban Review, 18,* 176–206.

Franklin, J. H. (1991, September 26). Illiberal education: An exchange. *New York Review of Books, 38,* 74–76.

Frazier, E. F. (1939). *The Negro family in the United States.* Chicago: University of Chicago Press.

Gates, H. L., Jr. (1988). *The signifying monkey: A theory of African-American literary criticism.* New York: Oxford University Press.

Gates, H. L., Jr. (1992). *Loose canons: Notes on the culture wars.* New York: Oxford University Press.

Genovese, E. D. (1972). *Roll Jordan roll: The world the slaves made.* New York: Pantheon.

Giroux, H. A. (1983). *Theory and resistance in education.* Boston: Bergin & Garvey.

Glazer, N. (1991, September 2). In defense of multiculturalism. *The New Republic,* 18–21.

Goodlad, J. I. (1984). *A place called school: Prospects for the future.* New York: McGraw-Hill.

Gordon, E. W. (1985). Social science knowledge production and minority experiences. *Journal of Negro Education, 54,* 117–132.

Gordon, E. W., Miller, F., & Rollock, D. (1990). Coping with communicentric bias in knowledge production in the social sciences. *Educational Researcher, 14*(3), 14–19.

Grant, C. A. (Ed.). (1992). *Research and multicultural education: From the margins to the mainstream.* Washington, DC: Falmer.

Gray, P. (1991, July 8). Whose America? *Time, 138,* 12–17.

Greenfield, G. M., & Cortés, C. E. (1991). Harmony and conflict of intercultural images: The treatment of Mexico in U.S. feature films and K–12 textbooks. *Mexican Studies/Estudios Mexicanos, 7,* 283–301.

Greer, S. (1969). *The logic of social inquiry.* Chicago: Aldine.

Gutman, H. G. (1976). *The Black family in slavery and freedom 1750–1925.* New York: Vintage.

Habermas, J. (1971). *Knowledge and human interests.* Boston: Beacon.

Hale-Benson, J. E. (1982). *Black children: Their roots, culture, and learning styles* (rev. ed.). Baltimore: John Hopkins University Press.

Harding, S. (1991). *Whose science? Whose knowledge? Thinking from women's lives.* Ithaca, NY: Cornell University Press.

Harding, V. (1981). *There is a river: The Black struggle for freedom in America.* New York: Vintage.

Heath, S. B. (1983). *Ways with words: Language, life and work in communities and classrooms.* New York: Cambridge University Press.

Hirsch, E. D., Jr. (1987). *Cultural literacy: What every American needs to know.* Boston: Houghton Mifflin.

hooks, b., & West, C. (1991). *Breaking bread: Insurgent Black intellectual life.* Boston: South End Press.

Howe, I. (1991, February 18). The value of the canon. *The New Republic,* 40–47.

Hoxie, F. E. (Ed.). (1988). *Indians in American history.* Arlington Heights, IL: Harlan Davidson.

Hoxie, F. E. (no date). *The Indians versus the textbooks: Is there any way out?* Chicago: The Newberry Library, Center for the History of the American Indian.

Kaplan, A. (1964). *The conduct of inquiry: Methodology for behavioral science.* San Francisco: Chandler.

King, J. E., & Mitchell, C. A. (1990). *Black mothers to sons: Juxtaposing African American literature with social practice.* New York: Lang.

Kuhn, T. S. (1970). *The structure of scientific revolutions* (2nd ed.). Chicago: University of Chicago Press.

Labov, W. (1975). *The study of nonstandard English.* Washington, DC: Center for Applied Linguistics.

Ladner, J. A. (Ed.). (1973). *The death of White sociology.* New York: Vintage.

Meier, A., & Rudwick, E. (1986). *Black history and the historical profession 1915–1980.* Urbana, IL: University of Illinois Press.

Merton, R. K. (1972). Insiders and outsiders: A chapter in the sociology of knowledge. *The American Journal of Sociology, 78,* 9–47.

Milner, D. (1983). *Children and race.* Beverly Hills, CA: Sage.

Minnich, E. K. (1990). *Transforming knowledge.* Philadelphia: Temple University Press.

Moynihan, D. P. (1965). *The Negro family in America: A case for national action.* Washington, DC: U.S. Department of Labor.

Myrdal, G. (with the assistance of R. Sterner & A. Rose). (1944). *An American dilemma: The Negro problem in modern democracy.* New York: Harper.

Nash, G. B. (1982). *Red, White and Black: The peoples of early America.* Englewood Cliffs, NJ: Prentice-Hall.

New York City Board of Education. (1990). *Grade 7, United States and New York state history: A multicultural perspective.* New York: Author.

New York State Department of Education. (1989, July). *A curriculum of inclusion* (Report of the Commissioner's Task Force on Minorities: Equity and excellence). Albany, NY: The State Education Department.

New York State Department of Education. (1991, June). *One nation, many peoples: A declaration of cultural interdependence.* Albany, NY: The State Education Department.

Ordovensky, P. (1992, July 7). Teachers: 87% White, 72% women. *USA Today,* p. 1A.

Philips, S. U. (1983). *The invisible culture: Communication in classroom and community on the Warm Springs Indian Reservation.* New York: Longman.

Phillips, U. B. (1918). *American Negro slavery.* New York: Appleton.

Ramírez, M., III, & Castañeda, A. (1974). *Cultural democracy, bicognitive development and education.* New York: Academic Press.

Ravitch, D., & Finn, C. E., Jr. (1987). *What do our 17-year-olds know? A report on the first national assessment of history and literature.* New York: Harper & Row.

Rivlin, A. M. (1973). Forensic social science. *Harvard Educational Review, 43,* 61–75.

Rorty, R. (1989). *Contingency, irony, and solidarity.* New York: Cambridge University Press.

Rosenau, P. M. (1992). *Post-modernism and the social sciences: Insights, inroads, and intrusions.* Princeton, NJ: Princeton University Press.

Schlesinger, A., Jr. (1991). *The disuniting of America: Reflections on a multicultural society.* Knoxville, TN: Whittle Direct Books.

Shade, B. J. R. (Ed.). (1989). *Culture, style and the educative process.* Springfield, IL: Thompson.

Shaver, J. P., Davis, O. L., Jr., & Helburn, S. W. (1979). The status of social studies education: Impressions from three NSF studies. *Social Education, 43,* 150–153.

Sleeter, C. E. (1991). (Ed.). *Empowerment through multicultural education.* Albany: State University of New York Press.

Sleeter, C. E., & Grant, C. A. (1987). An analysis of multicultural education in the United States. *Harvard Educational Review, 57,* 421–444.

Sleeter, C. E., & Grant, C. A. (1991a). Mapping terrains of power: Student cultural knowledge versus classroom knowledge. In C. E. Sleeter (Ed.), *Empowerment through multicultural education* (pp. 49–67). Albany: State University of New York Press.

Sleeter, C. E., & Grant, C. A. (1991b). Race, class, gender and disability in current textbooks. In M. W. Apple & L. K. Christian-Smith (Eds.), *The politics of textbooks* (pp. 78–110). New York: Routledge.

Smitherman, G. (1977). *Talkin and testifyin: The language of Black America.* Boston: Houghton Mifflin.

Sokol, E. (Ed.). (1990). *A world of difference: St. Louis metropolitan region, preschool through grade 6, teacher/student resource guide.* St. Louis: Anti-Defamation League of B'nai B'rith.

Stampp, K. M. (1956). *The peculiar institution: Slavery in the ante-bellum South.* New York: Vintage.

Takaki, R. T. (1979). *Iron cages: Race and culture in 19th-century America.* Seattle, WA: University of Washington Press.

Tetreault, M. K. T. (1993). Classrooms for diversity: Rethinking curriculum and pedagogy. In J. A. Banks & C. A. M. Banks (Eds.), *Multicultural education: Issues and perspectives* (2nd ed.) (pp. 129–148). Boston: Allyn & Bacon.

Thornton, R. (1987). *American Indian holocaust and survival: A population history since 1492.* Norman: University of Oklahoma Press.

Turner, F. J. (1989). The significance of the frontier in American history. In C. A. Milner II (Ed.), *Major problems in the history of the American West* (pp. 2–21). Lexington, MA: Heath. (Original work published 1894)

Van Sertima, I. V. (Ed.). (1988). *Great Black leaders: Ancient and modern.* New Brunswick, NJ: Rutgers University, Africana Studies Department.

Van Sertima, I. V. (Ed.). (1989). *Great African thinkers: Vol. 1. Cheikh Anta Diop.* New Brunswick, NJ: Transaction Books.

Wiggington, E. (1991/1992). Culture begins at home. *Educational Leadership, 49,* 60–64.

Williams, G. W. (1968). *History of the Negro Race in America from 1619 to 1880: Negroes as slaves, as soldiers, and as citizens* (2 vols.). New York: Arno Press. (Original work published 1892 & 1893)

Williams, C. (1987). *The destruction of Black civilization: Great issues of a race from 4500 B.C. to 2000 A.D.* Chicago: Third World Press.

Woodson, C. G. (1933). *The Mis-education of the Negro.* Washington, DC: Associated Publishers.

Woodson, C. G., & Wesley, C. H. (1922). *The Negro in our history.* Washington, DC: Associated Publishers.

Woodward, C. V. (1991, July 18). Freedom and the universities. *The New York Review of Books, 38,* 32–37.

Young, M. F. D. (1971). An approach to curricula as socially organized knowledge. In M. F. D. Young (Ed.), *Knowledge and control* (pp. 19–46). London: Collier-Macmillan.

Zinn, H. (1980). *A people's history of the United States.* New York: Harper & Row.

Investing in Our
CHILDREN:
A Struggle for America's Conscience and Future

"Too many young people of all races and classes are growing up unable to handle life, without hope or steady compasses to navigate a world that is reinventing itself technologically and politically at a kaleidoscopic pace."

Marian Wright Edelman

Ms. Edelman is president of the Children's Defense Fund, Washington, D.C.

THE 1990S' STRUGGLE is about the U.S.'s conscience and future. Many of the battles will not be as dramatic as Gettysburg or Vietnam or Desert Storm, but they are going to shape this nation's place in the 21st century. Every American in this last decade of the last century of this millennium must struggle to redefine success in the U.S., asking not "How much can I get?," but "How much can I do without and share?"; not "How can I find myself?," but "How can I lose myself in service to others?"; not just how I can take care of me and mine, but how I can help as one American to strengthen family and community values and help this great nation regain her moral and economic bearings at home and abroad.

When I was growing up, service was as essential as eating and sleeping and going to church and school. Caring black adults were buffers against the segregated outside world which told me that, as a black girl, I wasn't worth anything and was not important. However, I didn't believe it because my parents, teachers, and preachers said it wasn't so. The childhood message I internalized, despite the outside segregation and poverty all around, was that, as God's child, no man or woman could look down on me, and I could look down on no man or woman.

I couldn't play in segregated playgrounds or sit at drugstore lunch counters, so my father, a Baptist minister, built a playground and canteen behind our church. Whenever he saw a need, he tried to respond. There were no black homes for the aged in South Carolina at that time, so my parents began one across the street, and our entire family had to help out. I didn't like it a whole lot of the time, but that is how I learned that it was my responsibility to take care of elderly family members and neighbors, and that everyone was my neighbor.

I went everywhere with my parents and the members of my church and community who were my watchful extended family. The entire black community took responsibility for protecting its children. They reported on me when I did wrong, applauded me when I did well, and were very clear as adults about what doing well meant. It meant being helpful to others, achieving in school, and reading. We all finally figured out that the only time our father wouldn't give us a chore was when we were reading, so we all read a lot.

Children were taught, by example, that nothing was too lowly to do and that the work of our heads and hands were both valuable. As a child, I went with an older brother—I was eight or nine or 10 and remember the debate between my parents as to whether I was too young to go help clean the bedsores of a poor, sick woman—but I went and learned just how much the smallest helping hands can mean to a lonely person in need.

Our families, churches, and community made kids feel useful and important. While life often was hard and resources scarce, we always knew who we were and that the measure of our worth was inside our heads and hearts, not outside in material possessions or personal ambition. We were taught that the world had a lot of problems; that black people had an *extra* lot of problems, but that we could struggle and change them; that extra intellectual and material gifts brought with them the privilege and responsibility of sharing with others less fortunate; and that service is the rent each of us pays for living—the very purpose of life and not something you do in your spare time or after you have reached your personal goals.

I am grateful for these childhood legacies of a living faith reflected in daily service, the discipline of hard work, and stick-to-itiveness—a capacity to struggle in the face of adversity. Giving up, despite how bad the world was outside, simply was not a part of my childhood lexicon. You got up every morning and did what you had to do, and you got up every time you fell down and tried as many times as you had to until you got it right. I was 14 the night my father died. He had holes in his shoes, but he had two children who graduated from college, one in college, another in divinity school, and a vision that he was able to convey to me even as he was dying in an ambulance—that I, a young black girl, could be and do anything, that race and gender are shadows, and that character, self-discipline, determination, attitude, and service are the substance of life.

What kind of vision are we conveying to our children today as parents, political and business leaders, and professionals? Our children are growing up in an ethically polluted nation where instant sex without responsibility, instant gratification without effort, instant solutions without sacrifice, getting rather than giving, and hoarding rather than sharing are the too frequent signals of our mass media, popular culture, and political life.

The standard of success for far too many Americans has become personal greed, rather than common good. The standard for striving and achievement has become getting, rather than making an extra effort or service to others. Truth-telling and moral example have become devalued commodities. Nowhere is the paralysis of public or private conscience more evident than in the neglect and abandonment of millions of our shrinking pool of youngsters, whose futures will determine our nation's ability to compete economically and lead morally as much as any child of privilege and as much as any other issue.

We need to understand that investing in our children is not investing in a special interest group or helping out somebody else—it is absolutely essential to every American's well-being and future. Only two out of every 10 new labor force entrants in this decade will be white males born in the U.S. As an aging population with a shrinking pool of kids, we don't have a child to waste—we need every one of them. We either can decide to invest in them up front and give them a sense of nurturing and caring adults that are part of a community and a society that guarantees them a future, or we can continue to fear them, build more and more prisons, and worry about them shooting at us. We don't have a choice about investing in our children, only when we are going to invest and whether it's going to be positive or negative investment.

Every 16 seconds of every school day, as we talk about a competitive workforce in the future, one of our children drops out of school. Every 26 seconds of every day, an American child runs away from home. These are not just poor or black children— they are all of our children. This is not something affecting just a few families— these are national problems. Every 47 seconds, a youngster is abused. Every 67 seconds, a teenager has a baby. We produce the equivalent of the city of Seattle each year with children having children. Every seven minutes, a child is arrested for a drug offense. Every 30 minutes, one of our children is charged with drunken driving. Every 53 minutes, in the richest land on Earth, an American child dies because of poverty.

It is disgraceful that children are the poorest Americans and that, in the last year alone, 840,000 youngsters fell into poverty and that there has been a 26% increase since 1979 in poverty among children. The majority of poor youngsters in America are not black and not in inner cities. They are in rural and suburban areas and in working and two-parent families. A lot of folk who were middle class last year around the country are now in poverty and on food stamps. It can happen to any of us.

We are in a sad state when the American Dream for many middle-class young people has become a choice between a house and a child. They are worrying about how their offspring are going to make it through college, pay off their higher education loans, and get off the ground and form families. We have to begin investing in all of our kids and all of our families. I believe we have lost our sense of what is important as a people. Too many children of all races and classes are growing up unable to handle life, without hope or steady compasses to navigate a world that is reinventing itself technologically and politically at a kaleidoscopic pace. Too many are growing up terribly uncertain and fearful about the future.

Despite the global realities the nation faces and a lot of the economic and moral uncertainty of the present, there are some enduring values we have lost sight of. I agree with poet Archibald MacLeish that there is only one thing more powerful than learning from experience and that is *not* learning from experience. It is the responsibility of every adult—parent, teacher, preacher, professional, and political leader—to make sure that youngsters hear what adults have learned from the lessons of life. Author James Baldwin wrote some years back that children really don't ever do what we tell them to do, but they almost always do what we do.

Americans have to move away from the idea of being entitled to something because they are men, or wealthy, or white, or black. It is time to come together to work quietly and systematically toward building a more just America and ensuring that no child is left behind. We should resist quick-fix, simplistic answers and easy gains that disappear as fast as they come. I am sick of people talking big and making great promises, then not following up and getting it done. Too often, we get bogged down in our ego needs and lose sight of deeper community and national needs.

Family values vs. hypocrisy

As a nation, we mouth family values we do not practice. Seventy countries provide medical care and financial assistance to all pregnant women and to children—the U.S. is not one of them. Seventeen industrialized nations have paid maternity/paternity leave programs—the U.S. is not one of them. In 1992, Pres. George Bush vetoed an unpaid leave bill that would have allowed parents to stay at home when a child is sick or disabled. We need to stop the hypocrisy of talking about families when all our practices are the opposite. It is time for parents to have a real choice about whether to remain at home or work outside the home without worrying about the safety of their children.

Many families have had to put a second parent into the workforce in order to make ends meet. Even when both parents work, a vast number are not able to meet their basic housing and health care needs.

The new generation of young people must share and stress family rituals and values and be moral examples for their children, just as this generation must try even harder to be. If people cut corners, their children will too. If they are not honest, their children will not be either. If adults spend all of their money and tithe no portion of it for colleges, synagogues or churches, and civic causes, their children won't either. If they tolerate political leaders who don't tell the truth or do what they say, their children will lose faith as too many are doing in the political process.

If we snicker at racial and gender jokes, another generation will pass on the poison that our generation still has not had the will to snuff out. Each of us must counter the proliferating voices of racial, ethnic, and religious division that separates us as Americans. It's important for us to face up to, rather than ignore, our growing racial problems, which are America's historic and future Achilles' heel. Whites didn't create black or brown people; men didn't create women; Christians didn't create Jews—so what gives anybody the right to feel entitled to diminish another?

We need to ask ourselves as Americans—how many potential Martin Luther King, Jrs. or Colin Powells, Sally Rides or Barbara McClintocks our nation is going to waste before it wakes up and recognizes that its ability to compete in the new century is as inextricably intertwined with poor and non-white children as with its white and privileged ones, with girls as well as its boys? As Rabbi Abraham Heschel put it, "We may not all be equally guilty for the problems that we face, but we are all equally responsible" for building a decent and just

America and seeing that no child is left behind.

People who are unwilling or unable to share and make complicated and sometimes hard choices may be incapable or taking courageous action to rebuild our families and community and nation. Nevertheless, I have great hopes about America and believe we can rebuild community and begin to put our children first as a nation. It is going to require that each of us figure out what we're going to be willing to sacrifice and share.

Many whites favor racial justice as long as things remain the same. Many voters hate Congress, but love their own Congressman as long as he or she takes care of their special interests. Many husbands are happier to share their wives' added income than share the housework and child care. Many Americans deny the growing gap between the rich and the poor, and they are sympathetic and concerned about escalating child suffering as long as somebody else's program is cut.

Americans have to grow up beyond this national adolescence. Everybody wants to spend, but nobody wants to pay. Everybody wants to lower the deficit, but also to get everything that they can. We have to ask ourselves how we're going to come together as a people to begin to make sure that the necessities of the many are taken care of and that every child gets what he or she needs to achieve a healthy start in life. If we're not too poor to bail out the savings and loan institutions, if we're not too poor to build all those B-2 bombers, we're not too poor to rescue our suffering children and to ensure that all youngsters get what they need.

In a time of economic uncertainty and fear about the future, of rising crime, rising costs, and rising joblessness, we must never give in to the urge to give up, no matter how hard it gets. There's an old proverb that says, "When you get to your wits end, remember that God lives there." Harriet Beecher Stowe once said that, when you get into a "tight place and everything goes against you, till it seems as though you could not hang on for a minute longer, never give up then, for that is just the place and the time when the tide will turn."

We can not continue as a nation to make a distinction between our children and other people's kids. Every youngster is entitled to an equal share of the American Dream. Every poor child, every black child, every white child—every child living everywhere—should have an equal shot. We need every one of them to be productive and educated and healthy.

Let me end this article with a prayer, written by a schoolteacher in South Carolina. She urges us to pray and accept responsibility for children who sneak popsicles before supper, erase holes in math workbooks, and never can find their shoes, but let's also pray and accept responsibility for children who can't bound down the street in a new pair of sneakers, who don't have any rooms to clean up, whose pictures aren't on anybody's dresser, and whose monsters are real. Let each of us commit to praying and accepting responsibility for children who spend all their allowance before Tuesday, throw tantrums in the grocery store, pick at their food, shove dirty clothes under the bed, never rinse out the tub, squirm in church or temple, and scream in the phone, but let's also pray and accept responsibility for those children whose nightmares come in the daytime, who will eat anything, who have never seen a dentist, who aren't spoiled by anybody, who go to bed hungry and cry themselves to sleep all over this rich nation. Let's commit to praying and accepting responsibility for children who want to be carried and for those who must be carried. Let's commit to protecting those children whom we never give up on, but also those children who don't get a second chance. Let each of us commit to praying and voting and speaking and fighting for those children whom we smother, but also for those who will grab the hand of anybody kind enough to offer it.

The AAUW Report: How Schools Shortchange Girls — Overview —

— Why a Report on Girls? —

The invisibility of girls in the current education debate suggests that girls and boys have identical educational experiences in school. Nothing could be further from the truth. Whether one looks at achievement scores, curriculum design, or teacher-student interaction, it is clear that sex and gender make a difference in the nation's public elementary and secondary schools.

The educational system is not meeting girls' needs. Girls and boys enter school roughly equal in measured ability. Twelve years later, girls have fallen behind their male classmates in key areas such as higher-level mathematics and measures of self-esteem. Yet gender equity is still not a part of the national debate on educational reform.

Research shows that policies developed to foster the equitable treatment of students and the creation of gender-equitable educational environments can make a difference. They can make a difference, that is, if they are strongly worded and vigorously enforced.

V. Lee, H. Marks and T. Knowles, "Sexism in Single-Sex and Coeducational Secondary School Classrooms," paper presented at the American Sociological Association annual meeting, Cincinnati, OH, August 1991; S. Bailey and R. Smith, *Policies for the Future,* Council of Chief State School Officers, Washington, DC, 1982.

Neither the *National Education Goals* issued by the National Governors Association in 1990 nor *America 2000,* the 1991 plan of the President and the U.S. Department of Education to "move every community in America toward these goals" makes any mention of providing girls equitable opportunities in the nation's public schools. Girls continue to be left out of the debate—despite the fact that for more than two decades researchers have identified gender bias as a major problem at all levels of schooling.

Schools must prepare both girls and boys for full and active roles in the family, the community, and the work force. Whether we look at the issues from an economic, political, or social perspective, girls are one-half of our future. We must move them from the sidelines to the center of the education-reform debate.

A critical step in correcting educational inequities is identifying them publicly. The *AAUW Report: How Schools Shortchange Girls* provides a comprehensive assessment of the status of girls in public education today. It exposes myths about girls and learning, and it supports the work of the many teachers who have struggled to define and combat gender bias in their schools. The report challenges us all—policymakers, educators, administrators, parents, and citizens—to rethink old assumptions and act now to stop schools from shortchanging girls.

Our public education system is plagued by numerous failings that affect boys as negatively as girls. But in many respects girls are put at a disadvantage simply because they are girls. *The AAUW Report* documents this in hundreds of cited studies.

When our schools become more gender-fair, education will improve for all our students—boys as well as girls—because excellence in education cannot be achieved without equity in education. By studying what happens to girls in school, we can gain valuable insights about what has to change in order for each student, every girl and every boy, to do as well as she or he can.

What Do We Teach Our Students?

• The contributions and experiences of girls and women are still marginalized or ignored in many of the textbooks used in our nation's schools.
• Schools, for the most part, provide inadequate education on sexuality and healthy development despite national concern about teen pregnancy, the AIDS crisis, and the increase of sexually transmitted diseases among adolescents.

• Incest, rape, and other physical violence severely compromise the lives of girls and women all across the country. These realities are rarely, if ever, discussed in schools.

Curriculum delivers the central messages of education. It can strengthen or decrease student motivation for engagement, effort, growth, and development through the images it gives to students about themselves and the world. When the curriculum does not reflect the diversity of students' lives and cultures, it delivers an incomplete message.

Studies have shown that multicultural readings produced markedly more favorable attitudes toward nondominant groups than did the traditional reading lists, that academic achievement for all students was linked to use of nonsexist and multicultural materials, and that sex-role stereotyping was reduced in students whose curriculum portrayed males and females in non-stereotypical roles. Yet during the 1980s, federal support for reform regarding sex and race equity dropped, and a 1989 study showed that of the ten books most frequently assigned in public high school English courses only one was written by a woman and none by members of minority groups.

The "evaded" curriculum is a term coined in this report to refer to matters central to the lives of students that are touched on only briefly, if at all, in most schools. The United States has the highest rate of teenage childbearing in the Western industrialized world. Syphilis rates are now equal for girls and boys, and more teenage girls than boys contract gonorrhea. Although in the adult population AIDS is nine times more prevalent in men than in women, the same is not true for young people. In a District of Columbia study, the rate of HIV infection for girls was almost three times that for boys. Despite all of this, adequate sex and health education is the exception rather than the rule.

Adolescence is a difficult period for all young people, but it is particularly difficult for girls, who are far more likely to develop eating disorders and experience depression. Adolescent girls attempt suicide four to five times as often as boys (although boys, who choose more lethal methods, are more likely to be successful in their attempts).

Despite medical studies indicating that roughly equal proportions of girls and boys suffer from learning disabilities, more than twice as many boys are identified by school personnel as in need of special-education services for learning-disabled students.

U.S. Department of Education, Office for Civil Rights, 1988.

Perhaps the most evaded of all topics in schools is the issue of gender and power. As girls mature they confront a culture that both idealizes and exploits the sexuality of young women while assigning them roles that are clearly less valued than male roles. If we do not begin to discuss more openly the ways in which

ascribed power—whether on the basis of race, sex, class, sexual orientation, or religion—affects individual lives, we cannot truly prepare our students for responsible citizenship.

These issues are discussed in detail and the research fully annotated in Part 4/Chapters 1 and 3 of The AAUW Report.

How Do Race/Ethnicity and Socioeconomic Status Affect Achievement in School?

• Girls from low-income families face particularly severe obstacles. Socioeconomic status, more than any other variable, affects access to school resources and educational outcomes.
• Test scores of low-socioeconomic-status girls are somewhat better than for boys from the same background in the lower grades, but by high school these differences disappear. Among high-socioeconomic-status students, boys generally outperform girls regardless of race/ethnicity.
• Girls and boys with the same Math SAT scores do not do equally well in college—girls do better.

In most cases tests reflect rather than cause inequities in American education. The fact that groups score differently on a test does not necessarily mean that the test is biased. If, however, the score differences are related to the validity of the test—for example, if girls and boys know about the same amount of math but boys' test scores are consistently and significantly higher—then the test is biased.

A number of aspects of a test—beyond that which is being tested—can affect the score. For example, girls tend to score better than boys on essay tests, boys better than girls on multiple-choice items. Even today many girls and boys come to a testing situation with different interests and experiences. Thus a reading-comprehension passage that focuses on baseball scores will tend to favor boys, while a question testing the same skills that focuses on child care will tend to favor girls.

These issues are discussed in detail and the research fully annotated in Part 3 of The AAUW Report.

Why Do Girls Drop Out and What Are the Consequences?

• Pregnancy is not the only reason girls drop out of school. In fact, less than half the girls who leave school give pregnancy as the reason.
• Dropout rates for Hispanic girls vary considerably by national origin: Puerto Rican and Cuban American girls are more likely to drop out than are boys from the same cultures or other Hispanic girls.
• Childhood poverty is almost inescapable in single-parent families headed by women without a high school diploma: 77 percent for whites and 87 percent for African Americans.

In a recent study, 37 percent of the female drop-outs compared to only 5 percent of the male drop-outs cited "family-related problems" as the reason they left high school. Traditional gender roles place greater family responsibilities on adolescent girls than on their brothers. Girls are often expected to "help out" with caretaking responsibilities; boys rarely encounter this expectation.

There has been little change in sex-segregated enrollment patterns in vocational education: girls are enrolled primarily in office and business-training programs, boys in programs leading to higher-paying jobs in the trades.

U.S. Department of Education, 1989.

However, girls as well as boys also drop out of school simply because they do not consider school pleasant or worthwhile. Asked what a worthwhile school experience would be, a group of teenage girls responded, "School would be fun. Our teachers would be excited and lively, not bored. They would act caring and take time to understand how students feel. . . . Boys would treat us with respect. If they run by and grab your tits, they would get into trouble."*

Women and children are the most impoverished members of our society. Inadequate education not only limits opportunities for women but jeopardizes their children's—and the nation's—future.

These issues are discussed in detail and the research fully annotated in Part 2/Chapters 4 and 6 of The AAUW Report.

The research reviewed in this report challenges traditional assumptions about the egalitarian nature of American schools. Young women in the United States today are still not participating equally in our educational system. Research documents that girls do not receive equitable amounts of teacher attention, that they are less apt than boys to see themselves reflected in the materials they study, and that they often are not expected or encouraged to pursue higher level mathematics and science courses. The implications are clear; the system must change.

We now have a window of opportunity that must not be missed. Efforts to improve public education are under way around the nation. We must move girls from the sidelines to the center of educational planning. The nation can no longer afford to ignore the potential of girls and young women. Whether one looks at the issues from an economic, political, or social perspective, girls are one-half of our future.

Significant improvements in the educational opportunities available to girls have occurred in the past two decades. However, twenty years after the passage of Title IX, the achievement of sex- and gender-equitable education remains an elusive dream. The time to turn dreams to reality is now. The

---

*As quoted in *In Their Own Voices: Young Women Talk About Dropping Out,* Project on Equal Education Rights (New York, National Organization for Women Legal Defense and Education Fund, 1988), p. 12.

current education-reform movement cannot succeed if it continues to ignore half of its constituents. The issues are urgent; our actions must be swift and effective.

— The Recommendations —

Strengthened Reinforcement of Title IX Is Essential.

1. Require school districts to assess and report on a regular basis to the Office for Civil Rights in the U.S. Department of Education on their own Title IX compliance measures.
2. Fund the Office for Civil Rights at a level that permits increased compliance reviews and full and prompt investigation of Title IX complaints.
3. In assessing the status of Title IX compliance, school districts must include a review of the treatment of pregnant teens and teen parents. Evidence indicates that these students are still the victims of discriminatory treatment in many schools.

Teachers, Administrators and Counselors Must Be Prepared and Encouraged to Bring Gender Equity and Awareness to Every Aspect of Schooling.

4. State certification standards for teachers and administrators should require course work on gender issues, including new research on women, bias in classroom-interaction patterns, and the ways in which schools can develop and implement gender-fair multicultural curricula.
5. If a national teacher examination is developed, it should include items on methods for achieving gender equity in the classroom and in curricula.
6. Teachers, administrators, and counselors should be evaluated on the degree to which they promote and encourage gender-equitable and multicultural education.
7. Support and released time must be provided by school districts for teacher-initiated research on curricula and classroom variables that affect student learning. Gender equity should be a focus of this research and a criterion for awarding funds.
8. School-improvement efforts must include a focus on the ongoing professional development of teachers and administrators, including those working in specialized areas such as bilingual, compensatory, special, and vocational education.
9. Teacher-training courses must not perpetuate assumptions about the superiority of traits and activities traditionally ascribed to males in our society. Assertive and affiliative skills as well as verbal and mathematical skills must be fostered in both girls and boys.
10. Teachers must help girls develop positive views of themselves and their futures, as well as an understanding of the obstacles women must overcome in a society where their options and opportunities are still limited by gender stereotypes and assumptions.

6. EQUAL OPPORTUNITY IN EDUCATION

The Formal School Curriculum Must Include the Experiences of Women and Men From All Walks of Life. Girls and Boys Must See Women and Girls Reflected and Valued in the Materials They Study.

11. Federal and state funding must be used to support research, development, and follow-up study of gender-fair multicultural curricular models.

12. The Women's Educational Equity Act Program (WEEAP) in the U.S. Department of Education must receive increased funding in order to continue the development of curricular materials and models, and to assist school districts in Title IX compliance.

13. School curricula should deal directly with issues of power, gender politics, and violence against women. Better-informed girls are better equipped to make decisions about their futures. Girls and young women who have a strong sense of themselves are better able to confront violence and abuse in their lives.

14. Educational organizations must support, via conferences, meetings, budget deliberations, and policy decisions, the development of gender-fair multicultural curricula in all areas of instruction.

15. Curricula for young children must not perpetuate gender stereotypes and should reflect sensitivity to different learning styles.

Girls Must Be Educated and Encouraged to Understand That Mathematics and the Sciences Are Important and Relevant to Their Lives. Girls Must Be Actively Supported in Pursuing Education and Employment in These Areas.

16. Existing equity guidelines should be effectively implemented in all programs supported by local, state, and federal governments. Specific attention must be directed toward including women on planning committees and focusing on girls and women in the goals, instructional strategies, teacher training, and research components of these programs.

17. The federal government must fund and encourage research on the effect on girls and boys of new curricula in the sciences and mathematics. Research is needed particularly in science areas where boys appear to be improving their performance while girls are not.

18. Educational institutions, professional organizations, and the business community must work together to dispel myths about math and science as "inappropriate" fields for women.

19. Local schools and communities must encourage and support girls studying science and mathematics by showcasing women role models in scientific and technological fields, disseminating career information, and offering "hands-on" experiences and work groups in science and math classes.

20. Local schools should seek strong links with youth-serving organizations that have developed successful out-of-school programs for girls in mathematics and science and with those girls' schools that have developed effective programs in these areas.

Continued Attention to Gender Equity in Vocational Education Programs Must Be a High Priority at Every Level of Educational Governance and Administration.

21. Linkages must be developed with the private sector to help ensure that girls with training in nontraditional areas find appropriate employment.

22. The use of a discretionary process for awarding vocational-education funds should be encouraged to prompt innovative efforts.

23. All states should be required to make support services (such as child care and transportation) available to both vocational and prevocational students.

24. There must be continuing research on the effectiveness of vocational education for girls and the extent to which the 1990 Vocational Education Amendments benefit girls.

Testing and Assessment Must Serve as Stepping Stones Not Stop Signs. New Tests and Testing Techniques Must Accurately Reflect the Abilities of Both Girls and Boys.

25. Test scores should not be the only factor considered in admissions or the awarding of scholarships.

26. General aptitude and achievement tests should balance sex differences in item types and contexts. Tests should favor neither females nor males.

27. Tests that relate to "real life situations" should reflect the experiences of both girls and boys.

Girls and Women Must Play a Central Role in Educational Reform. The Experiences, Strengths, and Needs of Girls From Every Race and Social Class Must Be Considered in Order to Provide Excellence and Equity for All Our Nation's Students.

28. National, state, and local governing bodies should ensure that women of diverse backgrounds are equitably represented on committees and commissions on educational reform.

29. Receipt of government funding for in-service and professional development programs should be conditioned upon evidence of efforts to increase the number of women in positions in which they are underrepresented. All levels of government have a role to play in increasing the numbers of women, especially women of color, in education-management and policy positions.

30. The U.S. Department of Education's Office of Educational Research and Improvement (OERI) should establish an advisory panel of gender-equity experts to work with OERI to develop a research and dissemination agenda to foster gender-equitable education in the nation's classrooms.

31. Federal and state agencies must collect, analyze, and report data broken down by race/ethnicity, sex, and some measure of socioeconomic status, such as parental income or education. National standards for use by all school districts should be developed so that data are comparable across district and state lines.

32. National standards for computing dropout rates should be developed for use by all school districts.

33. Professional organizations should ensure that women serve on education-focused committees. Organizations should utilize the expertise of their female membership when developing educational initiatives.

34. Local schools must call on the expertise of teachers, a majority of whom are women, in their restructuring efforts.

35. Women teachers must be encouraged and supported to seek administrative positions and elected office, where they can bring the insights gained in the classroom to the formulation of education policies.

A Critical Goal of Education Reform Must Be to Enable Students to Deal Effectively with the Realities of Their Lives, Particularly in Areas Such as Sexuality and Health.

36. Strong policies against sexual harassment must be developed. All school personnel must take responsibility for enforcing these policies.

37. Federal and state funding should be used to promote partnerships between schools and community groups, including social service agencies, youth-serving organizations, medical facilities, and local businesses. The needs of students, particularly as highlighted by pregnant teens and teen mothers, require a multi-institutional response.

38. Comprehensive school-based health- and sex-education programs must begin in the early grades and continue sequentially through twelfth grade. These courses must address the topics of reproduction and reproductive health, sexual abuse, drug and alcohol use, and general mental and physical health issues. There must be a special focus on the prevention of AIDS.

39. State and local school board policies should enable and encourage young mothers to complete school, without compromising the quality of education these students receive.

40. Child care for the children of teen mothers must be an integral part of all programs designed to encourage young women to pursue or complete educational programs.

**The AAUW Report:
How Schools Shortchange Girls**

A startling examination of how girls are disadvantaged in America's schools, grades K–12. Prepared by the Wellesley College Center for Research on Women, the book includes recommendations for educators and policymakers, as well as concrete strategies for change. 128 pages/1992. $14.95 AAUW members/$16.95 nonmembers. Bulk prices available.

Serving Special Needs and Concerns

Providing educational services to one's fellow human beings is the primary mission of a teacher. People learn under many different sets of circumstances. There are many categories of concern relating to the education of persons, both within schools and in other alternative learning contexts. Each year we include in this section several articles on a variety of special topics that we believe our readers will find interesting and relevant.

Home schooling is a major alternative educational phenomenon in the United States. Although less than 1 percent of American elementary and secondary school students are taught in their homes, the commitment and dedication to the idea of educating children at home on the part of those parents who choose to do so are amazing. And these home schoolers are very well organized; they have active national and state organizations, and they frequently link up with other home schoolers at the local level to socialize, carry out field trips for their children, and share expertise in and questions on the challenges of educating them. Furthermore, these parents have access to several home school service organizations that provide books, lesson plans, inquiry and experiment packages, testing services, and support materials for assisting parents in the instruction of their

children from kindergarten through twelfth grade. This correspondence school organization enables parents to offer great breadth and depth to their children's education.

One idea regarding schooling that represents a major departure from traditional practice is the idea of going to school throughout the year. Thus far, year-round schooling is being done only by a relatively small number of school districts across the nation, but it has become very popular as an educational option in California, Texas, and North Carolina. In a year-round school students still get about 90 days a year in vacation time, but instead of being out of school all summer, students and teachers take three 30-day vacation breaks spread throughout the year (including one in the summer) or two 45-day breaks. The theory behind this is that students will retain more of what they learn in school if they take shorter vacation breaks. Teachers don't have to do as much review teaching each fall semester, and students retain school learning more efficiently.

As we explore other special topics in this unit this year, we review several other issues of general interest. A Nobel laureate in physics discusses what outside intervention by experts in various academic fields can contribute to extending the breadth and depth of teachers' repertoires of knowledge in academic areas of study. Another article reviews controversy surrounding the educational and commercial implications of *Channel One* news broadcasting in American public schools. The development and targeting of youth markets are discussed as well as the educational trade-offs evolving from commercial marketing of products to students in the schools. Resources are identified in economic education for teachers to use in teaching their students about economic concepts and issues.

Several issues are raised when people begin to consider whether commercial advertising should be used in schools. Some argue against it; others argue that it is beneficial for students to learn to be discriminating, knowledgeable consumers while they are still in elementary school. Students are exposed to heavy doses of commercial advertising from radio and television as well as outside the home. The educational issues related to this phenomenon spark interesting discussions among educators, parents, and people in business.

Jocelyn Elders, the former U.S. surgeon general, has contributed an excellent article on how violence in society becomes a health hazard to children and youth. Young persons who are poor and who live in economically marginal and multiproblematic neighborhoods are at greater risk of physical injury and even death. Elders points out how social violence increases greatly the risks to the health and safety of our youth. The rates of occurrence of several types of social violence in the United States are several times higher than in other industrialized nations.

"Blowing up the Tracks," by Patricia Kean, is a criticism of ability grouping in schools. The author is clearly in favor of inclusion of all students into a heterogeneous pattern of scheduling their classes in school without regard to traditional ways of defining ability. She supports optimum levels of inclusivity of students. One major movement toward a more inclusive scheduling of students—and away from ability grouping—is really an offshoot of the "mainstreaming" concept of the 1970s and 1980s, when all physically and cognitively handicapped students were required to be integrated into regular classes based on the criterion of "the least restrictive environment" possible for each child. This movement, in turn, has been a controversial issue since the United States made its commitment to mass universal secondary education in the teens of this century; that issue is the controversy over "heterogeneous versus homogeneous" grouping (ability "tracking") of students. Advocates of inclusion today favor heterogeneously scheduling students in schools without regard to ability on the primary premise that all students will learn from one another. Academically, they will benefit from being in classes with fellow students who represent a broad range of abilities and interests.

The next topic addresses certain assumptions that teachers should try to avoid in sex education or wherever discussion of sex and sexual orientation develops in school. Mary Krueger makes some very valuable observations in her essay on human sexual exceptionality.

Since first issued in 1973, this ongoing anthology has sought to provide discussion of special social or curricula issues affecting the teaching-learning conditions in schools. Fundamental forces at work in our culture during the past several years have greatly affected millions of students. The social, cultural, and economic pressures on families have produced several special problems of great concern to teachers. Serving special needs and concerns requires greater degrees of individualization of instruction and greater attention paid to the development and maintenance of healthier self-concepts by students.

Looking Ahead: Challenge Questions

What are the strengths of home schooling? Why do parents do it? What are the disadvantages, if any, to it?

What would be the principal arguments in favor of year-round schools? What are the arguments against it?

Is there a role for outside experts in improving the knowledge bases of teachers?

What are the issues surrounding *Channel One* broadcasting in schools?

What economic concepts should all students learn?

How does social violence affect youth? Why are children at risk?

What happens when violence breaks out at school? How would you react to having to attend a school plagued with violent incidents? Did you? How would you respond to violent behavior in school?

What are the pros and cons of inclusion in the scheduling of students in schools?

What does it mean to say that everyone is an exception when it comes to gender? What assumptions should be avoided?

—F. S.

HOME SWEET SCHOOL

Seeking excellence, isolation or just extra "family time," more and more parents are doing the teaching themselves

home schooling pg. 211 303-305

NANCY GIBBS

WHEN BONNIE VAUTROT REALIZED her daughter was dead bored in school, she decided to take on the system. She became the PTA president at the Williamsburg, Virginia, elementary school and challenged the teachers to challenge the kids. "I would go in and beg the teachers: 'What can I do?' If you have a curriculum that says you're in third grade now, but your child is ready for fourth-grade material, you hit a brick wall." The response, she recalls, was, "Well, obviously you've got nothing better to do. Why don't you teach your kids at home?" So she did. Thus was born another home school.

Beverly and Brad Williams had similar reasons but different circumstances. They were not only unimpressed with their local schools, they were scared of them as well. The idea of sending their four children through the cross fire of South Central Los Angeles was too harrowing. With ruthless budgeting, they managed to pay for private schools for six years, but tuition was just too high, and they were not satisfied with what it bought. So the couple converted their basement into a classroom with three desks, bulletin boards and two computers. Now their children get dressed every morning as if headed to school and are re-

quired to report to the basement by 9 a.m. Brad, who doesn't start work as a Federal Express delivery man until 3 p.m., handles most of the teaching. They work until 1:30, then break for the day.

If the Williamses and Vautrots do not seem like traditional home schoolers, that may be because there's no such thing anymore. A movement once reserved largely for misanthropes, missionaries and religious fundamentalists now embraces such a range of families that it has become a mainstream alternative to regular public or private education. In inner cities and rural farm towns all across the country, periodic tables hang on the dining-room walls, and multiplication tables are taped to the back of car seats for practice during field trips. Home schoolers hold conventions at which hundreds of companies offer curriculum guides, textbooks and support groups. There are home-school chat sessions on the Internet, even home-school proms and graduation ceremonies.

Since the late 1970s, when roughly 12,500 children were taught at home, the number has grown as high as half a million. It remains true that most parents who choose to withdraw their children from the school system, or never send them in the first place, do so for religious reasons, seeking to shape

their children's learning in accordance with their spiritual values. In addition, there are still the hermits and occasional hate-mongers, observes Joe Nathan, director of the University of Minnesota's Center for School Change, "people who have made it clear that the reason they educate at home is that they don't want their children exposed to people of different races, or that they don't want their children exposed to ideas with which they disagree."

More and more parents, however, are embracing home schooling for secular reasons. "I've also seen people who are very progressive or liberal," Nathan adds, "and think children are not well served by schools that are too stifling." Others, like the Williamses, are concerned mainly about the safety and the quality of public schools. Parents stress the chance to design a curriculum that is challenging, flexible and tailored to their particular child; to escape the "hidden agenda"—ranging from capitalist conformity to secular humanism—that they believe is promoted in public schools; and to have a teacher utterly devoted to their children's welfare.

For years the courts treated children who were kept home as truants; but home schooling is now legal in every state. Thir-

pertain

ty-four states have passed specific statutes and regulations, and 29 require standardized testing for home-schooled students to ensure that they are passing muster. Last June the Texas Supreme Court upheld a ruling that exempted home-schooled children from the state's compulsory-attendance laws. As long as parents use a curriculum that includes written materials and meets "basic education goals," the court ruled, the state has no authority over the matter.

If there was a turning point in the public image of home schooling, it came in 1987, when Grant Colfax got into Harvard after having been taught by his parents his entire life. Grant graduated magna cum laude, became a Fulbright scholar and graduated from Harvard Medical School. One by one, his home-schooled brothers followed suit. "Our kids were more or less the guinea pigs," says Micki Colfax, who along with husband David home schooled all four Colfax children from their home in Boonville, California (pop. 750). "Their going to Harvard validated what home schooling was all about."

The Colfaxes make compelling spokespeople for the movement they did so much to legitimize. "We feel every parent is qualified to teach," Micki says. "If it doesn't work, fine, go on to something else. Even within one family, the learning skills might be different, so one [child] might work at home, the other might work at school. But I think the more the government gets involved, the less freedom parents have."

Some critics of the movement argue that parents may have too much freedom under current laws. Only 10 states require parents to have a high school diploma or General Equivalency Diploma to be able to teach. "It's a giant step backward," argues Thomas Shannon, executive director of the National School Boards Association, which represents more than 15,000 public-school boards across the country. "People tend to think, as one old basketball coach said, that everybody can boil water and coach basketball, and they kind of feel the same way about teaching. They just don't know what they're talking about." If these parents spent their time supplementing their children's educations rather than substituting for it, he adds, "their children would be remarkably well off."

But home-school advocates counter that a teacher's certificate is no guarantee of success. They cite study after study showing that home-schooled children excel on standardized tests. While the national average is in the 50th percentile, the average home-schooled students register between the 65th and 80th percentiles. Nor is this unconventional background necessarily a disadvantage when students apply for college. With no grade-point averages or class ranks, no chance to edit the yearbook or captain the soccer team, home-schooled students must have top test scores to win admission to the most selective schools. But many colleges are eager to welcome freshmen who bring different experiences of learning. "What it really boils down to is getting a sense of a student's intellectual drive," says Jon Reider, associate director of admissions at Stanford.

But critics are also concerned about lessons that can't be measured on exams. A home-schooled child, they note, is not exposed to the diversity of beliefs and backgrounds that a child would encounter in many public schools and is deprived of an opportunity for "socialization." The after-school baseball leagues and Boy Scouts and dance classes don't make up the difference. "When you send them out to soccer and scouting, you're usually sending them out to a very select group of people who share, to a considerable extent, your own values," says Shannon. "That's a controlled group. The problem is, when they finally do get to working, they won't be in that controlled group."

Home-school parents retort that the socialization children experience in schools is not necessarily healthy: it may be competitive, even intimidating and violent. "I do not think that gang membership is proper social development," says Donna Nichols-White, who has home schooled her three children after having to teach herself how to write. "Whenever people mention the problem of gang membership, I mention that the common factor amongst all gang members is that they attended school at some time in their lives."

Do the children miss out on something essential? They don't seem to think so. "Sometimes I like playing school," confides Lydia Kiefer, 6. "I'll get up in the morning, get my backpack, put some books in it, come downstairs, and sit down at my little brown table and pretend I have a teacher and other kids next to me." She pauses to think. "But I'm not so sure it would be so fun in real life."

—Reported by Dan Cray/
Los Angeles, Scott Norvell/Atlanta and Bonnie I. Rochman/Williamsburg

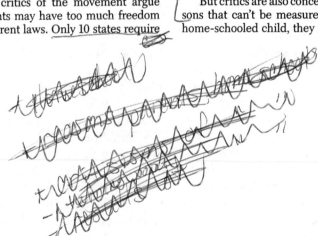

Year-Round School

The Best Thing Since Sliced Bread

Elaine Warrick-Harris

Elaine Warrick-Harris is Assistant Principal/Year-Round Coordinator, Balfour Elementary School, Asheboro, North Carolina. She is a member of the ACEI Executive Board.

Teachers, I ask you two questions. How many of your students helped to harvest crops last year? And how many mothers of students in your classroom stayed at home? It is true that some communities still depend heavily on agriculture, but modern farming's sophistication is such that children no longer carry the responsibilities that they once did. Fewer family situations today include a stay-at-home mother. Most teachers would probably answer the above questions by saying "none" or "very few." Therefore, a reasonable follow-up question would be, "Why do we continue to organize learning schedules for students based on the agricultural practices of 100 years ago?"

The outdated and agriculturally sensitive school calendar has other disadvantages. For example, vandalism to empty school buildings, especially over the summer months, is a growing problem. Students who have nothing to do during summer too often turn to mischief, or worse. On the other hand, Brekke (1984) and Ballinger (1987) indicate that schools operating on a year-round schedule have been able to reduce the incidence of vandalism and burglary.

Year-Round Education (YRE) is an excellent solution to the problems of vandalism, loss of productive learning time and unsupervised children. The term "year-round" is actually misleading. Other more descriptive terms might be "continuous learning," "all-seasons learning" or even "four-seasons school." "Year-round school" is the term most frequently associated with the organizational system that uses the school facility during every season. The year-round school is *not*, however, an alternative curriculum for learning. Quinlan, George and Emmett (1987) define YRE as a reorganization of the school calendar into instructional blocks and vacations distributed across the calendar year to ensure continuous learning. The single-track schedule, for example, offers nine weeks of instruction followed by a three-week break.

Traditional curriculum content continues to be used within the year-round schedule. Students' learning in a year-round school, however, can progress with less of an interruption during the summer months. Students retain more information during four short breaks than they would after the normal ten-week summer vacation. This continuity of instruction, along with remedial reviews offered during the breaks, helps reduce the number of students who must be retained in grade.

In addition, the year-round schedule leads to less teacher stress and burnout. Rather than the feast-or-famine break schedule practiced by most schools, teachers benefit from a cycle of evenly spaced vacations.

Parents, too, gain from YRE. Families have more options for arranging vacations and can enjoy off-season rates and less-crowded vacation sites. In addition, many working parents favor a YRE schedule because it provides them with an opportunity for child care most of the year.

With so many benefits associated with YRE, it is logical to ask, "Why doesn't everyone have year-round school?"

One School's Story

Tradition is one reason why more schools have not adopted a year-round schedule. It is not easy to replace a practice that has been in place for decades with an alternative that could disrupt teachers' and parents' social and familial patterns. Usually, a change this drastic is associated with broader and potentially problematic circumstances. The initiation of YRE at Balfour Elementary School, in Asheboro, North Carolina, fits this description.

Five years ago, Balfour Elementary School, built in 1926, was representative of the small community school of long ago. The majority of the 312 students walked to school and only one bus was needed. By 1989, however, the school's enrollment and costs were both spiraling out of control. Essentially, the building was too old and too small.

A successful school bond referendum enabled the Board of Education to fund construction of a spacious new school within a mile

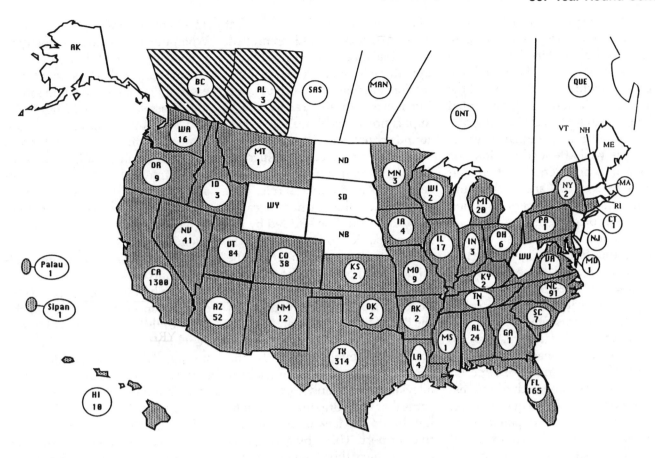

Number of Public/Private Schools with Year-Round Programs by State, Territory and Province 1994-95.
Source for all figures: National Association for Year-Round Education.

of the old structure. During the planning stage for the new school, the system superintendent challenged Balfour's principal and staff to explore the concept of year-round education. They visited other year-round schools in North Carolina and read published research on YRE. One report in particular (Ballinger, Kirschembaum & Poimbeauf, 1987), had great impact as it indicated that the continued flow of learning engendered by YRE was beneficial to students at all levels. These researchers found that no year-round school had reported a drop in academic achievement; in fact, all showed a higher gain in academic scores when compared to schools following the August-June structure. It seemed apparent that this new schedule would benefit Balfour's students. The faculty voted to accept the year-round plan.

After much exploration, discussion and debate, the Board of Education unanimously voted to offer the plan as an option. Part of the school would continue on the traditional August-June schedule, and an alternate path would be established for year-round school. Parents could choose from either option.

Staffing

After developing a clear concept of how the school would function, the next major task was to devise a staffing schedule for the year-round plan. Since faculty representatives had already visited year-round schools, read extensively on the topic and helped develop the reorganization plan, they were well aware of the new schedule's demands. They were asked to declare their scheduling preference—traditional or year-round. Some readily agreed to the 12-month schedule, some had conflicting family obligations and others were willing to teach under either pattern. Eventually, slots for each grade level were filled.

Allowing the staff to study the organizational plan and choose whether they wanted to participate ensured successful implementation of the plan. The competitiveness that can occur when new practices and old systems operate simultaneously was kept at a minimum, helping everyone to feel some investment in the project.

Community Support

A committee of faculty members

187

developed a plan for distributing information to help parents make informed choices. First, they wrote a series of articles for the local newspaper in which they explained the YRE plan. In addition, they printed and distributed flyers inviting parents to an informational meeting. At this well-attended session, the principal and central office staff gave an overview, and teachers and school board members supplied information gathered from their research and school visits. Advantages and disadvantages of the two systems were discussed, and parents were walked through a typical year-round calendar.

After the presentations, the parents were divided into small discussion groups. A teacher, principal, school board member or superintendent monitored each group discussion and answered questions. At the close of the session, parents were asked to respond to a survey about the new plan to show if they were interested, uncertain or preferred the traditional plan. The year-round plan would be implemented if at least 100 students could be enrolled. The initial level of interest fell short, but after releasing additional information and holding a second meeting we eventually received 175 applications. Asheboro's first year-round school was set.

Several factors led to the successful recruitment effort. First, the teachers played a central role. Parents trusted the teachers because they, too, would be affected by the new schedule, and would have to make as many adjustments as the students and parents. The teachers' endorsement gave the plan credence. Second, the involvement of the Board of Education and the Superintendent of Schools communicated high-level support for the project. Their participation helped alleviate parents' and teachers' concerns that the reorganization might fail due to the lack of administrative support. Third, by giving parents a choice, those who opted for the new plan had an investment in ensuring its success.

The New School
When the new Balfour Elementary School opened on July 13, 1992, 154 students and eight classroom teachers followed the year-round schedule. Class sizes ranged from 19-26, and enrollment stayed constant throughout the year. New students were placed in a traditional classroom unless they had previously attended another year-round school. This practice allowed them to meet the state's 180-day school attendance law.

As with any new program, challenges arose, especially the first time we had to accommodate students from both programs in the same building. Blending 398 students on two different schedules was a *real* challenge. Suddenly, we had to be mindful of the two schools in all areas. For example, class pictures could not be taken before the traditional students arrived. The Southern Association Accreditation team could not visit when the year-round faculty was on their three-week break. Faculty from both systems learned to be very flexible. When the year-round students were away, for example, lunch schedules had to be changed.

Another area of concern was teacher morale. The new year-round schedule often attracted media attention. To avoid unnecessary rivalry, the administration took extra steps to show *all* the teachers that their efforts were appreciated.

Unique Qualities of the Plan
The success of the year-round concept depended on the united effort of teachers, administrators and parents. But no matter how hard a group works, the effort will fail if the plan is not positive. Balfour's year-round concept succeeds because of the opportunities it offers to students and families. Some of the components of the year-round schedule that help make it successful follow:

Growth of Public Year-Round Education in the United States over a Ten-Year Period				
School Year	States	Districts	Schools	Students
1985-86	16	63	410	354,087
1986-87	14	69	408	362,669
1987-88	Data Not Collected			
1988-89	16	95	494	428,961
1989-90	19	115	618	520,323
1990-91	22	152	859	733,660
1991-92	23	204	1,646	1,345,921
1992-93	26	301	2,017	1,567,920
1993-94	33	366	1,941	1,407,377
1994-95	35	414	2,214	1,640,929

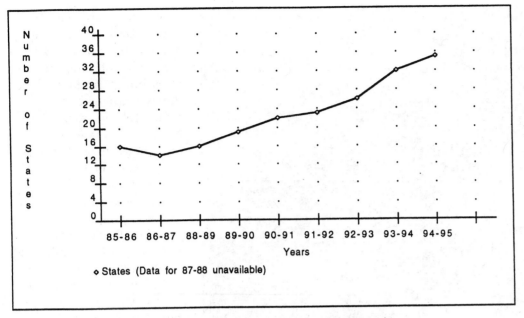

States with YRE Schools (Public and Private)

program provided by the school. During the first week of intersession, child care is available from 6:30 a.m. until 6:00 p.m. (preregistration ensures adequate staff allocation). Lunch is available, as usual, at the regular price; children on free or reduced lunch programs continue to receive this benefit.

During the second week of intersession, called Discovery Plus, children can participate in enrichment activities. Discovery Plus is available from 8:00 a.m. until noon. Early morning child care continues. Parents pay a $25.00 fee for five mornings of field trips, crafts and learning projects. At the end of the morning session, students are picked up by parents or remain in the school's child care program.

Learning Plus is offered in the third week of intersession. Students who need help can receive academic remediation. Free bus transportation is provided and the

The Single-Track Calendar. School begins in mid-July and ends in early June. Throughout the year, students go to school for nine weeks and then have a three-week break. This is known as the 45-15 single track. Students still attend school for 180 days, but their vacations are paced more evenly than in the August-June system. This allows students to be monitored more closely throughout the entire year and keeps in place necessary support services. In addition, students have less time to forget concepts and skills.

Child Care—Before and After School. Many of the school's students have two working parents. The school offers child care before and after school hours. A child care coordinator is available beginning at 6:30 a.m. and she oversees activities until the bell rings at 8:00 a.m. The cost is $2.00 per morning.

The child care coordinator leaves the campus during the day,

returns at 2:30 p.m. and continues until 6:00 p.m. After-school care includes a snack and the cost is $3.00 per child, per afternoon. Parents can choose the days they need the service and budget costs are minimized.

Intersession—The Three-Week Break. After the nine weeks of academic classes, the year-round students have a three-week break called "intersession." They either spend the time with their families or take advantage of a structured

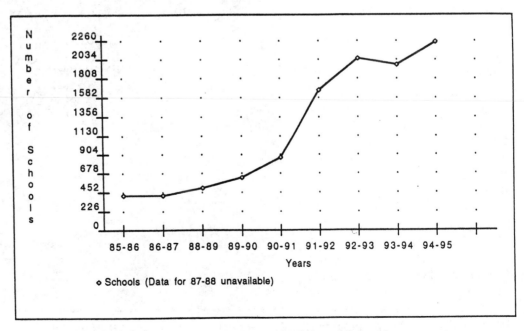

Schools with YRE Schools (Public and Private)

Photos courtesy of author

William Luck, 7, puts his book bag on the coat/bag rack in Mrs. Hardin's room on the first day of school at Balfour.

they return to school. Parents appreciate the high-quality activities and the availability of child care services during the three-week intersession vacation period. Teachers, too, benefit from the intersession. If they choose to teach during the Learning Plus week they earn extra income. But most of all, whether they teach in the intersession or not, they recognize the advantages of extra help for the children. Teachers taking advantage of the intersession break frequently use this time to develop course materials or relieve stress by taking a trip or relaxing at home.

program runs on a half-day schedule. The year-round teachers are offered the opportunity to teach in the Learning Plus program and receive additional pay for their participation. Other certified teachers are added as necessary. The Learning Plus program is financed with summer school funds appropriated by the state. Those who need remediation receive it every nine weeks, and thereby show improvement throughout the year. Even better, they do not have to wait for summer school to receive help. Consequently, they return to class better prepared than if they had been on vacation for ten weeks. The students appear to retain information better and take less time to readjust to the school routine. Charles Ballinger (1987) of the National Association for Year-Round Education explains, "Remediation can occur throughout the year by using more frequent vacation periods, rather than limiting it to summer school after nine months of failure and frustration."

The three-week intersession can be credited for much of the program's wide acceptance. Everyone benefits!

Children enjoy the positive social opportunities and the change of pace from the normal school routine. In addition, their confidence levels rise as they experience greater academic success when

Possible Disadvantages of Year-Round Education

We are creatures of habit and tradition. A great majority of parents, students and teachers have never known a school schedule other than the August-June agricultural one. Anything different represents a

First day of the new year at Balfour School. School secretary Margaret Womick shows 2nd-grader Lucia Mata (7) to her classroom.

break in tradition and a disruption. Parents with older children who are not on the year-round schedule may have to deal with separate calendars for the school year. Most camps, and other organized recreational activities, are planned only for the summertime. Teachers who want to earn an advanced degree may be unable to attend college classes during the summer.

Program Adjustments

Charles Ballinger (1987) says that "Schools need to allow at least a year or two for people to get accustomed to the idea." After the program's initial year, Balfour did make adjustments in several areas, mostly by responding to the increased demand for enrollment. Parents from other schools within the system also began requesting a year-round schedule. In response, two additional elementary schools and one middle school began offering the plan. Now children from kindergarten through 8th grade are on a year-round schedule. All four schools participate in the three-week intersession of Child Care, Discovery Plus and Learning Plus at one site.

Growth. More states are offering year-round education. The figures on pages 187–189 indicate the growth of this education innovation.

Conclusion

I was reared on a farm in eastern North Carolina, one of five children who helped plant, cultivate and harvest corn, tobacco, cotton and watermelons. These crops were our livelihood and each member of the family worked long hours. School never began before Labor Day and was finished by late May. In the spring, my father instructed my brothers to leave school at noon and walk the dusty roads home to help with the planting. My mother worked in our home; her never-ending duties included planting,

growing, harvesting and preserving vegetables and fruits to last our family the whole year. Our mother was always waiting for us when we came home at the end of the school day.

These are warm memories of a family working together. But times have changed. Many children come home to an empty house and spend the summer days trying to find something to do. Social and academic pressures, too, are higher for today's children. One way for schools to respond to today's shift in societal structures and academic expectations is to implement Year-Round Education.

Worthen and Zsiray (1994) summarize the important educational implications of the year-round program. They state that a year-round schedule has much to offer students. Nevertheless, they advise educators to advance "carefully, competently, and compassionately." Based on my research and three years' experience with the year-round school, I heartily agree with both points.

All in favor of year-round education, say "Aye."

References

Ballinger, C. E., Kirschembaum, N., & Poimbeauf, R. P. (1987). The various year-round plans. In *The year-round school: Where learning never stops* (pp. 16-24) (Fastback 259). Bloomington, IN: Phi Delta Kappa.

Ballinger, C. (1987). Unleashing the school calendar. *Thrust for Educational Leadership, 16*(4), 16-18.

Ballinger, C. (1988). Rethinking the school calendar. *Educational Leadership, 45*(5), 57-61.

Brekke, N. R. (1984). Year-round education: Cost saving and educationally effective. *ERS Spectrum, 2*(3), 25-30.

Quinlan, C., George, C., & Emmett, T. (1987). *Year-round education: Year-round opportunities: A study of year-round education in California.* Sacramento, CA: California State Department of Education.

Thomas, J. B. (1991). Year-round schools: How a new calendar would change life for your kids. *Better Homes and Gardens, 69*(12), 36.

Worthen, B. R., & Zsiray, S. W. (1994). *What twenty years of educational studies reveal about year-round education.* Chapel Hill, NC: NC Education Policy Research Center, The University of North Carolina.

Additional Readings on Year-Round Education

Archibald, R. S. (1992). The president's message. *The Year-Rounder*, p. 1. (Available from National Association for Year-Round Education, P.O. Box 11386, San Diego CA 92171-1386)

Forte, L. (1994). Going year-round. *The Education Digest, 59*(9), 7-9.

Glines, D. (1992). Year-round education: What lies ahead? *Thrust for Educational Leadership, 21*(6), 19-21.

Gregory, S. S. (1994). Everyone into the school. *Time, 144*(5), 48-49.

Grotjohn, D. K., & Banks, K. (1993, April). *An evaluation synthesis: Year-round schools and achievement.* Paper presented at the 1993 annual meeting of the American Educational Research Association, Atlanta, GA.

National Association for Year-Round Education. (1992). *Nineteenth reference directory of year-round education programs for the 1992-93 school year.* San Diego, CA: Author.

Shuster, T., & Rodger, P. L. (1992). *Concerning year-round education: A final report of an evaluative survey.* Logan, UT: Department of Psychology, Utah State University.

White, W. D. (1993, February). *Year-round education from start to finish.* Paper presented at the annual conference of the National Association for Year-Round Education, Las Vegas, NV.

For more information, write: National Association for Year-Round Education, P.O. Box 711386, San Diego CA 92171-1386, or call 619-276-5296.

BLACKBOARD BUNGLE

A Nobel laureate finds that intervention in the schools is a study in the realities of urban life

LEON LEDERMAN

LEON LEDERMAN is chairman of the Teachers Academy for Mathematics and Science (TAMS) in Chicago. He is also a 1988 Nobel laureate in physics, director emeritus at the Fermi National Accelerator Laboratory (Fermilab) in Batavia, Illinois, and professor of science at the Illinois Institute of Technology in Chicago. This article is adapted from a talk he gave to the section on science education at the New York Academy of Sciences, November 11, 1994.

IN 1983 THE NATIONAL COMMISSION ON EXcellence in Education, responding to a request from the secretary of education, reported on the quality of education in America. The report was also presented as an open letter to the American public under the title: *A Nation At Risk: The Imperative of Educational Reform*. It began without mincing words:

Our Nation is at risk. Our once unchallenged preeminence in commerce, industry, science, and technological innovation is being overtaken by competitors throughout the world. . . . We report to the American people that . . . the educational foundations of our society are presently being eroded by a rising tide of mediocrity that threatens our very future as a Nation and a people.

The body of the report was only slightly less chauvinistic than the introduction, but the purple prose and military metaphors of the former had the desired shock effect on the nation: its bugle call to action became front-page news, and for many weeks afterward there was a great outpouring of blame, anxiety and indignation on the editorial pages and the talk shows. The media attention generated by the crisis rhetoric kept the public focused on the educational predicament far more effectively than did the more specific, and more alarming, facts recited by the report inside.

But, of course, public attention moved on. Twelve years after *A Nation At Risk* the United States is still at risk. The educational systems at the federal, state and local levels are, by and large, dysfunctional. One cannot exaggerate the lack of preparation of primary school teachers for the teaching of mathematics and science. Less than 1 percent of the school budget in Chicago has normally been allocated to the ongoing professional enhancement of teachers, and little or no time is allowed during the school day for collegial interactions in urban schools in the U.S. Compare that with the corresponding statistic in Japan, where, by one estimate, the budget number is 40 percent: Japanese teachers spend nearly half their time in collegial activities, in improving curriculum, and in studying and advancing their knowledge of the teaching arts.

In 1989 a national convention of U.S. governors was convened by "the education president," George Bush, and a set of ambitious goals was set out to be achieved "by the year 2000." Yet by any measure one can devise, not much has been accomplished in advancing the "center of mass" of an enterprise that includes some fifty million students and two million teachers. And after personally spending the past five years immersed in the school-reform business, I can certainly understand the pessimism that most people have about the future of American schools—especially the large public school systems that serve most of the nation's disadvantaged children. Indeed, my own sobering experience has led me to conclude that the schools cannot heal themselves. Outside intervention, help and support are essential.

ABOUT FIVE YEARS AGO I BECAME INVOLVED IN a consortium of universities to organize a new venture in Chicago, a private, not-for-profit intervention in the public school system designed to assist, if not to rescue, the schools. A board of directors was created, made up of teachers, principals, other educators, university presidents, scientists from universities and national laboratories, community group leaders and a number of strong participants from the private sector. We had the organizational backing of all the academic institutions in Chicago, including some fourteen universities and four-year colleges. The goal was professional enhancement: training the primary school teachers in Chicago to teach science and mathematics.

As a physicist, I hardly need to be persuaded of the value of an education in science and mathematics. But all of us taking part in the Chicago schools intervention also care deeply about reading and writing and geography. So why the focus on science and mathematics? Experience with students from kindergarten age through fourth grade demonstrates that science and mathematics, taught in the right way, engage children, resonate with their own natural curiosity and open a door to the joy of learning. Children exposed to such teaching also develop their communications skills—a key to future learning. A positive introduction to the study of science and mathematics serves as a foundation for an interest in those topics throughout a person's lifetime. And as for the relevance of the curriculum, the engines that drive the changes in contemporary society are science and science-based technology.

Our target customers were some 17,000 teachers who teach science and mathematics, among other subjects, to students in kindergarten through the eighth grade. Our "mission possible" was to train the teachers in those disciplines as well as in new pedagogical techniques. We were encouraged at the outset by indications that there would be some financial support. And indeed, in 1990, with funding from the National Science Foundation, the U.S. Department of Energy, private philanthropy and the state of Illinois, we opened the Teachers Academy for Mathematics and Science (TAMS) on the campus of the Illinois Institute of Technology, near the south side of Chicago. That was the beginning of a learning process.

Historical Antecedents

WE ARE, OF COURSE, NOT THE FIRST TO EMBARK ON EDucational reform. Educational crises do have a history, and perhaps by reviewing that history one can learn how to make reform succeed.

In the 1860s a revolutionary educational movement emerged in the U.S. to promote "object teaching," a method introduced by the early nineteenth-century Swiss educational reformer Johann Heinrich Pestalozzi. Instead of merely lecturing to children, the teacher was to give them real objects with which to experiment and make observations. Object teaching sought to develop student thinking and deemphasize the memorization of facts. I wonder if that sounds familiar.

Also in the mid-1800s the industrialization of the U.S. led to the creation of a public high school system. Industry demanded a workforce that could read and communicate—and a workforce trained in such practical scientific subjects as technology, zoology, surveying, mechanics, mineralogy and engineering. Does that sound familiar?

In 1890, at Cornell University, a nature-study movement originated as a reaction against the growing urbanization of America. The basic fear was that city children would have no chance to learn which end of the cow to milk. Cornell leaflets of the day stressed birds, flowers, insects and trees. At about the same time science in the high schools was dominated by the needs of college curriculums—the style and content of both lectures and laboratories were essentially designed for the college bound. Then,

> THE REVOLUTION BEGUN
> *by the splendid high school*
> *textbooks that appeared after Sputnik*
> *was allowed to dangle and wither away.*

in 1893, a national "Committee of Ten" set standards for high school science that reduced the influence of colleges. In its report the committee wrote:

> Every subject which is taught at all in secondary school should be taught in the same way and to the same extent to every pupil so long as he pursues it—no matter what the probable destination of the pupil may be, or at what point his education is to cease.

Does that, too, sound familiar?

In the early 1900s H. G. Wells, the noted English historian, novelist and futurist wrote: "More and more, the future of society is a race between education and catastrophe."

In general, efforts to reform science education in the U.S. have gotten their greatest boost after a war. The most dramatic instance was the famous report *Science, the Endless Frontier,* prepared in 1945 by Vannevar Bush, director of the Office of Scientific Research and Development under President Franklin Delano Roosevelt. Bush's report described science education as an essential component of a new relation between the state and the scientific and technological community. By the mid-1950s some of the postwar activity to reform science education had begun to fade, only to be shocked into greater frenzy by the 1957 success of the Soviet *Sputnik I.* I recall many of my colleagues and teachers pausing in their research activities at the time to write splendid high school textbooks in all fields of science. Yet as the years passed, the impact of those textbooks diminished, because their authors picked up their slide rules and resumed their research, leaving the revolution they had started to dangle and wither away.

The New Pedagogy

AS A SCIENTIST ENGAGED IN SCIENCE EDUCATION, I NATUrally relate our efforts at TAMS to science itself. I relate the future of science education to the future of science. And I relate the way children learn about the world to the way scientists learn about the world. There is a lot more here than metaphor.

Let me try to be more specific. Science is a process of observation, measurement and synthesis. That sequence has been adopted in many of the hands-on science-education programs that are known to be most successful. What we scientists observe and what we choose to measure are constrained by what we already know and by what we think we understand. The creative insight comes about when we learn to acquire intuitions and then recognize the preconceptions that limit those intuitions—which is quite similar to what children do with the intuitions they acquire and accumulate in their explorations.

Consider Galileo's great discovery, immortalized as Newton's first law of motion: an isolated body will continue its state of motion forever. Boy, if that isn't counterintuitive! Galileo's creative act was in realizing that ordinary intuition is irrelevant because in ordinary experience objects are never isolated. Balls stop rolling, horses must pull carts to keep the carts in motion. But Galileo's deeper intuition suspected simplicity in the law governing moving bodies, and his insightful surmise was that if you *could* isolate the body, it would continue moving forever. So he polished the block and he polished the table, and the block moved much farther. He knew he could not achieve complete isolation, but perhaps he could get close enough to sniff out the underlying simplicity.

But Galileo was also confronting a powerful tradition. In 1600 it was just "common sense" that rest was the natural state. Aristotle had said so almost 2,000 years earlier, and so it was—until Galileo's new intuition. But for the past 300 years Galileo and his followers have insisted that scientists must construct new intuitions in order to learn how the world works.

Now listen to the educational psychologist Howard E. Gardner of Harvard University, writing in 1994:

We argue that, during the early years of life, children form extremely powerful theories or sets of beliefs about how the world works—theories of mind, theories of matter, theories of life. . . . These . . . become so deeply entrenched in the human mind, that they prove very difficult to eradicate in favor of the more comprehensive and more veridical views that have been painstakingly constructed in and across the disciplines.

What Gardner says about children can be said about Yale graduates, congressmen, judges . . . and schoolteachers.

Replacing the powerful misconceptions children bring with them to the classroom is the art of science education. Children need the same "intuition-modifying" experiences that scientists need, but where scientists need access to devices such as a synchrotron light source, a mass spectrometer, a particle accelerator, children need the chance to use their own hands, to consort with their own small collective in order to confront artfully contrived experiential processes.

As *they* polish the block and simonize the table, the block will go progressively farther; as they accumulate a large number of such examples, science as a way of thinking will begin to crystallize. But make no mistake: the process is difficult and time consuming. To change children's ways of thinking, one must first change teachers' ways of thinking. And even for teachers who love children and love teaching, that is a major challenge: it is literally a change in the teaching culture. The role of scientists in the task should be obvious. It is critical that we get involved.

professionals, and given time for collegial interactions and professional development. Those teachers must be empowered to make decisions based on sound professional judgment;

• a basic understanding that there is a collaboration between the school, the parents, the principal and the local community, including local industry, universities and laboratories.

In the past four years we have learned that, even in the most embattled schools in the inner city, there is a love of children and a passion for teaching. Given the opportunity to be better teachers, the response is overwhelmingly enthusiastic. At TAMS we live by all the buzzwords: hands-on, minds-on, activity-based, inquiry methods, cooperative learning—the constructivist approach. The teacher is taught to confess that she does not know the answers to questions the children raise. Her approach is to help them find the answers. The students work in teams, and they learn from one another.

All our teacher training is in-service, or in other words provided to full-time teachers, during school hours as well as on weekends, in the evenings and during the summer. In the past four years we have introduced seventy-two schools and some 3,200 teachers to our program—and some of them have been with us for as many as three years. On average, they have received roughly 120 hours of instruction in science, 140 hours in mathematics and more than 140 hours of additional close teaching supervision. That leaves only . . . 420 schools and 14,000 teachers to go.

Changing culture is never easy. That so much time and effort (and money) are needed should be no surprise to the funding agencies, but it is. We estimate that to sustain the efforts we have begun in Chicago will probably take an in-

THE EDUCATIONAL SYSTEM CANNOT HEAL ITSELF. OUTSIDE INTERVENTION— *evolutionary, systemic and sustained—will be essential.*

What Makes Good Schools?

ANYONE WHO HAS SPENT TIME WORKING WITH LARGE numbers of schools knows that the struggle to improve them can seem nearly impossible. What makes that particularly frustrating is that what it takes to make schools work better is well known; good schools do exist, and those of us working with TAMS know from experience what makes them and what common attributes they share:

• a belief that all children can learn, though they may learn differently;

• an environment that is caring, personal, considerate and respectful of both children and adults;

• an educational mission that is shared by the entire school community;

• a clear set of priorities that place children's learning needs at the center of every activity;

• high expectations of everyone—children, teachers, parents and principals;

• a competent, well-trained staff of teachers who are rewarded with reasonable salaries, accorded the status of

vestment of between $3,000 and $4,000 a year per teacher for perhaps three to four years. That expense includes the necessary costs of bringing in all the important groups that have a stake in education. The total is equivalent to the tuition for one year at a mid-priced university. Yet one of the curious and inexplicable frustrations of our work has been the difficulty of getting the money to sustain it.

Hopeful Signs—and Obstacles

DOES THE PROGRAM WORK? YES! TEACHERS LOVE IT. AND when it is well managed, it creates an intense, joyous learning process. Such interventions also lead to a greatly energized teaching corps, in which the new teaching style spreads to other subjects and brings with it technology that can fruitfully enhance the teacher's effectiveness.

Could it work elsewhere—in New York City, for instance? Again, yes, but it is impossible to overestimate the difficulties. In number of students, New York City's school system is two and a half times the size of Chicago's, and New York administers 1,017 public schools. Yet there is a shot that this kind of intervention, suitably replicated in many styles and variations in, say, twenty-five cities, could begin to restore to the nation what was once a superb system of public schools.

Successful intervention requires the support, encouragement and commitment of those in the environment of the teacher: principal, parents, school councils, community groups. It needs leadership of competent and visionary school superintendents. It needs the collaboration of state and public school administrators in adopting the new tough standards coming out of Washington. And it will need, for a long time to come, the support of everyone who has a stake in the outcome of education: scientists and educators, future employers, college authorities.

What are the chief obstacles to educational reform? I have mentioned the difficulty of obtaining funding. That goes hand-in-hand with what seems to be the near impossibility of sustaining (expensive) interventions long enough to change the culture of teaching. Finding excellent staff people to carry out interventions can become a long and vexing process. Learning to collaborate with systemic obstacles to systemic reform, the central offices of education, the state regulators, the unions and bureaucracy in general can be slow and immensely frustrating, but it must be done with persistence, determination—and humor. Finally, one

can only wonder at the slowness with which the education of educators has changed.

GIVEN THOSE OBSTACLES AND THE CURRENT crisis in the public schools, I do not believe we can fix them, even if we do know how, until we can make them a priority. Unfortunately, that has not yet been done in these United States, and there is enough blame for that truly sorry state of affairs to go all around. Furthermore, I must emphasize again that I do not think our educational systems can heal themselves. Outside intervention is essential. The interventions must be evolutionary and systemic, insofar as they involve parents, the community and indeed all the education stakeholders. Above all, the interventions must be sustained, so that it becomes clear the reform is working. Only then will the funding become politically irresistible. Time and again, solid and sensible reform has been aborted too soon.

Who can intervene? It seems to me that it comes down to a partnership of universities and the private sector. Today, few university presidents give much priority to precollege education. But a sustained effort by universities could begin to show results. The payback to the universities would be a population of scientifically literate students that would raise statues to university presidents and deans.

The Commercialization Of Youth

Channel One in Context

Channel One is merely part of a much larger explosion in youth-oriented marketing strategies, according to Ms. Wartella, who provides examples to bolster her claim.

Ellen Wartella

ELLEN WARTELLA is dean and holds the Walter Cronkite Regents Chair in Communication at the University of Texas, Austin.

MUCH OF THE controversy regarding the adoption of Channel One by public schools has centered on the two minutes of youth-oriented advertising in each day's telecast. My goal here is to place the controversy in the broader context of the commercialization of youth culture that has taken place in the 20th century and particularly during the past 20 years. I will examine the inroads the commercial mass media have made on children's leisure time and how the media have marketed advertisers' wares to successive generations of youth culture. A more focused examination of the changes in the consumer environment for children during the past 20 years will demonstrate that Channel One is part of a much larger explosion in youth-oriented marketing strategies.

The Commercialization of Youth

In an examination of the history of how American children have spent their leisure time during the 20th century, I have reached the conclusion that each successive major mass medium — film, radio, and television — has been instrumental in targeting and marketing to successive generations of American youth.[1] Moreover, to a large extent these media (and others — such as magazines, popular music, and outdoor advertising — as well as American business in general) catered to and helped to define successive generations of American youth culture. Throughout the 20th century, independent, autonomous youth cultures developed around leisure-time activities, and the mass media became the social catalyst — promoting, sustaining, and commercializing each group's use of leisure. During the course of the 20th century, younger and younger age groups have become the focus of media attention and commercialization, until today even preschoolers are a target for American marketers.

In a wonderful history titled *The Damned and the Beautiful*, Paula Fass makes a compelling argument that college students of the 1920s constituted the first identifiable youth culture.[2] The college student "flappers" of the 1920s represented an American subcultural group that was distinctly different in values and behaviors from its parents' generation. The flappers had their own styles of dress (bobbed hair, short skirts, raccoon coats). They had their own set of peer-related activities at college, which included not only fraternity parties, going to movies, and attending college sporting events but also premarital sex, which they adopted much more openly than had their parents.

All of these social pursuits were portrayed in movies, music, radio, magazines, and popular fiction. The American media consciously created the image of the flapper and college student and then proceeded to sell to young people the accoutrements of that image: cigarettes, movies and other media, and raccoon coats and other distinctive attire.

By the 1940s a younger, "teenage" culture had developed, which became the new target for the mass media and marketing. During the depression of the 1930s and the war years of the 1940s, American teenagers were increasingly spending time outside of their homes with their peers, and the mass media were becoming increasingly aware of the growing youth culture. The inauguration of *Seventeen* magazine in 1944 signaled how important teenagers' culture had become and would remain.

In the 1940s adolescents were more likely than earlier generations to attend and stay in high school, and this fact abetted the development of a youth culture. Popular culture began to cater to this autonomous youth culture by providing the bobby-soxers of the 1940s and 1950s with their own music (first Frank Sinatra and then rock-and-roll), their own teen movies and teen magazines, and — during the 1950s — their own hangouts (the drive-ins). By the 1950s high school students constituted a clearly separate subcultural group in American life. They had their own language, style of dress, values, and behaviors. Teenagers also provided an attractive market for new products and businesses such as the early fast-food restaurants.

Since the 1960s television has been the primary medium for bringing commercialization into the lives of younger children. The Sixties and Seventies saw the development of the "kidvid" phenomenon: Saturday morning cartoon shows interspersed

 From *Phi Delta Kappan*, February 1995, pp. 448-451.

with heavy doses of advertising for cereal, snack food, and toys. Kidvid was clearly aimed at grade school children and, as it continued to grow, even at preschoolers. Since the mid-Seventies the consumer environment for the under-12 group has exploded.

The New Consumer Environment

In the mid-1970s, when I was conducting research for the book *How Children Learn to Buy*,[3] the major and almost sole advertising medium for children was television — predominantly Saturday morning kidvid. Since the mid-1970s there have been major changes in the child-oriented TV market, and I will focus on three of them. The first change has been the rise of independent television stations and cable networks, such as Nickelodeon, the children's channel, to challenge the dominance of the three commercial broadcasting networks (ABC, CBS, and NBC). Cable television not only offers children more choices of channels to watch but also offers advertisers new venues for their messages.

The second change was the arrival in the early 1980s of a new kind of marketing device—the program-length commercial, a television show in which the main character is modeled after a toy product. The entire program is built around showing children how to play with the toy and encouraging them to buy it. "He-Man, Masters of the Universe" was the first of this genre, followed by "Ghostbusters," "Strawberry Shortcake," and, more recently, "Teenage Mutant Ninja Turtles." According to a 1988 content analysis of children's advertising, 64% of all toy ads on television were for dolls or other accessories related to children's programming.[4] In an analysis of children's television in Champaign-Urbana, Illinois, in 1989, I found that the majority of syndicated weekday and network shows for children were toy-related.[5]

A third important change in television advertising has been the proliferation of new products aimed at children: videotapes; 900-number information services; a wider range of food products, including children's TV dinners and other convenience foods that children can prepare on their own; and an expanded list of apparel, such as jeans and running shoes. We are also seeing an increasing number of travel ads, such as those for Walt Disney World and Disneyland, which are aimed explicitly at children and which are intended to get them to influence their parents' vacation choices.

Perhaps the best recent survey of the changes in TV advertising practices is a report by Dale Kunkel and Walter Gantz for the Children's Advertising Review Unit of the Council of Better Business Bureaus, published in January 1991.[6] Kunkel and Gantz conducted an analysis of the nature and extent of nonprogram content presented during children's television time. Their sample consisted of 607 hours of television videotaped in February and March 1990 in seven U.S. cities (Boston, Los Angeles, Detroit, Indianapolis, Portland, New Orleans, and Austin). Seven channels, including network affiliates, independent stations, and cable channels, were taped at each site.

In their content analysis of the advertising embedded in the children's programs, Kunkel and Gantz found that about 66% of the 16,024 nonprogram messages were commercials for products. Each program hour averaged about 10 minutes of nonprogram content; the networks averaged the most minutes per hour of product advertisements (10.05), and independent stations averaged the largest number of nonprogram minutes

per hour (13.26). Cable channels had the least product ad time (6.48 minutes per hour) and least overall nonprogram time (10.38 minutes per hour). Public service announcements averaged less than one minute per hour and were more likely to be found on the networks.

Kunkel and Gantz found that, as in earlier decades, three types of products predominated in television advertising: toys, cereals, and sugared snacks/drinks accounted for 75% of all commercials. Toys were more likely to be found on the independent stations (42% of all ads) than on the networks (17.3%) or cable (24%). Premiums, such as toys in cereal boxes, were mentioned in 10% of the ads.

Kunkel and Gantz noted that, since the research studies of the 1970s, several new product types had emerged in television advertising. For example, entertainment products, such as videotapes and 900-number telephone services, accounted for 7% of all ads (more of them on cable than on the networks or independent stations). Finally, just over half (51%) of the ads had disclaimers, but only 18% of those ads employed both audio and visual elements to convey such messages.

Kunkel and Gantz also looked at violations of the self-regulatory guidelines established by the Children's Advertising Review Unit. They found that 385 commercials (4% of the ads) violated some guidelines. Cable TV had the greatest number of violations; network TV, the least. About a third of the violations stemmed from making the premium primary in the ad and the product secondary (by virtue of the amount of time spent discussing premiums as opposed to products). Another 19% of the violations stemmed from presenting products in an unrealistic light, such as demonstrating toys being used in a way that a child could not duplicate or being vague about what a purchase buys when a product has multiple parts.

In addition to these changes in the television marketplace for children, there have been considerable changes in the larger consumer environment for young people. First, there is now increased interest in trying to "target" marketing to child consumers, and that means going where children can be found. Second, there is now a greater use of nonadvertising venues to market products. This whole area of promotions outside of advertising is growing at the expense of traditional advertising. For instance, 20 years ago about two-thirds of all marketing dollars went into advertising. Today 80% of marketing dollars go into other types of promotions.[7] Both of these new marketing strategies are particularly relevant to the issue of the commercialization of the American public schools.

The most obvious example of targeting is Channel One, the 12-minute daily newscast originally developed by Whittle Communications, in which two minutes of advertisements for various products geared toward young people are embedded. Channel One is now in some 12,000 schools in the U.S. and reaches 40% of children in grades 6 through 12. The appeal of Channel One to advertisers is that it guarantees that they will reach the target audience — what critics have called the "captive audience" — since subscriber schools are required to show the program every day to all children.

But Channel One is only one example of such targeting strategies. There has also been an enormous increase in the use of direct-mail marketing to children and their parents. According to Gary Wojtas, an upsurge in births parallels this increase.[8] He notes that in 1990, Standard Rate and Data Service had more than 200 different lists of children's names in its publication, with most of those lists renting for $50 per thousand names. He discusses the introduction of "kid grocery stores" with child-friendly displays and child-sized shopping carts, all intended to lure children. The model example of this approach may be Sears' McKids, a strategy that combines McDonald's characters with a clothing boutique in order to attract children and not just parents.

A dizzying variety of new, sophisticated, and often expensive products aimed at preteens have been introduced: toiletries, designer clothes, electronics, foods, and even travel programs. There has also been a boom in licensing and celebrity endorsements. According to Wojtas, advertisers targeting young people are increasingly turning to venues other than television. In particular, there has been a proliferation of children's magazines (*Sports Illustrated for Kids, Topps, Ladybug, Cricket,* and *Zillions,* a children's version of *Consumer Reports*) and student periodicals (e.g., *Scholastic News*) distributed through schools. All of this, Wojtas says, is aimed at "reaping profits from the piggy bank."[9] Also during the past two years, radio for children has emerged across the country, not necessarily because young children listen to a lot of radio but because advertisers are seeking new ways to target youth.

The marketing of products to children involves not only instore promotions such as the McKids sections of Sears but, increasingly, promotional activities through the schools. Kids' clubs and other marketer-sponsored school activities have been discussed by Donna Perkinson as effective selling devices.[10] Other examples of school-related promotions during the past several years abound. For instance, several small restaurant chains (e.g., Spaghetti Factory in the Southeast and Little Kings in the West) sponsor reading projects with local libraries or schools, through which children receive a free meal at a restaurant once they have read a certain number of books. In 1991 Minute Maid (a manufacturer of various fruit juice drinks popular with children), in conjunction with Scholastic, Inc. (the publisher of more than 30 school periodicals reaching 23 million students and one million teachers in 95,000 schools nationwide), co-sponsored a literacy program. Through the schools, they distributed reading charts and a letter encouraging parents to help their children "Take the Minute Maid Challenge" and read a book a week over the summer. The materials sent home included coupons for Minute Maid products. Last year Armour also ran a program with Scholastic to help students "say no to drugs," and AT&T and Scholastic teamed up to teach communication skills to children.[11] All of these programs include an effort to market various products to the students.

In short, American schools have become another marketing venue for companies that find it increasingly difficult to reach their young target audience through television advertising alone. Indeed, one might predict that the increased fractionalization of the television marketplace — with more cable channels, video games, and programming on demand in the future — will make promotional targeting through the schools even more attractive. Furthermore, by coupling marketing practices with the promise of advancing teaching goals (such as encouraging literacy or providing direct support for school programs), marketers become important "partners" in American education. In turn, the schools become partners in the increasing commercialization of American youth.

Why the Focus on Children?

What makes children so attractive to marketers today? The recent interest in targeting children aged 12 and younger has followed an explosion in spending on and by them. As of 1990 there were 32 million children in the U.S. between the ages of 4 and 12, and births that year hit four million, the highest total since 1964, the last year of the post-World War II baby boom.[12] In 1987 James McNeal reported that children between the ages of 4 and 12 had a total annual income of $4.7 billion.[13] In early 1992 McNeal revised his estimate and reported the income of children to have risen to nearly $9 billion in just five years.[14] With manufacturers eager to take advantage of this market, advertising to children has taken a corresponding leap. In 1991, for example, the ad revenues of Nickelodeon, the cable television channel that targets preteens, jumped 34% to $78.5 million. Advance sales of ad time for children's television as a whole jumped 15% in 1990 to an all-time high of $450 million.

Marketers are not responding simply to an increase in the number of children, for the baby boomlet leveled off in about 1987 at 52.5 million children under the age of 15. By the year 2000 that number is expected to reach around 55.9 million.[15] What has made children of such interest to marketers is a change in children's influence on purchases. Children either directly make or influence more purchases than ever before. While McNeal estimated children's direct purchasing power at $9 billion a year, he also estimated that children aged 12 and under now influence $132 billion in purchases each year.

The changing sociology of American families offers many potential explanations as to why today's children have gained so much consumer influence. Parents are having fewer children, thus increasing the influence — and affluence — of each child. There is an ever-increasing number of one-parent families in which children must do some of their own shopping. More women are delaying childbearing, and by the time they decide to have children they generally have more money to spend than they did when they were younger. And finally, in nearly 70% of U.S. households both parents work, thus forcing children to become more self-reliant at earlier ages. According to Penny Gill, a child "now buys products and services that were at one time targeted solely to adults, such as televisions, VCRs, personal computers, and automobiles. In terms of influence over their families' purchasing decisions, children have the most influence in buying products that they can enjoy themselves, such as electronics, sports, recreation equipment, and vacation/travel."[16] Moreover, when one reads the industry press, it becomes clear that marketers now believe that children today are wiser, more sophisticated, and much more capable consumers than were children in the past. However, these assumptions regarding the new child consumer have yet to be put to an empirical test.

What is clear is that many parents and even school officials have not taken on the debate about these new practices for commercializing childhood. Television advertising, rather than other promotional practices, is the focus of whatever critical concern does exist, and even here most adults will compromise on their stance about advertising when they think that the ads are coupled with good programming. According to McNeal, 64% of American parents would prefer television without commercials.[17] In one study I conducted in 1989, 80% of the parents surveyed said that there are too many commercials on television.[18] But according to Jerome Johnston, nearly 75% of teachers surveyed agreed with the statement that ads on Channel One were acceptable considering the programming they received in return.[19]

My argument in this piece is simple. American young people in recent years have come to be more and more sought after as consumers. They have been targeted through network and cable television and through other media such as radio and magazines. They have been targeted through direct mail to their homes and through displays in various retail stores. And they have been targeted as well through partnerships between the American public schools and various marketers and businesses. Channel One is not the only advertising vehicle for reaching children, and it should be examined within the larger context of the commercialization of youth.

1. Ellen Wartella and Sharon Mazzarella, "An Historical Comparison of Children's Use of Time and Media: 1920s to 1980s," in Richard Butsch, ed., *For Fun and Profit* (Philadelphia: Temple University Press, 1990), pp. 173-94.

2. Paula Fass, *The Damned and the Beautiful: American Youth in the 1920s* (New York: Oxford University Press, 1977).

3. Scott Ward, Daniel Wackman, and Ellen Wartella, *How Children Learn to Buy* (Beverly Hills, Calif.: Sage Publications, 1976).

4. John C. Condry, Patricia Bence, and Cynthia Scheibe, "Non-Program Content of Children's Television," *Journal of Broadcasting and Electronic Media*, Summer 1988, pp. 255-70.

5. Ellen Wartella et al., "Television and Beyond: Children's Video Media in One Community," *Communication Research*, February 1990, pp. 45-64.

6. Dale Kunkel and Walter Gantz, "Children's Television Advertising in the Multi-channel Environment," *Journal of Communication*, Autumn 1991, pp. 134-52.

7. Esther Thorson, School of Journalism, University of Missouri, personal communication, February 1994.

8. Gary Wojtas, "Consumer Kids: A New Marketing Frontier," *Direct Marketing*, August 1990, pp. 49-52.

9. Ibid., p. 52.

10. Donna Perkinson, "Promoting Reading," *Restaurant Business*, 10 February 1989, p. 94; and Wojtas, op. cit.

11. Penny Newcomb, "Hey Dude, Let's Consume," *Forbes*, 11 June 1990, pp. 126-31.

12. S. K. List, "The Right Place to Find Children," *American Demographics*, February 1992, pp. 44-48.

13. James U. McNeal, *Children as Consumers: Insights and Implications* (Lexington, Mass.: Lexington Books, 1987).

14. James U. McNeal, "The Littlest Shoppers," *American Demographics*, February 1992, pp. 48-53.

15. Peter Gill, "Treating Kids as Customers," *Stores*, March 1989, pp. 13-26.

16. Gill, p. 17.

17. McNeal, *Children as Consumers*, p. 108.

18. Wartella et al., op. cit.

19. Jerome Johnston, Evelyn J. Brzezinski, and Eric M. Anderman, *Taking the Measure of Channel One: A Three-Year Perspective* (Ann Arbor: Institute for Social Research, University of Michigan, January 1994).

Enhancing K–12 Economic Education with Contemporary Information Resources

FRED M. CARR

Fred M. Carr is the director of the Center for Economic Education, The University of Akron, Akron, Ohio.

An enlightened society's decision-making process depends on an ever-increasing understanding of economic influences. Since the oil embargo of 1973, the effort to understand these economic influences on society has grown, leading to the publication of many economically oriented magazine and newspaper articles. These articles can be used by teachers across grade levels and instructional disciplines to enrich their students' education.

Historical Analysis

If one accepts the premise that students trained in economic decision making eventually will have a beneficial effect on society, then effective instruction becomes increasingly important. The unfortunate lack of economic literacy among secondary students, however, has been well documented (Walstad and Soper 1987; Walstad 1988). One of the best ways to address the economic illiteracy problem is to instruct teachers K–12 in economic concepts so that they can then instruct their own students in these concepts. The most effective way for these teachers to learn about economics, however, is not known because the perfect empirical measurement instrument of effective instruction has yet to be created (Becker, Greene, and Rosen 1990). It is known that the students of teachers who discuss economics in the classroom do benefit when the teacher enrolls in academic instruction in economic methodologies. A 1984 study found that "teacher participation in an economics inservice workshop has a . . . positive impact on economics achievement of students in subsequent economics classes that they teach" (Schober 1984, 292). It may be logical to conclude that teachers will also increase their knowledge of social issues by regularly reading newspaper and magazine articles about economics.

In addition to exposure to economics, teachers also need materials about economics that they can use with students. Twenty years ago, effective classroom resources were called for, and in recent years this call to university educators involved with economic education was reiterated (McKenzie 1971, 30; Buckles 1991, 312). The need for relevant instructional resources complements the findings in two other studies. The first study states that "teachers can learn some economics by being exposed to economic curricular materials which they can use in their own classrooms" (Thornton and Vredeveld 1977); the second finds that teachers have a high interest in current events (Yankelovich, Skelly and White, Inc. 1981). This combination of teacher interest in current events, the potential contribution of newspaper and magazine articles to the curriculum, and the constant need for relevant classroom resources develops a justification for teachers to use current articles as instructional resources.

Using Articles in the Classroom

The teacher can use newspaper and magazine articles in a number of ways:

• Articles provide easy access to economic topics and issues. The teacher can bring in relevant newspapers and magazines from home or have students check them out of the library.

• Articles can be used to clarify complicated issues and help the teacher who has been receiving conflicting or incomplete information. Use of multiple resources promotes the analysis of differing opinions on a particular issue.

• Articles can be a source of graph or table data that is historically comprehensive and readily understand-

From *The Clearing House*, July/August 1994, pp. 348-353. © 1994 by the Helen Dwight Reid Educational Foundation. Reprinted by permission Heldref Publications, 1319 Eighteenth Street, NW, Washington, DC 20036-1802.

able by the instructor and students. Students can be taught critical analytical skills by having to interpret the tables.

• The data and analyses in current articles generally are based on up-to-date information and often come from authorities or parties closest to the issues. Students react positively to such relevant material.

It is important to note that exploration of social issues through current articles need not replace the regular curriculum; it can be a beneficial supplement. Teachers, regardless of grade level, who teach social studies, science, mathematics, history, language arts, music, or physical education—as well as economics or consumer economics—can use the list of articles, "Resources on Current Economic Topics," to develop an economic component for their courses.

Background on the List of Resources

I would like to explain how the list of resources came into being. From 1992 to 1994, I filed articles from a variety of popular magazines and news sources that would be readily available to educators throughout the United States. I chose my topics based on subjects that were of great interest to teachers at various inservice workshops and courses I have led. The selected articles explain the topic in understandable layman language and refer to economic concepts and charts that can be presented in the classroom.

I have included local newspapers in the list on the assumption that educators could substitute similar news sources from their particular areas. There is no intention on my part to promote or endorse any particular publication. Neither is the list meant to be comprehensive, as many media print sources contain articles on economics. An article may be listed under more than one topic if it contains information on the different topics. Where databases on particular topics are cited, they are found in the appropriate category as *database*, instead of by a title.

A Cautionary Note

Educators who use contemporary articles on economics to supplement their classroom instruction should be aware of several concerns. First, teachers should have a working knowledge of the basic economic concepts and principles involved in the topic being discussed, which can be obtained through a college-level economics course. Second, the educator should be aware that popular articles often contain condensed versions of current thought related to varius topics and may not include all relevant variables. The teacher should try to review all pertinent articles as an economic issue develops and the articles on it are published. Third, the educator should be cognizant that liberal or conservative ideas may influence certain data in the articles. Authors of popular economic articles may focus on one or two studies that may have been financed or sponsored by politically or topically biased organizations, and so the teacher should try to ascertain the primary origin of all table and graph data. Of course, articles with biased views still can provide relevancy and insight that can heighten class interest. When this is the case, the instructor should note the bias of the data and present opposing viewpoints to the class.

REFERENCES

Becker, W., W. Green, and S. Rosen. 1990. Research on high school economic education. *Journal of Economic Education* 21 (Summer):231–45.

Buckles, S. 1991. Visions for the future. In *Effective economic education*, edited by W. B. Walstad and J. C. Soper. Washington, D.C.: Joint Council on Economic Education and National Education Association.

McKenzie, R. B. 1971. An exploratory study of the economic understanding of elementary school teachers. *Journal of Economic Education* 3(Fall):26–31.

National Center for Research in Economic Education. 1992. *A national survey of American economic literacy*. New York: National Center for Research in Economic Education.

Schober, H. M. 1984. The effects of inservice training on participating teachers and students in their economic classes. *Journal of Economic Education* 15(Fall):282–95.

Thornton, D. L., and G. M. Vredeveld. 1977. In-service education and its effect on secondary students: A new approach. *Journal of Economic Education* 8(Spring):93–99.

Walstad, W. B. 1988. Economic literacy in the schools. Paper presented at the annual meeting of the American Economic Association, New York (December).

Walstad, W. B., and J. C. Soper. 1987. *Test of economic literacy: Examiner's manual*. New York: National Council on Economic Education.

Yankelovich, Skelly and White, Inc. 1981. *National Survey of Economic Education*. New York: Phillips Petroleum Co.

Resources on Current Economic Topics

Drugs/Crime

Accident price tag: $137 billion in 1990. 1992. *Akron Beacon Journal* (October 10): B8.
The crime scene. 1992. *Forbes* (September 14): 306.
Database. 1993. *U.S. News & World Report* (March 1): 8.
Dilulio, J. J., Jr. 1992. The value of prison. *Wall Street Journal* (May 13): A14.

The economic crisis of urban America. 1992. *Business Week* (May 18): 38–43.
Ellis, A. 1992. A glaring contrast. *Wall Street Journal* (May 14): A15.
Madigan, K. 1992. You want "family values"? They'll cost billions. *Business Week* (September 28): 88.
Merline, J. 1993. Clinton's new war on drugs. *Investor's Business Daily* (February 18): 1–2.

7. SERVING SPECIAL NEEDS AND CONCERNS

Staley, S. 1992. The war on drugs escalates urban violence. *Wall Street Journal* (August 13): A13.

The young and the violent. 1992. *Wall Street Journal* (September 23): A16.

Education

Back to school. 1992. *Forbes* (September 14): 310.

Bennett, W. J. 1993. Quantifying America's decline. *Wall Street Journal* (March 15): A10.

Blinder, A. S. 1992. Adam Smith meets Albert Shanker. *Business Week* (December 14): 20.

Brimelow, P., and L. Spencer. 1993. When quotas replace merit, everybody suffers. *Forbes* (February 4): 80–102.

Brownstein, V. 1992. Economic intelligence: The wages of education. *Fortune* (November 30):23.

Database. 1991. *U.S. News & World Report* (November 11): 14.

Database. 1992. *U.S. News & World Report* (September 28): 15.

Database. 1992. *U.S. News & World Report* (September 14): 16.

The economic crisis of urban America. 1992. *Business Week* (May 18): 38–43.

Henkoff, R. 1992. Where will the jobs come from. *Fortune* (October 19): 58–64.

Hood, J. 1993. What's wrong with head start. *Wall Street Journal* (February 19): A12.

Kramer, F. 1992. CEO briefing on management and leadership. *Investor's Business Daily* (October 26): 4.

Nazario, S. L. 1992. Move grows to promote failing pupils. *Wall Street Journal* (June 16): B1, B8.

Reynolds, A. 1992. Who gained in the 1980s? Everybody. *Wall Street Journal* (May 7): A14.

Samuelson, R. J. 1993. Rhetoric over reality. *Newsweek* (March 1): 30–31.

Sheler, J. L. 1992. The gospel on sex. *U.S. News & World Report* (June 10): 58–64.

Stewart, T. A. 1992. U.S. productivity: First but fading. *Fortune* (October 19): 54–57.

Stout, H. 1992. SAT scores rise but remain near lows. *Wall Street Journal* (August 27): B1, B8.

Trying harder. 1992. Survey. *The Economist* (November 21): 3–18.

Vonada, D. 1993. Matters of fact. *Ohio Magazine* (January): 7.

Waldman, S., and K. Springen. 1992. Too old, too fast? *Newsweek* (November 16): 80–88.

Environment

Beguile, S. 1992. Seeing red over little green lies. *Newsweek* (October 12): 90.

Environmentalism runs riot. 1992. *The Economist* (August 8): 11–12.

Feshbach, M. 1992. Russia's farms, too poisoned for the plow. *Wall Street Journal* (May 14): A14.

Fumento, M. 1991. Is recycling really worth it? *Investor's Business Daily* (November 27): 1–2.

Hong, P., and D. Jones. 1992. Tree-huggers vs. jobs. *Business Week* (October 19): 108–109.

Kiplinger Washington Editors. 1992. *The Kiplinger Washington Letter* (November 20): 2.

Landfills and forests. 1992. *Forbes* (September 14): 316.

Littman, D. 1992. The cost of regulation, counted in jobs. *Wall Street Journal* (April 21): A16.

Family Economics

Blinder, A. S. 1993. Why the cost of services is soaring. *Business Week* (November 16): 22.

Blonston, G. 1992. Are U.S. citizens better off? *Akron Beacon Journal* (August 30): A6.

Cunniff, J. 1991. Americans loaded with "stuff," debt. *Akron Beacon Journal* (December 19): B8.

Database. 1991. *U.S. News & World Report* (October 21): 18.

Database. 1991. *U.S. News & World Report* (September 20): 14.

Duignan-Cabrera, A., J. Seligmann, and T. Barrett. 1993. The art of flying solo. *Newsweek* (March 1): 70–73.

Glionna, J. M. 1992. America's second currency. *Akron Beacon Journal* (December 27): A2.

Hawkins, D. 1992. A depressing time at home. *U.S. News & World Report* (October 19): 60.

Kiplinger Washington Editors. 1992. *The Kiplinger Washington Letter* (November 20): 2.

Madigan, K. 1992. You want "family values"? They'll cost billions. *Business Week* (September 28): 88.

McCormally, K. 1992. Why yields aren't always what they seem. *Kiplinger's Personal Finance Magazine* (November): 89–93.

Reynolds, A. 1992. Who gained in the 1980s? Everybody. *Wall Street Journal* (May 7): A14.

———. 1992. The worst lying about the economy. *Wall Street Journal* (October 21): A16.

Richman, L. S. 1993. How to protect your financial future. *Fortune* (January 25): 58–60.

Seligmann, J. 1992. What traditional family? *Newsweek* (December 7): 67.

Usdansky, M. L. 1992. 1990s' wedding bell blues. *USA Today* (December 9): 12A.

Waldman, S., and K. Springen. 1992. Too old, too fast? *Newsweek* (November 16): 80–88.

Will, G. F. 1992. Purring along the Potomac. *Newsweek* (November 30): 96.

Wiseman, P. 1992. Debit cards finally get a little credit. *USA Today* (November 9): 1B.

Foreign Trade

Corrigan, R. 1992. Will the trade pact cost jobs? *Investor's Business Daily* (October 26): 1–2.

Database. 1991. *U.S. News & World Report* (October 21): 18.

Database. 1992. *U.S. News & World Report* (September 7): 16.

Dornbush, R. 1993. 1-year free ride: It's time to end Asia's 30-year free ride. *Business Week* (March 1): 18.

The final frontier. 1993. *The Economist* (February 20): 63.

Freadhoff, C. 1991. Do taxes hold U.S. firms back? *Investor's Business Daily* (November 8): 1.

———. 1992. Europeans squabble over unity. *Investor's Business Daily* (September 9): 1.

———. 1993. The America in decline myth. *Investor's Business Daily* (January 29): 1–2.

Stewart, T. A. 1992. U.S. productivity: First but fading. *Fortune* (October 19): 54–57.

Stovall, R. H. 1992. Cashing in on the dollar's slide. *Financial World* (September 29): 78.

A survey of China: When China wakes. 1992. *The Economist* (November 28): 1–18.

The trade deal's key provisions. 1992. *Business Week* (August 24): 30.

Health Care

Accident price tag: $137 billion in 1990. 1992. *Akron Beacon Journal* (October 10): B8.

Adams, David. 1992. Jobs at top of everyone's list. *Akron Beacon Journal* (November 13): A1, A21.

Database. 1991. *U.S. News & World Report* (October 21): 18.

Database. 1993. *U.S. News & World Report* (February 22): 8.

Database. 1993. *U.S. News & World Report* (November 18): 22.

Doctors' pay hikes beat inflation. 1993. *U.S. News & World Report* (March 8): 19.

Eye on the issues. 1992. *U.S. News & World Report* (October 26): 19.

Farrell, C. 1993. Health-care costs. *Business Week* (March 15): 80.

Feshbach, M. 1992. Russia's farms, too poisoned for the plow. *Wall Street Journal* (May 14): A14.

Hale, D. 1992. For new jobs, help small business. *Wall Street Journal* (August 10): A10.

O'Reilly, B. 1992. How to take care of aging parents. *Fortune* (May 18): 108–12.

Outlook. 1992. *U.S. News & World Report* (August 10): 8.

Samuelson, R. J. 1993. What Clinton isn't saying. *Newsweek* (March 15): 38.

———. 1993. Health care: How we got into this mess. *Newsweek* (October 4): 31–49.

This short-term tonic has lethal long-term side effects. 1992. *Business Week* (December 14): 24.

Smith, L. 1992. The right cure for health care. *Fortune* (October 19): 88–89.

The vaccine scapegoat. 1993. *Wall Street Journal* (February 23): A16.

Wessel, D. 1992. The outlook. *Wall Street Journal* (May 1): A1.

Young are most lacking in health insurance. 1992. *Wall Street Journal* (August 12): B1.

Inflation

Blinder, A. S. 1993. Why the cost of services is soaring. *Business Week* (November 16): 22.

Zero inflation: How low is low enough? 1992. *The Economist* (November 7): 23–26.

Invention

Buderi, R., and J. Carey. 1993. American inventors are reinventing themselves. *Business Week* (January 18): 78–82.

National Debt

Adams, D. 1992. Jobs at top of everyone's list. *Akron Beacon Journal* (November 13): A1, A21.

Brimelow, P. 1993. Why the deficit is the wrong number. *Forbes* (March 15): 79–82.

Cunniff, J. 1991. Americans loaded with "stuff," debt. *Akron Beacon Journal* (December 19): B8.

Dalio, R. 1992. Depression, not recession. *Barron's* (October 12): 17–27.

Database. 1991. *U.S. News & World Report* (October 21): 18.

Database. 1992. *U.S. News & World Report* (October 19): 10.

Eye on the issues. 1992. *U.S. News & World Report* (October 26): 18.

Hawkins, D. 1992. A depressing time at home. *U.S. News & World Report* (October 19): 60.

Littmann, D. L. 1992. 2001: A farm odyssey. *Wall Street Journal* (September 14): A10.

McKenzie, R. B. 1992. The credit binge that wasn't. *Wall Street Journal* (October 22): A16.

McKinnon, R. I. 1992. A fiscal stimulus won't work. *Wall Street Journal* (December 24): 6.

Meltzer, A. H. 1993. The worst kind of short-term thinking. *Wall Street Journal* (February 22): A10.

Merline, J. 1992. Do U.S. deficits really matter? *Investor's Business Daily* (April 9): 1–2.

———. 1993. Can Congress give up its pork? *Investor's Business Daily* (January 27): 1–2.

Mitchell, D. J. 1992. The revolutionary ten-percent option. *Wall Street Journal* (August 24): A8.

Parshall, G. 1992. The great panic of '93. *U.S. News & World Report* (November 2): 70–72.

Rising debt is campaign's dark secret. 1992. *U.S. News & World Report* (October 5): 28.

Roberts, C. 1992. Mr. Clinton, the people said: "Think small." *Business Week* (November 30): 26.

Roberts, P. C. 1993. The only way out of the budget trap. *Business Week* (March 15): 16.

Samuelson, R. J. 1992. The truth about deficits. *Newsweek* (September 28): 31.

———. 1993. Rhetoric over reality. *Newsweek* (March 1): 30–31.

Smith, L. 1992. The tyranny of America's old. *Fortune* (January 13): 68–72.

Sperry, P. 1992. Is U.S. debt really a monster? *Investor's Business Daily* (November 25): 1–2.

Weinberger, C. W. 1992. The federal deficit—Is it all that bad? *Forbes* (July 20): 33.

Will, G. F. 1992. Purring along the Potomac. *Newsweek* (November 30): 96.

Poverty

Blonston, G. 1992. Are U.S. citizens better off? *Akron Beacon Journal* (August 30): A6.

Discrimination and the market. 1993. *The Economist* (February 27): 19–20.

The economic crisis of urban America. 1992. *Business Week* (May 18): 38–43.

Jenkins, Jr., H. 1992. The "poverty" lobby's inflated numbers. *Wall Street Journal* (December 14): A-1.

Paulett, T. 1993. Poverty spread in 1992 to total of 36.9 million. *Wall Street Journal* (October 5): A2.

Rector, R. America's poverty myth. 1992. *Wall Street Journal* (September 3): A10.

Usdansky, M. L. 1992. Reports say housing costs outpace poor's ability to pay. *USA Today* (November 25): 3A.

Productivity

Farrell, C. 1993. Health-care costs: Don't be too quick with the scalpel. *Business Week* (March 15): 80.

The final frontier. 1993. *The Economist* (February 20): 63.

Freadhoff, C. 1993. The 'America in decline' myth. *Investor's Business Daily* (January 29): A1–A2.

Reynolds, A. 1992. The worst lying about the economy. *Wall Street Journal* (October 21): A16.

Stewart, T. A. 1992. U.S. productivity: First but fading. *Fortune* (October 19): 54–57.

Two cheers for American productivity. 1992. *U.S. News & World Report* (October 26): 24.

Wealth in services. 1993. *The Economist* (February 20): 15–16.

Race/Gender

Database. 1992. *U.S. News & World Report* (November 30): 12.

Hale, D. 1992. For new jobs, help small business. *Wall Street Journal* (August 10): A10.

Koretz, G. 1993. In 1993, fewer businesses may go belly-up. *Business Week* (January 26): 20.

Meeks, F., and L. Sullivan. 1992. If at first you don't succeed. *Forbes* (November 9): 172–180.

Reynolds, A. 1992. Who gained in the 1980s? Everybody. *Wall Street Journal* (May 7): A14.

Selz, M. 1993. For many firms, upturn comes too late. *Wall Street Journal* (January 15): B1–2.

Women, minorities own more small businesses. 1992. *Wall Street Journal* (August 12): B1.

Working on it. 1993. *The Economist* (January 9): 26.

7. SERVING SPECIAL NEEDS AND CONCERNS

Regulation

America's parasite economy. 1992. *The Economist* (October 10): 21–24.

Ansberry, G. 1993. Hired out. *Wall Street Journal* (March 11): A1–A4.

Armey, D. 1992. Small business and the recession. *Wall Street Journal* (November 6): A1–A2.

Cohen, Warren. 1993. Sticking it to business. *U.S. News & World Report* (March 8): 59–61.

Database. 1992. *U.S. News & World Report* (September 21): 14.

Davis, B. 1992. Cost of regulation isn't easy to figure but estimates exist. *Wall Street Journal* (Sept. 23): A10.

Discrimination and the market. 1993. *The Economist* (February 27): 19–20.

Henkoff, R. 1992. Where will the jobs come from. *Fortune* (October 19): 58–64.

Hong, P., and D. Jones. 1992. Tree huggers vs. jobs. *Business Week* (October 19): 108–109.

Ignon, L. 1992. The tragedy of worker's compensation. *Investor's Business Daily* (October 16): 1–2.

Littman, D. 1992. The cost of regulation, counted in jobs. *Wall Street Journal* (April 21): A16.

Merline, J. 1992. Why price controls don't work. *Investor's Business Daily* (November 13): 1.

Novack, J. 1993. How about a little restructuring? *Forbes* (March 15): 91–96.

The origins of the workers' compensation crisis. 1993. *U.S. News & World Report* (March 8): 61.

Outlook. 1993. *U.S. News & World Report* (February 1): 9.

Paved with muzzy intentions. 1992. *The Economist* (October 10): 25.

Richman, L. S. 1992. Bringing reason to regulation. *Fortune* (October 19): 94–96.

Reuters. 1993. Are soaring benefit costs stifling economic growth? *Investor's Business Daily* (February 18): 4.

Spencer, L., and P. Brimelow. 1993. When quotas replace merit, everybody suffers. *Forbes* (February 15): 80–102.

Sperry, P. 1992. Can Uncle Sam run a business? *Investor's Business Daily* (December 14): 1–2.

———. 1993. Where are the full-time jobs? *Investor's Business Daily* (March 10): 1–2.

Two cheers for American productivity. 1992. *U.S. News & World Report* (October 26): 24.

Will, G. F. 1992. Purring along the Potomac. *Newsweek* (November 30): 96.

Religion

Charitable giving amid the recession. 1992. *U.S. News & World Report* (July 6): 20.

Database. 1991. *U.S. News & World Report* (December 9): 16.

Khalaf, R. 1992. The accounting games charities play. *Forbes* (October 26): 252–56.

Steinfels, P. 1991. Pope, in a letter on capitalism, urges work to repair injustices. *New York Times* (May 3): A1, A7.

Tooley, J. 1990. Keeping the faith. *U.S. News & World Report* (November 19): 16.

Small Business

Armey, D. 1992. Small business and the recession. *Wall Street Journal* (November 6): A12.

Saddler, J. 1992. Small businesses complain that jungle of regulations threatens their future. *Wall Street Journal* (June 11): B1.

Social Security

Anderson, J. 1993. Why should I pay for people who don't need it. *Parade Magazine* (February 24): 4–7.

Brimelow, P. 1993. Why the deficit is the wrong number. *Forbes* (March 15): 79–82.

Merline, J. 1993. Putting social security in play. *Investor's Business Daily* (February 11): 1, 2.

Taxation

Barlett, B. 1993. Raising corporate taxes won't raise revenues. *Wall Street Journal* (February 18): A18.

Benham, B. 1993. Next step: A consumption tax? *Investor's Business Daily* (March 9): 1–2.

Burns, S. 1993. Yes, it's time for flat tax and yes, it's doable. *Akron Beacon Journal* (December 28): D5.

Database. 1993. *U.S. News & World Report* (February 8): 13.

How tax assessments are figured. 1992. *Consumer Reports* (November): 723.

Merski, P. G. 1992. Soaking the rich just won't work. *Wall Street Journal* (August 5): A18.

Novak, M. 1993. A new party line? *Forbes* (January 18): 70.

Reynolds, A. 1993. Taxes, taxes, taxes. *Wall Street Journal* (February 18): A18.

Roberts, C. 1992. Mr. Clinton, the people said: "Think small." *Business Week* (November 30): 26.

Samuelson, R. J. 1993. What Clinton isn't saying. *Newsweek* (March 15): 38.

Sperry, P. 1992. What is Reagan's real legacy? *Investor's Business Daily* (November 24): 1–2.

Stein, H. 1993. Reflections in the top 1%. *Wall Street Journal* (May 26): A14.

Tax deform. 1993. *Wall Street Journal* (February 3): A20.

Underground Economy

Brimelow, P. 1993. Why the deficit is the wrong number. *Forbes* (March 15): 79–82.

A lot going on under the table. 1993. *U.S. News & World Report* (February 22): 13.

Pennar, K., and C. Farrell. 1993. Notes from the underground economy. *Business Week* (Feb. 15): 98–101.

Unemployment

Ansberry, C. 1993. Hired out. *Wall Street Journal* (March 11): A1, A4.

A big ho ho ho for America's retailers? 1992. *U.S. News & World Report* (December 7): 16.

Blonston, G. 1992. Are U.S. citizens better off? *Akron Beacon Journal* (August 30): A6.

Database. 1992. *U.S. News & World Report* (October 19): 10.

Eye on the issues. 1992. *U.S. News & World Report* (October 26): 18.

Henkoff, R. 1992. Where will the jobs come from. *Fortune* (October 19): 58–64.

Ignon, L. 1992. The tragedy of workers' comp. *Investor's Business Daily* (October 16): 1–2.

Koretz, G. 1992. The white-collar jobless could really rock the vote. *Business Week* (September 28): 16.

Littman, D. 1992. The cost of regulation, counted in jobs. *Wall Street Journal* (April 21): A16.

McCracken, P. W. 1992. The myth of "chronic" unemployment. *Wall Street Journal* (September 16): A14.

Novak, J. 1993. How about a little restructuring? *Forbes* (March 15): 91–96.

Novak, M. 1993. A new party line? *Forbes* (January 18): 70.

Reuters. 1993. Are soaring benefit costs stifling economic growth? *Investor's Business Daily* (February 18): 4.

Sperry, P. 1993. Where are the full-time jobs? *Investor's Business Daily* (March 10): 1–2.

The thirst for jobs. 1992. *Forbes* (September 14): 274.

Where the jobs are: Government. 1992. *U.S. News & World Report* (August 17): 13.

Zachary, P., and B. Ortega. 1993. Age of angst. *Wall Street Journal* (March 10): A1, A8.

Wealth

Blonston, G. 1992. Are U.S. citizens better off? *Akron Beacon Journal* (August 30): A6.

Donlan, T. G. 1992. Rich and poor: Does America suffer from an income gap? *Barron's* (October 5): 10.

Gordon, J. S. 1992. Numbers game. *Forbes* (October 19): 48–56.

Lindsey, L. B. 1992. The richest people in America. *Forbes* (October 19): 89.

———. 1992. Why the 1980s were not the 1920s. *Forbes* (October 19): 78–80.

Measuring the comforts of life. 1992. *Forbes* (September 14): 288.

Michaels, J. W. 1992. Oh, our aching angst. *Forbes* (September 14): 47–54.

Munk, N. 1992. A convenience-of-living index? *Forbes* (September 14): 218–230.

Reynolds, A. 1992. The worst lying about the economy. *Wall Street Journal* (October 21): A16.

———. 1992. Who gained in the 1980s? Everybody. *Wall Street Journal* (May 7): A14.

Rudnitsky, H., and M. Schifrin. 1992. The inheritors. *Forbes* (October 26): 150–152.

Stein, H. 1993. Reflections in the top 1%. *Wall Street Journal* (May 26): A14.

Zaldivar, R. A. 1992. Taxing the rich: Where to start? *Akron Beacon Journal* (March 8): A8.

Violence as a Public Health Issue for Children

Joycelyn Elders

Joycelyn Elders is [a former] Surgeon General of the United States. The statistics in this article were based on data collected by the Centers for Disease Control and Prevention.

The Surgeon General's primary role is to make the people of the United States aware of serious health threats. One does not have to look far into the home, school or community to realize that a major threat to our health is violence. I would like to share with *Childhood Education* readers my views on the public health consequences of violence, and to discuss prevention efforts and the implications for health and child care professionals.

The problem of violence in this country has increased markedly in recent years, including extraordinary increases in homicide and suicide rates among our young people. Since the 1950s, suicide rates among our youth have almost quadrupled. Homicide rates among young men are 20 times as high as most other industrialized countries. Concurrently, the average age of perpetrators and victims has fallen. We now have the problem of children killing children. On the day you read this, 14 children in America under the age of 19 will die in suicides, homicides or accidental shootings and many more will be injured.

The violence has spilled over into the schools. In increasing numbers and proportions, kids are carrying guns to school. In 1989, an estimated 430,000 students took a weapon to school to protect themselves from attack or harm at least once during a six-month period.

Also, much of today's violence occurs in the home. In 1990, there were over 500,000 reported and confirmed cases of child abuse (physical and sexual) in the U.S. Evidence suggests that this figure may be only one-third the actual incidence—much of which results from drug and alcohol abuse. Furthermore, research shows that approximately 30 percent of the adult population experiences some form of spousal violence. Twenty to 30 percent of emergency room visits by women are the result of domestic violence.

Our children are learning to use violence to solve problems. Violent behavior is being modeled in our homes, schools, neighborhoods and in the media. If we are to have confidence in health care reform, we must restore security in our homes, our schools, our streets and our nation. It is time for us to roll up our sleeves and rid this country of the hideous, highly infectious, yet preventable problem of violence.

Public Health Consequences

The costs of violence to this country are clearly too great to ignore:

- Firearm injuries represent nearly $3 billion a year. The cost of firearm injuries alone to our health care system is nearly $3 billion a year.
- The vast majority (85 percent) of the hospital costs for treatment of firearm injuries is unreimbursed care.
- In the District of Columbia, the cost to hospitals of criminal violence totaled $20.4 million in 1989.

- The total medical cost of all violence in the U.S. was $13.5 billion in 1992—$3 billion due to suicides and suicide attempts and $10.5 billion due to interpersonal violence.
- In 1988, one out of six pediatricians nationwide treated a young gunshot victim.

The public health toll, however, is not just financial. We can clearly document the immediate adverse psychological and physical consequences of violence, including family violence and rape. The long-term effects of such violence include trauma-related disorders (including post-traumatic stress disorder, especially for rape victims), personality disorders, addictive disorders and even physical disorders. We also know that many violent individuals were victims themselves of child abuse.

Drug use is a leading cause of America's crime and violence. Research suggests that 40 percent of all homicides are related to drugs. In Washington, D.C., 80 percent of homicide victims had evidence of cocaine in their bodies. Likewise, in 65 percent of all homicides, the perpetrator and/or the victims had been drinking. Alcohol is a factor in at least 55 percent of all domestic disputes.

An estimated 1.2 million elementary-age children have access to guns in their homes. Having a handgun in the home constitutes a very real and serious threat. A recent study in the *New England Journal of Medicine* reported that if you have a gun at home:

- You are eight times more likely to be killed by, or to kill, a family member or intimate acquaintance.
- You are three times more likely to be killed or to kill someone in your home.
- You or a family member are five times more likely to commit suicide.

With its roots in poverty, violence has a disproportionately greater effect on racial and ethnic minorities. One of two African American children is poor and one out of three Hispanic children is poor. Up to 90 percent of all Native American children live in poverty. The violence exhibited in our society is not, however, the result of any racial or ethnic risk factor. Rather, it reflects an association between violence and poverty.

Although African Americans constitute 12 percent of the population, 50 percent of murder victims are African American. This is not interracial violence. In 1990, 93 percent of African American murder victims were killed by other African Americans. The vast majority of violence committed in this country is between people who know each other.

The media depiction of violence weaves its way throughout these factors. By portraying violence as the normal means of conflict resolution, the media gives youth the message that violence is socially acceptable and the best way to resolve problems. After more than 10 years of research, we know that a correlation exists between violence on television and aggressive behavior by children.

Perhaps even more important than the violence children view on television is the violence that they see in their own homes and communities and on the streets. I believe that this "real" violence is even more frightening and disruptive and leaves scars that can last a lifetime.

Let me now turn to what we in public health can do to help solve this enormous threat. We can't call out the military, we can't enforce gun control laws, we can't go on foot patrols in our neighborhoods. What we can do is help *prevent violence before it starts!*

Prevention Efforts

As President Clinton has said, one of the things our health care reform package and the anti-crime and anti-drug initiatives have in common is a focus on prevention. Although I want to focus primarily upon the role of public health in preventing violence, I also want to assure you that the Department of Health and Human Services is working on this problem at all levels with other Cabinet agencies—particularly the Departments of Justice, Education, HUD, Labor and the Office of National Drug Control Policy. Collectively, we are looking at five aspects of violence—family violence, youth violence, sexual assault, media violence and firearms.

Violence prevention, from a public health perspective, means two things: reducing our children's risk of facing violence in the future and preventing the *immediate* threat of violence to our adolescents and young children. Let me add that we must deal not only with the individual child, but also with the family, the social environment and the community in a coordinated fashion. Furthermore, what we do must be *long-term*—since violent behavior is persistent throughout adolescence and young adulthood.

Violence prevention means offering prenatal parenting classes and guidance, particularly to teen mothers and other parents at risk. *It means starting early.* That is why we must fully fund early childhood education programs like Head Start. Children who successfully complete Head Start are less likely as adults to be incarcerated or to be on welfare and more likely to have high school diplomas.

I am convinced that school offers us the best and easiest way to reach as many children as possible. That is why I personally have supported comprehensive school health education in junior and senior high school as an element of the health care reform package. I add my voice to those calling for passage of the Safe Schools Act, an act that would provide schools the means to choose their own "weapons" against drugs and violence. Obviously, such an effort requires a violence prevention curriculum as an integral part of a comprehensive health curriculum.

Since I became Surgeon General last spring, I have worked with the Department of Education to put together a plan for health care reform that would first provide funds for comprehensive health education in schools of highest need. Later, we hope we can do the same in all schools. Research has shown that comprehensive school health education is effective in influencing youths' behaviors and establishing a pattern of healthy behavior in the future.

Comprehensive school health education means, in part, a focus on safety and the prevention of injuries every day, in every grade and in age-appropriate ways. The most effective interventions with young children involve shaping their attitudes, imparting knowledge and modifying behaviors while the children are still open to positive influences. *We must teach children how to resolve conflicts peacefully,* especially those children at highest risk. We must work especially hard with young minority males in the inner cities.

It is also important to support families by providing parenting classes and helping parents become part of their communities. We know that individuals and families who feel connected to their communities are less likely to be abusive.

We must develop programs to train young people and make jobs available for them. Adolescents must become part of our society with clear, positive roles to perform. I am concerned that children today are not learning the skills they need to be employable and productive in today's modern work force. I am worried because one quarter of all African American males ages 20 to 29 are incarcerated, on probation or on parole, and only one fifth are enrolled in higher education.

This type of violence prevention education must be available for families in order to break the so-called "intergeneration cycle" of violence. When children regularly witness abuse and violence and know that they are likely victims, they often grow up to become violent themselves. We know that men who witness parental violence as children are much more likely to physically abuse their partners than men who have not. We must break that cycle.

Violence prevention means revitalizing our neighborhoods and making them safe and cohesive places. Communities should collectively share the burden of raising children by providing social structure and positive, peaceful role models. Violence prevention also means understanding why gangs flourish in our cities—what needs do they fill, and what security do they offer young people? We need to understand what kind of guidance these youth are seeking and what they will accept from their elders.

Violence prevention means removing the tools of violence and providing opportunities for our children to make the transition into adulthood. We can prevent violence and offer a hopeful future by providing community support, realistic role models, education and training, and the knowledge that jobs will be available. I fervently hope that the media will become part of the solution by airing prosocial programming, helping with public service announcements, showing the true conse-

quences of violence and giving us all hope that we can turn this around.

Implications for Health and Child Care Professionals

I join with my predecessor Surgeon Generals in urging our colleagues to recognize violence as a public health threat. When I talk about "health and child care professionals," I am speaking in the broadest sense to include physicians, school nurses, social workers, psychologists, mental health workers and, especially, teachers.

On a day-to-day basis, these professionals can:

- Become familiar with the AMA's effort to train health care professionals to identify and report domestic violence. A key part of this training is learning to refer patients to appropriate social service agencies and shelters.

- Use the emergency room as a place to intervene by identifying persons who are victims or perpetrators of violence and referring them to needed services such as conflict resolution training, family counseling, problem-solving training, substance abuse counseling and treatment and other mental health and social services.

- Become trained in and offer expectant parents prenatal counseling and guidance about early childhood growth and development.

- Participate with schools to develop curricula designed to promote healthful behaviors and prevent violence and other destructive behaviors.

- Recognize and determine the immediate risk factors facing students—with questions about gun storage at home, safety at school, aggressive be-

havior patterns at home or in school, and substance abuse.

- Become a credible source of information for students about preventing these problems.

Conclusion

Violence does not have to be a fact of life. Although it is now an epidemic, we can prevent it. We need to focus on the *prevention* of violence. To do this, we need to focus our efforts on children and teach them carefully at school and at home. We need to provide them with education and job opportunities, mentors and a chance to grow up without access to alcohol and other drugs. We can revitalize our neighborhoods.

By the time this issue is published, we will have announced details for establishing "empowerment zones" and "enterprise communities" in which designated communities receive cash assistance, federal tax incentives and coordinated economic and human development services. We need to concentrate less on fixing the results of violence, and more on preventing it. Violence is a complex problem that will not yield to simple solutions. Violence prevention will require all of us to work together—doctors and judges, teachers and police officers, scientists and community organizers.

Finally, I want to tell you that there is hope and there *is* a solution to this problem. We must not retreat behind locked doors. We must become even more involved with our children and our communities. We must empower ourselves to make needed changes. To do anything else is to sit back and let our children die. As Surgeon General, I know that this is a preventable problem and I am committed to help lead us to the solution.

Editor's note: Joycelyn Elders served 15 months as U.S. Surgeon General in the Clinton administration. She resigned in December 1994.

Blowing up the Tracks

Stop segregating schools by ability and watch kids grow

Patricia Kean

Patrician Kean is a writer in New York City.

It's morning in New York, and some seventh graders are more equal than others.

Class 7-16 files slowly into the room, prodded by hard-faced men whose walkie-talkies crackle with static. A pleasant looking woman shouts over the din, "What's rule number one?" No reply. She writes on the board. "Rule One: Sit down."

Rule number two seems to be an unwritten law: Speak slowly. Each of Mrs. H's syllables hangs in the air a second longer than necessary. In fact, the entire class seems to be conducted at 16 RPM. Books come out gradually. Kids wander about the room aimlessly. Twelve minutes into class, we settle down and begin to play "O. Henry Jeopardy," a game which requires students to supply one-word answers to questions like: "O. Henry moved from North Carolina to what state—Andy? Find the word on the page."

The class takes out a vocabulary sheet. Some of the words they are expected to find difficult include popular, ranch, suitcase, arrested, recipe, tricky, ordinary, humorous, and grand jury.

Thirty minutes pass. Bells ring, doors slam.

Class 7-1 marches in unescorted, mindful of rule number one. Paperbacks of Poe smack sharply on desks, notebooks rustle, and kids lean forward expectantly, waiting for Mrs. H. to fire the first question. What did we learn about the writer?

Hands shoot into the air. Though Edgar Allen Poe ends up sounding a lot like Jerry Lee Lewis—a boozehound who married his 13-year-old cousin—these kids speak confidently, in paragraphs. Absolutely no looking at the book allowed.

We also have a vocabulary sheet, drawn from "The Tell-Tale Heart," containing words like audacity, dissimulation, sagacity, stealthy, anxiety, derision, agony, and supposition.

As I sit in the back of the classroom watching these two very different groups of seventh graders, my previous life as an English teacher allows me to make an educated guess and a chilling prediction. With the best of intentions, Mrs. H. is teaching the first group, otherwise known as the "slow kids," as though they are fourth graders, and the second, the honors group, as though they are high school freshmen. Given the odds of finding a word like "ordinary" on the SAT's, the children of 7-16 have a better chance of standing before a "grand jury" than making it to college.

Tracking, the practice of placing students in "ability groups" based on a host of ill-defined criteria—everything from test scores to behavior to how much of a fuss a mother can be counted on to make—encourages even well-meaning teachers and administrators to turn out generation after generation of self-fulfilling prophecies. "These kids know they're no Einsteins," Mrs. H. said of her low-track class when we sat together in the teacher's lounge. "They know they don't read well. This way I can go really slowly with them."

With his grades, however, young Albert would probably be hanging right here with the rest of lunch table 7-16. That's where I discover that while their school may think they're dumb, these kids are anything but stupid. "That teacher," sniffs a pretty girl wearing lots of purple lipstick. "She talks so slow. She thinks we're babies. She takes a year to do anything." "What about that other one?" a girl named Ingrid asks, referring to their once-a-week student teacher. "He comes in and goes like this: Rail (pauses) road. Rail (pauses) road. Like we don't know what railroad means!" The table breaks up laughing.

Outside the walls of schools across the country, it's slowly become an open secret that enforced homogeneity benefits no one. The work of researchers like Jeannie Oakes of UCLA and Robert Slavin of Johns Hopkins has proven that tracking does not merely reflect differences—it causes them. Over time, slow kids get slower, while those in the middle and in the so-called "gifted and talented" top tracks fail to gain from isolation. Along the way, the practice resegregates the nation's schools, dividing the middle from the lower classes, white from black and brown. As the evidence piles up, everyone from the Carnegie Corporation to the National Governors Association has called for change.

Though some fashionably progressive schools have begun to reform, tracking persists. Parent groups, school boards, teachers, and administrators who hold the power within schools cling to the myths and wax apocalyptic about the horrors of heterogeneity. On their side is the most potent force known to man: bureaucratic inertia. Because tracking puts kids in boxes, keeps the lid on, and shifts responsibility for mediocrity and failure away from the schools themselves, there is little incentive to change a nearly-century old tradition. "Research is research," the principal told me that day, "This is practice."

Back track

Tracking has been around since just after the turn of the century. It was then, as cities teemed with immigrants and industry, that education reformers like John Franklin Bobbitt began to argue that the school and the factory shared a common mission, to "work up the raw material into that finished product for which it was best adapted." By the twenties, the scientific principles that ruled the factory floor had been applied to the classroom. They believed the IQ test—which had just become popular—allowed pure science, not the whims of birth or class, to determine whether a child received the type of education appropriate for a future manager or a future laborer.

It hasn't quite worked out that way. Driven by standardized tests, the descendants of the old IQ tests, tracking has evolved into a kind of educational triage premised on the notion that only the least wounded can be saved. Yet when the classroom operates like a battleground, society's casualties mount, and the results begin to seem absurd: Kids who enter school needing more get less, while the already enriched get, well, enricher. Then, too, the low-track graduates of 70 years ago held a distinct advantage over their modern counterparts: If tracking prepared them for mindless jobs, at least those jobs existed.

The sifting and winnowing starts as early as pre-K. Three-year old Ebony and her classmates have won the highly prized "gifted and talented" label after enduring a battery of IQ and psychological tests. There's nothing wrong with the "regular" class in this Harlem public school. But high expectations for Ebony and her new friends bring tangible rewards like a weekly field trip and music and computer lessons.

Meanwhile, regular kids move on to regular kindergartens where they too will be tested, and where it will be determined that some children need more help, perhaps a "pre-first grade" developmental year. So by the time they're ready for first grade reading groups, certain six-year-olds have already been marked as "sparrows"—the low performers in the class.

In the beginning, it doesn't seem to matter so much, because the other reading groups—the robins and the eagles—are just a few feet away and the class is together for most of the day. Trouble is, as they toil over basic drill sheets, the sparrows are slipping farther behind. The robins are gathering more challenging vocabulary words, and the eagles soaring on to critical thinking skills.

Though policies vary, by fourth grade many of these groups have flown into completely separate class-rooms, turning an innocent three-tier reading system into three increasingly rigid academic tracks—honors, regular, and remedial—by middle school.

Unless middle school principals take heroic measures like buying expensive software or crafting daily schedules by hand, it often becomes a lot easier to sort everybody by reading scores. So kids who do well on reading tests can land in the high track for math, science, social studies, even lunch, and move together as a self-contained unit all day. Friendships form, attitudes harden. Kids on top study together, kids in the middle console themselves by making fun of the "nerds" above and the "dummies" below, and kids on the bottom develop behavioral problems and get plenty of negative reinforcement.

> It's easier for educators to tinker with programs and make cosmetic adjustments than it is to ask them to do what bureaucrats hate most: give up one method of doing things without having another to put in its place. Tracking is a system; untracking is a leap of faith.

By high school, many low-track students are locked out of what Jeannie Oakes calls "gatekeeper courses," the science, math, and foreign language classes that hold the key to life after twelfth grade. Doors to college are slamming shut, though the kids themselves are often the last to know. When researcher Anne Wheelock interviewed students in Boston's public schools, they'd all insist they were going to become architects, teachers, and the like. What courses were they taking? "Oh, Keyboarding II, Earth Science, Consumer Math. This would be junior year and I'd ask, 'Are you taking Algebra?' and they'd say no."

Black marks

A funny thing can happen to minority students on the way to being tracked. Even when minority children score high, they often find themselves placed in lower tracks where counselors and principals assume they belong.

In Paula Hart's travels for The Achievement Council, a Los Angeles-based educational advocacy group, she comes across district after district where black and Latino kids score in the 75th percentile for math, yet never quite make it into Algebra I, the classic gatekeeper course. A strange phenomenon occurs in inner city areas with large minority populations—high track classes shrink, and low track classes expand to fit humble expectations for the entire school population.

A few years ago, Dr. Norward Roussell's curiosity got the best of him. As Selma, Alabama's first black school superintendent, he couldn't help but notice that "gifted and talented" tracks were nearly lily white in a district that was 70 percent black. When he looked for answers in the files of high school students, he discovered that a surprising number of low track minority kids had actually scored higher than their white top track counterparts.

Parents of gifted and talented students staged a full-scale revolt against Roussell's subsequent efforts to establish logical standards for placement. In four days of public hearings, speaker after speaker said the same thing: We're going to lose a lot of our students to other schools. To Roussell, their meaning was clear: Put black kids in the high tracks and we pull white kids out of the system. More blacks and more low-income whites did make it to the top under the new criteria, but Roussell himself was left behind. The majority-white school board chose not to renew his contract, and he's now superintendent in Macon County, Alabama, a district that is overwhelmingly black.

Race and class divisions usually play themselves out in a more subtle fashion. Talk to teachers about how their high track kids differ from their low track kids and most speak not of intelligence, but of motivation and "family." It seems that being gifted and talented is hereditary after all, largely a matter of having parents who read to you, who take you to museums and concerts, and who know how to work the system. Placement is often a matter of who's connected. Jennifer P., a teacher in a Brooklyn elementary school saw a pattern in her class. "The principal put all the kids whose parents were in the PTA in the top tracks no matter what their scores were. He figures that if his PTA's happy, he's happy."

Once the offspring of the brightest and the best connected have been skimmed off in honors or regular tracks, low tracks begin to fill up with children whose parents are not likely to complain. These kids get less homework, spend less class time learning, and are often taught by the least experienced teachers, because avoiding them can become a reward for seniority in a profession where perks are few.

With the courts reluctant to get involved, even when tracking leads to racial segregation and at least the appearance of civil rights violations, changing the system becomes an arduous local battle fought school by school. Those who undertake the delicate process of untracking need nerves of steel and should be prepared to find resistance from every quarter, since, as Slavin notes, parents of high-achieving kids will fight this to the death. One-time guidance counselor Hart learned this lesson more than a decade ago when she and two colleagues struggled to introduce a now-thriving college curriculum program at Los Angeles' Banning High. Their efforts to open top-track classes to all students prompted death threats from an unlikely source—their fellow teachers.

Off track betting

Anne Wheelock's new book, *Crossing the Tracks*, tells the stories of schools that have successfully untracked or never tracked at all. Schools that make the transition often achieve dramatic results. True to its name, Pioneer Valley Regional school in Northfield, Massachusetts was one of the first in the nation to untrack. Since 1983, the number of Pioneer Valley seniors going on to higher education jumped from 37 to 80 percent. But, the author says, urban schools continue to lag behind. "We're talking about unequal distribution of reform," Wheelock declares. "Change is taking place in areas like Wellesley, Massachusetts and Jericho, Long Island. It's easier to untrack when kids are closer to one another to begin with."

It's also easier for educators to tinker with programs and make cosmetic adjustments than it is to ask them to do what bureaucrats hate most: give up one method of doing things without having another to put in its place. Tracking is a system; untracking is a leap of faith. When difficult kids can no longer be dumped in low tracks, new ways must be found to deal with disruptive behavior: early intervention, intensive work with families, and lots of tutoring. Untracking may also entail new instructional techniques like cooperative group learning and peer tutoring, but what it really demands is flexibility and improvisation.

It also demands that schools—and the rest of us —admit that some kids will be so disruptive or violent that a solution for dealing with them must be found *outside* of the regular public school system. New York City seems close to such a conclusion. Schools Chancellor Joseph Fernandez is moving forward with a voluntary "academy" program, planning separate schools designed to meet the needs of chronic troublemakers. One of them, the Wildcat Academy, run by a non-profit group of the same name, plans to enroll 150 students by the end of the year. Wildcat kids will attend classes from nine to five, wear uniforms, hold part-time jobs, and be matched with mentors from professional fields. Districts in Florida and California are conducting similar experiments.

Moving away from tracking is not about taking away from the gifted and talented and giving to the poor. That, as Wheelock notes, is "political suicide." It's not even about placing more black and Latino kids in their midst, a kind of pre-K affirmative action. Rather, it's about raising expectations for everyone. Or, as Slavin puts it: "You can maintain your tracking system. Just put everyone into the top track."

That's not as quixotic as it sounds. In fact, it's

long been standard practice in the nation's Catholic schools, a system so backward it's actually progressive. When I taught in an untracked parochial high school, one size fit all—with the exception of the few we expelled for poor grades or behavior. My students, who differed widely in ability, interest, and background, nevertheless got Shakespeare, Thoreau, and Langston Hughes at the same pace, at the same time—and lived to tell the tale. Their survival came, in part, because my colleagues and I could decide if the cost of keeping a certain student around was too high and we had the option of sending him or her elsewhere if expulsion was warranted.

The result was that my honor students wrote elegant essays and made it to Ivy League schools, right on schedule. And far from being held back by their "regular" and "irregular" counterparts, straight-A students were more likely to be challenged by questions they would never dream of asking. "Why are we studying this?" a big-haired girl snapping gum in the back of the room wondered aloud one day. Her question led to a discussion that turned into the best class I ever taught.

In four years, I never saw a single standardized test score. But time after time I watched my students climb out of whatever mental category I had put them in. Tracking sees to it that they never get that chance. Flying directly in the face of Yogi Berra's Rule Number One, it tells kids it's over before it's even begun. For ultimately, tracking stunts the opportunity for growth, the one area in which all children are naturally gifted.

Everyone Is an Exception: Assumptions to Avoid in the Sex Education Classroom

More often than not, the teachers who are assigned to teach courses in sex education have little or no professional preparation to do so. Taking account of the difficulties inherent in the situation, Ms. Krueger provides helpful advice about how not *to proceed.*

....

MARY M. KRUEGER

MARY M. KRUEGER is the director of health education and an adjunct professor of public health at Emory University, Atlanta.

UNFORTUNATE though it may be, most public school teachers rarely have the opportunity (or luxury) to devote significant time to students as individuals. Such is the nature of our work — the classroom is made up of *groups* of people, and the moments in a school day when we can interact with our students one-to-one are infrequent at best. As a result, and in order to function with some degree of consistency, teachers usually develop and act on a set of generalizations and assumptions regarding students.

However, the unique nature of sex education — a field of growing importance as more and more states mandate its incorporation into the public school curriculum — necessitates a reexamination of some of these assumptions. To date 34 states have passed legislation requiring sex education in the schools, and additional state mandates are pending.[1] Nonetheless, there are no undergraduate de-

gree-granting programs in the discipline, nor do any state boards of education certify teachers in sex education; most frequently, in fact, sex education courses are assigned to teachers with little or no professional training in the area.[2] Such teachers — who have been, in effect, *dumped* into the sex education classroom — are not only undertrained in methodology and curriculum design but expected to facilitate activities and discussions in an exquisitely sensitive area. It is truly ironic that the sex education issues that are the most difficult for teachers (particularly undertrained teachers) to address are those in which teachers' assumptions have the potential to do the greatest disservice to students.

Regardless of their personal awkwardness or inexperience, sex education teachers have a special responsibility to avoid causing students embarrassment or pain. Above all, they have a duty to remember that their students are *individuals* with varying family backgrounds, experiences, and values.

During more than 12 years of experience in sex education, I have learned that sex education efforts are more effective

when teachers respect students' individuality and interact with students in ways that make them feel unique and special. I have also become familiar with the most common (and dangerous) assumptions that teachers of sex education hold about students. I list them here, along with suggestions about how to avoid them. If teachers refrain from making these assumptions, their students will feel that their individuality is being honored and will thus be more willing to participate fully in and gain from lesson activities.

ASSUMPTIONS TO AVOID

1. *All students come from traditional nuclear families.* This misconception is especially relevant to the sex education classroom, with its (one hopes) frequent references to and encouragement of family communication about sexuality. Teachers who automatically refer to students' families with such phrases as "mom and dad" deny the experience of the majority of their students, as well as the realities of modern American culture.

In almost every region of the U.S., two-parent, traditionally structured families are now the exception.[3] Families no longer consist solely of nuclear groupings of heterosexual married couples and their biological children. Students' families may comprise such aggregations as single parents with children; married parents with children from the current and previous marriages; single or married parents with foster or adopted children; or cohabiting heterosexual or homosexual couples with biological, adopted, or foster children. If teachers are successfully to facilitate the full participation of students in activities that involve parent/child communication and the clarification and validation of family values, we owe it to our students to remember that daily access to "mom and dad," in the traditional sense, is a fact of life for less than 20% of today's children.[4]

2. *All students are heterosexual.* Ten percent of students are *not* heterosexual, regardless of whether they have consciously internalized the fact yet.[5] It is common, yet potentially alienating to gay and lesbian students, to make unthinking references to male students' "girlfriends" or female students' "boyfriends." Such practices send a clear message to gay students that their sexual orientation is, at best, to be hidden and, at worst, abnormal and shameful.

In addition to promoting inclusive language with regard to sexual orientation, the field of sex education has an ethical obligation to condemn homophobic harassment and intimidation of gay, lesbian, and bisexual students. As one of society's most potent agents of socialization, schools are duty-bound to take a stand against hatred and ignorance and to allow all students to learn in a safe and nurturing environment. The denial of such an environment in the past has contributed to a suicide rate for gay and lesbian teenagers that is two to six times higher than that of heterosexual teens.[6] Gay and lesbian teens are also more likely than their heterosexual peers to drop out of school, become runaways, and abuse alcohol and other drugs.[7] Such self-destructive behavior is often the result of feeling overwhelmed by the challenge of learning to like oneself in a hostile world. Much of the self-doubt and inner turmoil that too often diminish the quality of life for these students can be averted by early and consistent messages of acceptance from adult authority figures. Sex education teachers are in a position to take significant steps toward that end.

3. *All students are sexually involved.* Many students are not sexually involved, and they need support for that decision. While we adults frequently wring our hands in concern over (and probably disapproval of) the percentage of "sexually active" teens, we must keep in mind that, in certain age groups and in many parts of the country, students who are not sexually involved are in the majority. However, they (like us) have been profoundly influenced by television, films, and the popular press, all of which send the message that "everyone" is having sex. Because adolescence is a stage of life that so strongly emphasizes conformity, young people may respond to these societal pressures by feeling that virginity is something to be hidden — a source of embarrassment. In an environment that bombards teens at every turn with incentives to become involved with sex, the decision to resist — when one wants above all else to "fit in" — is difficult indeed.

In classroom presentations that address sexual behavior, teachers may unwittingly reflect this "of-course-all-teenagers-are-having-sex" mindset by, for example, phrasing references in the second person ("when you have sex, you need to be responsible"). Training oneself to speak almost exclusively in the third person when presenting lessons will allow students who choose abstinence to feel supported, normal, and comfortable with their decision (and respected for their courage in resisting peer pressure and acting in accordance with their own values).

4. *No students are sexually involved.* Despite all efforts to the contrary on the part of parents, teachers, and other concerned adults, students are becoming involved in sexual behavior with partners at increasingly younger ages. They need the skills to clarify their decisions and to protect their health. Surveys of American teenagers have found that the average age of first intercourse is 16. More than half of high school students have had intercourse at least once, and many participate in intercourse on a regular basis.[8]

With regard to these students, sex education teachers face another dilemma. While generally preferring that students avoid premature sexual involvement, with all its concomitant emotional and medical risks, savvy teachers realize that their preferences are irrelevant to the fact that significant numbers of young people are already involved in sexual behavior that

was formerly considered the exclusive domain of adults. No truly caring teacher can choose to ignore the realities that accompany a young person's decision to be involved in sexual activity simply because the teacher is unwilling to face the fact that it is happening.

Teachers best serve the needs of sexually involved students by helping them to clarify their decisions and improve their decision-making skills, rather than making decisions for them; by educating them regarding the risks of early sexual activi-

> More than half of high school students have had intercourse at least once, and many participate in intercourse on a regular basis.

ty, without excluding the positive aspects of human sexual expression; and by expressing concern for their students' welfare, rather than standing in judgment of their behavior.

5. *All students' sexual involvements are consensual.* The faces we see in our classrooms every day include, by even the most rudimentary statistical calculations, more than one victim of sexual violence. It is estimated that 27% of girls and 16% of boys are sexually abused before they reach age 18.[9] Among adolescents, sexual abuse is the most common form of child abuse.[10] In addition, 50% of all rape victims are between the ages of 10 and 19, with half of that number under the age of 16.[11] Up to one-fourth of all college women report having experienced acquaintance rape.[12] (We must extrapolate from that figure to reflect the experience of junior high and high school girls, since the vast majority

of research on acquaintance rape has focused on university populations.) Indeed, young people are being sexually exploited with frightening regularity.

Perhaps the best service a teacher can provide to students who have been sexually victimized is to be approachable, and certainly a sex education class offers a natural venue for students to approach a caring adult with questions and concerns. Among adolescents who have been sexually abused, 27% disclose the fact on their own initiative[13] — a figure that tells us that few adults are diligently looking for indicators of abuse or assertively seeking information from survivors. By remembering that, for many students, sexual experience is, in fact, rape experience, sex education teachers can help students begin the necessary healing process, perhaps by putting students in touch with intervention services.

6. *Students who are "sexually active" are having intercourse.* A large number of young people are participating in sexual behaviors other than penis/vagina intercourse, thus rendering moot the overused and ill-defined catch phrase "sexually active." The most common expression of sexuality among teens is solo masturbation;[14] thus class discussions of sexual behavior that focus only on the risk of pregnancy or disease transmission exclude those students who are "sexually active" but not involved in behavior that puts them at medical risk.

Other nonintercourse behaviors, such as oral sex, partner masturbation, variations of "petting," and even such benign activities as kissing and hugging are part of the sexual repertoire of most adolescents. Ninety-seven percent of teenagers have kissed someone by the time they are 15; by age 13, 25% of girls have had their breasts touched by a partner. At least 40% of teens participate in partner masturbation.[15] By age 17, 41% of girls have performed fellatio on a partner, and 33% of boys have performed cunnilingus on a partner. Overall, 69% of young people who are sexually involved with a partner include oral sex in their behavior.[16]

When adults deny the full range of human sexual expression and regard only intercourse as "sex," students are denied an important educational opportunity. Many young people believe that there is no acceptable form of sexual behavior other than intercourse.[17] Operating under that assumption, students may put themselves at risk for unwanted pregnancy or sexually transmitted disease by engaging in intercourse when less risky sexual behavior would have been equally fulfilling. The myth that intercourse is the only way to act on one's sexual feelings has surely contributed significantly to such negative phenomena as premature pregnancy and the spread of sexually transmitted diseases (including AIDS). Clearly, ignorance is anything but bliss where sexual health is concerned. Teachers who help young people learn that intercourse is not required to enjoy one's sexuality not only broaden their students' horizons, but also impart knowledge that may help lower rates of adolescent pregnancy and sexually transmitted disease by lowering the rate of adolescent intercourse.

SCHOOLS ARE increasingly expected to address social problems that were formerly the province of the family, religious organizations, and social agencies. Understandably, teachers often feel overwhelmed by the prospect of dealing with sexuality, pregnancy, sexual abuse, and other complex issues facing young people. Complicating matters further are teachers' fears that sex education curricula are necessarily controversial, that they will incite negative community reaction, and that the majority of parents will disapprove. Indeed, both prospective and current sex education teachers are vociferous in expressing doubts about their ability to deal with potential objections to their curricula.[18]

Since the likelihood of avoiding all controversy when operating a school-based sex education program is slim, the best approach may be to expect and accept diversity of opinion among members of the community, to respect well-intentioned questioning of curricula and methodology, and to operate with unflagging vigor despite any limitations that may result from controversy.[19] Teachers' primary concern, however, *must* remain the well-being of the students, and the work of sex educators needs to be steeped in an awareness of the unique manner in which sexuality and well-being interact. If teachers know their material, believe in the importance of the program, and have clearly defined goals and objectives (one of which is the best possible quality of life for students), then they will be able to comfortably defend those curricular approaches that protect students' health, life, and individuality.

The sweeping alterations in American lifestyles, family structures, and interpersonal mores that have marked recent decades have been mind-boggling indeed. Precisely because modern society is so complicated, family organization so tenuous, and support systems so capricious, students need more than ever to be viewed as individuals. As teachers dealing with topics of an especially personal and sensitive nature, let us remember that, in one way or another, each of our students is an exception. Let us celebrate and respect the uniqueness of our students — because, when we do, we earn for ourselves the right to expect the same kind of treatment in return.

1. Debra Haffner, "1992 Report Card on the States: Sexual Rights in America," *SIECUS Report,* February/March 1992, pp. 1-7.

2. Mary M. Krueger, "Sex Education by State Mandate: Teachers' Perceptions of Its Impact" (Doctoral dissertation, University of Pennsylvania, 1990).

3. Steven Mintz and Susan Kellogg, *Domestic Revolutions: A Social History of American Family Life* (New York: Free Press, 1988); and Mary S. Calderone and Eric W. Johnson, *The Family Book About Sexuality* (New York: Harper & Row, 1985).

4. Calderone and Johnson, op. cit.

5. A. Damien Martin, "Learning to Hide: The Socialization of the Gay Adolescent," *Adolescent Psychiatry,* vol. 10, 1982, pp. 52-64.

6. "Suicide Major Cause of Death for Homosexual Youth," *Contemporary Sexuality,* September 1989, p. 3.

7. Laura Pender, "Growing Up Gay," *Cincinnati Magazine,* February 1990, pp. 26-29.

8. Mark O. Bigler, "Adolescent Sexual Behavior in the Eighties," *SIECUS Report,* October/November 1989, pp. 6-9.

9. Calderone and Johnson, op. cit.

10. Janet Eckenrode et al., "The Nature and Substantiation of Official Sexual Abuse Reports," *Child Abuse and Neglect,* vol. 13, 1988, pp. 311-19.

11. Donald E. Greydanus and Robert B. Shearin, *Adolescent Sexuality and Gynecology* (Philadelphia: Lea and Febiger, 1990).

12. Robin Warshaw, *I Never Called It Rape* (New York: Harper & Row, 1988); and Jean Hughes and Bernice Sandler, *Friends Raping Friends: Could It Happen to You?* (Washington, D.C.: Project on the Status and Education of Women, Association of American Colleges, 1987).

13. Warshaw, op. cit.

14. Kenneth R. Sladkin, "Counseling Adolescents About Sexuality," *Seminars in Adolescent Medicine,* vol. 1, 1985, pp. 223-30.

15. Robert Coles and Geoffrey Stokes, *Sex and the American Teenager* (New York: Harper & Row, 1985).

16. Susan F. Newcomer and J. Richard Udry, "Oral Sex in an Adolescent Population," *Archives of Sexual Behavior,* vol. 14, 1985, pp. 41-46.

17. Sladkin, op. cit.

18. Ione J. Ryan and Patricia C. Dunn, "Sex Education from Prospective Teachers' View Poses a Dilemma," *Journal of School Health,* vol. 49, 1979, pp. 573-75; and Krueger, op. cit.

19. Peter Scales, *The Front Lines of Sexuality Education* (Santa Cruz, Calif.: Network Publications, 1984).

The Profession of Teaching Today

There are several exciting attempts going on across the United States to use the knowledge bases on teaching to create alternative forms in schools. The essays in this unit report on several fascinating efforts by teachers to "reinvent" the school. Our nation's youth will be the beneficiaries of these efforts.

We continue the dialogue over what makes a teacher "good." There are numerous external pressures on the teaching profession today from a variety of public interest groups. The profession continues to develop its knowledge base on effective teaching through ethnographic and empirical inquiry on classroom practice and teacher behavior in elementary and secondary classrooms across the nation. Concern continues over how best to teach to enhance insightful, reflective student interaction with the content of instruction. We continue to consider alternative visions of literacy and the roles of teachers in fostering a desire for learning within their students.

All of us who live the life of a teacher are aware of those features that we associate with the concept of a good teacher. In addition, we do well to remember that the teacher-student relationship is both a tacit and an explicit one—one in which teacher attitude and emotional outreach are as important as student response to our instructional effort. The teacher-student bond in their assent into the teaching/learning process cannot be overemphasized; teaching is a two-way street. We must maintain an emotional link in the teacher-student relationship that will compel students to want to accept instruction and attain an optimal learning performance. What, then, constitute those most defensible standards for assessing good teaching?

The past decade has yielded much in-depth research on the various levels of expertise in the practice of teaching. We know much more now about specific teaching competencies and how they are acquired than in the 1970s. Expert teachers do differ from novices and experienced teachers in terms of their capacity to exhibit accurate, integrated, and holistic perceptions and analyses of what goes on when students try to learn in classroom settings. We can now pinpoint some of these qualitative differences.

As the knowledge base on our professional practice continues to expand, we will be able to certify with greater precision what constitute acceptable ranges of teacher performance based on more clearly defined procedures of practice, as we have, for example, in medicine and dentistry. Medicine is, after all, a practical art as well as a science—and so is teaching. The analogy in terms of setting standards of professional practice is a strong one. Yet the emotional pressure on teachers that theirs is also a performing art, and that clear standards of practice can be applied to that art, is a bitter pill to swallow for many of them. Hence, there is intense reaction against external competency testing and any rigorous classroom observation standards. The writing, however, is on the wall: the profession cannot hide behind the tradition that teaching is a special art, unlike all others, and therefore should not be subjected to objective observational standards, aesthetic critique, or to a core knowledge base. Those years are behind us. The public demands the same standards of practice as are demanded of those in the medical arts.

Likewise, we have identified certain approaches to working with students in the classroom that have been effective. Classroom practices such as cooperative learning strategies have won widespread support for inclusion in the knowledge base on teaching. The knowledge base of the social psychology of life in classrooms has been significantly expanded by collaborative research between classroom teachers and various specialists in psychology and teacher education. This has been accomplished by using anthropological field research techniques to ground theory of classroom practice into demonstrable phenomenological perspectives. Many issues have been raised—and answers found—by basic ethnographic field observations, interviews, and anecdotal record-keeping techniques to understand more precisely how teachers and students interact in the classroom. A rich dialectic is developing among teachers regarding the description of ideal classroom environments. The methodological insight from this research into the day-to-day realities of life in schools is transforming what we know about teaching as a professional activity and how to best advance our knowledge of effective teaching strategies.

Creative, insightful persons who become teachers will usually find ways to network their interests and concerns with other teachers and will make their own opportunities for creative teaching in spite of external assessment procedures. They acknowledge that the science of teach-

ing involves the observation and measurement of teaching behaviors but that the art of teaching involves the humanistic dimensions of instructional activities, an alertness to the details of what is taught, and equal alertness to how students receive it. Creative, insightful teachers guide class processes and formulate questions according to their perceptions of how students are responding to the material.

To build their hope as well as their self-confidence, teachers must be motivated to an even greater effort for professional growth in the midst of these fundamental

revisions. Teachers need support, appreciation, and respect. Simply criticizing them while refusing to alter social and economic conditions that affect the quality of their work will not solve their problems, nor will it lead to excellence in education. Not only must teachers work to improve their public image and the public's confidence in them but the public must confront its own misunderstandings of the level of commitment required to achieve teacher excellence—and their share of responsibility in that task. Teachers need to know that the public cares about and respects them enough to fund their professional improvement in a primary recognition that they are an all-important force in the life of this nation. The articles in this unit consider the quality of education and the status of the teaching profession today.

Looking Ahead: Challenge Questions

What is "expertise" in teaching?

What are some ways in which teacher-student classroom interaction can be studied?

What do you think of efforts to "reinvent" schools? What are your own visions of what is possible in schooling?

Should teachers encourage students to develop their own visions of social reality and to locate themselves in the context of their own lives and social circumstances?

Why has the knowledge base on teaching expanded so dramatically in recent years?

List by order of importance what you think are the five most vital issues confronting the teaching profession today. What criteria did you use in ranking these issues? What is your position on each of them?

What does gaining a student's assent to a teacher's instructional effort mean to you?

What are the most defensible standards to assess the quality of a teaching performance?

What is the role of creativity in the classroom?

What political pressures do teachers in the United States face today?

Can teachers be sufficiently imaginative in their teaching and still get students to meet standardized objective test requirements? What are the issues to be considered regarding assessment of student learning?

—F. S.

Reflection and Teaching: The Challenge of Thinking Beyond the Doing

PEGGY RAINES and LINDA SHADIOW

Peggy Raines is an assistant professor and Linda Shadow is a professor, both at the Center for Excellence in Education, Northern Arizona University, Flagstaff.

She soon discovered that knowing something and teaching it are as different as dreaming and waking.
—May Sarton, *The Small Room*

Preservice teachers embarking on their student teaching semester often express the belief that sustained day-to-day classroom experience is exactly what they will need to complete their "knowledge" of teaching. In a more sophisticated but similar vein, teachers who return to a university for advanced coursework or for professional development nod their heads approvingly during discussions of the benefits of "reflective teaching" and then agree that as a natural part of their planning for teaching, they indeed are all "reflective practitioners." The two words *reflection* and *practice* are a part of everyone's general vocabulary, so it is easy to reduce the complexities and challenges of the phrase to something like "thinking about the doing." Because no one wants to be accused of *not* thinking about the doing, educators—whether novice or veteran—are usually unanimous about their being reflective practitioners.

One consequence of this automatic agreement—that by virtue of being a teacher one is already a reflective teacher—can be an unproductive superficiality: "reflection with no experience is sterile and generally leads to unworkable conclusions, while experience with no reflection is shallow and at best leads to superficial knowledge" (Posner 1989, 22). The challenge for educators is to move beyond the literal meaning of this seemingly simplistic phrase—reflective teacher—to an understanding of its pedagogical implications, which encompass (1) a respect for teachers' ongoing profes-sional growth (beyond learning more "things to do"), (2) a mutually beneficial dialogue between elements of one's theory and practice (beyond a simple recounting of one's successes), and (3) a potential for more critically deliberative classroom practices.

The concepts of *reflection*, *reflective teaching*, and *reflective practitioner* have gained much recent attention in the professional education literature, but a cursory reading can overlook frequent references to the work of John Dewey (and others), which provided a substantive base for reflective practices. Although a comparison of the first paragraphs of many of these teacher-as-thinker articles illustrates the observation that "there is no generally accepted definition of these concepts" (Korthagen 1993, 133), the substantive aims share a theoretical foundation that, if ignored, suggests at best a partial use and at worst a misuse of a powerful concept for teachers using their own work as "text." The term *reflective teacher* in its theoretical context is more likely to provide teachers with a sense of the mindfulness and thoughtfulness from which a list of promising reflective practices is drawn and with a glimpse of the deliberative pedagogy to which it can lead. A teacher's "'intelligent practice' in a classroom . . . develops *in action* rather than by application of rules learned outside the context of practice" (Russell and Johnston 1988, 1). Teachers' "intelligent action" is subsequently strengthened through the "development of the *capacity for self-directed learning*" so teachers emerge as their own teacher educators (Korthagen 1993, 136).

Reflective Action and Routine Action

The distinction between *reflective action* and *routine action* is one that respects teachers as professionals whose technical expertise goes beyond the application of pedagogical "treatments." Understanding this distinction can help teachers to penetrate the superficial agreement that can come too quickly and easily when, in either preser-

From *The Clearing House*, May/June 1995, pp. 271-274. © 1995 by the Helen Dwight Reid Educational Foundation.
Reprinted by permission of Heldref Publications, 1319 Eighteenth Street, NW, Washington, DC 20036-1802.

vice or inservice, teachers are asked about their use of reflective practice. One current writer, in fact, characterizes routine action and its reliance on thinking about methods in absence of context as "magical" because of the powers ascribed to their use (Bartolome 1994). The well-intentioned frenzy for identifying more and better ways of doing things, he says, constitutes a "methods fetish," and Lilia Bartolome agrees with Donaldo Macedo (1994) that an anti-methods pedagogy is more likely to encourage critical (or reflective) action. In 1933, Dewey made this same distinction and likened routine action to the stream of consciousness that accompanies everyday experience, in which the ends are taken for granted but the means for getting to those ends may be problematic (the goal or desired outcome of this routine action is unexamined and any procedural deviation can be tinkered with to improve the likelihood of the desired end). Reflective action, on the other hand, entails "active, persistent, and careful consideration of any belief or supposed form of knowledge in the light of the grounds that support it and the further conclusions to which it leads" (Dewey 1933, 9). In this sense, reflection is not a point of view but rather a process of deliberative examination of the interrelationship of ends, means, and contexts.

Vivian Gussin Paley engages in this reflective action in her book *White Teacher* (1979), in which she stands both within and above the stream of consciousness of her kindergarten teaching in a classroom with a diverse student population. She observes the children and the differences between what she expects of them and what their actions are, and then she critically questions (as Dewey's work suggests) the reliability and worth and value of the predetermined "ends" in order to validate, redirect, or modify both ends and means. In the preface to a later book, *Molly Is Three* (1986), Paley describes the inherent challenge of this level of reflection: "It is not easy to wait and listen. In my haste to display the real world, I offer the children solutions to unimagined problems. My neatly classified bits and pieces clamor for attention. . . . I try to stand aside . . . "(xv).

Fifty years after Dewey identified three attitudes—open-mindedness, responsibility, and wholeheartedness—that characterize reflective practice (attitudes evident in Paley's accounts), other writers are reiterating that reflective practice is "neither a solitary nor meditative process . . . . [It is] a challenging, demanding, and often trying process that is most successful as a collaborative effort" (Osterman and Kottkamp 1993, 19). Dewey defined *open-mindedness* as "an active desire to listen to more sides than one; to give heed to the facts from whatever source they come; to err in the beliefs that are dearest to us" (29). *Responsibility* he viewed as being a deliberative consideration of the consequences of actions, and *wholeheartedness* he equated with an abiding commitment to open-mindedness and responsibility. Taken together, these attitudes have much in common with the "believing

and doubting game" that Peter Elbow writes about in *Embracing Contraries* (1986)—an acceptance that "certainty evades us" (254)—and with the need to examine our certainty in order to move to a more thorough and substantive level of understanding.

The resulting reflective action, Dewey maintained, moves teachers away from impulsive and routine activity; reflective action thus places inquiry, not response, in the foreground. Such inquiry-oriented teaching places the teacher-as-*learner* in a prominent position while at the same time it challenges the teacher to delve deeper into the "doing" of teaching. Donald Schon (1983) voices the conviction that "competent practitioners usually know more than they can say" (viii), and teachers like Vivian Paley demonstrate that when deliberative reflection gives voice to one's knowing and not knowing, professional growth and development accelerates; thus reflection has the potential to benefit both the teacher and the taught. This view echoes the distinctions of "knowledge telling" and "knowledge transforming" (Bereiter and Scardamalia 1987), but it places an internal, rather than external, audience in the foreground.

Problem Solving and Problem Setting

The artificial but pervasive dichotomy of theory and practice presents an obstacle for viewing reflective practice as a powerful contributor to a teacher's professional development. Building partly on Dewey's notion of reflection, Schon (1983) proposes a reorganization of the way we think about professional practice and the relationship between theory and practice. He criticizes the still-prevailing model of technical rationality: "According to the model of Technical Rationality—the view of professional knowledge which has most powerfully shaped both our thinking about the professions and the institutional relations of research, education and practice—professional activity consists in instrumental problem solving made rigorous by the application of scientific theory and technique" (21).

Selection of a technique from a broad professional repertoire based solely on the matching of sets of pre-identified characteristics can serve to elevate teaching rituals, tradition, and decontextualized authority to unrealistic levels. On the other hand, actions based solely on intuition and one's own biography can result in an equally isolated (and idiosyncratic) approach. The potential for professional growth comes, in Schon's view, from a persistent and rigorous acknowledgment of both spheres, "a dialogue of thinking and doing through which I become more skillful" (1987, 31). One vehicle for engaging in this dialogue is the distinction between problem *solving* and problem *setting*:

> In real world practice, problems do not present themselves to the practitioner as given. They must be constructed from the materials of problematic situations that are puzzling, troubling, uncertain. When we set the problem, we select what we will treat as "things" of the situation, we set

the boundaries of our attention to it, and we impose upon it a coherence which allows us to say what is wrong and in what directions the situation needs to be changed. Problem setting is a process in which interactively, we name the things to which we will attend and frame the context in which we will attend to them. (Schon 1983, 40)

Problem setting demands a broader view than problem solving. In teachers' published accounts of their own growth, many, like Paley, engage in more than problem identification and, in fact, end up re-orienting their views of what a "problem" is and what theory and practice can both contribute to any kind of resolution. In *Uptaught* (1970), an account of his uneasiness with college teaching, Ken Macrorie provides a record of the reflection that led to changes in his approach to teaching (later developed as a text, *Writing to be Read*); similarly, Peter Elbow recounts his reflective journey in *Embracing Contraries* and in many ways places his earlier text, *Writing without Teachers* (1973), in the realm of problem setting; poet Richard Hugo shares a view of his growth and reflection as a teacher of creative writing in *Triggering Town* (1979); teacher educator William Ayers explores the intertwining of his own teaching, learning, and parenting in *To Teach: The Journey of a Teacher* (1993). It is not by accident that touchstones such as these were written by teachers of writing, people who are more practiced at putting a voice to the reflective process. These and other books, however, allow individual teachers (preservice or inservice) or groups of teachers from any grade or subject matter to eavesdrop on another educator's process of reflection. A newly developed group of educational cases (*Case Studies for Teacher Problem Solving* by Silverman, Welty, and Lyon [1992]; *Diversity in the Classroom: A Casebook for Teachers and Teacher Educators* by Shulman and Mesa-Bains [1993]) can be used in inservice sessions to help teachers develop skills in problem setting and recognizing the distinctions that Schon makes. The cases themselves can be used superficially where limited discussion is presumed to constitute "reflective practice." Basing case discussions primarily on one's experiences as a teacher and learner can deify experience, however, and the result is "telling" with little likelihood of "transforming" one's pedagogy (McAnnich 1993).

Books such as these also illustrate another distinction that belies the more simplistic definition of reflection. Schon differentiates between reflection-in-action and reflection-on-action (1983). Reflection-in-action is formative in that it is a part of the interactive phase of teaching in the presence of students. It is usually stimulated by some unpredictableness that prompts the teacher to respond with on-the-spot restructuring, spontaneous re-evaluation of past experiences, or deliberate testing of past knowledge in order to arrive at a solution to the immediate problem. Reflection-on-action happens at another level where a teacher engages in revising experiences and knowledge, in reformulating foundational structures

on which he or she bases classroom practice. This is not unlike Dewey's distinction between routine and reflective practice, but it seeks to make the two interdependent.

Doing and Thinking About the Doing

Experience in the absence of reflection is unstable (Schon 1983) because it contributes little to the deliberative development that is a part of the potential of reflective practice:

When we go about the spontaneous, intuitive performance of the actions of everyday life, we show ourselves to be knowledgeable in a special way. Often we cannot say what it is we know. When we try to describe it we find ourselves at a loss, or we produce descriptions that are obviously inappropriate. Our knowing is ordinarily tacit, implicit in our patterns of action and in our feel for the stuff with which we are dealing. It seems right to say that our knowing is *in* our action. (49)

Reflecting on this knowing-in-action is what identifies a master teacher, according to Schon. This is the "dialogue of the thinking and doing," the reflexive interchange between the immediate and the reflective that Schon has called reflection-in-action. The doing (teaching) is accompanied by a co-existing "thinking about the doing" (knowing-in-action), and then there are deliberate opportunities to think both about and beyond the doing (reflection-in-action).

Teachers, curriculum specialists, or professional development personnel who want to engage in reflection will be assisted by the recent work of several researchers and theorists. Freema Elbaz (1988), in her experiences with teachers examining their own knowledge, initially found that "autobiographical writing, combined with other types of writing, work on metaphors and imagery, and group discussion, enhanced teachers' awareness of their situations" (180). Later, Elbaz found that it was important for teachers to generate and exchange different views in a group process and to envision concrete alternative courses of action if they are to become self-sustaining in the reflective process. Henry Giroux's work explores the dialogue both within one's self as well as within one's context; his book *Teachers as Intellectuals: Toward a Critical Pedagogy of Learning* (1988) forges a persuasive description of the transformative potential that occurs when we combine the "language of critique with the language of possibility" (134).

Reflective practitioners often need help in developing observation skills and must be provided with opportunities for analyzing teaching (Wildman and Niles 1987). Necessary attitudes and resources, such as time and collegial support for nurturing reflection, are essential. Daily or weekly logs or some such method of recording events and personal reactions are effective tools for facilitating initial reflection. These and other reflective opportunities such as seminars, discussions, or reviews are needed to encourage reflection in and on action. Within the context of assessment, some districts and states are seeking the formalization of teaching portfolios that document action, thought, and thought-in-action for teachers seeking status as master teachers or for career ladder advancement. The National Board of Professional Teaching Standards is pursuing an evaluation process that will include components encompassing such reflection.

Thinking Both About and Beyond the Doing

In a far more structured way, the work of Gary Fenstermacher and Virginia Richardson has focused on skills that develop a "practical rationality," which they trace to the work of Aristotle and define as "a process of thought that ends in an action or an intention to act" (102). They criticize the calls for reflective practice as being "murky" and imprecise in that "it is not enough to provide answers [to why one teaches as one does]" but that "it is also important that the answers accord with a reasonable and morally defensible conception of what it means to educate a fellow human being" (101).

Reflective teaching is a concept that can, under the press of large class sizes, increasing extracurricular responsibilities, and vociferous calls for technical reform, be set aside as something so inherent in the profession of teaching as to not need deliberate attention or support. On the contrary, however, reflective practice goes beyond just thinking about one's teaching and opens doors to professional growth and collaboration that can contribute to teachers' having a clearer and more substantive role in reform, both locally and nationally. Thinking about teaching practices is only the beginning; describing perceived classroom successes and failures is an initial step. Reflection, in the most potent sense of the word, involves searching for patterns in one's thinking about classroom practices and interrogating the reasons for one's labeling some lessons as successes or failures; it challenges one not to stop with thinking *about* the doing.

During her first year of university teaching, the main character in the May Sarton novel *The Small Room* is faced with the realization that "knowing something and teaching it are as different as dreaming and waking" (44). Thinking-*beyond*-the-doing challenges teachers at all levels to learn from a more deliberate wakefulness about how and why we teach as we do and then to use what we discover about ourselves to benefit the students whom we teach.

REFERENCES

Ayers, W. 1993. *To teach: The journey of a teacher*. New York: Teachers College Press.

Bartolome, L. 1994. Beyond the methods fetish: Towards a humanizing pedagogy. *Harvard Educational Review* 64(2): 173–94.

Bereiter, C., and M. Scardamalia. 1987. *The psychology of written composition*. Hillsdale, N.J.: Lawrence Erlbaum.

Dewey, J. 1933. *How we think*. Boston: D. C. Heath.

Elbaz, F. 1988. Critical reflection on teaching: Insights from Freire. *Journal of Education for Teaching* 14(2): 171–81.

Elbow, P. 1973. *Writing without teachers*. New York: Oxford University Press.

———. 1986. *Embracing contraries: Explorations in learning and teaching*. New York: Oxford University Press.

Fenstermacher, G. D., and V. Richardson. 1993. The elicitation and reconstruction of practical arguments in teaching. *Journal of Curriculum Studies* 25(2): 101–14.

Giroux, H. 1988. *Teachers as intellectuals: Toward a critical pedagogy of learning*. New York: Bergin and Garvey.

Hugo, R. 1979. *Triggering town: Lectures and essays on poetry and writing*. New York: W. W. Norton.

Korthagen, F. A. J. 1993. The role of reflection in teachers' professional development. In *Teacher professional development: A multiple perspective approach*, edited by L. Kremar-Hayon, H. C. Vonk, and R. Fessler, 133–45. Amsterdam/Lisse: Swets & Zeitlinger, B. V.

Macedo, D. 1994. Preface. In *Conscientization and resistance*, edited by P. McLaren and C. Lankshear. New York: Routledge.

Macrorie, K. 1970. *Uptaught*. New York: Hayden.

———. 1984. *Writing to be read*. New Jersey: Boynton/Cook.

McAninch, A. R. 1993. *Teacher thinking and the case method: Theory and future directions*. New York: Teachers College Press.

Osterman, K. F., and R. B. Kottkamp. 1993. *Reflective practice for educators*. Newbury Park, Calif.: Corwin Press.

Paley, V. 1979. *White teacher*. Cambridge, Mass.: Harvard University Press.

———. 1986. *Molly is three*. Chicago: University of Chicago Press.

Posner, G. 1989. *Field experience: Methods of reflective teaching*. New York: Longman.

Russell, T., and P. Johnston. 1988. Teacher reflection on practice. Paper presented at the meeting of the American Educational Research Association, New Orleans, April 5–9.

Sarton, M. 1961. *The small room*. New York: W. W. Norton.

Schon, D. 1983. *The reflective practitioner*. New York: Basic Books.

———. 1987. *Educating the reflective practitioner*. San Francisco: Jossey-Bass.

Shulman, J., and A. Mesa-Bains. 1993. *Diversity in the classroom: A casebook for teachers*. New Jersey: Research for Better Schools and Lawrence Erlbaum.

Silverman, R., W. Welty, and S. Lyon. 1992. *Case studies for teacher problem solving*. New York: McGraw-Hill.

Wildman, T. M., and J. A. Niles. 1987. Reflective teachers: Tensions between abstractions and realities. *Journal of Teacher Education* 38(4): 25–31.

Phase II: Implementing a Design for Learning

A serious experiment is underway at the Elizabeth Street Learning Center in Los Angeles. The outcome may decide the future of American education

Students, students everywhere as they cross the Learning Center's wide-open central courtyard on their way to their next class.

Imagine a K-10 school with 2,500 students, close to 200 teachers and a computer in every classroom. But don't stop there. Imagine also that the school is open all year round, serves the student body breakfast and lunch, has education classes for parents five days a week, and is big on multiage classrooms and clusters of teachers.

That's just the beginning of what Los Angeles' Elizabeth Street Learning Center

is all about. There's more on the drawing board – a lot more – as the school develops a model of public education in urban, multi-ethnic communities.

School with a mission. The Elizabeth Street Learning Center is one of a handful of schools throughout the nation funded by the New American Schools Development Corporation (NASDC), a consortium formed by American corporate leaders to support the design and establishment of new, high performance schools. (For more on NASDC and its goals, see box).

Obviously, the Learning Center is not your typical neighborhood school. Far from it. There are a lot of people in Los Angeles, including the Center's teachers, who think of the project as a pioneering effort to do no less than reinvent America's schools.

Thoughts like that inevitably present a challenge to an education magazine. Either you shrug it off, or you put it in the future file, or you go to Los Angeles and see for yourself. *Teaching K-8* went.

One thing's for sure: Pioneering efforts at the Elizabeth Street Learning Center begin early in the morning. By the time we arrived shortly before 8 a.m., classes had been in session for more than half an hour.

Deborah Kagan's class was no exception. We were ushered into her classroom and found that she had already started a project to teach her sixth graders how to write,

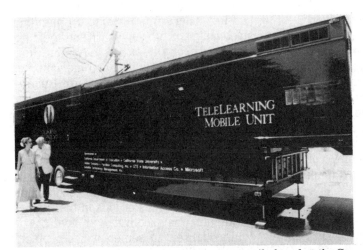

This mobile telecommunications unit, temporarily based at the Center, has 26 work stations that can be hooked into a statewide network.

Deborah shows her students a book she made. Before the morning's out, they'll be making their own books.

From left: Patricia Broderick, Teaching's editorial director; Deborah; Roberta Benjamin of LAEP; and Ian Elliot, Teaching's senior editor.

Teacher's aide Oscar Soto moves from child to child, offering advice and encouragement when needed.

Shown with Deborah are Gerardo Salazar (K-1) and Beverly Wanner (4-5). The three shared a cluster last year.

Judy Johnson of LAEP has a smile for the students. "They're all so healthy and self-confident," she said.

illustrate and produce their own books.

Almost all of Deborah's students are Latino and speak English as a second language. She told us that the children were there because they really wanted to be there. That was easy to see. They were low-keyed, interested and involved. Never once during the day did Deborah have to raise

Fast food? *Make that super fast. Breakfasts and lunches by the hundreds are served in a matter of minutes.*

Creative *people must be comfortable when they work. If this requires perching cross-legged on a chair, so be it.*

In a classroom *corner sit books and materials on Egypt used in the sixth graders' study of culture.*

Deborah *is big on personal attention, and that's a very good reason why her kids are eager to learn.*

her voice. Just the opposite, in fact. When she needed to get their attention, she lowered her voice slightly and, just like that, all eyes were on her. Another point worth noting: Not once did she have to consult notes or even pause to think about what came next. It was perfect planning all the way.

Deborah's approach to do-it-yourself book-making was smooth and subtle: from literature to creative movement to forms of energy to prewriting and finally to book assembly.

She began by reading aloud *On the Day You Were Born* by Debra Frasier (Harcourt Brace, 1991). After explaining that the author was a colleague she had met last summer, she showed a video featuring the author and her book. This was followed by a brief demonstration by Deborah of how *she* had made her own book.

For many teachers, this would have been the ideal time to let the students launch their publishing careers. Deborah, however, had other plans. She had the children use creative movement to strengthen the concepts – time, space and energy – presented in *On the Day You Were Born.*

First, there was a warm-up (bending, stretching, smooth and sharp energy); next, moving through space (heavy and light walking, smooth and sharp movements); finally, movement exploration (groups silently acting out elements of nature such as gravity, wind and tides, all featured in *On the Day You Were Born*).

One thing creative movement creates is a healthy appetite. Deborah's timing was perfect. Next stop: a quick breakfast in the Center's outdoor dining area. Feeding hundreds and hundreds of kids in the space of 20 minutes may seem like an invitation to total collapse, but somehow the people at Elizabeth Street made it look easy.

Following breakfast, the sixth graders got down to the job of producing their own books. They were shown a clip from a laserdisc and a videotape on Earth, and asked to write one-sentence answers to a series of open-ended questions about Earth.

"How does the earth look from space?" Deborah asked. "Tell something about its first minute.... Write a compliment – or a comment or a question – about Earth."

Finally, after several more questions, Deborah said, "Now pick three of the things you just wrote and put them together. That's page three of your book."

As a teacher's aide passed out materials, Deborah listed the other pages each child would produce – from title page and dedication to biographical note. The children went right to work. Never have young authors plied their craft more seriously.

Dream come true. After the morning session was over, we had a chance to talk with Deborah. We were joined by Roberta Benjamin, project director of the Los Angeles Educational Partnership (LAEP), which manages the Learning Centers.

We learned that like the sixth graders she teaches, Deborah was there because she wanted to be there.

"I'd been working as an educational consultant, and when I saw the design put out by the LAEP, I knew I'd enjoy the larger blocks of instructional time and the multiage grouping," she told us.

(Touch of irony: Like other sixth grade teachers, Deborah does *not* have a multiage class. She had one last year, and she'll have one next year, but this year it's sixth grade pure and simple.)

"This was the first job I interviewed for and I wasn't going to take no for an

Los Angeles Learning Centers

The Los Angeles Learning Centers are one of nine Designs selected by NASDC as part of a national effort to reinvent American schools. The Elizabeth Street Learning Center opened last March. A second Los Angeles Learning Center was launched this fall on the site of the Forshay Middle School.

The two Learning Centers are a collaborative project of the Los Angeles Unified School District, United Teachers Los Angeles and Los Angeles Educational Partnership (LAEP), which manages the project.

The Learning Center Design is built around a set of "Basic Concepts" that reflect advanced research and practice, as well as established methods. Addressing the needs of a highly diverse, multi-lingual population of students from pre-K through the equivalent of grade 12, the Design will:

- Provide several advocates for each child
- Utilize a state-of-the-art curriculum and new forms of assessment
- Provide for continual professional development for teachers and administrators
- Integrate advanced technology with instruction and curriculum
- Emphasize the use of in-depth thematic teaching
- Engage the community as a classroom and integrated resource
- Link teachers with their students for several years
- Utilize large blocks of time to permit in-depth learning
- Provide opportunities for colleagues to meet weekly to plan and to review student needs
- Restructure support services to enable the community to prevent and remove barriers to learning
- Prepare all students for the school-to-work transition

Faculty members attend a professional development session in Elizabeth Street's product development center.

As part of their book-making project, the children use creative movement to interpret one of the elements featured in Debra Frasier's book.

NASDC: Blueprint for Excellence

The New American Schools Development Corporation (NASDC) is a private, non-profit organization formed by American corporate leaders to restore American education to world prominence.

In July 1991, NASDC invited all citizens to become architects of a new generation of American schools that would bring every child up to world class standards in English, math, science, history and geography.

By February 1992, NASDC had reviewed nearly 700 design proposals from thousands of applicants from every state in the nation. Eleven Design Teams were chosen to receive funding for Phase I development.

After nearly one year of design work, nine Teams (including the Los Angeles Learning Centers) were selected to proceed with Phase II of their programs and test their designs in real school settings.

In Phase III, scheduled to begin sometime after next summer, NASDC will set in motion a national public education and technical assistance effort to make the work of the Design Teams available to every interested community in the nation.

The study of culture, which culminated in the book-making project, is celebrated on this bulletin board. The legends around the central design reveal the components the children studied: art, religion, celebrations, social structure, science, language, economics, technology, entertainment and politics. Above the board are books on some of the cultures they studied: China, the Greeks, the Aztecs and the Crusaders. The bulletin board was co-created and designed by Laura Cobabe, one of Deborah's fellow teachers.

Sixth graders celebrate Teaching K-8's visit with a welcoming dance and song. Leading the way is Deborah, who, before becoming a teacher, spent five years as a dancer and choreographer in Paris.

"With the resources of LAEP and the dollars that NASDC provides, the Elizabeth Learning Center teachers are discovering new paradigms of success, but most of all, their success is due to their great personal effort," says John Kershaw, principal.

Christina Doyle, director of the state's Telemation Project. She predicts that the project will bring in a new kind of professionalism. She says, "Every teacher with a computer, modem and a phone line can have her or his own account with the state's K-12 Telecommunications Network."

answer," Deborah continued. "I saw the Learning Center as a dream come true. There was support for teachers, a willingness to try new things and, well, just a chance to be part of the cutting edge."

This cutting edge includes working with "clusters" of teachers. One afternoon a week, the students go home early and clusters of teachers meet to think of themes and interdisciplinary activities to use with the themes. The end result might be something like this: How is past, present and future affected by natural and social patterns?

"Clusters can be really successful," Deborah said. "Students can go from classroom to classroom and hear the same concepts. They can hear a teacher say, 'I know you're working with these themes in Ms. Kagan's literature class. Now let's see how they're applied in math and science.'"

Teachers also work with each other in compiling portfolios. For example, teachers of students who were not in Deborah's class last year have sent her the children's portfolios so she can keep building a record of their accomplishments. She hopes one day to have portfolios that include audiotapes, videotapes and computer disks of students' work in word processing, spreadsheets, multimedia presentations and so on.

Heroes and holidays. Deborah's students – like almost all of the other students at the Learning Center – come from Mexican-American homes. This does not mean, however, that she stresses Latino culture.

"My brother Andrew suggested that I place less emphasis on the Egyptians, Greeks and Romans, and concentrate on the Aztecs, Mayas and Incas, who are part of the kids' heritage," she said. "I disagree. I certainly want the children to take pride in their heritage, but it's better to let them learn about other cultures they may not know about.

"I try to avoid the heroes and holidays approach to multicultural education. Rather, we have a more comprehensive approach all year long."

"All year long" means just that when

you're talking about the Learning Center. The school is in session 12 months a year, with students and teachers getting three breaks a year. The breaks are carefully scheduled so that at any given time, one-third of the school population is "off track."

At the Learning Center, off-track teachers are learning teachers. The school is big on professional development.

Roberta Benjamin noted, "There are 20 paid days annually when off-track teachers call upon people who can help them, either in one-on-one or small group situations. Their attitude is definitely not, 'I'm not working. I'm on vacation.' Teachers know that they're still learners, that professional development is part of their work."

On the drawing board. It would be a mistake to think of the Elizabeth Street Learning Center as a "finished product." It was never intended to be. Think of it, rather, as a Design that's being tested, evaluated and often modified. By this time next year, for example, the Center will have:

- Two additional secondary grade levels, making the Center a K-12 school.
- Increased educational opportunities for parents. At present, parents have classes in English, computer skills and sewing.
- More after-school activities for students and parents.
- Greater emphasis on health and human services in the school and community.

Roberta Benjamin sums it up this way: "We're hoping that next year other jurisdictions will have the opportunity of shopping through the NASDC Designs, including ours, and making choices as to ways to go.

"We hope to give schools such a variety of offerings that they can start making choices about how they want to allocate their resources. Maybe a school will decided to divide its time differently. Maybe a school will change the way it looks at the curriculum.

"They'll be able to do it because our new governing structure allows stakeholders to make their own decisions about every aspect of the program."

IAN ELLIOT

Toward Lives Worth Sharing:

A Basis for Integrating Curriculum

William H. Schubert

William H. Schubert, Ph.D., is Professor of Education and Coordinator of Graduate Curriculum Studies at the University of Illinois at Chicago and is a past president of the John Dewey Society.

KELTY HALEY

What is worth knowing? What is worth experiencing? What is worth doing, being, and sharing with others? Why? Whom does it help? Might it also hurt others? How should worthwhile knowledge, experience, modes of living, and sharing be acquired? Who decides? Who should decide? These are basic questions that must be addressed if education is to serve defensible purposes. Moreover, these questions are essential to the theory and practice of curriculum integration.

These are the questions that call me to learn, teach, and to do curriculum work.[1] They raise many other questions—both practical and theoretical ones. Parents since the dawn of time have asked such curriculum questions when trying to decide how to raise their children. Nations, states, communities, and tribes (throughout history) have pondered how to induct children as new members who would carry on and improve their society and culture. Most of the striving to answer these questions is lost in the winds of history. They were thought about, discussed, and acted upon, but no records of deliberations on their answers or reflections on their consequences in action remain. The notable exception, of course, is that the thoughtful caring and sharing of family, friends, and educators who have helped children grow is recorded in young people's very being and is passed on to subsequent generations.

There are, of course, more formal records of reflection on curriculum; the great artifacts of every culture—philosophical and social treatises, poems, stories, dance, music, art, mathematics, science, sport—do represent striving to reach some kind of coherence on powerful curriculum questions.[2] Only occasionally do such artifacts pertain directly to curriculum of schools. When they speak most broadly to education in individual and cultural life, profound messages are given to those who develop curriculum for schools. One such message deeply embedded in human beings and in the societies and cultures they create is a striving for meaning and purpose. This is the call to curriculum. It is a basic human seeking of integration. I suggest that this is integral to everyone's life. If this is so, then the central curriculum development problem for schooling (as it is for parenting and other spheres of life) is to capture that penetrating interest in creating a life worth living. I suggest further that a life worth living is a life worth sharing, and I come to that conclusion from the influences of curriculum history and from my own personal history as an educator.

I contend that the basis for integration or coherence, its organizing center,[3] is what human beings seek as they try to make their lives fit together. Yet this is too seldom central to schooling. A decade of investigating teacher and student lore has revealed this to me.[4] It is further confirmed by my own experience of nearly a decade of public school teaching and almost two decades of interaction with teachers and administrators through work as a professor and consultant. The daily press of events for teachers and administrators—the pressure to follow state and district guidelines, meet the newest sets of standards, prepare for standardized tests, practice the current fads, respond to the procession of special interests—takes such a toll on life in schools that it is rare when school experience addresses fundamental human concerns such as those noted above.

What is fundamentally curricular and what is fundamentally human are of the same fabric. They are woven into consciousness when individuals and communities authentically ask questions about the meaning, purpose, and consequence of who they are and what they do. This questioning has emerged for me as the much-sought-after and enigmatic organizing center of curriculum.

My position on what is worth knowing derives from a neglected form of curriculum history, the personal history that educators have lived through.[5] I will illustrate personal curriculum history by drawing upon my experiences in education as they speak to integration.

My experience in education has taught me that the key to coherence in curriculum is to integrate institutionalized curriculum with the personal search for a meaningful and worthwhile life. I have, therefore, tried to recollect salient instances in my own pathway to becoming an educator. I often ask the same question of participants in my graduate and undergraduate classes and in my consulting work. I recommend this exercise to those who develop inservice programs and staff development activities, and have invented variations on the theme,[6] too numerous to mention in this short article.

My earliest experience with integrated curriculum was the role of play and story in my childhood. My parents, grandparents, two aunts, and several other relatives were teachers. Sometimes they were my school teachers. In spite of the fact that they were often regarded as fine teachers, my most educative memories with them involve acts of imaginary play and the sharing of stories. We acted out stories, drawing upon widely varying realms of knowledge and experience. Characters faced problems that had to be

What is fundamentally curricular and what is fundamentally human are of the same fabric.

solved, and to solve them we encountered new ideas. As John Dewey advocated in his maxim of moving from the psychological to the logical, we moved from interest or concern to extant knowledge,[7] and back and forth on the continuum between them. Years later as a teacher, I tried to make acting and playfulness a central construct of my work with elementary school students. Story has a way of giving coherence to an array of subjects that bear upon it. Clearly, today this is a tenet of the whole language movement—especially approaches that build upon works of children's literature, stories children make up themselves, or experiences children shape into story form. Story naturally integrates. As I reflect upon the stories my parents, grandparents, and other relatives shared with me (their capacity for imaginary play and make-believe), I am increasingly aware of the vast array of knowledge sources that I encountered as a child.

When I was in elementary and high school my parents, grandparents, and great aunt took a lengthy vacation each summer, driving throughout a large part of the United States, Canada, and Mexico. Progressively, I was allowed to plan these trips—to decide what was worth visiting, why, and how we should get there. This task required considerable study that integrated the disciplines. It was not unlike what I would eventually learn to call "the project method."[8] Later, as an elementary school teacher I often developed units with students around the metaphor of travel. We "traveled" to different countries, or through the human body (as in the movie *Fantastic Voyage*), or in outer space, or in the lands of fictional characters.

With my own children as well as with my students, I have used both the travel and acting metaphors. Indirectly, I have found that experiences in fictionalized travel and acting out of make-believe stories have raised some of the deepest and most valuable questions in my life. Especially with my own children, in play, we have conjured up problematic events, novel ways of posing problems, unexpected interactions of characters, and surprising solutions to dilemmas that have given me great pause for reflection. Such experiences reveal the essence of coherence that brings together seemingly isolated topics around

common themes—the sense of meaning and purpose that helps one fashion a life in this world.

As a teenager I began to think about this issue directly. I wondered about a host of things. Given the usual tendency of teens to need a departure from adult authority, many of my conversations about fashioning a life in the world occurred with peers. In the conversational spaces dominated by talk of sports, relationships, youth organizations, and pop culture, we talked of life's meaning and what we wanted to do and be. Often our wonderings would race to the outer reaches of religious or metaphysical speculation. Rarely did school work tap this potential organizing center or basis for coherence. The poems memorized, the history studied, the mathematics and science encountered, the literature read—they all had the potential to cohere with our adolescent wonderings, with our desire to fashion a life.

Once in a while something did cohere, whether designed to do so or not. Such an event was an assignment for my sophomore English class. We were told of the Indiana State Poetry Contest and we were encouraged (perhaps even required) to enter. I still remember the chair on which I sat in our Indiana farmhouse when I told myself (probably at the last minute) that I had to write that poem. My parents were surprised that I took an interest in writing something (so was I, for that matter), for I was more interested in sports, popular culture, and peer interactions. But for some reason some of my wonderings poured out onto a piece of paper in just a few minutes. I found it recently in a scrapbook that my grandmother and great-aunt had put together in the 1960s. I include it here because it symbolizes some of the adolescent wonderings that could readily be the basis for integration in curriculum.

This is hardly the work of a budding Sandburg, Hughes, Dickinson,

or Wordsworth! Yet, it represents what was on my mind, and it was

Who Knows?

Who knows what lies in outer space;
Or how far the skies extend?
What will become of the human race?
When will life on earth end?

Who knows how God can live forever?
Why are we tempted to do wrong?
How has man progressed to the rocket
   from the lever?
What makes a nation strong?

Who knows exactly what happens after
   death?
Will we have another war?
If so, what will be left?
As for the future, what is in store?

These questions are by many people
   asked.
You may think them odd.
To answer these for one is a simple
   task—
He who knows is God.

recognized with the second place prize in the Serious Division of the Indiana State Poetry Contest that year (though I am not sure if there were many entries!). The point for coherence is that all subjects of the curriculum potentially speak to the deeply felt concerns of youth, but schools too seldom tap this rich resource that resides in their midst each day. Why is that so? Why is the idea that curriculum must be conjured up by adults and delivered to students so thoroughly ingrained in our image of what education and schooling is and should be?

Must the connection between life concerns and school subjects be discovered by the students? Or can such connections be made by curricular design? In continuing my trek through my own curricular experience, I do not think that I connected school subjects with the questions raised in my poem. I do, however, vividly recall several years later sitting at a long table in the library of a small liberal arts college trying to make sense of

Ibsen's *The Wild Duck* and Melville's *Billy Budd*. Both were among the readings for an introduction to literature class, and I was having difficulty with some of the symbolism. In my quest for interpretation I discovered literary criticism. As I read what the critics said, at first I felt guilty; I thought I located an answer key! Nevertheless, I was intrigued. Suddenly, these literary works were not just the stuff of assignments, bridges to credentials. Instead, they were currents in a river that could help me shape a more meaningful life. From that point onward I assessed each new course as an opportunity to grow, because I found reason to hope that therein I could find insights and perspectives that addressed some of my most valued questions. These questions were more than idle interests; they were about who I was becoming.

The realization of connections between what I studied and who I was becoming led me to want to share what I found with others. Thus, I decided to be a teacher. I wanted to help children learn how great literatures in all disciplines could unlock new vistas and enrich the lives they were building. Later, I learned in graduate study about John Dewey's many contributions to education,[9] and as an elementary school teacher I discovered the insight in Dewey's admonition to begin with students' current interests. I strove to build on those interests to help students coherently connect school with life. I found that when students are enabled to share their interests, concerns, and wonderings with each other, they begin to see that they are not alone. Under the surface seemingly disparate interests often connect like filings to a magnet. I learned that this enables groups of students to form projects, ones that draw from both practical knowledge and from knowledge of the disciplines. From such projects other projects emerge, continuously expanding and deepening perception, knowledge, and understanding with each new project.

In this Deweyan progressive understanding of curriculum resides what I contend is a firm basis for coherent curriculum. It begins with interests and concerns of students that grow out of their lives, and because it draws upon existing knowledge to illuminate those interests, it connects life with learning. In itself this goes a long way to overcome the frequent and legitimate complaint that school is not interesting. I want to add another dimension, as well, to the basis for coherent curriculum. It should cohere not only around students' interests, but also around what interests themselves cohere around. Interests are expressions of the desire to make sense of the world, to infuse activity with meaning, and to contribute to good purposes. In short, it is to create a life worth living, a life that the person wants to share with the world. Whenever possible as an elementary school teacher, I tried to provide coherent curricular experiences by drawing upon student interests and by encouraging students to reflect on the lives they were creating. It was not always possible because of the demands of the day, but it was rewarding indeed when it occurred.

It begins with interests and concerns of students that grow out of their lives, and because it draws upon existing knowledge to illuminate those interests, it connects life with learning.

Teaching in a somewhat homogeneous suburban area, however, prevented me from in-depth awareness of yet another realm of coherence. The complexity of problems and issues in our urban society was obscured somewhat by the rural and suburban environments I had experienced, though each of these holds its own insights as well. Exposure to the urban scene brought me new awareness and a heightened sense of possibility embedded in life in the city, one built on the interests, concerns, and potential projects of its participants and its resources.

I found that when students are enabled to share their interests, concerns, and wonderings with each other, they begin to see that they are not alone.

When I began my work as a faculty member at the University of Illinois in Chicago, I was immersed in the complexities, difficulties, and richness of urban life. In particular, I learned from Ann Lopez, my wife, as she taught students in the Westside barrio where she grew up. The diverse communities of Chicago (the teachers, administrators, parents, students), the continuous tension of educational reform effort, the ebb and flow of conflict and collaboration—all call for another kind of coherence. A huge proportion of that coherence involves integration in its more widely recognized connotation. Rather than integration as combining subjects in some interdisciplinary fashion, I refer here to integration of individuals who have not seen one another deeply because of differences in race, class, ethnicity, religion, gender, sexuality, and place. To perceive more clearly across such boundaries is a major step toward the creation of a life worth living in a world fraught with contention among diverse groups and individuals. This reality was brought into bold relief for me especially by the complexity of life in urban settings and by Lopez's[10] study of three urban contexts. She observed: "Urban [settings] are . . . places of value, diversity, freedom, possibility, and complexity rather than barren wastelands of filth, corruption, decay, and vice to be condemned, feared, and distrusted." To realize this potential requires great effort to keep alive a Deweyan faith[11] in the good intentions of humanity and the possibility of authentic democracy, which grows from the essence of sharing.

The foregoing is a neglected form of curriculum history—personal perspective. Here, it happens to be mine, but every educator has a personal curriculum history worth excavating. In reflecting on salient aspects of my own history as an educator, I am able to point out to myself and to readers some of the transformations in my conceptualization of what coherence means in curriculum. I encourage others to reconstruct their own pathways to their current image of coherence (or of any other significant educational idea). In fact, I strongly recommend that a large proportion of in-service education (or staff development) should focus precisely on the personal histories of educators. Having written about this elsewhere,[12] I am preparing a book with Ann Lopez, called *Curriculum Questions*, designed to stimulate reflections on curriculum through reflection by readers on their own personal histories as educators.

This hope for inservice education or staff development makes the medium the message, or massage as Marshall McLuhan[13] was wont to say. The message and the massage are the embodiment of a Deweyan image of curriculum as continuous movement between the psychological (interests and concerns of learners) and the logical (knowledge stored by human beings, e.g., in libraries). As noted earlier[14] this is also Dewey's message and massage for younger learners. But whatever the age of a learner, I argue that we should not forget that the most integrative force is the hope of human beings to create lives worth living. Indeed, if we conclude that this is not a fundamental human hope, then control-oriented purposes (and worse) assume prominence.

The essence of my position is that curriculum integration can be achieved best when an organizing center lies at the heart of human concerns and interests. To me the dominant educational interest is how to create a life worth living. But what makes a life worth living? Achievement? Accomplishment? Performance? Efficiency? Fame? Recognition? Based on nearly thirty years of experience as an educator, I conclude that having something worth sharing, or should I say being someone worth sharing, is the key. Put another way, to create a life worth living—because it is worth sharing—

The essence of my position is that curriculum integration can be achieved best when an organizing center lies at the heart of human concerns and interests.

should be our focus of attention.

The question of exactly what kind and quality of life is worthwhile, worth sharing, should never be answered with finality. It should always remain problematic. If it does remain problematic in the lived interactions of teachers and parents and students, it is indeed a powerful source of coherence. It connects interest and subject, school and home, subjects and other subjects, concern and effort, affect and cognition, individual growth and social commitment, theory and practice, thought and action, similarity and difference, self and other, and education and life. It is imperative to ask students and educators alike to consciously address the question: How can I make my life one worth living, a life worth sharing?

1. See William H. Schubert, *Curriculum: Perspective, Paradigm, and Possibility* (New York: Macmillan, 1986).
2. See primary source excerpts from classic philosophical and social treatises that deal with education and curriculum, e.g., Robert

Ulich, ed., *Three Thousand Years of Educational Wisdom* (Cambridge, Mass.: Harvard University Press, 1947).

3. Virgil E. Herrick, John I. Goodlad, Frank J. Estvan, and Paul W. Eberman, *The Elementary School* (Englewood Cliffs, N.J., 1956) for discussions of the concept of "organizing center."

4. See William H. Schubert and William C. Ayers, *Teacher Lore: Learning from Our Own Experience* (New York: Longman, 1992) and other writings on teacher lore cited in that book, and see a new book series with the State University of New York Press, under the title of *Student Lore*, edited by William H. Schubert.

5. See William H. Schubert, "Thoughts on the Future of SSCH," in *Curriculum History*, ed. Craig Kridel (Lanham, Md.: University Press of America, 1989), 19-23. This volume is a set of papers drawn from the first decade of conferences of the Society for the Study of Curriculum History (SSCH).

6. William H. Schubert, "The Question of Worth as Central to Curriculum Empowerment," in *Teaching and Thinking about Curriculum*, ed. James T. Sears and Dan Marshall (New York: Teachers College Press, 1990), 211-227; here, I present several different approaches for generating reflection on curriculum for use in preservice and inservice education.

7. The following books by John Dewey set forth his idea of moving from the "psychological" to the "logical": *The Child and the Curriculum* (Chicago: University of Chicago Press, 1902); *Democracy and Education* (New York: Macmillan, 1916); and *Experience and Education* (New York: Macmillan, 1938).

8. The "project" approach is usually credited to William H. Kilpatrick, "The Project Method," *Teachers College Record* 19 (September 1918): 319-335. Today it has resurfaced and again soared to popularity; for example, see: Heidi H. Jacobs, ed. *Interdisciplinary Curriculum: Design and Implementation* (Alexandria, Va.: Association for Supervision and Curriculum Development, 1989) and Susan M. Drake, *Planning the Integrated Curriculum* (Alexandria, Va.: Association for Supervision and Curriculum Development, 1993). In recent work the debt to Kilpatrick and other early progressives is often not acknowledged.

9. See again for example, the Dewey classics listed in note 7.

10. Ann L. Lopez, *Exploring Possibilities for Progressive Curriculum and Teaching in Three Urban Contexts* (Chicago: Unpublished Ph.D. dissertation at the University of Illinois at Chicago, 1993).

11. John Dewey, *A Common Faith* (New Haven, Conn.: Yale University Press, 1934).

12. See William H. Schubert and Ann L. Lopez, "Teacher Lore as a Basis for Inservice Education," *Teaching and Teacher's Work* 1 (December 1993), 1-8; Schubert and Ayers, *Teacher Lore*; and Schubert, "The Question."

13. Marshall McLuhan and Quentin Fiore, *The Medium Is the Massage* (New York: Bantam, 1967).

14. See again, Dewey citations in notes 7 and 9.

About Instruction: *Powerful New Strategies Worth Knowing*

Preston D. Feden

Preston D. Feden, Ed.D., is Associate Professor of Education at La Salle University in Philadelphia. A former special education teacher, he also consults widely with school districts on instructional practices.

Teaching involves many elements, and factors and conditions within schools have a significant effect upon teachers and learners. Teachers routinely deal with administrators who vary in leadership style and ability. Teachers also assume a wide range of non-instructional roles as they carry out school procedures and policies. Teachers must skillfully employ effective communication skills as they work with pupils and their parents. Nevertheless, *instruction* is central to the teaching process, and it is essential for teachers to refine their instructional skills continually. Even in the worst of situations, no teacher is in a position where he or she cannot apply, to some degree, powerful strategies that have recently emerged from cognitive science.

Ten years later, despite exciting new research findings, Howard Gardner laments that what we know about learning is still not reflected in current teaching practice.

Advances in the knowledge base for teaching and learning now require a fundamental reconceptualization of the type of instruction provided to students at all levels of American education. A decade ago, when the knowledge base had already become sophisticated, John Goodlad's extensive study of schools found that teachers used a limited repertoire of pedagogical approaches. Strategies consisted mostly of their own talk and monitoring seatwork.[1] Ten years later, despite exciting new research findings, Howard Gardner laments that what we know about learning is still not reflected in current teaching practice.[2] And he is not alone. There is a clear need for teachers to know and understand newly emerging knowledge, and to base their practice on it.

This "contemporary" knowledge base, firmly rooted in cognitive science and substantiated by empirical data, stands in sharp contrast to "traditional" views of learning and teaching. Traditional views reflect the factory model of production in American society. This model "provided fertile soil for the behavioral approach to learning, which has dominated educational practices for the past fifty years."[3] The techniques that emanate from the contemporary knowledge base and its associated research have the potential to transform our classrooms and to empower the pupils who will compose the next generation of American citizenry. As John Bruer claims: "Teaching methods based on [research in cognitive science] . . . are the educational equivalents of polio vaccine and penicillin. Yet few outside the educational research community are aware of these breakthroughs or understand the research that makes them possible."[4]

Others who apply research in cognitive science to instruction support this dramatic claim. For example, a synthesis of research on models of teaching from Bruce Joyce, Beverly Showers, and Carol Rolheiser-Bennett lists information processing theory and cooperative learning as producing moderate to substantial effects upon student achievement.[5] Both models are derived from cognitivist research.

A research-supported, contemporary view of teaching and learning questions the assumptions underlying the traditional view, among them:

- that learning is the process of accumulating bits of information and isolated skills;
- that the teacher's primary responsibility is to transfer knowledge directly to students;
- that the process of learning and teaching focuses primarily on the interactions between the teacher and individual students.[6]

James Nolan and Pam Francis point out that ". . . for most educators [these views] have remained largely implicit and unexamined."[7]

In contrast, a contemporary view of teaching and learning based on research in cognitive science holds that, among other things:

- all learning, except for simple rote memorization, requires the learner to actively construct meaning;
- students' prior understandings and thoughts about a topic or concept before instruction exert a tremendous influence on what they learn during instruction;
- the teacher's primary goal is to generate a change in the learner's cognitive structure or way of viewing and organizing the world;
- learning in cooperation with others is an important source of motivation, support, modeling, and coaching.[8]

Implications

What, then, from this emerging, contemporary knowledge base is now worth knowing about instruction? What follows are key concepts gleaned from research and translated into practice. These procedures, based upon applied cognitive science, can help teachers in preparing and presenting better lessons to their students. They are meant to be neither formulaic nor mistaken for an attempt to oversimplify the very complex task of teaching. As Bruer points out, "There is more to medicine than biology, but basic medical science drives progress and helps doctors make decisions that promote their patients' physical well-being. Similarly, there is more to education than cognition, but cognitive science can drive progress and help teachers make decisions that promote their students' educational well-being."[9]

Focus on core concepts.

Teachers should focus on the core concepts of the subject or subjects that they teach. Much recent criticism of schools focuses on their tendency to promote and reward rote memorization rather than true understanding of academic content. David Perkins notes that students, although they may acquire fragmented knowledge and isolated skills, often do not truly understand the knowledge and cannot really use the skills they acquire. Perkins goes on to explain what he means by "understanding"—essentially, the ability to carry out various performances, such as making predictions, generalizing, explaining, analogizing, providing supporting evidence, and applying concepts. Further, he says that the more of these performances a pupil displays, the more confident we can feel that the student understands a topic or concept.[10]

Because truly useful understanding takes time to develop, it is usually not possible for teachers to "cover" as much curriculum, or as many topics, as they typically attempt. Using the principle that "less is more,"(teachers should cover less content. The point is to lead pupils to a *deep* understanding of what *is* covered. Lessons and units of instruction designed around core concepts are more likely to produce conceptual change that moves learners along from novice to expert in subject matter content.

Core concepts are generally agreed upon by experts as those that stand the test of time and that are capable of generating new knowledge for those pupils who master them. Lauren Resnick and Leopold Klopfer offer several examples of core concepts: in reading and writing, concepts such as text structures and genre; in history and government, the nature of representative government; in arithmetic, the decomposability of numbers. They observe that these key concepts and principles organize and structure much specific information.[11] Perkins offers samples of core concepts gathered from practicing teachers, which he believes are especially capable of generating new knowledge. They include: *What Is a Living Thing?*; *Civil Disobedience*; *Ratio and Proportion*; and *Whose History?* Each of these topics, he asserts, is a powerful conceptual system that can help learners generate new knowledge, while at the same time connect information to realities in their own lives.[12]

Use advance organizers.

Teachers should begin each class with an advance organizer. These are statements, made by teachers just before presenting the day's lesson, that are usually presented at a higher level of abstraction than the content that will follow. Advance

---

The point is to lead pupils to a deep understanding of what is covered.

---

organizers help pupils activate prior knowledge, and they also provide an anchor for later learning. Richard Arends gives an example of an advance organizer for a teacher about to present information about the Vietnam war:

> I want to give you an idea that will help you understand why the United States became involved in the Vietnam war. *The idea is that most wars reflect conflict between peoples over one of the following: ideology, territory, or access to trade.* As I describe for you the United State's involvement in Southeast Asia between 1945 and 1965, I want you to look for examples of how conflict over ideology, territory, or access to trade may have influenced later decisions to fight in Vietnam.[13]

Recent research tells us that advance organizers are important because pupils need to locate themselves in the appropriate area of long-term memory to use prior knowledge effectively. Further, pupils who connect new knowledge to prior knowledge are much more likely to retain the new knowledge in an organized fashion, or to reorganize existing knowledge in a more expert way. Teachers who launch a lecture or any other form of instruction without first helping pupils draw upon prior knowledge risk reducing these pupils to mindless note-taking, as they attempt to copy the teacher's knowledge rather than construct their own.

Teach pupils strategies for learning.

Contemporary research clearly outlines the importance of several powerful techniques for teaching pupils strategies for learning. Teachers can instruct pupils on using these strategies, and then encourage their application as the year progresses. One of these strategies is *elaboration*. Elaboration is the process of generating new ideas related to the ideas being received from external sources. When pupils add to information taught, discussed in class, or read, they engage in elaborative rehearsal. Research indicates elaboration is much more powerful than memorization in promoting retention of information.[14]

Teachers can employ many strategies to enhance elaboration among their pupils, including the use of drawings, metaphors, and analogies. Teachers can also have pupils summarize information in their own words.[15] Summarization is particularly useful in conjunction with note-taking. Teachers might also re-examine the types of questions they ask during lecture and discussion, to ensure that the questions encourage elaboration. Jay McTighe and Frank Lyman provide very practical examples of different types of questions, and a summary in the form of a bookmark for teachers to use while guiding discussions.[16]

Another technique that helps pupils learn strategies for learning is *imagery*. There is truth to the saying that "one picture is worth a thousand words." Current research reaffirms what many teachers have suspected—that things we can see or picture in our minds are generally easier to learn and remember than things we cannot see or picture. Information processing research suggests that this is because our working memories can hold only seven or so chunks of information before some information is forgotten. Images, which form a continuous representation of information, therefore take up less space than things we cannot imagine. Consequently, many items can be "chunked" together as one image, leaving much more space in working memory for additional information or thought.[17] Teachers should

> *Research indicates elaboration is much more powerful than memorization in promoting retention of information.*

encourage children to form images or mental pictures whenever possible and appropriate. Furthermore, teachers should use abundant visual aids during lesson presentations.

Finally, *organization* can be a valuable aid in helping pupils to structure information and retain it. Recall the point above that learners can remember only about seven unrelated things at one time, because of limitations of working memory. But if material is "carefully divided into subsets, and the relations within and between subsets are noted,"[18] pupils can learn much information quickly and simulta-

neously increase their knowledge and understanding of that material. Teachers can assist pupils by instructing them in constructing and using traditional outlines or in concept mapping, an alternative using spatial organization of ideas.[19]

Teachers also need to carefully consider the organization of the content they plan to teach to their pupils. They cannot always rely upon textbooks to provide the organization scheme most appropriate for pupils. For example, history texts often organize events chronologically when core ideas or concepts might better relate to one another thematically.

Allow time and opportunity for practice.
Contemporary research indicates teachers should allow plentiful opportunities for their pupils to practice what they have been taught. Information processing researchers distinguish between two types of knowledge. Schools have typically devoted sufficient time to developing declarative knowledge—knowledge of facts, ideas, and concepts. Procedural knowledge is knowledge of how to do things. For example, knowing that a barometer and a thermometer are instruments used to predict weather is declarative knowledge; being able to actually read and interpret a barometer and thermometer is procedural knowledge. Schools typically do not devote ample time to the development of procedural knowledge.

Current research generally counsels resisting the temptation to move quickly through subject matter and to focus only on facts. When providing practice activities, teachers should not use activities that provide only rote practice. Rather, they should use activities that present problems or scenarios for pupils to analyze. Pupils should actually *do* the subject.[20] For example, during a unit on weather, pupils should try to predict the weather based upon instrument readings. Finally, research has made

clear that pupils learn procedural knowledge best through practice, followed by specific feedback from the teacher. Teachers can make it a point to provide frequent, specific feedback to pupils on their performances.

> *Schools typically do not devote ample time to the development of procedural knowledge.*

Use cooperative learning strategies.
Many teachers are now beginning to use cooperative learning assignments in their classrooms, and contemporary research supports the use of this pedagogical strategy. Cooperative learning is useful while pupils are learning facts, and it is also appropriate while pupils practice applying facts and ideas. Cooperative learning is not just another name for group work; instead, it emphasizes mutual interdependence among learners and individual accountability for mastery of information.[21]

There are many ways to organize cooperative work groups. One popular technique is *jigsaw*, where pupils receive pieces of information on which they become experts. They then meet with others to share their expertise so that everybody learns the material by putting it together.

Cooperative learning is wholly consistent with recent cognitivist research on learning, because pupils become active learners and assist each other in constructing knowledge. That most children learn better when interacting with others is well established by empirical research. Teachers who use cooperative strategies are taking full advantage of a powerful technique that also teaches pupils a great deal about democratic living and the power of community.

Use interactive lecturing.

Contemporary research shows that unless teachers gain and maintain the pupils' attention, little if any learning can occur.[22] This finding might sound obvious to the point of humor, except for the common misperception that pupils who quietly listen to the teacher are attending to what the teacher is actually saying. While pupils do attend to *something* during waking hours, the lesson at hand might not be that something. Further, studies on attention span indicate that after about fifteen or twenty minutes a lecture loses its effectiveness for most learners.[23]

Therefore, teachers who feel that a lecture is the best approach for a topic should consider using alternative formats. These formats should be interactive in order to combat pupil boredom and focus attention on relevant information. For example, in the *participatory lecture* pupils brainstorm to generate ideas that the teacher then organizes into a rational and coherent pattern. Sivasailam Thiagarjan provides an example:

Janice has the members of her audience brainstorm a list of characteristics which make a seminar interesting. She writes down the audience inputs on a flipchart. After five minutes of brainstorming, she classifies the items into seven major categories. She then lectures on each category. Later, she adds two categories missed by the audience (but considered important by researchers). She reports the research data on effective seminars.[24]

Another example of an alternative format is the Assigned Reading Activity. In this format, reading is assigned as preparation for class. When class convenes, pupils are given roles such as *supporter, critic, observer,* and *discussion leader.*[25] Essentially, the supporter must defend the position of the author of the reading, and the critic must find flaws in the position. The discussion leader manages the session and the debate, and the observer decides whether the supporters or the critics were more convincing. This works best for controversial readings. There are many more alternatives available for those seeking a different approach.[26]

Keep learning styles in mind.

Children (and adults) differ in learning style preferences. The pioneering work of Howard Gardner has even suggested that humans actually possess multiple intelligences.[27] Teachers who present information in various ways are more likely to meet diverse learner needs.

An excellent system for helping teachers plan lessons that are both consistent with the contemporary cognitivist models and with learning styles theory is Bernice McCarthy's 4MAT System.[28] McCarthy's system incorporates left brain/right brain research into an instructional system that identifies four different learning styles: the "innovative" learners who need to be given a reason to learn; the "analytical" learners who need facts and information; the "common sense" learners who need to try things out to see how they work; and the "dynamic" learners who like to go beyond the information given and engage in self-discovery.

The 4MAT system fits cognitivist approaches beautifully, and it is especially well connected to information processing research. 4MAT moves instruction from catching the pupil's attention, to helping pupils gain declarative knowledge, to helping pupils attain procedural knowledge, to assisting pupils in making connections to their lives and among and between other ideas, facts, and concepts.

Practice some of the newer strategies.

There are many promising pedagogical practices now emerging from the practical literature that are consistent with contemporary research. Many of these come under the umbrella of authentic learning.[29] One of the most interesting, and potentially most powerful practices, is problem-based learning (PBL). This type of learning, which emerged from the literature on the education of physicians, is now influencing gifted education and teaching in mathematics and sciences.[30] William Stepien and Shelagh Gallagher are leading the way in applying PBL techniques in classroom settings.[31]

Essentially, PBL provides pupils the opportunity to understand and resolve ill-structured problems under the guidance, rather than direction, of the teacher. "Ill-structured problems" are those for which necessary solution procedures are not readily apparent and for which necessary solution information is not given up front. These problems may actually change course and become more complex as pupils tackle them.[32] Pupils work in small groups and take an active role in their learning. They must use knowledge and skills from the discipline, or from several disciplines, to work on the problems presented to them. In this way, they are learning content and skills in the context of the types of problems encountered in the "real world."[33]

The case method, although not as new, is consistent with recent research and cognitivist approaches. Like PBL, the case method also requires active participation on the part of the learner. The case method is an instructional technique that employs case studies to engage pupils in problem-solving activity. Case studies describe a decision or problem, and they are typically written from the perspective of the person who must make the decision. Cases are presented and then end with a problem or dilemma that needs to be resolved.[34] The case method differs from PBL in that cases tend to be more clearly structured; the case problems tend to be of shorter duration; and the cases allow pupils to practice knowledge they have attained, rather than to actually learn content.[35]

Summary

Will Rogers once said, "Schools aren't as good as they used to be, but then they never were." Only in the past decade or two have we had the tools to study human learning in more precise ways than ever before. The acceptance of cognitive psychology by American educators has loosened the grip of behavioral psychology, which has dominated educational practice during much of this century. Although cognitive science has provided the empirical studies for the contemporary knowledge base in teaching and learning, the application of cognitive science to school learning is clearly the domain and the responsibility of teachers. This application will allow teachers to transform classrooms into vital, interesting places where children truly move from novice to expert behavior in discipline-specific knowledge. And teachers can rest assured that the techniques they are using are supported by empirical data and are the most powerful currently available in our pedagogical arsenal. [eH]

1. John Goodlad, "A Study of Schooling: Some Findings and Hypotheses," *Phi Delta Kappan* 64 (March 1983): 467. See also John Goodlad, *A Place Called School* (New York: McGraw-Hill, 1984) for an in-depth study of 1,016 classrooms.

2. See Howard Gardner, *The Unschooled Mind: How Children Think and How Schools Should Teach* (New York: Basic Books, 1991), for an empirically-based treatise that merges cognitive science and education.

3. Renate Nummela Caine and Geoffrey Caine, *Making Connections: Teaching and the Human Brain* (Alexandria, Va.: Association for Supervision and Curriculum Development, 1991), 15.

4. John T. Bruer, "The Mind's Journey from Novice to Expert," *American Educator* 17 (Summer 1993): 7–8.

5. Bruce Joyce, Beverly Showers, and Carol Rolheiser-Bennett, "Staff Development and Student Learning: A Synthesis of Research on Models of Teaching," *Educational Leadership* 45 (October 1987): 11–23.

6. James Nolan and Pam Francis, "Changing Perspectives in Curriculum and Instruction," in *Supervision in Transition*, ed. Carl Glickman (Alexandria, Va.: Association of Supervision and Curriculum Development, 1992), 45.

7. Ibid., 45.

8. Ibid., 47–48.

9. Bruer, "The Mind's Journey," 8.

10. David Perkins, "Teaching for Understanding," *American Educator* 17 (Fall 1993): 28–35.

11. Lauren Resnick and Leopold Klopfer, eds., *Toward the Thinking Curriculum: Current Cognitive Research* (Alexandria, Va.: Association for Supervision and Curriculum Development, 1989), 207–208.

12. Perkins, "Teaching for," 33.

13. Richard Arends, *Learning to Teach*, 2nd edition (New York: McGraw-Hill, 1991), 243. It should be mentioned, however, that schema theorists believe that organizers containing concrete examples (such as drawings, etc.) are better than abstract organizers.

14. See Ellen Gagne, Carol Walker Yekovich, and Frank Yekovich, *The Cognitive Psychology of School Learning*, 2nd edition (New York: Harper-Collins, 1993), 127–135 for a solid treatment of studies supporting the use of elaboration.

15. Richard Hamilton and Elizabeth Ghatala, *Learning and Instruction* (New York: McGraw-Hill, 1994), 118.

16. Jay McTighe and Frank Lyman, Jr., "Cueing Thinking in the Classroom: The Promise of Theory-Embedded Tools," *Educational Leadership* 45 (April 1988): 21.

17. Gagne, Yekovich, and Yekovich, *Cognitive Psychology*, 70–71.

18. Hamilton and Ghatala, *Learning*, 119.

19. For examples, see McTighe and Lyman, "Cueing Thinking," 21.

20. For a more detailed treatise on declarative and procedural knowledge, and very practical classroom examples of activities to promote each one, see Robert Marzano, *A Different Kind of Classroom: Teaching with Dimensions of Learning* (Alexandria, Va.: Association of Supervision and Curriculum Development, 1992).

21. Much of the cooperative learning research has been pioneered by David and Roger Johnson at the University of Minnesota, Minneapolis, and by Robert Slavin at Johns Hopkins University in Baltimore, Maryland.

22. Anita Woolfolk, *Educational Psychology*, 5th edition (Massachusetts: Allyn and Bacon, 1993), 247.

23. Peter Frederick, "The Lively Lecture—8 Variations," *College Teaching* 34 (Spring 1986): 44.

24. Sivasailam Thiagarjan, "25 Ways to Improve Any Lecture," *Performance and Instruction Journal* 24 (December 1985/January 1986): 22.

25. Nina Buchanan, "Assigned Reading Activity: An Alternative to Lecture/Discussion," *College Teaching* 34 (Summer 1986): 111–113.

26. See Frederick and Thiagarjan for additional alternative formats.

27. Howard Gardner, *Frames of Mind: The Theory of Multiple Intelligences* (New York: Basic Books, 1983).

28. Bernice McCarthy, *The 4MAT System: Teaching to Learning Styles with Right/Left Mode Techniques* (Illinois: EXCEL, 1980). EXCEL has many additional materials that teachers might find useful in lesson preparation, and the company offers several levels of training in the 4MAT System for teachers and other school personnel.

29. For many classroom examples of authentic learning, readers are encouraged to consult *Educational Leadership* 50 (April 1993), which was devoted to this topic.

30. David Aspy, Cheryl Aspy, and Patricia Quinby, "What Doctors Can Teach Teachers about Problem-Based Learning," *Educational Leadership* 50 (April 1993): 22–24.

31. William Stepien and Shelagh Gallagher, "Problem-Based Learning: As Authentic as It Gets," *Educational Leadership* 50 (April 1993): 25–28. Teachers who would like to purchase units of instruction in PBL format may obtain a list of available topics and ordering information from the Center for Gifted Education, 232 Jamestown Road, Williamsburg, Va. 23185.

32. John O'Neil, "What Is Problem-Based Learning," *Update* 34 (August 1992): 4.

33. Stepien and Gallagher, "Problem-Based," 26.

34. Theodore Kowalski, Roy Weaver, and Kenneth Henson, *Case Studies on Teaching* (New York: Longman, 1990), ix.

35. O'Neil, "What Is Problem-Based," 4.

Cultural Revolution

Real professional development encourages teachers to break old habits.

Paula Evans

Paula Evans is director of the National Re:Learning Faculty of the Coalition of Essential Schools, based at Brown University in Providence, R.I.

When I started out as a French teacher in the late 1960s, my department head gave me three commands: "Never talk to a student before class. Be sure the books have covers. Look for gum." I was assigned introductory courses of lower-level students. Our textbook, written in the 1940s, featured Jean-Paul, who wore knickers and wanted garden tools for his 16th birthday. My students hated French and told me so regularly. I just kept looking for gum and making sure their books were covered.

The habits I was cultivating reflected and reinforced the school's culture. All students will take a foreign language and will speak and write acceptable French after two years with Jean-Paul. Use one method of teaching for all kids. They are, after all, basically the same anyway. You, the teacher, have the knowledge and skills. Transmit them to the kids. New teachers get the lower-track kids (Camus will have to wait), and lower-track kids get the oldest books. Keep order. Maintain decorum.

I knew better. I had been trained in one of the country's most progressive graduate schools of education. Yet within six months, I had forgotten most of that training. The culture of the school and of the larger field of education proved far more powerful. I was learning to insist that students do as they were told,

no matter what—and to do likewise myself.

And in the 1990s, I continue to watch some of our strongest student teachers repeat my same pattern. "They don't call parents at this school, so how can I?" "I can't arrange the chairs differently; no one else does." "I don't give homework. The kids aren't allowed to take the books home." Culture and habits still shape practice.

In the late '60s, "professional development" consisted of a visit from my supervisor and advice to write at the board without turning my back to the class. Such inservice programming as existed was brought to us in occasional, one-shot workshops. Expertise lodged elsewhere; we were not to generate it but to absorb and apply it. It is still very hard to find schools where the development of teachers (and the principal) is seen as a true priority and is being pursued in meaningful ways—even in schools that claim to be restructuring.

We must provide teachers and principals opportunities for growth that lead not simply to small improvements on the edge of their practice but to basic changes as its core. Restructuring does not mean coming up with new techniques. It goes far beyond any one dimension of schooling—assessment, schedule, curriculum design, or student advising. And, unfortunately, there are no clear step-by-step formulas that work in the same sequence for all schools.

There are, however, schools across the country where the culture is changing and nurturing very different habits. Teacher collaboration has become the norm within these schools.

Teachers can't imagine not teaching with a team of colleagues, not developing and constantly refining their own curriculum. It is expected that they will question themselves and their colleagues, that they will be self-critical. It is understood that everyone will take a serious interest in the well-being of his or her students and that, of course, teachers will be in touch with parents and guardians. There are few rules in many of these schools, and the ones they have make sense. And so the habits people cultivate have little to do with checking for gum and book covers and much to do with making sure that students are engaged, pushed to think hard, respectful of each other, and given regular opportunities to show what they know and can do publicly.

We have learned from the work of these pioneering schools. We know that teacher-development programs are futile unless certain core conditions obtain. If teachers can't know their students well, for example, nothing else matters. The teacher-student load—how many kids a teacher has actual contact with—is critical. Unless the numbers are down, schools will not change. We know that our standards in schools across the country are far too low and that one of the ways to raise them is to come out of the closet, to assess students publicly, and to share student work among teachers. We know that teachers and principals, with their schools' kids, are at the heart of it all and that community and district support are critical.

Given these understandings and the demands of a changing school culture, how do we move beyond

From *Teacher* magazine, January 1995, pp. 40-41. © 1995 by Paula Evans. Reprinted by permission of the author.

our traditional lip service to truly link radical school change and professional development? Perhaps, most important, we begin by creating opportunities for "transformational" changes for teachers and principals, enabling them to see, feel, and experience teaching and learning and leading differently. And we reconceptualize professional development so that it is continuing, intensive, and encourages risk-taking by both participants and leaders.

It isn't enough to come together and have a good talk; we need to be jolted. Many teachers and principals have not experienced themselves what it means to be pushed intellectually, to exhibit knowledge publicly, to generate knowledge. Adults must experience that first-hand in order to change their thinking about teaching, curriculum, standards, and the role of students. Yes, we do need to give people tools and strategies and examples, but, even more important, people need the opportunity of working through for themselves what it means to develop authentic assessment, to structure the program differently for kids, to forgo the $45 anthology that kids aren't allowed to take home and purchase instead a series of paperback novels.

The Coalition of Essential Schools has opted to concentrate significant resources on the development of a core of teachers and principals who can then work with their colleagues out in the field. Called the National Re:Learning Faculty, this network of some 200 teachers, principals, and superintendents focuses on classroom and whole-school change—raising standards for all students, creating coherent, integrated curricula, redesigning assessment to meet clear goals. The faculty then shares this knowledge with colleagues.

Our goal is to build a network of practitioners committed to coaching or assisting their colleagues to restructure classrooms and schools based on the common principles of the coalition. These practitioners do not come into a school with a series of set workshops but rather spend time getting to know the school well. They then work with teachers and administrators over time on issues and concerns that they together have identified as central to their restructuring work.

Many teachers and principals have not experienced themselves what it means to be pushed intellectually.

After five years, we are seeing across the United States places where Re:Learning faculty members are assuming the leadership of teacher development in support of restructuring. Beginning where it makes the most sense, in their own schools and those nearby, they are helping shape the implementation of school reform locally, regionally, and nationally.

In the course of this work, we have learned some lessons:

- Teacher development must have a clear focus. We have chosen to concentrate on classroom and school practice. This emphasis has given our work direction and kept us honest. Others may take a different course, but the focus has to be clear and unambiguous.

- Outside perspective—a "third eye" or "critical friend"—can really help teachers and principals in their work. It is sometimes very hard to work within one's own school, and an outsider—particularly a credible, informed outsider—can play a crucial helping role.

- Practitioners are the most credible helpers. Consultants and "experts" may be good, but it makes a huge difference when those who design and lead professional development programs have had recent, direct experiences of change in their own classrooms and schools. Moreover, when practitioners lead the work, the learning is reciprocal.

- Relationships are key. There is no substitute for the opportunity to work, over time, with colleagues. Change is relationship-intensive and must be nourished by long-standing connections and commitments.

- Real change requires sustained support. No matter how enlightening a seminar or consultation, if there is not a continuing group at a teacher's home school, innovation falters. Wherever teachers or principals feel isolated, we hear, "I feel overwhelmed. I can't do this work. It's too much."

- Critical mass matters. Clusters of schools and networks of like-minded colleagues encourage and support school change. They provide sustenance and new knowledge about practice, school structure, and school program for each others. Similarly, good national support nurtures local change. A larger network can add useful leverage to good local work. For example, teachers in Chicago who are linked to colleagues across the country—through a vibrant e-mail network and at least yearly conferences or institutes—may have a more powerful voice in their own community.

There are clear gaps in the work of restructuring and professional development over which we still puzzle. Most immediately, we haven't figured out how to build in regular opportunities for practitioners to reflect, read, and write. And we haven't figured out how to nurture the political savvy that is required to permit schools to restructure. Too often, we leave the work of educating the school board, the legislature, and the public to others. That strategy is not helpful. Teachers and principals must somehow be party to the political context in which they work. Rethinking schooling is challenging. It's hard. It's exhilarating. It requires imagination, strength, courage, and perseverance. Already we have come a far distance from checking for chewing gum and book covers. We might just make a difference.

How to Make Detracking Work

Successful detracking is tantamount to school restructuring, the authors point out. Viewed and handled as such, it offers much promise both for ending an inequitable arrangement and for improving educational practice.

Richard S. Marsh and
Mary Anne Raywid

RICHARD S. MARSH is principal of Shubert Elementary School, Baldwin, N.Y. MARY ANNE RAYWID is a professor of administration and policy studies at Hofstra University, Hempstead, N.Y.

THE CASE for detracking the schools continues to be compelling, and the pressure to detrack is mounting steadily. It is still too early to cite a substantial research record on just how to go about it, but a recent study of 10 Long Island school districts with successful detracking efforts has yielded a number of suggestions.

We polled the area's more than 120 districts to learn which had been involved in such efforts. Then, to confirm and extend the reports, we visited those districts that had undertaken detracking. Conversations with key local figures — teachers and parents as well as administrators — revealed a number of suggestions on when and how to go about the process.

Illustration by Carol O'Malia

Tracking has a long history, growing out of early 20th-century efforts to prepare youngsters for the quite different careers and lifestyles awaiting them. As larger percentages of the nation's youth attended schools, their different talents, abilities, and destinies became increasingly apparent. Schools adapted to such an awareness first with differentiated programs (e.g., college preparatory and manual training) and later with tracking — the practice of separating youngsters into differentiated classes of low-, average-, or high-ability students.

Over the years, we have had cause to become increasingly aware of the negative effects and injustices of tracking. Today the evidence clearly calls for its elimination. Yet tracking remains standard practice in a large majority of the nation's schools, probably 80% or more.[1] And programs at both state and federal levels support and perpetuate the practice.

In New York, for instance, the very existence of two sets of state tests serves to endorse course differentiation and homogeneous grouping. Upper-track students take Regents Examinations; lower-track students take Regents Competency Tests. At the federal level, legislation providing for the handicapped and for compensatory education has entrenched the practice of separating youngsters for targeted instruction given by teachers specially prepared to offer it. Not surprisingly, then, teachers have come to endorse tracking, believing that they can deal effectively only with groups of youngsters whose abilities all fall into the same narrowly defined range.

Yet the sense that tracking is unacceptable has been growing for some years and has come to challenge the widespread practice. It has been almost two decades since the first major exposé of the extent of tracking in the schools and of the ills and injuries accompanying it.[2] And nearly a decade has now passed since Jeannie Oakes' classic *Keeping Track* was published in 1985, a study that both updated and underscored what we know about the harm done by tracking. We are now seeing works that look toward alternatives, such as Anne Wheelock's *Crossing the Tracks: How "Untracking" Can Save America's Schools.*[3]

But, despite growing agreement that tracking is unfair and injurious, it remains a prominent organizational feature of most American high schools as well as most junior high schools, where the practice begins in earnest. (Many elementary schools also have grouping arrangements that are tantamount to tracking, but in most districts it is in junior high school that the practice becomes formalized and official.)

Tracking has been standard procedure even where it is unannounced and not generally perceived. For example, in one school where the principal denied the existence of tracking, *nine* distinct tracks were identified and acknowledged by the guidance office that maintained them.[4]

Teachers have been especially skeptical about the feasibility of other arrangements, since they tend to assume that alternative setups would simply remove ability grouping without making any other changes. Understandably, they are dubious about making a classroom work under such circumstances. But the evidence points to at least eight major drawbacks inherent in grouping students by ability levels. The students assigned to lower tracks and even to average classes often suffer from these drawbacks.[5]

1. The best teachers are often assigned the ablest students, and the least-experienced — or least-favored — teachers are assigned the weakest and most challenging students.

2. There are differences in the content presented to the different groups, with less — and lesser — substance presented to low-ability students.

3. There are differences in the quality of instruction delivered to the different groups, with higher-order thinking reserved largely for high-ability classes.

4. Teachers of students assigned to low-ability classes expect and demand little of them.

5. Students excluded from high-ability classes encounter lower motivation among their peers and develop less motivation themselves; thus they achieve less.

6. Students in low-ability classes include such disproportionate numbers of minority youngsters that tracking often functions as a form of resegregation.

7. Students in average and low-ability classes are restricted in their subsequent educational and career opportunities.

8. Compounding the above inequities, there are many cases in which youngsters have been erroneously assigned to lower-track classrooms (often on the basis of standardized test scores).

Thus the evidence suggests that, for all but the youngsters in the highest track, the practice of tracking renders school less interesting, less productive, and less rewarding. The result, not surprisingly, is that the longer students remain in school, the greater the achievement gap between those enrolled in lower and upper tracks.[6]

THESE ARE grave charges. Why have they failed to prompt more frequent and more extensive attempts to change the system? Our examination of Long Island school districts that have successfully detracked suggests that context is important and that particular ways of conducting the undertaking will make success more likely.

First, in the districts we examined, detracking had not been launched as a separate project. It was adopted either as a part of the solution to a larger problem or as part of a broader reform effort. Detracking might be one feature of a school restructuring plan, or it might become part of an effort to pursue equity or excellence. We concentrated our search at the junior high school level because that is the point at which tracking becomes formal.

We found that in some districts detracking became part of the process of converting a junior high school into a middle school. In other districts it was prompted by revelations of inequity — such as the absence of minority students in upper-ability classes. In still other places, detracking began with districtwide efforts to improve student outcomes and performance.

The widespread move toward middle schools certainly fosters detracking. Both the concern of middle schools with youngsters and their needs and the middle school commitment to equal access to education are incompatible with efforts to track students. And the literature on middle schools, such as the influential *Turning Points*, vehemently rejects tracking as "one of the most divisive and damaging school practices in existence."[7] Thus districts that are adopting the middle school orientation are embarking on detracking.

Elsewhere among our 10 districts, examination of existing local data revealed that minority students were underrepresented in upper-ability classes and in extracurricular activities. Such data prompted some districts to consider detracking, as well as other measures.

In still other districts, detracking began with a concern about the dwindling number of students taking Regents Examinations. When studies suggested that some of the students in non-Regents classes could handle the exams, one district abolished the lower track in an effort to prepare all youngsters for Regents-level work. In addition, it obtained an agreement from the state that students who failed the Regents Examinations by less than 10 points would be considered to have passed the Regents Competency Tests. Thus, in the interests of encouraging more students to pursue an academic program, this district moved simultaneously to reduce tracking and to provide some reassurance for youngsters facing increased academic demands.

We found that a genuine and widespread understanding of the need for detracking was perhaps the most fundamental element of a successful detracking effort. Studies of change have recently begun to turn away from an exclusive focus on structures and practices, emphasizing instead the importance of the meaning of change proposals to the people involved.[8] The evidence suggests that unless those expected to implement a reform genuinely understand its meaning and the need for it — and unless they are personally committed to carrying it out — only minimal success can be expected.[9] This puts a premium on finding ways to change the culture of schools and districts.

We found leadership to be crucial in this regard. Although teacher leadership could prove important, it rarely emerged in relation to detracking — a venture in which the time and resources involved require strong administrative leadership anyway. But the administrative leadership could emerge from either the school or district level. To initiate detracking requires transformational leadership: the ability to articulate and communicate a vision in ways that convince others of both its desirability and its feasibility.

But convincing people of the desirability and feasibility of detracking is even harder and more complicated than merely getting them to take on new convictions; they must also be persuaded to reject and replace old ones. This sort of reeducation typically demands more than information and inspiration. We encountered some ingenious activities intended to make participants question their own beliefs.

For example, one assistant superintendent used a reasoning test to demonstrate the range in thinking ability among a group of youngsters assigned to high-ability classes. If some were capable of formal thought and others were not, just how homogeneous was this presumably similar group? And how important to

instructional effectiveness was the lack of homogeneity on this critical ability? Teachers and board members later took the test as well — which stimulated substantial reflection on the part of staff members and policy makers.

Another top administrator distributed Howard Gardner's *Frames of Mind* to his board and presented a seminar on Gardner's theory of multiple intelligences to challenge the conception of ability on which homogeneous grouping is typically based. In yet another district the assistant superintendent sponsored an open forum to which he invited members of the staff and community representatives to bring prepared position papers on heterogeneous grouping, both pro and con. Elsewhere, a new principal suggested that the school enter a national "school of excellence" competition, which required the staff to reflect collaboratively on school practices and achievements. Together they completed the application and were successful in winning recognition.

Generally, however, so fundamental a change in school culture as detracking demands more than collaborative reflection; it requires collective examination of a challenge to existing beliefs. Cultural change involves a modification of what has been assumed to be true and desirable. Such modification requires that somehow the taken-for-granted be redefined as problematic. The most effective way of accomplishing this goal appears to be the presentation of some sort of convincing challenge to the beliefs of group members.[10]

As such cultural change begins, two sorts of skeptics and resisters are not uncommon. One group doubts that classrooms can work effectively in the absence of ability grouping; the other believes that something important is lost with the elimination of ability grouping. People who have successfully detracked schools insist that the most effective way of convincing the first group of resisters is to take them to see successfully detracked schools. So visits to such schools, with opportunities to observe in classrooms and talk with the teachers involved, are often a part of the early phases of effective detracking efforts.

The resisters who fear to lose present advantages are another matter. Frequently these are the parents of children assigned to high-ability groups. And — given the advantages their children have enjoyed, as enumerated above — their concern is hardly surprising. Thus it is

important that these resisters, like doubting teachers, come to see that detracking is not simply a matter of substituting heterogeneous for homogeneous classes. They must come to see that much more is involved and that detracking holds promise for their children as well.

Some schools have combined the termination of grouping by ability with the substitution of grouping on the basis of interest. Thus they have introduced themed programs from which youngsters and their families can choose, such as a microsociety school, an aerospace school, or a service academy. Other districts have focused instead on instructional strategies associated with successful detracking, such as cooperative learning, reciprocal teaching, interdisciplinary content, and teaming.

Either way, doubters must be acknowledged, and some attempt must be made to deal with their concerns. This is especially true with the parents of high-ability youngsters, since they are likely to be vocal and influential. But it is also sometimes the case with families of lower-track students who fear that their children will be faced with challenges and demands that they cannot meet.

Under some circumstances, our informants reported, it may be best to lower the sights and strike compromises that limit the scope of detracking plans. Some districts made the decision to phase in detracking gradually, carefully examining its progress and reporting to the community. Thus they have, for example, detracked entering seventh-grade classes — or English and/or social studies or science classes — while retaining tracking elsewhere. Others have compromised by eliminating the lower track but maintaining a separation between groups of high and average ability. In all such cases, eventual full detracking seems to have remained the goal, but a gradual phasing in has been pursued as necessary to its initial acceptance.

One thing that all our informants emphasized was the need for careful planning and preparation prior to the implementation of a detracking proposal. Reluctant teachers in strictly tracked programs are probably correct in thinking that the instructional strategies most familiar to them will not work in heterogeneous classrooms. Thus a major need for successful detracking is to provide teachers with additional pedagogical strategies. This translates into increased staff development, especially in such areas as cooperative learning, workshop or learning laboratory techniques, and differentiation of content. They also need help in learning how to work with colleagues — always a particular need when teachers launch new programs and thus require both moral and intellectual support.

Nor do the requisites for successful detracking end with staff development. In addition to instructional and curricular changes, several of our respondents were convinced that new kinds of assessment were necessary to determine student progress. And new class-ranking arrangements might also be called for in some schools.

People in our 10 districts were convinced that a number of organizational changes play a vital role as well. Class size must be held to an absolute minimum. "Safety nets" — in the form of extra help and tutorial sessions — need to be created for students previously treated as marginal. As these changes imply, corresponding changes must be made in both student and teacher schedules. Staffing may also need to be adjusted. In one school one teacher was made the school math tutor and was available all day to students on an "as needed" basis. Elsewhere, the presence of a second teacher supervisor converted study halls into real, small-group study sessions.

If this sounds as though detracking is an expensive proposition, it need not be — although some new costs are surely involved. Any serious reform or restructuring effort requires staff development, and detracking is certainly no exception. In fact, where there are likely to be doubters and resisters, staff development may be even more crucial to detracking than to other changes. And for most districts, serious, sustained staff development of any kind will be an added expense. New materials may also be necessary for the regrouped classrooms. However, smaller classes and new staff roles may not prove as expensive as they might initially seem. The elimination of the lower-track classes, which are usually small, permits other class averages to decrease. In one case, a Minnesota elementary school that adopted a policy of total inclusion for all its youngsters, including special education students, managed thereby to *halve* class size throughout the school. This was a substantially changed staffing policy, but it did not add much expense.

As all this suggests, successful detracking is tantamount to school restructuring. Viewed and handled as such, it offers much promise both for ending an arrangement that has proven highly inequitable and for improving educational practice. But if it is to succeed, a detracking effort must acknowledge the magnitude of the changes involved. As our respondents suggested, it must be carefully planned and initiated, it must acknowledge and meet the concerns of skeptics and resisters, it must prepare teachers adequately for their new circumstances, and it must align organizational structures and practices to support the new grouping arrangements.

1. John O'Neill, "On Tracking and Individual Differences: A Conversation with Jeannie Oakes," *Educational Leadership*, October 1992, pp. 18-22; and Carol Spencer and Michael G. Allen, *Grouping Students by Ability: A Review of the Literature* (Washington, D.C.: U.S. Department of Education, 1988).

2. James E. Rosenbaum, *Making Inequality: The Hidden Curriculum of High School Tracking* (New York: Wiley, 1976).

3. Jeannie Oakes, *Keeping Track* (New Haven, Conn.: Yale University Press, 1985); and Anne Wheelock, *Crossing the Tracks: How "Untracking" Can Save America's Schools* (New York: New Press, 1992).

4. Rosenbaum, p. 33.

5. Emily Dentzer and Anne Wheelock, *Locked In/Locked Out: Tracking and Placement Practices in Boston Public Schools* (Boston: Massachusetts Advocacy Center, 1990); and Oakes, op. cit.

6. Thomas Hoffer, "Cumulative Effects of Ability Grouping on Student Achievement," paper presented at the annual meeting of the American Educational Research Association, New Orleans, April 1994.

7. Carnegie Council on Adolescent Development, *Turning Points: Preparing American Youth for the 21st Century* (Washington, D.C.: Carnegie Corporation of New York, 1989), p. 49.

8. Michael Fullan, *Change Forces: Probing the Depths of Educational Reform* (Bristol, Pa.: Falmer Press, 1993).

9. Ibid.; and Gary Wehlage, Gregory A. Smith, and Pauline Lipman, "Restructuring Urban Schools: The New Futures Experience," *American Educational Research Journal*, vol. 29, 1992, pp. 51-93.

10. William T. Pink, "Competing Views of Change: Reforming School Culture," paper presented at the annual meeting of the American Educational Research Association, New Orleans, April 1994.

Challenges to the Public School Curriculum: New Targets and Strategies

Conservative challenges to materials used in the public schools are no longer limited to isolated attacks against individual books. Ms. McCarthy alerts readers to the powerful tactics now being employed to influence all aspects of the curriculum.

Martha M. McCarthy

MARTHA M. McCARTHY is a professor of education at Indiana University, Bloomington.

EFFORTS to make fundamental changes in public schooling for the 21st century face a number of obstacles.[1] Among the significant threats to these efforts are challenges from conservative citizen groups objecting to particular instructional strategies and materials. Some of the best-known conservative groups are listed in the box on page 247.[2] Challenges by these groups to the public school curriculum are increasing dramatically; according to People for the American Way, the number of reported incidents was 50% higher in 1991-92 than in the previous school year.[3]

The conservative groups' most common complaint is that certain curricular materials or activities advance anti-Christian, anti-American doctrine, often referred to as "secular humanism" or, more recently, "New Age theology." Materials that encourage students to think critically, to examine alternatives, or to clarify values — in other words, to become more active learners — are alleged

to represent this anti-theistic belief.[4] The conservative groups contend that secular humanism and New Age theology are characterized by reliance on science and human nature instead of God and the Bible.[5] Humanistic, New Age materials and practices allegedly are founded on such doctrinal cornerstones as mysticism, occultism, globalism, moral relativism, internationalism, and hedonism.[6] "Secular humanism" and "New Age" have become catchall phrases, used by critics — much as "communism" was used in the 1950s and 1960s — to refer to everything that is considered a threat to traditional American values and institutions.[7]

Curriculum challenges are not a new phenomenon. However, recent efforts in this regard are particularly noteworthy, not only because of their increasing frequency, but also because of the shift in targets and the change in strategies used to influence the content of the public school curriculum.

NEW TARGETS

There have been subtle but important changes in the targets of curriculum challenges. Until the late 1970s the targets were usually individual books, such as *The Catcher in the Rye* and *Of Mice and Men*. Those making the charges were often parents acting on their own. While the list of individual books under attack continues to grow, recent protests — often orchestrated by national conservative groups — are more likely to focus on entire textbook series and components of the instructional program.

Currently, the most widely challenged textbook series is the Impressions reading series published by Harcourt Brace

Recent curriculum challenges are noteworthy for their frequency, new targets, and changed strategies.

Jovanovich. This 15-volume anthology for elementary grades contains selections by such noted authors as A. A. Milne, Maurice Sendak, and C. S. Lewis. The series, used by school districts in 34 states, embraces the whole-language approach to reading instruction. This approach is grounded in the belief that children learn to read as they learn to speak. Accordingly, the series focuses on reading for meaning, with selections that are believed to be of interest to children in the elementary grades. The conservative groups allege that the selections are depressing, morbid, and violent; invade students' privacy; attack traditional values; and promote Satanism, mysticism, and the occult.[8] Most of the challenges focus on the series' subject matter rather than on its pedagogical approach, but the controversy associated with Impressions may have implications for the future of whole-language instruction.

Courts try to defer to local school boards, whether the boards are defending or restricting the curriculum.

Because of California's influence on the textbook market nationwide, it is not surprising that the conservative groups have focused their attacks on the Impressions series in this state. Two closely aligned groups, Citizens for Excellence in Education (CEE) and the National Association of Christian Educators (NACE), both based in Costa Mesa, have distributed statewide mailings condemning the Impressions series. One letter begins with the following passage: "Before you read this letter, I want to warn you that it contains shocking and graphic quotes from a children's reading series used in classrooms across America. The good news is that God is doing wonderful things through His committed people. . . ."[9] Approximately 100 California school districts have adopted the Impressions series, and the series was challenged in about one-fourth of these districts between 1989 and 1990.[10] One in five of the school districts that have experienced challenges no longer uses the series.

Another recent popular target of the conservative groups is the Lions-Quest drug prevention curriculum, developed by Quest International and the Lions Club International. Lions-Quest consists of programs for elementary grades (Skills for Growing) and middle school students (Skills for Adolescence). A program for high school students (Skills for Living) is currently being revised. The asserted purposes of the programs are to develop character, citizenship, responsibility, and positive social skills.[11] The programs encourage students to make positive commitments to their families and communities and to lead healthy, drug-free lives.

The materials emphasize parent involvement and include exercises designed for students to complete at home with their parents. However, the conservative groups allege that the materials teach relative values and encourage students to make their own decisions rather than to rely on parental authority. In a 1992 study of challenges to the curriculum in Indiana, the Lions-Quest program was by far the most popular target of attacks, with 28 school districts reporting challenges to this program within the previous four years.[12]

Also challenged by conservative groups has been the program Tactics for Thinking, developed by Robert Marzano and distributed by the Association for Supervision and Curriculum Development. This program is designed to improve students' higher-level thinking skills and their ability to address complex problems. This thinking-skills program has been attacked as undermining Christian values and promoting New Age theology through practices that allegedly include meditation and mental imagery.[13] Such exercises as having children focus all their energy on an object for one minute and then describe their concentration process have been challenged as encouraging students to enter into self-hypnotic trances.[14]

Moreover, many course offerings (e.g., sociology, psychology, health, and biology) as well as instruction pertaining to values clarification, self-esteem, multicultural education,[15] evolution, AIDS education, and global education are being contested as anti-Christian, anti-American, or otherwise inappropriate. Several instructional strategies currently touted in the education literature, such as collaborative learning and thematic instruction, are being challenged because they shift to students some of the responsibility that was formerly lodged with the teacher.[16] Outcome-based education (OBE), a popular reform strategy intended to focus attention on school results in terms of what students actually learn, is being attacked by conservative groups as replacing factual subject matter with subjective learning outcomes.[17] OBE initiatives often emphasize higher-order thinking skills, problem solving, and content integration across subject areas. In states such as Iowa, Ohio, Oklahoma, and Pennsylvania, OBE programs have been modified or dropped because of serious opposition from conservative citizen groups.[18]

These recent challenges to textbook series, pedagogical approaches, and thinking-skills programs call into question some of the basic assumptions of school restructuring initiatives (e.g., that students should examine alternatives critically and take responsibility for their learning). Thus they pose far more serious threats to efforts to improve the public school program than do challenges to individual novels.

INCREASING USE OF GRASSROOTS STRATEGIES

In their efforts to influence the content of the public school curriculum, the conservative groups are using a number of strategies, ranging from litigation to personal persuasion. Recently, these groups have experienced setbacks in their attempts to influence state textbook adoptions.[19] They have also been unsuccessful with their litigation alleging that certain materials unconstitutionally advance an anti-theistic creed.[20] Although courts have upheld school boards' decisions to implement challenged programs, they have also upheld board efforts to *restrict* the curriculum, as long as the boards followed their own adopted procedures and based their decisions on legitimate pedagogical concerns.[21] In short, courts try to defer to local school boards, whether the boards are defending or restricting the curriculum.

Consequently, the conservative groups have focused their recent efforts on influencing school boards. They have attempted to marshal grassroots support and have boasted considerable recent success in rallying communities behind their attacks on particular aspects of the public school program. Often the campaigns are initiated by a few individuals who go door-to-door telling parents that, if they care about their children, they will join the crusade against the targeted materials or activities. When enough support is garnered, pressure is applied to the school board to bar the materials and courses from the curriculum.

As noted above, local attacks on curriculum materials are often orchestrated or at least influenced by national conservative groups. CEE, which has more than a thousand chapters nationwide, has produced "Public School Awareness" kits, which are distributed for $195 and contain materials to use in convincing parents of the "danger" of particular instructional materials. The organization's goal is to have such kits available in all Christian churches across the nation and to establish "Public School Awareness" committees in all communities.

The national conservative groups have also distributed to a wide audience a number of books condemning the allegedly anti-theistic orientation of public school offerings. These include such titles as *Secular Humanism: The Most Dangerous Religion in America*, by Homer Duncan; *Your Child and the Occult: Like Lambs to the Slaughter*, by Johanna Michaelsen; *Globalism: America's Demise*, by William Bowen, Jr.; and *Dark Secrets of the New Age*, by Texe Marrs. In addition, the national organizations' newsletters alert parents to "warning signs" of the New Age world view, among them such symbols as rainbows and unicorns and such phrases as "human potential" and "impersonal force."[22] These materials are designed to alarm parents and motivate them to take action.

As a result of the conservative groups' increasing numbers and greater identification with the mainstream, they are having a more significant impact on school board elections.[23] CEE has claimed that its chapters helped to elect approximately 2,000 school board members from 1989 to 1991, and the organization's goal was to elect 3,500 members by 1993.[24] Skipp Porteous, president of the Institute for First Amendment Studies, has noted that these well-organized conservative groups can have an impact on school board elections because of general voter apathy: "The fundamentalists are a minority, but they're an active minority. This is where the power is."[25]

CEE and NACE have distributed a book, *How to Elect Christians to Public Office*, in which Robert Simonds asserts, "We need strong school board members who know right from wrong. The Bible, being the only true source on right and wrong, should be the guide of board members. Only godly Christians can truly qualify for this critically important position."[26] Simonds has voiced optimism regarding the Religious Right's potential to "gain complete control of all local school boards. This would allow us to determine all local policy, select good textbooks, good curriculum programs, superintendents, and principals."[27]

IMPLICATIONS

Without question, challenges to the public school curriculum are more widespread, well-organized, and complex than many educators have realized. Until the

latter 1980s educators did not take such challenges very seriously. Those making the challenges were often viewed as the fundamentalist fringe, and courts consistently backed school boards in resisting censorship efforts. However, as noted above, current challenges to entire programs and textbook series are much more serious than isolated attacks on books. And the success rate of those initiating challenges has been rising.[28]

Educators have underestimated the political strength of those challenging the curriculum. Some of the conservative groups, viewing their activities as a divine crusade, sincerely believe that the materials and programs under attack pose a threat to the well-being of children. These groups have been effective in convincing parents that, if they are concerned about their children, they will not let them be exposed to the targeted "harmful" materials. Professional education associations have begun to recognize the magnitude of the challenges, but this professional awareness has come late. Many communities have become mobilized against particular instructional programs and materials, catching educators unprepared. Robert Marzano has asserted that "this movement is very powerful and growing at a geometric rate, and I don't think we realize what we have to lose as educators."[29]

Even if a school board does not remove a challenged program, the controversy itself can disrupt school operations and interfere with implementation of the program. Furthermore, challenges to the curriculum have a ripple effect, a fact that conservative organizations use to their advantage. When materials or programs are attacked in one school district, the controversy often affects other districts, as seen with the spreading challenges to the Impressions reading series in California.[30] Similarly, in the recent Indiana study, most of the reported challenges to the curriculum were geographically clustered.[31]

Moreover, a school board may be reluctant to adopt a specific program that has been challenged in a neighboring district. The board may decide that the educational benefits of the program are not worth the risk of a heated community controversy. Even without school board directives, educators may avoid materials they fear will offend influential conservative parent groups.[32] Such self-censorship by teachers and administrators in public schools is difficult to document be-

> *When materials are attacked in one school district, the controversy often affects other districts.*

cause it is simply handled informally and not reported. Henry Reichman has noted:

> Where sound formal policies and procedures are lacking, censorship efforts may quietly succeed. In these types of situations, teachers, librarians, or administrators may accede to pressure without any "incident" being registered. Perhaps more ominously, school personnel may initiate removals on their own, either to deter perceived threats or to impose their own values and orthodoxies on the educational process. In some cases, potentially controversial materials simply are not acquired in the first place.[33]

School personnel need to become more assertive in involving parents in efforts to restructure the instructional program. When innovative materials or strategies are adopted without parental participation, it is not surprising that suspicions are aroused. Educators need to explain

Selected Conservative Citizen Groups

American Coalition for Traditional Values (Tim LaHaye)
Christian Coalition (Pat Robertson)
Christian Educators Association (Forrest Turpen)
Citizens for Excellence in Education; National Association of Christian Educators (Robert Simonds)
Concerned Women for America (Beverly LaHaye)
Eagle Forum (Phyllis Schlafly)
Educational Research Analysts (Mel and Norma Gabler)
Family Research Council (Gary Bauer)
Focus on the Family (James Dobson)

Educators
*and policy makers
need to take a
stand that some
content, attitudes,
and skills shouldn't
be compromised.*

to parents the pedagogical justification for programs and materials. If parents become knowledgeable about the rationale for specific programs, they will be less likely to be persuaded by groups that have a "hit list" of materials and programs. Often parents are simply confused and do not understand the educational rationale for the questioned programs.[34] Many have not personally reviewed the materials they are challenging; instead, they rely on information distributed by the national organizations.

School boards often find, when the curriculum is challenged, that they have no procedures in place to handle such complaints. It is imperative for boards to establish a review process *before* a controversy arises. Critics of the curriculum deserve a forum in which to be heard, and some complaints may be valid. Challenges to materials and programs certainly have a "legitimate function in a democratic educational system."[35] But decisions regarding the fate of the challenged materials or programs should be based on educational considerations rather than on emotion, religious zeal, or political expediency. It is too late to establish a process when parents are storming the school with their list of "objectionable" materials. Challenges are twice as likely to be turned back in school districts with explicit procedures for handling curriculum complaints.[36]

Policy makers and educators must recognize that public schools cannot appease all groups. Public schools are not value-free, and the argument that they are value-neutral is destined to fail. For example, if critical thinking is emphasized, that is a value judgment. We must accept

that, for some groups, any material or strategy that does not promote reliance on Biblical absolutes is offensive. Indeed, trying to convince some fundamentalist groups of the religious neutrality of public schools simply fuels their allegations that Christianity is being denounced, because "neutral" instruction is viewed as anti-Christian.[37]

Instead of arguing that the challenged instructional programs are value-neutral or trying to sanitize the curriculum so that no groups are offended, policy makers and educators need to take a stand that some content (e.g., science), attitudes (e.g., respect for racial diversity), and skills (e.g., critical thinking) should not be compromised. Such instruction is necessary to ensure an educated citizenry in our democratic society, and educators should not have to defend the merits of teaching children how to think or how to get along with others from diverse backgrounds. If policy makers do not take a stand against the mounting threats to the public school curriculum, many school restructuring efforts may be doomed before they get off the ground. And, more significantly, we may produce a generation of citizens who lack the skills necessary to address the vexing dilemmas that will confront our nation in the 21st century.

1. A range of groups, from civil rights organizations to consumer activists, are condemning various curricular materials for being racist or sexist or for promoting bad health habits for students. And, of course, public schools have not been immune to the current debate over "political correctness." But most of the recent challenges have been mounted by conservative citizen groups. See *Attacks on Freedom to Learn* (Washington, D.C.: People for the American Way, 1992).

2. The conservative citizen groups — fundamentalist or evangelical Protestant in orientation — emerged in the 1970s and "coalesced with the political right in the 1980s." For an analysis of this movement, see Richard Pierard, "The New Religious Right and Censorship," *Contemporary Education*, vol. 58, 1987, p. 131.

3. Arthur J. Kropp, press release, People for the American Way, 1 September 1992, p. 3. See also Dianne Hopkins, "Challenges to Materials in Secondary School Library Media Centers: Results of a National Study," *Journal of Youth Services in Libraries*, vol. 4, 1991, pp. 131-40; and "Schools Face Increased Censorship," *School Board News*, 27 September 1989, p. 4.

4. See Charles Kniker, "Accommodating the Religious Diversity of Public School Students: Putting the 'Carts' Before the House," *Religion and Public Education*, vol. 15, 1988, p. 316.

5. See Edward Jenkinson, "Secular Humanism, Elitist Humanoids, and Banned Books," paper presented at the National Education Association Leadership Conference, Washington, D.C., February 1985, p. 5; and Christy Macy and Ricki Seidman, "Attacks on 'Secular Humanism': The Real Threat

to Public Education," *Kappa Delta Pi Record*, vol. 23, 1987, p. 77.

6. See Johanna Michaelsen, *Your Child and the Occult: Like Lambs to the Slaughter* (Eugene, Ore.: Harvest House, 1989).

7. James Wood, "Religious Fundamentalism and the Public Schools," *Religion and Public Education*, vol. 15, 1988, p. 51.

8. See Robert Simonds, *President's Report* (Costa Mesa, Calif.: National Association of Christian Educators/Citizens for Excellence in Education, June 1990), pp. 1-2.

9. Ibid., p. 1.

10. Louise Adler and Kip Tellez, "Curriculum Challenge from the Religious Right: The *Impressions* Reading Series," *Urban Education*, July 1992, pp. 152-73.

11. *Frequently Asked Questions* (Granville, Ohio: Quest International, n.d.); and Sue Keister, Judy Graves, and Dick Kinsley, "Skills for Growing: The Program Structure," *Principal*, vol. 68, 1988, p. 24.

12. See Martha McCarthy and Carol Langdon, *Challenges to the Public School Curriculum in Indiana's Public Schools* (Bloomington, Ind.: Indiana Education Policy Center, 1993).

13. See Debra Viadero, "Christian 'Movement' Seen Trying to Influence Schools," *Education Week*, 15 April 1992, p. 8.

14. Edward Jenkinson, "The New Age of Schoolbook Protest," *Phi Delta Kappan*, September 1988, pp. 66-69.

15. Children of the Rainbow, a multicultural curriculum adopted in the New York City School District, sparked a volatile controversy over the component of the program promoting tolerance toward homosexuals. See Peter Schmidt, "Fernandez Ousted as School Chief in New York City," *Education Week*, 17 February 1993, pp. 1, 14.

16. See Pamela Klein, "New Age Lessons Put Educators, Parents at Odds," *Indianapolis Star*, 3 December 1991, pp. 1, 4.

17. Phyllis Schlafly, "What's Wrong with Outcome-Based Education?," *Phyllis Schlafly Report*, May 1993.

18. Diane Brockett, "Outcome-Based Education Faces Strong Opposition," *School Board News*, 8 June 1993, pp. 1, 6.

19. See Edwin Darden, "Texas Adopts Textbook List: Ripple Effect May Be Felt Nationwide," *Education Daily*, 28 November 1988, p. 2; Robert Rothman, "Scientist, Creationist Each Claim Victory in Texas Evolution Vote," *Education Week*, 22 March 1989, pp. 1, 14; and Kent Ashworth, "Texas Board Repeals Rule on Evolution in Textbooks," *Education Daily*, 18 April 1984, p. 3. See also Franklyn Haiman, "School Censors and the Law," *Communication Education*, vol. 36, 1987, p. 337.

20. See *Mozert* v. *Hawkins County Pub. Schools*, 827 F.2d 1058 (6th Cir. 1987), *cert. denied*, 484 U.S. 1066 (1988); *Smith* v. *School Comm'rs of Mobile County*, 827 F.2d 684 (11th Cir. 1987); and *Grove* v. *Mead School Dist. No. 354*, 753 F.2d 1528 (9th Cir. 1985), *cert. denied*, 474 U.S. 826 (1985).

21. See *Virgil* v. *School Bd. of Columbia County*, 862 F.2d 1517 (11th Cir. 1989); and *Zykan* v. *Warsaw Community School Corp.*, 631 F.2d 1300 (7th Cir. 1980).

22. Andrea Priolo, "Principals Claim Most Parental 'Impressions' Problems Are Resolved," *Dixon Tribune*, 11 May 1990, p. 3.

23. See Viadero, p. 8. See also Erica Sorohan, "School Leaders Grapple with 'New Age' Accusations," *School Board News*, 1 October 1991, p. 5.

24. Sonia Nazario, "Crusader Vows to Put God Back into Schools Using Local Elections," *Wall Street Journal*, 15 July 1992, pp. A-1, A-5.

25. Quoted in Del Stover, "CEE's Goal: Gain Control of Local School Boards," *School Board News*, 1 September 1992, pp. 1, 5.

26. Robert Simonds, *How to Elect Christians to Public Office* (Costa Mesa, Calif.: National Association of Christian Educators/Citizens for Excellence in Education, 1985).

27. Quoted in J. Charles Park, "The Religious Right and Public Education," *Educational Leadership*, May 1987, p. 9.

28. Kropp, p. 3.

29. Quoted in Viadero, p. 8.

30. See Adler and Tellez, op. cit.

31. McCarthy and Langdon, op. cit.

32. For example, teachers in school districts in Virginia and Oregon refused to air Channel One's student news program the day it included a picture of Michelangelo's *David*, because they feared negative reactions to the statue's nudity. See "Schools Face Disputes Over Religious Issues," *Executive Educator*, November 1991, p. 11.

33. Henry Reichman, *Censorship and Selection* (Chicago and Arlington, Va.: American Library Association and American Association of School Administrators, 1988), p. 13. See also "Censorship Strips Teachers of Faith in Textbooks, Survey Says," *Education Daily*, 3 January 1990, p. 5; and Sissy Kegley and Gene Guerrero, *Censorship in the South — A Report of Four States 1980-1985* (New York: American Civil Liberties Union, 1985).

34. See William Carnes, "The Effective Schools Model: Learning to Listen," *Contemporary Education*, vol. 63, 1992, pp. 128-29.

35. Michelle Marder Kamhi, "Censorship vs. Selection — Choosing the Books Our Children Shall Read," *Educational Leadership*, December 1981, p. 211.

36. See Reichman, p. 13.

37. Martha McCarthy, "Secular Humanism and Education," *Journal of Law and Education*, vol. 19, 1990, pp. 495-96.

A Look to the Future

Which education philosophy is most appropriate for our schools as we approach the year 2000? This is a complex question, and we will as a free people come up with alternative visions of what it will be. Let us explore what might be possible as more students go on the Internet and the wonder of the cyberspace revolution opens to teachers and students. What challenges can we expect in using the technology of the cyberspace revolution in our schools? What blessings can we hope for? What changes need to occur in how people go to schools as well as in what they do when they get there?

The breakthroughs that are developing in new learning and communications technologies are really quite impressive. They will definitely affect how human beings learn in the very near future. Two new essays on this topic explore some of these new technologies. While we look forward with considerable optimism and confidence to these future educational developments, there are presently many controversies that will still be debated in the early years of the twenty-first century; the school choice issue is one. We will not attain all the goals that were set for us for the year 2000 by the governors of the states and former president George Bush in 1989, but we will make significant progress toward them. Some

very interesting new proposals for new forms of schooling, both in public schools and private schools, are developing. We can expect to see at least a few of these proposals practiced in the next few years.

Some of the demographic changes and challenges involving young people in the United States are staggering. Data sources tell us that 10 percent of all our female teenage population will become pregnant each year, the highest rate in the developed world. At least 100,000 American elementary school children get drunk once a week. Incidence of venereal disease has tripled among adolescents in the United States since 1965. The actual school dropout rate in the United States stands at 30 percent.

On other fronts, the student populations of North America reflect vital social and cultural forces at work to destroy our progress. In the United States, a massive secondary school dropout problem has been developing steadily through the past decade. The 1990s will reveal how public school systems will address this and other unresolved problems brought about by dramatic upheavals in demographics. For example, there is the issue of how great a shortfall in the supply of new teachers will be experienced in the 1990s. In the immediate future, we will be able to see if a massive teacher shortage is indeed beginning, and, if it is, how emergency or alternative certification measures adopted by states will affect achievement of the objectives of our reforms.

At any given moment in a people's history, several alternative future directions are open to them. Since 1970, North American educational systems have been subjected to one wave after another of recommendations for programmatic change. Is it any wonder that *change* is a sensitive watchword for persons in teacher education on this continent? What specific directions it will take in the immediate future depend on which recommendations of the reform agenda are implemented, which agencies of government (local, state/provincial, and federal) will pay for the very high costs of reform, and which shifts in perceived national educational priorities by the public will occur that will effect fundamental realignments of our educational goals.

Basic changes in society's career patterns should also be considered. It is estimated that in the United States the average nonagricultural worker now makes a major job change about five times in his or her career. The schools will surely be affected, indirectly or directly, by this major social phenomenon. Changes in the social structure due to divorce, unemployment, and job retraining efforts will also have an impact. Educational systems are integral parts of the broader social systems that created them; if the larger social system experiences fundamental change, this is reflected in the educational system.

In the area of information science and computer technologies applicable for use in educational systems, the development of new products is so rapid that we cannot predict what technological capacities may be available to schools 20 years from now. In addition, basic computer literacy is becoming more and more widespread in the population. We are entering—indeed we are in—a period of human history when knowledgeable people can control far greater information (and have immediate access to it) than at any previous time. As new information command systems evolve, this phenomenon will become more and more meaningful to all of us.

The future of education will be determined by the current debate concerning what constitutes a just, national response to human needs in a period of technological change. The history of technological change in all human societies since the beginning of industrial development clearly demonstrates that major advances in technology and breakthroughs in the basic sciences lead to more rapid rates of social change. Society is on the verge of discoveries that will lead to the creation of entirely new technologies in the dawning years of the twenty-first century. All of the social, economic, and educational institutions globally will be affected by these scientific breakthroughs. The basic issue is not whether schools can remain aloof from the needs of industry or the economic demands of society but how they can emphasize the noblest ideals of free persons in the face of inevitable technological and economic changes. Another concern is how to let go of predetermined visions of the future that limit our possibilities as free people. The schools, of course, will be called upon to face these issues. We need the most enlightened, insightful, and compassionate teachers ever educated by North American universities to prepare the youth of the future in a manner that will humanize the high-tech world in which they live.

All of the articles included in this unit can be related to discussions on the goals of education, the future of education, or curricula development. They also reflect highly divergent perspectives in the philosophy of education.

Looking Ahead: Challenge Questions

What might be the shape of school curricula by the year 2020?

What changes in society are most likely to affect educational change?

Based on all of the commission reports of recent years, is it possible to identify any clear directions in which teacher education in North America is headed? How can we build a better future for teachers?

How can information about population demographics, potential discoveries in the basic sciences, and the rate and direction of technological change assist in planning for our educational future?

How can schools prepare students to live and work in an uncertain future? What knowledge bases are most important? What skills are most important?

Will privatized schools represent an expansion of the educational opportunities for our children?

What is made possible in the classroom by the new learning and communications technologies that have been developed?

What can we expect to be the challenges confronting educators as more schools are enabled to go on the Internet and take advantage of the information technologies of the cyberspace age?

What should be the philosophical ideals for American schools in the fast-approaching twenty-first century?

—F. S.

A Philosophy of Education For the Year 2000

A conception of school as a moral equivalent of home is as responsive to societal conditions at the end of the 20th century as the factory model of schooling is unresponsive to them, Ms. Martin points out.

Jane Roland Martin

JANE ROLAND MARTIN is a professor of philosophy emerita at the University of Massachusetts, Boston. Most of the material in this article is drawn from her book The Schoolhome: Rethinking Schools for Changing Families *(Harvard University Press, 1992).*

AT THE TURN of this century — in 1899, to be exact — John Dewey started off a series of lectures in Chicago with a description of the changes in American society wrought by the Industrial Revolution. "It is radical conditions which have changed, and only an equally radical change in education suffices," he said.[1] One of those radical conditions was the removal of manufacture from households into factories and shops. It was Dewey's genius to see that the work that in the relatively recent past had been done at home had offered genuine educational benefits, which had become endangered. It was his great insight that some other educational agent could and should take over what had previously been one of the responsibilities of the home.

I draw attention to Dewey's analysis because in the United States today home and family have once more been trans-

formed. The critical factor now is the removal of parents from the household. With many households headed by a single parent, usually a mother, and most families in need of two salaries just to maintain a home, for many hours each day there is simply no one at home.

If nothing more were at stake than a child's misgivings about being home alone or a mother's exhaustion after working a double shift, educators might be justified in ignoring our changed reality.[2] But there are the three brothers, ages 12 to 15, in Lawrence, Massachusetts, who were arrested in February of 1994 for stealing their mother's jewelry to pay drug dealers for crack cocaine. "They looked like three little old men," said the police officer.[3] There are also the juveniles who were arrested two weeks before this incident for entering a roller rink in Boston and shooting seven children. "The police should have been there to take the gun away from my son before he went inside," said one mother.[4] And then there is the 4-year-old who, even as I was writing this, was discovered in unspeakable conditions in his own home. In tomorrow's newspaper, as on yesterday's television screen, there will be accounts of teenage shoot-outs, 5-year-olds toting guns, children in the drug trade.

I have no quarrel with those who point out that science and math and literacy education in the U.S. are not what they should be. I am as thoroughly convinced as anyone that the country's vocational education system needs overhauling. But this nation's political and educational leaders talk repeatedly about setting higher standards in the teaching of literacy, math, and science and about the schools' failure to develop a highly skilled work force — without ever seeming to notice that our changed social reality makes correspond-

ingly radical changes in schools imperative. To put it starkly, there is now a great domestic vacuum in the lives of children from all walks of life. In light of this radical change in conditions, once again the pressing question has become, What radical changes in school will suffice?

Needed: A Moral Equivalent Of Home

In the U.S., as in other industrialized societies, home has traditionally been the agency responsible for turning infants who are "barely human and utterly unsocialized" into "full-fledged members of the culture."[5] Sherry Ortner's words bring to mind the "Wild Boy" of Aveyron. Until he emerged from the woods, Victor had no exposure to the curriculum that inducts our young into human culture — not even to wearing clothes, eating food other than nuts and potatoes, hearing sounds, sleeping in a bed, distinguishing between hot and cold, or walking rather than running.[6] He had to be taught the things that people — other than parents of the very young and teachers of differently abled children — assume human beings instinctively know.

Shattering the illusion that what is called "second nature" is innate, Victor's case dramatically illustrates that what we adults learned at home as young children is far more basic than the school studies we call the basics. Years ago, one of the research questions I was asking was, What entitles us to call some studies rather than others "the basics"?[7] My answer was that reading, writing, and arithmetic are considered essential — hence basic — components of education because of their roles in preparing young people for membership in the public world — specifically, for enabling them to be citizens in a

From *Phi Delta Kappan*, January 1995, pp. 355-359. © 1995 by Phi Delta Kappa, Inc. Reprinted by permission.

democracy and to be economically self-sufficient individuals. In addition, we take the three R's to be fundamental because of the part they play in initiating our young into history, literature, philosophy, and the arts — "high" culture or Culture with a capital C. Bring the home's educational role into the picture, however, and one realizes that these three goals — achieving economic viability, becoming a good citizen, and acquiring high culture — make sense only for people who have already learned the basic mores of society.

Now there are some today who perceive the great domestic vacuum in children's lives, blame it on women, and would have us turn back the clock to a presumed golden age when mothers stayed home and took care of their young. These social analysts are simply oblivious to the present demands of economic necessity. They are also loath to acknowledge that it is not women's exodus from the private home each day that creates a vacuum in our children's lives. It is the exodus of *both* sexes. Had men not left the home when the Industrial Revolution removed work from that site — or had fathers not continued to leave the home each morning after their children were born — women's departure would not have the ramifications for children that it does.

The question is not, Whom can we blame? It is, What are we as a nation, a culture, a society going to do about our children?

In a widely read essay titled "A Moral Equivalent of War," written in 1910, William James introduced the concept of moral equivalency into our language. Given the great domestic vacuum in the U.S. today, the concept of a moral equivalent of home is as germane as James' moral equivalent of war ever was. Indeed, of the many things we can and should do for our children, perhaps the most important is to establish a moral equivalent of home for them.

To avoid misunderstanding, let me say that I am not proposing that home be abolished. When James spoke of a moral equivalent of war, he had in mind a *substitute* for war that would preserve those martial virtues that he considered the "higher" aspects of militarism.[8] When I speak of a moral equivalent of home, I have in mind the *sharing of responsibility* for those educative functions of home that are now at risk of extinction. Who or what will do the sharing? In accordance with Dewey's insight and in light of the

universality, ubiquitousness, and claims on a child's time that characterize schooling, there is no institution so appropriate for this task as school. Yet there can be no doubt that school is an overburdened institution. How then in good conscience can I or anyone ask it to take on more responsibilities? Moreover, will school even *be* school if it shoulders the functions of the home?

If one learns nothing else from the study of educational history, one discovers that education in general and schooling in particular are as subject to change, as much a part of the societal flux, as everything else.[9] Thus to suppose that school has some immutable task or function that it and only it must carry out and that other tasks contradict or defile its nature is to attribute to school an essential nature it does not have. Yes, school can add new functions without losing its identity. It can also shed old ones, as well as share some of these — for instance, vocational education with industry, or science education and history education with museums. After all, those old functions were themselves once brand new.

History, then, teaches that school can be turned into a moral equivalent of home without its becoming hopelessly overextended. It teaches that, even as we assign the school some of the old educative functions of the home, we can ask the many other educational agents that now exist to share the educational work that our culture currently assigns to school.

The Schoolhome

Because they think of school as a special kind of production site — a factory that turns out workers for the nation's public and private sectors — government officials, business leaders, granting agencies, and educational administrators focus today on standards. As they see it, the products of our nation's classrooms, like the automobiles on a General Motors assembly line and the boxes of cereal in a Kellogg's plant, should be made according to specifications. When minimum requirements are not met, the obvious remedy is to tighten quality control. Colleges and universities are apt to respond to this demand by raising entrance requirements. Public schools will launch efforts to improve testing, to hold teachers accountable for student performance, and to standardize curriculum.

In an age when the lives of all too many children bring to mind Dickens' novels, it is perhaps to be expected that young children in school are pictured as raw material, teachers as workers who process their students before sending them on to the next station on the assembly line, and the curriculum as machinery that over the span of 12 or so years forges the nation's young into marketable products. However, this conception of schooling totally ignores the needs and conditions of children, their parents, and the nation itself at the end of the 20th century.

At the very least, children need to love and be loved. They need to feel safe, secure, and at ease with themselves and others. They need to experience intimacy and affection. They need to be perceived as unique individuals and to be treated as such. The factory model of schooling presupposes that such conditions have already been met when children arrive in school, that the school's raw materials — the children — have, so to speak, been "preprocessed." Resting on the unspoken assumption that home is the school's partner in the educational process, the model takes it for granted that it is home's job to fulfill these basic needs. Thus the production-line picture derives its plausibility from the premise that school does not have to be a loving place, that the classroom does not have to have an affectionate atmosphere, and that teachers do not have to treasure the individuality of students because the school's silent partner will take care of all of this.

One consequence of the great domestic vacuum that exists in children's lives today is that we can no longer depend on home to do the preprocessing. Speaking generally, the home cannot be counted on to transmit the love; the three C's of care, concern, and connection; and the knowledge, skills, attitudes, and values that enable each individual born into this society to become a member of human culture in the broadest sense of that term. If for no other reason, then, the factory model of schooling is untenable. To be sure, one can irrationally cling to it. Insisting that the school's raw materials are so defective that they cannot possibly be turned into acceptable end products, one can blame and penalize the victims of the latest transformation of the home instead of insisting that the school respond to their plight. The nation's children will be far better served, however, if we change our conception of school. The nation also stands to gain from a new idea of school, for its continued well-being ultimately depends on the well-being of the next generation and of its successors.

The recent transformation of home and family belies the very model of schooling that our political and educational leaders tacitly accept. A conception of school as a moral equivalent of home, on the other hand, is as responsive to conditions at the end of the 20th century as the factory model is insensible to them. Thus I propose that we as a nation set ourselves the goal of turning our school*houses* into school*homes*.

Instead of focusing our gaze on abstract norms, standardized tests, generalized rates of success, and uniform outcomes, the idea of the schoolhome directs attention to actual educational practice. Of course, a schoolhome will teach the three R's. But it will give equal emphasis to the three C's of care, concern, and connection — not by designating formal courses in these fundamentals but by being a domestic environment characterized by safety, security, nurturance, and love.

In a schoolhome, classroom climate, school routines and rituals, teachers' modes of teaching, and children's ways of learning are all guided by a spirit of family-like affection. And so are the relationships between teachers and students and between the students themselves. The inhabitants of a schoolhome will learn science and literature, history and math. But they will also learn to make domesticity their business. Feeling that they belong in the schoolhome and, at the same time, that the schoolhome belongs to them, the children will take pride in their physical environment while happily contributing their own labor to its upkeep. Perhaps even more important, with their teachers' help, the pupils in a schoolhome will countenance no violence, be it corporal punishment or teacher sarcasm, the bullying of one child by others or the terrorization of an entire class, the use of hostile language about whole races or the denigration of one sex.

Now I realize that America's private homes were never idyllic sanctuaries and that at present they, like our streets, are sites of violence. When I propose that our schools be homelike, however, I have in mind *ideal* homes, not dysfunctional ones. Thus, in recommending that school be a moral equivalent of home, I assume a home that is warm and loving and a family that is neither physically nor psychologically abusive and that believes in and strives for the equality of the sexes.

Yet is home an appropriate metaphor for school in a nation whose population is as diverse as ours? It is, provided we recognize that, one century after Dewey's Chicago lecture, the question has become, How can we create a moral equivalent of home in which children of all races, classes, and ethnicities feel at home?

Needed: A New Curricular Paradigm

Surprisingly, those today who criticize this country's schools and make recommendations for their improvement pay little attention to the changed composition of the nation's population. I call them "restorationists" because, seemingly impervious to the pressing need our nation now has for a new inclusionary curriculum that will serve all our children, they want to restore the old outmoded one. Looking back with longing at the curriculum of their youth, they would reinstate a course of study designed for an earlier age and a different people.

It scarcely needs saying that a more inclusive curriculum is not necessarily a better one. Yet in a society in the process of changing color, can courses in African philosophy be considered frivolous? In a nation with a history of slavery and a continuing record of racial division and inequality, can the reading of slave narratives be irrelevant to the study of American history and literature? In a land in which rape is rampant, the victims of child sexual abuse are most often girls, and women are subjected to sexual harassment at home, at school, and at work, is it sensible to say that courses that represent and analyze women's history, lives, and experiences are parochial and take too subjective a point of view?

If all U.S. children are to feel at home in both school and society, then schools must reserve space in the curriculum for the works, experiences, and societal practices of women as well as men, poor people as well as the middle classes, and ethnic, racial, and other minorities. But even more than this is required.

Protesting a school curriculum very like that which the restorationists would piece back together — one whose subjects of study represent abstract bodies of knowledge divorced from the activities of everyday life — Dewey called on us to educate "the whole child." I, in turn, ask that we educate *all* our children in our *whole* heritage so that they will learn to live in the world together.[10] Because that

whole heritage includes ways of living as well as forms of knowing, societal activities and practices as well as literary and artistic achievements, we need more than a curriculum that honors diversity. We need a new curricular paradigm — one that does not ignore the disciplines of knowledge but assigns them their proper place in the general scheme of things as but one part of a person's education; one that integrates thought and action, reason and emotion, education and life; one that does not divorce persons from their social and natural contexts; one that embraces individual autonomy as but one of many values.[11]

Unfortunately, even when this nation's heritage is defined multiculturally, it is too easy for school to instruct children *about* it without ever teaching them to be active and constructive participants in living — let alone how to make the world a better place for themselves and their progeny. This is especially so when the school's business is thought to be the development of children's minds, not their bodies; their thinking and reasoning skills, not their emotional capacities or active propensities. Yet a nation that cannot count on home to perform its traditional educative functions dare not settle for so narrow a definition of the school's task.

We need to ask ourselves if turn-of-the-21st-century America is well-served by a population of onlookers. In 1989, in a letter to the *Boston Globe,* a school-teacher wrote, "I used to wonder if my adolescent boys would remember my lessons once they left my classroom; now I wonder if they will live to remember them." At about that same time a Boston gang member was reminiscing: "When I was 12, I carried a .38 everywhere. I sold drugs in great balls. I was carryin' the gun just to be carryin' it. I wanted to be someone big. To me, a gun changes a person. It makes 'em brave. Sometimes I would go on the roof and shoot in the air. I felt like, let 'em come up on me. I'd be like Hercules. I even said, 'Let a cop come. I'll get 'em.'"[12]

Five years later the violence in the U.S. is all-pervasive, yet the school's critics and reformers seem as unaware of it as they are unconscious of the transformation of the home and of our changed population — or, if they are aware of the violence, they are quite confident that it is not education's concern. Mindless imitation is, however, the easiest path for someone to follow who has not been trained to bring intelligence to bear on living. In the best of cases, education for spectatorship teaches students to lead divided lives — to apply their intelligence when observing the world but to be unthinking doers. In the worst of cases, it consigns them to the nasty, brutish, and short life that the philosopher Thomas Hobbes long ago attributed to the state of nature.

Choosing Integrative Activities of Living

It is sheer folly to expect our young to live and work together at home and in the world if they have never, ever learned to do so. Yet the restorationists would devote little or no curriculum space to the enormous range of ways of acting and forms of living that the young of any nation need to learn. In contrast, in the schoolhome, mind and body, thought and action, reason and emotion are all educated. Furthermore, if the occupations that children pursue there are well-chosen, they will integrate these elements in such a way that they in turn can be integrated into the lives those young people lead both in school and in the world.

When school is a surrogate home, children of all ages and both sexes not only engage in the domestic activities that ground their everyday lives there — e.g., planning, cooking, and serving meals and cleaning, maintaining, and repairing the physical plant — but they also participate in one or more of the integrative endeavors that stand at the very center of the curriculum.

Let me briefly list the integrative potential of two such activities — theater and newspaper. To begin with, theater and newspaper spin webs of theoretical knowledge in which students can be "caught." One thinks immediately of language, literature, and social studies, but serious ethical and legal questions also arise in the course of producing plays and publications. Moreover, for those who engage in these activities, mathematical, scientific, and technical knowledge loom large. Furthermore, besides spinning webs of knowledge, theater and newspaper spin webs of skills, such as reading, writing, speaking, listening, drawing, designing, and building. In so doing, they connect

mind and body, thought and action. By reaching out to every human emotion, they also join both head and hand to heart.

The webs of knowledge and skill that theater and newspaper weave and the integration of thought and action and of reason and emotion that they effect might in themselves justify placing these activities at the center of curriculum. Their integrative claims are enhanced, however, by the fact that social interdependence is built into them from the start. Through the demands of the shared task as well as the realization that everyone's efforts not only count but are vitally important, participants become bonded to one another. These two activities have the added integrative advantage that their products — the plays performed, the newspapers published — can be designed to speak to everyone's experience and to be seen or read by everyone. Tying together the shared emotions that derive from common experiences, the activities can weave young people of different races, classes, ethnicities, physical abilities, and sexual orientations into their own webs of connection.

The Objectives of the Schoolhome

Since there are numerous activities that can be integrative in these several different ways, the decision as to which ones to make the linchpins of any particular schoolhome curriculum must, I think, be based on local considerations, not the least of which are the interests and talents of both the teaching staff and the students. This, of course, means that, as local conditions change, so perhaps will the choice of integrative activities.

I also want to stress that, although theater and newspaper — or, for that matter, farming and building a historical museum — easily lend themselves to vocationalism and professionalism, these are not the interests that the schoolhome represents. Its concern is that the children in its care receive an education for living and working together in the world. Thus the schoolhome is not a training ground for actors, architects, or journalists. Its students put

on plays, raise crops, or put out a newspaper not to win competitions or add to their résumés. The best student actor by Broadway or Hollywood standards does not necessarily play the lead; the best feature writer or cartoonist does not necessarily get published. Rather, the schoolhome is a moral equivalent of home where this nation's children can develop into constructive, contributing members of culture and society — individuals who want to live in a world composed of people very different from themselves and who have practiced doing so. As I envision it, the schoolhome is also a place that possesses and projects a larger point of view: that of this nation itself — and ultimately the whole world of nations and the planet Earth — as a moral equivalent of home.

1. John Dewey, *The School and Society* (Chicago: University of Chicago Press, 1956), p. 12.

2. The material in this paragraph is drawn from Jane Roland Martin, "Fatal Inaction: Overcoming School's Reluctance to Become a Moral Equivalent of Home," paper presented at the American Montessori Society Seminar, Detroit, April 1994.

3. Kevin O'Leary, "Police: 3 Boys Dealing Cocaine," *Boston Globe*, 10 February 1994.

4. Mike Barnicle, "Dropping Our Eyes at True Evil," *Boston Globe*, 25 February 1994.

5. Sherry B. Ortner, "Is Female to Male as Nature Is to Culture?," in Michelle Zimbalist Rosaldo and Louise Lamphere, eds., *Women, Culture, and Society* (Stanford, Calif.: Stanford University Press, 1974), pp. 67-87.

6. Harlan Lane, *The Wild Boy of Aveyron* (Cambridge, Mass.: Harvard University Press, 1979).

7. Jane Roland Martin, "Two Dogmas of Curriculum," *Synthese*, vol. 51, 1982, pp. 5-20.

8. William James, "A Moral Equivalent of War," in Richard A. Wasserstrom, ed., *War and Morality* (Belmont, Calif.: Wadsworth, 1970), pp. 4-14.

9. See, for example, Bernard Bailyn, *Education in the Forming of American Society* (New York: Vintage, 1960); and Lawrence Cremin, *The Genius of American Education* (New York: Vintage, 1965).

10. There is an implicit value judgment in the notion of heritage as I use it. In the broad sense of the term, murder, rape, and so on are part of our heritage. I speak here, however, only of that portion of it that is worthwhile.

11. Jane Roland Martin, "Needed: A New Paradigm for Liberal Education," in Jonas P. Soltis, ed., *Philosophy and Education: 80th NSSE Yearbook, Part I* (Chicago: National Society for the Study of Education, University of Chicago Press, 1981).

12. Linda Ann Banks, letter to the editor, *Boston Globe*, 14 June 1989; and Sally Jacobs and Kevin Cullen, "Gang Rivalry on the Rise in Boston," *Boston Globe*, 16 March 1989.

Preparing for the 21st Century:
The EFG Experiment

Joel A. Barker

Joel Barker is a consultant and expert in future studies. A former educator himself, he works with corporations and organizations around the world to communicate his principles—including the importance of "vision" and the paradigm shift.

As I stood at the door of the school on August 29, 1994, I realized that what I had started talking about sixteen years ago was now a reality. The first EFG School in the world was beginning its first day.

I considered all the history that had transpired to make this day happen:

- The five-page essay I had delivered at a global education conference at the Aspen Institute in the summer of 1978 and the initial rejection of the concept by almost everyone there.
- The call from Barbara Barnes in 1988 to speak to a group of teachers in California, and her immediate commitment to the idea.
- The five summer workshops that Barbara then organized from 1989 to 1994—Irvine; Tahoe; Erie; Doncaster, U.K.; and then Chattanooga—where teachers and administrators came on their own time and with their own money to carefully measure the EFG concept and then develop working units. Each of the schools had gone back and implemented one or more of the units within their traditional school systems.
- And now, in Chattanooga, the first school totally committed to applying the EFG curriculum concepts, called the 21st Century Preparatory School. It was initiated under the leadership of Dr. Harry Reynolds, the city school's superintendent, and with the constant tutelage and support of Barbara Barnes, who worked with the new faculty and administration.

What makes this school so different from other schools? Two major assumptions; one about competency and one about curriculum.

Assumption #1:
Education is NOT a race to be won
but a pathway to be climbed.

Without this beginning premise, education in America cannot change. For too long, we have focused on a time-oriented school structure in which, at the end of a given time, we see where our students are in their competencies. Those who have fulfilled the goals within the set time are given A's. And the remainder of the grades are parceled out based on their distance from the competencies we set as targets.

We have justified this kind of evaluation based on "the real world." And, if you have taught all your life and never been out in the real world, it makes sense. But it is a false picture of what goes on out there.

Especially with the advent of total quality and continuous improvement, the real world now actively understands and practices the following behavior:

Don't release a new product or service until it does what it is supposed to do in a consistent and competent way.

Ford Motor Company made a decision *not* to release the newly designed Thunderbird before year-end in 1982 because it did not yet meet their quality standards. Ford knew that a December release would allow them to compete for

 From *Educational Horizons*, Fall 1994, pp. 12-17. © 1994 by Pi Lambda Theta, Inc. Reprinted by permission.

"Car of the Year," and the Thunderbird was the best new American car. They also knew that award would increase sales as much as 10 percent. And that meant hundreds of millions of dollars of extra revenue.

Yet they did not release the car until it met their specifications for quality. It came out in January 1983, too late for the award, but truly qualified for the customer.

We release our children with a diploma that is measured by the race, not the pathway. Ford was following a pathway and the time issue was not the critical issue; the performance was.

How many of our children would be ready for life if they only had another year in school focusing on the weaknesses that needed special attention? But when you race, you *cannot* spend the extra time, because you are using time as the separator.

The EFG School focuses on giving its students competencies, however long it takes. So there is not a K-12 structure in the school. It is, instead, K-Competency.

Think about it: if your goal is to climb the mountain, do you care if you take an extra day to get there compared to others on the pathway?

K-Competency is about climbing the mountain. Think about it: if your

goal is to climb the mountain, do you care if you take an extra day to get there compared to others on the pathway? Of course not. You will get to the top.

This point of view—the pathway view—allows for great variability in student differences without having the "slower" ones feel judged. Schools with a pathway view are implicitly saying to their students, "We want you to be competent in important skills of life and we will take whatever time it requires to help you become competent."

Outward Bound Schools now routinely take people with physical handicaps on expeditions such as canoe trips, hiking trips, sailing trips, mountaineering trips. When they first started thinking about doing these kinds of trips, "normal" people thought they were crazy. "How are you going to get a wheelchair in a canoe?" was a common question. But the Outward Bound schools understood that such a question missed the essence of the event. You see, the correct answer to such a question is simply "whichever way we can." And then you go and do it. Because it is the trip that counts, not the specific dilemmas you have to overcome to take the trip.

Pathways can be found to the top of the mountain if you start with the assumption that it is worthwhile for everyone to get to the top. So what if some students have to spend more time learning statistics than other students? What you want in the end is that all students have high-level understanding and application skills of statistics.

Jaime Escalante, the heroic calculus teacher in East Los Angeles, proved exactly that point when he took barrio students—*who should not even have been in a calculus class according to the norms of the school*—and with their consent spent extraordinary amounts of time leading them up the pathway to the calculus summit. He helped them become competent because he did not follow

time formulas for their learning. He followed pathway formulas. We must never forget:

The cost of competency is always cheaper than the alternative.

Assumption #2:
Curriculum must be obviously connected to the real world of the 21st Century

Or to put it another way: The best technology in the world cannot make an irrelevant curriculum successful.

I started my work as a teacher in 1966. I taught for seven years. Then I left teaching and moved into the real world. I call it the real world because there was no tenure; you could not close your door and leave the world outside; almost all the work was tied to teams; and performance was measured by outcomes. If you did not meet the outcomes set by you and your management, you could lose your job. And if you did make your objectives, you were given accolades and pay raises. Performance counted for more than any other single variable. In almost every aspect, the real world was the opposite of the world of secondary education teaching.

What did I learn out there in the real world? Simply that education should prepare students to be active citizens by teaching them *directly* about those elements of the world they will most often encounter and be responsible for. Thus the EFGs were developed: Ecological Education, Futures Education, and Global Education.

Ecological Education
Ecological Education focuses on the first of three crucial relationship questions: *What is the relationship between the human species and the rest of the living creatures on this planet?*

The test for the utility of Eco Ed can be performed by asking a single question: Do we believe our children will have to make important and frequent decisions about the environment in the 21st century?

When I ask children this question, they give an emphatic "Yes." When I ask their parents this question, they also say yes. When I ask top executives of major corporations if they think their future employees will have to do that, they laugh and say, "We need them to do that now!"

Here is an example of why ecological education is so needed. In *The Ecology of Commerce*, Paul Hawken writes on the dangers of organochlorines that have been manufactured by humans during the past century. He speaks to their universality and their danger and explains to his readers that they are not metabolized by naturally occurring organisms: "Biologically speaking, our metabolic processes have little or no effect on rendering these substances into more harmless forms, because whales, swordfish, polar bears, and human beings have never in their evolutionary history encountered chemicals similar to organochlorines."[1] Hawken claims that these manmade chemicals are uniquely new in the biological history of the world and environmentally disastrous.[2]

A student [in] an EFG school would understand what organochlorines and organohalogens (part of the family, so to speak) are and would also know the following:

Immense quantities of organochlorines and other organohalogen chemicals occur *naturally* in our biosphere. . . . Tetrachloroethylene, chloroform, carbon tetrachloride, methylene chloride, and several natural CFCs have been detected in the emissions of the Santiaguito volcano of Guatemala and Kamchatka volcanoes of Siberia. . . . Chlorine is as natural to our world as carbon, oxygen, and hydrogen.[3]

These words were written, not by some PR flack for Union Carbide, but by Gordon W. Gribble, professor of chemistry at Dartmouth College.[4] So what is the point? Without solid understanding of the sciences of biology, chemistry, and physics along with systems thinking and statistics, claims like Paul Hawken makes can only be taken on faith.

Ecologically educated students will not be fooled into taking partial accounts as the whole account. And that means our children will make wiser decisions about our environment and not be panicked, through scientific ignorance, into making unwise ones.

> *. . . [O]ur children will make wiser decisions about our environment and not be panicked, through scientific ignorance, into making unwise ones.*

By the way, I am not suggesting that we ought to ignore the consequences of spreading nasty chemicals indiscriminately across the planet. I am suggesting that only an educated populace can keep people who take extreme positions from misrepresenting the situation.

What makes up Ecological Education? It is the sciences plus mathematics, driven strongly by statistics. But these elements are taught not as chemistry five days per week, one hour each day; rather, environmental projects are begun and whatever chemistry, physics, biology, statistics, or botany needed for the project is taught within that context.

The accumulation of chemistry knowledge will occur over the entire pathway of education. And I believe students will know much more chemistry and biology and physics because they will have always learned it within the context of an important community environmental question.

At the Chattanooga school, the first Eco Ed project, "Water—H20H," focuses on the river because Chattanooga is a river city. Students will be measuring rate of flow, water analysis, and biota analysis. They will examine the living creatures that live around the river as well as those living in the river. They will examine the kinds of elements now being put in the river by the city, by run-off from farmland, by factories, by nature herself. This river project will last about a month and will involve students of ages ranging from four years old to fourteen years old—the entire age range of the school. Their goal is to produce a document they can present to the city to help the city think about the river's present state, its future, and its relationship to the future of the city.

Futures Education

Futures Education is the second domain of the EFGs. Its focus is on *the human relationship with time—past, present, and future*. Where did we come from? Where are we going? How do we prepare for the life ahead?

The test question for the relevance of this domain is: Do we believe that our children will have to anticipate the future, understand the implications of emerging trends, make decisions about new innovations, and plan for the future with greater care than we did? Everyone I ask answers yes.

Futures education is made up of many elements, including the study of history. But at Chattanooga, we plan to study history backward. We will start with 1994 and ask, How did we get here? What decisions were made that brought about the

EFG Curriculum Competencies:

Ecological Domain

An ecologically educated person:
• has a working knowledge of the planet
• understands his or her own role within an ecosystem
• understands the positive and negative effects he or she can have on the planet
• can use their knowledge and skills to improve the environment

Futures Domain

A futures-educated person:
• understands the relationship between past, present, and future actions
• has learned and can apply a broad range of futures thinking tools
• understands the responsibility for thinking about long-term implications of actions and innovations before instituting them
• feels empowered to effect, adapt to, and respond to change

Global Domain

A globally educated person:
• has broad knowledge of the cultures of the world
• has deep knowledge of a culture other than one's own
• is fluent in a language other than one's own
• accepts responsibility for helping establish global stability, justice, and peace

1994 we are now experiencing? Then we will step back and ask those questions again, always looking for the results of decisions made further back in history that led to the historical time we are studying.

This approach is especially useful because the students will always see the connection with their own time. Typically, the study of history keeps the punch line of connection until the end of the year. Too often, the class runs out of time before they make it to the present, so the connections are never really completed.

Besides history, Futures Ed will also include the following:

Economics—it determines so much of the world's behavior today and attempts, usually unsuccessfully, to forecast the future.

Philosophy—why are we here?

Psychology—trying to understand ourselves and how we look at the world around us.

The study of paradigms and paradigm shifts—helps explain how the future gets discovered and how many options still remain to be discovered.

The study of innovation and technology—both have become key drivers in our world.

Futures thinking tools—TIPS Teams™, trend tracking, the Implications Wheel™, the Strategy Matrix™, the cross-impact matrix, scenario writing, visioning, forecasting, anticipation trees™.[5] Many of these tools are now being taught only to managers of major institutions. But in the 21st century they will be part of the normal skills of any employee, just as adding and subtracting are now.

Nutrition and physical education—how taking care of yourself today allows you to shape your own future.

Science fiction—not as a predictive source of information, but to see how coherent stories of the future can be told and to examine how *wrong* most sci-

ence fiction writers have been about the future.

Music making, studio arts—both activities reinforce the creative skills needed to imagine and represent images of the future.

Community service—because to help the community as an adult, our children must practice that behavior as students. This is not about volunteerism, which is another kind of activity altogether. It is about being part of shaping the future at a neighborhood level.

The overall goal of futures education is to give students an understanding of how we got here, where we could go, and how many choices will have to be made to get there.

The first Futures Ed project at Chattanooga will focus on wellness and integrate many of the specific elements above into a multi-week program. The program will involve personal assessment and prediction and lots of nutrition education, including computer analysis and re-design of school lunches (with the active help of the food service staff) to make them more healthful. The school will also visit the Tennessee Valley Authority wellness center and talk to adults about why they keep fit and what the benefits are.

The overall goal of futures education is to give the students an understanding of how we got here, where we could go, and how many choices will have to be made to get there.

Global Education

The third domain of this curriculum deals with *the relationship with all other people on the planet.*

The test question for utility of this domain is: Do we believe our children are going to have to interact in significant ways with people from other cultures around the world? Or another way to ask the question is: how many calls a week, in the 21st century, do you believe our children will receive from places other than the United States of America?

It is clear that if we want our children to be full participants in the world of the 21st Century they must have much greater global knowledge than they have now.

The components of this domain are:

- Foreign languages
- Political geography
- World history (yes, this is a repeat)
- Anthropology
- Sociology
- Social studies
- World literature
- World music
- World art
- Study of the world's religions
- World travel

For many the word religion raises a red flag. All of us who have been working on the EFG curriculum believe that without clear understanding of the religions of the world and their histories, it is impossible to understand what is going on out there. It is time to stop the debate about whether or not religion should be taught in the school and make sure we start teaching *about* religions if we expect our children to be wise and thoughtful world citizens.

At the Chattanooga school, the faculty decided to start their global education emphasis by focusing on foreign languages. Eight languages will be introduced during the school year. The goal is to give children exposure to these languages and a "marketplace" vocabulary that would let them get along at a minimum level in the culture speaking that language. The languages to be taught are: American standard English, Russian, German, Spanish, Chinese, Japanese, French, and Portuguese.

The Blends and the Core

E, F, and G are the major domains of the curriculum. If you look at the Venn diagram that represents the relationship of these three domains, you see the "blends": EF, FG, GE. These shared spaces capture more of the real world where several kinds of relationships occur at the same time.

As an example, Motorola is planning to put up a universal satellite communications system called Iridium. This project has huge implications for the future of communications and also has a direct impact on many cultures that do not have modern communications. That's an FG blend discussion.

At the center of the diagram is the core. The core represents all those skills needed in all the other domains and blends. Many of the core skills are from the universal school of all ages; others are completely new for the 21st century— word processing; data base management; thought presentation via computer graphics; total quality; and continuous improvement skills. The values of the community and values discussions based on Stephen Covey's work also appear in the core.

The two major assumptions of the school about competency and curriculum have driven its design. There are also many smaller pieces to the puzzle that are being fine-tuned even as you read this.

The EFG school does not pretend that it has all the answers. But what we do know *for sure* is that if America does not determine what is the best education for the 21st century, we cannot expect our children to be ready to accept the responsibilities awaiting them.

It is our responsibility to find an answer, and the sooner, the better.

1. Paul Hawken, *The Ecology of Commerce*, (Harperbusiness, 1993).
2. Ibid.
3. Letters, *Science News* (23 April 1994): 259.
4. Ibid.
5. Joel Barker, Infinity Limited, Inc.

SEARCHING FOR TERMS

Rick Wilber

Rick Wilber is a journalism professor at the School of Mass Communications at the University of South Florida.

S it down at your computer keyboard, move that mouse around on its pad, click on an icon or two, and log onto a good data base. Now, type in a few search terms that have to do with education and its use of emerging technologies.

If that didn't make any sense to you, just ask your children for help. They'll know what it means. More than 97 percent of American elementary schools and high schools have computers for student use these days,[1] so you can bet your children will be comfortable—probably a lot more comfortable than you are—with the digital future. To them, a mouse is a device you use to move a cursor around on a computer screen, and the idea of using particular search terms to dive into a data base seems quite the ordinary way to do a little research for that high school term paper.

To research the new technologies and their impact on our children's education, try terms like *elementary* and *education* and *technology,* or *elementary* or *secondary* and *technology,* or if you want to narrow things down, add the words *future* and *quality* or the catch-phrase *multimedia.* Anything similar to those terms should jog the enormous memory of the data base.

Wait a few seconds, and watch what comes up on the screen. When I tried the first few terms recently on Nexis (a leading data base that collects full text from thousands of newspapers, magazines, and other sources), I confined the search to recent magazine articles and still had more than a thousand "hits," or stories where the terms were used. Limiting the search by adding the terms *quality* and *future* narrowed things down some, but there were still hundreds of hits.

THE INFORMATION AGE: A HOT TOPIC NOW

N ot only does my little exercise in modern research show how quick and effective a data base search can be these days, but it also shows how hot this topic is. Educators nationwide are working hard to find the best ways to make use of the new technologies to improve the way we teach our children.

We all know the bad news—the horrific anecdotes and statistics of violence and fear in some schools, of illiterate high school graduates, of declining test scores and the subsequent dumbing down of America.

Some of this is media hyperbole. The percentage of high school graduates who enrolled in a college or university, after all, was at an all-time high of 63 percent in 1992. And the percentage of high school students who graduated was just over 71 percent. So the news is not all bad.[2]

But are those graduates ready for the work force or college? And what of the 29 percent who didn't graduate, some four hundred thousand young people who dropped out? What kind of future do they face?

1. World Almanac and Book of Facts, 1994.

2. World Almanac.

These are compelling worries. Something has to be done, or America's very future will be in doubt.

There must be a way to revive America's educational system, a way to raise the standards, do a better job of teaching, produce better students, better citizens.

Maybe the information age (coming right at you on the newly minted information highway) offers us that something, that answer. After all, many of the educational experts say, computer technology has the ability to lower costs while increasing educational quality. All we have to do is make the initial investment and wait for the educational and societal profits to roll in.

Elementary students, these experts promise us, will learn the basics better if only we use these new tools properly. And at the high school level, the information highway and its technological side streets will help today's students prepare better for the needs of the workplace of tomorrow.

As a longtime professor of journalism who has watched the writing skills of our entering students decline for some two decades, I certainly hope these experts are right. And as a writer of science fiction stories, I find these new technologies fascinating and full of promise. They are a kind of science fictional future rushing into reality so quickly that the futurists can barely stay ahead of the game.

But it is as the father of a three-year-old girl that I find the entire issue of education and technology of preeminent importance. Like most parents, my wife and I worry for little Samantha's educational future. Will her schooling be safe, interesting, useful, exciting, and worthwhile? Will it help us prepare her for what lies ahead in a world that promises to be very different from the one we are in now?

THESE TECHNOLOGIES IN ELEMENTARY AND SECONDARY EDUCATION

There are, it seems to me, several ways that these technologies promise to have a positive impact—perhaps a dramatic one—on elementary and secondary education.

But there are also several major roadblocks—some of them financial, some institutional, some just personal reluctance on the part of teachers and administrators—in the way of realizing this promise.

And one major issue that the information age brings to us seems to me, as a writer, a teacher, and a parent, to be so profound that it threatens to change one of the most basic tenets of education as we've known it for two hundred years. Article after article in magazines like *Technology Review*, *PC World*, *T.H.E.* (Technological Horizons in Education) *Journal*, and *CD-ROM World* point out that if today's students don't have the skills to navigate properly, they will be, literally and metaphorically, lost while driving down that information highway at breakneck speed.

A few of the "new" technologies having an impact in current education aren't really very new at all. There is a flurry of interest at the college level in televised (and videotaped) lectures, for instance. The relatively low cost of equipment combined with improvements in quality have prompted renewed interest in television during this era of tight budgets and demand for increased teacher productivity.

The televised lecture has some obvious advantages. Such classes are not necessarily time- or space-dependent, for one thing. On many campuses, a student can either watch the lecture live from a remote location or have access to a videotape of the class. The videotape means that the student can replay the lecture at his leisure, stopping and starting as needed to make note taking easier and to help understand particularly difficult information or concepts.

Also, using even low-cost television production techniques can provide appealing, if minimal (at most campuses), special effects to enhance the presentation of the material. It's quite possible, as a matter of fact, that a lecture as seen on the TV screen may be more effective than the live presentation in the lecture hall.

But there are significant drawbacks to the televised lecture, too, even at the college level.

When students watch a lecture on videotape, they can't interact with the lec-

PRÉCIS

With the recent arrival of video and new computer technologies, the opportunity is at hand for enormous change and dramatic improvement in the U.S. education system. The changes may be so profound, in fact, that the very need for literacy is eliminated.

On the college level, televised lectures are becoming a reality on many campuses. Instead of gathering at a central lecture hall, students may go to several satellite rooms to see the professor, or master teacher, on a video monitor as he delivers his lecture. The presentation becomes interactive through a video camera and microphones in each satellite room that are linked to the professor, who is able to answer the students' questions.

On the elementary and secondary school levels, the computer—with its ability to retrieve vast quantities of information through CD-ROMs and on-line databases—is beginning to assume the position of a master teacher, replacing the traditional classroom teacher. The computer's software is able to present information in an entertaining, informative way to the student, and the classroom teacher becomes an assistant to the electronic teacher, helping students understand the presented material, while occasionally expanding on it.

Ultimately, it may transpire that most entertainment and communication will be accomplished without the need for reading and writing, making literacy a less important social and professional value.

The problem of interaction is at least partially solved by requiring students to see the lecture live at their remote site, where graduate assistants or other teachers should be available to answer questions. In these cases the on-screen lecturer serves as a sort of master teacher, using available visuals to enhance the lecture and counting on the on-site teachers to explain or clarify as needed.

Indeed, at many universities the format uses the "teleconferencing" idea, in much the same way that corporate America does. A centrally televised presenter lectures, and microphones at each remote site allow for questions to be asked of the principal lecturer. A camera at each site, and some extra monitors at the central location, mean the lecturer can see the questioner as well as hear the request.

This method is effective, in terms of both communication and cost, at the college level, but even teleconferencing doesn't solve all the problems, especially from the students' perspective. Even with interaction, televised lectures can be both intimidating and distant for too many students. They don't have the courage to stand up in front of a camera and ask a question, and they miss the relative personal warmth of a real live person in the front of the lecture hall.

Another problem is that televised lectures are heavily dependent on the entertainment skills of the master teacher to communicate through this medium. The best informed teacher, unfortunately, is not always the best entertainer, and few things are as tedious as a poorly presented television lecture.

Still, the televised lecture works and is again in vogue on many campuses, perhaps primarily because administrators love it for its cost effectiveness, if nothing else.

At elementary and high school levels the televised lecture has a whole new set of problems, compounded by the relative immaturity of the audience and the inability of the teacher to have constant interaction with each student.

CD–ROM TECHNOLOGY

Other technologies, though, hold great promise for younger students. CD–ROMs, on-line services, and the data bases that

turer—they can't immediately ask questions or get clarification as they can in real time. It is ironic that video's lack of interaction should be such a stumbling block at exactly the same time as the newer multimedia technologies—CD-ROMs and computer networks, principally—gain a major part of their appeal from being interactive.

CD–ROMs, on-line services, and the data bases that come with both form the troika of new technology that is poised to lead our elementary and high school education system into dramatic change.

come with both form the troika of new technology that is poised, if we let it (or even if we don't), to lead our elementary and high school education system into dramatic change.

CD–ROMs (compact *d*isk, *r*ead *o*nly *m*emory) are disks that can store hundreds of millions of characters' worth of information that a special disk player (attached by cable to a computer) can read by laser. When you use a CD–ROM you may read text, hear music or other sounds, and see visual images, some of them in motion.

When the three-year-old in our home, for instance, wanted to learn something about elephants we might, in the past, have described one to her, drawn a picture, looked up a picture in a book, or, best case, have taken her to a zoo that has an elephant. But alas, our local zoo has no elephants, and the animals were surprisingly hard to find in the dozens of books lining the shelves in her room.

Enter the new family computer with its CD–ROM. We looked up "elephant" in the encyclopedia disk that slides into the CD–ROM with a gentle click and quickly found information in the form of text. Also on the screen were a number of other choices for other kinds of information. With a quick move of the mouse and a click or two, we saw a picture of an elephant, heard its bellow, and then watched it amble off into the thicket with the rest of the herd.

Now that sort of multimedia approach is undeniably an effective way to teach a child about elephants or electrons, government, geography, or anything else you can think of.

CD–ROM technology offers an incredible array of knowledge available at the touch of a keyboard or the slight movement of a mouse and a double click, and the number of CD–ROMs is rapidly increasing. But they aren't the only new thing out there.

COMPUTER NETWORKS

Many educators these days extol the benefits of teachers and students joining computer networks.

There are a number of cases now where students in one elementary or high school communicate regularly with students from another via computer. They can share information, work on projects together, or even gossip through e-mail (electronic mail).

Also, there are a number of on-line services, companies that offer access to a wide variety of data bases, computer bulletin boards, special on-line publications, and much more—the list of possibilities seems to grow daily.

These services range from the vast Internet through the growing, prosperous on-line services like Prodigy, America Online, Genie, CompuServe, and others all the way down to local bulletin boards, where relatively few people in one town can share information.

Computers interconnected in this way offer a powerful means of sharing information and knowledge. Using our computers, another writer and I are collaborating on a novel, sending chapters back and forth to each other through computers connected by telephone lines—a process that takes only a few minutes instead of the several days it would take by mail.

Such computerized collaboration has the added advantage of the chapters being instantly incorporated into our computer software (in our case, WordPerfect, a popular word-processing program), so that we already have them stored and can edit or print them out as needed.

Teachers, administrators, and students, of course, are already doing much the same thing with research, bureaucratic paperwork, term papers, and more.

Many educators these days extol the benefits of teachers and students joining computer networks.

From the computer networks you can also find access to the data bases, like Nexis/Lexis. There are a number of these, and they all offer quick access to information that would have taken days to uncover just a few years ago. Now it is the work of minutes.

IMPROVING QUALITY WHILE CUTTING COSTS

One example of the way that technology could be used to improve quality and cut cost is offered by Lohn O'Looney in an article in *Phi Delta Kappan* magazine.[3]

O'Looney suggests an alternative to the current heavily stratified, top-down educational structure, where one teacher routinely spends a relatively short time with a student and then passes him on to the next teacher, and where various administrative levels handle the paperwork associated with each student, rarely giving the teacher a look but amassing a lot of paperwork that has little educationally useful information.

His case management system, based on current trends in corporate America, depends heavily on generalist teachers who would stay with students for longer periods of time than the traditional semester or year.

"Shared data bases and expert systems, in combination with a redesigned work environment, could help generalist teachers educate children more effectively," he argues.

Using this computer-dependent approach, he says, "A single teacher could: (1) use data bases and computer networks both to enter and to extract information that would be of actual use to that teacher and to other teachers, as well as infor-

mation that is currently compiled and processed by administrators; (2) teach a group of children for as long a period of time as the bonds of teacher/student relationship appear to warrant; and (3) teach—or, perhaps more accurately, facilitate—lessons in a variety of subject-matter areas. This facilitation would make use of an assortment of computer-based instructional systems, individual diagnostic programs, and support from expert systems."

O'Looney believes the case management approach can eliminate numerous administrative positions, counter the "alienation of teachers who feel they have no control over their work environment or the outcome of their work, make creative and powerful use of information technologies" that are often poorly used, and finally, promote "more stable and more psychologically productive teacher/student/parent relationships."

It's a grand idea. As he points out, data bases, interactive CD–ROMs, on-line services, and the rest mean that students will have ready access to the factual information they need to progress through a body of knowledge at their own pace. So teachers, in effect, will spend most of their time helping students acquire the knowledge from the computer, not lecturing on the material. In this sense, the teacher becomes a kind of coach, a facilitator, for students, and if a solid teacher-student bond is formed, there is no reason why one teacher could not spend several years with a particular student or group of students.

THE ONE-ROOM SCHOOLHOUSE

This idea seems to be, in some ways, a return to the days of the rural one-room schoolhouse, and perhaps that's good. One hundred fifty years ago, a single teacher with a

3. Lohn O'Looney, "Redesigning the Work of Education," *Phi Delta Kappan*, January 1993, 375.

group of students ranging in ability and age from those just starting their education to those ready for high school or college could meet the needs of each one as long as the number of students wasn't overwhelming. After all, the body of knowledge was much smaller, the competitive pressures less acute on both students and teacher, and the bond between them often a productive one that encouraged learning.

But the one-room schoolhouse couldn't compete with mass production. The current school structure follows a pattern that has its roots in the Industrial Revolution, one based on mass production techniques. Anyone who has read Charles Dickens' *Hard Times* has seen what this system can be like carried to its extreme. Still, it served us well in its time, doing an average job for the average student and generally educating the masses to a level that society found useful. Most adults today went through an educational system based, for the most part, on these techniques.

O'Looney raises the argument that just as industry has had to retool and rethink how to produce products—abandoning, in many cases, the principles of assembly line mass production—the educational system must do the same, and computer-based case management techniques hold great promise.

PROBLEMS WITH INCORPORATING THESE TECHNOLOGIES INTO THE SCHOOL SYSTEM

There are, as you might suspect, some problems with incorporating case management style into the educational setting. The first is reluctance on the part of administrators, who see it not only as expensive and experimental (two words that do not make a typical administrator happy), but also as a threat. For if successful, the case management approach would mean fewer administrators are needed and perhaps a smaller support staff all around. That sounds pretty menacing to current school administrators.

But an equally troublesome problem is reluctance on the part of teachers. This new system asks something very different of the typical elementary or high school teacher from what has been asked before. Under the new system, there is no need to pour information into the students—the computers do that. Instead, the teacher must learn new techniques to help the students learn.

These new techniques are interpersonal, and just learning how to work with students in this new way will be a challenge for many teachers. There are serious technological hurdles as well. Teachers will have to be on comfortable, even expert, terms with the computers themselves if they are to expect their students to use them daily as the major source of information.

Teachers who can't show students how to use the computer to find information, or can't help them work their way through a particularly demanding piece of educational software, will not be of much use as facilitators.

THE VIDEO-CLASS APPROACH

In a sense, this new approach is reflective of the video-class approach that has been around for some time. The computer and its software become the master teacher, presenting information in an entertaining, informative way to the student. And the classroom teacher becomes an assistant to the electronic master teacher, helping students understand the material presented, expanding on it from time to time but primarily helping the student to learn through the ongoing encounter with the software.

This new system asks something very different of the typical elementary or high school teacher from what has been asked before.

A number of such software packages already exist, and many more are in the works, though slow acceptance of the new technology by school systems has, in turn, slowed the software makers' progress. But the numbers suggest, as we'll see in a bit, that the interactive future is, for the most part, already here. The educational establishment, like it or not, is going to have to deal with an information age future.

If one looks a little further ahead, an even more ambitious variant of how we might use computers is possible, one where each student will have access to virtually any information he could need to learn almost anything.

Seymour Papert, Lego Professor of Learning Research at the MIT Media Laboratory, asserts that the new technologies make it possible at last for the educational establishment to undertake dramatic, effective change in the way we teach our children. "No technical obstacle stands in the way of making a machine—let's call it the Knowledge Machine—that would put the power to know what others know [into the hands of students]," he writes. Having this material readily available, he adds, means a typical elementary student, for instance, could,

> using speech, touch, or gestures, . . . steer the machine to the topic of interest, quickly navigating through a knowledge space much broader than the contents of any printed encyclopedia. Whether she is interested in giraffes or panthers or fleas, whether she wants to see them eating, sleeping, running, fighting, or birthing, she would be able to find her way to the relevant sounds and images. This availability will one day extend to experiencing the smell and touch of being with animals.[4]

Imagine its capacity to teach.

THE DECLINE OF READING?

But think of some of the implications, too. On the negative side, this near-future world of Knowledge Machines, or CD–ROMS, data bases, and on-line information, spells

danger to those who think that reading is the main route to learning. For the fact is that reading and writing, or at least some elements of both skills, are terribly threatened by this new technology.

With a CD–ROM, you can be informed and entertained at great depth, and yet you don't really have to read much and have little need to memorize. It's that simple. Reading and retention skills aren't really necessary.

Of course, some minimal skills are useful. But the idea of teaching a high school student to write a cogent three-page essay seems terribly irrelevant in an age where no one needs that approach to sharing information or entertaining. With multimedia computerized sources of information, the acquisition of knowledge becomes something that is entertaining, easy, and powerful—and it doesn't require that you read much.

One of the major difficulties in teaching reading and writing skills to current elementary and secondary students is that they have little need to apply those skills outside the classroom setting. For them, most forms of entertainment and communication are accomplished without reading and writing skills.

CD–ROMs, just now making their way into many homes, add a whole new level of difficulty for the teacher who wants to impart some reading and writing skills. For most students, reading is likely to become more and more of an academic activity, like geography or mathematics or history—something learned for its own sake, not for its actual utility in the lives of the students.

As Papert points out,

> Written language is not likely to be abandoned. But we need to think anew about the position assigned to it as the prerequisite to children's accumulation of knowledge. Children who grow up with the opportunity to explore the jungles and the cities and the deep oceans and ancient myths and outer space will be even less likely than the players of video games to sit quietly through anything even vaguely resembling the elementary school curriculum as we now know it. And why should they?[5]

---

4. "The Children's Machine," *Technology Review,* July 1993, 28. This article was adapted from Seymour Papert's book *The Children's Machine: Rethinking School in the Age of the Computer* (New York: Basic Books, 1993).

5. Seymour Papert, "The Children's Machine" *Technology Review,* July 1993, 28.

In a few years, perhaps, someone putting together an article like this will not need a keyboard at all, but instead will pull together a wide variety of illustrations, sound bites, graphs, charts, and copy to get the same information across to the reader, er, user.

Clearly, what Papert and others are pointing out is that the opportunity is there for great change in the educational system. The new technologies offer the chance for dramatic improvements in the ways we teach, while also containing some very real threats to the methods we have thought most basic for some two centuries. Literacy, in effect, may no longer be necessary.

HOW SOON WILL ALL THIS HAPPEN?

One could argue that it won't happen all that fast, that teachers' reluctance and administrators' fear will slow the acceptance of this approach in schools. It might be said that it is all still too expensive, and that it discriminates between the more affluent students able to afford it at home and the less affluent, who will be forced to make do with the archaic idea of teachers lecturing them and then reading material in books or using the occasional computer found these days in even the most underfunded of school districts.

And there is some merit to that argument. After all, while 97 percent of schools nationwide have computers, only 20 percent of students have access to their own computer, and only a little over 10 percent of personal computers currently have a CD–ROM drive.[6]

6. Don Menn, "Multimedia in Education," *PC World*, October 1993, M52.

However, not only is the number of home CD–ROM units rising fast (there should be nearly 8.8 million by the end of 1994), but there is also the near-future possibility of CD–ROM-style interactive availability without even owning a personal computer.

The fiber-optic promise of 500-or 1,000-channel television (yes, the information highway's off-ramp right into the home) is one way that this material might be brought into every home.

When that happens—when Everyman's cable television hookup brings some form, at least, of interactive multimedia into the home—the change will be profound. And it won't be just the children who won't need to read very much or very well; it will be all of us.

Perhaps, of course, this isn't a problem—it may be merely a shift in our social paradigm. Mass literacy, after all, has been around for only a couple centuries, and maybe its time is now past.

In a few years, perhaps, someone putting together an article like this will not need a keyboard at all, but instead will pull together a wide variety of illustrations, sound bites, graphs, charts, and a few brief paragraphs of copy to get the same information across to the reader, er, user.

It will no doubt be much more informative and a lot more fun. And only some of us, the real dinosaurs, will miss all those words.

THE
Plug-In School

A LEARNING ENVIRONMENT FOR THE 21ST CENTURY

**New technologies make it possible for learning to take place anywhere.
The Plug-In School may show the way.**

*Text and Illustrations
By David Pesanelli*

David Pesanelli is an advanced planner and conceptual designer who develops communications, environments, and products. His address is David Pesanelli and Company, 14508 Barkwood Drive, Rockville, Maryland 20853, telephone 301/871-7355.

The Plug-In School concept was developed with his collaborator on education projects, Bill Raxsdale, who is an educator, author, and researcher based in Lafayette, Louisiana, telephone 318/232-5025.

In the future, technologies will allow learning to take place virtually everywhere. School buildings as they now exist could even be eliminated, replaced with a ubiquitous array of stimulating, interactive, and flexible learning technologies embedded in all human habitats.

While eliminating the school is a revolutionary change in the distribution of education services that deserves serious consideration, it is also fruitful to examine ways in which the educational physical plant might shed its "factory school" format and emerge in new forms. We can then begin to see how the classroom could become a precursor of

"The Morning Surprise" (Scenario One) awaits students in the "Plug-In School" of the twenty-first century. Transporters (left, rear) bring learning packages to an unloading dock. The modules are unpacked and checked in the preview area. Two students (right) assemble a robot, which guides them in the process. Others (center, rear) check out the portable planetarium. One student (far left) uses a touch-screen monitor to log in to a database to receive information on an upcoming careers class. A video screen suspended from the ceiling provides timely information on special events at the school.

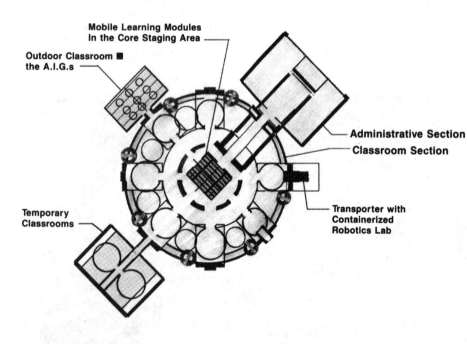

**PLUG-IN SCHOOL
CONCEPTUAL PLAN**

In "Afternoon Career Class" (Scenario Two), students gather around a Mobile Learning Module. Video screens on the rear wall show close ups of the project they are working on. The elements in the room are all mobile, including work stations, project work benches, the learning modules, and the soft partitions connected to tracks in the ceiling. This allows the room to be reconfigured to meet the class's varying needs.

true twenty-first-century environments, a prototype for the evolving workplace and home.

New, integrated technologies enrich the learning experience by giving students access to encyclopedic amounts of information and data in any of their subject areas, integrated with rich images and animation. Curriculums enhanced by these exciting technologies could help teachers expose students to history and its meanings: Names and dates of historical events and actors come alive in full costumes of the times, embellished by period music.

The advanced physical learning environment would also teach students about life in the twenty-first century—at work, at home, and in places yet to be imagined.

Child sits at brightly colored work station when in class. The module can easily be moved and has an adjustable seat, a rear storage compartment, and a snap-in computer that the student can take home for assignments.

The school, the workplace, and the home are clearly integrating. Responsibilities, functions, activities, and tasks that once occurred exclusively within each domain are crossing over into the other environments. Corporate workers have home offices, students and older learners take cable-access university courses, and parents bring their toddlers to day-care learning centers at work sites. It may no longer be sensible to think about the school, the office, and the home as separate from one another. These three once-distinct entities are breaking apart, combining, and overlapping in new and unexpected ways. The next-generation school can lead this process of blending aspects of learning, living, and working.

The School as Change Agent

Dramatic and pervasive changes are occurring in the workplace, to which the advanced school environment can help orient students. Organization charts are flattening, team assignments are becoming prevalent, off-site work is increasing, and teleconferencing is expanding. Just beneath the surface of these visible transformations are powerful change-themes such as "fluidity," "mobil-

ity," "flexibility," and "adaptability." These underlying qualities can guide the planning and design of advanced schools.

For example, children could easily rearrange colorful and mobile work stations in the classroom as they switch from teacher-led programs to individual assignments to team projects to distance-learning via satellite or cable broadcasts. These flexible learning situations have parallels in the ways that office and factory work are evolving.

The Plug-In School

The "Plug-In School" is a possibile first step toward the flexible learning environments of the twenty-first century. As now envisioned, this facility serves as a hub for receiving learning modules "injected" into its classrooms. The school has a physical structure that opens its walls to become part of the library, museum, science center, planetarium, laboratory, and corporation that is plugged in to it. Yet, the school never loses its own identity as the students' and teachers' environment.

The Plug-In School is conceived as a facility that, in addition to its traditional roles, functions at the center of a delivery and distribution system

for education "packages." A key goal is to strengthen the school's relationships with informal learning centers and with employers to create both academic and career-oriented instructional programs.

Transporters deliver containerized modules to school facilities. These "packages" are planned, designed, and manufactured at science centers and museums. They might contain interactive exhibits or materials that will be used for pursuing creative problem-solving exercises. Corporations could create stimulating, career-oriented modules. An architectural firm might send models of buildings accompanied by optical discs showing computer-aided design. An industrial laboratory could provide a module that demonstrates state-of-the-art laser applications.

These education and career packages need not be exclusively high tech. A crafts company might send an entire section of a woodworking shop, complete with work benches and tools for the students to use in creating artistic and personal objects. Some containerized modules might literally plug in to openings in the school walls, and the craft shop or robotics lab or architectural studio would become a walk-in extension of the classroom.

At the center of the Plug-In School is a storage and staging core, where the school's own mobile learning modules are prepared for classroom use. Teachers request combinations of models, mockups, specimens, interactive devices, and media to enhance course experiences.

What might it be like to spend some time in this dynamic facility?

Scenario One: The Morning Surprise

The young children have been waiting impatiently for this morning's "surprises" to appear. And now their wait is over. Two sleek transporters have arrived, and their drivers unload containerized "packages" at one of the school's loading bays. One module is from Chicago's Adler Planetarium. Tina, Beverly, and Tom—a student teaching assistant—eagerly assemble the traveling planetarium. The projection instrument is a compact model designed to be transported easily. The inflatable dome will soon be in place and swept with galaxies, quasars, and galactic black holes.

The second vehicle brings a robotics lab from the National Institute of Science and Technology. Jimmy and Quan insert a program card into the instructor robot, which launches into a comedy routine while instructing the boys on assembling a mini-manufacturing plant to be used in the classroom this morning. A second section of the robotics lab, including microbots and videos depicting careers in the field, is loaded onto a mobile learning module and delivered to the school's storage core. Later, it will be sent to a physics class for a career-oriented program.

Scenario Two: Afternoon Career Class

The sun-drenched classroom is filled with bright, gregarious 15- to 17-year-old students, who chatter excitedly as they rearrange the room for the afternoon's career class. They reposition soft partitions and program the track lighting, then decide how to arrange their work stations for the two-hour session's rigorous agenda. The "stations" hold the snap-in computers that they will carry home in backpacks and use for their homework assignments.

As the session on robotics careers begins, a section of the classroom wall slides aside, and the students grow quiet. The teacher and a robotics expert enter the environment just ahead of a self-guided mobile unit. The "package" that it carries arrived earlier that day after being picked up at another school complex in the next county.

A teaching assistant slides back the cover of the mobile learning module. Inside are a laboratory's

Young student interacts with AIG (Artificial Intelligence Grounder), a personal learning environment that responds individually to each student. The personal environment could be integrated into the future "Plug-In School."

products—microbots. The module's video camera scans the array of electronic and mechanical marvels, and enlarged images appear on a suspended video screen. The lab expert explains how microbots are developed and manufactured, as well as what they can do.

After taking turns manipulating the microbots, the students watch a video on careers in the rapidly expanding robotics field and related disciplines. Interested students press a module section and receive a printout that identifies robotics labs and corporations in the region where interns are employed during vacation breaks.

The career-oriented session ends, and some of the class members eagerly rearrange their work stations for a team project. Others reconfigure the classroom area for a distance-learning course taught by a robotics engineer broadcasting via satellite from an upstate New York laboratory.

Everywhere Learning

Learning environments of the future should provide a context for technologies as well as a counterpoint to them. The "little red schoolhouse" of yore will disappear, re-

placed with a more futuristic design in which brilliant technologies seem natural and not overwhelming or intimidating. But at the same time, this high-tech environment should embrace its natural surroundings. The classrooms, for instance, might have large windows to give students a view of trees, meadows, and lakes, providing a serene visual respite for kids spending many hours with computer screens and electronic devices of one type or another.

The Plug-In School is but one potential concept for a twenty-first-century school. Students—and adult learners as well—will likely use several facilities of different sizes and complexity, including study environments in the home and workplace. In the twenty-first century, it will be possible for all of us to plug in to "schools"—wherever we may be.

Credits/ Acknowledgments

Cover design by Charles Vitelli

1. How Others See Us and How We See Ourselves
Facing overview—Dushkin Publishing Group/Brown & Benchmark Publishers photo. 7—Photo by Wendy Ewald. 27, 30-31—Illustrations by David Suter.

2. Rethinking and Changing the Educative Effort
Facing overview—United Nations photo by Y. Nagata.

3. Striving for Excellence
Facing overview—AP/Wide World photo by Jim Gerberich.

4. Morality and Values in Education
Facing overview—Photo by Pamela Carley.

5. Managing Life in Classrooms
Facing overview—New York Times Pictures photo by Sara Krulwich.

6. Equal Opportunity in Education
Facing overview—United Nations photo by Y. Nagata.

7. Serving Special Needs and Concerns
Facing overview—United Nations photo by Marta Pinter.

8. The Profession of Teaching Today
Facing overview—Westinghouse Electric Corporation photo. 222-226—Photos by Jon Alcorn.

9. A Look to the Future
Facing overview—AP/Wide World photo by Carlos Osorio.

ANNUAL EDITIONS ARTICLE REVIEW FORM

■ NAME: _____ DATE: _____

■ TITLE AND NUMBER OF ARTICLE: _____

■ BRIEFLY STATE THE MAIN IDEA OF THIS ARTICLE: _____

_____

■ LIST THREE IMPORTANT FACTS THAT THE AUTHOR USES TO SUPPORT THE MAIN IDEA:

_____

_____

_____

_____

_____

_____

■ WHAT INFORMATION OR IDEAS DISCUSSED IN THIS ARTICLE ARE ALSO DISCUSSED IN YOUR TEXTBOOK OR OTHER READING YOU HAVE DONE? LIST THE TEXTBOOK CHAPTERS AND PAGE NUMBERS:

_____

_____

_____

_____

_____

_____

■ LIST ANY EXAMPLES OF BIAS OR FAULTY REASONING THAT YOU FOUND IN THE ARTICLE:

_____

_____

_____

_____

■ LIST ANY NEW TERMS/CONCEPTS THAT WERE DISCUSSED IN THE ARTICLE AND WRITE A SHORT DEFINITION:

_____

_____

_____

_____

_____

ANNUAL EDITIONS: EDUCATION 96/97
Article Rating Form

Here is an opportunity for you to have direct input into the next revision of this volume. We would like you to rate each of the 52 articles listed below, using the following scale:

1. **Excellent: should definitely be retained**
2. **Above average: should probably be retained**
3. **Below average: should probably be deleted**
4. **Poor: should definitely be deleted**

Your ratings will play a vital part in the next revision. So please mail this prepaid form to us just as soon as you complete it.
Thanks for your help!

Annual Editions revisions depend on two major opinion sources: one is our Advisory Board, listed in the front of this volume, which works with us in scanning the thousands of articles published in the public press each year; the other is you—the person actually using the book. Please help us and the users of the next edition by completing the prepaid article rating form on this page and returning it to us. Thank you.

Rating	Article	Rating	Article
	1. Education for Conflict Resolution		30. *Turning Points* Revisited: A New Deal for Adolescents
	2. Will Schools Ever Get Better?		31. The Canon Debate, Knowledge Construction, and Multicultural Education
	3. Full-Service Schools: Ideal as Reality		
	4. Public School Lifts Kids Off New York's Mean Streets		32. Investing in Our Children: A Struggle for America's Conscience and Future
	5. America Skips School: Why We Talk So Much about Education and Do So Little		33. The AAUW Report: How Schools Shortchange Girls
	6. The 27th Annual Phi Delta Kappa/Gallup Poll of the Public's Attitude toward the Public Schools		34. Home Sweet School
			35. Year-Round School: The Best Thing Since Sliced Bread
	7. Shifting the *Target* of Educational Reform		36. Blackboard Bungle
	8. How Our Schools Could Be		37. The Commercialization of Youth: Channel One in Context
	9. A Class of Their Own		
	10. Rebel with a Cause		38. Enhancing K–12 Economic Education with Contemporary Information Resources
	11. Schools That Do More Than Teach		
	12. An Evolving Strategy for Middle Grade Reform		
			39. Violence as a Public Health Issue for Children
	13. On Lasting School Reform: A Conversation with Ted Sizer		
			40. Blowing up the Tracks
	14. Towards Excellence in Education		41. Everyone Is an Exception: Assumptions to Avoid in the Sex Education Classroom
	15. Not All Standards Are Created Equal		
	16. Wrong Problem, Wrong Solution		
	17. Somebody's Children		42. Reflection and Teaching: The Challenge of Thinking Beyond the Doing
	18. Making America's Schools Work		
	19. A Morally Defensible Mission for Schools in the 21st Century		43. Phase II: Implementing a Design for Learning
			44. Toward Lives Worth Sharing: A Basis for Integrating Curriculum
	20. A De-Moralized Society: The British/American Experience		
			45. About Instruction: Powerful New Strategies Worth Knowing
	21. The Return of Character Education		
	22. What Are Your Family Values?		46. Cultural Revolution
	23. Teaching Values		47. How to Make Detracking Work
	24. Routines and the First Few Weeks of Class		48. Challenges to the Public School Curriculum: New Targets and Strategies
	25. Waging Peace in Our Schools: Beginning with the Children		
			49. A Philosophy of Education for the Year 2000
	26. How to Create Discipline Problems		
	27. A Lesson Plan Approach for Dealing with School Discipline		50. Preparing for the 21st Century: The EFG Experiment
			51. Searching for Terms
	28. Challenging the Myths about Multicultural Education		52. The Plug-In School: A Learning Environment for the 21st Century
	29. Time to See, Tell, and Do about Bigotry and Racism		

(Continued on next page)

ABOUT YOU

Name _____ Date _____

Are you a teacher? ❑ Or student? ❑

Your School Name _____

Department _____

Address _____

City _____ State _____ Zip _____

School Telephone # _____

YOUR COMMENTS ARE IMPORTANT TO US!

Please fill in the following information:

For which course did you use this book? _____

Did you use a text with this Annual Edition? ❑ yes ❑ no

The title of the text? _____

What are your general reactions to the Annual Editions concept?

Have you read any particular articles recently that you think should be included in the next edition?

Are there any articles you feel should be replaced in the next edition? Why?

Are there other areas that you feel would utilize an Annual Edition?

May we contact you for editorial input?

May we quote you from above?